Software Engineering for Secure Systems:
Industrial and Research Perspectives

Haralambos Mouratidis
University of East London, UK

INFORMATION SCIENCE REFERENCE

Hershey · New York

Director of Editorial Content:	Kristin Klinger
Director of Book Publications:	Julia Mosemann
Acquisitions Editor:	Lindsay Johnston
Development Editor:	Christine Bufton
Typesetter:	Michael Brehm
Production Editor:	Jamie Snavely
Cover Design:	Lisa Tosheff

Published in the United States of America by
Information Science Reference (an imprint of IGI Global)
701 E. Chocolate Avenue
Hershey PA 17033
Tel: 717-533-8845
Fax: 717-533-8661
E-mail: cust@igi-global.com
Web site: http://www.igi-global.com

Library of Congress Cataloging-in-Publication Data

Software engineering for secure systems : industrial and research perspectives
/ Haralambos Mouratidis, editor.
    p. cm.
  Includes bibliographical references and index.
  Summary: "This book provides coverage of recent advances in the area of
secure software engineering that address the various stages of the development
process from requirements to design to testing to implementation"--Provided by
publisher.
  ISBN 978-1-61520-837-1 (hardcover) -- ISBN 978-1-61520-838-8 (ebook) 1.
Computer security. 2. Software engineering. I. Mouratidis, Haralambos, 1977-
  QA76.9.A25S6537 2010
  005.8--dc22
                                    2010017214

British Cataloguing in Publication Data
A Cataloguing in Publication record for this book is available from the British Library.

All work contributed to this book is new, previously-unpublished material. The views expressed in this book are those of the authors, but not necessarily of the publisher.

Editorial Advisory Board

Table of Contents

Chapter 1

 Bill Whyte, Independent Consultant, UK
 John Harrison, LanditD, UK

Section 1
Security Patterns

Chapter 2

 Eduardo B. Fernandez, Florida Atlantic University, USA
 Nobukazu Yoshioka, GRACE Center, National Institute of Informatics, Japan
 Hironori Washizaki, Waseda University, Japan
 Jan Jurjens, Technical University of Dortmund, Germany
 Michael VanHilst, Florida Atlantic University, USA
 Guenther Pernul, University of Regensburg, Germany

Chapter 3

 Holger Schmidt, Technical University Dortmund, Germany
 Denis Hatebur, University Duisburg-Essen and ITESYS Institut für Technische
  Systeme GmbH, Germany
 Maritta Heisel, University Duisburg-Essen, Germany

Section 2
Methodologies and Frameworks

Section 3
Privacy and Trust

Section 4
Secure Code Analysis

Detailed Table of Contents

Chapter 1

Bill Whyte, Independent Consultant, UK
John Harrison, LanditD, UK

In this chapter the authors present a synthesis of expert views on some important actions to improve the state of practice in secure software. The authors base their study on experiences as panel moderators, rapporteurs and report writers involved in drafting the views of experts.

Section 1
Security Patterns

Chapter 2

Eduardo B. Fernandez, Florida Atlantic University, USA
Nobukazu Yoshioka, GRACE Center, National Institute of Informatics, Japan
Hironori Washizaki, Waseda University, Japan
Jan Jurjens, Technical University of Dortmund, Germany
Michael VanHilst, Florida Atlantic University, USA
Guenther Pernul, University of Regensburg, Germany

In this chapter the authors present work on the use of patterns for the development of secure software systems. Their work applies the pattern paradigm to various parts of the software systems development from analysis to design to testing.

Chapter 3

Holger Schmidt, Technical University Dortmund, Germany

Denis Hatebur, University Duisburg-Essen and ITESYS Institut für Technische
Systeme GmbH, Germany

Maritta Heisel, University Duisburg-Essen, Germany

In this chapter, the authors discuss a security engineering process based on security problem frames and concretized security problem frames. The presented process is supported by formal models that are used to prove that the solution approaches are correct solutions to the security problems. Furthermore, the formal models of the solution approaches constitute a formal specification of the software to be developed.

Chapter 4

Armstrong Nhlabatsi, The Open University, UK

Arosha Bandara, The Open University, UK

Shinpei Hayashi, Tokyo Institute of Technology, Japan

Charles B. Haley, The Open University, UK

Jan Jurjens, The Open University, UK

Haruhiko Kaiya, Shinshu University, Japan

Atsuto Kubo, National Institute of Informatics, Japan

Robin Laney, The Open University, UK

Haralambos Mouratidis, University of East London, UK

Bashar Nuseibeh, The Open University, UK & Lero, Ireland

Thein T. Tun, The Open University, UK

Hironori Washizaki, Waseda University, Japan

Nobukazu Yoshioka, National Institute of Informatics, Japan

Yijun Yu, The Open University, UK

The authors of this chapter present evaluation results of a study that examined the extent to which constructs provided by security requirements engineering approaches can support the use of security patterns as part of the analysis of security problems. Their analysis was based on a specific pattern and it employ a number of existing security modelling approaches.

Section 2
Methodologies and Frameworks

Chapter 5

C. Blanco, University of Cantabria, Spain

D. G. Rosado, University of Castilla-La Mancha, Spain

C. Gutiérrez, Correos Telecom, Spain

A. Rodríguez, University of Bio-Bio, Chile

D. Mellado, Spanish Tax Agency, Madrid, Spain

E. Fernández-Medina, University of Castilla-La Mancha, Spain

J. Trujillo, University of Alicante, Spain

M. Piattini, University of Castilla-La Mancha, Spain

In this chapter the authors discuss the problem of integrating security into the software development process, paying more attention to the requirements engineering discipline and the software design stage, and they present their efforts to integrate security considerations into the software systems development process in various domains such as software product lines, business processes, web services, and databases and data warehouses.

Chapter 6

Siv Hilde Houmb, Telenor GBDR Platform for Service Innovation Group, Norway

Geri Georg, Colorado State University, USA

Dorina C. Petriu, Carleton University, Canada

Behzad Bordbar, University of Birmingham, UK

Indrakshi Ray, Colorado State University, USA

Kyriakos Anastasakis, University of Birmingham, UK

Robert B. France, Colorado State University, USA

The authors present the Aspect-Oriented Risk Driven Development (AORDD) methodology, which integrates the analysis of two quality properties, namely security and performance, into the development process of critical systems. The approach is illustrated using a transactional web e-commerce benchmark (TPC-W) originally developed by the Transaction Processing Performance Council.

Chapter 7

S. P. Maj, Edith Cowan University, Australia

This chapter presents an approach concerned with the configuration and management of network devices. In particular, the paper demonstrates how the State Model Diagram method is useful for the configuration and management of complex security protocols and devices.

Section 3
Privacy and Trust

    Christos Kalloniatis, University of the Aegean, Greece
    Evangelia Kavakli, University of the Aegean, Greece
    Stefanos Gritzalis, University of the Aegean, Greece

In this chapter the authors identify a number of privacy requirements that should be considered during system analysis and design. They also present and analyse 10 methods from the area of secure requirements engineering. They then compare these methods based on their initial set of privacy requirements.

    Alberto Coen-Porisini, Università degli studi dell'Insubria, Italy
    Pietro Colombo, Università degli studi dell'Insubria, Italy
    Sabrina Sicari, Università degli studi dell'Insubria, Italy

In this chapter, the authors present their work on the development of a conceptual model to support the definition of privacy policies. The presented model introduces a set of concepts concerning privacy and defines the existent relationships among those concepts along with the interfaces for the definition of privacy related mechanisms. The assessment of the model is presented with the aid of an example from the health domain.

    Piotr Cofta, BT (British Telecom), UK
    Hazel Lacohée, BT (British Telecom), UK
    Paul Hodgson, BT (British Telecom), UK

In this chapter, the authors discuss how the "designing for trust" paradigm leverages trust governance into the design practices of ICT systems by complementing security-based methodologies. In particular, they argue about the need to consider trust as part of the software systems development process, they present three different (but complimenting) views of the notion of trust and they discuss how trust governance and security management can benefit from an integration.

Section 4
Secure Code Analysis

Chapter 11

Alexandros Loizidis, Aristotle University of Thessaloniki, Greece
Vasilios Almaliotis, Aristotle University of Thessaloniki, Greece
Panagiotis Katsaros, Aristotle University of Thessaloniki, Greece

In this chapter the authors investigate recent advances in theory and tool support for static program analysis of security critical applications. Based on their investigation they then present an approach for automatic verification of critical application based on the domain of smart cards.

Chapter 12

Kézia de Vasconcelos Oliveira, Federal University of Campina Grande, Brazil
Kyller Gorgônio, Federal University of Campina Grande, Brazil
Angelo Perkusich, Federal University of Campina Grande, Brazil
Antônio Marcus Nogueira Lima, Federal University of Campina Grande, Brazil
Leandro Dias da Silva, Federal University of Alagoas, Brazil

In this chapter the authors present a method to increase the confidence in the behavior of critical control systems. The presented method automatically generates the timed automata models from the specification ISA 5.2 Binary Logic Diagrams, and the implementation Ladder programs, for model-based analysis. The method is based on the use of the Uppaal tool and the Uppaal-TRON testing tool.

Foreword

As Information Technology (IT) is permeating more and more functions of society, and digital information is becoming a key asset of every organization; software systems security is growing in importance and urgency. The massive amount of security flaws that keep emerging in various software systems indicate that security has not been given sufficient attention in software engineering education and research.

But security is also difficult. A secure software system needs to withstand all attacks, while an attacker only needs to beat the system's security once, possibly out of thousands of tries. In large complex software systems, it is unlikely that there will not be a single vulnerability. Hence, security needs to be addressed in a holistic way, at multiple levels to provide defence in depth, and from multiple angles to avoid bias to one particular type of threat.

This book delivers such a needed multiplicity, having interesting contributions from a number of excellent researchers within the area of software systems security. With parts about security patterns, development methods and frameworks, privacy and trust, and code analysis, it covers a large part of the lifecycle, from high level threats and early user requirements to intricate technical details; and it covers both process (e.g., development methods) and product (e.g., patterns, architecture).

All in all, this anthology provides a very important view of where the research front stands today on various issues related to software engineering for security and privacy. The reader who has little knowledge about the topic will find good introductions to the various challenges, as well as a wealth of references pointing to further readings. The expert will find detailed contributions by top researchers in the field, which will inspire further research and hopefully provide a crucial and needed input for industrial practice, aiming to provide the foundations for better software systems security and privacy in the years to come.

Prof. Guttorm Sindre
Norwegian University of Science and Technology
January 2010

Guttorm Sindre *(b.1964) holds a Ph.D. in Computer from the Norwegian Institute of Technology (NTH), 1990 and is currently professor in information systems at the Norwegian University of Science and Technology (NTNU) in Trondheim, Norway. He has published around 100 peer-reviewed papers in journals, books, and conferences since 1987, and has been involved in several national and international research projects. He has been on the program committee of several international conferences and was program co-chair of CAiSE '07, posters & demos chair of RE '08, and organizational co-chair of REFSQ '09. In recent years his research has focussed on conceptual modelling and early stage requirements techniques, especially related to security and safety, and he is currently project manager of REQSEC, a funded by the Norwegian Research Council to investigate techniques for security requirements.*

Preface

The security of software systems in recent years has been transformed from a mono-dimensional technical challenge to a multi-dimensional technico-social challenge, due to the wide usage of software systems in almost every area of the human life. This situation requires a different and more holistic approach to the development of secure software systems. Recent research argues that it is essential for security to be considered from the early stages and throughout the software development life-cycle; thus, sound software engineering methodologies and practices need to be developed that support the simultaneous analysis of both security and software requirements, their transformation to an appropriate design and the implementation of that design. Towards this direction, a number of relevant challenges have been identified[1] ranging from the development of appropriate security requirements techniques to security modelling languages to secure code analysis. On the other hand, a number of research-led and industrial-led projects have been presented in the literature aiming to provide some answers to these challenges and successfully integrate security considerations during the development of software systems starting from the early stages of the development process. This area of researh and development, widely termed in the literature as secure software engineering[2], is currently very active and fast moving.

This book aims to capture the essential elements of this area and provide a forum for presenting the most recent and innovative lines of research and industrial practice related to secure software engineering. The book provides coverage of recent advances in the area of secure software engineering that address the various stages of the development process from requirements to design to testing to implementation. The contributions of this book are three-fold: it provides a comprehensive understanding of the curent state of the art in the area of secure software engineering; it inspires and motivates further research and development; and it bridges the gap between academic research and industrial practice.

BOOK AUDIENCE

The book is addressed to a wide range of industrial and professional audiences from project managers to security engineers and software developers; and anyone else in an industrial context who is involved with any aspects of secure software systems. The book is also addressed to researchers who are involved in creating the future theories, methods, methodologies and tools for secure software engineering. Finally, the book is addressed to university lecturers and professors developing programmes of studies in secure software systems engineering and their students (especially at master level).

ORGANISATION OF THE BOOK

The book is organised into twelve (12) chapters. The first chapter provides an overview of the state-of-practice in the area of secure software and it presents a synthesis of expert views on some important actions needed to improve the state of practice in secure software. The authors base their study on experiences as panel moderators, rapporteurs and report writers involved in drafting the views of experts. The rest of the chapters are organised into four (4) sections.

Section 1 is on *Security Patterns* and it includes three (3) chapters. Together, these three chapters form a comprehensive introduction to security patterns for the novice reader but also give novel insights about recent research to the expert reader. The concept of security patterns has achieved prominence as an important vehicle for sharing and reusing security knowledge among developers, accessible even to those with limited security expertise assisting them in the construction of secure software systems. Chapter 2 (*Using Security Patterns to Develop Secure Systems*) by Fernandez et. al. provides an overview of how security patterns can be used in various development stages from analysis to design to testing. Chapter 3 (*A Pattern-Based Method to Develop Secure Software*) by Schmidt et. al., presents a security engineering process based on security problem frames and concretized security problem frames. The presented process is supported by formal models that are used to prove that the solution approaches are correct solutions to specified security problems. Chapter 4 (*Security Patterns: Comparing Modeling Approaches*) by Nhlabatsi et. al. presents a comparative analysis and evaluation of a number of secure software systems approaches, by examining the extent to which their constructs can support the use of security patterns as part of the analysis of security problems.

Section 2 is on *Methodologies and Frameworks* and it includes 3 chapters. Chapter 5 (*Security over the Information Systems Development Cycle*) by Blanco et. al., discusses the problem of integrating security into the software development process, paying more attention to the requirements engineering discipline and the software design stage. They present their efforts to integrate security considerations into the software systems development process in various domains such as software product lines, business processes, web services, and databases and data warehouses. Chapter 6 (*Balancing Security and Performance Properties During System Architectural Design*) by Houmb et. al., presents the Aspect-Oriented Risk Driven Development (AORDD) methodology, which integrates the analysis of two quality properties, namely security and performance, into the development process of critical systems. The approach is illustrated using a transactional web e-commerce benchmark (TPC-W) originally developed by the Transaction Processing Performance Council. Chapter 7 (*State Model Diagrams – a universal, model driven method for network system configuration and management*) by Maj presents an approach concerned with the configuration and management of network devices. In particular, the paper demonstrates how the State Model Diagram method is useful for the configuration and management of complex security protocols and devices.

Section 3 is on *Privacy and Trust*. Two topics very related to security itself. Privacy sometimes is considered as a sub-factor of security, while other times the two might also be seen as opposites, since security mandates the recording of information (e.g., users' details) whereas privacy might motivate anonymity. On the other hand, trust and security are also closely related. This is the case for a number of reasons. For example, security always assumes some degree of trust in its mechanisms. Consider, for instance, a software system that is based on passwords to provide access to an account. The software engineers may have assumed that each user is trustworthy and will not make their passwords freely available to potential attackers of the system. Further, the system and its administrator are assumed to be trusted not to divulge, alter or remove passwords. However, it is only when such trustworthiness is demonstrated, that the security can properly assumed. Chapter 8 (*Designing Privacy Aware Information Systems*) by Kalloniatis et. al. identifies a number of privacy requirements that should be considered during system analysis and design. The authors also present and analyse 10 methods from the area of secure requirements engineering. They then compare these methods based on their initial set of privacy requirements. Chapter 9 (*Privacy aware systems - from models to patterns*) by Coen-Porisini et. al., presents work on the development of a conceptual model to support the definition of privacy policies. The presented model introduces a set of concepts concerning privacy and defines the existent relationships among those concepts along with the interfaces for the definition of privacy related mechanisms. An assessment of the model is presented with the aid of an example from the health care domain. Chapter 10 (*Incorporating social trust into design practices for secure systems*) by Cofta et. al., discusses how the "designing for trust" paradigm leverages trust governance into the design practices of ICT systems developers by complementing security-based methodologies. In particular, they argue for the need to consider trust as part of the software systems development process; they present three different (but complimentary) views of the notion of trust and they discuss how trust governance and security management can benefit from integration.

Section 4 is on *Secure Code Analysis*. There is a large collection of well established analysis techniques and recent research developments, and the two chapters in this section complement the existing literature. Chapter 11 (*Static program analysis of multi-applet JavaCard applications*) by Loizidis et. al., investigates recent advances in theory and tool support for static program analysis of security critical applications. Based on their investigation the authors present an approach for automatic verification of critical application based on the domain of smart cards. Chapter 12 (*Automatic Timed Automata Extraction from Ladder Programs for Model-Based Analysis of Control Systems*) by Vasconcelos Oliveira et. al., presents a method to increase the confidence in the behaviour of critical control systems. The presented method automatically generates the timed automata models from the specification ISA 5.2 Binary Logic Diagrams, and the implementation Ladder programs, for model-based analysis. The method is based on the use of the Uppaal tool and the Uppaal-TRON testing tool.

Haralambos Mouratidis
University of East London, UK

ENDNOTES

[1] H. Mouratidis and P. Giorgini (2006), Integrating Security and Software Engineering: Advances and Future Visions, Idea Group Publishing, pages 290.

[2] The term secure software engineering is defined by Mouratidis and Giogini (see footnote 1 above for full reference details) as a branch of research investigating the integration of security concerns into software engineering practices, which draws from expertise from the security and softtware engineering community. It is thought of as an umbrella term under which the areas of security requirements engineering, security modelling and secure sofware development lie. It is worth noting that there are also alternative names used in the literature, which refer to the same area of research and development, such as software security engineering, software engineering for security, software engineering for secure systems.

Acknowledgment

I would like to take this opportunity to thank a number of people who have contributed in various ways in the development process of this book. First of all the authors of all the chapters that are presented in this book, as well as the authors of the chapters submitted but did not quite made it to the final chapter selection. The large interest shown by all of them indicate that the area is indeed very active. I would like also to thank all the reviewers of the chapters as well as the members of the editorial advisory board for their assistance in ensuring the quality of the publication. Thank you also goes to the development team at IGI Global, and especially Christine Bufton for all the support throughout the book development process.

Haralambos Mouratidis
University of East London, UK

Chapter 1
State of Practice in Secure Software:
Experts' Views on Best Ways Ahead

Bill Whyte
Independent Consultant, UK

John Harrison
LanditD, UK

ABSTRACT

The authors present a synthesis of expert views on some important actions to improve the state of practice in secure software. The main conclusions are: the skill base is lacking; business cases for security good practice are poorly developed: choosing between different 'good practices' is difficult; research will only have impact if compatible with the commercial environment of developers and their existent skills. The study is grounded on experiences as panel moderators, rapporteurs and report writers involved in drafting the views of experts. Some research directions are indicated.

INTRODUCTION

Although some organisations are proficient in and committed to good-practice software development that promotes resilience against security-attacks, it is widely recognised that they are very much the minority, with a long tail of developers who lack either the skill or motivation to do so. Here we present a synthesis of expert views on some of the most important actions for the medium and long-term in order to improve the overall state of practice in secure software. An important aspect of our study is that it is grounded significantly on

our experiences as panel moderators, rapporteurs and report writers involved in drafting the views of a number of experts and submission of these drafts to the experts for approval through a series of iterations. By this means we believe we have identified several areas of expert consensus and disagreement, with minimal interpretation by ourselves. Furthermore these have been crosschecked against other independent sources.

A large majority of the experts involved agreed that a very significant, if not the most significant, positive impact on secure software development would be concentration on measures that improve the overall quality of the 'state of practice' rather than the 'state of the art' in secure

DOI: 10.4018/978-1-61520-837-1.ch001

software development. They further concluded that this necessarily involves not just new research and development in good-practice security life-cycle methodology but also measures to support business-case development. Furthermore, these should take into account the knowledge-base, (professional development and university education), on which any better-practice developments would have to be based. However good in itself is any research activity, clearly its eventual adoption by these segments of the software industry must depend on its clear contribution to their business case and, at the very least, their ability to use and understand it.

This text, therefore, does not attempt a deep analysis of secure software research development in terms of its detailed scientific and technological excellence or its theoretical basis, but rather attempts to identify specific characteristics which it should possess in order to meet the needs particularly of the 'average' (and lower than average) development teams and those under significant commercial pressure.

BACKGROUND

Proper selection of methodology for acquiring, authoritative views in the area of applied technology is often insufficiently addressed, with a failure to employ research methods that are properly grounded, with issues such as 'observation' versus 'theory' [O'HEAR] not separated out. At worst, observation simply consists of an unrepresentative sampling of journal papers or online search, and theory simply the biased views of the enquirer, and in neither case with the investigator's views subject to proper 'closed-loop' feedback. To avoid this as far as possible and although we do make use of open-loop sources, our findings are weighted towards first-hand encounters with a number of peer-reviewed activities involving experts in secure software development. In the course of these encounters we have sometimes

been involved in drafting (and redrafting) reports summarizing consensus views on the subject. What is, and what is not, said, and the manner in which the discussions proceed during this consensus building, can give additional insight into the debate.

Prominent among these was participation in a UK Department of Trade and Industry (DTI) Global Watch Initiative, in January 2006 [GWM]. The Global Watch team comprised a small body of experts who met a wide range of influential academic and governmental representatives and senior staff in leading software companies in California and Washington State.

One consequence of the report back from the Global Watch Mission was the setting up in March 2007 of a Special Interest Group on Secure Software Development (SSDSIG). This is one of a number of working groups established by the Cyber Security Knowledge Transfer Network of the UK Department of Business, Enterprise and Regulatory Reform. SSDSIG has as its aims that of identifying the principle barriers to secure software development and to make recommendations to address them. Membership is open to all interested persons and has operated via a number of mechanisms: well-attended, face-to-face meetings of industry and academic practitioners, active email discussions between members and also other interested parties, approaches to outside bodies for information acquisition and knowledge transfer. SSDSIG sponsored a report into the state of undergraduate education on software security, has run a very successful open workshop and published its first White Paper in June 2008 [WHYTE, HARRISON]. SSDSIG'S executive are now concentrating on taking forward the recommendations contained in that paper.

Following on from the above activities, SSDSIG was invited to be represented at a meeting held jointly by the European Research Consortium for Informatics and Mathematics (ERCIM) and the F5 'Security Unit' of the European Commission Directorate for the Information Society. The meeting (full title *EC-ERCIM Strategic Seminar on ICT Security "Engineering Secure Complex Software Systems and Services'*, 16 October 2008, Brussels) was intended to be a significant influence in the direction of European-funded research and technology developments. It provided an opportunity to present the views of SSDSIG and to review them against the opinions of a different, and cross-European, peers.

All in all, the number of experts involved in the views put forward below, well exceeds one hundred. In addition to the input from consensus views described above and later, we also cite a number of 'open-loop' resources. It should be noted that this open-loop material has been used for illustration and clarification only. Unless we quote it explicitly as output from consensus-moderated sources, it should not be assumed to be an example of 'expert agreement'.

STATE OF PRACTICE: CREATING MAXIMUM IMPACT

There are a number of preconditions necessary for the creation of change. There must be some motivation and there must be some ability to implement the change. In the case of secure software development, security experts and some others all agree that one motivation should be that much that is produced today is highly vulnerable to security attacks, and they further agree that current good practice can lead to significant improvements, in the short and medium term. Therefore they overwhelmingly agree that maximum impact could be gained by invoking this good practice in a way to raising the overall standard of the state of practice, rather than that of the cutting edge. They also acknowledge that there are still serious deficiencies in the tools and techniques, resulting in a need for further research. But much more can

be achieved with what already exists and there remain two serious questions: why have these good practices not been taken up, and how does one decide the direction of the research agenda?

The experts' conclusions regarding the lack of take-up of good practice can be summed up as follows:

- The business case for security good practice as a whole has not been demonstrated
- The skill base required for adopting much current good practice is not there
- The choice between 'good practices' is fraught with risk

And they further considered that:

- Research will only have significant impact if it is compatible with the commercial environment of developers and their existent skills

Business Case Support

Experts agreed that the benefits of good practice in secure software development have not been acknowledged by a large portion of industry and its clients, driven as they are by other perceived priorities: capital cost, training/recruitment, delay in product launch, and so on, with security activities often perceived as antagonistic to these.

A minority of experts voiced opinion that this is inevitable: it is often difficult, if not impossible to demonstrate gains from actions that have avoided loss; data is inherently too fuzzy to gather; business agendas will ignore everything else in favour of arguments based on immediately perceived functionality, time-to-market etc. However, the majority do agree on the possibility of demonstrating cost-benefits to some degree or other and they suggest a number of issues and solutions:

Need to be Cost-Effective and Measurable

Some work has been carried out into how to develop security business cases e.g. [SEI] but in general more attention is required to found them on harder evidence, with adequate metrics, measurement and empirical data, and taking cost into account. Moreover it should involve all stakeholders, and complexity issues should be investigated, not just on a technical, systems-of-systems basis, valuable though this extension to current practice might be, but also to including the environment in which the systems operate. It should be (business -) risk-based and include the issue of trustworthiness as a whole. It is agreed that significant further research is required in these areas.

Security measures should be proportionate to nature of the application. It is best to provide a range of solutions, each equated to a different level of risk and cost. In this regard, it is felt that many of the existing approaches are too heavy-weight for commercial use, where risks are less critical. For example, there may be a need for light-weight alternatives to Common Criteria [ComCrit], although it is recognised that making these more or less compulsory might be a difficult issue. One option, it is thought, might be through the inclusion of security clauses in purchasing contracts.

There is however some opposition from a number of commercial experts for a proliferation of security 'kite-marks', thus requiring conformance to yet another set of criteria.

Investment Appraisal, Obsolescence and Lock-In

A point made repeatedly by the industry-side experts, is that researchers and other theorists sometime fail to realise that business does not necessarily see the development of a new idea or a new tool as a good thing. The emergence for something novel indicates problems with exist-

ing infrastructure whose investment may not yet been recouped from the market. Indeed, it often asks for new investment decisions in the light of insufficient evidence. Should the organisation scrap current practices for something new, with upfront cost and the possibility of delay to product launch? Should developers with obsolete skills be laid off, or at least is additional recruitment needed to achieve a new skill-set? Is this, in any case the right change of path? Is there a danger of lock-in or of incompatibility with associated partners or systems? To minimise these problems, our experts again recommended better metrics, but also vendor-neutral approaches to tools and techniques and more effort on codes of practice and standards.

Balance across the Lifecycle

At present, security 'solutions' tend to be offered on a point-by-point basis, with little or no prioritisation across the entire lifecycle. The right place(s) and relative resource allocation within the life-cycle for the various security activities need to be made explicit. More attention than in the past should be given to the long and expensive support and maintenance phases, and there is also the need to include third party and legacy software. This will require further research.

Validation and Credibility

Researchers and 'improvers' need to accept that organisations will be reluctant to change unless presented with evidence (a) that it is needed and (b) that the proposed course of action will be successful. As noted earlier, experts were not uniformly in agreement that this could always – or even, often – be achieved, but recognised that there is a lack of good case-study material, and consideration could be given to the feasibility of creating and maintaining a catalogue of such material.

Education and Competence

As the UK Global Watch Mission worked its way across the software organizations of west coast USA, it became increasingly clear that few of them admitted to having a structured secure software development process. To the repeated question, 'What then do you do to ensure your software is secure?' almost invariably the answer was, 'We rely on good people.'

Is this a sustainable position? In the opinion of the US President's IT Advisory Committee [PITAC] and by many other experts, it is not. The solution, then, must lie with either an improvement in the competence of the average developer through some form of training or education or the provision of processes and tools which allow the less skilled to do a better job. General opinion seems to be that all of these must be improved.

Professional Training

Overall, the experts agree that there are isolated instances of professional training, in-house or externally provided that offer a reasonable background to a professional's need for security expertise. As regards in-house activities, the Microsoft decision to include a strong element of security in its structured training for its software development lifecycle programme, was welcomed as one of a number of improved attitudes by major developers, but like the others, this will inevitably tend to be vendor-specific. The experts noted that organisations such as the [SafeCode] alliance and the Open Web Applications Security Project [OWASP] both produce educational material that is more 'open'. However these are seldom if ever made mandatory within any software vendor's skill-set.

It is in fact extremely difficult to gather credible material on the actual uptake of training outside that made essentially mandatory by the employer; moreover there is no industry-wide professional standard for secure software development. We can get some idea of uptake by looking at a relatively

long-established approximation, the Certified Information Security Specialist qualification, [CISSP], which is more concerned with business-related aspects of information security than with software development. The Global Watch experts noted that, of an estimated 1.4 million information security professionals worldwide, only about 3% had the CISSP qualification. Among the experts there are some advocates for some means of proving 'certified secure software developer' professional status, but there does not appear to be any strong consensus that this would be either feasible or desirable, except perhaps if it could be made part of the entrance qualifications for membership of a professional association (IEEE, IET, EurEng etc.),

University Education: Postgraduate Programmes

Although several experts in the US echoed the views of PITAC, mentioned above, regarding the relatively few graduates in security-related subjects, one stating that only 23 security-related PhDs were issued in 2005 [GWM], others state there are signs that the situation is improving a little, although mainly in specific areas such as security for service oriented architectures.

In terms of Masters and similar qualifications, the *Guardian* newspaper issues yearly a list of postgraduate courses in the UK. Concentrating on courses that probably can legitimately be described as possessing a high degree of secure software design, as opposed to, eg, computer forensics or cryptography specialisms, we find around 17 out of 340 computing courses in total, ie 5%, for 2008 and a similar figure for 2009. Given other competing specialisms, this is probably as good as one can expect. Although obviously greater in depth than undergraduate security education, the course content in the great majority is similar in form, being highly pragmatic and lacking a structured approach to software engineering. The cultural divide between reliability/formal method approaches and 'computer security' is present at Masters as well as undergraduate level.

It would be reasonable to assume that embryonic secure software experts might be represented in these figures and estimating 10-20 students per course, we would end up with around 150 – 200 graduating per year.

Undergraduate Education

Perhaps then we might expect to get more security-aware students from undergraduate programmes? But:

'Why don't universities do a better job [in teaching secure software]?' asks Mary Ann Davidson, Chief Security Officer, Oracle, [DAVIDSON].

'The reality is that most universities do not teach secure software... You cannot assume that anyone you hire understands how to build secure defences, comment Microsoft's Michael Howard and Steve Lipner [HOWARD, LIPNER}, and many other experts in the software industry.

Howard and Lipner appear to be correct. A report commissioned by SSDSIG into the state of education of computing undergraduates in England in the subject of security [WHYTE] confirmed anecdotal evidence in the UK, the European Union and the United States, that few computing students receive anything like enough teaching to have an effective insight into the subject. Taking the case of England specifically, the SSDSIG study looked in detail at nearly all university courses in the broad area of 'computing', for evidence of software security topics in their online prospectuses. Even taking into account some necessary limitations in this approach, which are frankly acknowledged, the author asserts confidently that 80% of the undergraduates receive less than 6 hours teaching on the subject. Many receive nothing at all. The findings of the report have been quite widely publicised in the technical press and presented in

a number of specialist forums. The author is not aware of any dissenting opinions; the only comments received have supported the conclusions.

On the subject of undergraduate education, the experts widely agree that it is a problem, but do not think that it is feasible to provide sufficient time in a standard degree course to present an in-depth education in security, bearing in mind the needs of other subjects. However, the experts are strongly in favour of ensuring that the vast majority of computing undergraduates should be given a basic awareness, say 10 hours minimum, in the subject. Opinions were divided as to whether this should be a specific, standalone module, or spread across the various units within the course. In the latter case, security could be used as an interesting and approachable way to explaining more general concepts of computer science. For example, in the teaching of the PHP language, students could be made aware of the dangers of any language that was slack in initialling variables [PHP], [PHPLX]. As another example, security problems with code injection in tiered architectures could be used as illustrations of generic issues of emergent properties of complex systems.

Interestingly, though, there seems little enthusiasm for teaching very formal methods as part of 'basic awareness', and this is also seen in outline syllabi proposed internationally, for example in the quite detailed *Bodies of Knowledge* produced by the Association for Computing Machinery [ACM] and, in the UK, the *Computing Subject Benchmark for Security and Privacy* by the Quality Assurance Agency for Higher Education [QAA]. These are highly pragmatic and unformalised. In Table 1, we give an exemplar representing the typical security content of a 'computing/computer engineering' programme, wherein a reasonable level of programming skill might be expected.

It is noted that, where advertised in the degree prospectuses, broadly this same content is offered across the spectrum, from 'Computer science' programmes to those on 'information systems'. Also, there is some evidence that formal methods

Table 1. Example of 10 credit module on 'Secure Computing' (by kind permission of School of Computing, University of Leeds)

Business context; terminology and evolution of standards; symmetric and public key cryptography; standard cryptographic algorithms, e.g. DES, AES, RSA; digital signatures; limitations of cryptography; security review of low- and high-level Internet protocols; classic attacks; case studies of malicious software such as the Morris worm, Melissa, Nimda, SQL Slammer; threat modelling: functional decomposition, STRIDE, attack trees, risk assessment; secure system design principles; firewalls, tunnelling and VPNs; cryptographic key management; software audits; source code vulnerabilities, e.g. buffer overruns, TOC-TOU problems, lack of randomness, malicious input; system operation and maintenance issues, such as password management, virus scanning, intrusion detection, incident response.

teaching tends to occur in courses directed towards high reliability computing, rather than in a security context.

Why is Secure Software so Seldom Taught?

We are not aware of any detailed study into the reasons for the lack of teaching of secure software development, but the experts voiced reasonably consistent opinions. It was often mentioned that, unlike cryptography and forensic computing, or on major initiatives such as the NSA program for Centers of Academic Excellence in Information Assurance Education, teaching or research grant funding for secure software – indeed software development as a whole - is relatively poor. Consequently there are few active research groups, which in turn leads to a shortage of staffing willing or able to teach the subject. There are also the added difficulties of designing and running safe laboratories, as well as the cost [HU], [IRVINE].

However, there are a number of experts who believe that industry itself is at least in part responsible for the lack of security-related teaching, as the needs is not put forcibly enough to the universities. 'We teach what we think is wanted,'

was a common remark made by course directors and heads of departments.

Experts agree that further investigation into the reasons for the shortfall in teaching are required and they also support the idea of defining an outline syllabus that should be taught as part of the basic awareness proposal.

Improving Operational Security by Peer-to-Peer Information Exchange

Education and training in end-to-end security must, by definition, include operational issues. This has been a rather under-researched area. Current approaches are pragmatic and include warnings, alerts and advisories generated by vendors, government-inspired and user organisations. Historically, this information under names such as CERT or CCIRT, etc has predominantly issued from a knowledgeable centre out to less knowledgeable consumers. More recently, peer-to-peer, mechanisms with by-directional information flow have emerged, usually operating under conditions of limited disclosure. See for example, the various surveys and guides produced by the European Commission's European Network and Information Security Agency [ENISA].

The most common approach involves non, standardized, human-readable natural language exchanges, but work is underway to develop standardized, possibly machine-processable, ontologies for security messages, for instance within the [OASIS] Emergency Data Exchange Language Resource Messaging activity.

Communicating Security-Awareness to the Citizen and the Policy-Maker

Experts, particularly at European level, are also aware of a need to develop a semantic bridge between the security community and the lay public, as users and policy-makers. One example cited was the misguided belief in 'the false alternatives of security and privacy', as shown by some senior policy makers.

Secure Software Development 'Good Practice'

We have seen that business aspects and educational realities must influence the nature of secure software good practice. It is now appropriate to look specifically at defining the components of good practice itself, both in terms of what is happening (or not happening now) and with a view to proposing some pointers to longer term developments.

Top Level View of Good Practice

Beginning with a top-down look at good practice in secure software development, we find experts in complete agreement over one aspect: whatever form its individual components might take: good practice as a whole needs to be end-to-end – business opportunity and requirements, concept, outline design, build, validation, installation, operation and maintenance, and right up to product withdrawal – and comprising the full vertical stack, from coding, functional (and security) architecture, testing, specification and modelling and so on, with language and meta-language tools at the design stages, followed by static and dynamic testers, plus penetration and audit-trail etc in the operational phases. Currently there are many gaps in the armoury, both vertically and phase-wise, plus heated debate regarding the components and the degree of formality.

Lifecycle and Risk-Based Issues

Experts agree that security engineering is not at present well-integrated with software engineering practices as a whole, nor is risk properly managed within the s/w development lifecycle. In this regard, it was noted that frequently security problems arise at development boundaries and with outsourcing. Moreover, there is a need to

be more explicit as to the right places within the life-cycle for the various security activities, and, echoing comments made by the experts on business case support, the right balance of these activities also needs identification. This is significantly hindered by a lack of commonly agreed security metrics. Also experts note that while there is a body of knowledge regarding software costing, for example Boem's **CO**nstructive **CO**st **MO**del [BOEM], more research is required on the security aspects.

One approach welcomed by most experts is 'threat modelling', which has its roots in high level business perspectives but can also go into significant technical detail. Perhaps the best-known example is from Microsoft. A review of this and a number of alternatives has been conducted by the Open Web Application Security Project [OWASP]. Threat modelling might best be described as semi-structured and dependent on a degree of expert value-judgement, often expressed in natural language rather than purely formal. As such, connecting it rigorously with more mechanistic or automated lower-level tools is not without some problems.

A Word on 'Formal Methods'

At this point, it is probably worthwhile to include a few comments on 'formal methods'. One of the most difficult tasks we faced in writing consensus reports was getting agreement on this topic. What the term means, and what are its most profitable aspects, both cause considerable and quite impassioned debate. Some take it to mean 'highly mathematically rigorous', though none were prepared to state that techniques exist today that can give definitive 'secure' or 'insecure' proofs for most large-scale commercial systems. There seems to be a continuum of views regarding the beginning and end of the 'formal' spectrum, and similarly at where the term can be used and the techniques applied, from high-level specification, protocol and security policies, through provable coding, down to operating system, and from an early in the lifecycle, correct-by-specification-and-design approach to later-phase detect-and-correct approaches based on dynamic, run-time validation or penetration testing. See, for example, [WING]. Perhaps one can best get some idea of the past and current balance of topics by looking at the programmes for major conferences, e.g. [FSME05], [FM2006], [FSME08].

But however the definition is cut and employed by experts in formal methods, there seems to remain a degree of scepticism among a number of experts in other fields of software security, especially those in the commercial areas not dominated by specifications demanding highly secure solutions. This division of opinion is also apparent in the university sector where, as we noted earlier, most undergraduate security courses do not give much attention to the topic. In neither case is the reason for this clear, by it might be because, historically, formal methodology was associated with high reliability computing, an important, but somewhat niche, area of computer science.

Many of our experts do however place at least some limited support for an increasing use of more structured cum 'lightweight' formal methods, and they observe there are some indications that even the pragmatists are becoming somewhat more aware of potential benefits But they do agree that that the formal methods lobby needs to provide further explanation and justification to the unconverted. In the subsections that follow, we shall briefly outline some of the consensus views on a few of these, in order to give an outline of where things are going. Whether or not these are merely 'structured' or strictly 'formal' is left to the reader's opinion!

Modeling

The use of structured modeling methods in design specification and their associated development environments is generally welcomed. (For one example, see the Model-Driven Security with SecureUML activities at ETH Zurich [ETH]). Experts mostly support building the security modelling on top of well-established model-languages such as UML (e.g. [PELARTI], as these are more approachable by developers with less expertise in secure development, and, certainly in the case of UML, increasing taught as standard to computing undergraduates. There are, however, some dissenting views regarding the imprecision of UML, particularly from experts with a belief in techniques that are more rigorously based, and with integrating some semantic concepts of security modelling languages with, for example, UML (mis)use cases. (For some discussion on this, see [CABOT] or [MOURATIDIS]).

The semantic issue in general is one that causes some debate among experts. One example is where there exists a reasonably well-defined analysis of business risk, in terms of information assets, say. But what *is* an information asset in functional specification terms? How can it be rigorously captured for incorporation in a code-proving tool, say?

Safer Languages and Meta-Languages

Catching errors in design as early as possible is generally considered a good thing, and this is one area where 'structured', perhaps even quite 'formal' approaches are used. One active approach to a formal methodology is that of 'language-based (verifiable) security.' Mindful of comments made earlier, it is probably advisable to give an approximate definition. Roughly, it is concerned to operate mainly above operating system level, principally concerned with developing applications that are to a degree, provably robust. The key components include interpreters, rewriters, and compilers, with emphasis on issues such as strong typing, 'sandbox-like' memory constraints, proof systems, and on tools such as static analysers for checking correctness and detecting weaknesses. A comprehensive tutorial on recent language-based security is available in [MORRISETT].

Language-based security is an active research area whose current state-of-play appears to be a mixture of formal proof and pragmatics. The widespread use of JAVA and other modern languages which include elements of language-based security has improved the visibility and acceptability outside the expert community, which previously had been based on more strictly formal and less-commercially accepted languages (e.g. ADA) and specification (meta-)languages such as Z., CSP. However, even among those experts who believed very strongly in its principles, there appears to be a realization that something of a gulf still exists between theorists and their theories and most commercial software developers. As with other security approaches, it is realized that more must be done, in terms of ease-of-use, automated tools and building upon accepted practices and languages, rather than advocating drastic changes with significant commercial risk and cost.

Testing and T

In the past few years a number of tools have been offered, some commercially, to assist in the testing of systems for security flaws, at various parts in the lifecycle.

Even a rapid scan of online resources reveals many statements such as 'Web application security testing is a recent concern, its automated tools are relatively immature', [GOKHALE]. Again, 'Testing of security functions…. is often given a low priority….due to combination of cost and technical considerations, except in the case of high assurance products.' [CHANDRAMOULI].

Comments such as these are very similar to those frequently made in debates among our experts. Also, considerable difference of expert opinion on the relative merits of specific tools and their underlying approaches.

This should not be taken as a criticism, but rather as an indication that the state of the art is such as to be somewhat premature for mass-market entry. Acknowledging this, and also that all tools

had a long way to go before they could pick up most of the weaknesses in badly designed code, experts still strongly believe in the value of tools for testing software security even today. Examples mentioned (without necessarily endorsing the specific product) were vulnerability scanners (IBM), model-driven security management tools (ObjectSecurity, E2E, iO), and code property proof tools (Microsoft). They agree that tools such as these are useful but only if used correctly. This caveat is important: the experts also acknowledge that the use is inhibited by lack of skill on behalf of many users, often down to problems of usability with the tools themselves. A more automated approach is called for, but always bearing in mind that the limitations of the tool in detecting vulnerabilities (or in generating false positives) are made visible. It is generally felt that goals should be modest and the expectation should be towards automated assistance to augment human abilities, not to replace them completely.

Credibility

Adoption of a good-practice package of measures can be simply a local team leaders' choice or, as we have seen with Microsoft, mandated by senior management. But in any case, someone has had to decide that the specific measures to be adopted have demonstrated that they are reasonably cost-effective, before full roll-out. To do so, they need to have sufficient, credible evidence Experts agree that insufficient effort has been given to providing such. Clearly vendors will tend to promote their own solutions and, hopefully, more often in future provide reference sites and other open evidence, but as far as vendor-neutral advice is concerned, too little is currently available. If one looks for it, one is usually directed to academic material which, although often meeting other criteria of scientific method, has been trialed in somewhat artificial circumstances.. For example, [SOBEL], is highly regarded and frequently referenced but is based on experiments with teams of students, not software professionals.

It is recommended that in evaluating whether to fund research projects in secure software development good practice, consideration should be given to whether the project plan includes good validation procedures that are likely to be seen as credible, for example by leaders of commercial software teams.

Good-Practice Repositories

The general lack of security expertise among developers and their managers has been referred to several times. Experts welcome the idea of the creation of (online) repositories of good practice for secure development. Apart from giving encouragement and advice, these could also improve the credibility issue mentioned in the previous subsection.

EMERGING ISSUES AND SOME POINTERS TO FURTHER RESEARCH

Although the focus of this report has been on areas of current practice that experts consider require attention, including further research (some of which we have referred to), we should also briefly mention some emerging technical issues that they identified as having near-term impact upon the commercial scene and which also require more research. This short list is, of course, by no means exhaustive.

New Devices and Their Networks

The proliferation of programmable devices and their increasing complexity, raise for their designers the need to develop appropriate security measures for which the 'traditional' computing solutions may not be ideal. Past history tells us that mobile devices in particular have at best a patchy record on security. [ANDERSON]. Sometimes

the faults are 'simply' lack of appreciation of the dangers by designers unversed in the insecurity of the Internet or other public networks (another warning regarding poor education appropriate here?) or sometimes vulnerabilities inherent in the networks themselves. Many new devices may be totally unattended for most of the operational lives: one area of research receiving much attention is in networks of sensors,. See for example [FINTEU]. There is also an increasing possibility of hybrid hardware/software attacks; examples include the several successful power analysis attacks on smartcards. [KOCHER]

Technical Complexity and Compositional and Abstraction Problems

The growing complexity of systems and the interworking of distributed architectures, tiers and provisioning of service present new security challenges to designers. Ownership of data and of the administration of the systems that store, transport and compute with it, are no longer monolithic. So-called 'cloud computing' and the principles of purchasing information and computing services from third parties in general, call for new algorithms, protocols and paradigms throughout the vertical and horizontal layers and life-cycle.

Environmental Complexity

It is not just the technical complexity of individual systems or of systems-of-systems that will present new challenges, but also the total environment in which the systems operate, in particular human and organisational aspects. 'Security' methods are insufficient in dealing with this: the emphasis needs to be on preserving 'trustworthiness' as a whole. Integral with this is a shift of emphasis towards risk-driven secure software development, at all stages of the lifecycle.

Qualitative/Probabilistic Notions of Security and Trust

Furthermore, more attention needs to be given to research into technical level for managing situations where trust is no longer a binary, all-or-none, concept, for example in trading relationships and social networking.

CONCLUSION AND RECOMMENDATIONS

Experts agree that, although some have appreciated the benefits of structured, secure software development good-practice many, probably most, developers of software are either insufficiently skilled to do so, or are simply skeptical about its added value. Furthermore, experts agree that initiatives to improve the state of practice at the lower end, would have significant impact on the security of software in the short and medium term, probably greater than activities directed at the state of the art. The lack of security education at university level is recognised and, as the causes are not clear, these should be investigated further and followed by remedial action.

Acknowledgement of this lack of adequate education and understanding of security issues in the profession needs to be a major driver of research into new tools and practices: wise developers will not use what they cannot understand, whereas foolish ones will misinterpret the results. Thus (naïve) user-friendliness and automation are important.

However, these measures alone will not sufficiently tackle the problem: there is a need to address the lack of willingness, even among the competent, to accept the benefits of secure software development good practice. Experts agree that more needs to be done to provide credible, unbiased evidence that there is a sound business case for secure software development good practice, even in areas under severe commercial pressures. Apart from demonstrating that tangible shorter-term gains can be achieved by incremental changes to existing practices, preferably mainly using existing staff, languages and tools, the consideration of benefits must extend backwards in time to embrace legacy systems and forwards to avoid costly obsolescence or lock-in. Research therefore should to be biased towards vendor neutrality, compatibility with commercially exploited platforms and languages (or at least, graceful, relatively pain-free evolution from them). Suggested improvements need to slot together to cover the whole development life-cycle and the balance of resource allocation across this lifecycle needs to be explicit. Above all, validation of proposed solutions needs to be much more credible than at present.

In short, research agendas into secure software development good practice need to take serious cognisance of the limited skill base of the mass of developers and the scepticism of many of their team leaders and business managers regarding the benefits that might accrue to their bottom line.

REFERENCES

Anderson, R. (2001). Security Engineering. New York: Wiley.

Association of Computing Machinery. (2001) *Computer Science Body of Knowledge*. Retrieved January 2009 from Online at http://www.sigcse.org/cc2001/cs-csbok.html

Boem, B. (1981). *Software engineering economics*. Englewood Cliffs, NJ: Prentice-Hall.

Cabot, J. & Zannone, N. (n.d.). *Towards an Integrated Framework fo rModel-driven Security Engineering* Work supported by the Spanish Ministry of Education and Science (project TIN2005-06053) the Hyperion project founded by Canada's NSERC.

Carnegie-Mellon Software Engineering Institute. (n.d.). *Making the Business Case for Software Security*. Retrieved January 2009 from http://www.sei.cmu.edu////sr001.cfm

Chandramouli, R., & Blackburn, M. (2004). *Automated Testing of Security Functions using a combined Model & Interface driven Approach*. Proceedings of the 37th Hawaii International Conference on System Sciences.

Code, S. (n.d.). Retrieved January 2009 from http://www.safecode.org/

Criteria, C. (n.d.). Retrieved January 2009 from http://www.commoncriteriaportal.org/.html

Davidson, M. A. (2006). *The case for information assurance*. Edinburgh: Keynote Address.

ENISA (European Network and Information Security Agency). (2009). Retrieved January 2009 from http://www.enisa.europa.eu/

European Future Internet Portal. (2009). Retrieved January 2009 from http://www.future-internet.eu//-projects.html

European Future Internet Portal. (2010). Retrieved January 2009 from http://www.future-internet.eu//-projects.html

Global Watch Mission Report, D. T. I. (2006). *Changing nature of information security: A UK perspective on US experiences*. Anon.

Howard M. & Lipner S.(2006). *The Security Development Lifecycle*. Microsoft Publications Jun 28, 2006

Hu, J. H. Dirk C., Christoph M.(2004). A Virtual Laboratory for IT Security Education. In *Proceedings of the Conference on Information Systems in E-Business and EGovernment* (EMISA), Luxembourg, pp. 60-71

Irvine, C. E. (1999) Amplifying Security Education in the Laboratory. In *Proceedings of the 1st World Conference on Information Security Education* (IFIP TCII WC 11.8), pp. 139-146.

Kocher, P., & Joshua Ja, E. Benjamin Jun. (1999). *Differential Power Analysis*. Retrieved January 2009 from http://www.cryptography.com//.//.pdf

Linuxsecurity.com. (n.d.). Retrieved January 2009 from http://www.linuxsecurity.com/////

Logan, P. Y. (1997). Crafting an Undergraduate Information Security Emphasis Within Information Technology. *Journal of Information Systems Education, 13*(3).

Morriset, G. (2003). *Tutorial on language-based security*, given at the 2003 ACM PLDI San Diego. Retreived January 2009 from http://www.cs.cornell.edu/////.ppt#256,1,Tutorial on Language-Based Security

Mouratidis, H., & Giorgini, P. (2006). *Integrating Security and Software Engineering: Advances and Future Vision*. Hershey, PA: IGI Global.

O'Hear, A. (1991). *An Introduction to the Philosophy of Science*. New York: Oxford University Press.

OASIS. (2009). Retrieved January 2009 from http://www.oasis-open.org//_home.php?wg_abbrev=emergency

O.M.G. (2010).Retrieved January 2009 from http://www.omg.org//

OWASP. (n.d.). Retrieved January 2009 from http://www.owasp.org and threat modeling can be found at http://www.owasp.org/.php/_Risk_Modeling#Alternative_Threat_Modeling_Systems

Peralta, K. P., & Alex, M. Orozco, Avelino F. Zorzo, Flavio M. Oliveira.(2008) Specifying Security Aspects in UML Models. In *Proceedings of the 2008 International Conference on Model Driven Engineering Languages and Systems*. Toulouse, France, September 28, 2008

PHP. (2009). Retrieved January 2009 from http://www.php.net/

President's Information Technology Advisory Committee. (2007) *Cyber Security: A Crisis of Prioritization.*

Proceedings of. *3rd ACM Workshop on Formal Methods in Security Engineering: From Specifications to Code.* (2005, November). Alexandria, VA, USA. Retrieved January 2009 from http://www.ti.informatik.uni-kiel.de/~kuesters//.html

Proceedings of. *14th International Symposium on Formal Methods. Hamilton, Canada,* (2006, August) LNCS. New York: Springer Berlin/Heidelberg

Proceedings of. *6rd ACM Workshop on Formal Methods in Security Engineering.* (2008, October). Alexandria, VA, U.S.A. Retrieved January 2009 from http://www.cs.utexas.edu/~shmat//

Quality Assurance Agency. (n.d.). *Subject benchmark statements: Computing.* (undated) Retrieved January 2009 from http://www.qaa.ac.uk////.asp

Rajendra, G., & Madhura, H. *(n.d.). A New Approach to Application Security Testing Tool Design* Retrieved January 2009 from http://www.aztecsoft.com//Aztecsoft_Whitepaper_Approach_to_Application_Security_Testing_Tool_Design.pdf

Security Transcends Technology, I. S. C. (n.d.). Retrieved January 2009 from http://www.isc2.org/

Sobel, A E Kelly & Clarkson, M R.(2002), Formal Methods Application: An Empirical Tale of Software Development. *IEEE Trans on Software Development, 28*(3).

Swiss Federal Institute of Technology. (n.d.). Retrieved January 2009 from http://www.infsec.ethz.ch/people/doserj/mds

Whyte, B. (2008).*The teaching of security issues to computing undergraduates in England: a cause for concern?* Retrieved January 2009 from http://www.ktn.qinetiq-

Whyte, B., & Harrison, J. (2008). *Secure Software Development: a White Paper (Software Security Failures: who should correct them and how).* Cyber Security Knowledge Transfer Network. Retrieved January 2009 from www.ktn.qinetiq-tim.net/content/files/groups/securesoft/SSDSIG_softwareSecurityFailures.pdf

Wing, J. M.(1998). *A Symbolic Relationship Between Formal Methods And Security.* Carnegie Mellon University report CMU-CS-98-118.

Section 1
Security Patterns

Chapter 2
Using Security Patterns to Develop Secure Systems

Eduardo B. Fernandez
Florida Atlantic University, USA

Nobukazu Yoshioka
GRACE Center, National Institute of Informatics, Japan

Hironori Washizaki
Waseda University, Japan

Jan Jurjens
Technical University of Dortmund, Germany

Michael VanHilst
Florida Atlantic University, USA

Guenther Pernul
University of Regensburg, Germany

ABSTRACT

This chapter describes ongoing work on the use of patterns in the development of secure systems. The work reflects a collaboration among five research centers on three continents. Patterns are applied to all aspects of development, from domain analysis and attack modeling to basic design, and to all aspects of the systems under development, from the database and infrastructure to policies, monitoring, and forensics. The chapter, provides an overview of the method of development involving the full range of patterns, and describes many recent contributions from the many research threads being pursued within the collaboration. Finally, future directions of research in the use of patterns are described.

INTRODUCTION

We initiated an international collaboration between our security groups a few years ago, centered on methodologies to build secure systems using patterns. We describe here where we are now and where we are going. This chapter should be considered a survey of our work and not an attempt to present new work or to introduce in detail the

DOI: 10.4018/978-1-61520-837-1.ch002

models presented here, for that we refer the reader to our previous publications. We also provide a section comparing our work to others but again in each paper we relate our work to others in more detail. In particular, we have worked or we are working on:

- **Secure software development methodology:** We have worked on a general methodology to build secure systems and have produced until now some specific aspects of it, which are described below. Of course, these aspects have value independently of this methodology and can be applied to other methodologies or on their own.

- **Modeling and Classification of security patterns:** We have tried to provide a precise characterization of security patterns that can be used as a basis for classification. A good classification makes the application of the patterns much easier along the software lifecycle. It also helps understand the nature and value of the patterns. Another objective is to identify which patterns are missing.

- **Misuse patterns:** A misuse pattern describes, from the point of view of the attacker, how a type of attack is performed (what units it uses and how), analyzes the ways of stopping the attack by enumerating possible security patterns that can be applied for this purpose, and describes how to trace the attack once it has happened by appropriate collection and observation of forensics data. They can be used in the lifecycle to prevent the occurrence of known types of attacks and to evaluate a completed system.

- **Characterization and selection of access control models:** Access control is a fundamental aspect of security. There are many variations of the basic access control models and it is confusing for a software developer to select an appropriate model

for her application. We have defined a way to clarify their relationships and a way to guide designers in selecting an appropriate model.

- **Databases in secure applications:** Most applications need to include databases to store the persistent information, which constitutes most of the information assets of the institution. We have studied the effect of databases on the security of a system under development.

The following sections describe these aspects in detail.

SECURE SOFTWARE DEVELOPMENT METHODOLOGY

A good methodology for design is fundamental to produce secure systems. In Fernandez, Yoshioka, Washizaki & Jürjens (2007) we defined some requirements for such a methodology. Principles to build secure systems have been defined in some classical papers (Saltzer & Schroeder, 1975) and textbooks (Viega & McGraw, 2001), patterns may apply them implicitly. Specific requirements include:

- At each stage, there is guidance on where to apply and how to select appropriate security patterns.
- There are guidelines for pattern selection to satisfy functional requirements or restrictions at each stage.
- There are guidelines to find vulnerabilities and threats in a system.
- There are guidelines to select patterns to mitigate the identified threats.
- The models of the patterns should be relatively detailed and precise, using languages such as UML and OCL to describe the solutions.

- There should be a clear way to apply formalizations at least to specific parts of the design.

Based on these requirements we chose object-oriented design as the most appropriate software methodology because of its ability for abstraction, well-defined life cycle, intuitive nature, and being known by many developers. While it has some limitations, the fact that it is a methodology known to many developers makes it of practical value.

We had proposed in the past separate methodologies (Fernandez, Larrondo-Petrie, Sorgente & VanHilst, 2006, Jürjens, 2004, Yoshioka, 2006). We found that they have many common and complementary aspects and we proposed a combination of them in Fernandez, Yoshioka, Washizaki & Jürjens, (2007). This methodology appears to satisfy all the requirements described above, although it is still not complete. A main idea in the proposed methodology is that security principles should be applied at every stage of the software lifecycle and that each stage can be tested for compliance with security principles. Another basic idea is the use of patterns at each stage. A security pattern describes a solution to a recurrent problem and providing a complete set of them, appropriately classified, can be very useful to developers with little experience on security. The methodology includes the following stages:

- **Domain analysis stage:** A business model is defined. Legacy systems are identified and their security implications analyzed. Domain, institutional, and regulatory constraints are identified. These constraints become policies that apply to the complete system and can be defined in the domain model in the form of patterns. From business goals or institutional points of view, assets in the domain are identified. The suitability of the development team is assessed, possibly leading to added training. This phase is performed only once for each

new domain. The possible selections for specialized database architectures and other specific platform requirements should be determined at this point.

- **Requirements stage:** Use cases define the required interactions with the system. Applying the principle that security must start from the highest levels, it makes sense to relate attacks to use cases. Activity diagrams indicate access to existing and created objects and are a good way to determine which data should be protected. Threats in each activity define misuse activities, which might threaten assets which we need to protect. Since many possible threats may be identified we should apply risk analysis to prune them according to their impact and probability of occurrence. Any requirements for degree of security should be expressed as part of the use cases. We then determine which policies would stop these attacks. These include aspects such as mutual authentication to stop impostors, authorization based on roles, need for logging accesses, etc. From the use cases we can also determine the needed rights for each actor and thus apply a need-to-know policy. The security test cases for the complete system are also defined at this stage.

- **Analysis stage:** Analysis patterns can be used to build the conceptual model in a more reliable and efficient way. The policies defined in the requirements can now be expressed as abstract security models, e.g. access matrix, represented as patterns (Schumacher, Fernandez, Hybertson, Buschmann, & Sommerlad, 2006). The model selected must correspond to the type of application; for example, multilevel models have not been successful for medical applications. One can build a conceptual model where repeated applications of a security model pattern realize the rights determined from use cases.

In fact, analysis patterns can be built with predefined authorizations according to the roles in their use cases. Instances of patterns for authentication, logging, and secure channels are also applied at this level (Fernandez & Yuan, 2007). Note that the model and the security patterns should define precisely the requirements of the problem, not its software solution. UML is a good semi-formal approach for defining policies, avoiding the need for ad-hoc policy languages. The addition of OCL (Object Constraint Language) can make the approach more formal. An alternative is the use of UMLSec (Jürjens, 2004), which adds stereotypes to UML to describe the security requirements of the application.

- **Design stage:** When we have found the needed policies and added their pattern representation to the conceptual model, we can select mechanisms that correspond to their concrete software realizations. A specific security model, e.g. Role-Based Access Control (RBAC), is now implemented in terms of software units. Misuse patterns at the design level are useful to analyze how the attacks operate and the security patterns related to the attacks are used to implement the policies. User interfaces should correspond to use cases and may be used to enforce the authorizations defined in the analysis stage when users interact with the system. Components can be secured by using authorization rules for Java or .NET components. Security restrictions can be applied in the distribution architecture; for example, access control for web services. Deployment diagrams can define secure configurations to be used by security administrators. System behavior fragments can be used to consider also performance aspects. A multilayer architecture is needed to enforce the security constraints defined at the application level.

In each level we use patterns to represent appropriate security mechanisms. Security constraints must be mapped between levels. Iteration of the application of misuse patterns and security patterns may be useful to remove security holes. The persistent aspects of the conceptual model are typically mapped into relational databases. The design of the database architecture is performed according to the requirements from the uses cases for the level of security needed and the security model adopted in the analysis stage.

- **Implementation stage:** We now reflect in the code the security rules defined in the design stage. Because these rules are expressed as classes, associations, and constraints, they can be implemented as classes in object-oriented languages. In this stage one can also select specific security packages or COTS components, e.g., a firewall product or a cryptographic package. Some of the patterns identified earlier in the cycle can be replaced by COTS components (these can be tested to see if they include a similar pattern). Performance aspects become now important and may require iterations. Attack scenarios derived from attack patterns and test cases are useful to examine systems to find security holes.

An important aspect for the complete design is assurance. We could verify each pattern used but this does not verify that the system using them is secure. We can still say that since we used a careful and systematic methodology with verified and tested patterns, the design should provide a good level of security. The set of patterns can be shown to be able to stop or mitigate the identified threats (Fernandez, Yoshioka & Washizaki, 2009b).

MODELING AND CLASSIFICATION OF SECURITY PATTERNS

A fundamental tool for any methodology based on patterns is a good catalog. This catalog should be not only complete, covering every stage and architectural level, but also organized in such a way that the designer can find the right pattern at the right moment in the development cycle.

The solution section of a pattern must be given in a generic form and be an abstraction of best practices. It must also provide enough detail and guidance for developers to incorporate them in their applications. This implies that the solution should be expressed as precisely as possible and be complemented with textual descriptions and examples. As indicated earlier, a good way to present the solution is in the form of UML models, which are understood by most software developers and can be easily converted into executable code. UML models can be enhanced with OCL constraints for greater precision (Warmer & Kleppe, 2003). Our patterns in Fernandez & Pernul (2006) and Morrison & Fernandez (2006) are examples of our style. Purely formal definitions of the solution have the problem that most software developers cannot understand them. In addition, there are many formal notations, without any of them becoming an accepted standard. Other authors take the opposite view and prefer short (thumbnail) pattern descriptions, indicating mostly the general idea of the pattern. This approach could be useful to provide a perspective of what is available for a particular domain and a catalog of this type of patterns could complement a more detailed catalog to serve as a roadmap. A requirement for a pattern is that the solution it describes has been used in at least three real systems (Buschmann, Meunier, Rohnert, Sommerlad & Stal, 1996, Gamma, Helm, Johnson & Vlissides, 1994). This is consistent with the idea of patterns as best practices. However, a pattern can also describe solutions that have not been used (or have been used only once) but appear general

and useful for several situations. Because of this, we have included sometimes both types: good practices patterns and useful solutions patterns.

Patterns can be defined at several levels of abstraction. The highest level is typically a principle or a very fundamental concept, e.g. the concept of Reference Monitor, which indicates that every access must be intercepted and checked. Another example shows that firewalls, database authorization systems, and operating system access control systems are special cases of access control systems. Figure 1 shows a generalization hierarchy showing that a Firewall pattern is a concrete version of a Reference Monitor. There are four basic types of firewalls, which filter at different architectural levels: the Application (User level) Firewall, the Proxy Firewall (system application), the Stateful Firewall, and the Packet Filter Firewall. An XML Firewall is a specialized type of Application Firewall. One can combine Stateful firewalls with Proxy or Packet Filter firewalls to produce even more specialized types of firewalls such as Stateful Proxy firewall, which combines aspects of both Proxy and Stateful firewalls (Schumacher, et al., 2006). Descriptions of all these patterns can be found in the website of the F.A.U.'s Secure Systems Research Group (2009).

We started with an initial classification (Fernandez, Washizaki, Yoshioka, Kubo & Fukazawa, 2008), where we used three aspects or dimensions to classify patterns: the architectural layers where the patterns belong, the security concerns considered by the patterns, and relationships between the patterns' textual descriptions. Figure 2 shows some patterns classified according to these criteria. Each column describes some concern; in particular we show three concerns: Filtering (using firewalls), Enforcement of access control (using variations of the Reference Monitor), and Authentication. Each concern may appear in multiple levels; for example, we may authenticate at the operating system level or the web service level, or the distribution level.

Figure 1. Firewall patterns generalization hierarchy

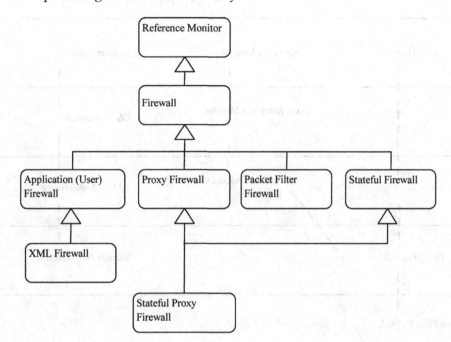

We then developed a multidimensional approach, which provides a finer classification (VanHilst, Fernandez & Braz, 2009a, VanHilst, Fernandez & Braz, 2009b). We address pattern classification and problem coverage through the use of a multi-dimensional matrix of concerns. Each dimension of the matrix presents a range of concerns along a single continuum, with a simple concept defined by two polar opposites, like internal and external or begin and end. The categories along each dimension should be easily understood and represent widely used and accepted classifications with respect to that concept. In addition to the dimensions mentioned earlier, another dimension would be a list of lifecycle activities, covering domain analysis, requirements, problem analysis, design, implementation, integration, deployment (including configuration), operation, maintenance and disposal. A pattern applies to a lifecycle stage if a developer could use knowledge from the pattern in performing tasks at that stage. Another dimension is component source, ranging for completely internal new

code, to completely external, like a web service. In-between categories include legacy code, library components, outsourced, and COTS. Response to stages of attack is a third dimension, from avoidance of an initial intent, through deterrence, prevention, detection, mitigation, recovery, and investigation (or forensics).

As an example of the use of multiple dimensions, the classification of the XACML Access Control Evaluator pattern is shown in Figure 3. This pattern defines the reference monitor for XACML rules. The classification includes the dimensions mentioned early and also dimensions for domains and constraints (mechanism, human (operator or developer), organizational, and regulatory). Distinctions on the Component Source dimension were considered not significant – hence all are valid. The XACML Access Control Evaluator pattern is part of a pattern language and is related to an XACML protocol pattern for the domain analysis stage, and a more general Access Control abstract pattern for the analysis stage. Early experience indicates that this clas-

Figure 2. Types of patterns based on levels, concerns, and relationships

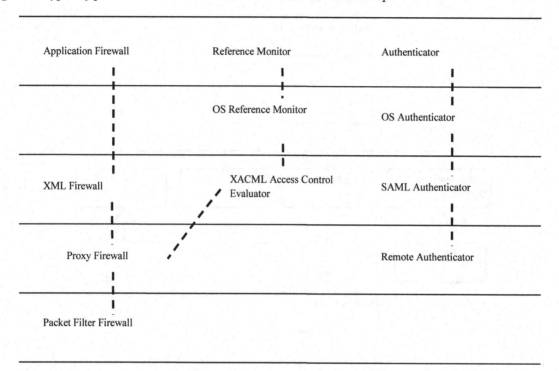

Figure 3. Classifications of the XACML access control evaluator

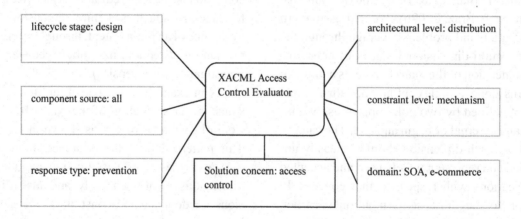

sification approach is feasible and offers many desirable properties.

We introduced the concept of Dimension Graph (DG), to formalize this classification (Washizaki, Fernandez, Maruyama, Kubo, & Yoshioka, 2009). DGs describe patterns in a multidimensional space relating each pattern to a set of dimensions of interest, i.e. they formalize the multidimensional classification defined earlier. Therefore, DGs are useful to understand properties of each pattern, and to classify precisely the pattern. DGs can be modeled by using details of the target pattern documents and expertise in the patterns.

Figure 4. Metamodel for pattern representation

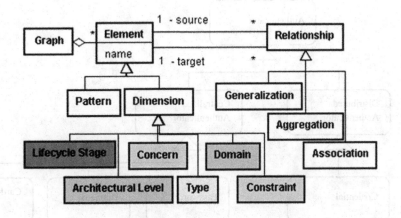

A property of a pattern can be considered as a relationship between the pattern and one of all possible classification dimensions, such as the lifecycle stage (i.e. when to use a pattern) and the concern (i.e. what kind of concerns a pattern addresses). We defined a metamodel to describe the relationships of pattern-to-dimension and pattern-to-pattern uniformly. Figure 4 shows a metamodel to represent patterns as a UML class diagram. The relations of pattern-to-dimension and pattern-to-pattern can be modeled uniformly at the instance level, by using two associations between Element and Relationship, and a generalization hierarchy whose root is Element. In the hierarchy, Element has two children: Pattern and Dimension; therefore it is possible to model both relationships between patterns and between patterns and dimensions. Moreover, it is also possible to describe relationships between dimensions

In the analysis stage of software development we are trying to make the problem precise, we are not concerned with software aspects. From a security point of view we only want to indicate which specific security mechanisms are needed, not their implementation. For this purpose, we introduced the idea of abstract security patterns which define abstract security mechanisms incorporating only the fundamental functions of the specific mechanism. Abstract patterns can also

help for classification and systematization of patterns. Figure 5 shows an abstract Authentication pattern which defines the basic functions of any authentication mechanism. More concrete or specialized patterns are defined for specific environments, e.g. credentials for any types of distributed environments (Morrison & Fernandez, 2006). X.509 certificates for computer distributed environments, and SAML assertions for web services are special types of credentials. The specialized patterns all have the basic properties of the abstract authentication pattern but they perform this authentication process in specific ways. This idea can also be used to relate different types of patterns as shown in Figure 2 (Figure 1 was another example, where Firewall ia an abstract pattern).

MISUSE PATTERNS

A misuse pattern describes, from the point of view of an attacker, a generic way of performing an attack that takes advantage of the specific vulnerabilities of some environment or context. It also presents a way to counteract its development as well as a way to trace back the information needed at each stage of the attack. We introduced this concept in Fernandez, Pelaez, & Larrondo-Petrie

Figure 5. The authentication hierarchy

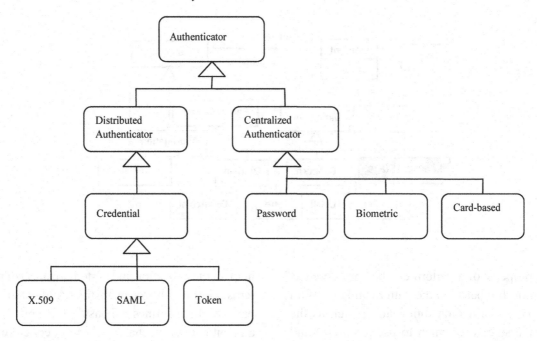

(2007) under the name of attack pattern. Independently, the NII group had developed a similar concept (Yoshioka, Honiden & Finkelstein, 2004) and we merged the two approaches in Fernandez, Yoshioka & Washizaki (2009a). We adopted the name "misuse" pattern because the name attack pattern had already been used for a slightly different concept. A misuse is an unauthorized use of information and our emphasis is in how the misuse is performed, i.e., the steps of the attack and the system units used to perform the misuse.

Figure 6 presents a UML model that describes the sections of a misuse pattern. We describe below the components of the Misuse Pattern class, which correspond to sections of the template used for its desciption.

Intent or thumbnail description: A short description of the intended purpose of the pattern (which problem it solves for an attacker). The context describes the generic environment including the conditions under which the misuse may occur. This may include minimal defenses present in the system as well as typical vulnerabilities of the system. The context is specified using a de-

ployment diagram of the relevant portions of the system as well as sequence or collaboration diagrams that show the normal use of the system.

Problem: From a hacker's perspective, the problem is how to find a way to attack the system The forces indicate what factors may be required in order to accomplish the attack and in what way. The solution describes how the misuse can be accomplished and the expected results of the attack. UML class diagrams describe the relevant portions of the system under attack. Sequence or collaboration diagrams show the exchange of messages needed to accomplish the attack. State or activity diagrams may add further detail. Attack patterns which are necessary for the misuse are also listed here (an attack pattern is a specific action, e.g. a buffer overflow). **Known uses:** This section describes specific incidents where this attack has been used. **Consequences:** Discusses the benefits and drawbacks of a misuse pattern from the attacker's viewpoint. The section on **Countermeasures and Forensics** describes the security measures necessary in order to stop, mitigate, or trace this type of attack. This im-

Figure 6. UML class model for misuse patterns

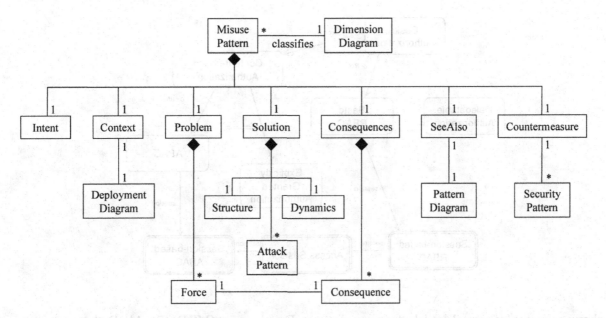

plies an enumeration of which security patterns are effective against this attack. From a forensic viewpoint, it describes what information can be obtained at each stage tracing back the attack and what can be deduced from this data in order to identify this specific attack. Finally, it may indicate what additional information should be collected at the involved units to improve forensic analysis. Each pattern may also carry information about the time it takes to apply its solution (Yoshioka, Honiden & Finkelstein, 2004). **Related Patterns (See also):** Discusses other misuse patterns with different objectives but performed in a similar way or with similar objectives but performed in a different way. It also considers patterns of complementary misuses o patterns of attacks that support the misuse. These patterns can be related using a misuse pattern diagram.

We have applied this approach to the construction of a catalog of the most typical attack patterns in VoIP (Pelaez, Fernandez, & Larrondo-Petrie, 2009). We need to expand this catalog to make it of more general use. Note that as usual, patterns provide only guidelines, not plug-in solutions; that

is, for each new application the patterns provide guidelines about what to expect, where to look, and how to start, their solutions must be tailored to the specific environment.

CHARACTERIZATION AND SELECTION OF ACCESS CONTROL MODELS

Access control is a fundamental aspect of security. Because of its importance there are many variations of the basic access control models, emphasizing different aspects. It is confusing for a software developer to select an appropriate model for her application (Fernandez, Pernul & Larrondo-Petrie, 2008). In practice, this confusion results in designers adopting only simple models and missing the richness of other models. We have tried to clarify this panorama through the use of patterns. A pattern diagram shows relationships between patterns (represented by rectangles with rounded corners). In particular, we use pattern diagrams to navigate the pattern space. Figure 7

Figure 7. Relationships between access control patterns

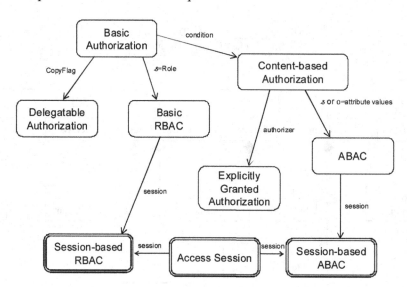

shows some access control models; for example, a Basic Authorization pattern has components *(s,o,t)*; making *s* a role we get the Basic Role-Based Access Control (RBAC) pattern. Adding sessions we obtain Session-based RBAC, and so on. A subproduct of our work is the analysis of which patterns are available for use and which need to be written. The goal here is to provide the designer of a secure system with a navigation tool that she can use to select an appropriate pattern from a catalog of security patterns. Our examples show how to compose new access control models by adding features to an existing pattern and how to define patterns by analogy. The patterns with a double border are the ones discussed in (Fernandez & Pernul, 2006).

Using our approach of mapping relationships, we can study complex models, e.g. Attribute-Based Access Control (ABAC), where the attributes of the subject and object determine access, and relate them to simpler patterns (Priebe, Fernandez, Mehlau, & Pernul, 2004). We can combine access control with auxiliary functions such as sessions (Fernandez & Pernul, 2006). Pattern maps are also useful to perform semi-automatic model transformations as required for Model-Driven Development (MDD). For MDD, they can serve as metamodels of possible solutions being added at each transformation.

A pattern in the pattern diagram shows how it is related to other patterns. We believe that this perspective can help developers to align their needs with the selection of appropriate access control models. The selected access control pattern not only guides the conceptual security of the application but later it also guides the actual implementation of the model. We can navigate the pattern diagram because patterns are composable with respect to features, i.e. adding a feature (perhaps embodied by another pattern) produces a new pattern with extra features. This aspect of their composition can be understood in terms of object-oriented models, where a new feature implies the addition of a new class or of a class attribute.

Our focus on the relationships among access control models and patterns has led us also to discover the need for new security patterns: Subject, Object, Labeled Security, DAC, MAC. These are concepts with models for which there are no patterns or which are needed to precisely represent some aspects of existing patterns. For example, Labeled Security is necessary to implement mandatory multilevel models. Access control patterns give us also the possibility of evaluating commercial products: we can see if the product contains the corresponding pattern in its design.

ADDING DATABASES TO THE SECURE METHODOLOGY

A design aspect which is interesting and not much studied is the incorporation of databases as part of the secure architecture (Fernandez, Jürjens, Yoshioka & Washizaki, 2008). The database system is a fundamental aspect for security because it stores the persistent information, which constitutes most of the information assets of the institution. We presented some ideas on how to make sure that the database system has the same level of security as the rest of the secure application.

An interesting problem in when incorporating database management systems is the mapping from the conceptual security model (that may apply to a collection of DBMSs) to the authorization system of a specific database. For example, security constraints defined in a conceptual UML model defining authorizations in terms of classes (Fernandez & Yuan, 2007) must be mapped to an SQL-based authorization system which defines authorizations in terms of relations. Clearly, whatever is defined in the common conceptual model must be reflected in the DBMS.

RELATED WORK

A general methodology for developing security-critical software which has common aspects with this methodology has been proposed in Jürjens (2004). It makes use of an extension of the Unified Modeling Language (UML) to include security-relevant information, which is called UMLsec. The approach is supported by extensive automated tool-support for performing a security analysis of

the UMLsec models against the security requirements and has been used in a variety of industrial projects (Best, Jürjens, & Nuseibeh, 2007). As mentioned earlier, we are incorporating some parts of this model in our methodology.

Mouratidis and his group use the Secure Tropos methodology to model security. Their work includes modeling requirements (Mouratidis, Jürjens & Fox, 2006, Mouratidis & Giorgini, 2004). They have also considered other stages; for example how to test security along the life-cycle (Mouratidis & Giorgini, 2004). They use patterns. However, instead of UML, they use special diagrams expressed in a special notation, which has its advantages and disadvantages. By connecting security requirements to misuse patterns, our approach provides more context on the specific threats to a protected resource. However, this approach is complementary to ours in several respects.

There have been several attempts to classify security patterns. Hafiz, Adamczyk & Johnson (2007) proposed several classification dimensions to organize security patterns. One of these is based on security objectives, such as confidentiality, integrity, and availability. Their dimensions are subsumed in our set of dimensions (concerns). Rosado, Gutierrez, Fernandez-Medina, & Piattini (2006) related security requirements to security patterns, and classified security patterns into just two categories: architectural patterns and design patterns. Weiss and Mouratidis (2009) have looked at the issue of selecting security patterns for fulfilling security requirements.

Unfortunately, much of the work by others on classifying security patterns has been motivated by a desire to create taxonomies with which to group or distinguish patterns. As a result, the proposed classifications have dealt with only a few dimensions of classification and arranged them hierarchically, rather than treating them uniformly as independent properties of facets. It is difficult with those approaches for users to select and/or find appropriate patterns from a number of patterns with any precision, or from the viewpoints of both pattern relations and properties. Our multidimensional classification is an attempt to improve on the other approaches.

CONCLUSIONS AND FUTURE WORK

Although this collaboration has been unstructured and between people far apart, it has resulted in a significant amount of work. This is due in part to the similarities of our interests and objectives. On his part, the first author and his group have produced a variety of security patterns (Secure Systems Research Group, 2009), fundamental to the application of the methods proposed here.

Future work includes:

- **Formalization and model checking.** As shown by the template of Figure 6 and by the templates normally used to describe patterns, patterns include textual descriptions as well as precise models. The textual descriptions are important for usability, so a pattern should not be fully formalized. However, the solution section and perhaps the related patterns sections can be formalized. How then do we incorporate formal methods into our secure methodology? We are investigating to augment patterns in ways that aid the process of producing formally verifiable systems, or at least formalizing aspects of systems.
- **Verification of security.** We cannot prove formally that a system produced in our approach is secure, due to the complexity of the applications we consider. We can however, verify that all identified threats are covered. Preliminary ideas are shown in Fernandez, Yoshioka & Washizaki (2009b).
- **Tool support.** Threat enumeration and the application of patterns following an MDA approach are highly desirable (Delessy

& Fernandez, 2008). We need to develop tools to make development systematic.

- **Once we have enumerated the threats of a system, we define the policies needed to stop or mitigate them.** However, it is not simple to go from these policies to security patterns that describe the actual configuration of the system (Braz, Fernandez & VanHilst, 2008), this aspect needs more work.
- **Run-time monitoring.** How do we measure if a design is actually keeping a system secure? To date, there is little work on this topic (Nagaratnam, Nadalin, Hondo, McIntosh & Austel, 2005).

REFERENCES

Best, B., Jürjens, J., & Nuseibeh, B. (2007). Model-Based Security Engineering of Distributed Information Systems Using UMLsec. In *Proceedings of the 29th International Conference on Software Engineering* (pp. 581-590). New York: ACM.

Braz, F., Fernandez, E. B., & VanHilst, M. (2008). Eliciting security requirements through misuse activities. In *Proceedings of the 19th International Workshop on Database and Expert Systems Applications* (pp. 328-333). Los Alamitos, CA: IEEE Computer Society.

Buschmann, F., Meunier, R., Rohnert, H., Sommerlad, P., & Stal, M. (1996). Pattern-Oriented Software Architecture: *Vol. 1. A System of Patterns*. West Sussex, England: John Wiley & Sons.

Delessy, N., & Fernandez, E. B. (2008). A pattern-driven security process for SOA applications. In *Proceedings of the 3rd International Conference on Availability, Reliability, and Security* (pp. 416-421). Washington DC: IEEE Computer Society.

Fernandez, E. B., Jürjens, J., Yoshioka, N., & Washizaki, H. (2008). Incorporating database systems into a secure software development methodology. In *Proceedings of the 2008 19th International Conference on Database and Expert Systems Application* (pp. 310-314). Washington DC: IEEE Computer Society.

Fernandez, E. B., Larrondo-Petrie, M. M., Sorgente, T., & VanHilst, M. (2006). A Methodology to Develop Secure Systems Using Patterns. In Mouratidis, H., & Giorgini, P. (Eds.), *Integrating Security and Software Engineering: Advances and Future Vision* (pp. 107–126). Hershey, PA: IDEA Group.

Fernandez, E. B., Pelaez, J. C., & Larrondo-Petrie, M. M. (2007). Attack patterns: A new forensic and design tool. In P. Craiger & S. Shenoi (Eds.) *Advances in Digital Forensics III: Proceedings of the Third Annual IFIP WG 11.9 International Conference on Digital Forensics* (pp. 345-357). Berlin, Germany: Springer.

Fernandez, E. B., & Pernul, G. (2006). Patterns for session-based access control. In *Proceedings of the Conference on Pattern Languages of Programs*. Hillside Group. Retrieved November 25, 2009, from http://hillside.net/plop/2006/.

Fernandez, E. B., Pernul, G., & Larrondo-Petrie, M. M. (2008). Patterns and pattern diagrams for access control. In S. Furnell; S.K. Katsikas, & A. Lioy (Eds.) *LNCS 5185: Trust, Privacy and Security in Digital Business: 5th International Conference on Trust and Privacy in Digital Business* (pp. 38-47). Heidelberg, Germany: Springer.

Fernandez, E. B., Washizaki, H., Yoshioka, N., Kubo, A., & Fukazawa, Y. (2008). Classifying security patterns., In Y. Zhang, G. Yu, & E. Bertino (Eds.) *LNCS 4976 Progress in WWW Research and Development: Proceedings of the 10th Asia-Pacific Web Conference* (pp. 342-347). Heidelberg, Germany: Springer.

Fernandez, E. B., Yoshioka, N., & Washizaki, H. (2009a). Modeling misuse patterns. In *Proceedings of the International Conference on Availability, Reliability and Security* (pp. 566-571). Los Alamitos, CA: IEEE Computer Society.

Fernandez, E. B., Yoshioka, N., & Washizaki, H. (2009b). Security patterns and quality. In H. Washizaki, N. Yoshioka, E.B.Fernandez, & J. Jürjens (Eds.) *Proceedings of the Third International Workshop on Software Patterns and Quality* (pp. 46-47).*)*, in conjuction with OOPSLA 2009. Retrieved November 25, 2009 from http://grace-center.jp/downloads/GRACE-TR-2009-07.pdf.

Fernandez, E. B., Yoshioka, N., Washizaki, H., & Jürjens, J. (2007). Using security patterns to build secure systems. *Proceedings of the 1st International Workshop on Software Patterns and Quality*, Retrieved November 25, 2009, from http://apsec2007.fuka.info.waseda.ac.jp/parts/W3SPAQu.pdf.

Fernandez, E. B., & Yuan, X. Y. (2007). Securing analysis patterns. In D. John and S.N. Kerr (Eds.) *Proceedings. of the 45th ACM Southeast Conference* (pp. 288-293), New York: ACM.

Gamma, E., Helm, R., Johnson, R., & Vlissides, J. M. (1994). *Design Patterns: Elements of Reusable Object-Oriented Software*. Reading, MA: Addison-Wesley Professional.

Hafiz, M., Adamczyk, P., & Johnson, R. E. (2007). Organizing security patterns. *IEEE Software*, *24*(4), 52–60. doi:10.1109/MS.2007.114

Jürjens, J. (2004). *Secure Systems Development with UML*. Heidelberg, Germany: Springer.

Morrison, P., & Fernandez, E. B. (2006). The credential pattern. In *Proceedings of the Conference on Pattern Languages of Programs*. Hillside Group. Retrieved November 25, 2009, from http://hillside.net/plop/2006/.

Mouratidis, H., & Giorgini, P. (2004). Analysing security in information systems. Presented at the *Second International Workshop on Security in Information Systems*, Porto Portugal. Retrieved November 25, 2009, from http://www.dit.unitn.it/~pgiorgio/papers/ICEISWorkshop04.pdf

Mouratidis, H., Jürjens, J., & Fox, J. (2006). Towards a Comprehensive Framework for Secure Systems Development. In *LNCS 4001: Proceedings of the 18th Conference on Advanced Information Systems,* (pp. 48-62). Heidelberg, Germany: Springer.

Nagaratnam, N., Nadalin, A., Hondo, M., McIntosh, M., & Austel, P. (2005). Business-driven application security: From modeling to managing secure applications. *IBM Systems Journal, 44*(4), 847–867. doi:10.1147/sj.444.0847

Pelaez, J., Fernandez, E. B., & Larrondo-Petrie, M. M. (2009). Misuse patterns in VoIP. *Security and Communication Networks*. Wiley InterScience. Retrieved November 25, 2009 from http://www3.interscience.wiley.com/journal/122324463/abstract.

Priebe, T., Fernandez, E. B., Mehlau, J. I., & Pernul, G. (2004). A pattern system for access control. In C. Farkas and P. Samarati (Eds.) *Research Directions in Data and Applications Security XVIII: Proceedings of the 18th. Annual IFIP WG 11.3 Working Conference on Data and Applications Security* (pp. 25-28). Amsterdam, Netherlands: Kluwer Academic Publishers.

Rosado, D. G., Gutierrez, C., Fernandez-Medina, E., & Piattini, M. (2006). Security patterns related to security requirements. In E. Fernandez-Medina and M. Inmaculada (Eds.) *Security in Informaiton Systems: Proceedings of the 4th International Workshop on Security in Information Systems*. Setúbal, Portugal: INSTICC Press.

Saltzer, J. H., & Schroeder, M. D. (1975). The protection of information in computer systems. *Proceedings of the IEEE, 63*(9), 1278-1308. Retrieved November 25, 2009 from http://web.mit.edu/Saltzer/www/publications/protection/index.html

Schumacher, M., Fernandez, E. B., Hybertson, D., Buschmann, F., & Sommerlad, P. (2006). *Security patterns: Integrating security and systems engineering*. Hoboken, NJ: John Wiley & Sons.

Secure Systems Research Group. (2009). Florida Atlantic University. Retrieved November 25, 2009 from http://security.ceecs.fau.edu/

VanHilst, M., Fernandez, E. B., & Braz, F. (2009a). A multidimensional classification for users of security patterns. *Journal of Research and Practice in Information Technology, 41*(2), 87–97.

VanHilst, M., Fernandez, E. B., & Braz, F. (2009b). Building a concept grid to classify security patterns. In H. Washizaki, N. Yoshioka, E.B.Fernandez, & J. Jürjens (Eds.) *Proceedings of the Third International Workshop on Software Patterns and Quality* (pp. 34-39). Tokyo:NII. Retrieved November 25, 2009 from http://grace-center.jp/downloads/GRACE-TR-2009-07.pdf.

Viega, J., & McGraw, G. (2001). *Building secure software: How to avoid security problems the right way*. Boston: Addison-Wesley.

Warmer, J., & Kleppe, A. (2003). *The object constraint language* (2nd ed.). Boston: Addison-Wesley.

Washizaki, H., Fernandez, E. B., Maruyama, K., Kubo, A., & Yoshioka, N. (2009). Improving the classification of security patterns. In *Proceedings of the International Workshop on Database and Expert Systems Applications* (pp. 165-170). Los Alamitos, CA: IEEE Computer Society.

Weiss, M., & Mouratidis, H. (2008) Selecting security patterns that fulfill security requirements, *Proceedings of the 16th IEEE International Conference on Requirements Engineering (RE'08)*, IEEE Computer Society, pp. 169-172

Yoshioka, N. (2006, March 29). A development method based on security patterns. Presented at National Institute of Informatics. Tokyo, Japan.

Yoshioka, N., Honiden, S., & Finkelstein, A. (2004) Security patterns: A method for constructing secure and efficient inter-company coordination systems. In *Proceedings of the Eighth IEEE International Enterprise Distributed Object Computing Conference* (pp. 84-97). Los Alamitos, CA: IEEE Computer Society.

Chapter 3
A Pattern–Based Method to Develop Secure Software

Holger Schmidt
Technical University Dortmund, Germany

Denis Hatebur
University Duisburg-Essen and ITESYS Institut für Technische Systeme GmbH, Germany

Maritta Heisel
University Duisburg-Essen, Germany

ABSTRACT

The authors present a security engineering process based on security problem frames and concretized security problem frames. Both kinds of frames constitute patterns for analyzing security problems and associated solution approaches. They are arranged in a pattern system that makes dependencies between them explicit. The authors describe step-by-step how the pattern system can be used to analyze a given security problem and how solution approaches can be found. Afterwards, the security problems and the solution approaches are formally modeled in detail. The formal models serve to prove that the solution approaches are correct solutions to the security problems. Furthermore, the formal models of the solution approaches constitute a formal specification of the software to be developed. Then, the specification is implemented by generic security components and generic security architectures, which constitute architectural patterns. Finally, the generic security components and the generic security architecture that composes them are refined and the result is a secure software product built from existing and/or tailor-made security components.

INTRODUCTION

It is acknowledged that a thorough requirements engineering phase is essential to develop a software product that matches the specified requirements. This is especially true for *security requirements*.

We introduce a security engineering process that focuses on the early phases of software development. The process covers engineering of security requirements, security specifications, and security architectures. The basic idea is to make use of special *patterns* for security requirements analysis and development of security architectures.

DOI: 10.4018/978-1-61520-837-1.ch003

Security requirements analysis makes use of patterns defined for structuring, characterizing, and analyzing *problems* that occur frequently in security engineering. Similar patterns for functional requirements have been proposed by Jackson (2001). They are called *problem frames*. Accordingly, our patterns are named *security problem frames*. Furthermore, for each of these frames, we have defined a set of *concretized security problem frames* that take into account generic security mechanisms to prepare the ground for solving a given security problem. Both kinds of patterns are arranged in a pattern system that makes dependencies between them explicit. We describe how the pattern system can be used to analyze a given security problem, how solution approaches can be found, and how dependent security requirements can be identified.

Security specifications are constructed using the formal specification language CSP (Communicating Sequential Processes) by Hoare (1986). We present a procedural approach to construct formal CSP models for instances of security problem frames and concretized security problem frames. These models serve to formally express security requirements. Afterwards they are used to formally prove a *refinement* between the CSP model of a security problem frame instance and a corresponding CSP model of a concretized security problem frame instance. This refinement must *preserve the security requirements* to ensure that the constructed specification realizes the security requirements.

Once we have shown that the selected generic security mechanisms solve the security problems, we develop a corresponding security architecture based on platform-independent *generic security components* and *generic security architectures*. Each concretized security problem frame is equipped with a set of generic security architectures that represent the internal structure of the software to be built by means of a set of generic security components. After a generic security architecture and generic security components are

selected, the latter must be refined to platform-specific security components. For example, existing component frameworks can be used to construct a platform-specific security architecture that realizes the initial security requirements.

The rest of the chapter is organized as follows: First, we introduce problem frames and present a literature review. Second, we give an overview of our security engineering process. Then we present the different development phases of the process in detail. Each phase of our process is demonstrated using the example of a secure text editor application. Finally, we outline future research directions and give a summary and a discussion of our work.

BACKGROUND

In the following, we first present problem frames and second, we discuss our work in the context of other approaches to security engineering.

Problem Frames

Patterns are a means to reuse software development knowledge on different levels of abstraction. They classify sets of software development problems or solutions that share the same structure. Patterns are defined for different activities at different stages of the software life-cycle. *Problem frames* by Jackson (2001) are a means to analyze and classify software development problems. *Architectural styles* are patterns that characterize software architectures (for details see (Bass & Clements & Kazman, 1998) and (Shaw & Garlan (1996)). *Design patterns* by Gamma, Helm, Johnson, and Vlissides (1995) are used for finer-grained software design, while *idioms* by Coplien (1992) are low-level patterns related to specific programming languages.

Using patterns, we can hope to construct software in a systematic way, making use of a body of accumulated knowledge, instead of starting from scratch each time. The problem frames defined by

Figure 1. Simple workpieces problem frame

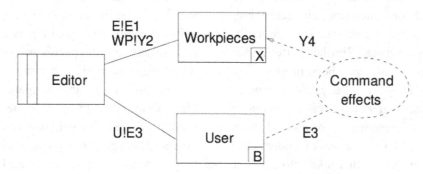

Jackson (2001) cover a large number of software development problems, because they are quite general in nature. Their support is of great value in the area of software engineering for years. Jackson (2001) describes them as follows: „A problem frame is a kind of pattern. It defines an intuitively identifiable problem class in terms of its context and the characteristics of its domains, interfaces, and requirement." (p. 76). Jackson introduces five basic problem frames named *required behaviour*, *commanded behaviour*, *information display*, *simple workpieces*, and *transformation*.

Problem frames are described by frame diagrams, which basically consist of rectangles and links between these. As an example, Figure 1 shows the frame diagram of the problem frame *simple workpieces*.

The task is to construct a *machine* that improves the behavior of the environment it is integrated in.

Plain rectangles denote problem domains (that already exist), and a rectangle with a double vertical stripe denotes the machine to be developed. Requirements are expressed as a dashed oval, which contains an informal description of the requirements. The connecting lines represent interfaces that consist of shared phenomena. Shared phenomena may be events, operation calls, messages, and the like. They are observable by at least two domains, but controlled by only one domain. For example, if a user types a password to log into an IT-system, this is a phenomenon shared by the user and the IT-system. It is controlled by the user. A dashed line between the dashed oval that contains the requirements description and a domain represents a requirements reference. This means that the requirements description refers to the domain. An arrow at the end of a requirements reference indicates that the requirements constrain the domain. Such a constrained domain is the core of any problem description, because it has to be controlled according to the requirements. Hence, a constrained domain triggers the need for developing a new software (the machine), which provides the desired control.

Furthermore, Jackson distinguishes causal domains that comply with some physical laws, lexical domains that are data representations, and biddable domains that are usually people. Côté & Hatebur & Heisel & Schmidt & Wentzlaff (2008) introduced display domains that represent output devices, e.g., video screens.

In the frame diagram depicted in Figure 1, a marker "X" indicates that the corresponding domain is a lexical domain and "B" indicates a biddable domain. A causal domain is indicated by "C" and a display domain is indicated by "D". The notation "E!E1" means that the phenomena of interface "E1" between the domains "Editor" (abbreviated "E") and "Workpieces" are controlled by the "Editor" domain.

Software development with problem frames proceeds as follows: first, the environment in which the machine will operate is represented by a context diagram. Like a frame diagram, a context diagram consists of domains and interfaces. However, a context diagram contains no requirements (see Figure 4 for an example). Then, the problem is decomposed into subproblems. If ever possible, the decomposition is done in such a way that the subproblems fit to given problem frames. To fit a subproblem to a problem frame, one must instantiate its frame diagram, i.e., provide instances for its domains, phenomena, and interfaces. The instantiated frame diagram is called a *problem diagram*. Furthermore, relevant *domain knowledge* about the domains contained in the frame diagram must be elicited, examined, and documented. Domain knowledge consists of *facts* and *assumptions*. Facts describe fixed properties of the environment irrespective of how the machine is built, e.g., that a network connection is physically secured. Assumptions describe conditions that are needed, so that the requirements are accomplishable, e.g., we assume that a password selected by a user is not revealed by this user to other users.

Successfully fitting a problem to a given problem frame means that the concrete problem indeed exhibits the properties that are characteristic for the problem class defined by the problem frame. A problem can only be fitted to a problem frame if the involved problem domains belong to the domain types specified in the frame diagram. For example, the "User" domain of Figure 1 can only be instantiated by persons, but not for example by some physical equipment like an elevator.

Since the requirements refer to the environment in which the machine must operate, the next step consists in deriving a specification for the machine (see Jackson & Zave (1995) for details). The specification describes the machine and is the starting point for its construction.

Related Work

In this section, we discuss our work in connection with a selection of other approaches to engineering of security requirements, security specifications, and security architectures.

Security Requirements Engineering

To elicit security requirements, the threats to be considered must be analyzed. Lin & Nuseibeh & Ince & Jackson (2004) use the ideas underlying problem frames to define so-called anti-requirements and the corresponding abuse frames. The purpose of anti-requirements and abuse frames is to analyze security threats and derive security requirements. Hence, abuse frames and security problem frames complement each other.

Gürses & Jahnke & Obry & Onabajo & Santen & Price (2005) present the MSRA (formerly known as CREE) method for multilateral security requirements analysis. Their method concentrates on confidentiality requirements elicitation and employs use cases to represent functional requirements. The MSRA method can be useful to be applied in a phase of the security requirements engineering process that mainly precedes the application of security problem frames.

SREF - Security Requirements Engineering Framework by Haley & Laney & Moffett & Nuseibeh (2008) is a framework that defines the notion of security requirements, considers security requirements in an application context, and helps answering the question whether the system can satisfy the security requirements. Their definitions and ideas overlap our approach, but they do not use patterns and they do not give concrete guidance to identify and elicit dependent security requirements.

Moreover, there exist other promising approaches to security requirements engineering, such as the agent-oriented Secure Tropos methodology by Mouratidis & Giorgini (2007) and the goal-driven KAOS - Keep All Objectives Satisfied approach by van Lamsweerde (2004).

A comprehensive comparison of security requirements engineering approaches (including the one presented in this chapter) can be found in

(Fabian, B. & Gürses, S. & Heisel, M. & Santen, T. & Schmidt, H., to appear).

Formal Security Specifications

Li & Hall & Rapanotti (2006) use an extended CSP version by Lai & Lai & Sanders (1997) to systematically derive a specification from requirements. Their work does not consider non-functional requirements such as security requirements. Furthermore, biddable domains are not formalized. Since biddable domains are used to model unpredictable parts of the environment (such as honest and malicious users), we believe that this is a key feature to security requirements engineering.

KAOS by van Lamsweerde (2004) addresses security requirements by means of anti-goals. A linear real-time temporal logic is used to formalize these goals. The goals and further ingredients such as domain properties as well as pre- and post-conditions form patterns that can be instantiated and negated to describe anti-goals. Furthermore, Mouratidis & Giorgini (2007) added this formal approach to Secure Tropos.

Haley & Laney & Moffett & Nuseibeh (2008, 2004) consider the notion of a *trust assumption*: "… the requirements engineer trusts that some domain will participate 'competently and honestly' in the satisfaction of a security requirement in the context of the problem." (pp. 4) in their SREF approach. To decide whether a system can satisfy the security requirements, Haley & Laney & Moffett & Nuseibeh (2005) make use of structured informal and formal argumentation. A two-part argument structure for security requirement satisfaction arguments consisting of an informal and a formal argument is proposed. In combination with trust assumptions, satisfaction arguments facilitate showing that a system can meet its security requirements.

In a stepwise development process, it is essential that security requirements specified in a certain step are preserved in later steps. This concept corresponds to the *stepwise refinement* concept of formal methods. Moreover, *information flow properties* represent a class of security properties that can be used to formally express informal security requirements. In contrast to safety and liveness properties, information flow properties are generally not preserved under refinement. Mantel (2003) gives an overview of using information flow properties for security requirements specification and preserving information flow properties under refinement.

In contrast to our work, KAOS with anti-goals, Secure Tropos, and SREF with trust assumptions do not allow to express security requirements in terms of information flow properties. Thus, the refinement of security requirements to specifications is only considered based on informal techniques.

Security Architectures

Architectural patterns named architectural styles are introduced by Bass & Clements & Kazman (1998) and Shaw & Garlan (1996). These patterns do not consider security requirements, and they are not integrated in a security engineering process.

Similarly, the AFrames by Rapanotti & Hall & Jackson & Nuseibeh (2004) do not consider security requirements. These patterns correspond to the popular architectural styles Pipe-and-Filter and Model-View-Controller (MVC), which the authors apply to Jackson's problem frames for transformation and control problems.

Hall & Jackson & Laney & Nuseibeh & Rapanotti (2002) extend machine domains of problem diagrams by architectural considerations. They do not deal with security requirements and they do not derive software architectures explicitly. Instead, their extension of the problem frames approach allows one to gather architectural structures and services from the problem environment.

There exist several techniques to evaluate the security properties of architectures, e.g., formal proving of security properties (Moriconi & Qian & Riemenschneider & Gong, 1997), analysis by means of petri nets and temporal logics (Deng & Wang & Tsai & Beznosov, 2003), or evaluation of used security patterns (Halkidis & Tsantalis & Chatzigeorgiou & Stephanides, 2008).

Choppy & Hatebur & Heisel (2005, 2006) present architectural patterns for Jackson's basic problem frames. The patterns constitute layered architectures described by UML (Unified Modeling Language) composite structure diagrams (UML Revision Task Force, Object Management Group (OMG), 2007). The authors also describe how these patterns can be applied in a pattern-based software development process. Hatebur & Heisel (2005) describe similar patterns for security frames. These frames are comparable to security problem frames, which are enhancements of the original security frames presented in (Hatebur & Heisel, 2005). Compared to the architectural patterns presented in this chapter, the mentioned papers do not consider behavioral interface descriptions and operation semantics. Furthermore, only a vague general procedure to derive components for a specific frame diagram is given. Architectural patterns especially for the problem class of confidential data storage using encryption are not described. And as a last difference, a refinement to implementable architectures is not considered. Nevertheless, the papers by Choppy & Hatebur & Heisel (2005, 2006) and Hatebur & Heisel (2005) as well as the idea to systematically preserve quality requirements from early requirements engineering to software design presented by Schmidt & Wentzlaff (2006) constitute the basis for the enhancements presented in this chapter.

Patterns for Security Engineering

Patterns for security engineering are mainly used during the phase that follows the phases presented in this chapter, i.e., they are applied in fine-grained design of secure software. Many authors advanced the field of security design patterns for years, e.g., (Schumacher & Fernandez-Buglioni & Hybertson

& Buschmann & Sommerlad, 2005) and (Steel & Nagappan & Lai, 2005). A comprehensive overview and a comparison of the different existing security design patterns is given by Scandariato & Yskout & Heyman & Joosen (2008). Fernandez & Larrondo-Petrie & Sorgente & Vanhilst (2007) propose a methodology to systematically use security design patterns during software development. The authors use UML (UML Revision Task Force, 2007) activity diagrams to identify threats to the system, and they use security design patterns during fine-grained design to treat these threats. Mouratidis & Weiss & Giorgini (2006) present an approach to make use of security design patterns that connects these patterns to the results generated by the Secure Tropos methodology by Mouratidis & Giorgini (2007). Moreover, Weiss and Mouratidis (2009) have produced an approach to select security patterns that fulfill specific security requirements.

The relation between our concretized security problem frames, which still express problems, and security design patterns is much the same as the relation between problem frames and design patterns: the frames describe problems, whereas the design/security patterns describe solutions on a fairly detailed level of abstraction. Furthermore, since security design patterns are more detailed than our generic security components and architectures, they can be applied after a composed generic security architecture is developed.

Furthermore, the security standard Common Criteria (International Organization for Standardization (ISO) and International Electrotechnical Commission (IEC), 2009) and KAOS make use of patterns for security engineering. The Common Criteria introduces security functional requirements, which are textual patterns to express security mechanisms on an abstract level. They are comparable to concretized security problem frames. KAOS provides formal patterns to describe security goals specified using a linear real-time temporal logic. These patterns can be compared to the effects of security problem frames.

OVERVIEW OF A SECURITY ENGINEERING PROCESS USING PATTERNS

We present in this chapter a *security engineering process using patterns* (SEPP). SEPP is an iterative and incremental process that consists of three phases. It follows a top-down and platform-independent approach until a generic security architecture is selected in phase three. Then, it takes a bottom-up and platform-specific approach to search for given security components that realize the generic security architecture.

Phase 1: Security Requirements Analysis

This phase starts with an initial set of security requirements, which is analyzed in detail by incrementally and iteratively processing six analysis steps. The result of this phase is a consolidated set of security requirements including solution approaches.

- **Step 1. Describe Environment:** The environment in which the software development problem is located is described in detail, developing a context diagram and expressing domain knowledge about the domains that occur in the context diagram. The domain knowledge describes the environment of the machine. This concerns especially potential attackers. The distinction of facts and assumptions is particularly important for security requirements. A machine usually cannot satisfy security requirements unconditionally. It can provide security mechanisms that contribute to system security, but cannot enforce system security on its own.
- **Step 2. Select and Instantiate Security Problem Frames:** The software development problem is decomposed into smaller subproblems. The security-relevant sub-

problems are analyzed and documented based on security problem frames (SPF).

- **Step 3. Select and Instantiate Concretized Security Problem Frames:** Generic solution approaches are selected for the previously documented security problems. The generic solution mechanisms are documented based on concretized security problem frames (CSPF).
- **Step 4. Check for Related SPFs:** Based on a pattern system of SPFs and CSPFs, SPFs that are commonly used in combination with an already used CSPF can be found.
- **Step 5. Analyze Dependencies:** Based on the pattern system, dependent security problems are identified, which can be either assumed to be already solved or they have to be considered as new security requirements to be solved by generic security mechanisms.
- **Step 6. Analyze Possible Conflicts:** the pattern system shows possible conflicts between security requirements and generic solution mechanisms. If a conflict is relevant, it must be resolved.

Phase 2: Security Specifications

A formal CSP model is developed for each instantiated (C)SPF. These models are used to formally express the security requirements and to prove refinements that preserve the specified security requirements. The result is a set of formal behavioral security specifications of the machines and their environment. Moreover, the refinement proofs guarantee that the generic solution approaches selected in phase one are sufficient to realize the security requirements.

- **Step 1. Construct Formal CSP Models:** A formal CSP model is constructed for each (C)SPF instance.

- **Step 2. Formally Express Security Requirements:** The informally described security requirements are expressed formally based on the CSP models.
- **Step 3. Show Security-Requirements Preserving Refinements:** For each SPF instance and the corresponding CSPF instance, the previously constructed CSP models are used to show that the CSPF CSP model refines the SPF CSP model. This refinement proof comprises the functional refinement and the preservation of the formally specified security requirement.

Phase 3: Security Architectures

Generic security architectures are selected and realized using existing security components from APIs or component frameworks. The result of this phase is a platform-specific and implementable security architecture that realizes the machines of the instantiated CSPFs.

- **Step 1: Select Generic Security Architectures:** A generic security architecture that consists of a set of generic security components is selected for each CSPF instance, based on domain knowledge and constraints of the application domain.
- **Step 2: Combine Generic Security Architectures:** The selected generic security architectures are combined to a single generic security architecture based on relations between the CSPF instances.
- **Step 3: Refine Generic Security Architecture:** The combined generic security architecture is refined to a platform-specific security architecture based on, e.g., existing security components.
- **Step 4: Connect Security Components:** Glue code is written to connect the components according to the chosen generic security architecture.

The process is described as an *agenda* (Heisel, 1998) that summarizes the input development artifacts, the output development artifacts, and validation conditions for each step. Furthermore, each step is complemented by a method describing how to develop the output artifacts from the input artifacts.

USING PROBLEM FRAMES FOR SECURITY REQUIREMENTS ENGINEERING

We present security problem frames, concretized security problem frames, the pattern system, and the process steps for security requirements engineering. The described techniques are then applied to the secure text editor case study.

Security Problem Frames

Jackson (2001) states that his five basic problem frames are "... far from a complete or definitive set" (p. 76). To meet the special demands of software development problems occurring in the area of security engineering, we introduced *security problem frames* (Hatebur & Heisel & Schmidt, 2006). SPFs are a special kind of problem frames, which consider *security requirements*. Similarly to problem frames, SPFs are *patterns*. The SPFs we have developed strictly refer to the *problems* concerning security. They do not anticipate a solution. For example, we may require the confidential storage of data without being obliged to mention encryption, which is a means to achieve confidentiality. The benefit of considering security requirements without reference to potential solutions is the clear separation of problems from their solutions, which leads to a better understanding of the problems and enhances the re-usability of the problem descriptions, since they are completely independent of solution technologies.

Each SPF consists of a name, an intent, a frame diagram with a set of predefined interfaces, an informal description, a security requirement template, and an effect. The latter is a formal representation of the security requirement template. Effects are expressed as formulas in Z notation (Spivey, 1992) based on a metamodel for problem frames developed by Hatebur & Heisel & Schmidt (2008). The metamodel formally specifies problem frames and problem frame constituents such as domains and interfaces by means of a UML class diagram (UML Revision Task Force, Object Management Group (OMG), 2007) and OCL (Object Constraint Language) constraints (UML Revision Task Force, Object Management Group (OMG), 2006). We use the instances of the classes of the metamodel as types for the formulas representing effects.

As an example, we present in detail the *SPF confidential data storage,* which describes the problem class of confidentially storing data:

Name

SPF confidential data storage

Intent

Conceal data (e.g., files, folders, metadata, etc.) stored on some storage device (e.g., hard disks, memory cards, smartcard, etc.).

Frame Diagram

Figure 2 shows the frame diagram of the SPF confidential data storage.

Predefined Interfaces

The interfaces of the SPF confidential data storage are defined as follows:

$E1 = \{OperationsOnStoredData_{HS}\}$
$Y2 = \{ContentOfStoredData\}$
$E3 = \{OperationsOnStoredData_{MS}\}$
$Y4 = \{Obervations_{SM}\}$

$Y5 = \{Obervations_{CSM}\}$
$Y6 = \{ContentOfStoredData, Observations\}$
$E7 = \{SpyOperations\}$
$Y8 = \{OperationsOnStoredData\}$

Informal Description

The malicious environment is represented by the domains *Malicious subject, Spy machine, and Malicious subject display.* The domain *Stored data* represents the data to be protected against the malicious environment. The *Malicious subject* domain uses the interface MS!E7 (between *Malicious subject* and *Spy machine*) to spy (*SpyOperations*) on the *Stored data* domain. The interface SM!Y4 (between *Malicious subject* and *Spy machine*) is used by the *Malicious subject* domain to receive some observations (*Obervations_{SM}*), e.g., meta-information about *Stored data* such as its length or type, from the *Spy machine* domain. The *Spy machine* domain is connected directly to the *Stored data* domain via interfaces SD!Y4 and SM!E7 to represent that the *Malicious subject* domain is not restricted to only access the *Stored data* domain through the machine domain *Confidential storage machine.* For example, access to the *Stored data* domain can also be possible via the operating system.

The *Malicious subject* domain can execute some operations (*OperationsOnStoredData_{MS}*) on the *Stored data* domain using the machine domain via interface MS!E3 (between *Malicious subject* and *Confidential storage machine*). Similarly, the honest environment represented by the domains *Honest subject* and *Honest subject display* can execute some operations (*OperationsOnStored-Data_{HS}*) on the *Stored data* domain using the machine domain via interface HS!E1 (between *Honest subject* and *Confidential storage machine*).

According to the commands from the (malicious or honest) environment, the machine accesses the domain *Stored data* via interfaces CSM!E1 and CSM!E3. The content of *Stored data* (*ContentOfStoredData*) is received by the machine

Figure 2. (C)SPF confidential data storage (using password-based encryption)

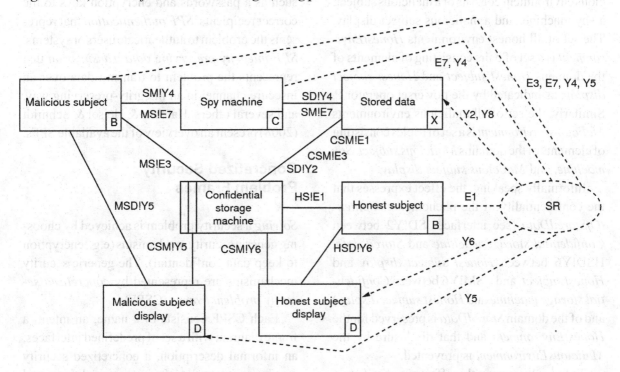

domain using the interface SD!Y2. Afterwards, the content of *Stored data* and some observations (*Obervations*) is shown to the domain *Honest subject* using the *Honest subject display* domain (via interface CSM!Y6 between *Confidential storage machine* and *Honest subject display* and via interface HSD!Y6 between *Honest subject display* and *Honest subject*).

The domain *Malicious subject* can possibly make some observations (*Obervations*_{CSM}), e.g., meta-information about *Stored data* such as its length or type, using the *Malicious subject display* (via interface CSM!Y5 between *Confidential storage machine* and *Malicious subject display* and via interface MSD!Y5 between *Malicious subject display* and *Malicious subject*).

Security Requirement Template

The security requirement template (SR) is described as follows: Preserve confidentiality of *Stored data* for honest environment (consisting of *Honest subject* and *Honest subject display*) and prevent disclosure to malicious environment (consisting of *Malicious subject*, *Spy machine*, and *Malicious subject display*).

Effect

```
HonestEnvironment: P(HonestSubject ×
HonestSubjectDisplay)
MaliciousEnvironment:
P(MaliciousSubject × SpyMachine × Ma-
liciousSubjectDisplay)
∀ cosd: ContentOfStoredData; he: Hon-
estEnvironment; me: MaliciousEnviron-
ment ·
              conf(cosd, he, me)
∀ sd: StoredData; he: HonestEnviron-
ment; me: MaliciousEnvironment ·
              conf(sd, he, me)
```

An honest environment consists of an honest subject and an honest subject display, whereas a malicious environment consists of a malicious subject, a spy machine, and a malicious subject display. The set of all honest environments *HonestEnvironment* is a set of pairs consisting of elements of the domains *Honest subject* and *Honest subject display*, as indicated by the powerset operator P. Similarly, the set of all malicious environments *MaliciousEnvironment* is a set of triples consisting of elements of the domains *Malicious subject, Spy machine,* and *Malicious subject display.*

Informally speaking, the effect expresses that the confidentiality of the phenomenon *ContentOfStoredData* (see interfaces SD!Y2 between *Confidential storage machine* and *Stored data*, HSD!Y6 between *Honest subject display* and *Honest subject*, and CSM!Y6 between *Confidential storage machine* and *Honest subject display*) and of the domain *StoredData* is preserved for the *HonestEnvironment* and that disclosure by the *MaliciousEnvironment* is prevented.

To formally express this effect, we specify two versions of a relation *conf*. One version of *conf* deals with the confidentiality of a phenomenon, another version deals with the confidentiality of a lexical domain. We define *conf* as a set of triples of a phenomenon (or a lexical domain), an honest environment, and a malicious environment. Each triple describes that the confidentiality of the phenomenon (or of the lexical domain) is preserved for the honest environment and that disclosure by the malicious environment is prevented.

The universally quantified formulas that express the effect make use of the relation *conf*: the first formula expresses that the confidentiality of each possible instance *cosd* of the phenomenon *ContentOfStoredData* is preserved for each possible instance *he* of the *HonestEnvironment* and that disclosure by each possible instance *me* of the *MaliciousEnvironment* is prevented. The second formula expresses a similar condition for each possible instance *sd* of the lexical domain *StoredData.*

Further SPFs exist, e.g., *SPF distributing secrets* that represents the problem to deliver secrets such as a passwords and encryption keys to the correct recipients, *SPF authentication* that represents the problem to authenticate users or systems, *SPF integrity-preserving data transmission* that represents the problem to transmit data over an insecure channel in an integrity-preserving way, and several others. Hatebur & Heisel & Schmidt (2008) present an overview of the available SPFs.

Concretized Security Problem Frames

Solving a security problem is achieved by choosing generic security mechanisms (e.g., encryption to keep data confidential). The generic security mechanisms are represented by *concretized security problem frames* (CSPF).

Each CSPF consists of a name, an intent, a frame diagram with a set of predefined interfaces, an informal description, a concretized security requirement template, necessary conditions, and a list of related SPFs. The necessary conditions must be met by the environment for the generic security mechanism that the CSPF represents to be applicable. If the necessary conditions do not hold, the effect described in the according SPF cannot be established. The necessary conditions are expressed in Z notation. A *concretized security requirements template* refers to the effect described in the according SPF and the necessary conditions. More precisely, it is expressed as an implication: if the necessary conditions hold, then the effect is established. The effects of the SPFs and the necessary conditions of the CSPFs serve to represent dependencies between SPFs and CSPFs explicitly. The list of related SPFs serves to exhibit security problems that often occur when the security mechanism represented by the CSPF at hand is applied.

As an example, we present in detail the *CSPF confidential data storage using password-based encryption*. This CSPF represents the generic security mechanism password-based encryption according to the password-based cryptography standard PKCS #5 v2.0 (RSA Laboratories, 1999), which can be used to solve problems that fit to the SPF confidential data storage problem class. Another CSPF that solves such a security problem is the *CSPF confidential data storage using encryption key-based encryption.*

Name

CSPF confidential data storage using password-based encryption

Intent

Conceal data (e.g., files, folders, metadata, etc.) stored on some storage device (e.g., hard disks, memory cards, smartcard, etc.) using a password-based encryption mechanism.

Frame Diagram

The frame diagram of the CSPF confidential data storage using password-based encryption is similar to the frame diagram of the SPF confidential data storage shown in Figure 2. For this reason, we do not explicitly show it here. Instead, we briefly describe the differences between the two frame diagrams: The domain *Stored data* is replaced by the domain *Encrypted stored data.* Furthermore, the usage of a password-based encryption mechanism leads to modifications of the interfaces (see informal description for details).

Predefined Interfaces

The interfaces of the CSPF confidential data storage using password-based encryption are defined as follows:

E1= {OperationsOnEncryptedStoredData$_{HS}$, Password}
Y2= {EncryptedContentOfStoredData}
E3= {OperationsOnEncryptedStoredData$_{MS}$, WrongPassword}

Y4= {EncryptedContentOfStoredData, Obervations$_{SM}$}
Y5= {Obervations$_{CSM}$}
Y6= {ContentOfStoredData, Observations}
E7= {SpyOperations}
Y8= {OperationsOnEncryptedStoredData}

Informal Description

Since the domain *Stored data* is replaced by the domain *Encrypted stored data*, the interface SD!Y4 is replaced by the interface ESD!Y4. Compared to the SPF confidential data storage, the phenomenon *ContentOfStoredData* of the interfaces SD!Y2 (between *Confidential storage machine* and *Encrypted stored data*), ESD!Y4 (between *Encrypted stored data* and *Spy machine*), and SM!Y4 (between *Spy machine* and *Malicious subject*) is replaced by the phenomenon *EncryptedContentOfStoredData.* Accordingly, the phenomenon *OperationsOnStoredData*$_{HS}$ of the interfaces HS!E1 (between *Honest subject* and *Confidential storage machine*) and CSM!E1 (between *Confidential storage machine* and *Honest subject*) is replaced by the phenomenon *OperationsOnEncryptedStoredData*$_{HS}$. These interfaces additionally contain the phenomenon *Password* that represents a password used by the honest environment for encryption and decryption. Furthermore, the phenomenon *OperationsOnStoredData*$_{MS}$ of the interfaces MS!E3 (between *Malicious subject* domain and *Confidential storage machine*) and CSM!E3 (between *Confidential storage machine* and *Malicious subject*) is replaced by the phenomenon *OperationsOnEncryptedStoredData*$_{MS}$. These interfaces additionally contain the phenomenon *WrongPassword* that represents a password used by the malicious environment for encryption and decryption.

Finally, the phenomenon *OperationsOnStoredData* of the phenomena set Y8 (at the requirement reference connected to *Encrypted stored data*) is replaced by the phenomenon *OperationsOnEncryptedStoredData.*

43

Concretized Security Requirement Template

The concretized security requirement template (CSR) is described as follows: If *Password* is unknown to malicious environment, then confidentiality of *Stored data* is preserved for honest environment and disclosure to malicious environment is prevented.

Necessary Conditions

```
HonestEnvironment: P(HonestSubject ×
HonestSubjectDisplay)
MaliciousEnvironment:
P(MaliciousSubject × SpyMachine × Ma-
liciousSubjectDisplay)
RightPasswords: P PasswordWrongPass-
words: P PasswordRightPasswords ∩
WrongPasswords = ∅
∀ pwd: Password; he: HonestEnviron-
ment; me: MaliciousEnvironment ·
              conf(pwd, he, me)
    ∀ pwd: Password; he: HonestEnvi-
ronment; me: MaliciousEnvironment ·
              int(pwd, he, me)
```

Passwords used by the honest environment must be different from the ones used by the malicious environment. Otherwise, a password-based encryption mechanism is not applicable. In practice, this necessary condition has to be assumed. That is, we have to assume that the malicious environment does not guess the right password. It cannot be fulfilled by a security mechanism. This necessary condition is formally expressed based on a set *RightPasswords* that represents the valid passwords chosen by the honest environment, and a set *WrongPasswords* that represents the invalid passwords chosen by the malicious environment. Thus, we formally express the necessary conditions by stating that these two sets are disjoint.

Furthermore, passwords used by the honest environment must not be known by the malicious environment. This necessary condition is formally described by the first universally quantified formula which expresses that the confidentiality of each possible instance *pwd* of the phenomenon *Password* is preserved for each possible instance *he* of the *HonestEnvironment* and that disclosure by each possible instance *me* of the *MaliciousEnvironment* is prevented.

Moreover, passwords used by the honest environment must be transmitted to the machine domain in an integrity-preserving way. To formally express this necessary condition, we specify a relation *int* as a set of triples of a phenomenon (or a lexical domain), an honest environment, and a malicious environment. Each triple describes that the integrity of the phenomenon (or of the lexical domain) is preserved for the honest environment and that modification by the malicious environment is prevented. Consequently, the second universally quantified formula expresses the mentioned necessary condition using the relation *int*: the integrity of each possible instance *pwd* of the phenomenon *Password* is preserved for each possible instance *he* of the *HonestEnvironment* and that modification by each possible instance *me* of the *MaliciousEnvironment* is prevented.

Related SPFs

SPF Integrity-Preserving Data Storage

Further CSPFs exist, e.g., *CSPF distributing secrets using negotiation* that represents the generic security mechanism to deliver secrets using a negotiation mechanism, *CSPF authentication using passwords* that represents the generic security mechanism to authenticate users by passwords, *CSPF integrity-preserving data transmission using symmetric mechanism* that represents the generic security mechanism to transmit data over an insecure channel in an integrity-preserving way using a symmetric mechanism, and serveral others. Hatebur & Heisel & Schmidt (2008) present an overview of the available CSPFs.

Table 1. (C)SPF pattern system

	...	SPF confidential data storage	SPF confidential data transmission	SPF integrity-preserving data storage	SPF integrity-preserving data transmission	SPF Distributing Secrets	...
⋮							
CSPF confidential data storage using password-based encryption		C	D	R	D		
CSPF confidential data storage using encryption key-based encryption		C, D	D	R	D	D	
⋮							

Pattern System

We developed a catalog of SPFs and CSPFs. Both kinds of frames are arranged in a *pattern system* (Hatebur & Heisel & Schmidt, 2007), which indicates dependent, conflicting, and related frames. The pattern system is represented as a table and is partly shown in Table 1. The complete pattern system can be found in (Hatebur & Heisel & Schmidt, 2008).

The pattern system is constructed by analyzing the necessary conditions of the different CSPFs and the effects of the different SPFs. We check the necessary conditions of a CSPF and syntactically match them with the effects of all SPFs. For example, the necessary conditions of the CSPF confidential data storage using password-based encryption and the CSPF confidential data storage using encryption key-based encryption require integrity-preserving and confidential paths for the passwords and the encryption keys, respectively. The effect of the SPF integrity-preserving data transmission provides an integrity-preserving path

and the effect of the SPF confidential data transmission provides a confidential path. For this reason, the mentioned CSPFs depend on the SPF integrity-preserving data transmission and the SPF confidential data transmission. Consequently, the rows that belong to these CSPFs in Table 1 are marked at the positions of the columns that belong to the SPF integrity-preserving data transmission and the SPF confidential data transmission with the letter "D". Furthermore, the necessary conditions of the CSPF confidential data storage using encryption key-based encryption require that encryption keys must be distributed and that these encryption keys are confidentially stored. Thus, this CSPF depends on the SPF confidential data storage and on the SPF distributing secrets. The row that belongs to this CSPF in Table 1 is marked at the positions of the columns that belong to the SPF confidential data storage and SPF distributing secrets with the letter "D".

The fact that a CSPF concretizes an SPF is represented in Table 1 by the letter "C". For example, in the row of the CSPF confidential data storage using password-based encryption is a letter "C" at the position of the column of the SPF confidential data storage.

Furthermore, the "Related" sections of the CSPFs are represented in Table 1 by the letter "R". The rows of the CSPFs confidential data storage using password-based encryption and using encryption-key based encryption are marked with the letter "R" at the positions of the column of the SPF integrity-preserving data storage. The "Related" sections are helpful, since they indicate at an early stage of software development possible security problems that commonly occur in combination with the generic solution mechanism at hand and the security problem it solves.

Additionally, possible interactions between generic security mechanisms represented as CSPFs and security requirements represented as SPFs are indicated by the pattern system. We do not discuss this part of the pattern system here. Hatebur & Heisel & Schmidt (2008) describe this part of the pattern system in detail based on a case study of a software to handle legal cases.

The (C)SPFs we developed form a self-contained pattern system: for any necessary condition of a CSPF covered by the pattern system, there exists at least one SPF contained in the pattern system that provides a matching effect. Therefore, the (C)SPFs contained in the pattern system can be used to *completely* analyze a given security problem, whose initial security requirement is covered by one of the frames.

The explicit knowledge of the dependencies between the security SPFs and their concretized counterparts increases the value of our approach. The guidance provided by the dependency relations of the pattern system helps to structure the security requirements engineering process, to avoid confusion, and to analyze security problems and their solution approaches in depth. Hence, the security requirements engineering process will result in a consolidated set of security requirements and solution approaches, which is complete with respect to the initial set of secu-

rity requirements. Compared to the initial set of security requirements, the final set of security requirements additionally contains dependent and related security requirements that may not have been known initially.

Security Requirements Analysis Method

Figure 3 shows an overview of SEPP's security requirements analysis lifecycle. The arrows are annotated with inputs or with conditions (in square brackets). The latter must be true to proceed with the step the arrow under consideration is pointing at. The arrow pointing at the "End" state is annotated with SEPP's overall output of the first phase. Each of the steps is described according to the following template:

- Input: artifacts necessary to accomplish the step
- Output: artifacts that are created or modified during the execution of the step
- Validation conditions: necessary semantic conditions that an output artifact must fulfill in order to serve its purpose properly (Heisel, 1998)

Before we explain SEPP step-by-step, we note that some activities to be executed for a comprehensive security requirements analysis are not explicitly mentioned in the descriptions of SEPP's security requirements analysis steps. These activities concern the maintenance of the following development artifacts:

- **attacker model** describes assumptions about potential attackers. For example, the Common Evaluation Methodology (CEM) (International Organization for Standardization (ISO) and International Electrotechnical Commission (IEC), 2006) defines the attack potential of a potential attacker as a function of time, expertise,

Figure 3. SEPP's security requirements analysis lifecycle

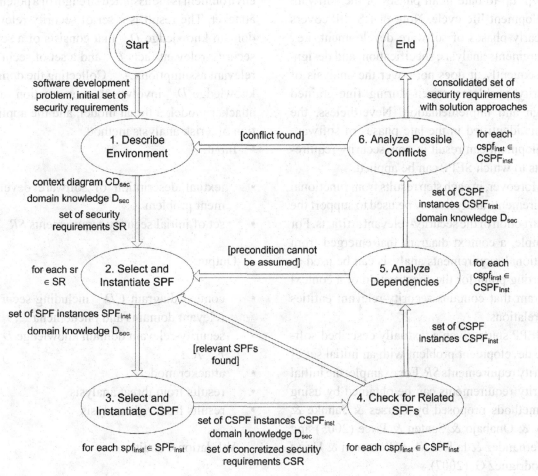

knowledge, and equipment. It also identifies two numeric values for each of these factors. The first value is for identifying and the second one is for exploiting a vulnerability. By assuming values for the input variables of the function, we can calculate the attack potential.

- **results from threat analysis** represent potential threats. For example, attack trees by Schneier (1999) can be applied.
- **results from risk analysis** represent the risk of an attack and the resulting loss. For example, a risk analysis method such as CORAS by Braber & Hogganvik & Stølen & Vraalsen (2007) can be applied.

- **glossary** contains all used names, type information (if applicable), and references to artifacts that contain the names.

These artifacts are initially constructed in SEPP's first step. After every refinement step, i.e., the steps from requirements analysis and specification to architectural and fine-grained design and finally implementation, new threats can arise. For example, the decision for a particular security mechanism, the definition of a certain length for cryptographic keys, and the usage of a specific security component of a component framework enlarge the attack surface of the system to be developed. Hence, the attacker model as well as the results from threat and risk analysis must be kept up-to-date in all phases of the software development life-cycle. Note that SEPP covers the early phases of software development, i.e., requirements analysis, specification, and design. Consequently, it does not cover the analysis of security problems arisen during fine-grained design and implementation. Nevertheless, the threats identified in the late phases of software development can result in new security requirements to which SEPP can be applied.

Moreover, in each step results from functional requirements analysis may be used to support the construction of the security-relevant artifacts. For example, a context diagram that emerged from functional requirements analysis can be used as a starting point for the construction of a context diagram that contains security-relevant entities and relations.

SEPP starts given a textually described software development problem with an initial set of security requirements *SR*. For example, the initial security requirements can be obtained by using the methods proposed by Gürses & Jahnke & Obry & Onabajo & Santen & Price (2005) and by Fernandez & la Red M. & Forneron & Uribe & Rodriguez G. (2007).

Step 1: Describe Environment

All security-relevant entities contained in the environment and relations between them are modeled. Given a context diagram that emerged from functional requirements analysis, it is extended by security-relevant entities and relations. The result is a context diagram CD_{sec}. An example is shown in Figure 4. The hatched area named "Malicious environment" represents the extension by security-relevant entities and relations.

Domain knowledge, i.e., facts and assumptions, about the environment in which the software development problem is located is collected and documented. Especially, domain knowledge about the malicious environment is considered. An example for domain knowledge about a malicious

environment is the assumed strength of a potential attacker. The result is a set of security-relevant domain knowledge D_{sec} that consists of a set of security-relevant facts F_{sec} and a set of security-relevant assumptions A_{sec}. Collecting the domain knowledge D_{sec} involves the construction of an attacker model, a threat model, and the application of a risk analysis method.

Input:

- textual description of software development problem
- set of initial security requirements *SR*

Output:

- context diagram CD_{sec} including security-relevant domains and phenomena
- security-relevant domain knowledge $D_{sec} \equiv F_{sec} \land A_{sec}$
- attacker model
- results from threat analysis
- results from risk analysis

Validation Conditions:

- domains and phenomena of context diagram CD_{sec} must be consistent with *SR* and D_{sec}
- context diagram CD_{sec} must contain malicious environment

Step 2: Select and Instantiate SPF

This step must be executed for each security requirement $sr \in SR$. To determine an SPF that is appropriate for the given environment and the security requirement $sr \in SR$, the latter is compared with the informal descriptions of the security requirement templates of the SPFs contained in our pattern system. The result is a set of SPFs candidates from which the SPF to be instantiated is selected by considering the security-relevant

Figure 4. Context diagram "secure text editor"

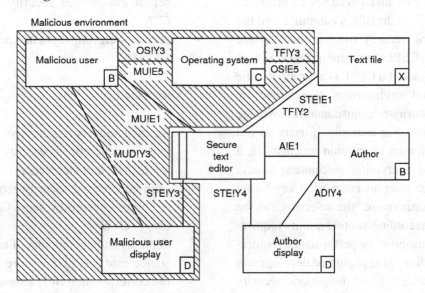

environment represented by CD_{sec} and the security-relevant domain knowledge D_{sec}.

More precisely, the context diagram CD_{sec} represents the environment of a complex problem, which is decomposed into subproblems that fit to SPFs using decomposition operators such as "leave out domain" or "combine several domains into one domain". Thus, an SPF candidate that fits to the decomposed environment of the corresponding subproblem is selected.

Afterwards, the SPF is instantiated by assigning concrete values to the domains, phenomena, interfaces, effect, and the security requirement template. The instantiation of an SPF may result in additional security-relevant domain knowledge, which is added to the set of security-relevant domain knowledge D_{sec}. For example, if in the course of the problem decomposition a domain is split into several domains, domain knowledge about these new domains is collected and documented.

After this step is executed for each security requirement $sr \in SR$, the result of this step is a set of security problems SPF$_{inst}$ represented as instantiated SPFs. Furthermore, the set of security-relevant domain knowledge D_{sec} may be updated.

Input:

• all results of step 1

Output:

• set of SPF instance SPF_{inst}
• security-relevant domain knowledge added to D_{sec}

Validation Conditions:

• each security requirement $sr \in SR$ is covered by some SPF instance $spf_{inst} \in SPF_{inst}$
• each SPF instance $spf_{inst} \in SPF_{inst}$ can be derived from the context diagram CD_{sec} by means of certain decomposition operators

Step 3: Select and Instantiate CSPF

This step must be executed for each SPF instance $spf_{inst} \in SPF_{inst}$. To solve a security problem characterized by an instance of an SPF, a generic security mechanism based on the CSPFs linked to the applied SPF is chosen. The pattern system indicates the CSPFs linked to an SPF by positions marked with "C" in the SPF's column. From the different generic security mechanisms that are represented by CSPFs, an appropriate CSPF is selected. To decide if a CSPF is appropriate, the security-relevant environment represented by CD_{sec} and the security-relevant domain knowledge D_{sec} is considered. For example, if users should select secrets for an encryption mechanism, a password-based encryption mechanism should take precedence over an encryption-key based mechanism. Furthermore, the selection can be accomplished according to other quality requirements such as usability or performance requirements or according to the presumed development costs of the realizations of the generic security mechanisms represented by the different CSPFs.

After a CSPF is selected, it is instantiated by assigning concrete values to the domains, phenomena, interfaces, necessary conditions, and the concretized security requirement template. Normally, domains and phenomena contained in the SPF instance are re-used for the instantiation of the corresponding CSPF. The instantiation of a CSPF may result in additional security-relevant domain knowledge, which must be added to the set of security-relevant domain knowledge D_{sec}, e.g., domain knowledge about passwords or encryption keys.

After this step is executed for each SPF instance $spf_{inst} \in SPF_{inst}$, the result is a set of CSPF instances $CSPF_{inst}$ and a corresponding set of concretized security requirements CSR. Furthermore, the security-relevant domain knowledge D_{sec} may be updated.

Input:

- all results of step 2

Output:

- set of CSPF instances $CSPF_{inst}$

- set of concretized security requirements CSR

- security-relevant domain knowledge added to D_{sec}

Validation Conditions:

- for each security requirement $sr \in SR$ there exist a concretized security requirement $csr \in CSR$, and vice versa
- each concretized security requirement $csr \in CSR$ is covered by some CSPF instance $cspf_{inst} \in CSPF_{inst}$
- domains and phenomena of each CSPF instance $cspf_{inst} \in CSPF_{inst}$ are re-used from the corresponding SPF instance

Step 4: Check for Related SPFs

This step must be executed for each CSPF instance $cspf_{inst} \in CSPF_{inst}$. SPFs that are commonly used in combination with the described CSPF are indicated in the pattern system by positions marked with "R" in the CSPF's row. This information helps to find missing security requirements right at the beginning of the security requirements engineering process.

After this step is executed for each CSPF instance $cspf_{inst} \in CSPF_{inst}$, the result of this step is a set of related security requirements and a corresponding set of SPFs. The related security requirements are added to the set of security requirements SR and the SPFs are instantiated by returning to step 2.

Input:

- all results of step 3

Output:

- related security requirements added to the set of security requirements SR

- set of SPFs that correspond to the related security requirements

Validation Conditions:

- the new security requirements are relevant for the given software development problem

Step 5: Analyze Dependencies

This step must be executed for each CSPF instance $cspf_{inst} \in CSPF_{inst}$. The necessary conditions of a CSPF instance are inspected to discover dependent security problems. Two alternatives are possible to guarantee that these necessary conditions hold: either, they can be *assumed* to hold, or they have to be established by instantiating a further SPF, whose effect matches the necessary conditions to be established. Such an SPF can easily be determined using the pattern system: the corresponding positions in the row of the instantiated CSPF are marked with "D".

Only in the case that the necessary conditions *cannot* be assumed to hold, one must instantiate further appropriate SPFs. Then, steps 2 - 4 must be applied to the dependent SPFs.

The security-relevant domain knowledge D_{sec} helps to decide whether the necessary conditions can be assumed to hold or not. For example, assumptions on the strength of passwords chosen by honest users lead to the assumption that malicious users cannot guess the honest user passwords. In contrast, if encryption keys must be delivered to the correct recipients over an insecure network, additional security mechanisms to authenticate the recipients and to transmit the encryption keys in a confidential and integrity-preserving way must be taken into consideration.

This step is executed for each CSPF instance $cspf_{inst} \in CSPF_{inst}$ until all necessary conditions of all CSPF instances can be proved or assumed to hold. The result of this step is a set of dependent

security requirements and a corresponding set of SPFs.

Input:

- all results of step 4

Output:

- dependent security requirements added to the set of security requirements SR
- set of SPFs that correspond to the dependent security requirements

Validation Conditions:

- each necessary condition of each $cspf_{inst} \in CSPF_{inst}$ is either assumed to hold or treated by some SPF
- if a necessary condition is assumed, a justification is stated

Step 6: Analyze Possible Conflicts

This step must be executed for each CSPF instance $cspf_{inst} \in CSPF_{inst}$. The pattern system indicates possible conflicts between the SPF instances and the CSPF instances by rows marked with "I" (for "interaction"). If a possible conflict is discovered, it must be decided if the conflict is relevant for the application domain using D_{sec}. In the case that it is relevant, the conflict must be resolved by modifying or prioritizing the requirements. An example of relaxing security requirements for the benefit of usability requirements can be found in Schmidt & Wentzlaff (2006). This step can result in modified sets of security requirements and concretized security requirements. In such a case, all previous steps must be re-applied to the modified security requirements.

This step is executed for each CSPF instance $cspf_{inst} \in CSPF_{inst}$ until all possible conflicts are analyzed and all relevant conflicts are resolved. Finally, we obtain a set of CSPF instances $CSPF_{inst}$ that can solve the security problems represented by the SPF instances as well as modified sets of security requirements *SR* and concretized security requirements *CSR* with all conflicts resolved.

Input:

- all results of step 5

Output:

- consolidated set of security requirements *SR*
- consolidated set of concretized security requirements *CSR*
- security-relevant domain knowledge added to D_{sec}

Validation Conditions:

- the set of security requirements *SR* contains no more conflicts and is complete with respect to the initial set of security requirements
- the set of concretized security requirements *CSR* contains no more conflicts and is complete with respect to the initial set of security requirements

All in all, the security requirements analysis method results in a consolidated set of security problems and solution approaches that additionally cover all dependent and related security problems and corresponding solution approaches, some of which may not have been known initially.

Case Study: Secure Text Editor

We now apply the techniques introduced in the previous sections to the following software development problem:

A graphical secure text editor should be developed. The text editor should enable a user to create, edit, open, and save text files. The text files should be stored confidentially.

The informal security requirement (*SR*) can be described as follows:

Preserve confidentiality of Text file except for its file length for honest environment and prevent disclosure to malicious environment.

Note: We decide to focus on confidentially storing text files. The given software development problem can also be interpreted such that the security requirement also covers confidential editing operations, e.g., confidential clipboard copies. For reasons of simplification, this is not covered in the security requirements analysis. For the same reason, the create and edit functionality of the secure text editor is not covered in our case study. Practically, it is very difficult to develop 100% confidential systems. Hence, as an example, we discuss a SR that allows the secure text editor to leak the file length.

According to the first step of our security requirements analysis method, the context diagram of this software development problem shown in Figure 4 is developed. Note: we do not show the interfaces of the context diagram explicitly, since they are similar to the interfaces of the instantiated SPF confidential data storage shown in Figure 5. Furthermore, the attacker model and the results of the threat and risk analysis are not shown explicitly. For example, the attacker model comprises assumptions on the strength and the abilities of potential attackers and an analyzed threat covers the usage of the domain *Operating system* to access the domain *Text file*.

In the second step, we instantiate the SPF confidential data storage as shown in Figure 5 to capture the *SR*. The interfaces of the SPF confidential data storage are instantiated as follows:

E1 = {Save, Open}
Y2 = {TextFile}
Y3 = {LengthOfTextFile}
Y4 = {TextFile, LengthOfTextFile}
E5 = {Spy}

Figure 5. Instantiated SPF confidential data storage "secure text editor"

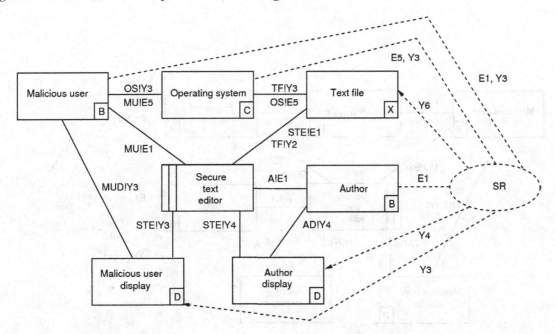

Y6 = {Saving, Opening}

According to the commands from the (malicious and honest) environment, the machine accesses the domain *Text file*, and opens a file or saves one. An opened file is shown to the domain *Author* using the *Author display* domain. We assume that the domain *Malicious user* can at most observe the length of the opened file via the domains *Malicious user display* and *Operating system*.

In the third step, we decide to use a password-based encryption mechanism to conceal text files. For such an encryption mechanism, passwords are necessary. The passwords should be generated and memorized by the users. Since the users must memorize the passwords, a symmetric encryption mechanism is to be preferred over an asymmetric one. This is a trade-off between the usability and the security of the password-based encryption mechanism: asymmetric encryption keys must be much larger compared to symmetric keys to achieve a similar level of encryption strength. Because of the encryption key lengths, it is more

difficult for users to memorize asymmetric keys than symmetric ones.

Using passwords for encryption leads to the assumptions that the users do not reveal their passwords and that they choose passwords that guarantee a certain level of security.

Note that the latter assumption can be transformed into a requirement: the users should not be able choose trivial passwords. Such a requirement can be realized by password checking mechanisms to prevent users from choosing trivial passwords, e.g., words from dictionaries, proper names, and so on.

According to the pattern system, we decide to select the CSPF confidential data storage using password-based encryption. The structure of the CSPF instance shown in Figure 6 is similar to the instantiated SPF confidential data storage shown in Figure 5 with the difference that the domain *Text file* is replaced by the domain *Encrypted text file*. The differences between the SPF instance and the CSPF instance are located in the interfaces. The interfaces of the CSPF instance are instantiated as follows:

Figure 6. Instantiated CSPF confidential data storage using password-based encryption "secure text editor"

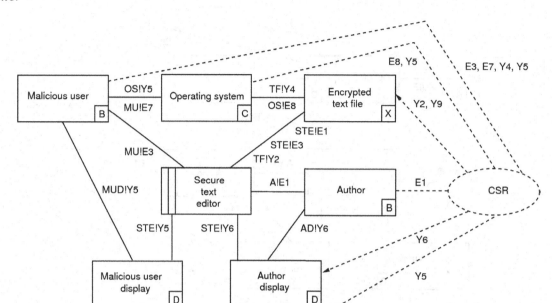

E1= {Save, Open, Password}

Y2= {EncryptedContentOfTextFile}

E3= {Save, Open, WrongPassword}

Y4= {EncryptedContentOfTextFile, LengthOfTextFile}

Y5= {WrongContentOfTextFile, LengthOfTextFile}

Y6= {TextFile, LengthOfTextFile}

E7= {Spy, WrongPassword}

E8= {Spy}

Y9= {Saving, Opening}

Since the text files are encrypted by the encryption mechanism, the interfaces TF!Y2 (between *Confidential storage machine* and *Text file*) and TF!Y4 (between *Text file* and *Operating system*) contain the phenomenon *EncryptedContentOfTextFile*. The authors can enter passwords for encrypting and decrypting text files. Therefore, the interfaces A!E1 (between *Author* and *Confidential storage machine*) and STE!E1 (between *Confidential storage machine* and *Text file*) contain the phenomenon *Password*. The malicious users can

also enter passwords under the assumption that they cannot guess passwords of authors. Therefore, the interfaces MU!E3 (between *Malicious user* and *Confidential storage machine*), STE!E3 (between *Confidential storage machine* and the *Text file*), and MU!E7 (between *Malicious user* and *Operating system*) contain the phenomenon *WrongPassword*. The concretized security requirement (*CSR*) derived from the *SR* is phrased as follows:

If *Password* is unknown to malicious environment, then confidentiality of *Text file* except for its file length for honest environment is preserved and disclosure to malicious environment is prevented.

In step four, the pattern system is inspected to check for related security problems. According to the pattern system, the SPF integrity-preserving data storage is related to the CSPF confidential data storage using password-based encryption. This SPF is indeed relevant in the given application context: the integrity of text files stored by authors should be preserved and modification by malicious environment should be prevented.

However, for reasons of simplification, this related SPF is not considered here.

In step five, the instantiated necessary conditions (not shown, since they are similar to the necessary conditions of the CSPF except for the types) of the instantiated CSPF are inspected. The first necessary condition is assumed to hold, because we assume that a malicious user cannot guess passwords of an author. The second necessary condition is assumed to hold, because we assume that an author does not reveal passwords to a malicious user. The third necessary condition is assumed to hold, because we assume that there is no malicious user able to intercept and modify passwords of an author.

In step six, our security requirements engineering method proceeds with an analysis of potential conflicts between security requirements. Since only one SPF (and one CSPF) is instantiated, it is not necessary to analyze any potential conflicts between security requirements.

No further SPFs must be instantiated, because each necessary condition is covered by an assumption.

DEVELOPMENT OF A SECURITY SPECIFICATION

According to Jackson (2001), a specification is "an optative description: it describes the machine's behaviour at its interfaces with the problem domains" (p. 55). In contrast to the requirements, a machine specification gives an answer to the question: "How should the machine act, so that the system, i.e. the machine together with the environment, fulfills the requirements?" Specifications are descriptions that are sufficient for building the machine. They are implementable requirements.

SEPP supports two methods of constructing a security specification:

- Construction of a semi-formal security specification based on *generic security*

protocols (Hatebur & Heisel & Schmidt, 2006), which are expressed using UML sequence diagrams (UML Revision Task Force, Object Management Group (OMG), 2007).

- Construction of a formal security specification according to Schmidt (2009) expressed in CSP (Communicating Sequential Processes) (Hoare, 1986).

In the following, we discuss the second method of constructing a security specification in detail. The software development principle of *stepwise refinement* is popular in software engineering, and is also well supported by *formal methods*. When performing stepwise refinement, software is developed by creating intermediate levels of abstraction. Starting with the requirements, an abstract *specification* is constructed, which is refined by a more concrete *implementation*. Then, the implementation must be verified against the specification, and further refinement steps are accomplished until the desired level of abstraction is reached.

We consider the step from the instantiation of an SPF to the instantiation of a corresponding CSPF a refinement step that not only preserves functional correctness but also the security requirement. To prove this refinement, we apply formal techniques to the (C)SPF approach. Refinement is traditionally either data-refinement or behavior-refinement. Since the (C)SPFs deal with interfaces and communicating domains rather than with states, we decided to describe them using CSP.

CSP is a process algebra that can be used to describe parallel processes that communicate synchronously via message passing. Furthermore, with the model-checker FDR2 (Failure-Divergence Refinement) from Formal Systems (Europe) Limited, sophisticated tool support is available for CSP.

Applying CSP and stepwise refinement to the (C)SPF approach has several benefits:

- CSP models of the (C)SPF instances enable a developer to formally express security requirements captured by (C)SPF instances.
- The CSP models provide a point of contact to the formal probabilistic (and possibilistic) security requirement descriptions by Santen (2008).
- Since problem frames and (C)SPFs as such only provide a static view of a system, we obtain an understanding of the dynamic aspects of (C)SPF instances.
- The CSP models allow a developer to verify that the functional and the security requirements of an SPF are *correctly* implemented by an associated CSPF, i.e., that the functionality and the security requirement are preserved.
- Verification is tool-supported by the model-checker FDR2.

Introduction to CSP$_M$

We make use of the CSP ASCII notation named CSP$_M$ since this is a prerequisite for formal verification using the model-checker FDR2. Using CSP$_M$ notation, we define *processes* that interact only by communicating. Communication takes the form of visible *events* or *actions*. A sequence of events produced by a process is called a *trace*. The set of all traces that can be produced by a process P are denoted *traces*(P). Let a be an action and P be a process; then $a \rightarrow P$ is the process that performs a and behaves like P afterwards. This is called *prefixing*. A process can have a name, e.g., $Q = a \rightarrow P$. *Recursion* makes it possible to repeat processes and to construct processes that go on indefinitely, e.g., $Q = a \rightarrow Q$.

We can make use of input and output data: the expression *in*?x binds the identifier x to whatever value is chosen by the environment, where x ranges over the type of the *channel in*. The expression *out*!y binds an output value to the identifier y, where y ranges over the type of channel *out*. The

variables x and y can then be used in the process following the prefix. By convention, ? denotes input data and ! denotes output data.

A process acts in a *nondeterministic* way when its behavior is unpredictable because it is allowed to make internal decisions that affect its behavior as observed from outside. The *replicated internal choice operator* $|\sim|$ models these internal decisions: let P be a process and X a finite and non-empty data type, then $|\sim| a: X \cdot P(a)$ behaves according to the selected a. This operator gives the environment no control over which data item is chosen. In contrast, the *replicated external choice operator* [] models external decisions: [] $a: X \cdot P(a)$ behaves according to the a selected by the environment.

Security Specification Method

The security specification method consists of three steps, which are discussed in detail in the following.

Step 1: Construct Formal CSP Models

This step must be executed for each SPF and CSPF instance. To formalize a given (C)SPF instance, we describe each of its domains as a recursive CSP process. The interfaces and the control direction of the shared phenomena (control flow) of a domain are translated into CSP channels as well as input and output events. For lexical shared phenomena, we define data types and declare the corresponding channels to be of one of these data types.

Note that when using a model-checker such as FDR2 to analyze real-world problems, we have to address the state explosion problem. A common approach to keep the model-checking effort manageable is to simplify the system to be analyzed. For that reason, we usually must define simplified data types.

We describe a (C)SPF instance as a CSP process consisting of the CSP processes of all of its domains. The processes are combined using *synchronized parallel communication* denoted by [| |]. The synchronization is accomplished over the channels modeling the interfaces that connect the domains.

Finally, the CSP models are checked using the model-checker FDR2 to prove that they are deadlock-free and livelock-free. The model-checker can also be used to debug CSP models.

After this step executed for each SPF and CSPF instance, the result is a set of CSP models that formally specify the (C)SPF instances.

Input:

- all results of phase one

Output:

- set of CSP models of SPF instances CSP_{spf}
- set of CSP models of CSPF instances CSP_{cspf}

Validation Conditions:

- each domain is described by at least one CSP process
- each interface is described by exactly one channel
- each phenomenon is described by an event or an element of a data type
- for each (C)SPF instance, one CSP process expresses a (C)SPF instance by combining all corresponding domains using synchronized parallel communication over those channels that represent the interfaces of the (C)SPF
- all CSP processes are deadlock-free and livelock-free (to be checked using FDR2)

Step 2: Formally Express Security Requirements

SEPP's security requirements analysis phase currently covers integrity and confidentiality requirements. Integrity requirements can be for-mally expressed as correctness properties, since they require to preserve the correctness of data.

Confidentiality requirements can be expressed as *information flow properties* of two flavors:

- *possibilistic:* based on the fact that an ICT system has a system behavior, which pro-duces observations visible to the environ-ment, there must exist at least one alterna-tive possible system behavior that produces the same observation.
- *probabilistic:* stochastic system behavior is taken into account.

This step must be executed for each SPF instance CSP model $csp_{spf} \in CSP_{spf}$. In the fol-lowing, we focus on confidentiality requirements in terms of *possibilistic* information flow proper-ties. In general, we call the formal description of a confidentiality requirement a *confidentiality property*. To formally specify a confidentiality requirement, we apply the framework for the specification of confidentiality requirements by Santen (2008). There does not exist *the* confiden-tiality property that allows us to express every (informal) confidentiality requirement. Instead, an adequate confidentiality property depends on the confidentiality requirement that it formalizes. Mantel (2003) gives a comprehensive overview of possibilistic information flow properties. Further-more, the framework by Santen (2008) discusses different confidentiality properties that formalize different confidentiality requirements.

We apply the techniques presented by Santen (2008) to a CSP model that formally specifies an SPF instance. First, a confidentiality property that fits the informal security requirements description is chosen. Second, the confidentiality property is expressed based on the CSP model of the SPF instance, and it is proven that the CSP models fulfills the confidentiality property.

Note: since confidentiality properties are predicates on *sets* of traces of a CSP model, they cannot be modeled directly in CSP, and thus cannot be verified using FDR2. Nevertheless, we can mathematically specify a confidentiality property and prove that a given machine and environment (i.e., an SPF instance) satisfy the property.

After this step executed for each informal security requirement description, the result is a set of formal security requirement descriptions.

Input:

- informal security requirement description *sr*
- CSP models of SPF instances $csp_{spf} \in CSP_{spf}$

Output:

- formal descriptions of security requirements *SR*

Validation Conditions:

- each formal description of a security requirement $sr \in SR$ refers to traces that are produced by the CSP model of the corresponding SPF instance

Step 3: Show Security-Requirements Preserving Refinements

Refinement is the transformation of an abstract specification into a concrete specification (implementation). CSP supports three types of process refinements:

- **Trace refinement** A process Q trace-refines a process P, if all the possible sequences of communications, which Q can perform, are also possible in P: $traces(Q) \subseteq traces(P)$
- **Failure refinement** Trace refinement extended by consideration of deadlocks.
- **Failure-divergence refinement** Failure refinement extended by consideration of livelocks.

This step must be executed for each formal security requirement description. First, it is proven on a functional level that the CSPF instance failure-divergence refines the SPF instance. Since all structural elements of the SPF are preserved in an associated CSPF, we can show a failure-divergence refinement after we reduce the structural additions of the CSPF instance to the SPF instance structure:

- We hide events that can only be communicated in the CSPF instance model using the *hiding* operator \ of CSP
- We map those events that have a more concrete structure in the CSPF instance model to events that are compatible with events of the SPF instance model. This mapping constitutes a *data refinement*. The mapping is accomplished using the *relational renaming* operator [[<-]] of CSP.

This refinement proof is tool-supported by the model-checker FDR2.

Second, it is proven that the confidentiality requirement is preserved in the CSPF instance. This proof depends not only on the CSP models of (C)SPF instances but also on the confidentiality property. For this proof, tool support is not available. For example, to prove that the confidentiality property *concealed behavior* (Santen, 2008) is satisfied by a given CSPF instance, a set inclusion of sets of traces must be proven.

After this step is executed for each formal security requirement description, the result is a set of functional and confidentiality-preserving refinement proofs.

Input:

- all results of steps 1 and 2

Output:

- refinement proofs of functional requirements (e.g., using FDR2)

- refinement proofs of confidentiality-preserving refinement

Validation Conditions:

- for each pair consisting of the CSP model of an SPF instance $csp_{spf} \in CSP_{spf}$ and the CSP model of the corresponding CSPF instance $csp_{cspf} \in CSP_{cspf}$ $csp_{cspf} \sqsubseteq_{FD} csp_{spf}$ must hold (the concrete CSPF instance model failure-divergence refines the abstract SPF instance model)

CASE STUDY: SECURE TEXT EDITOR

According to step one of the previously described method to construct security specifications, we develop CSP models for the instantiated SPF confidential data storage and the instantiated CSPF confidential data storage using password-based encryption of the secure text editor case study. In the following, the suffix _S (for specification) of a process or channel name denotes that it is part of the CSP model of the abstract SPF instance, whereas the suffix _I (for implementation) denotes that it is part of the CSP model of the concrete CSPF instance.

Construction of the CSP Model of the Instantiated SPF Confidential Data Storage

The basic ingredients of a CSP model are type and function definitions as well as channel declarations. We define a simple data type named *Plaintext* with four values *p1, p2, p3, p4*:

```
datatype Plaintext = p1 | p2 | p3 |
p4
```

Then, we declare the channel *TextFile_Y2_S* that corresponds to the interface TF!Y2 in Figure

5 to be of this data type, i.e., all events communicated over this channel are *p1, p2, p3,* or *p4*. Furthermore, we model a *spy* command by a data type *SpyCommand* with only one action *spy* that represents an operating system command to open a text file:

```
datatype SpyCommand = spy
```

We declare the channels *MaliciousUser_E5_S* and *OperatingSystem_E5_S* to be of this type. We model the user command *open* to securely open text files:

```
datatype UserCommand = open
```

We declare the channels *Author_E1_S, MaliciousUser_E1_S*, and *SecureTextEditor_E1_S* to be of this type.

We represent the interfaces MUD!Y3, OS!Y3, STE!Y3, and TF!Y3 (see Figure 5) by channels of the datatype *Length*:

```
datatype Length = short | long
```

The data items leaked over this channel are defined by a *leakage function f*:

```
f(p) = if p==p1 or p==p2
            then short
            else long
```

As an example, the leaked data items are *short* and *long*, and they correspond to the lengths of the plaintexts sent over the channel *TextFile_Y2_S*.

The interfaces AD!Y4 and STE!Y4 are represented by channels of the datatype *Plaintext. Length*, i.e. the plaintext and its length concatenated to it.

We describe each domain as a recursive CSP process, e.g., the process *HonestUser_S* that represents the *Author* domain:

```
Author_S = (|~| ucmd: UserCommand @
Author_E1_S!ucmd -> Author_S)
   [] (AuthorDisplay_Y4_S?pt ->
Author_S)
```

This process arbitrarily chooses a user command *ucmd* and sends this command over the channel *Author_E1_S* or it receives a plaintext *pt* over the channel *AuthorDisplay_Y4_S*. Afterwards, the recursive call of *Author_S* ensures that the process is repeated.

We specify the instantiated SPF in Figure 5 as a process *SecureTextEditor_ SPF_CONFIDENTIAL_DATA_STORAGE(pt)* that combines all formalized domains of the instantiated SPF confidential data storage. It has a parameter *pt* that is initialized by an arbitrary chosen element of *Plaintext*. For example, the process

```
(Author_S [| {|AuthorDisplay_Y4_S|}
|] AuthorDisplay_S)
```

combines the processes *Author_S* and *AuthorDisplay_S*. They synchronize over the channel *AuthorDisplay_Y4_S*, or, informally speaking, the domain *Author* reads data from the domain *Author display*.

Construction of the CSP Model of the Instantiated CSPF Confidential Data Storage Using Password-Based Encryption

Instead of describing the instantiated CSP model of the CSPF confidential data storage using password-based encryption completely, we present those parts that are responsible for the usage of the password-based encryption mechanism.

We introduce data types *Password* and *Ciphertext*, and the functions *encr* and *decr*:

```
datatype Ciphertext = c1 | c2 | c3 |
c4
datatype Password = pwd1 | pwd2 |
```

```
pwd3 | pwd4
encr(p1,pwd1) = c1      ...
decr(c1,pwd1) = p1      ...
encr(p1,pwd2) = c2      ...
decr(c1,pwd2) = p2      ...
encr(p1,pwd3) = c1      ...
decr(c1,pwd3) = p1      ...
encr(p1,pwd4) = c2      ...
decr(c1,pwd4) = p2      ...
```

Note: the definitions of the *encr* and *decr* functions are not complete. The functions *encr* and *decr* model a length-preserving cryptographic mechanism.

The implementation of the previously presented process *Author_S* makes use of the declared passwords:

```
Author_I(password) = (|~| ucmd: User-
Command @
   Author_E1_I!ucmd.password ->
Author_I(password))
   [] (AuthorDisplay_Y6_I?pt ->
Author_I(password))
```

The process *Author_I(password)* is parameterized by the *password* selected by the author. This password is passed together with the user command *ucmd* over the channel *Author_E1_I* to the *SecureTextEditor_I* process. The type of the channel *Author_E1_I* is *UserCommand.Password*.

The process *OperatingSystem_I* makes use of the declared ciphertexts and decryption function:

```
OperatingSystem_I = (MaliciousUs-
er_E7_I?scmd.pwd -> OperatingSystem_
E8_S!scmd
   -> OperatingSystem_I_mempwd(pwd))
OperatingSystem_I_mempwd(password) =
OperatingSystem_I
   [] (TextFile_Y4_I?ct
   -> OperatingSystem_
Y5_I!decr(ct,password).
   f(decr(ct,password)))
```

```
-> OperatingSystem_I)
```

The process *OperatingSystem_I* receives a spy command *scmd* and a password *pwd* over the channel *MaliciousUser_E7_I*. The spy command *scmd* is passed over to the process *TextFile_I* representing the *Text file* domain via the channel *OperatingSystem_E8_S*. Then, the process *OperatingSystem_I* behaves as defined by the process *OperatingSystem_I_mempwd*(*password*).

This process either behaves as defined by the process *OperatingSystem_I* or it behaves as follows: it receives a ciphertext *ct* over the channel *TextFile_Y4_I*. The operating system applies the decryption function to the ciphertext using *decr*(*ct,password*) to obtain the (wrong) plaintext. Furthermore, it calculates the length of this plaintext using *f*(*decr*(*ct,password*)). The plaintext and the result of the length calculation are concatenated and sent over the channel *OperatingSystem_Y5_I* to the *MaliciousSubject_I* process, which represents the *Malicious subject* domain.

The role of the channel between the malicious user and the operating system has changed: the channel *OperatingSystem_Y5_I* not only leaks the lengths of the transferred data items to the environment, but also the (wrong) plaintext obtained by applying the *decr* function to the ciphertext *ct* using the password *pwd*. Under the assumption that the password *pwd* selected by the malicious user is unequal to the password selected previously by the author to encrypt the plaintext yielding the ciphertext *ct,* the malicious user will only be able to decrypt the ciphertext *ct* to a wrong plaintext.

In summary, we constructed CSP models of the instances of the SPF confidential data storage and the corresponding CSPF confidential data storage using password-based encryption. Using FDR2, we successfully verified that the presented CSP models are deadlock-free and livelock-free.

Formally Expressing the Confidentiality Requirement

Following step two of phase two, we formally express the confidentiality requirement according to Schmidt (2009). The concept of indistinguishable traces presented by Santen (2008) is the foundation for defining confidentiality properties. Given a set of channels W, two traces $s, t \in traces(P)$ of a process P are *indistinguishable* by W (denoted $s \equiv_W t$) if their projections to W are equal: $s \equiv_W t \Leftrightarrow s \upharpoonright W = t \upharpoonright W$, where $s \upharpoonright W$ is the projection of the trace s to the sequence of events on W. The *indistinguishability class* $J_W^{P,k}(o)$ contains the traces of P with a length of at most k that produce the observation o on W.

Applied to the previously presented CSP models, this means that any distinction (e.g., data item length is *short* or *long*) the malicious subject can make about the internal communication of the system (e.g., appearance of different plaintexts and ciphertexts) based on the observations on, e.g., *OperatingSystem_Y3_S* and *OperatingSystem_Y4_I* is information revealed by the system. Conversely, any communication that cannot be distinguished by observing, e.g. *OperatingSystem_Y3_S* and *OperatingSystem_Y4_I* is concealed by the system. We can determine two indistinguishability classes: one that contains those traces that produce the observation *short* on the monitoring channel, and another one that contains those traces that produce the observation *long* on the monitoring channel.

An *adversary model* according to Santen (2008) is a system model that consists of the machine to be developed, the honest environment, the malicious environment, and their interfaces. The previously presented CSP models constitute valid adversary models.

A *mask м* for an adversary model is a set of subsets of the traces over the alphabets (i.e., the events supported by a process) of the processes modeling the machine to be developed, the honest user environment, and the malicious environment such that the members of each set are indistinguishable by observing the monitoring channels (i.e., the channels that leak the wrong plaintexts and the lengths) of the adversary environment W:

$$\forall M: M \cdot \forall t_1, t_2: M \cdot t_1 \equiv_W t_2$$

All traces of the form

```
t_0(pt) =
< TextFile_Y3_S.f(pt), OperatingSys-
tem_Y3_S.short>      if pt ∈ {p1,
p2},
< TextFile_Y3_S.f(pt), OperatingSys-
tem_Y3_S.long>      else,
```

A mask M_0 supporting the confidentiality requirement needs to require that for a given length l all variations of plaintexts pt in the parameter list of the trace t_0 are possible causes of the observation *OperatingSystem_Y3_S.l*.

Therefore, the sets $M_0 = \{t_0(p1), t_0(p2)\}$ and $M_1 = \{t_0(p3), t_0(p4)\}$ should be members of M_0. If the traces in a set $M \in M$ are indistinguishable by observing the monitoring channels, then the differences between these traces are kept confidential. This confidentiality property is named *concealed behavior* (Santen, 2008). It is formalized based on a set inclusion $M \subseteq J_W^{QE,k}(o)$, where the process QE is a *variant*, i.e., a purely deterministic process, of the adversary model. It is required that members of M are either completely contained in an indistinguishability class, or not at all. One says that the set of indistinguishability classes I covers M.

In general, a given adversary model satisfies a confidentiality property, which is defined based on a *basic confidentiality property* (Santen, 2008), if there exists a probabilistic deterministic realization of a machine that satisfies the basic confidentiality property in all admissible environments. In the case of concealed behavior, the question is if there is an adversary model that covers a given mask.

To show that the adversary model represented by the CSP model of the SPF instance conceals

the mask M_0, a deterministic machine realization must be found such that its composition with all realizations of the environment covers M_0.

We choose the implementation of the CSP model of the SPF instance that resolves all nondeterministic choices by probabilistic choices with equal probabilities for all alternatives.

The admissible environments consist of realizations that deterministically produce traces according to the pattern $t_0(pt)$, where $pt \in Plaintext$. The members M_0 and M_1 of M_0 are covered by the indistinguishability classes of all resulting variants of the CSP model of the SPF instance, because the chosen machine realization does not exclude any of the traces $t_0(pt)$, where $pt \in Plaintext$.

In summary, we presented a formal description of the informal confidentiality requirement description of the instance of the SPF confidential data storage.

Proving Confidentiality-Preserving Refinement

The next and last step of phase two comprises the verification of a confidentiality-preserving refinement based on the CSP model of the (C)SPF instances and the formally specified confidentiality requirement.

To prove the functional refinement, we prove that the CSP model of the CSPF instance failure-divergence refines the CSP model of the SPF instance using the model-checker FDR2.

Based on the CSP model of the CSPF instance, we create a re-abstracted CSP model by hiding events that can only be communicated in the CSPF model, e.g., *Password* and *WrongPassword*, and we map those events that have a more concrete structure in the CSPF model to events that are compatible with the events of the SPF model, e.g., *Ciphertext* events are substituted by *Plaintext* events. The data refinement is characterized by the fact that a plaintext is refined by a pair consisting of a ciphertext and a password. The resulting CSP process failure-divergence refines the CSP process that models the SPF instance, which can be verified using FDR2.

To prove the confidentiality-preserving refinement, we calculate the indistinguishability classes of the CSP model of the CSPF instance. As an example, we present the indistinguishability class

$$J^{QE,2}_{OperatingSystem\_Y4\_I}(OperatingSystem\_Y5\_I.p1.l)$$

$$J^{QE,2}_{OperatingSystem\_Y4\_I}(OperatingSystem\_Y5\_I.p1.l)=$$

$\{< TextFile\_Y4\_I.c1, OperatingSystem\_Y5\_I.p1.short >,$
$< TextFile\_Y4\_I.c2, OperatingSystem\_Y5\_I.p2.short >,$
$< TextFile\_Y4\_I.c3, OperatingSystem\_Y5\_I.p1.long >,$
$< TextFile\_Y4\_I.c4, OperatingSystem\_Y5\_I.p2.long >\}$

Since the confidentiality property concealed behavior refers to both, the monitoring channel *OperatingSystem_Y5_I* and the data, we must relate the concrete monitoring channel and the data back to the abstract ones originally referred to by the confidentiality property. Applied to concealed behavior, this general concept provides a basis for defining *refined concealed behavior*. After the re-abstraction, we must check if the re-abstracted traces are members of M_0 and M_1, respectively.

We find out that the re-abstracted traces are the same traces as the abstract ones. For this reason, they are contained in the sets M_0 and M_1. Hence, the CSP model of the CSPF instance conceals the mask M_0, and the confidentiality property concealed behavior is preserved in the CSP model of the CSPF instance. Therefore, the CSP model of the CSPF instance comprises a valid specification for the machine to be developed.

DEVELOPMENT OF A SECURITY ARCHITECTURE

In the following, we move on to the design phase of software development, i.e., the construction of a software architecture using:

- *architectural patterns* to construct a *platform-independent* secure software architecture that realizes the specified security requirements and
- a method to construct a *platform-specific* secure software architecture based on a previously developed platform-independent secure software architecture and a component framework or an application programming interface (API).

Generic Security Components and Architectures

Software components are reusable software parts. We represent software components by means of UML composite structure diagrams (UML Revision Task Force, Object Management Group (OMG), 2007) and *interface specifications*. The latter consist of several parts: structural and syntactic descriptions are expressed as UML class diagrams (interface classes). Semantic descriptions of the operations provided and used by the components' interfaces are expressed as OCL pre- and postconditions. Behavioral descriptions are expressed as UML sequence diagrams.

The generic security components discussed in this section constitute special software components that realize concretized security requirement templates. We call them "generic", because they are a kind of conceptual pattern for software components. They are platform-independent. An example for a generic security component is an encryption component defined neither referring to a specific encryption mechanism such as AES or DES nor specific encryption keys, such as encryption keys with a certain length.

We use generic security components to structure the machine domain of a CSPF. They describe the machine's interfaces to its environment and the machine-internal interfaces of its components. Each CSPF is linked to a set of generic security components.

A machine domain of a CSPF can be structured by means of generic security components according to the following principles:

- Each interface of the machine with the environment must coincide with an interface of some component.
- Components of the same purpose can be combined, e.g., several storage management components can be combined to one such component.
- For each interface between the machine and a biddable or display domain a user interface component must be introduced. Interfaces to another display or machine domain can result in an additional user interface component (especially if such an interface is security-critical, e.g., an interface to enter a password).
- For each interface from the machine to a lexical domain, a storage management component must be introduced. Symbolic phenomena correspond to return values of operations or to getter/setter operations.
- For each interface of the machine domain with a causal domain, a driver component must be introduced. Causal phenomena correspond to operations provided by driver components.
- For password or encryption key handling, key management components or key negotiation components must be introduced.
- For encryption key generation, random number generator and encryption key generator components must be introduced.
- For symmetric / asymmetric encryption / decryption, corresponding encryptor / decryptor components must be introduced.
- For integrity mechanisms, hash and MAC calculation components must be introduced.

Following the described principles, we developed a catalog of generic security components for each available CSPF. These components can be combined to obtain a set of generic security architectures that realize the concretized security requirement template of a CSPF.

The generic security components constructed for a CSPF can be combined to obtain generic security architectures according to the following principles:

- An adequate basic software architecture to connect the generic security components has to be selected, e.g., a layered architecture.
- If components can be connected directly, one connects these components.
- If components cannot be connected directly (e.g., because a component provides incompatible input for another component), additional components to interconnect them must be introduced.
- Interfaces between the machine and its environment must be introduced in the generic security architecture according to the generic security components that provide or use these interfaces.

As examples, we present generic security components and architectures for the CSPF confidential data storage using password-based encryption.

Generic Security Components for CSPF Confidential Data Storage Using Password-Based Encryption

Figure 7 shows on the left-hand side a generic security component for handling passwords expressed as a UML composite structure diagram and a class diagram.

The component *PasswordReader* provides an interface *PwdRIf*. It consists of the operations *readPassword()* and *destroyPassword()*.

The behavior of the *PasswordReader* component is described using the UML sequence diagram in Figure 8. After the operation *readPassword()*

Figure 7. Generic security components "PasswordReader" and "SecretManagement" with interfaces classes

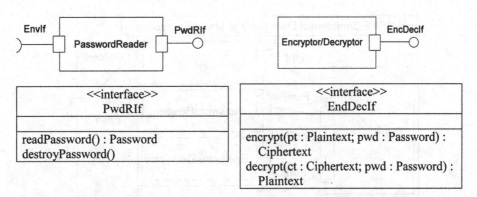

is called via the interface *PwdRIf*, the component calls the operation *showPasswordDialog()* via the used interface *EnvIf* that shows a dialog to the user and requests a password from her/him. Then, the user can submit a password *pwd* to the component, which returns this password to the caller of the operation *readPassword()*. Afterwards, this password must be wiped out from memory using the operation *destroyPassword()*.

OCL pre- and postconditions can be used to enrich the generic security component *PasswordReader* with security-relevant operation semantics. For example, constraints on the quality of the password captured by the operation *readPassword()*: e.g., a minimal password length, occurrence of special characters, etc. can be expressed.

The generic security component Encryptor/Decryptor described on the right-hand side of Figure 7 provides an operation *encrypt(pt: Plaintext; pwd: Password)* that encrypts a plaintext *pt* using a password *pwd* to a ciphertext *ct*. Additionally, it provides an inverse operation *decrypt(ct: Ciphertext; pwd: Password)* that calculates the plaintext *pt* given the ciphertext *ct* and the password *pwd*.

The generic security components described previously must be combined to obtain generic security architectures. Since generic security components are platform-independent, so are generic security architectures. Each CSPF is linked to a

Figure 8. Behavior of the generic security component "PasswordReader"

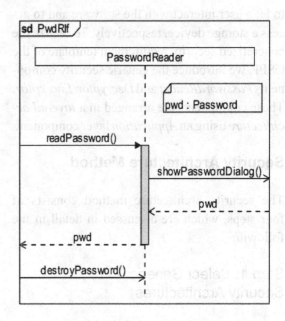

set of generic security architectures that realize the concretized security requirement template.

As an example, we present a generic security architecture for the CSPF confidential data storage using password-based encryption in Figure 9.

According to the previously presented general procedure to set up a generic security architecture of a CSPF's machine domain, we introduce *UserInterface* and *StorageManager* components

Figure 9. Generic security architecture "CSPF Confidential Data Storage Using Password-Based Encryption"

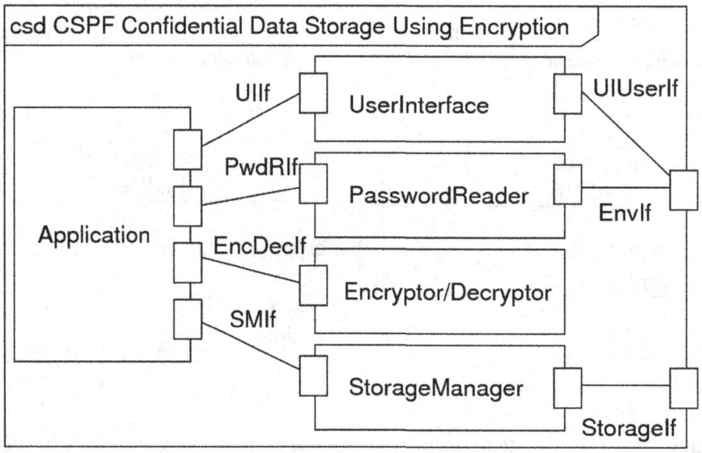

to let a user interact with the software and to access a storage device, respectively. To realize the concretized security requirement template of the CSPF, we introduce the generic security components *PasswordReader* and *Decryptor/Encryptor*. These components are arranged in a *layered architecture* using an *Application* layer component.

Security Architecture Method

The security architecture method consists of four steps, which are discussed in detail in the following.

Step 1: Select Generic Security Architectures

A generic security architecture that consists of a set of generic security components is selected for each CSPF instance, based on domain knowledge and constraints of the application domain.

Input:

- all results of phase one

Output:

- set of generic security architectures including sets of generic security components

Validation Conditions:

- the set of generic security architectures is suitable to realize the concretized security requirements *CSR*

Step 2: Compose Generic Security Architectures

Generic security architectures can also be applied to software development problems of higher complexity, i.e., problems that are divided into several subproblems, by composing the according sub-architectures. Note that we refer to generic security architectures as generic security sub-architectures if a software development problem described by more than one CSPF is considered. Choppy & Hatebur & Heisel (2006) developed for a set of subproblems a corresponding set of sub-architectures that solve these subproblems.

Moreover, the sub-architectures are composed based on dependencies between the subproblems. The authors identified three different kinds of dependencies:

• parallel subproblems
• sequential subproblems
• alternative subproblems

For subproblems that are instances of CSPFs, sequential dependencies can be identified based on the effects and necessary conditions of the subproblems. If a necessary condition of an instantiated CSPFA is considered as an additional security requirement, then a CSPFB that solves this security requirement depends on CSPFA. More precisely, the effect of CSPFB that solves the new security requirement must be established before the mechanism represented by CSPFA can work correctly.

According to Choppy & Hatebur & Heisel (2006), we must "decide if two components contained in different subproblem architectures should occur only once in the global architecture, i.e., they should be merged". We adopt the principles to merge components presented by Choppy et al. to our approach. We consider the dependencies of functional subproblems (e.g., problem frame instances) and security subproblems (CSPF instances). The principles to merge components contained in generic security sub-architectures are as follows (Choppy & Hatebur & Heisel, 2006):

• Two components that belong to sequential or alternative subproblems should be merged into one component.
• Two components that belong to parallel subproblems and that share some output phenomena should be merged into one component, because the output must be generated in a way satisfying both subproblems.

• If two components that belong to parallel subproblems and that share some input phenomena do not share any output phenomena, one can merge the components or keep them separate. In the latter case the common input must be duplicated.
• Two components that belong to parallel subproblems and that do not share any phenomena should be kept separate.

The result of the composition procedure is a platform-independent global generic secure software architecture. To show that the components in a global generic security architecture work together in such a way that they fulfill the security requirements corresponding to the different subproblems, one can model the global generic security architecture with UMLsec by Jürjens (2003). It can then be analyzed using the tool suite provided for UMLsec (see (Jürjens, 2003, pp. 133) for details) to check if the security requirements are fulfilled in the global generic security architecture.

Especially, confidentiality requirements must be treated carefully, since composition of incompatible components can lead to non-fulfillment of confidentiality requirements (see (Santen & Heisel & Pfitzmann, 2002) for details).

Input:

• all results of step one

Output:

• a generic security architecture that combines all generic security architectures selected in step one

Validation Conditions:

• the combined generic security architecture is suitable to realize the concretized security requirements *CSR*

Step 3: Refine Generic Security Architecture

In the following, we consider the refinement of the platform-independent generic security architecture to a platform-specific and implementable security architecture. It consists of several substeps:

1. Select an adequate component framework or API, e.g., the security APIs BouncyCastle or Sun's javax.crypto.*.
2. Select given components from the chosen component framework or API:
    a. Compare the interfaces, the operation semantics, and the behavioral description of the generic security components with the documentation of the component framework or API to find adequate existing components.
    b. Normally, several existing components must be used to realize one generic security component; in this case glue code must be written to connect the existing components in such a way that the specification of the generic security component is fulfilled.
    c. In the rare case that the specification of an existing component matches the specification of a generic security component, the existing component can be used without customization.
    d. Those generic security components that cannot be treated by the selected component framework or API must be implemented from scratch, based on the specification of the generic security component.

Input:

•   combined generic security architecture from step two

Output:

•   a refined security architecture including a set of refined security components

Validation Conditions:

•   each generic security component is either realized using an existing security component or it is developed from scratch

Step 4: Connect Security Components

Glue code is written to connect the components according to the refined generic security architecture.
Input:

•   all results of step three

Output:

•   a security architecture that realizes the concretized security requirements *CSR*

Validation Conditions:

•   the refined security component are connected according to the refined security architecture

CASE STUDY: SECURE TEXT EDITOR

In step one of phase three, we select a generic security architecture for each applied CSPF. For the secure text editor case study, the generic security architecture shown in Figure 9 is adequate, since it comprises a component for password-based encryption/decryption and a component to obtain a password from a user.

It is not necessary to apply step two, because we selected only one generic security architecture.

Figure 10. Refined "PasswordReader" component

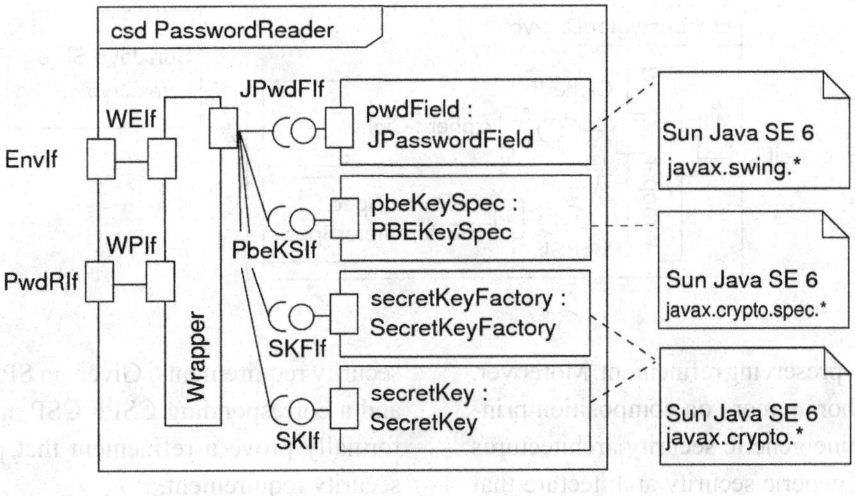

We refine this generic architecture in step three using the Java Standard Edition 6 API provided by Sun. As examples, we present the refined *PasswordReader* component in Figure 10 and the refined *Encryptor/Decryptor* component in Figure 11. The refined *PasswordReader* component consists of a Wrapper component that represents the glue code necessary to combine the components pwdField, *pbeKeySpec*, *secretKeyFactory*, and *secretKey* provided by Sun's Java Standard Edition 6 API. The *pwdField* component provides a graphical text field to retrieve a password from a user. It makes the user input unreadable, while the password is entered into text field.

The other components are used to construct a symmetric encryption key compliant to a specific password-based cryptography specification (e.g., PKCS #5) from the user password.

The refined *Encryptor/Decryptor* component is constructed similarly. It also consists of a *Wrapper* component that connects the components *cipher* and *pbeParamSpec* from Sun's Java Standard Edition 6 API. The *cipher* component provides the functionality of a cryptographic cipher for encryption and decryption. The *pbeParamSpec* component is necessary to construct a parameter set for password-based encryption as defined in the PKCS #5 standard.

Due to space limitations, we do not describe the component-internal interfaces in detail and we do not show the other refined security components. The result of SEPP's last phase applied to the secure text editor case study is a security architecture that makes use of given components provided by Sun's Java Standard Edition 6 API. The next last step of phase three is programming the *Wrapper* components and the glue code to connect the refined generic security components. Finally, testing and deployment have to be performed.

We implemented two versions of the case study, one based on the BouncyCastle API and another one based on Sun's javax.crypto.* API. Both versions re-use existing modules of the APIs according to the refined security components shown in Figure 10 and Figure 11.

The amount of glue code to implement the wrapper components ranges between 20 to 50 lines of code per component.

FUTURE RESEARCH DIRECTIONS

In the future, we intend to find new patterns to extend the catalogue of SPFs and CSPFs.

We would like to consider probabilistic confidentiality properties and the compositionality of

Figure 11. Refined encryptor/decryptor component

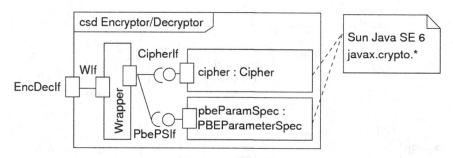

confidentiality-preserving refinement. Moreover, we plan to elaborate more on composition principles to combine generic security architectures to a combined generic security architecture that preserves the security requirements of the different generic security subarchitectures.

Furthermore, we intend to describe the generic security components and the generic security architectures using CSP models. We would like to formally show refinements between the CSPFs and the generic security components/architectures.

CONCLUSION

We presented SEPP, a security engineering process that makes use of different kinds of patterns. It covers security requirements engineering, formal security specifications, and the construction of security architectures.

SEPP starts with an extensive security requirements engineering phase, which is based on SPFs and CSPFs. These special kinds of problem frames are arranged in a pattern system. They serve to structure, characterize, analyze, and finally solve software development problems in the area of software and system security. SEPP supports to obtain a complete set of security requirements by analyzing the necessary conditions of the used CSPFs and deciding if they can be assumed or must be established by applying more frames.

Afterwards, formal security specifications in CSP are developed based on instantiated (C)SPFs. These models can be used to formally express

security requirements. Given an SPF CSP model and a corresponding CSPF CSP model, we can formally prove a refinement that preserves the security requirement.

SEPP's final phase covers the development of security architectures, which are constructed based on generic security architectures and generic security components. The generic security architectures are refined using existing or tailor-made security components. The results are platform-specific and implementable software architectures that realize the specified security requirements.

REFERENCES

Bass, L., Clements, P., & Kazman, R. (1998). *Software Architecture in Practice* (1st ed.). Reading, MA: Addison-Wesley.

BouncyCastle API. (n.d.). Retrieved June 24, 2009, from http://www.bouncycastle.org/.

Braber, I. F., Hogganvik, M. S. L., Stølen, K., & Vraalsen, F. (2007). Model-based security analysis in seven steps - a guided tour to the CORAS method, (pp.101-117). *BT Technology Journal, 25*(1). doi:10.1007/s10550-007-0013-9

Choppy, C., Hatebur, D., & Heisel, M. (2005). *Architectural patterns for problem frames. IEEE Proceedings - Software, Special Issue on Relating Software Requirements and Architecture* (pp. 198–208). Washington, DC: IEEE Computer Society.

Choppy, C., Hatebur, D., & Heisel, M. (2006). Component composition through architectural patterns for problem frames. *In Proceedings of the Asia Pacific Software Engineering Conference (APSEC)* (pp. 27-34). Washington, DC: IEEE Computer Society.

Coplien, J. O. (1992). *Advanced C++ programming styles and idioms*. Reading, MA: Addison-Wesley.

Côté, I., Hatebur, D., Heisel, M., Schmidt, H., & Wentzlaff, I. (2008). A systematic account of problem frames. *In Proceedings of the European Conference on Pattern Languages of Programs (EuroPLoP)* (pp. 749-767). Universitätsverlag Konstanz.

Deng, Y. & Wang, J. & Tsai, J. J. P. & Beznosov, K. (2003). An approach for modeling and analysis of security system architectures, (pp. 1099 - 1119). *IEEE Transactions on Knowledge and Data Engineering, 15*(5). Washington, DC: IEEE Computer Society.

Fabian, B., Gürses, S., Heisel, M., Santen, T., & Schmidt, H. (to appear). A comparison of security requirements engineering methods. *Requirements Engineering*.

Failure-Divergence Refinement (FDR) 2 by Formal Systems (Europe) Limited.(n.d.). Retrieved June 24, 2009, from http://www.fsel.com/index.html.

Fernandez, E. B., & la Red, M. D. L. & Forneron, J. & Uribe, V. E. & Rodriguez G., G. (2007). A secure analysis pattern for handling legal cases. *In Latin America Conference on Pattern Languages of Programming (SugarLoafPLoP)* (2007). Retrieved June 24, 2009, from http://sugarloafplop.dsc.upe.br/wwD.zip.

Fernandez, E. B., Larrondo-Petrie, M. M., Sorgente, T., & Vanhilst, M. (2007). In Mouratidis, H., & Giorgini, P. (Eds.), *Integrating security and software engineering: Advances and future visions* (pp. 107–126).

Gamma, E., Helm, R., Johnson, R. E., & Vlissides, J. (1995). *Design patterns - elements of reusable object-oriented software*. Reading, MA: Addison Wesley.

Gürses, S., Jahnke, J. H., Obry, C., Onabajo, A., Santen, T., & Price, M. (2005). Eliciting confidentiality requirements in practice. *In Proceedings of the Conference of the Centre for Advanced Studies on Collaborative Research (CASCON)*, (pp. 101-116). New York: IBM Press.

Haley, C. B., Laney, R., Moffett, J., & Nuseibeh, B. (2004). Picking battles: The impact of trust assumptions on the elaboration of security requirements. In C. D. Jensen & S. Poslad & T. Dimitrakos (Ed.), Proceedings of the International Conference on Trust Management (iTrust), (pp. 347-354).LNCS 2995. Springer Berlin / Heidelberg / New York.

Haley, C. B., Laney, R., Moffett, J., & Nuseibeh, B. (2005). Arguing security: Validating security requirements using structured argumentation. *In Proceedings of the Symposium on Requirements Engineering for Information Security (SREIS)*.

Haley, C. B. & Laney, R. & Moffett, J. & Nuseibeh, B. (2008). Security requirements engineering: A framework for representation and analysis, (pp. 133-153). *IEEE Transactions on Software Engineering, 34*(1). Washington, DC: IEEE Computer Society.

Halkidis, S. T. & Tsantalis, N. & Chatzigeorgiou, A. & Stephanides, G. (2008). Architectural risk analysis of software systems based on security patterns, (pp. 129 - 142). IEEE Transactions on Dependable and Secure Computing, 5(3). IEEE Computer Society.

Hall, J. G., Jackson, M., Laney, R. C., Nuseibeh, B., & Rapanotti, L. (2002). Relating Software Requirements and Architectures using Problem Frames. *In Proceedings of IEEE International Requirements Engineering Conference (RE)*, (pp. 137-144). IEEE Computer Society.

Hatebur, D., & Heisel, M. (2005). Problem frames and architectures for security problems. In B. A. Gran & R. Winter & G. Dahll (Ed.), *Proceedings of the International Conference on Computer Safety, Reliability and Security (SAFECOMP)* (pp. 390-404). LNCS 3688. Springer Berlin / Heidelberg / New York.

Hatebur, D., Heisel, M., & Schmidt, H. (2006). Security engineering using problem frames. In G. Müller (Ed.), *Proceedings of the International Conference on Emerging Trends in Information and Communication Security (ETRICS)* (pp. 238-253). LNCS 3995. Springer Berlin / Heidelberg / New York.

Hatebur, D., Heisel, M., & Schmidt, H. (2007). A pattern system for security requirements engineering. *In Proceedings of the International Conference on Availability, Reliability and Security (AReS)* (pp. 356-365). IEEE Computer Society.

Hatebur, D., Heisel, M., & Schmidt, H. (2008). A formal metamodel for problem frames. *In Proceedings of the International Conference on Model Driven Engineering Languages and Systems (MODELS)* (pp. 68–82). LNCS 5301. Springer Berlin / Heidelberg / New York.

Heisel, M. (1998). Agendas - a concept to guide software development activities. In Proceedings of the IFIP TC2 WG2.4 working Conference on Systems Implementation: Languages, Methods and Tools (pp. 19-32). Chapman & Hall London.

Hoare, C. A. R. (1986). Communicating Sequential Processes. Prentice Hall. Retrieved June 24, 2009, from http://www.usingcsp.com.

International Organization for Standardization (ISO) and International Electrotechnical Commission. *(IEC)* (2006). Common evaluation methodology 3.1, ISO/IEC 18405. Retrieved June 24, 2009, from http://www.commoncriteriaportal.org.

Jackson, M. (2001). *Problem Frames. Analyzing and structuring software development problems.* Reading, MA: Addison-Wesley.

Jackson, M., & Zave, P. (1995). Deriving Specifications from Requirements: an Example. In Proceedings of the Internation Conference on Software Engineering (SE) (pp. 15-24). New York: ACM Press.

Java Standard Edition, S. U. N. *6 API.*(n.d.). Retrieved June 24, 2009, from http://java.sun.com/javase/6/docs/api/overview-summary.html.

Jürjens, J. (2003). *Secure systems development with UML.* New York: Springer Berlin / Heidelberg.

Laboratories, R. S. A. (1999). *Password-Based Cryptography Standard PKCS #5 v2.0.* Retrieved June 24, 2009, from ftp://ftp.rsasecurity.com/pub/pkcs/pkcs-5v2/pkcs5v2-0.pdf

Lai, L., Lai, L., & Sanders, J. W. (1997). A refinement calculus for communicating processes with state. *In Proceedings of the Irish Workshop on Formal Methods: Electronic Workshops in Computing.* Berlin / Heidelberg / New York:Springer

Li, Z., Hall, J. G., & Rapanotti, L. (2008). From requirements to specifications: a formal approach. *In Proceedings of the International Workshop on Advances and Applications of Problem Frames (IWAAPF)* (pp. 65-70). New York: ACM Press.

Lin, L., Nuseibeh, B., Ince, D., & Jackson, M. (2004). Using abuse frames to bound the scope of security problems. *In Proceedings of IEEE International Requirements Engineering Conference (RE)* (pp. 354-355). Washington, DC: IEEE Computer Society.

Mantel, H. (2003). *A Uniform Framework for the Formal Specification and Verification of Information Flow Security.* Unpublished doctoral dissertation, Universität des Saarlandes, Saarbrücken, Germany.

Moriconi, M., Qian, X., Riemenschneider, R. A., & Gong, L. (1997). Secure software architectures. *In Proceedings of the IEEE Symposium on Security and Privacy* (pp. 84–93). IEEE Computer Society.

Mouratidis, H., & Giorgini, P. (2007). Secure Tropos: A security-oriented extension of the Tropos methodology, (285-309). *International Journal of Software Engineering and Knowledge Engineering, 17*(2). doi:10.1142/S0218194007003240

Mouratidis, H., Weiss, M., & Giorgini, P. (2006). Modelling secure systems using an agent oriented approach and security patterns. [IJSEKE]. *International Journal of Software Engineering and Knowledge Engineering, 16*(3), 471–498. doi:10.1142/S0218194006002823

Rapanotti, L., Hall, J. G., Jackson, M., & Nuseibeh, B. (2004). Architecture Driven Problem Decomposition. *In Proceedings of IEEE International Requirements Engineering Conference (RE)*, (73-82). Washington, DC: IEEE Computer Society.

Santen, T. (2008). Preservation of probabilistic information flow under refinement, (pp. 213-249). *Information and Computation, 206*(2-4). doi:10.1016/j.ic.2007.07.008

Santen, T., Heisel, M., & Pfitzmann, A. (2002). Confidentiality-preserving refinement is compositional - sometimes. *In Proceedings of the European Symposium on Research in Computer Security (ESORICS)*, (pp. 194-211). LNCS 2502. Springer Berlin / Heidelberg / New York.

Scandariato, R., Yskout, K., Heyman, T., & Joosen, W. (2008). *Architecting software with security patterns (Report No. CW515)*. Katholieke Universiteit Leuven - Department of Computer Science.

Schmidt, H. (2009). Pattern-based confidentiality-preserving refinement. *In Engineering Secure Software and Systems - First International Symposium (ESSoS)*, (pp. 43-59). LNCS 5429. Springer Berlin / Heidelberg / New York.

Schmidt, H., & Wentzlaff, I. (2006). Preserving software quality characteristics from requirements analysis to architectural design. *In Proceedings of the European Workshop on Software Architectures (EWSA)*, (pp. 189-203). LNCS 4344/2006. Springer Berlin / Heidelberg / New York.

Schneier, B. (1999). *Attack trees*. Dr. Dobb's Journal. Retrieved June 24, 2009, from http://www.schneier.com/paper-attacktrees-ddj-ft.html.

Schumacher, M., Fernandez-Buglioni, E., Hybertson, D., Buschmann, F., & Sommerlad, P. (2005). *Security Patterns: Integrating Security and Systems Engineering*. Washington, DC: Wiley & Sons.

Shaw, M., & Garlan, D. (1996). *Software Architecture - Perspectives on an Emerging Discipline*. Upper Saddle River, NJ: Prentice-Hall.

Spivey, M. (1992). *The Z Notation - A Reference Manual*. Upper Saddle River, NJ: Prentice Hall. Retrieved June 24, 2009, from http://spivey.oriel.ox.ac.uk/mike/zrm.

Steel, C. & Nagappan, R., & Lai, R. (2005). Core security patterns: Best practices and strategies for J2EE, web services, and identity management.

SUN javax.crypto.* API. (n.d.). Retrieved June 24, 2009, from http://java.sun.com/javase/6/docs/api/javax/crypto/package-summary.html.

UML Revision Task Force, Object Management Group (OMG). (2007). OMG Unified Modeling Language: Superstructure. (n.d.). Retrieved June 24, 2009, from http://www.omg.org/spec/UML/2.1.2/.

UML Revision Task Force, Object Management Group (OMG) (2006). Object Constraint Language Specification. Retrieved June 24, 2009, from http://www.omg.org/docs/formal/06-05-01.pdf.

van Lamsweerde, A. (2004). Elaborating security requirements by construction of intentional anti-models. *In Proceedings of the International Conference on Software Engineering (ICSE)*, (pp. 148-157). Washington, DC: IEEE Computer Society.

Weiss, M., & Mouratidis, H. (2008). Selecting Security Patterns that Fulfill Security Requirements. *Proceedings of the 16th IEEE International Conference on Requirements Engineering (RE'08)*, IEEE Computer Society, pp. 169-172.

Chapter 4
Security Patterns:
Comparing Modeling Approaches

Armstrong Nhlabatsi
The Open University, UK

Arosha Bandara
The Open University, UK

Shinpei Hayashi
Tokyo Institute of Technology, Japan

Charles B. Haley
The Open University, UK

Jan Jurjens
The Open University, UK

Haruhiko Kaiya
Shinshu University, Japan

Atsuto Kubo
National Institute of Informatics, Japan

Robin Laney
The Open University, UK

Haralambos Mouratidis
University of East London, UK

Bashar Nuseibeh
The Open University, UK & Lero, Ireland

Thein T. Tun
The Open University, UK

Hironori Washizaki
Waseda University, Japan

Nobukazu Yoshioka
National Institute of Informatics, Japan

Yijun Yu
The Open University, UK

ABSTRACT

Addressing the challenges of developing secure software systems remains an active research area in software engineering. Current research efforts have resulted in the documentation of recurring security problems as security patterns. Security patterns provide encapsulated solutions to specific security problems and can be used to build secure systems by designers with little knowledge of security. Despite this benefit, there is lack of work that focus on evaluating the capabilities of security analysis approaches for their support in incorporating security analysis patterns. This chapter presents evaluation results of a study we conducted to examine the extent to which constructs provided by security requirements engineering approaches can support the use of security patterns as part of the analysis of security problems. To achieve this general objective, the authors used a specific security pattern and examined the challenges of representing this pattern in some security modeling approaches. The authors classify the

DOI: 10.4018/978-1-61520-837-1.ch004

security modeling approaches into two categories: problem and solution and illustrate their capabilities with a well-known security patterns and some practical security examples. Based on the specific security pattern they have used our evaluation results suggest that current approaches to security engineering are, to a large extent, capable of incorporating security analysis patterns.

1. INTRODUCTION

The collective experience of engineering secure software systems indicates that potential considerations for vulnerabilities in system design are both broad and deep. Anything from a single line of program code, the level of power consumption by the computer, to lapses in human memory may invite security breaches. Security engineers, therefore, need an array of tools at their disposal in dealing with diverse security problems. An integral part of the toolkit is the ability to access transferable design knowledge. Very often it is convenient to document this transferable knowledge in a pattern. A *pattern* is a description of a recurring problem and its corresponding successful solution (Gamma *et al.*, 1996). As a pattern describes the identified recurring problem and its solution in principle, it (pattern) can be described in different languages. We call the description of a pattern using a specific modelling language, such as UML, its *representation*. Security patterns are well-understood solutions to recurring security problems (Schumacher *et al.*, 2005). They enable engineers to recognise, with relative ease, known vulnerabilities in their design and potential solutions. Several security patterns have been reported by practitioners and researchers, and there are lively and ongoing discussions about the discovery, documentation and application of security patterns.

Although many security patterns are documented in the public domain, they are often specifically tied to the language and the method in which they are expressed. Since security engineers do not have a common language and method to model, analyse and implement systems, it is important to know whether a particular security pattern can be expressed and applied in their own approach. This chapter aims to examine some of the languages in which security patterns may be expressed and the methods in which they are applied, with a view to articulating their relative strengths and weaknesses.

In this survey, we will focus primarily on the languages for modelling and methods for applying security patterns in early requirements analysis and designs. This choices are both principled and practical: principled because earlier patterns are less understood compared to those at the implementation level and because early prevention of security vulnerabilities is thought to be less costly than remedial actions taken later; and practical because further expanding the scope of the survey would open up issues that are too many to be discussed in this chapter.

The main contribution of this chapter is an evaluation of security pattern modelling approaches. Our evaluation builds on the survey of security patterns by Yoshioka et al. (Yoshioka *et al.*, 2008). We compare approaches from the following three categories because these approaches are repeatedly referred as representative ones that address security in models (Mayer *et al.*, 2007; Cabot and Zannone, 2008): object-oriented design (UML, SecureUML, UMLsec, Misuse Cases), goal-oriented (KAOS, Secure Tropos, i*), and problem-oriented (problem frames, abuse frames). In comparing and contrasting these different approaches, we adopt the widely acknowledged security pattern, Roll-Based Access Control (RBAC), and a familiar example to illustrate different aspects of each approach using a common set of evaluation criteria to judge the pros and cons of each approach. The general objective of this survey is to evaluate how security patterns can be described in selected requirements engineering approaches: in particular whether all key properties of RBAC can be expressed in those approaches. In other words, we are evaluating what each RE approach is able (and not able) to describe. Evaluation results should be useful for the following stakeholders: security pattern designers can use the results to find out what languages are appropriate for modeling their patterns; and application designers can use security patterns to develop their applications with desired quality characteristics including security. Since the evaluation results characterise the attributes of existing security patterns, they can also be used to improve the understanding of these security patterns that are modelled by any one of the approaches evaluated in the chapter. This survey aims to examine some of the languages in which security patterns may be expressed partially or entirely.

The chapter is structured as follows. Section 2 defines the main characteristics of security patterns using the well-known dimensions of pattern languages, focusing on what makes a security pattern distinctive from general ones. In Section 3, we present a running example consisting of a security problem from the banking domain and RBAC as an example of a security pattern. Based on the security pattern evaluation criteria introduced in section 2, Section 4 reviews security modelling approaches and evaluate their capabilities to representing security patterns using the RBAC and the banking example introduced in section 3. Section 5 presents a comparative summary of the evaluation results from section 4. Finally, section 6 presents our conclusions, identifying open research issues in security pattern modelling and articulate an agenda for further research.

2. CHARACTERISING SECURITY PATTERNS

In software engineering a pattern documents an abstract relationship between a recurring software development problem that arises in a specific context and a well-proven schema for its solution (Buschmann *et al.*, 1996; Gamma *et al.*, 1996; Jackson, 2001). Similarly, in security engineering a security pattern documents the description of a solution to a recurring security problem in a specific context (Fernandez and Pan, 2001; Schumacher *et al.*, 2005). In essence, security patterns are abstraction of real security problems and are identified through an analysis of real systems. In this section we present basic attributes of security patterns. By discussing these attributes we aim to address a question fundamental to the rest of the presentation of the rest of the chapter. This fundamental question is *what makes a security pattern*?

2.1 Characteristics of Security Patterns

According to Fernandez et al. (Fernandez and Pan, 2001; Fernandez *et al.*, 2007), a security pattern has five main attributes, namely: the problem, context, forces, solution, and consequences. Besides these main attributes, others exist in a pattern template such as 'know uses' and 'related patterns'. In this survey chapter we will focus on the five main attributes as these are more relevant to our main objective. Worth noting from these main pattern attributes is the fact that each pattern is specific to a given type of generic problem, solution, and context. The rest of the section describes each of these attributes in detail and their rationale.

Problem: The problem part of a security pattern captures the *intention* of the patterns as a specific recurring problem that it is aimed at addressing; that is, what is it for? The problem at which the pattern is aimed can be classified by the type of security goals such as confidentiality, integrity, availability, or accountability. Depending on the type of security goal, security patterns capture different concerns; for example, the set of challenges relevant to a confidentiality problem are different from those of an availability problem. For this reason, a security pattern must be specialised to certain types of security problems that it is intended to address. Being able to capture and analyse a security problem is an important characteristic of a security pattern modelling language.

Context: The characteristics of a security problem are influenced by its environment referred as its *context*. Context defines the conditions or situation under which a security problem may occur. It can be specified in terms of: the type of *attack* that could exploit vulnerabilities resulting from the identified security problem; the types of *assets* that could be affected (whether tangible or intangible) by an attack; and the type of *harm* or loss on assets that could occur as a result of a successful attack. Context is an essential characteristic in a security pattern as it enables the user of a pattern to evaluate its relevance and limitations to its application in a particular domain. Also worth noting is that a security problem may raise different concerns, depending on the context in which it considered. For example, addressing the integrity goal in a database of medical records may present different security issues from addressing integrity in a nuclear plant control system. Attack, assets, and harm are security-specific attributes of context. There is also the *generic* aspect of context, that is, context in general without reference to security.

Forces: A security problem may have several potential solutions. Forces document the rationale for selecting one of these solutions. They state reasons for selecting a particular security solution from several potential solutions and capture the pros and cons (advantages and disadvantages) of applying the solution. Forces are critical for evaluating alternative solutions and for understanding the costs and benefits of applying the pattern. Such rationale helps the user of a pattern to appreciate why the particular solution was chosen to be part of the pattern.

Solution: A solution is a description of the machine (plan, task, action or structure) whose ex-

ecution (or application to the context) can mitigate the security problem. The solution is well-proven in the sense that it has been validated to address the security problem adequately in previous context in which the problem was encountered. For example one solution to confidentiality of data transmitted over a public network is to use an encryption mechanism which reduces the risk of confidential information being disclosed to an attacker tapping on the communication medium. In the context of protecting data stored on a computer an authentication mechanism may be a more appropriate solution. The solution part does not need to describe a particular concrete solution to a security problem, because a pattern is like a template that can be applied in different situations. Instead, it describes how a general arrangement of elements solves the corresponding security problem in the pattern. This confidentiality example also demonstrates the role of context in selecting a suitable security solution to a security problem. Documenting the solution-part of a security pattern is important as it facilitates the reuse of solutions to commonly recurring problems. This serves the essence of having a security pattern.

Consequences: The application of a security pattern may result in changes in the context of application. Such changes are due to the fact that security requirements often conflicts with functional requirements and as a result the application of a security pattern may impact a system's flexibility, extensibility, portability, or usability. Consequences document the impact of the changes brought about by the application of pattern explicitly and help a security analyst understand and evaluate the capabilities of the given pattern.

2.2 Patterns of Problems vs. Patterns of Solutions

In addition to the criterion described above, our evaluation of each security pattern modelling approach would also discuss the phase of application of the approach. In the context of software engineering approaches, security patterns can largely be classified into two categories, depending on the phase of software development where they can be applied. They can either be classified as patterns of security problems, patterns of security solutions, or both problem and solution. Patterns of security problems document recurring structures in analysis of software development problems in the problem space.

Examples of problem patterns are Jackson's problem frames (Jackson, 2001) and their abuse frame extension (Lin *et al.*, 2003; Lin *et al.*, 2004). Once the security problem to be solved by the envisioned software system is well-understood, the next step is to move into the solution space to design the security solution. Designing and developing a security solution has its own set of problems which are determined by the characteristics of the chosen solution. The problem in the solution space should not be confused with the problem of understanding the security needs of stakeholders in the problem space. Patterns of security solutions document recurring structures of problems and their solutions in the solution space. Examples of solution patterns include architectural patterns such as pipe-and-filter (Hoare, 1983) or design patterns in object-oriented software development (Fernández-Medina *et al.*, 2009).

We will use these characteristics of security patterns and evaluation criteria for comparing and contrasting approaches to security engineering. Our evaluation will look at the extent to which each approach is capable of supporting each of the attributes of security patterns discussed in section 2.1.

3. RUNNING EXAMPLE

This section presents a running example consisting of a security problem from the banking domain and RBAC as an example of a security pattern. We use this running example in the rest of the chapter for illustrating and comparing requirements languages that may be used in representing patterns.

3.1 Banking Problem Example

We use the "open account" use case in the bank example described by Fernandez et al. (Fernandez *et al.*, 2008) to illustrate the features of the security analysis approaches surveyed. The execution of the use case involves the participation of two actors: a bank customer and bank manager. The example is about a bank customer opening a bank account securely.

The use case has the following main steps: (1) the customer provides personal information to the bank manager; (2) the bank manager performs credit checks; (3) if the customer has a good credit record, the bank manager creates an account; (4) the customer then makes an initial deposit into the account; (5) the bank manager creates authorisation and issues a card to the customer. Each of the steps in fulfilling the requirement of opening the bank account presents potential security vulnerabilities.

3.2 Role-Based Access Control

The selected security pattern example is Role-Based Access Control (RBAC). In RBAC, access control policy is embodied in user-role and role-permission relationships for achieving Separation of Duties (SoD). Users and permissions are not directly bound but indirectly associated via roles. When a user acts one of his/her roles under a session, he/she does not have any permission bounded with the other roles. For the sake of valuable comparison, RBAC pattern described in this paper includes the functionalities of the authorization.

For briefly understanding the structural aspect of RBAC, we explain $RBAC_0$ (Sandhu *et al.*, 1996), - a simpler variant of the RBAC which

Figure 1. Structure of RBAC$_0$ (from Sandhu et al., 1996)

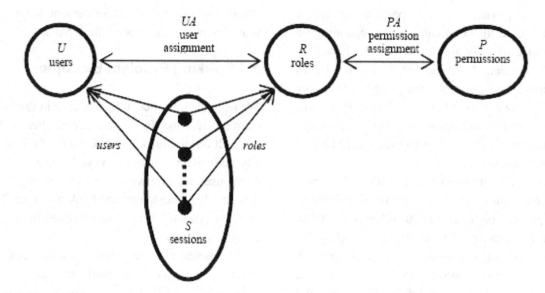

is rich enough for our discussions. The structure of RBAC$_0$ is illustrated in Figure 1. RBAC$_0$ is formalised as the four sets, two relationships, and two functions. The sets of entities *U*, *R*, *P*, and *S* denote users, roles, permissions, and sessions, respectively. The relationship between users and roles, called *user assignment*, is denoted by *UA* $\subseteq$ U $\times$ R. The *permission assignment, PA $\subseteq$ P $\times$ R*, also denotes the relationship between permissions and roles. Here, suppose that a session s_i $\in$ *S* is given; the associated users and roles are determined by the following functions: *user*(s_i) $\in$ *U* and *roles*(s_i) $\subseteq$ R. Consequently, the session s_i has all the permissions of {*p* | (*p*, *r*) $\in$ *PA* } for all *r* $\in$ roles(s_i).

RBAC is a well-understood and widely used security pattern. A unified model for RBAC is published as the National Institute of Standards and Technology (NIST) RBAC model (Ferraiolo *et al.*, 2001) and adopted as an ANSI/INCITS standard (ANSI/INCITS, 2004). RBAC is implemented in a variety of commercial systems, such as Sun's J2EE and Microsoft Windows.

4. SECURITY MODELLING APPROACHES

In this section we review security modelling approaches and evaluate their capabilities to representing security patterns using the RBAC and the banking example introduced in section 3 and the security pattern evaluation criteria introduced in section 2. For each modelling approach we introduce only the aspects that are sufficient for the evaluation. As stated in the introduction, the main objective of this chapter is to survey requirements approaches to security patterns. We classify the approaches into three categories: design, goal-oriented, and problem-oriented. Under each category we selected several representative requirements engineering techniques such as problem frames, goals, and UML. In evaluating support for security patterns in each approach we assign an integer value in the range 0 to 3. At the lower end, the value 0 implies that an approach offers no support for a particular attribute of a security pattern. On the higher end of the scale, the value 3 implies that an approach fully supports the given attribute of security patterns.

4.1 Design Approaches

Design approaches are based on the notion that models help requirements analysts in understanding complex software problems and identifying potential solutions through abstraction (Fernández-Medina *et al.*, 2009). For example, models have been successfully for abstracting source code into class diagrams in reverse engineering. Such abstractions make it easier to understand the behaviour of a software system and how it might be improved. In this section we review four representative design approaches in security engineering, namely: UML, SecureUML, UMLsec, and Misuse Cases.

4.1.1 UML

In this subsection we summarize the UML approach, and show how it may be applied to illicit the security concerns.

(i) Overview of UML
Unified Modelling Language (UML) (OMG, 2009) is a widely used model notation method for mainly software and systems. UML defines several diagrams to express different aspects of software and systems in an abstract way, such as the class diagram for the static structural aspect and the sequence diagram for dynamic behavioural aspect.

Although UML does not originally cover nonfunctional characteristics including security in an explicit way, it is possible to analyse and represent vulnerabilities in the target system and the vulnerabilities can be mitigated from the viewpoints of structure and dynamic behaviour.

(ii) Representing a Security Pattern in UML
In this subsection we show how the RBAC security pattern can be represented in UML. We also illustrate its application on the banking example. Our modelling of RBAC in UML is based on a meta-model proposed in Fernandez et al. (Fernandez and Pan, 2001; Schumacher *et al.*, 2005).

The RBAC pattern describes how to assign precise access rights to roles in an environment where control of access to computing resources is required such that confidentiality and availability requirements are preserved, and where there are a large number of users and a variety of resources. Rights of access to resources are assigned to roles instead of users directly through an authorization policy and users are assigned to roles. An object-oriented class structural model provided by the solution of RBAC is shown in Figure 2. The User, Role, Right classes describe the users registered in the system, the predefined roles in the system, and the types of access rights to the protected computing resources (described by the ProtectionObject class), respectively.

The user-to-role and right-to-role relations are many-to-many assignments. Among these relations, the separation of duties can be represented as an additional constraint on the user-to-role relationship. The Right class has accessType (such as "read only") as its attribute, and a function for checking rights (i.e. permission) as its method (checkRights()). Usually the function receives an access request and returns the result of checking whether the request is permitted according to the accessType. The Session class describes temporal situations where the users activate a subset of the roles they belong to (Sandhu *et al.*, 1996). Each session must belong to a single user.

The application of RBAC to the bank domain is as shown Figure 3. In this example, the main roles are the bank customer and the bank manager. Different rights are assigned to different actors (i.e. roles). For example, customers are granted to full access (including the transfer operation) to only their own accounts. Meanwhile, the bank manager is granted access to the customers' accounts in restricted ways.

(iii) Evaluation of Security Pattern Support in UML
In this subsection we evaluate the extent to which UML supports the representation of security

81

Figure 2. Structure provided by the solution, in the form of the UML class diagram (Schumacher et al., 2005)

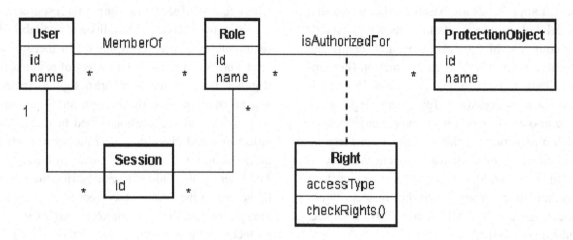

Figure 3. Structure of the analysis model of the bank domain with RBAC

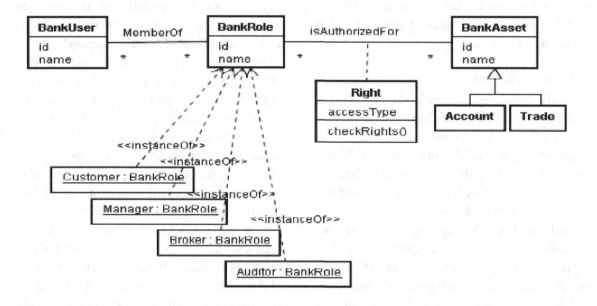

concerns using the generic characterization of security patterns.

Problem: It is hard to model high-level security goals explicitly with UML. This is due to the fact that UML is a language for communicating designs rather than analyzing software problems.

Context in General: Although UML does not have any feature specific to security patterns, the structural and behavioural aspects of attacks and assets can be modelled by UML.

Context for Attack (Threat): It is possible to model concrete structures and behaviour of specific attack scenarios as threats with UML. This is achieved by using the dynamic behavioural constructs of UML such as sequence diagrams.

Table 1. Evaluation of support for security patterns in UML

Problem	Context				Forces	Solution	Consequences
	General	Attack	Assets	Harms to Assets			
1	2	0	0	0	0	3	1

Context for Assets: It is possible to model dependencies among tangible and/or intangible assets and other entities from the viewpoint of structure or behaviour with UML. However it is hard to clarify the type of each asset.

Context for Harms to assets: It is hard to model characteristics and/or degree of certain harms to assets explicitly with UML.

Forces: It is hard to model reasons or rationales affected for the choice of the certain security solution from potentially several solutions with UML. Moreover, UML is not appropriate for modelling complex dependencies including alternative solutions.

Solution: It is possible to model structures and behaviour of the machine with UML. Moreover constraints (excluding temporal logics) on the machine and its environment can be represented by OCL included in UML 2.0 or later.

Consequences: It is hard to model tradeoffs and/or effects on quality characteristics including security explicitly with UML. The application of the RBAC pattern on a target environment makes it possible to control access to computing resources precisely while keeping high maintainability and low complexity because typically there are much more users than roles.

Table 1 presents a summary of the evaluation of the support for security patterns in UML based on the discussion above. UML tends to be used for modelling solutions mainly because it can capture structural and behavioural aspects of security functions and/or constraints on the environment, and sometimes referring to problems.

UML provides a special diagram notation for representing parameterized collaboration, which can be used for modelling structure and behaviour of the solution of any pattern. Moreover, UML provides a built-in generic extension mechanism called UML Profile to customize UML models for particular domains by using additional stereotypes, tagged values and constraints for specific model elements. There are several UML profiles for patterns such as the UML Profile for Patterns as a part of the UML Profile for Enterprise Distributed Object Computing (EDOC) specification (OMG, 2004). However, these existing diagram and profile are not specific to security patterns so that they are incapable of representing security concerns with precise semantics explicitly.

4.1.2 SecureUML

(i) Overview of SecureUML
Lodderstedt *et al.* (Lodderstedt *et al.*, 2002) present a modelling language, based on UML, called SecureUML. SecureUML focuses on modelling access control policies and how these (policies) can be integrated into a model-driven software development process. It is based on an extended model of role-based access control (RBAC) and uses RBAC as a meta-model for specifying and enforcing security. RBAC lacks support for expressing access control conditions that refer to the state of a system, such as the state of a protected resource. In addressing this limitation, SecureUML introduces the concept of authorisation constraints. Authorisation constraints are preconditions for granting access to an operation.

The combination of the graphical capability of UML, access control properties of RBAC, and authorisation constraints makes it possible to base

Figure 4. SecureUML meta-model (from Lodderstedt et al., 2002)

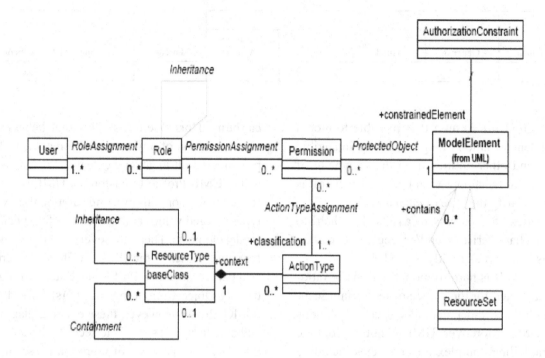

access decision on dynamically changing data such as time. Similar to its parent modelling language UML, SecureUML focuses on the design phase of software development.

(ii) Representing Security Patterns in SecureUML

The representation of security patterns in SecureUML inherits features from both UML and RBAC and is based on the following concepts: Role, Permission, ResourceSet, ModelElement, ActionType, and AuthorisationConstraints (Lodderstedt *et al.*, 2002). Figure 4 is a meta-model that illustrates how these concepts are related. The concepts of Role, Permission, ResourceRType, and ActionType are from RBAC and they are described in section 3. Meanwhile ModelElement is a UML concept.

SecureUML introduced the concepts of ResourceSet and AuthorisationConstraint. A ResourceSet represents a user-defined set of model elements used to define permissions or authorisa-

tion constraints. An authorisation constraint is a part of an access control policy that expresses a precondition imposed on every call to an operation on a resource. AuthorisationConstraint is derived from the UML core type Constraint. The precondition depends on the dynamic state of the resource, the current operation call, or the environment.

Figure 5 illustrates an authorisation constraint which states that a manager can update and view a bank account, but such operations are limited to business hours only. As shown in the Figure, in SecureUML, authorization constraints are tagged with the stereotype <<secureuml.constraint>>. A role is identified with the stereotype <<secureuml.role>>. The Account class is an abstraction of the asset to be protected and it is identified with the <<object>> stereotype.

(iii) Evaluation of Patterns Support in SecureUML

Problem: SecureUML does not explicitly model security goals but focuses on modelling solutions

Figure 5. Example of SecureUML constraints

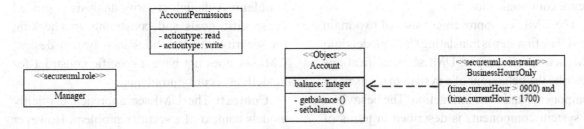

Table 2. Evaluation of support for security patterns in SecureUML

Problem	Context				Forces	Solution	Consequences
	General	Attack	Assets	Harms to Assets			
1	2	1	2	1	1	3	2

to security problems. Its foundation of on RBAC implies that it is specific to security goals relating to controlling access to shared resources.

Context: The modelling of context in SecureUML is similar to RBAC. However, the context only captures assets that may be harmed in the event of an attack. It does not model scenarios of attacks and possible harm to assets.

Forces: There is no construct for capturing and modelling forces in SecureUML.

Solution: Yes. The combination of RBAC with UML and the authorization constraints extension is the bases of a security solution in SecureUML.

Consequences: Yes. The consequences of using SecureUML is a solution to an access control problem in access rights to resource are assigned to roles and users are assigned to roles with specific authorization constraints. The evaluation of security pattern support in this approach is summarized in Table 2.

4.1.3 UMLsec

(i) Overview of the UMLsec
UMLsec (Jurjens, 2004) is an extension of UML which allows an application developer to embed security-related functionality into a system design

and perform security analysis on a model of the system to verify that it satisfies particular security requirements. Security requirements are expressed as constraints on the behaviour of the system and the design of the system may be specified either in a UML specification or annotated in source code.

Automated theorem proving or model checking is used to establish whether security requirements hold in the design. If the design violates security requirements, a Prolog-based tool is used to generate a scenario (in the form of attack sequences) of how security requirements may be violated by the design and countermeasures are taken to remove the vulnerability. In essence, UMLsec assumes that requirements have already been elicited and there exists some system design to satisfy them. Its objective is to establish whether the system design satisfies security properties. The design is then progressively refined to ensure that it satisfies security requirements.

(ii) Representing Security Patterns in UMLsec
UMLsec defines several new stereotypes towards formal security verification of elements such as: fair exchange to avoid cheating for any party in a 2-party transaction; secrecy/confidentiality of information; secure information flow to avoid

partial leaking of sensitive information; and, secure communication links.

The UMLsec approach consists of two main steps. The first step is translating UML models into UMLsec specifications. UMLsec specifications describe the behaviour of a system in terms of its components and their interaction. The behaviour of system components is described in terms of the messages they exchange in communication links between them. The formal semantics of the communication between components are similar to Hoare's communication sequential processes (CSP) (Hoare, 1983).

The next step, security analysis, involves eliciting ways by which an adversary may modify the contents of the data exchanged in communication link queues that may compromise the integrity of system behaviour. The analysis focuses on a consideration specific types of adversaries that may attack a system in a specific way. An example of such an attack on a communication link between components is breach of confidentiality, which state that some information will only become known only to legitimate parties. UMLsec specifications are checked for vulnerability to types of threats on contents of a communication link such as delete, read, and insert. The types of threats are adversary actions associated with particular adversary types. *Delete* means that an adversary may delete messages from a communication link queue. *Read* allows an adversary to read messages in the link queue, while *insert* allows the adversary to insert messages in the communication link.

The above discussion illustrates how security patterns are supported in UMLsec. In summary, first, UMLsec specifications are described based on component behaviour and patterns of interaction between system components. Secondly, the analysis for security vulnerabilities is guided by specific types of adversaries with specific classes of threats on contents of communication links. The classes of threats are also associated with specific types of security goals that an adversary may violate.

(iii) Evaluation of Patterns Support in UMLsec

Problem: Although security analysis is guided by specific goals and constraints in checking for security vulnerabilities in a system design, UMLsec does not have a specific construct for modelling security problems.

Context: The UMLsec approach explicitly models context of a security problem. However this context is limited to system design components, their interactions, and adversary models.

Forces: Once security vulnerabilities have been identified the system design is progressively refined to eliminate the threat. The rationale for selecting a particular solution of refining a design is not explicitly captured and it is not explicit whether alternative solutions are explored. It is possible though that such alternative security solutions can be explored in the refinement process based on the native UML design.

Solution: UMLsec provides an explicit refinement of design in order to ensure that they satisfy security constraints. Once a design has undergone refinement its ability to satisfy security requirements is re-verified. The refinement continue until it can be demonstrated that the vulnerability of the design to attacks is eliminated

Consequences: When a design has been found to violate security requirements, UMLsec provides for the generation of scenarios, in the form of attack sequences, which explain how security requirements may be violated by the design. The results (consequences) of refining a system design in order to address security vulnerabilities are captured in the revised version of the design and assessed against security requirements. A summary of evaluation results of UMLsec is presented in Table 3.

4.1.4 Misuse Cases

(i) Overview of the Misuse Cases

Use cases document functional requirements of a system by exploring the scenarios in which the system may be used (Jacobson, 1992). Scenarios

Table 3. Evaluation of support for security patterns in UMLsec

Problem	Context				Forces	Solution	Consequences
	General	Attack	Assets	Harms to Assets			
1	2	3	2	3	2	3	2

Figure 6. Use case and misuse cases in the banking example

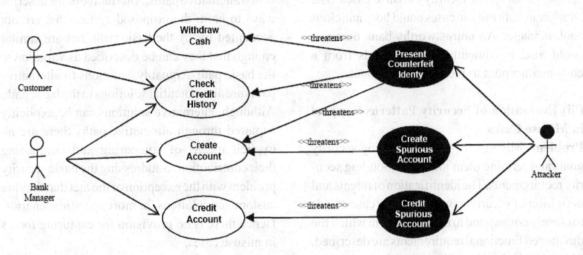

are useful for eliciting and validating functional requirements (Weidenhaupt *et al.*, 1998; Sindre and Opdahl, 2005), but are less suited for determining security requirements – which describe behaviours not wanted in the system. Similar to anti-goals (van Lamsweerde, 2004), misuse cases are a negative form of use cases and thus are use cases from the point of view of an actor hostile to the system (Alexander, 2002; Alexander, 2003). They are used for documenting and analysing scenarios in which a system may be attacked. Once the attack scenarios are identified, countermeasures are then taken to remove the possibility of a successful attack.

Although misuses cases are not entirely design-oriented as they represent aspects of both problems and solutions, they have become popular as a means of representing security concerns in system design. Worth noting is that they are limited by the fact that they are based only on scenarios. Completeness of requirements analysed through

scenarios is not guaranteed as other scenarios by which the security of a system could be exploited may be left out.

(ii) Representing Security Patterns in Misuse Cases

Figure 6 shows some of the use cases and misuse case in the bank account example. Use cases are represented as clear ellipses while misuse cases are represented with the shaded ellipses. The <<threatens>> stereotype implies that the given misuse case is a threat to the satisfaction of the requirements of the corresponding use case. The notation we use for misuse cases is based on requirements engineering process proposed by Sindre and Opdahl (Sindre and Opdahl, 2005).

As illustrated in Figure 6, the security threats described in misuse cases are based on the functional requirements described in use cases. For example, the "create account" use case can be threatened by the "create spurious account" and

Table 4. Evaluation of support for security patterns in misuse cases

Problem	Context				Forces	Solution	Consequences
	General	Attack	Assets	Harms to Assets			
2	2	3	1	3	1	2	2

"present counterfeit identity" misuse cases. The attacker in both misuse cases could be a malicious bank manager. An untrustworthy bank manager could also fraudulently transfer funds from a customer account to the spurious account.

(iii) Evaluation of Security Patterns Support in Misuse Cases

Problem: Misuses focus on describing security goals and refining them into corresponding security requirements. The identification of threats and definition of security goals in misuse cases tends to closely correspond to the use cases in which the threatened functional requirements are described. This bounds the identification of threats only to known functional requirements.

Context: Context is not explicitly captured in the high-level descriptions of misuse cases. It is possible though to describe assumptions about the states of the environment that make the misuse case possible. In the bank account example the "create spurious account" misuse case is possible if a user playing the role of a bank manager is untrustworthy. Similarly, the credit spurious account misuse case is based on the assumption that entities playing the role of a bank clerk may potentially divert funds from a genuine account to a fraudulent account. Hence, misuse cases describe assumptions about the problem context although these assumptions are oversimplified and do not explicitly capture the context and the assets that can be harmed in the event of a successful attack (Arlow, 1998).

Forces: Apart from the basic solution to satisfying a security goal, misuse cases have constructs for capturing alternative solutions called alternative paths. Alternative paths describe ways to harm the proposed system that are not accounted for by the basic path, but are similar enough that they can be described as variation to the basic path. Arguably, solutions to alternative paths are also potential solutions to the basic path. Although, alternative solutions can be explicitly captured through alternative paths there are no explicit means of comparing and contrasting their contribution to addressing the basic security problem with the exception of the fact that they are customized solutions for more specific scenarios. Hence there is no provision for capturing forces in misuse cases.

Solution: Misuse cases capture solutions for addressing security goals through *mitigation points* (Sindre and Opdahl, 2005). Mitigation points identify actions in a basic or alternative path where misuse threats can be mitigated and potential mitigation strategies that should be taken.

Consequences: The guaranteed outcome of mitigating a misuse case is described in a *mitigation guarantee* (Sindre and Opdahl, 2005). In this respect, a mitigation guarantee captures the consequences of applying a security patterns. The description in a mitigation guarantee depends on the level of detail of the description in mitigation points. If mitigation points are not specified in detail, then a mitigation guarantee describes the level of security required from the mitigating use cases to be described later. On the other hand if mitigation points have been described in detail, then a mitigation guarantee captures the strongest possible security guarantee that can be made.

Figure 7. A model showing the context of a security pattern in i*

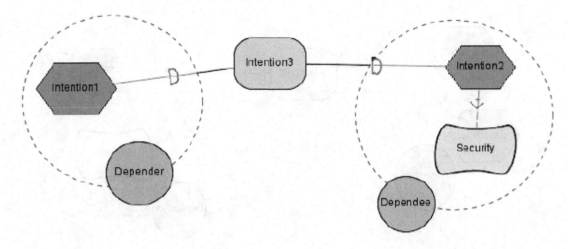

4.2 Goal-Oriented Requirements Approaches

4.2.1 Secure i*

(i) Overview
Distributed intentions, also known as the i* representations (Yu, 1997) are used to model and explore goal-oriented requirements of stakeholders in the problem space. Tropos is a process (Castroa *et al.*, 2002) that applies i* to analyse early requirements in order to come up with a validated list of specifications (tasks or plans) for a solution.

In i*, distributed stakeholders are categorised as agents, actors, roles and positions. Two kinds of relations among the goals of stakeholders are often analysed, one concerns the strategic rationale (SR) of individual stakeholders with AND-OR refinement respectively through decomposition and means-ends links; the other concerns the strategic dependencies (SD) among different stakeholders. Four types of intentions, namely goals, softgoals, tasks, resources, can appear in the SR model as nodes on the AND-OR refinement trees, or appear in the SD model as the dependum of the dependencies. Goals represent the desired states of the stakeholders, whilst soft-goals model

quality requirements that do not have clear-cut Yes/No answers, such as security. The goals/tasks connect to softgoals through four types of contribution links (HELP +, HURT -, MAKE ++ or BREAK –) (Yu, 1997).

(ii) Security Patterns in i*
Figure 7 is an example i* diagram where intentions such as goals are shown as labelled ovals, tasks as hexagons, resources as rectangles, softgoals as clouds. The decomposition links are shown with arrowheads, whilst the means-ends links are shown with a mark of line segment, and the contribution links are shown with a type label. Agents are shown by dotted circles that enclose the intentions they contain. On the border of these circles are circular icons that indicate the type of the agent, such as Roles as shown in this figure. Strategic dependencies between two intentions of different agents are shown by arrows connecting them with an intention node beyond the boundaries of any agents. These dependency arrows have a D-shaped mark in the middle to emphasise their difference to decomposition/contribution links. Figure 7 is also an example i* diagram representing the RBAC security pattern (Yu *et al.*, 2008).

Figure 8. The security pattern in i* to enforce responsibility

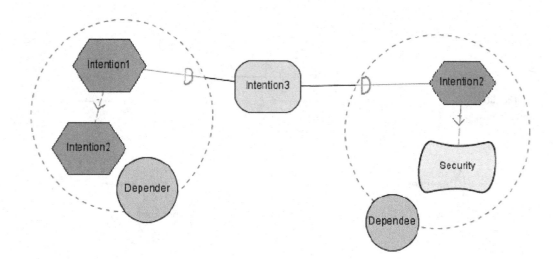

One of the important issues in RBAC (Arlow, 1998) is to clarify the responsibilities of two different roles. This can be represented by using two dependent roles "Depender" and "Dependee", and the "Dependee" contains a soft-goal "Security" in its SR model (Figure 7). The achievement of "Intention2" of "Dependee" depends on the achievement of "Intention1" through a dependum "Intention3". If the role "Depender" may achieve "Intention1" by itself, there is no need for the role "Dependee" to achieve "Intention1". According to the RBAC security requirement, however, only the role "Dependee" is allowed to achieve "Intention1" to separate the duty. To avoid a violation of the separation of duty requirement in RBAC, one therefore must prevent "Intention1" from being executed by the role "Depender".

Hence, we introduce the following security pattern in i* by adding a negative contribution (HURT or BREAK) from "Intention1" to "Intention2", as introduced in Figure 8. Since one cannot have "Intention2" both satisfied and denied when "Intention1" is satisfied, it avoids the vulnerability in the model. This is the consequence of the security pattern in i*.

Figure 9 illustrates a realistic context for opening a bank account where the security pattern in Figures 7 and 8 can be applied. A task "manage PIN" may be achieved by a "Bank Clerk", but it seems to be insecure because "Bank Clerk" can maliciously manage the PIN by, e.g., issuing a very simple PIN or leaking the PIN. Consequently, the task "mange Personal Info" cannot be achieved by "Bank Clerk" because otherwise the personal information could have been abused to open the account by the malicious bank manager.

To prevent this from happening, we apply the security pattern that results in a new securer model in Figure 10, which satisfies the security property by the RBAC requirement.

(iii) Evaluation of Patterns Support in i*

This subsection presents an evaluation of the extent to which security pattern modelling is supported in the i* approach. Table 5 presents a summary of the evaluation results based on the examples representing security patterns presented in the subsection 4.2.1(ii).

Problem: Supported. The security goals are represented natively as softgoals in the i* approach in addition to the dependencies among them. This is a strength in the i* approach for security patterns. The vulnerability in the context is specified

Figure 9. A part of a model for opening bank account

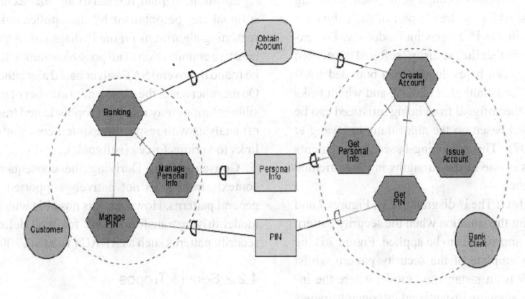

Figure 10. A new secure model

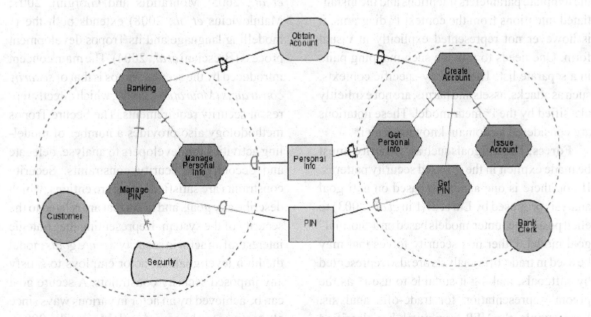

Table 5. The strength of support of security pattern using the i* approach

Problem	Context				Forces	Solution	Consequences
	General	Attack	Assets	Harms to Assets			
3	1	0	1	1	2	1	1

in the i* diagrams through goal-based reasoning analysis, which is already part of the validation process in the i*/Tropos methodology. For example, whether the "security" softgoal is satisfied or denied can be evaluated by a bounded SAT-solver (Sebastiani *et al.*, 2004), and which tasks prevent the softgoal from being satisficed can be diagnosed based on the algorithms in (Wang *et al.*, 2007). The reasoning-based requirements analysis is one of the strengths in goal-oriented approaches.

Context: The i* diagrams (e.g., Figures 7 and 9) present the situation when the security pattern of an i* approach is to be applied. Figure 7 is the general template of the security pattern whilst Figure 9 is an instantiated model where the intention names are instantiated by concrete names (e.g., Intention1="account opened"). Although it is possible to identify such a relationship between the template parameters intentions and the instantiated intentions from the context i* diagrams, it is however not represented explicitly in visual form. One needs to provide such mapping pairs in a separate list. The security-specific contexts, such as attacks, assets and harms, are not explicitly classified by the i* meta-model. These notations are considered as domain knowledge in i*.

Forces: The softgoals such as "Security" must be made explicit in the i* based security patterns. If not, there is one approach based on anti-goal analysis proposed by Liu et al (Liu *et al.*, 2003) to elicit possible counter-models based on a "normal" goal model. Other non-security forces that may be used in trade-offs analysis are also represented by softgoals, making it suitable to use i* as the pivotal representation for trade-offs analysis. For example, the NFR framework has classified Security further into Availability, Confidentiality, Authentication, etc. Such decomposition patterns are a strength of i* approach. One limitation of such analysis in the qualitative reasoning based on the i* meta-model can be improved by its extension, Secure Tropos, using quantitative evaluations for risk management (Giorgini *et al.*, 2002).

Solution: A plan for satisfying the security softgoal can be obtained by the application of reasoning algorithms on the i* diagrams. An exhaustive enumeration of all possible solutions can be found by several SAT-solver based algorithms. On the other hand, the exponential number of possible solutions may require a sophisticated trade-off analysis with respect to explicit contribution links to various forces (softgoals).

Consequences: Deriving the consequence contexts from i* is not natively supported for general patterns. However, it is possible with the model-driven transformations for well-defined security patterns such as RBAC (Yu *et al.*, 2008).

4.2.2 Secure Tropos

(i) Overview of Secure Tropos

Secure Tropos (Mouratidis, 2004; Mouratidis *et al.*, 2005; Mouratidis and Giorgini, 2007; Matulevicius *et al.*, 2008) extends both the i* modelling language and its Tropos development process (Bresciani *et al.*, 2004). The main concept introduced by the secure Tropos is that of *security constraints (Mouratidis, 2004)*, which directly represent security requirements. The Secure Tropos methodology also provides a number of modelling activities for developers to analyse, delegate and decompose security constraints. Security constraints are satisfied by secure entities, which describe any goals and tasks that are related to the security of the system. Representing the strategic interests of an actor in security, *secure goals* model the high level goals an actor employs to satisfy any imposed security constraints. A secure goal can be achieved by an actor in various ways since alternatives can be considered (Mouratidis, 2004).

The precise definition of how the secure goal can be achieved is given by a *secure task*. *Secure dependency* introduces security constraint(s) that must be respected by actors for the dependency to be satisfied. Both the depender and the dependee must agree for the fulfilment of the security constraint(s) in order for the secure dependency

Figure 11. A Secure Tropos model

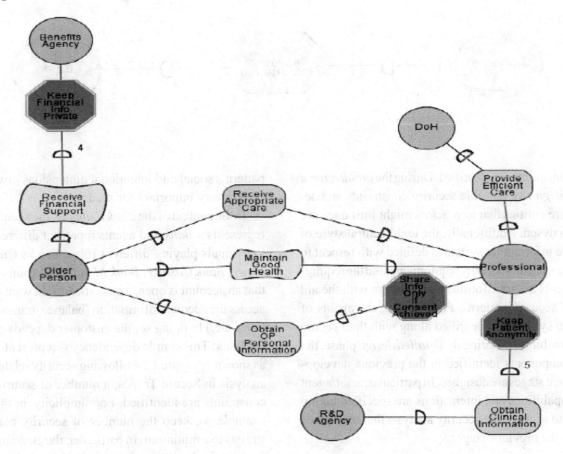

to be valid. This means the depender expects the dependee to satisfy the security constraint(s) and also that the dependee will make an effort to deliver the dependum by satisfying the security constraint(s). A graphical representation of a Secure Tropos model with the above concepts is shown in Figure 11.

The process of Secure Tropos analyses the security needs of the stakeholders and the system in terms of secure dependencies and security constraints imposed to the stakeholders and the system; of identifying secure entities that guarantee the satisfaction of the security constraints; and of assigning capabilities to the system towards the satisfaction of the secure entities (Mouratidis, 2004). This process is spread out into four main phases: early requirements analysis, late require-

ments analysis, architectural design, and detailed design. During the *early requirements analysis* phase the secure dependencies between the various stakeholders of the system are analysed. In particular, secure dependencies and security constraints are identified for the various actors. During this stage, imposed security constraints are expressed, initially as high-level statements which are later further analysed. Then secure goals and entities are introduced to the corresponding actors to satisfy the security constraints.

During the *late requirements analysis* phase, security constraints are imposed on the system under development. These constraints are further analysed according to the analysis techniques of secure Tropos and secure goals and entities necessary for the system to guarantee the security

Figure 12. A simple dependency for the bank example

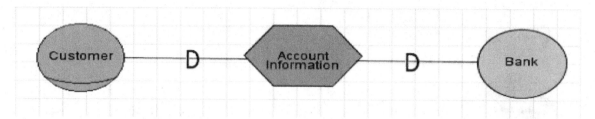

constraints are identified. During the *architectural design* any possible security constraints and secure entities that new actors might introduce are analysed. Additionally, the architectural style of the information system is defined with respect to the system's security requirements and the requirements are transformed into a design with the aid of security patterns. Furthermore, the agents of the system are identified along with their secure capabilities. During the *detailed design* phase, the components identified in the previous development stages are designed. In particular, actor/agent capabilities and interactions are specified taking into account the security analysis that took place in the previous stages.

(ii) Representing Security Patterns

In Secure Tropos, patterns are normally used to assist developers to identify a network of actors or a set of agents to solve specific security problems based on the security requirements of the system. In doing so, patterns are documented using a template that it is mostly based on the Alexandrian format. Each pattern is described in terms of its problem (intent), context, forces, solution and consequences. Depending on the targeted solution paradigm (network of actors or set of agents) developers can describe the patterns using standard or agent-oriented terminology and concepts (e.g. agency: the place where an agent resides). The solution proposed by any pattern in Secure Tropos is described in terms of social dependencies and intentional elements. This makes it possible to achieve a good understanding of the

pattern's social and intentional dimensions - two factors very important for security.

In the context of the *Bank Example*, the agency represents a *Bank* and agents represent different individuals playing different roles such as *Customer, Bank Cashier, Bank Manager*. Assuming that an account is open, a customer might want to access the account information (balance, transactions, etc.) In doing so, the customer depends on the Bank. This simple dependency is represented as shown in Figure 12. Following security related analysis in Secure Tropos, a number of security constraints are identified. For simplicity, in this example we keep the number of security constraints to a minimum. In particular, the customer is given the security constraint "to Keep Account Information Secure" and the Bank is required to maintain two security constraints "to Keep Customer Information Private" and "to Allow Account Access Only to Authorised Customers" as shown in Figure 13. Once security constraints have been identified, it is important that a design is developed to fulfil such security constraints. It is at this stage that security patterns are applied.

In particular, the RBAC pattern can be used to create a design that satisfies the "Allow Account Access Only to Authorised Customers". The rest of the subsection illustrates how the RBAC pattern is represented using the Secure Tropos approach and how the pattern assist in developing a design that fulfils the appropriate security constraint. It is worth mentioning that Secure Tropos adopts agent-oriented terminology and concepts when describing the pattern. This enables us to demon-

Figure 13. A secure dependency for the bank example

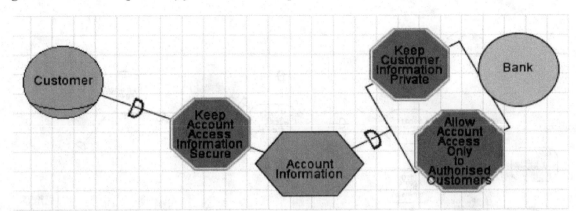

strate how the approach deals with agent related security patterns and it also provides a slightly different view of the pattern as described in the rest of the approaches. This, in turn, allows us to demonstrate a wider application domain for the Secure Tropos approach and its representation of patterns, and enables us to evaluate the approaches described in this chapter in a wider context.

Problem: Allow an agency to provide access to its resources, according to its security policy, based on the roles that each agent plays. Agents belonging to an agency might try to access resources that are not allowed. Allowing this to happen might lead to serious problems such as disclosure of private information or alteration of sensitive data. How can the agency make sure that agents only access resources which they are allowed to access?

Context: Many agents exist in an agency. These agents often play different roles and most likely will require access (according to the role they play) to some of the agency's resources in order to achieve their operational goals.

Forces: It is unlikely that the access control facilities of all internal resources are activated and configured appropriately. In particular, out-of-the box installations offer standard services that can be misused by malicious agents. Even if there are restrictions to access, it is unlikely that they are consistent, especially when more than one

administrator is involved and there are no "global" guidelines. Even worse, it could be assumed that most internal resources are not hardened. Experience shows that patches are not applied in time and that many, often unneeded services are running. Furthermore, it might happen that attacks cannot even be detected, as one cannot ensure that the audit facilities of the internal resources are activated and configured appropriately.

Solution: Each agent is allowed access to a resource according to the role they play. A Role Controller agent exists in the Agency to enforce the role based policy of the Agency. Thus, when an agent, playing a specific role, requests access to a resource; this request is forwarded to the Role Controller agent. The Role Controller checks the role based policy against the agent's role and determines whether the access request should be approved or rejected. If the access request is approved the Role Controller forwards the request to the Resource Manager. The graphical representation of the pattern dependencies is shown in Figure 14. The Requester Agent depends on the Resource Manager for the resource, and the Agency depends on the Role Controller for checking the request. The Role Controller depends on the Agency for receiving the role based policy and for forwarding the request, which is forwarded to the Resource Manager in case it is approved.

Figure 14. Pattern solution representation

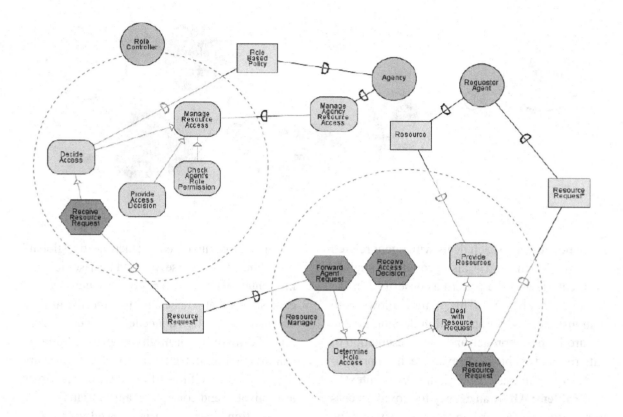

Consequences: Agency's resources are accessed only by agents which playing specific roles. Different role based policies can be used for accessing different resources. However, a possible attack is that, if this fails the role base access control system fails.

4.2.2.3 Evaluation of Security Patterns Support in Secure Tropos

As mentioned before, security patterns can assist developers to develop a design that satisfies specific security constraints. Therefore, the use of security patterns in Secure Tropos is particularly encouraged during the architectural design stage of the methodology. Although an extended Alexandrian format is used to represent the security patterns in Secure Tropos, the real novelty of the pattern representation template used above is based on the presentation of the solution in terms of social dependencies of the actors. Such representation enables one to directly fit security patterns to Secure Tropos models. Going back to the *Bank Example*, the *Requester Agent* of the pattern solution representation is effectively the *Customer*, the *Agency* represents the *Bank* and the *Resource Manager* and *Role Controller* represent roles within the bank that are required for the RBAC to work such as *Account Manager* and *Bank Cashier* (or an electronic system in case request is made online or through a system).

It is now well recognized that security is not just a technical issue but it also demonstrates a social dimension. Therefore, to completely represent security patterns, it is important that Secure Tropos model the social dependencies that a security pattern introduces as part of its solution. Moreover, since the security aware concepts of the methodology contribute to the various security

Table 6. Summary of evaluation of pattern support in the Secure Tropos approach

Problem	Context				Forces	Solution	Consequences
	General	Attack	Assets	Harms to Assets			
3	3	2	3	3	3	1	2

related analysis (attacks, assets, harm etc), the Secure Tropos allows one to specify contexts or applicability of the pattern and to quantify the risks. It is also important to mention that the methodology supports not only the representation of individual security patterns, but the representation of security pattern languages and the formalization of the properties of the patterns that belong to the language as demonstrated in (Mouratidis *et al.*, 2006). A number of guidelines on the application of patterns have also been defined (Mouratidis *et al.*, 2006). Moreover, an approach has been developed and integrated into Secure Tropos that supports the search for a combination of security patterns that will meet given security requirements (Weiss and Mouratidis, 2008). Table 6 summarises the support provided by the Secure Tropos approach to the representation of security patterns.

Secure Tropos is an improvement over i* on the Forces and Context attributes. Forces in Secure Tropos fully consider the quantified risks. It also improves partially the Context attribute of security constraints by providing additional contexts for security patterns.

4.2.3 KAOS

(i) Overview of KAOS

Introduced by van Lamsweerde at al., the KAOS is a requirements engineering framework that supports patterns of goal refinement that allow high-level goals to be stated in terms of a combination of lower level ones (van Lamsweerde *et al.*, 1995; Darimont and Lamsweerde, 1996; van Lamsweerde, 2004). A goal is defined as statements that express the intended behaviour of the system under development, and in general it is expected that this behaviour will be achieved through the cooperative interaction of the agents that make up the system. Agents are the active components of the system, be they humans, devices, existing software or software-to-be, that will play some role in satisfying the goals of the system.

The goals can be specified in KAOS using both a formal and informal notation. The informal definition is specified is natural language whilst the formal definition uses the temporal logic notation introduced by (Manna and Pnueli, 1992). KAOS provides reusable patterns of goal refinement that are formally proven in terms of temporal logic expressions. The approach taken for proving a given pattern is to assume that each of the sub-goals holds and then show that it is possible to infer the truth of the base goal from the conjunction (or disjunction) of the sub-goals. The patterns ensure that each stage of the elaboration process is correct, i.e. achieving the low level goals is equivalent to achieving the higher-level one; consistent, meaning that it is possible to satisfy all the low-level goals; and minimal, i.e. there are no redundant goals in the refined set.

KAOS represents each goal as a Temporal Logic rule and then makes use of refinement patterns to decompose these goals into a set of sub-goals that logically entail the original goal (Figure 15). Obstacles were introduced into the KAOS framework in order to help identify scenarios that might cause goal violations. Obstacles are essentially negated goals that are used to prompt thinking about requirements in terms of states that the system should not achieve. Like goals, obstacles will at first be defined at a high-level and need to be elaborated into more precise definitions. The KAOS methodology provides techniques for resolving these lower-level obstacles by introducing new goals that ensure that the obstacles are avoided.

Once a goal has been elaborated to the level of a system-level requirement (i.e. an operational goal), the final stage of the procedure is to assign each of the refined goals to a specific object/operation such that the final system will meet the original requirements. KAOS defines a library of domain-independent refinement patterns, backed up by logical proofs that can be used to refine goals and obstacles (Figure 16).

Once a refinement pattern has been derived, it can be applied to any matching scenario without the need to recreate the proof again. When applying a goal elaboration pattern, the system will present the user with the set of patterns that are valid for the given higher-level goal. Then it is up to the user to select a pattern that can be instantiated with meaningful values for each of the missing goal properties in the sub-goal formulae.

(ii) Representing a Security Pattern in KAOS

The KAOS approach provides support for security goal specification in terms of a number of specialised meta-classes of goal, namely, *Confidentiality, Integrity, Availability, Privacy, Authentication* and *Non-repudiation* goal subclasses. In order to support the concepts of attacker knowledge, the formal language of goals is extended with the epistemic operators, $KnowsV_{ag}$, which is defined as follows:

```
KnowsV   (v) = ∃x: Knows  (x=v)
      ag                ag
("knows value")
Knows  (P) = Belief   (P) ∧ P
     ag             ag
("knows property)
```

The operational semantics of the epistemic operator $Belief_{ag}(P)$ is defined as "P being one of the properties stored in the local memory of agent

Figure 15. KAOS goal elaboration process

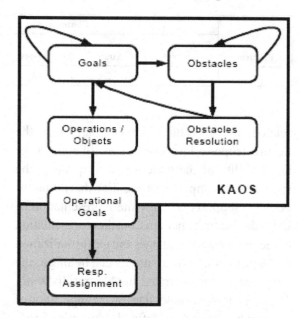

ag". The knowledge of a value of a property at a given point depends on both the agent having a value for the property in its local memory *and* that property value actually holding at the given point in time.

The use of obstacles for security goals makes obstacle refinement trees analogous to the threat trees that are used for modelling potential attacks security-critical systems. However, obstacles neither capture the goals and knowledge of a potential attacker; or the vulnerabilities in software systems. The notions of anti-goals and anti-models were introduced to the KAOS framework in order to deal with these problems (van Lamsweerde, 2004). Combining with the epistemic operators described above, allows security patterns to be expressed in the KAOS framework. We illustrate this using the RBAC example presented previously.

In the banking example, the requirement is to ensure that only authorized users are allowed to perform particular operations on bank assets, such as accounts. We can document this requirement as the following top-level goal

Figure 16. Example of KAOS goal elaboration pattern

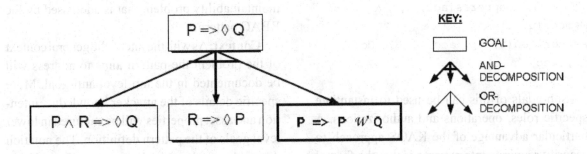

```
Goal Maintain        [OperationOfAc-
countOnlyByAuthorizedUser]
InformalSpec         If user performs an
operation on an account, they must be
authorised to do so
FormalSpec          ∀ acc:Account,
op:Operation, u: User
           Supports(acc, op) ∧
Authorized(u, op, acc) => CanDo(u,
op, acc)
```

A security pattern that documents a solution to satisfying this high-level goal, must take into account the potential attacks on the system that would negate the above, as shown in the following anti-goal.

```
AntiGoal Achieve        [UnauthorizedU-
serOperatesAccount]
InformalSpec        A user performs an
operation on an account, with no au-
thority to do so
FormalSpec         ∃ acc:Account,
op:Operation, u:User
           Supports(acc, op) ∧
Unauthorized(u, op, acc) => CanDo(u,
op, acc)
```

This top level anti-goal identifies the asset and the capabilities of the attacker, and provides the general context for the security requirement being modelled. By decomposing the anti-goal, we can elaborate particular threats that would lead to the unauthorised operation of an account. The maintainability problem of the direct user-permission assignment model is highlighted by the following anti-goal:

```
AntiGoal Achieve        [FormerEmloyee-
AuthorizationUnrevoked]
InformalSpec        A user retains per-
mission to perform operation even
after leaving employment
FormalSpec         ∃ acc:Account,
op:Operation, u:User
           [ExEmployee(u) =>
Unauthorized(u, op, acc)] ∧
[Supports(acc, op) ∧ Unauthorized(u,
op, acc) => CanDo(u, op, acc)]
```

RBAC provides a countermeasure to the above anti-goal by decoupling users from permissions using roles. Thus, permission revocation can be achieved by simply removing a user from a particular role. We can document the RBAC goal as follows:

```
Goal Maintain        [RBACModelForBank]
InformalSpec        Maintain a role-
based access control model for the
bank
FormalSpec          ∀ acc:Account,
```

```
op:Operation, u: User, ∃ r: Role
            Supports(acc, op) ∧
Member(u, r) ∧
Authorized(r, op, acc) => CanDo(u,
op, acc)
```

Sub-goals of this can be used to instantiate specific roles, operations and authorizations. A particular advantage of the KAOS approach to security requirements patterns is that the formal specification can be used to formally prove the correctness of the goal refinement. This allows the final pattern to be reused with confidence.

(iii) Evaluation of Security Pattern Support in KAOS

The KAOS framework allows security requirements patterns to be expressed in terms of the goals of the attacker (anti-goals) and vulnerabilities of the system under study. Patterns can also include a definition of the solution, or counter-measure, to the attack in terms of goals that avoid a given vulnerability. In this subsection we evaluate the extent to which KAOS the representation of security patterns using the generic characterization presented in section 2.

Problem: The intent of a security requirements pattern expressed in KAOS is documented in the top-level goal of the pattern. The meta-class of the top-level goal will identify if the pattern pertains to a confidentiality, integrity, availability, privacy, non-repudiation or authentication concern. The anti-goal model that forms part of the pattern definition can be used to identify the problem addressed by the pattern. In the example given above, the low-level anti-goal relating to permission revocation presents the permission maintainability problem that is addressed by the RBAC pattern.

Context: As with the intent, the general context of the problem the pattern aims to address will be documented in the top-level anti-goal. More specific details of the attacker knowledge, intention and asset properties will be captured in lower level goals of the pattern definition. The notation does not provide an explicit means of specifying harms to assets, although these can be captured as annotations to the anti-goal model.

Forces: The KAOS pattern notation does not provide an explicit means of capturing the forces that might influence the selection of a particular refinement pattern. However, requirements engineers are able to use the preconditions specified in the formal definition of goals to determine the suitability of a give pattern for the problem at hand.

Solution: The KAOS pattern notation allows specification of the solution to the initial problem in the form of sub-goals that satisfy the original goal. In the RBAC example, the solution is denoted by the RBACModelForBank sub-goal, which can be further refined into specific instances of roles, operations and authorisations for a given scenario.

Consequences: The consequence of a KAOS refinement pattern is to satisfy the original, high-level goal. If a pattern is specified using the formal notation provided by KAOS, the entailment relation between the sub-goals and top-level goal can be formally proven. This ability to validate that the consequences specified for a given pattern are correct is particularly useful in the domain of security patterns.

Table 7. Evaluation of support for security patterns in KAOS

	Context						
Problem	General	Attack	Assets	Harms to Assets	Forces	Solution	Consequences
3	2	3	3	0	0	2	2

4.3 Problem-Oriented Approaches

Problem oriented approaches (Jackson, 1995; Hall *et al.*, 2007; Hall *et al.*, 2008), bring informal and formal aspects of software development together in a single theoretical framework for software engineering design – presenting software development as the representation and step-wise transformation of software problems. This theoretical framework allows for: identification and clarification of system requirements; the understanding and structuring of the problem world; the structuring and specification of a machine that can ensure satisfaction of the requirements in the problem world; and the construction of adequacy arguments, to convince both developers and other stakeholders that the system will provide what is needed. In this section we review two problem-oriented approaches, namely: problem frames (Jackson, 2001) and abuse frames (Lin *et al.*, 2003; Lin *et al.*, 2004).

4.3.1 Problem Frames

In this subsection we summarize the Problem Frames approach, and show how it may be applied to illicit the privacy and security concerns.

(i) Overview of Problem Frames
Introduced by Jackson (Jackson, 2001), the Problem Frames approach (PF) provides a intellectual structure for analyzing software problems in the problem space. There are a few principles that are relevant this discussion. First, PF emphasizes the need for separating three descriptions: *specification*, *problem world domains*, and the *requirement*. Roughly, a specification (S) is a description of a software system that, within the context of certain problem world domains (W), satisfies a requirement (R). A problem diagram describing the relationship between W, S and R are typically described as shown in Figure 17. P_s is the phenomena shared between the machine and problem world, while P_r is the requirements phenomena. Second, in PF, a complex problem is decomposed by fitting its subproblems into of known problem patterns called problem frames. A frame captures the contextual structure of a problem and concerns associated with the frame. One of such concern is the 'proof obligation' to show $W, S \vDash R$.

The philosophy of problem frames is that some software development problems are recurring. Based on this premise, the main idea of problem frames is to document classes of commonly recurring problem structures and their solutions in problem-solution patterns. When a problem that matches a well known problem structure is encountered, it becomes easier to find a solution that solves the problem at hand.

(ii) Representing a Security Pattern in Problem Frames
The way patterns or frames are represented in PF has the following characteristic. Each frame is a generalization of some instances of recurring software problems. Frames tend to focus on the structure of problems rather than the solutions, although some work has been done to explore how the problem and solution structures are related. In each frame, there are three descriptions: the requirement, the problem world domains and

Figure 17. Separation of descriptions in problem frames

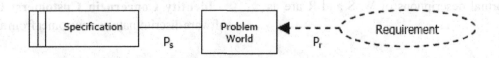

Figure 18. Workpiece frame and some known concerns

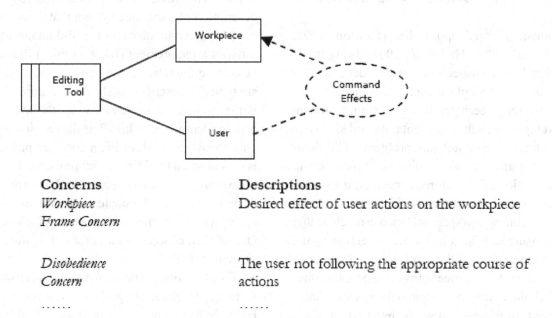

Concerns	Descriptions
Workpiece Frame Concern	Desired effect of user actions on the workpiece
Disobedience Concern	The user not following the appropriate course of actions
......	......

the machine. A potential security vulnerability may be identified as a "concern", which may be attached to either the frame, the machine, the problem world domains and their connections, or the requirements itself. It means that vulnerability may arise from any of the elements.

One of the several problem frames currently recognized is called *workpiece frame*. Figure 18 shows the structure of software certain problems in which an operator needs to use a computer program to edit a lexical object such as a text document, a picture, or a variable. The main concern of the problem is to take in certain commands from the operator, interpret them appropriately, and if the commands are valid, operate on the lexical object accordingly.

In PF, the account opening problem fits the Workpiece frame. Figure 19 shows how the problem of "opening of a bank account" may be represented in PF.

Informal descriptions of W, S and R are as follows:

R   "opening of a bank account": if the customer is new, create a new bank account with the customer's details.

W   *Customers*: people who provide their details to open a new bank account.
Managers: people who use the software to open a new back account.
Account Details: a storage where the details of the customer who opened a bank account is kept.

S   The software examines whether the system already has opened an account for the customer, and if not, opens a new one.

Once a problem is fitted to a frame, problem frames provides a way of methodically checking whether W, S ⊨ R holds and how this relationship may be broken. Here are some standard concerns that may be applied to illicit security vulnerabilities in the subproblem:

Identity Concern in Customers: Can the software discriminate one customer from another?

Figure 19. Problem diagram for "Opening a bank account"

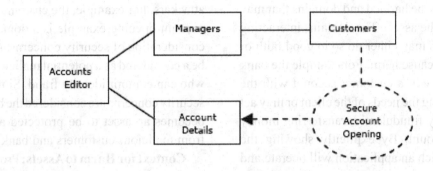

If someone turns up and say s/he is an existing customer, or provide some details purporting to be an existing customer, can the software determine whether the claim is true? The answer is clear `no'. This environmental assumption is too weak. We may strengthen it by saying that the manager should check that a customer is who they say they. Again, this is not foolproof, but may be the best one can do. This assumption that the manager can really verify customer details is an important assumption in our proof obligation.

Credibility Concern in Managers: Will the manager always input the customer details faithfully? Can the manager act maliciously by fraudulently transferring money from a customer's account to their personal accounts or those of their associates? Although it may be impossible or very difficult for the software to prevent such malicious actions, it is important for a requirements analyst to be aware that this is possible.

Interception Concern: All connections between the customers, managers, software and the database may be intercepted. For example if the customer has subscribed to online banking, there is a possibility that information sent or received from the bank server may be intercepted by attackers and replayed later. The analysis of this problem needs to take into account the possibility that this may occur and identify appropriate solutions to address this concern.

(ii) Evaluation of Security Pattern Support in Problem Frames

Problem Frames are a way of structuring software development problems, and concerns associated with the frames raise important security and other dependability issues. In this subsection we evaluate the extent to which problem frames support the representation of security concerns using the generic characterisation of security patterns presented in section 2.

Problem: The security goal analysed through a given problem frame depends on the concerns that are associated with that problem frame. For example the structuring of the bank account opening example as a workpiece raises confidentiality and accountability concerns of bank customer and managers, respectively. This illustrates that the structuring of software problems using problem frames leads to the identification and analysis of specific security concerns associated with the given frame/pattern. Therefore, although the intention of problem frames is classification of recurring software development problems, these patterns can be used to elicit associated security goals. It is also worth noting that even though security concerns can be identified from generic frame concerns, such identification of security goals depends on the specific problem represented in the problem frame.

Context in General: Explicit modelling of physical context and phenomena shared between domains is one of the core characteristics of problem frames. The context may represent the assets that may be harmed and domains that may interact with the assets. The domains interacting with the assets may either do so in good faith or with intent to cause harm. For example the bank manager may edit a customer account with the intent of serving the needs of the client or may act maliciously by fraudulently transferring money from the account. By explicitly showing the context in which an application will operate and relationships between domains, problem frames enables requirement analyst to assess potential threats that may arise.

Context for Attack: Potential attacks may be identified through frame concerns. However, there is no explicit risk analysis; that is, assessment of the probability of an attack occurring and the extent of the resulting damage that may be incurred. Hence frames concerns are sufficient for identifying potential attack, such as how do we authenticate the customer in order to ascertain that he is who he claims to be and is the legitimate owner of the bank account. In this respect, frames concerns allow requirements analysts to ask "what if" questions about the behaviour of the domains in a problem structure with respect to violation of security goals. Although, frame concerns may help surface potential attacks on assets, they are not detailed enough to explain scenarios by which a security goal may be violated. This may be achieved by elaborating the identified security concerns with scenario-based approaches such as misuse cases (Alexander, 2003; Whittle *et al.*, 2008).

Context for Assets: As earlier stated, problem frames provide explicit modelling of the context in which a system will operate but this context is general and not specific to security. From a security perspective the general context can be seen as the assets that may be harmed and their potential attackers. It is worth mentioning that, initially, in a problem frame these assets and attackers are modelled as domains. It is only when security issues are taken into account that these

domains can be classified as assets or potential attackers. For example, the customer in the bank account opening example is a domain but upon consideration of security concerns, s/he can also be a considered as a potential malicious customer who can commit identity fraud. Similarly, when security concerns are considered the bank account becomes an asset to be protected against harm from malicious customers and bank managers.

Context for Harm to Assets: Problem frames do not provide explicit modelling for harms to assets. It is possible, though to describe such harm as a security requirement in a different problem description once vulnerability has been identified.

Forces: Although there is no explicit support for trade-off analysis in problem frames, alternative solutions can be evaluated by re-analysing a problem with different context as demonstrated in the work on context-awareness (Salifu *et al.*, 2007). The selection of a problem pattern depends on the characteristics of the problem at hand.

Solution: The emphasis in the problem frames approach is on structures of problems rather than solutions. In a problem frame, the solution is modelled as an abstract machine without going into details about its dynamic behaviour. In order to model the dynamic behaviour of a machine, problem frames is often complemented with behavioural languages such as the Event Calculus (Shanahan, 1999).

Consequences: The consequences for applying a given problem frame for analyzing a security problem can be evaluated through the concerns associated with the problem pattern. An adequacy argument is then used to demonstrate that the behaviour of the security solution (S) in the problem context (W) satisfies the security requirements.

The classification and structuring of problems with problem frames provides a systematic way of capturing recurring software development problems. The frames also document standard concerns that should be addressed when a problem that fits a given pattern is encountered. Identifi-

Table 8. Evaluation of support for security patterns in problem frames

Problem	Context				Forces	Solution	Consequences
	General	Attack	Assets	Harms to Assets			
3	3	0	0	0	1	1	2

cation and reasoning about the concerns of each frame provides a means to identifying potential security issues that need to be addressed for a given problem as illustrated by the security engineering process based on patterns proposed in (Hatebur *et al.*, 2007). Table 8 presents a summary of the evaluation of the support for security patterns in problem frames based on the discussion above.

4.3.2 Abuse Frames

(i) Overview of Abuse Frames

Lin et al. (Lin *et al.*, 2003; Lin *et al.*, 2004) proposed abuse frames, an approach to analysing security problems in order to determine security vulnerabilities. This approach is based on Jackson's problem frames approach to structuring and analysing software development problems (Jackson, 2001). While problem frames are aimed at analysing the requirements to be satisfied, in contrast, abuse frames are based on the notion of an anti-requirement. An anti-requirement is the requirement of a malicious user that can subvert an existing requirement (similar to the concept of an anti-goal (van Lamsweerde, 2004)).

Abuse frames represent the notion of a security threat imposed by malicious users and a means for bounding the scope of security problems in order to provide early focus for security threat analysis. Binding the scope of a security problem makes it possible to describe it more explicitly and precisely. Such explicit and precise descriptions facilitate the identification and analysis of threats, which in turn drive the elicitation and elaboration of security requirements.

(ii) Security Patterns in Abuse Frames

Abused frames are based on the notion of an anti-requirement. An anti-requirement defines a set of undesirable phenomena imposed by a malicious user that ultimately cause the system to reach a state that is inconsistent with its requirement. The representation of security analysis patterns in abuse frames share the same notion as problem frames. However, in abuse frame frames the domains are associated with a different meaning. An abuse frame consists of three domains: *vulnerability machine*, *asset*, and *malicious user*; as shown in Figure 20. Phenomenon P1 represents undesirable effects on the asset resulting from an attack and phenomenon P3 represents abuse actions sent by the vulnerability machine to the asset on behalf of the malicious user. Similarly, phenomenon P4 represents interaction between the malicious user and the vulnerable machine during an attack.

A vulnerability machine domain describes the behaviour that a malicious user exploits to make an attack possible. The asset domain represents the asset that will be harmed if an attack succeeds, while the malicious user domain represents a potential attacker. Similar to problems frames, each abuse frame is associated with a set of abuse frame concerns which need to be addressed to minimise possibility of an attack from being successful. Figure 21 is an abuse frame describing a possible attack on the bank account. The attack scenario described is one where a malicious bank manager transfers funds from an account without authorisation for the account owner.

Figure 20. Generic abuse frame describing a threat

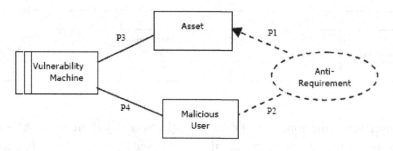

Figure 21. Abuse frame describing possible attack on a bank account

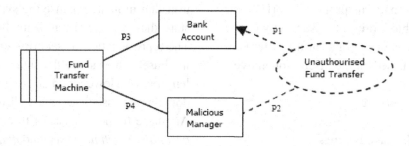

(iii) Evaluation of Patterns Support in Abuse Frames

Support for patterns in abuse frames is very similar to problem frames. The difference is that abuse frames have specific constructs for security analysis, while problem frames are generic patterns of software development problem. Table 9 presents a summary of the evaluation of security pattern support in abuse frames.

As shown in the table, abuse frames provide explicit support for modelling potential attackers, assets, and harms to assets. By modelling the behaviour of an attacker, the properties assets, and the specification of a vulnerable machine that an attacker could use to harm assets; abuse frames provides systematic means of eliciting security requirements.

5. COMPARING MODELLING APPROACHES

Table 10 presents a summary of the evaluation results presented in section 4. Our evaluation re-

sults suggest that approaches to security analyses are similar in their capabilities to capturing and modelling security analysis patterns. The differences between the features of the approaches are dependent on the different concerns they were originally meant to address. This suitability of each security analysis approach to specific security concerns makes it possible for the approaches to complement each other in a number of ways.

Problem-oriented and goals oriented approaches document problem structures in the problem space; while design approaches document solution patterns. Goal-based approaches are useful in documenting security goals at a higher-level of abstraction than problem-oriented approaches. Goal-based approaches are useful for capturing and refining security goals. Problem-oriented approaches further analyse the security goals structuring them into problem structures whose solutions can be identified with design approaches.

Table 9. Evaluation of support for security patterns in abuse frames

Problem	Context				Forces	Solution	Consequences
	General	Attack	Assets	Harms to Assets			
3	3	3	3	3	1	1	2

Table 10. Comparison of modelling approaches

Modelling approaches		Problem	Context				Forces	Solution	Consequences
			General	Attack	Assets	Harms to Assets			
Design-Oriented	UML	1	2	0	0	0	0	3	1
	SecureUML	1	2	1	2	1	1	3	2
	UMLsec	1	2	3	2	3	2	3	2
	Misuse Cases	2	2	3	1	3	1	2	2
Goal-Oriented	Secure i*	3	1	0	1	1	2	1	1
	Secure Tropos	3	3	2	3	3	3	1	2
	KAOS	3	2	3	3	0	0	2	2
Problem-Oriented	Problem Frames	3	3	0	0	0	1	1	2
	Abuse Frames	3	3	3	3	3	1	1	2

6. CONCLUSION AND FURTHER WORK

Security remains a key challenge in the development of software systems and the goal of developing secure software systems has remained an area of active research. Research in security engineering has resulted in the realization that documenting recurring security problems and their solutions as security patterns is an important advancement as it allows software designers with little knowledge of security to build secure systems. When a designer encounters a security problem that match a given pattern, they can reuse the solution part of the pattern or use the pattern to guide them in finding a solution to the problem at hand. In this chapter we have reviewed approaches to security analysis. Our review focused on evaluating the capabilities of these approaches to supporting security analysis patterns and is based on a set

of evaluation criteria for characterising security patterns.

Although the approaches reviewed were originally aimed at addressing specific security concerns our evaluation results suggest that these approaches are, to a large extent, overwhelmingly similar in their capabilities to capturing and modelling security analysis patterns. The minor differences in their capabilities to modelling security patterns seem to imply that these approaches complement each other in a number of ways. Problem-oriented approaches document problem structures in the problem space; while design approaches document solution patterns. Goal-based approaches are useful in capturing and refining security goals at a higher-level of abstraction than problem-oriented approaches. On the other hand, the explicitness of context modelling in problem-oriented approaches make them more suited to further analyses of security goals, structuring them (security goals) into problem structures whose solutions can be identified with design approaches. This systematic structuring of security problems could potentially result in more clearly defined structures of common security goals such as confidentiality, integrity, etc, into generic problem structures that can be instantiated for analysing security problems in different application domains.

Although our conclusion is based on the evaluation representation of a single security patterns with different languages, we believe that our results may be generalized to other security patterns. Part of our future work is validating the extent to which the conclusions we have draw here can be generalized.

ACKNOWLEDGMENT

We are grateful for financial support of the EU for the SecureChange project, the Science Foundation Ireland (SFI grant 03/CE2/I303_1), and the National Institute of Informatics. We are very thankful to the anonymous reviewers for their useful critic that helped us improve and enrich the ideas in this chapter.

REFERENCES

Alexander, I. (2002). Initial industrial experience of misuse cases in trade-off analysis. *Proceedings of IEEE Joint International Conference on Requirements Engineering.*

Alexander, I. (2003). Misuse cases: use cases with hostile intent. *IEEE Software, 20*(1), 58–66. doi:10.1109/MS.2003.1159030

ANSI/INCITS (2004). Information Technology - Role Based Access Control. *InterNational Committee for Information Technology Standards.*2008.

Arlow, J. (1998). Use cases, UML visual modelling and the trivialisation of business requirements. *Requirements Engineering, 3*(2), 150–152. doi:10.1007/BF02919976

Bresciani, P., Perini, A., Giorgini, P., Giunchiglia, F., & Mylopoulos, J. (2004). Tropos: An Agent-Oriented Software Development Methodology. *Autonomous Agents and Multi-Agent Systems, 8*(3), 203–236. doi:10.1023/B:AGNT.0000018806.20944.ef

Buschmann, F., Meunier, R., Rohnert, H., Sommerlad, P., & Stal, M. (1996). Pattern-Oriented Software Architecture: *Vol. 1. A System of Patterns*. Chichester, United Kingdom: John Wiley & Sons.

Cabot, J., & Zannone, N. (2008). *Towards an Integrated Framework for Model-driven Security Engineering.* Proceedings of the Workshop on Modeling Security (MODSEC08), Toalose, France.

Castroa, J., Kolp, M., & Mylopoulos, J. (2002). Towards requirements-driven information systems engineering: the Tropos project. *Information Systems, 27*(6), 365–389. doi:10.1016/S0306-4379(02)00012-1

Darimont, R., & Lamsweerde, A. v. (1996). Formal refinement patterns for goal-driven requirements elaboration. *ACM SIGSOFT Software Engineering Notes, 21*(6), 179–190. doi:10.1145/250707.239131

Fernandez, E., Ballesteros, J., Desouza-Doucet, A., & Larrondo-Petrie, M. (2007). Security Patterns for Physical Access Control Systems. *Data and Applications Security, XXI*, 259–274. doi:10.1007/978-3-540-73538-0_19

Fernandez, E., G. Pernul & M. Larrondo-Petrie (2008). Patterns and Pattern Diagrams for Access Control. *Trust, Privacy and Security in Digital Business*, 38-47.

Fernandez, E. B., & Pan, R. (2001). *A pattern language for security models*. Proceedings of 8th Conference on Pattern Languages of Programs (PLoP), Monticello, Illinois, USA.

Fernández-Medina, E., Jurjens, J., Trujillo, J., & Jajodia, S. (2009). Model-Driven Development for secure information systems. *Information and Software Technology, 51*(5), 809–814. doi:10.1016/j.infsof.2008.05.010

Ferraiolo, D. F., Sandhu, R., Gavrila, S., Kuhn, D. R., & Chandramouli, R. (2001). Proposed NIST standard for role-based access control. *ACM Transactions on Information and System Security, 4*(3), 224–274. doi:10.1145/501978.501980

Gamma, E., Helm, R., Jonson, R., & Vlissides, J. (1996). *Design Patterns: Elements of Reusable Object Oriented Software*. Buam, Holland: Addison Wesley.

Giorgini, P., Mylopoulos, J., Nicchiarelli, E., & Sebastiani, R. (2002). Reasoning with Goal Models. *Proceedings of the 21st International Conference on Conceptual Modeling*, Springer-Verlag: 167-181.

Hall, J. G., Rapanotti, L., & Jackson, M. (2007). *Problem Oriented Software Engineering: A design-theoretic framework for software engineering*. 5th IEEE International Conference on Software Engineering and Formal Methods.

Hall, J. G., Rapanotti, L., & Jackson, M. A. (2008). Problem Oriented Software Engineering: Solving the Package Router Control Problem. *IEEE Transactions on Software Engineering, 34*(2), 226–241. doi:10.1109/TSE.2007.70769

Hatebur, D., Heisel, M., & Schmidt, H. (2007). *A Security Engineering Process based on Patterns*. 18th International Conference on Database and Expert Systems Applications (DEXA), Regensburg, Germany.

Hoare, C. A. R. (1983). Communicating sequential processes. *Communications of the ACM, 26*(1), 100–106. doi:10.1145/357980.358021

Jackson, M. (1995). *Software Requirements and Specifications: A Lexicon of Practice, Principles and Prejudices*. London, United Kingdom: Addison-Wesley.

Jackson, M. (2001). *Problem frames: analysing and structuring software development problems*. Harlow: Addison-Wesley.

Jacobson, I. (1992). *Object-Oriented Software Engineering: A Use Case Driven Approach*. London, England: Addison-Wesley Professional.

Jurjens, J. (2004). *Secure Systems Development with UML*. Heidelberg: German, Springer-Verlag.

Lin, L., Nuseibeh, B., Ince, D., & Jackson, M. (2004). *Using abuse frames to bound the scope of security problems*. Proceedings of 12th IEEE International Requirements Engineering Conference.

Lin, L., Nuseibeh, B., Ince, D., Jackson, M., & Moffett, J. (2003). *Introducing abuse frames for analysing security requirements*. Proceedings of 11th IEEE International Requirements Engineering Conference.

Liu, L., Yu, E., & Mylopoulos, J. (2003). *Security and privacy requirements analysis within a social setting*. 11th IEEE International Requirements Engineering Conference.

Lodderstedt, T., D. Basin & J. Doser (2002). SecureUML: A UML-Based Modeling Language for Model-Driven Security. *«UML» 2002: The Unified Modeling Language*: 426-441.

Manna, Z., & Pnueli, A. (1992). *The Temporal Logic of Reactive and Concurrent Systems*. Springer Verlag.

Matulevicius, R., Mayer, N., Mouratidis, H., Dubois, E., Heymans, P., & Genon, N. (2008). Adapting Secure Tropos for Security Risk Management in the Early Phases of Information Systems Development. *Proceedings of the 20th international conference on Advanced Information Systems Engineering.* Montpellier, France, Springer-Verlag: 541-555.

Mayer, N., Heymans, P., & Matulevicius, R. (2007). *Design of a Modelling Language for Information System Security Risk Management.* 1st International Conference on Research Challenges in Information Science (RCIS), Ouarzazate, Morocco.

Mouratidis, H. (2004). A Security Oriented Approach in the Development of Multiagent Systems: Applied to the Management of the Health and Social Care Needs of Older People In England (PhD Thesis), Department of Computer Science, University of Sheffield, Sheffield, UK.

Mouratidis, H., & Giorgini, P. (2007). Secure Tropos: A Security-Oriented Extension of the Tropos methodology. *International Journal of Software Engineering and Knowledge Engineering, 27*(2), 285–309. doi:10.1142/S0218194007003240

Mouratidis, H., Giorgini, P., & Manson, G. (2005). When security meets software engineering: a case of modelling secure information systems. *Information Systems, 30*(8), 609–629. doi:10.1016/j.is.2004.06.002

Mouratidis, H., Weiss, M., & Giorgini, P. (2006). Modelling Secure Systems Using An Agent Oriented Approach and Security Patterns. *International Journal of Software Engineering and Knowledge Engineering, 16*(3), 471–498. doi:10.1142/S0218194006002823

OMG (2004). UML Profile for Patterns Specification. *UML Profile for Enterprise Distributed Object Computing (EDOC) specification.* 2009.

OMG (2009). *Unified Modeling Language (UML).* 2009.

Salifu, M., Yu, Y., & Nuseibeh, B. (2007). *Specifying Monitoring and Switching Problems in Context.* Proceedings of the 15th IEEE International Conference in Requirements Engineering (RE '07), New Delhi, India.

Sandhu, R. S., Coyne, E. J., Feinstein, H. L., & Youman, C. E. (1996). Role-based access control models. *Computer, 29*(2), 38–47. doi:10.1109/2.485845

Schumacher, M., Fernandez-Buglioni, E., Hybertson, D., Buschmann, F., & Sommerlad, P. (2005). *Security Patterns: Integrating Security and Systems Engineering.* West Sussex, England: John Wiley & Sons.

Sebastiani, R., P. Giorgini & J. Mylopoulos (2004). Simple and Minimum-Cost Satisfiability for Goal Models. *Advanced Information Systems Engineering:* 20-35.

Shanahan, M. (1999). *The Event Calculus Explained. Artificial Intelligence Today: Recent Trends and Developments* (pp. 409–430). Berlin, Heidelberg: Springer.

Sindre, G., & Opdahl, A. L. (2005). Eliciting security requirements with misuse cases. *Requirements Engineering, 10*(1), 34–44. doi:10.1007/s00766-004-0194-4

van Lamsweerde, A. (2004). *Elaborating security requirements by construction of intentional anti-models.* Proceedings of the 26th International Conference on Software Engineering (ICSE). Edinburgh Scotland, IEEE Computer Society: 148-157.

van Lamsweerde, A., Darimont, R., & Massonet, P. (1995). *Goal-directed elaboration of requirements for a meeting scheduler: problems and lessons learnt.* Proceedings of the 2nd IEEE International Symposium on Requirements Engineering. York, England, IEEE Computer Society: 194.

Wang, Y., McIlraith, S. A., Yu, Y., & Mylopoulos, J. (2007). An automated approach to monitoring and diagnosing requirements. *Proceedings of the 22nd IEEE/ACM international conference on Automated software engineering*. Atlanta, Georgia, USA, ACM: 293-302.

Weidenhaupt, K., Pohl, K., Jarke, M., & Haumer, P. (1998). *Scenario usage in system development: a report on current practice.* Proceedings of the 3rd International Conference on Requirements Engineering.

Weiss, M., & Mouratidis, H. (2008). Selecting Security Patterns that Fulfill Security Requirements. *Proceedings of the 16th IEEE International Conference on Requirements Engineering (RE'08),* IEEE Computer Society, pp. 169-172

Whittle, J., Wijesekera, D., & Hartong, M. (2008). *Executable misuse cases for modeling security concerns.* ACM/IEEE 30th International Conference on Software Engineering.

Yoshioka, N., H. Washizaki & K. Maruyama (2008). A survey on security patterns. *Progress in Informatics*(5): 35-47.

Yu, E. S. K. (1997). *Towards modelling and reasoning support for early-phase requirements engineering.* Proceedings of the 3rd IEEE International Symposium on Requirements Engineering.

Yu, Y., Kaiya, H., Washizaki, H., Xiong, Y., Hu, Z., & Yoshioka, N. (2008). Enforcing a security pattern in stakeholder goal models. *Proceedings of the 4th ACM Workshop on Quality of Protection.* Alexandria, VA: ACM, 9-14.

Section 2
Methodologies and Frameworks

Chapter 5
Security Over the Information Systems Development Cycle

C. Blanco
University of Cantabria, Spain

D. G. Rosado
University of Castilla-La Mancha, Spain

C. Gutiérrez
Correos Telecom, Spain

A. Rodríguez
University of Bio-Bio, Chile

D. Mellado
Spanish Tax Agency, Madrid, Spain

E. Fernández-Medina
University of Castilla-La Mancha, Spain

J. Trujillo
University of Alicante, Spain

M. Piattini
University of Castilla-La Mancha, Spain

ABSTRACT

Information security is currently considered to be a crucial aspect of systems development. However it has traditionally been considered during the final stages of development, once the main components of the system have been developed and therefore provides solutions which are inappropriate for security integration. Software engineering has traditionally been separated from security engineering, and security issues have not usually been included in software engineering processes, activities, techniques, models, and so on. Furthermore, security engineering has not been aligned with information systems, and has focused rather on the definition of protocols, cryptographic algorithms, access control policies, etc. However, the scientific community is beginning to realize the importance of aligning software

DOI: 10.4018/978-1-61520-837-1.ch005

engineering and security engineering in order to develop more secure systems. Security in software engineering is a branch of research in which many contributions dealing with security integration from the early development stages have recently appeared. This chapter discusses some of the most interesting contributions in this area, and also provides a summary of our contributions through the development of various research lines dealing with different strategies to integrate security into information systems development as early in the development stages as is possible.

1. INTRODUCTION

Software Engineering is defined as the area of engineering which applies a systematic, disciplined and quantifiable approach in order to develop software systems (IEEE, 1990). Software Engineering has thus improved the development process through methodologies, techniques, models and tools which provide systems that are close to the client's needs and have a predictable cost and time. However, the complexity of the software systems to be developed has increased dramatically, thus making their development more difficult.

System requirements, which are the kernel of the development process, specify the functions that the system or system components should perform. Requirements in the development process therefore need to be identified as soon as possible in order to be able to develop analysis models which represent these requirements, design models which integrate the requirements in the high level solution, and finally, carry out an implementation which respects these needs through an integrated and robust solution.

If requirements are not identified and integrated during the first stages of the development process, the needs they represent will not be appropriately integrated into the system and the development will be less robust, more expensive and its maintenance will be more complex. It is therefore crucial to analyze, elicit, specify and model information system requirements from the early stages of development. These functional requirements represent the functionality of the system and describe what the software will do,

but too many manners in which to provide this functionality exist.

Nonfunctional requirements are, moreover, important since they describe how the software will carry out its purpose, and they involve several issues such as security constraints, performance requirements or quality attributes. These non functional requirements should therefore also be identified during the first stages of the software development process for the reasons previously mentioned. Furthermore, security is considered to be an important aspect in the development of quality software (Devanbu and Stubblebine, 2000, Ferrari and Thuraisingham, 2000, Ghosh et al., 2002), so by improving the security, we also improve the quality of the software. Indeed, the ISO 9126 standard includes security as a characteristic of software quality which contains the following properties: availability, confidentiality, integrity, non-repudiation, accountability, authenticity and compliance.

However, although security is an important type of requirement, Software Engineering and Security Engineering have traditionally been independent of each other (Giorgini et al., 2007). On the one hand, software engineering is focused on the systematic development of information systems, and does not consider security as an important issue. It recognizes the importance of security as a nonfunctional requirement, but software engineering techniques and methods do not incorporate security. On the other hand, security engineering is focused on the definition of formal and theoretical methods (such as protocols, cryptographic algorithms, access control policies or information flow control), which are not usually aligned with the processes of software development, software modeling, etc.

Security in Software Engineering is an open research topic (Giorgini et al., 2007). During the last decade there has, therefore, been a clear explosion in this research area, the main contributions being related to the integration of security into requirements engineering, software architectures, system models and information system development processes (Jürjens, 2002, Jürjens, 2005, Basin et al., 2006, Hafner et al., 2006).

We have principally organized the remainder of this chapter into two sections. The following section will discuss the problem of integrating security into the software development process, paying more attention to the requirements engineering discipline and the software design stage, and finally introducing the model driven development approach as a possible means to represent security requirements in software models. The third section will summarize some of the approaches that have been developed by the Alarcos Research group since 1998, in order to integrate security into the software development process. Proposals dealing with security requirements engineering for software product lines, security in business processes, security in web services, and security in databases and data warehouses will also be considered in this section.

2. SECURITY OVER SOFTWARE DEVELOPMENT PROCESS

In this section, we discuss how the scientific community is providing solutions to the problem of the software engineering and security engineering alignment. In the first subsection we discuss some of the most interesting approaches which attempt to integrate security into the entire software development process. We then focus our attention on specific stages of the software development process, each of which has specific problems, and proposals to deal with their security (software

analysis and design). We conclude this section by introducing the Model Driven Development approach as a promising software engineering discipline which is being used both to accommodate security requirements in software models, and to automatically generate code, including solutions to the security requirements specified in these models.

2.1. Security over the Development Process

The growing need to construct secure systems, mainly as a result of the new vulnerabilities which have arisen from the use of the Internet and caused by applications distributed in heterogeneous environments, has encouraged the scientific community to demand a clear integration of security into the development processes (Bass et al., 2004, Breu et al., 2003, Haley et al., 2006, Jürjens, 2005, Lodderstedt et al., 2002, Mouratidis and Giorgini, 2006, Giorgini et al., 2007, Villarroel et al., 2005). The main reason for this is that, traditionally, security aspects are only considered during the implementation stages, signifying that security solutions are not perfectly coupled with the design and the remaining requirements of the system (Artelsmair and Wagner, 2003).

Software Engineers consider security as a non-functional requirement, but unlike other non-functional requirements, such as reliability and performance, security has not been fully integrated into the development lifecycle and is still principally considered after the design of the system. However, security introduces not only quality characteristics but also constraints under which the system must operate (Mouratidis, 2004). Ignoring such constraints during the development process could lead to serious problems (Anderson, 2001), since security mechanisms would have to be fitted into a pre-existing design, therefore leading to design challenges that usually translate into software vulnerabilities (Artelsmair and Wagner, 2003, Mouratidis and Giorgini, 2006, Giorgini et al., 2007). An enormous amount of money and valuable time are also required to overcome these problems once they have been identified (a major rebuild of the system is usually necessary).

There are at least two reasons for the lack of support for security engineering (Lampson, 2004) (Mouratidis and Giorgini, 2006):

- Security requirements are generally difficult to analyze and model. A major problem in analyzing non-functional requirements is that there is still a need to separate functional and non-functional requirements, while individual non-functional requirements may also relate to one or more functional requirements. If non-functional requirements are stated separately from functional requirements, it is sometimes difficult to see the correspondence between them. If stated with functional requirements, it may be difficult to separate functional and non-functional considerations.
- Developers lack expertise in secure software development. Many developers, who are not security specialists, must develop systems that require security features. Without an appropriate methodology to guide those developers in the development processes, it is likely that they will fail to produce effective solutions (McDermott and Fox, 1999).

By considering security only at certain stages of the development process it is probable that, security needs will come into conflict with the system's functional requirements. Taking both security and the functional requirements into consideration throughout the development stages helps us limit the cases of conflict, by identifying them very early in the system development, and finding ways to overcome them.

One of the ways to overcome these problems is by ensuring that security plays an integral role in the training of software developers. In particular,

software engineers must be conditioned to consider the security of their software products from the early stages of architecture and design. Architectures must be formulated with security in mind, and a skilled developer or designer must be able to translate these architectures and requirements into early software design artifacts that include some notion of security, at least in principle, if not at the level of detailed descriptions of necessary security mechanisms. The developer must then take advantage of this preliminary work in the early software lifecycle model and implement that system with security in mind during all phases of development, testing, and maintenance (Sachitano et al., 2004).

Finally, in recent years, the scientific community has increased its interest in incorporating security into software engineering, in order to build robust secure information systems in which security is not improvised and incorporated once the system has been completely built. Literature contains many interesting approaches related to the secure development of information systems, but here we shall present only those approaches that we consider to be most relevant and which indicate the current interest and importance of security in software engineering:

- **Secure Unified Process** (Steel et al., 2005b) is a methodology for the integration of security into software systems, and is based on the Unified Process (Kruchten, 2000). Security is represented as a set of features that fortify the entire application or service with safeguards and countermeasures for potential risks and vulnerabilities. The incorporation of fundamental security principles plays a vital role during software design and architecture, and it also helps to identify and eliminate risks and threats in the early phases of the software development cycle;
- **Secure Tropos** (Giorgini et al., 2007) is a security oriented extension of Tropos

(Bresciani et al., 2004) which is a software development methodology tailored to describe both the organizational environment of a system and the system itself. This extension includes security related concepts such as a security constraint which is defined as a restriction related to security issues, such as privacy, integrity and availability, which may influence the analysis and design of the information system under development. In addition to security constraints, Secure Tropos also defines secure dependencies which introduce the security constraint(s) that must be fulfilled for the dependency to be satisfied;

- **CLASP** (Graham, 2006) is an activity driven, role-based set of process components guided by formalized best practices. It is designed to help software development teams build security into the early stages of existing and new-start software development lifecycles in a structured, repeatable, and measurable manner. This process is presented through five high-level perspectives which allow users to quickly understand the process, including how process components interact and how to apply them to a specific software development lifecycle;

- **Model Driven Security** (Basin et al., 2003) was conceived as a new approach towards building secure information systems, in which designers specify high-level system models along with their security properties and use tools to automatically generate system architectures from the models, including security infrastructures. Models help us to understand a complex problem and its potential solutions through abstraction (Fernández-Medina et al., 2009). Model building is a standard practice in software engineering. The construction of models during requirements analysis and system design can improve the quality of the re-

sulting systems by providing a foundation for early analysis and fault detection. The main advantage of integrating security into the model-driven architecture (MDA) is that security will become an essential part of the system development process rather than being an add-on feature. We can find clear examples of the integration of software engineering and security engineering such as SecureUML (Lodderstedt et al., 2002) which is a methodology for modeling access control policies and their integration into a model driven software development process, and is a modeling language which is designed to integrate information relevant to access control into application models defined with UML; SECTET (Hafner et al., 2006), a model driven security engineering framework that facilitates the design and implementation of secure inter-organizational workflows; and UMLSec (Jürjens, 2005, Best et al., 2007) which proposes a security extension of UML to consider security aspects in the design phase in distributed system environments. They encapsulate knowledge about prudent security engineering and target developers who are not specialists in security;

- **AEGIS** (Flechais et al., 2007) is a secure software engineering method that integrates security requirements elicitation, risk analysis and context of use, bound together through the use of UML. This method uses context regeneration and risk analysis as tools to assist developers in representing and addressing security and usability requirements in system design. By involving stakeholders in the high-level risk analysis and selection of countermeasures, their understanding of the need for security countermeasures and their motivation to contribute to security are likely to be improved. Finally, AEGIS uses UML to provide a uniform basis which can be used to discuss and bind the separate areas of usability, risk management and technical design.

From the above it clear that this area has evolved very rapidly, and that many interesting approaches have been proposed. However, if this area is to be considerably more effective, research must mature and reach industry.

2.2. Security Requirements Engineering

Software Security Engineering, a practice through which to address software security issues in a systematic manner, is known to be an extremely important part of the software development process through which to achieve secure software systems. Nevertheless, we believe that Security Requirements Engineering is particularly important within this discipline since it provides techniques, methods and norms for tackling this task during the early stages of the IS (Information System) development cycle. The building of security during the early stages of the development process is also cost-effective and brings about more robust designs (Kim et al., 2005). It should involve the use of repeatable and systematic procedures in an effort to ensure that the set of requirements obtained is complete, consistent, easy to understand and analyzable by the different actors involved in the development of the system. A good requirements specification document should include both functional requirements (related to the services that the software or system should provide), and non-functional requirements (related to what are known as features of quality, performance, portability, security, etc) (McDermott and Fox, 1999). In our contemporary Information Society, depending as it does on a huge number of software systems which have a critical role, it is absolutely vital to ensure that IS are safe from the very beginning.

Extensive work has been carried out on security requirements in recent years. Some of the most relevant current proposals are listed as follows:

*   In "Modelling Security and Trust with Secure Tropos" (Mouratidis and Giorgini, 2007) (Giorgini et al., 2007) the authors propose the Tropos methodology whose intention is to support all the analysis and design activities in the software development process. Tropos rests on the idea of building a model of the system-to-be and its environment, which is incrementally refined and extended, providing a common interface to various software development activities, along with a basis for the documentation and evolution of the software. Work from the same authors has enhanced the methodology with an approach to develop and evaluate various attack scenarios (Mouratidis and Giorgini, 2007b). This methodology is based on social hierarchies and adapts components of the i* framework (Yu et al., 2007). This uses the concepts of actors, goals, tasks, resources and social dependencies to define the obligations of actors (dependees) towards other actors (dependers).
*   Firesmith's "Specifying Reusable Security Requirements" (Firesmith, 2004b) offers certain steps which allow security requirements to be defined from reusable templates. The author's analysis of security requirements is founded on two basic principles obtained from OCTAVE (Operationally Critical Threat, Asset, and Vulnerability Evaluation) based on resources and risk-driven development. The author proposes security use cases as a technique that should be used to specify the security requirements that the application will successfully fulfil to protect itself from its relevant security threats.

- In "Security Quality Requirements Engineering (SQUARE) Methodology" (Mead and Stehney, 2005) and "Security Requirements Engineering for Software Systems: Case Studies in Support of Software Engineering Education" (Mead and Hough, 2006) the authors propose a process which provides a means to elicit, categorize, and prioritize security requirements for information technology systems and applications. This methodology seeks to build security concepts into the early stages of the development lifecycle. The model may also be useful for documenting and analyzing the security aspects of fielded systems, and could be used to steer future improvements and modifications to these systems.

- Haley et al.'s "Security Requirements Engineering: A Framework for Representation and Analysis" (Haley et al., 2008) suggests a framework which unifies the concepts of the two disciplines of requirements engineering and security engineering. The concepts of functional goals, which are operationalised into functional requirements with appropriate constraints, are taken from requirements engineering, and the concepts of assets, together with threats of harm to those assets are taken from security engineering. Security goals aim to protect the system from these threats, and are operationalised into security requirements, which take the form of constraints on the functional requirements..

- In "UMLsec: extending UML for secure systems development" (Jürjens, 2002) and "Automated Analysis of Permission-Based Security Using UMLsec" (Jürjens et al., 2008b) the authors presents a methodology to specify requirements regarding confidentiality and integrity in analysis models based on UML. Multilevel security and mandatory access control are the security

models highlighted in this proposal. This approach considers a UML extension to develop secure systems. In order to analyse the security of a subsystem specification, the behaviour of the potential attacker is modelled; specific types of attackers that can attack different parts of the system in a specific way are thus modelled. Finally, "Risk-Driven Development Of Security-Critical Systems Using UMLsec" (Jürjens and Houmb, 2004) makes use of a risk-driven approach to develop security-critical systems based on UMLsec in which risk-driven development is risk-driven in that it focuses on assessing risks and proposing treatments through a set of activities focusing on security requirements and the allocation of security requirements.

- Mellado et al.'s "A Common Criteria Based Security Requirements Engineering Process for the Development of Secure Information Systems" (Mellado et al., 2007) and "Towards security requirements management for software product lines: a security domain requirements engineering process" (Mellado et al., 2008b) propose a standard-based process, named SREP (Security Requirements Engineering Process), that deals with the security requirements during the early stages of software development in a systematic and intuitive manner which is based on the reuse of security requirements by providing a Security Resources Repository. It also deals with the integration of both the Common Criteria (ISO/IEC 15408) and the SSE-CMM (ISO/IEC 21827), thanks to the CC_SSE-CMM approach (Lee et al., 2003), into the software lifecycle model, and furthermore conforms to ISO/IEC 17799:2005 with regard to security requirements.

- In "Experimental comparison of attack trees and misuse cases for security threat identification" (Opdahl and Sindre, 2008) the authors present a systematic approach for eliciting security requirements by extending traditional UML use cases to also cover misuse, and it is potentially useful for several other types of extra-functional requirements beyond security. The Sindre et al. approach focuses solely on the activities directly related to reuse. The authors propose a reuse-based approach for determining security requirements. Development for reuse involves identifying security threats and associated security requirements during application development and abstracting them into a repository of generic threats and requirements. Development with reuse involves identifying security assets, setting security goals for each asset, identifying threats to each goal, analysing risks and determining security requirements, based on the reuse of generic threats and requirements from the repository.

- "A Social Ontology for Integrating Security and Software Engineering" (Yu et al., 2007) states that understanding the organizational context and rationales (the "Whys") that lead up to systems requirements can be just as important for the ongoing success of the system. Most existing requirements techniques are intended more for the later phase of requirements engineering, which focuses on completeness, consistency, and automated verification of requirements. In contrast, the early phase aims to model and analyze stakeholders' interests and how they might be addressed, or compromised, by various system-and-environment alternatives. The authors therefore argue that a different kind of modelling and reasoning support is needed for the early phase, and so provide i* framework, which was developed to model and reason about organiza-

tional environments and their information systems.

After performing a comparative analysis of the various aforementioned relevant proposals concerning IS security requirements in (Mellado et al., 2006b), we concluded that these proposals did not reach the desired level of integration into the development of IS, nor were they sufficiently specific for a systematic and intuitive treatment of IS security requirements during the early stages of software development. We shall therefore briefly present the Security Requirements Engineering Process (SREP) (Mellado et al., 2007) which describes how to integrate security requirements into the software engineering process in a systematic and intuitive manner. Moreover, as an evolution of our previous "generic" security requirements engineering process (SREP), we shall also propose a security requirements engineering framework for Software Product Lines (SPL), and we shall thus provide a complete explanation of the Security Requirements Engineering Process for SPL (SREPPLine).

2.3. Security in the Architectural Design

In a typical application development environment, architects and developers share similar experiences. They deploy business applications in a highly compressed time frame, making applications work, testing functionality at all levels, ensuring that they meet expected system performance or service levels, and wrapping applications with attractive client presentation and user documentation. Ensuring the security of the application at all levels has usually been considered in the last phase of the development process (Steel et al., 2005b).

For decades, the security community has undertaken detailed research into specific areas of security, while largely ignoring the design process. Security aspects cannot be "blindly" inserted into an IT-system, but the overall system development must take security aspects into account. The result of a well-engineered security system must be an architecture that ensures the fulfillment of specific security aspects and security requirements analyzed and specified in the analysis stage (Artelsmair and Wagner, 2003).

In development environments or processes, the architecture and design phase represents a critical time during which security flaws must be identified and prevented before they become part of the software. As the connectivity, complexity, and extensibility of software increase, the importance of effectively addressing security concerns as an integral part of the architecture and design process becomes even more critical. During this phase of the software development effort, architects, designers, and security analysts have an opportunity to ensure that requirements are appropriately interpreted through a security lens and that appropriate security knowledge is leveraged to give the software structure and form in a way that minimizes security risk (Allen et al., 2008).

Therefore, we can conclude that the main artefact of the design phase is the software architecture which has emerged as an important sub-discipline of software engineering, particularly in the realm of large system development. There are many definitions of software architecture (Garlan and Anthony, 2002, Bass et al., 2003), but what these definitions have in common is their emphasis on architecture as a description of a system, as a sum of smaller parts, and how those parts relate to and cooperate with each other to perform the work of the system. Architecture provides us with intellectual control over the very complex by allowing us to substitute the complex with a set of interacting pieces, each one of which is substantially simpler than the whole (Bachmann et al., 2000). Thus, from this definition, we can define security architecture as being a collection of security software and security components along with their position and relationships to the system's components, connections, and constraints, and

how the integration of the security components with the system's own components, connections, and constraints would satisfy the requirements of corporate security policy (Ramachandran, 2002).

As we have already stated, the software architecture for a system plays a central role both in system development and in the organization that produces it. Architecture serves as the blueprint for both the system and the project developing it. It defines the work assignments that must be carried out by design and implementation teams and is the primary carrier of system qualities such as performance, modifiability, and security, none of which can be achieved without a unifying architectural vision. Architecture should be analysed at an early stage to ensure that the design approach will yield an acceptable system. In short, architecture is the conceptual glue that holds every phase of the project together for all of its many stakeholders (Bass et al., 2003).

Moreover, the architecture must be documented to communicate how it achieves properties such as performance, reliability, security, or modifiability. Fundamentally, architecture documentation may have three different functions (Bachmann et al., 2000): a) A means of education. Typically, this means introducing people to the system. These people may be new members of the team, external analysts, or even a new architect. b) A vehicle for communication among stakeholders. A stakeholder is someone who has a vested interest in the architecture. The documentation's use as a communication vehicle will vary according to which stakeholders are communicating. c) A basis for system analysis. If it is to support analysis, documentation must provide the appropriate information for the particular activity being performed.

On the other hand, the aim of the industrial and research communities' recent interest in software security is to prevent security problems by building software without the so-called security holes. One way in which to achieve this goal is by applying security patterns which enable us to immediately incorporate a level of security in the design phase of a software system. There has recently been a growing interest in identifying security patterns in software-intensive systems since they provide techniques for considering, detecting and solving security issues from the beginning of their development life-cycle (Cheng et al., 2003, Schumacher et al., 2005, Schumacher and Roedig, 2001, Yoder and Barcalow, 1997). Security patterns work together to form a collection of coordinated security countermeasures, thereby addressing host, network and application security.

The reason for using patterns is to create a reusable design element. Each pattern is useful in and by itself. The combination of patterns assists those responsible for implementing security to produce sound, consistent designs that include all the operations required, and so assure that the resulting implementations can be efficiently completed and will perform effectively (Blakley et al., 2004).

Security patterns are proposed as a means to bridge the gap between developers and security experts, and are intended to capture security expertise in the form of worked solutions to recurring problems. Security patterns are also intended to be used and understood by developers who are not security professionals (Kienzle and Elder, 2005) by providing techniques to identify and solve security issues. They work together to form a collection of best practices (to support a security strategy) and they address host, network and application security. The first person to use the pattern approach was Christopher Alexander (Alexander et al., 1977). In his book he indicates that each pattern describes a problem which occurs over and over again in our environment, and he then states the core of the solution to that problem in such a way that this solution can be used a million times over, without ever using it the same way twice. The "Gang of Four" book, as it is commonly known, defines design patterns as "descriptions of communicating objects and classes that are customized to solve a general design problem in a particular context" (Gamma et al., 1994).

One of the most useful aspects of patterns is that they exhibit known quality attributes, and it is for this reason that the architect chooses a particular pattern and not one at random. Some patterns represent known solutions to performance problems, others lend themselves well to high-security systems, and yet others have been successfully used in high-availability systems. Choosing a pattern is often the architect's first major design choice (Bass et al., 2003), and design strategies which determine which application tactics or design patterns should be used for particular application security scenarios and constraints are used to assist in this choice (Steel et al., 2005a). A possible relationship between typical security requirements and security patterns can also be used (Rosado et al., 2006). Moreover, as literature has shown security patterns can be used to fulfill security requirements (Weiss and Mouratidis, 2008).

Therefore, by using security patterns, which drive and guide us both towards a secure development and towards security software architecture, we can be certain that our design based on these patterns fulfils and guarantees the security requirements specified in the analysis stage through the design and implementation of security solutions that provide reliable security services.

2.4. MDE for Developing Secure Information Systems

Models help us to understand a complex problem and its potential solutions through abstraction. Model Driven Development (MDD) has been proposed as a means to support the software development process through the use of a model-centric approach, improving productivity, quality, and platform independence. MDD can be used to develop high level (platform independent) models which can be transformed into more specific (according to the specific platforms) models which can in turn be transformed into code dependent models. This successive model transformation provides a basis for mapping between analysis and design models, and for its traceability.

Model Driven Architecture (MDA, 2003) is an Object Management Group standard (OMG, 2003) for software development under the Model Driven Engineering framework which proposes models at different abstraction levels to separate the specification of the system functionality and its implementation. As Figure 1 shows, MDA allows us to define three viewpoints of a system: i) the Computation Independent Model (CIM), which is used by the business analyst, and is focused on the context and requirements of the system without considering its structure or processing, ii) the Platform Independent Model (PIM), which is used by software architects and designers, and is focused on the operational capabilities of a system outside the context of a specific platform, and iii) the Platform Specific Model (PSM), which is used by software developers and programmers, and includes details relating to the system for a specific platform (Harmon, 2004). Transformations between models are also supported by the definition of transformation rules. OMG proposes Query / Views / Transformations (QVT) (OMG, 2005) as an intuitive language with which to implement transformations between Meta Object Facility (MOF) compliant models.

Developing information systems by applying the MDA approach improves productivity, thus saving time and effort, and provides support for system evolution, integration, interoperability, portability, adaptability and reusability. Many applications of MDA therefore exist in the development of information systems: databases and data warehouses, since central MDA models (PIM and PSM) fit perfectly with conceptual and logical data models; web software development, including concepts of content, navigation, process and presentation; software product lines which model the commonality and variability of CIM

Figure 1. The MDA development sequence (Harmon, 2004)

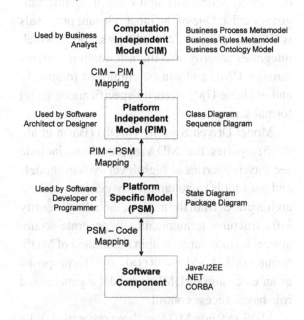

models; and other types of systems such as embedded real-time systems.

Furthermore, the scientific community has advocated that security engineering and software engineering should be integrated in order to build robust secure information systems in which security is not improvised and incorporated once the system has been completely built (Fernández-Medina et al., 2009). The use of Model Driven Development for secure information systems is one of the most intuitive strategies through which to achieve this goal since it permits the definition of secure models at different abstraction levels (for each development stage). However, the philosophy of model driven engineering when applied to the development of secure information systems is different to that of traditional security models which describe the protection needs of the systems. Security models are therefore embedded in and scattered throughout the high level system models, meaning that these integrated models can be transformed into implementation models according to the MDA strategy.

Several works dealing with the integration of security with UML and other modeling languages exist. One of the most relevant proposals is UMLsec (Jürjens, 2005, Jürjens, 2002), which integrates security into the information systems through UML and can be employed to specify and evaluate UML security specifications using formal semantics.

Model Driven Security (MDS) (Basin et al., 2006) applies the MDA approach to include security properties in high-level system models and uses tools to automatically generate system architectures from the models, including security infrastructures to automatically generate secure system architectures. Within the context of MDS, SecureUML (Lodderstedt et al., 2002) is proposed as an extension of UML to model a generalized role based access control.

MDS extends MDA in three respects: (i) the system models are enriched with primitives and rules to integrate security into the development process, (ii) the model transformation techniques are extended to ensure that these security details are also transformed, and (iii) the system is obtained, including the security properties and the corresponding security mechanisms. In order to fulfill this goal, the authors consider dialects which provide a bridge by defining the connection points with which to integrate elements of the security modeling language with elements of the system design modeling language.

The philosophy of Model-Driven Security has been applied to many research works providing frameworks for B2B workflows, specifying role and constraint based access control policies, dealing with trust management, and also to UMLsec (Best et al., 2007, Jürjens et al., 2008a), thus defining three abstraction levels (requirements, models and code), and providing both direct and reverse engineering, verification, configuration, etc., thanks to a rich set of tools (Jürjens and Shabalin, 2007, Jürjens, 2008).

3. OUR SPECIFIC PROPOSALS

This section provides a summary of some of the most interesting proposals that we have developed in order to integrate security into the software development process. We shall begin by presenting a process developed to consider specific security requirements in the development of web service based applications. We shall then present our contribution in the area of security requirements engineering, summarizing two processes developed to deal with security requirements in software and software product lines analysis respectively. Finally we shall present three proposals which use the basis of the Model Driven Development in order to integrate security into software models, starting with business process models, and finishing with databases and data warehouses models.

3.1. Software Process for Web Services Security Development

In the field of Web Services (hereafter, WS) Security Architectures, the PWSSec (Process for Web Services Security) framework (Gutiérrez et al., 2006) (Figure 2) provides a WS-based security architecture meta-model that can be instantiated to implement a security architecture that ensures the correct implementation of security requirements (Gutiérrez et al., 2007).

The present-day business environment demands optimized efficiency and rapid adaptability to its continuous changes. New channels, new competitors, new technologies and globalization are forcing companies to learn to see change as the only permanent state of their businesses (Buecker et al., 2007). Said companies have discovered that the IT function is paramount to attaining this objective, and have in particular discovered that Service Oriented Architectures actually promote the achievement of these goals. There has consequently been an increase in the adoption of Service Oriented Architectures, both

Figure 2. Sub-processes and main security artifacts of the PWSSec process

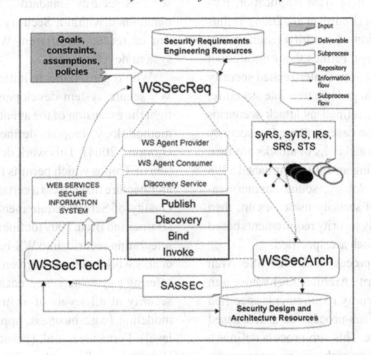

in industry and academia, and of its main implementation technology: Web Services technology.

Web service-based specifications, standards, technologies and tools have shown a spectacular growth in the last few years. This evolution has principally been motivated by their widespread adoption and promotion by the major vendors in the industry (Gutiérrez et al., 2004). This overwhelming amount of new business and technological literature, together with its rapid evolution and instability, has caused this technology's target users to show a very reticent attitude towards its practical application in mission-critical software-intensive systems. The main rationale behind this issue is that the general approach has been based on a bottom-up approach, which lacks a development process with which to establish a general security framework and facilitate the systematic integration of security into all stages of the existing WS-based software development life-cycle. As Vinoski states (Vinoski, 2004), so far, the approach followed by WS (security) specifications' main actors has been driven by self interest, with a greater focus

on filling the WS (security) stack for their own (commercial) purposes than providing a global architectural (WS-Architecture) solution.

To fill this gap, we proposed the PWSSec process (Gutiérrez et al., 2006) (Figure 2). PWSSec is intended to facilitate and guide the development of Web Service-based security systems in order to permit the easy integration of a complimentary security software development stage comprising security in each of the traditional stages for the construction of this kind of systems (Endrei et al., 2004).

PWSSec accomplishes the following main stages of secure system development: risk-based security engineering, pattern-oriented security architecture and standard-centered security design.

The first sub-process, WSSecReq (Web Services Security Requirements), applies a business-, application-centered approach which identifies the set of security threats to the system. This approach sets out by identifying the IBM Business Pattern problem the system to be built should solve and then, depending on the Business Pattern problem, states the corresponding IBM Application Pattern that addresses it (Endrei et al., 2004). It thus enables the definition of security requirements from these threats and refines them throughout the construction of a set of inter-related security artifacts: threats arranged in a tree-like structure; the threats are next refined as attack scenarios by specifying misuse cases gathered in security profiles; the impact and risks of attacks are then computed by applying an ISO-compliant 15408 risk analysis methodology; sound countermeasures in the form of security use cases are then identified; and finally security requirements based on a reusable approach are specified.

The second sub-process is called WSSecArch (Web Service Security Architecture) whose aim is to allocate the security requirements specified in the WSSecReq sub-process to a WS-based security architecture. This sub-process defines a Web services security architecture meta-model that can be instantiated to fulfill the security requirements specified in the previous sub-process. As a result, a Web services security architecture will be designed which will be equipped with the necessary security architectural mechanisms to achieve the identified security requirements. A case study demonstrating how this WS-based security architecture can be designed was presented in (Gutiérrez et al., 2009).

The third sub-process, denominated as WS-SecTech (Web Services Security Technologies), has the main objective of identifying the set of WS-based security standards that will implement the architectural security mechanisms identified in the WSSecArch sub-process. As mentioned earlier, a considerable amount of Web services-based security, and sometimes overlapping, standards have been developed and released in recent years. This sub-process attempts to assist developers to identify the most suitable Web services security standards to be used to implement the security mechanisms specified by the security architecture. It does so by mainly defining which security mechanisms can be implemented by which Web

services security standards. This knowledge is maintained within a Security Repository which can be reused in different Web services-based system developments.

With regard to the definition of processes for WS secure system development, we can highlight the extension of the agent and goal-oriented methodology Tropos, defined in (Aiello and Giorgini, 2004). This work describes an adaptation of Tropos which permits the definition of an architecture that covers a certain set of WS-based Quality-of-Service requirements. Hafner and Breu (Hafner and Breu, 2009) define another method for integrating security into WS-based systems. Breu et al.'s work is a model-driven oriented approach offering a systematic approach for incorporating security at all levels of abstraction of systems modeling (e.g.: business, application, technical level). Fernandez et al. (Fernandez et al., 2007, Delessy and Fernandez, 2008), have recently proposed a pattern-centered security methodology for the development of SOA systems. This approach is aligned to the PWSSec framework but does not provide specific security artifacts that facilitate the integration of security aspects during the security requirements engineering stage. Neither does it provide traceability between security requirements and security architecture, nor a security reference architecture from which a WS-based approach can be designed.

3.2. Security Requirements Engineering Proposals

In the area of security requirements engineering, we have proposed two different processes. The first is SREP (Security Requirements Engineering Process), a general security requirements engineering process which is applicable to the analysis of any information system. We have also developed SREPPLine (Security Requirements Engineering Process for Software Product Lines), which has been defined to analyze, model, elicit and specify security requirements for software product lines,

Figure 3. SREP overview

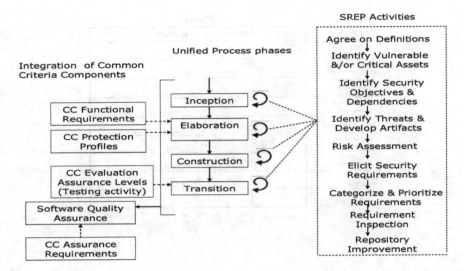

exploiting the specific characteristics of these types of information systems.

3.2.1. SREP

SREP (Mellado et al., 2007) is an asset-based risk-driven method for the establishment of security requirements in the development of secure Information Systems which focuses on building security concepts during the early phases of the development lifecycle. This process basically describes how to integrate the Common Criteria into the software lifecycle model together with the use of a security resources repository to support the reuse of security requirements (modeled with UMLSec (Popp et al., 2003), or expressed as security use cases or as plain text with formal specification), assets, threats (which can be expressed as misuse cases, threat/attack trees, UMLSec diagrams) and countermeasures.

Figure 3, in which we provide a brief outline of SREP, shows that the Unified Process (UP) lifecycle is divided into a sequence of phases, each of which may include many iterations. Each iteration is like a mini-project and may contain all the core workflows (requirements, analysis, design, implementation, and test), but with dif-

ferent emphasis depending on where the iteration is in the lifecycle. Moreover, the core of SREP is a micro-process, made up of nine activities which are repeatedly performed at each iteration throughout the iterative and incremental development, but also with different emphasis depending on what phase of the lifecycle the iteration is at. The model chosen for SREP is thus iterative and incremental, and the security requirements evolve throughout the lifecycle, so that each iteration coincides with an iteration in a phase of the UP. This is because the UP lifecycle is divided into a sequence of phases, which may include many iterations, each of which concludes with a major milestone. This allows us to take into account changing requirements, it facilitates reuse and corrects errors over several iterations, risks are discovered and mitigated earlier, and the process itself can be improved and refined along the way. Therefore, the result is a more robust IS.

The nine activities of which the micro-process for security requirements engineering are formed are summarized below (for more details see (Mellado et al., 2007)):

- **Activity 1:** Agree on definitions. The organization's first task is to define the stake-

Figure 4. Amount of work per SREP iteration

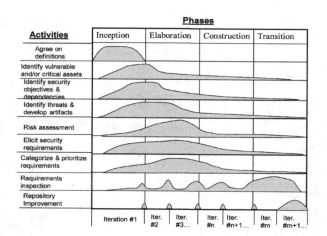

holders and to agree upon a common set of security definitions, along with the definition of the organizational security policies and the security vision of the IS.

- **Activity 2:** Identify vulnerable and/or critical assets. This is where the SRR (Security Resources Repository) is used for the first time and consists of the identification of the different kinds of valuable or critical assets, along with vulnerable assets, by the requirements engineer.

- **Activity 3:** Identify security objectives and dependencies. The SRR can also be used in this activity. Otherwise the organization's security policy, along with legal requirements and other constraints, will be considered in order to determine the security objectives.

- **Activity 4:** Identify threats and develop artifacts. Each asset is targeted by threat/s that may prevent the security objective from being achieved.

- **Activity 5:** Risk assessment. Risk must normally be determined from application to application. The final goal is to achieve 100% risk acceptance.

- **Activity 6:** Elicit security requirements. The SRR is again used. For each threat retrieved from the repository, one or more

associated clusters of security requirements may be found.

- **Activity 7:** Categorize and prioritize requirements. Each requirement is categorized and prioritized in a qualitative ranking such that the most important requirements (in terms of impact and likelihood) are handled first.

- **Activity 8:** Requirements inspection. Requirements inspection is carried out in order to validate all the generated artifacts (all the documents, requirements, the modified model elements and the new generated model elements), and is generated as a Validation Report.

- **Activity 9:** Repository improvement. The new model elements (threats, requirements, etc.) found throughout the development of the previous activities and which are considered as likely to be used in forthcoming applications and are of sufficient quality (according to the Validation Report) are introduced into the SRR.

Moreover, as Figure 4 shows, the core of SREP is performed during the earlier phases, and therefore in the earlier iterations, although requirements are reviewed during later phases and it may be necessary to introduce any new ones that appear during the IS development process.

Common Criteria Components are simultaneously introduced into the software lifecycle, signifying that SREP uses different Common Criteria Components according to the phase and activity, although the Software Quality Assurance activities (product evaluation and process monitoring) are performed throughout all the phases of the software development lifecycle. According to (Kam, 2005), it is in these Software Quality Assurance activities that the Common Criteria Assurance Requirements could be incorporated.

Finally, SREP applicability has been validated in real case studies, such as that described in (Mellado et al., 2006a).

3.2.2. SREPPLine

A software product line is a set of software-intensive systems sharing a common, managed set of features (Kang et al., 1990) which satisfy the specific needs of a particular market segment or mission and which are developed from a common set of core assets in a prescribed way (Clements and Northrop, 2002). The software product line engineering paradigm differentiates two processes: domain engineering, the process of SPL engineering in which commonality and variability of the product line are defined and performed; and application engineering, the process of SPL engineering in which the applications of the product line are built by reusing domain artifacts and exploiting the product line variability (Pohl et al., 2005).

Software engineering methodologies and the standard proposals of Software Product Line (SPL) engineering have traditionally ignored security requirements and security variability issues. The few recent proposals which deal with security in SPLs are either principally focused on the design of the implementation aspects of SPL development or include only a few security requirements activities, such as prevention, detection, or recovery (Arciniegas et al., 2006, Faegri and Hallsteinsen, 2006). In addition, after analyzing the most relevant current "generic" security requirements related proposals in (Mellado et al., 2006b) and (Mellado et al., 2006c), we concluded that none of them are either sufficiently specific or are tailored to the SPL development paradigm. We therefore developed the Security Requirements Engineering Process for Software Product Lines (SREPPLine) as an evolution of our previous "generic" security requirements engineering process (SREP) (Mellado et al., 2007).

SREPPLine (security quality requirements engineering process for software product lines) (Mellado et al., 2008b) is an add-in of activities, which can be incorporated into an organization's SPL development process model providing it with a security requirements engineering approach. We have therefore defined the key activities that must be part of each SPL process. The order in which they are performed depends on the particular process that is established in an organization. Thus, the sub-processes and their activities can be combined with existing development methods such as RUP (Rational Unified Process), or other development processes.

It is a security features or security goals based process which is driven by risk and security standards (concretely ISO/IEC 27001 (ISO/IEC, 2005b) and Common Criteria (ISO/IEC, 2005a)) and deals with security requirements and their related artifacts from the early stages of SPL development in a systematic and intuitive manner especially tailored to SPL based development. It is based on the use of the latest and most widely validated security requirements techniques, such as security use cases (Firesmith, 2003) or misuse cases (Sindre and Opdahl, 2005), along with the integration of the Common Criteria (CC) components and ISO/IEC 27001 controls into the SPL lifecycle in order to facilitate SPL products security certification. Moreover, our proposed process suggests the use of a method to carry out the risk assessment which conforms to ISO/IEC 13335 (ISO/IEC, 2004), and it concretely uses MAGERIT (López et al., 2005) for both SPL risk assessment and SPL products risk assessment.

Furthermore, the aim of SREPPLine is to minimize knowledge of the necessary security standards along with security expert participation during SPL product development. To this end, it provides a Security Core Assets Repository to facilitate security artifact reuse and to implement the Security Reference Meta Model, which is composed of the Security Variability Sub-Meta Model and the Security Requirement Decision Sub-Meta Model, that assist in the management of the variability and traceability of the security requirements related artifacts of the SPL and its products. This metamodel is the basis through which the activities of SREPPLine capture, represent and share knowledge about security requirements for SPL and help to certify them against security standards. In essence, it is a knowledge repository with a structure to support security requirements reasoning in SPL engineering.

This Variability Sub-Meta Model relates the defined variability to other software development models such as feature models, use case or misuse case or security use case models, design models and test models. It thus provides a cross-cutting view of the security requirements variability across all security development artifacts and assists in maintaining the different views of variable security requirements artifacts consistent.

As is shown in Figure 5, our process is composed of two sub-processes: a Product Line Security Domain Requirements Engineering (PLSecDomReq) sub-process and a Product Line Security Application Requirements Engineering (PLSecAppReq) sub-process. According to (Kotonya and Sommerville, 2000) these sub-processes cover the four basic phases of requirements engineering: requirements elicitation; requirements analysis and negotiation; requirements documentation; and requirements validation and verification. They must therefore at least be performed for each iteration of the Domain or Application Requirements Engineering Process of the SPL respectively (Mellado et al., 2008b).

Tools are important for an effective method deployment in the particular context of industrial scale SPLs and they help by automating many operations which may, if carried out manually, seriously hinder the quality and efficient analysis of large scale systems (Djebbi et al., 2007). We have therefore developed a prototype of a CARE (Computer Aided Requirements Engineering) tool, called SREPPLineTool, to support SREPPLine. This is a first approximation that will help to obtain experience in the problem through its application in real case studies in order to refine it and obtain a definitive version. SREPPLineTool prototype permits us to apply the SREPPLine process in an SPL development by providing its activities with automated support. This tool implements the Security Reference Meta Model by means of dynamic repositories of security artifacts, and guides the user in the execution of the process in a sequential manner. It is thus able to propose related security artifacts in each of the SREPPLine activity tasks depending on the domain categories of the SPL project artifacts. SREPPLineTool also facilitates both the management and the visualization of the artifacts variability and traceability links and the generation of the security documents of the SPL, which could be generated in XML with the characteristics variability model in order to facilitate other tools' use of the information generated and their extension of this tool., along with integration with other functional and non-functional requirements and features.

This prototype has been developed with .NET technology and implemented with C#, using a SQL Server 2005 database and is linked with the IBM Rational RequisitePro tool by means of a Visual Basic.NET interface to retain the advantages of a requirements management tool, thus permitting it to read the requirements and features from a RequisitePro project and also to send the gener-

Figure 5. SREPPLine framework

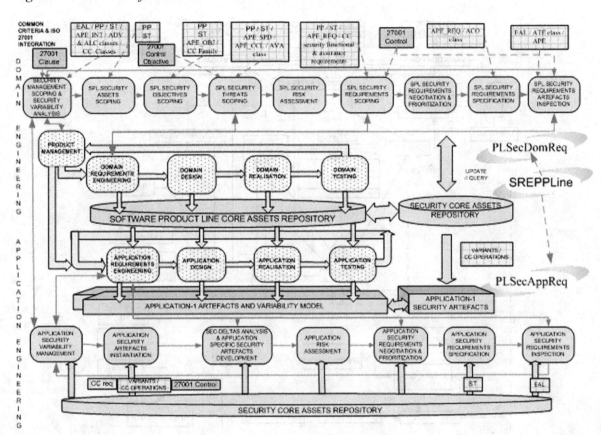

ated documents to a RequistePro project. The architecture is shown in Figure 7.

Finally, SREPPLine and SREPPLineTool applicability has been validated in real case studies, such as those described in (Mellado et al., 2008a) and (Mellado et al., 2009) respectively.

3.3. Developing Secure Information Systems from Secure Business Processes

Software development constitutes a permanent challenge for researchers and professionals. Both have been searching for new techniques with which to lower the costs and improve the quality of software products. One way in which to improve the process of information systems creation, and consequently the end product, is to consider the

early specification of requirements, in this case paying special attention to security aspects from the business analyst perspective.

In this section we have used a model driven approach to develop our proposal. We shall first explain how business process models can be specified by allowing the users who define these processes to specify security requirements, and we shall then present model transformations which allow us to obtain UML artifacts that are closer to the software implementation.

3.3.1. Secure Business Process Definition

In order to specify a secure business process it was necessary to extend the expressiveness of the Unified Modeling Language (Object Management

Figure 6. Security reference meta model

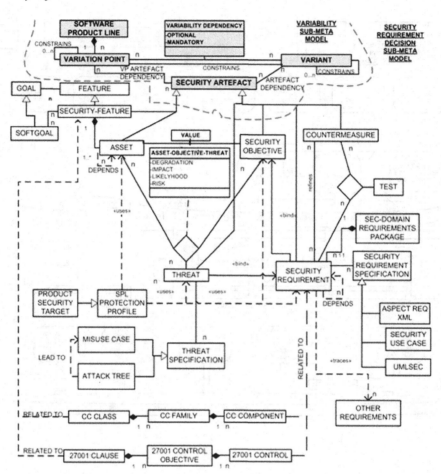

Figure 7. SREPPLineTool architecture

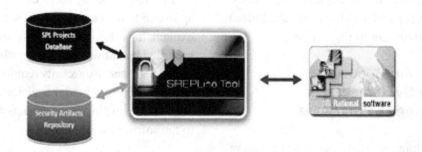

Group, 2007) and the Business Process Modeling Notation (BPMN, 2006), the two main standards used to specify business processes in industry (Lonjon, 2004). Said extension has been specified for the UML activity diagram (UML 2.0-AD) in (Rodriguez et al., 2007) and for the BPMN business process diagram (BPMN-BPD) in (Rodríguez et al., 2007b). In both cases an extension has been

Figure 8. Icons used to represent security requirement in secure business process

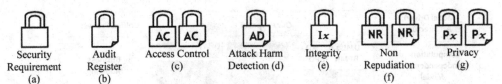

| Security Requirement (a) | Audit Register (b) | Access Control (c) | Attack Harm Detection (d) | Integrity (e) | Non Repudiation (f) | Privacy (g) |

defined as a UML profile, which we have called BPSec, and which is composed of stereotypes, restrictions and labeled values.

The central idea is to enable business experts to express certain limitations or restrictions with regard to determined elements of which a business process is composed. This perspective should be exempt from the technicalities involved in the implementation of security in software systems since it cannot otherwise be considered as a part of the computation independent model.

Three security objectives have traditionally been identified: confidentiality, integrity, and availability, and authenticity has also recently been added to this list (Haley et al., 2004). It is also possible to use classifications which consider secret, integrity, availability and responsibility (Lampson, 2004), or aspects such as authorization, auditing, anonymity or the separation of duties (Atluri, 2001).

We have considered security requirements definitions which are understandable to business analysts and are not ambiguous for security experts. We have taken as a reference the taxonomy proposed by (Firesmith, 2004a). This has been used to select a subset of requirements, taking into consideration (i) clarity of definition, (ii) potential significance in a business environment and (iii) the extent to which the definition is not related to security specific solutions. The subset of security requirements used in our proposal (which is unlimited) is composed of: Access Control, Attack Harm Detection, Security Auditing, Integrity, Non repudiation and Privacy.

Since the specification of security requirements in our proposal is performed by a business

analyst, we have paid particular attention to the graphical representation of these requirements. To do so, we have chosen a padlock, considered a de facto standard associated with security. Figure 8 (a) shows the basic symbol over which a determined security requirement is specified. In Figure 8 (b), the same symbol but with one of the edges folded, associated with the symbol used to represent a comment, annotation or register, is used to represent a security requirement which also requires audit register.

These symbols are associated with the component elements of UML 2.0-AD and BPMN-BPD and represent secure business processes. Both the specification of secure business processes and the later obtaining of UML artefacts which consider security form part of a method. This method, which we have denominated as M-BPSec (Rodríguez et al., 2007c), allows us to define business processes, incorporate security into them, refine said definitions and finally obtain UML artifacts in a systematic and ordered manner.

3.3.2. An MDA Approach for Mapping Secure Business Process to UML Artifacts

Model-driven approaches have favoured the way in which software development is carried out. In particular, Model Driven Architecture (MDA) (OMG, 2003) offers a framework based on the identification of models at various levels of abstraction. Since these models represent a different abstraction from the system itself, an integration/transformation mechanism is required to establish how to move from one level (e.g. CIM) to another

Figure 9. MDA approach for secure business process (SBP)

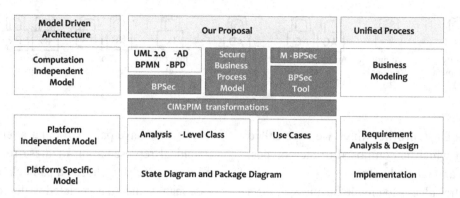

(e.g. PIM). Transformations are thus a core element in the MDA. According to MDA, a transformation is the process of converting one model into another model belonging to the same system.

The essential element of our proposal is that it considers obtaining analysis level classes (Rodríguez et al., 2007a) and use cases (Rodríguez et al., 2007d) by taking the definition of a secure business process as a reference. The model driven approach is used in our proposal (Rodriguez et al., 2007) because it establishes that a business process corresponds to a computation independent model, while UML artifacts such as analysis classes and use cases correspond to platform independent models. Thus, a model transformation from a secure business process to analysis level classes and use cases is totally MDA compliant. Figure 9 shows all the details of our proposal (colored in dark grey): (i) BPSec; the UML 2.0-AD or BPMN-BPD extension previously presented in detail in this work, (ii) M-BPSec, a method designed for the ordered and systematic construction of secure business processes, (iii) BPSec-Tool, a prototype that supports M-BPSec application, (iv) the Secure Business Process model which is obtained from the application of the method supported by the tool and (v) a set of rules described using QVT, that have been incorporated into the method and the tool and which describes the transformation from CIM to PIM.

The CIM2PIM transformations shown in Figure 9 permit us to obtain a set of UML artifacts (analysis level classes and use cases) that correspond to PIM models from a Secure Business Process description (in CIM). The work flows of the unified process are shown in the last column of Figure 9. Our purpose is to show that not only SBP specification but also analysis level classes and use cases can be used in a complementary manner in a consolidated and successful software development process such as the Unified Process. Thus, taking into consideration a certain parallelism between our proposal and the Unified Process, the SBP model will be built in the "Business Model" stage and the analysis level classes and use cases will be defined and refined in the "Requirements" and "Analysis & Design" stages.

In general terms the rules are defined by using QVT to express the equivalence between the component elements of a Secure Business Process model with analysis level classes and use cases. Table 1 shows a set of transformations which allows us to map a set of analysis level classes, including those security aspects specified by the business analyst, from a Secure Business Process. In said specifications note, for example, that it is possible (see Rule 4) to map a UML 2.0-AD Action with an analysis level class Operation. Additionally, all security requirement specification in SBP will be mapped to an analysis level class.

Table 1. Mapping between activity diagrams and class diagrams elements

transformation ActivityDiagram2ClassDiagram

top relation R1 // from Activity Partition to Analysis-Level Class
{
checkonly domain uml_ActivityDiagram ap:ActivityPartition {name=n}
enforce domain uml_ClassDiagram c:Class {name = n}
where { ap.containedNode → forAll(cn:Action|R4(cn))}
}

top relation R2 // from Interruptible Activity Region to Analysis-Level Class
{
checkonly domain uml_ActivityDiagram iar:InterruptibleActivityRegion {name = n}
enforce domain uml_ClassDiagram c:Class {name = n}
where { ap.containedNode → forAll(cn:Action|R4(cn))}
}

top relation R3 // from Data Store Node to Analysis-Level Class
{
checkonly domain uml_ActivityDiagram dsn:DataStoreNode {name = n}
enforce domain uml_ClassDiagram c:Class {name = n}
}

relation R4 // from Action to Operation in Analysis-Level Class
{
checkonly domain uml_ActivityDiagram ac:Action {name = n, inPartition=ap}
enforce domain uml_ClassDiagram
op:Operation {name=n, ownerClass=c:Class{name=ap.name}}
}

Table 2 shows some of the transformations specified in QVT which allow us to obtain use cases. For example, Rule 3 specifies the way in which an Actor is obtained from the Lane specification in the definition that was made from the secure business process using BPMN-BPD.

3.3.3. An Illustrative Example

A graphic specification of a Secure Business Process model specified using the BPSec-Tool is shown in Figure 10. The example describes a typical business process for the admission of patients to a health-care institution. In the "Admission of Patients" business process specification, the business analyst has specified «Privacy» (anonymity) for the Patient ActivityPartition, with the aim of preventing the disclosure and storage of sensitive information about Patients. «Nonrepudiation» has been defined for the control flow that goes from the Fill Admission Request action to the Capture Insurance Information and Check Clinical Data

actions with the aim of avoiding the denial of the Admission Request reception. «AccessControl» and «Privacy» (confidentiality) have been defined for the Interruptible Activity Region. A «SecurityRole» can be derived from this specification. Admission/Accounting will be another role. All objects in an interruptible region must be considered for permission specification. The Access Control specification has been complemented with an audit requirement. This implies that it must register information about the security role and security permissions. An «Integrity» (high) requirement has been specified for the Clinical Information DataStore and finally, the business analyst has specified «AttackHarmDetection» for the Medical Evaluation DataStore, signifying that all events related to the attempt or success of attacks or damages are registered.

After the application of the QVT rules it is possible to obtain one analysis level class diagram and six use case diagrams. Figure 11 shows a graphical representation of the analysis-level

Table 2. Mapping between BPMN-BPD and use case elements

```
transformation BusinessProcessDiagram2UseCaseDiagram

top relation R1 // from Pool to Actor
{
checkonly domain bpmn_BusinessprocessDiagram p:Pool {name = n}
enforce domain uml_UseCaseDiagram a:Actor{name = n}
where { ap.containedNode → forAll(cn:Activity|R4(cn)) }
}

top relation R2 // from Lane to Actor
{
checkonly domain bpmn_BusinessprocessDiagram l:Lane {name = n}
enforce domain uml_UseCaseDiagram a:Actor{name = n}
where { ap.containedNode → forAll(cn:Activity|R4(cn)) }
}

top relation R3 // from Group to Actor
{
checkonly domain bpmn_BusinessProcessDiagram g:Group {name = n}
enforce domain uml_UseCaseDiagram a:Actor {name = n}
where { ap.containedNode → forAll(cn:Activity|R4(cn)) }
}

relation R4 // from Activities to UseCase
{
checkonly domain bpmn_BusinessProcessDiagram ac:Activity {name = n, inPartition=ap}
enforce domain uml_UseCaseDiagram uc:UseCase {name = n, subject= ACTORS: Set(Actor)};
where { ACTORS→including (a:Actor{name=ap.name}) }
}
```

classes derived from Secure Business Process specification. The analysis-level class derived from the security requirement specification is shown in the dark-colored areas.

Figure 12 shows use cases related to the security requirements Non Repudiation specified in the Patient Admission Business Process.

In the MDA approach the business processes constitute computation independent models (CIM) since they are created by business analysts who do not specify computation aspects in the model. However, the Analysis Classes and Use Cases are considered to be computation dependent models, although they are platform independent (PIM). The platform is not specified in these models, but the decision has already been made to construct a computational system which implements the business model. The transformations that we have presented can therefore be classified as being C2P, that is, from CIM to PIM. The result of said transformations is an analysis class and use case

model in which security is considered and which satisfy a first approximation for the description of the models which definitively represent the problem.

3.4. Developing Secure Databases

Information in databases is vital for companies and also for individuals, since these databases frequently store individuals' private or personal details (such as medical data, ideologies or religious beliefs). Database protection is therefore a serious requirement that must be carefully considered, not as an isolated aspect, but as an element present in all stages of the database life cycle.

Fernández-Medina and Piattini (Fernandez-Medina and Piattini, 2005) have thus proposed a methodology with which to build databases taking into consideration aspects of confidentiality from the earliest stages to the end of the development process. Since MDA had not been consolidated

Figure 10. Patients' admission to a medical institution with security requirement

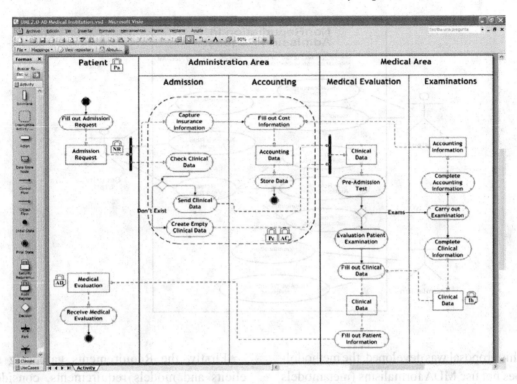

Figure 11. Analysis-level class from patient admission

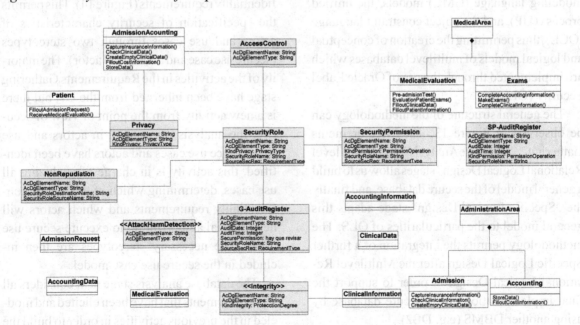

Figure 12. Patient admission and access control/privacy use cases specification

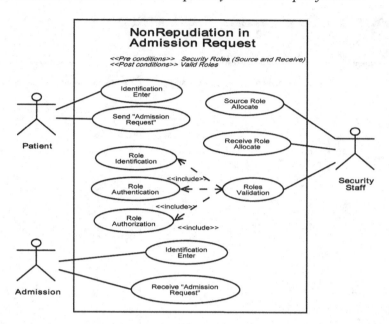

when this proposal was developed, the methodology does not use MDA formalisms (metamodels and semiautomatic transformations) but is based on ideas close to MDD. This methodology extends some well-known models such as various unified modeling language (UML) models, the unified process (UP), and the object constraint language (OCL), thus permitting the creation of conceptual and logical models of multilevel databases which are implemented through the use of Oracle Label Security (OLS).

The general structure of the methodology can be observed in Figure 13. The "Requirements Gathering", "Database Analysis", and "Multilevel Relational Logical Design" stages allow us to build a general model of the secure database, and finally the "Specific Logical Design" stage adapts this general model to the particularities of OLS. The methodology permits the integration of a further Specific Logical Design after the Multilevel Relational Logical Design in order to support the final implementation of the secure database by using another DBMS (e.g. DB2).

Firstly, the Requirements gathering stage elicits and models requirements, considering security issues. This goal is achieved through the use of the secure use case model, which is an extension of the use case model considering confidentiality requirements (Figure 14). This permits the specification of security characteristics of actors and use cases through two stereotypes (secure use case and authorized actor). The majority of the activities in the Requirements Gathering stage have been inherited from the UP, but there is a new activity from the point of view of security: the analysis of security in actors and use cases. Once use cases and actors have been identified, this activity is in charge of analyzing all use cases, determining which of them have confidentiality requirements and which actors will need special authorization to execute secure use cases. The necessary stereotypes are then included in the secure use case model.

The database analysis stage next considers all the requirements that have been elicited and modeled in the previous activities in order to build the database conceptual model by using secure class

Figure 13. Methodology for secure databases

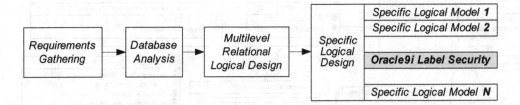

Figure 14. Secure use case diagram for secure databases

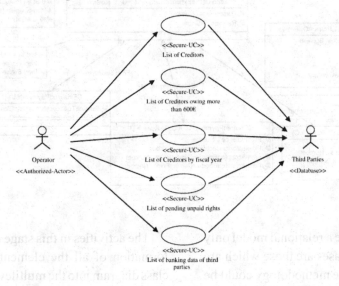

models and a set of security constraints. The secure class model (Figure 15) makes it possible to specify security information in classes, attributes and associations, indicating the conditions that the users will have to fulfill in order to access them.

In order to allow the specification of security constraints by using the Object Constraint Language (OCL), an extension called Object Security Constraint Language (OSCL) has been defined. OSCL permits the definition of the information concerning the security of classes, attributes or associations to be specified depending on a particular condition. This methodology supports mandatory (MAC) and role-based (RBAC) access control policies in their basic models, by defining levels of security and user

roles which represent an organizational classification of users.

A new activity, "Security Analysis", is included in the Unified Process (UP) in this stage, and is composed of the following tasks: specification of the valid security levels; definition of the user roles hierarchy; assignation of security levels to classes, attributes and associations; classification of classes, attributes and associations in different authorized roles; specification of security constraints; analysis of other kinds of security constraints; definition of the user authorization information; and revision of the security aspects defined.

The Multilevel Relational Logical Design stage represents a general logical model and is the bridge between the database conceptual model and the database specific logical design model. It

Figure 15. Secure class model for secure databases

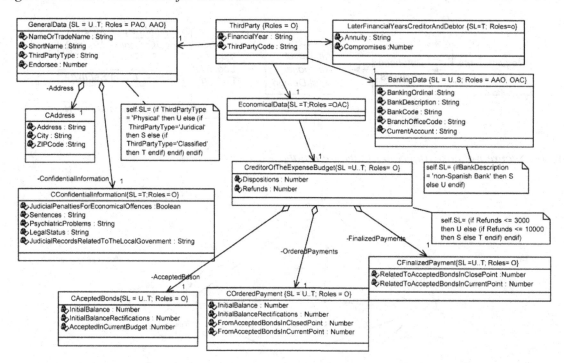

has been considered to be a relational model only because relational databases are those which are most widely used, but the methodology could be adapted in order to develop secure object-relational or object oriented databases by including other Specific Logical Designs.

There are three components in this stage:

- the database relational model which includes the definition of each relation of the database, considering the attributes which are necessary to represent the confidentiality information.
- a meta-information tuple associated with each relation including the datatype of the attributes, and the valid values of the attributes related to the tuple and attribute security information
- security constraints defined from the conceptual model which are specified in this model without loss or modification of their semantics.

The activities in this stage deal with the transformation of all the elements from the secure class diagram into the multilevel relational model in a similar way to the common transformation between conceptual and logical models, but considering security information.

Table 3 shows these components: (a) the database relational model which is defined as a set of n relations, where RELi is the name of the relation i, RLi and RRi are attributes that will respectively contain the security level and role of each row of relation i, Aij is the name of the attribute j, and Lij and Rij are attributes that will, respectively, contain the security level and role of the attribute Aij; (b) meta-information defined as a set of tuples, where RELi is the name of the relation i, ILi and SRi are the interval of security levels and the set of user roles that has been respectively defined for this relation i, Aij is the name of the attribute j, DTij is the datatype of Aij, and VLij and VRij are the interval of security levels and the set of user roles that has been respectively defined for Aij; and (c)

Table 3. Multilevel relational model for secure databases

(a)	$REL_1 (RL_1, RR_1, A_{11}, L_{11}, R_{11}, \ldots A_{1m}, L_{1m}, R_{1m})$ ... $REL_n (RL_n, RR_n, A_{n1}, L_{n1}, R_{n1}, \ldots A_{nm}, L_{nm}, R_{nm})$
	BankingData(Id, BankingOrdinal, BankDescription, BankCode, BranchOfficeCode, CurrentAccount, TFinancialYear, TThirdPartyCode, Security Level)
(b)	$<REL_1, IL_1, SR_1, A_{11}, DT_{11}, VL_{11}, VR_{11}, \ldots A_{1m}, DT_{1m}, VL_{1m}, VR_{1m}>$ ... $<REL_n, IL_n, SR_n, A_{n1}, DT_{n1}, VL_{n1}, VR_{n1}, \ldots A_{nm}, DT_{nm}, VL_{nm}, VR_{nm}>$
	<BankingData, U..S, AAO, OAC, Id: VarChar, BankingOrdinal: VarChar; BankDescription: VarChar; BankCode: VarChar; BranchOfficeCode: VarChar; CurrentAccount: VarChar; TFinancialYear: VarChar; TThirdPartyCode: VarChar; Security Level: SL>
(c)	Context REL_k inv: SecurityAttribute = OSCLExpression
	Context BankingData inv: Self.SecurityLevel = (if Self.BankDescription = "Non-Spanish bank" then S else U endinf)

security constraints, where RELk is the name of the associated relation, SecurityAttribute is the name or the attribute that the security constraint defines and the OSCLExpression is the condition that determines the value of the SecurityAttribute.

Finally, the Specific Logical Design stage specifies the secure database in a particular model. This methodology (Fernandez-Medina and Piattini, 2005) deals with the final implementation by using Oracle Label Security which is part of one of the most important DBMS and permits the implementation of label-based databases. Furthermore, this architecture was improved (Vela et al., 2006) by including another Specific Logical Design model based on XML which permits its eventual implementation in XML databases.

3.5. Developing Secure Data Warehouses

A Data Warehouse (DW) is a repository that manages a vast amount of a business' historical information which is integrated from different data sources (Inmon, 2002). This information is usually organized by following a multidimensional approach, using facts or cubes (for example, a product sale) and related dimensions with classifications per subject (for instance, departments, cities or product categories). A typical DW architecture is composed of several layers: heterogeneous Data Sources (DS); ETL (extraction/transformation/load) processes which extract and transform data from these DSs and load the information into the DW; the main part of the architecture, the DW repository in which the data are stored; and Data Base Management Systems (DBMS) and On-Line Analytical Processing (OLAP) tools which analyze data.

The data in DWs are highly sensitive since they involve vital business information which is used to support the strategic decision making process, and may also manage personal information protected under law. The differences between data sources and user requests make a better flexibility and information confidentiality control necessary, which is a critical aspect for the survival of enterprises. In order to avoid unauthorized accesses to information it is therefore necessary to consider the privacy problem in all layers and operations of the DW, from the early stages of development as a strong requirement, to the final implementation in Data Base Management Systems (DBMS) or On-Line Analytical Processing (OLAP) tools (Thuraisingham et al., 2007).

The most interesting proposal through which to achieve this goal is the methodology of Priebe and Pernul (Priebe and Pernul, 2001) in which

Figure 16. MDA architecture for secure DWs

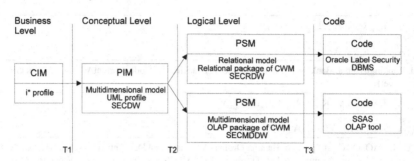

the authors analyze security requirements and their implementation in commercial tools by hiding multidimensional elements such as cubes, measures, slices and levels. They extend their proposal with a DW representation at the conceptual level with ADAPTed UML, but do not establish the connection between levels in order to allow automatic transformations.

Our research efforts are focused on developing DWs, considering security from early stages of the development process by using an access control and audit model specifically designed for DWs. We have therefore defined models at different abstraction levels which have been improved with security capabilities. Our proposal is aligned with an MDA architecture. It considers security issues in business (CIM), conceptual (PIM) and logical (PSM) models and defines transformation rules for the final implementation according to the MDA strategy. This architecture (Figure 16) provides two paths: a relational path for implementation in DBMS and a multidimensional path for OLAP tools. The automatic transformations between models (T1, T2 and T3) are achieved by executing set of transformation rules. This proposal uses Query/View/Transformation (QVT) rules for model to model transformations (T1 and T2) and MofScript for the final model to code transformation that generates the implementation (T3).

A computational independent metamodel (CIM) supports an early definition of the security requirements at the business level. This metamodel (Trujillo et al., 2009b, Trujillo et al.,

2009a) defines both functional and non functional requirements for DWs by using a UML profile based on the i* framework (Yu, 1997), which is an agent oriented approach towards requirements engineering centering on the agents' intentional characteristics.

For DW secure modeling at the conceptual level a Platform Independent Metamodel (PIM) called Secure Data Warehouse (SECDW) (Villaroel et al., 2006, Fernández-Medina et al., 2007b, Fernández-Medina et al., 2007a) has been defined which is composed of a UML profile specifically created for DWs (Luján-Mora et al., 2006) and an Access Control and Audit (ACA) model focused on DW confidentiality (Fernández-Medina et al., 2006). The transformation from secure CIM models has also been dealt with in (Trujillo et al., 2009a), in which the MDA methodology for secure DWs is described by using the OMG Software Process Engineering Metamodel Specification standard (SPEM).

The SECDW metamodel (Figure 17) permits the specification of structural aspects of DWs such as facts, dimensions, base classes, measures or hierarchies, many-to-many relations, degenerated dimensions, multiple classifications or alternative paths of hierarchies. This model is complemented by the ACA model which allows security constraints to be specified. The ACA model classifies authorization subjects and objects into security roles (SecurityRole) which organize users into a hierarchical role structure according to the responsibilities of each type of

Figure 17. Conceptual metamodel for decure DWs (SECDW)

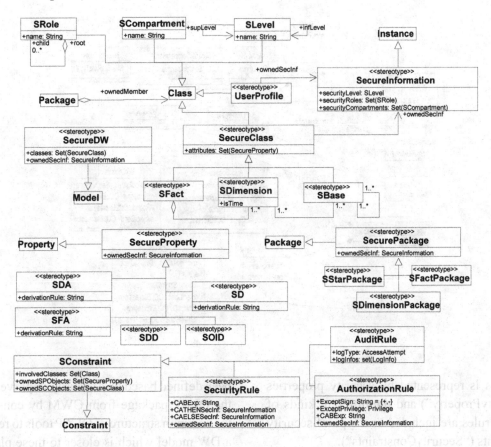

work, levels (SecurityLevel) which indicate the user's clearance level, and compartments (SecurityCompartment) which classify users into a set of horizontal compartments or groups.

The definition of several kinds of security rules related to the multidimensional elements of DWs is also permitted by using stereotypes and Object Constraints Language (OCL) expressions. Sensitive information assignment rules (SIAR) specify multilevel security policies and allow sensitivity information to be defined for each element in the multidimensional model; authorization rules (AUR) permit or deny access to certain objects by defining the subject that the rule applies to, the object that the authorization refers to, the action that the rule refers to and the sign describing whether the rule permits or denies access; and

audit rules (AR) ensure that authorized users do not misuse their privileges.

Multidimensional modeling at the logical level depends on the tool finally used and can thus be principally classified into online analytical processing by using relational (ROLAP), multidimensional (MOLAP) and hybrid (HOLAP) approaches. A relational approach has therefore been followed to define a Specific Platform Metamodel (PSM) called Secure Relational Data Warehouse (SECRDW) (Soler et al., 2008) as an extension of the relational package from the Common Warehouse Metamodel (CWM, 2003). SECRDW (Figure 18) models secure relational elements such as tables, columns or keys, and when related to these elements express the security issues defined at the conceptual level. The classification into security levels, compartments

Figure 18. Logical relational metamodel for secure DWs (SECRDW)

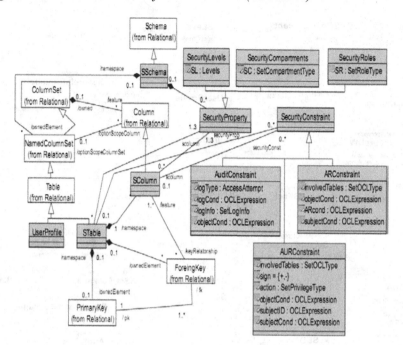

and roles is represented by security properties ("SecurityProperty") and the different kinds of security rules are included as a type of security constraints ("SecurityConstraints").

Moreover, the automatic transformation from conceptual models into relational logical models (transformation T2 in Figure 16) has been implemented by using QVT (Soler et al., 2009). Figure 19 shows a transformation rule in its graphical notation and its application to a simple example. The transformation is "SFact2Stable" and transforms fact classes and their properties into secure tables with a primary key and columns. The eventual implementation in Oracle Label Security has been dealt with in order to complete this relational path for DBMS (transformation T3).

Since most DWs are managed by OLAP tools using a multidimensional approach (MOLAP), this MDA architecture has been improved by including a new multidimensional path. A secure multidimensional logical metamodel (PSM), called Secure Multidimensional Data Warehouse (SECMDDW) (Blanco et al., 2009), has therefore

been defined based on a security improvement of the OLAP package from CWM by considering the common structure of OLAP tools to represent a DW model which is closer to these platforms than conceptual models.

The SECMDDW metamodel (Figure 20) is composed of: a security configuration metamodel which represents the system's security configuration by using a role-based access control policy (RBAC); a cube metamodel which defines both structural cube aspects such as cubes, measures, related dimensions and hierarchies, and security permissions for cubes and cells; and a dimension metamodel with structural issues of dimensions, bases, attributes and hierarchies, and security permissions which are related to dimensions and attributes. With regard to the abstraction gap between the conceptual and logical levels, security rules from conceptual models are represented by using a set of permissions (for cubes, cells, dimensions and attributes) related to certain security roles and positive and negative expressions ("AllowedSet" and "DeniedSet" attributes)

Figure 19. Transformation from PIM to relational PSM

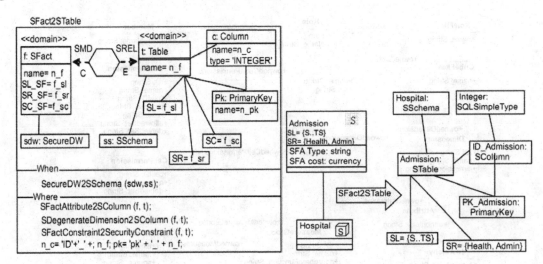

in order to establish the information that must be shown or hidden for that role.

Several sets of QVT transformation rules (Figure 21) have also been defined to automatically obtain secure logical multidimensional models from conceptual models (Blanco et al., 2009) (transformation T2 in Figure 16). Three main sets of transformations obtain each kind of target model from the source conceptual model: the security configuration model (SECDW2Role transformation), the cube model (SECDW2Cube) and the dimension model (SECDW2Dimension), and the remaining sets of transformations are focused on security rules (SECDWSecurityRules-2CubePermissions and SECDWSecurityRules-2DimensionPermissions). Obtaining secure multidimensional code from our secure multidimensional PSM is a simple task since both consider structural and security issues by using a multidimensional approach and the vast majority of the destination concepts are defined in our source metamodel. The final secure implementation has been also carried out by developing the corresponding Model-to-Text (M2T) rules in

order to automatically obtain secure code for a specific OLAP platform, SQL Server Analysis Services (SSAS) (transformation T3).

4. CONCLUSION

Software engineering has not traditionally integrated security in an appropriate manner, but the importance of developing secure software has been recognized. Software engineering methods and techniques, which integrate security issues during the entire development process are, therefore, now demanded, and in order to achieve this goal and develop quality systems in which security solutions fit perfectly in the system design it is extremely important to integrate security requirements from the early stages of the development process.

As we have shown in this chapter, a great number of proposals dealing with this problem can be found in literature. However, this discipline is not sufficiently mature, these proposals are not yet consolidated in commercial solutions, and a

Figure 20. Logical multidimensional metamodel for decure DWs (SECMDDW)

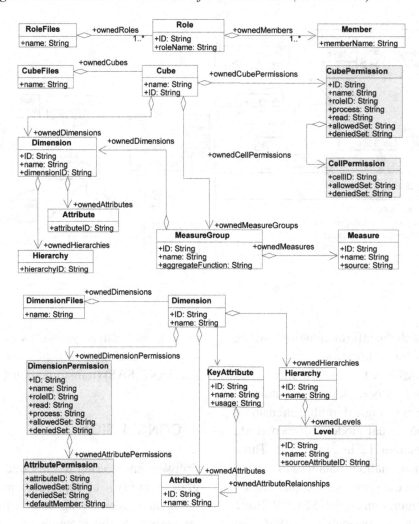

Figure 21. Transformation from PIM to multidimensional PSM

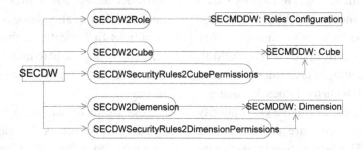

greater research effort by the scientific community in this field is still needed. In fact the majority of these proposals are partial solutions, dependent on a particular software engineering technique or modeling notation, specific to a technology, etc. We can therefore conclude by saying that although a global secure software engineering solution for secure information system development has not yet been obtained, the scientific community has identified the problem and is working towards this goal. In this respect, the number of scientific events focused on the integration of security into software engineering is therefore increasing exponentially, thus demonstrating that this is one of the most active research areas in the scientific community.

ACKNOWLEDGMENT

This research is part of the BUSINESS (PET2008-0136) Project financed by the "Ministerio de Ciencia e Innovación" (Spain), the PEGASO (TIN2009-13718-C02-01) Project financed by the "Ministerio de Ciencia e Innovación" (Spain), the SISTEMAS (PII2I09-0150-3135) Project financed by the "Consejería de Educación y Ciencia de la Junta de Comunidades de Castilla-La Mancha" (Spain), the QUASIMODO (PAC08-0157-0668) Project financed by the "Viceconsejería de Ciencia y Tecnología de la Junta de Comunidades de Castilla-La Mancha" (Spain) and the MEDUSAS (IDI-20090557) Project financed by the "Centro para el Desarrollo Tecnológico Industrial. Ministerio de Ciencia e Innovación (CDTI)" (Spain).

REFERENCES

Aiello, M., & Giorgini, P. (2004). Applying the Tropos Methodology for Analysing Web Services Requirements and Reasoning about Qualities of Services. *UPGRADE, 5*, 20–26.

Alexander, C., Ishikawa, S., & Silverstein, M. (1977). *A pattern language: towns, builings, construction*. New York: Oxford University Press.

Allen, J. H., Barnum, S., Ellison, R. J., Mcgraw, G., & Mead, N. R. (2008). *Software Security Engineering: A Guide for Project Managers*. Addison Wesley Professional.

Anderson, R. (2001). *Security Engineering: A Guide to Building Dependable Distributed Systems*. Jonh Wiley & Sons, Inc.

Arciniegas, J. L., Dueñas, J. C., Ruiz, J. L., Cerón, R., Bermejo, J., & Oltra, M. A. (2006). Architecture Reasoning for Supporting Product Line Evolution: An Example on Security. In Käkölä, T., & Dueñas, J. C. (Eds.), *Software Product Lines: Research Issues in Engineering and Management*. Springer.

Artelsmair, C., & Wagner, R. (2003). Towards a Security Engineering Process. *In:* Nagib Callaos, W. L., Belkis Sánchez, Elizabeth Hansen (eds.), The 7th World Multiconference on Systemics, Cybernetics and Informatics, July 27-30, 2003 2003 Orlando, Florida, USA. 22-27.

Atluri, V. (2001). Security for Workflow Systems. *Information Security Technical Report, 6*(2), 59–68. doi:10.1016/S1363-4127(01)00207-2

Bachmann, F., Bass, L., Carriere, J., Clements, P., Garlan, D., Ivers, J., Little, R. & Nord, R. (2000). Software Architecture Documentation in Practice: Documenting Architectural Layers CMU/SEI-2000-SR-004.

Basin, D., Doser, J., & Lodderstedt, T. (2003) Model Driven Security for Process-oriented Systems. *In:* ACM Symposium on Access Control Models and Technologies, 2003 Como, Italy. ACM Press, 100-109.

Basin, D., Doser, J., & Lodderstedt, T. (2006). Model Driven Security: from UML Models to Access Control Infrastructures. *ACM Transactions on Software Engineering and Methodology, 15*, 39–91. doi:10.1145/1125808.1125810

Bass, L., Bachmann, F., Ellison, R. J., Moore, A. P., & Klein, M. (2004). *Security and Survivability Reasoning Frameworks and Architectural Design Tactics*. SEI.

Bass, L., Clements, P., & Kazman, R. (2003). *Software Architecture in Practice*. Addison-Wesley.

Best, B., Jürjens, J., & Nuseibeh, B. (2007) Model-Based Security Engineering of Distributed Information Systems Using UMLsec. *In:* International Conference on Software Engineering, Minneapolis, MN, USA. 581-590.

Blakley, B., & Heath, C. The Open Group. (2004). *Technical Guide*. Security Design Patterns.

Blanco, C., García-Rodríguez de Guzmán, I., Rosado, D., Fernández-Medina, E., & Trujillo, J. (2009). Applying QVT in order to implement Secure Data Warehouses in SQL Server Analysis Services. *Journal of Research and Practice in Information Technology*, *41*, 135–154.

BPMN. (2006). *Business Process Modeling Notation Specification* [Online]. OMG Final Adopted Specification, dtc/06-02-01. Available: http://www.bpmn.org/Documents/OMG%20Final%20Adopted%20BPMN%201-0%20Spec%2006-02-01.pdf [Accessed].

Bresciani, P., Giorgini, P., Giunchiglia, F., Mylopoulos, J., & Perini, A. (2004). Tropos: Agent-Oriented Software Development Methodology. *Journal of Autonomous Agents and Multi-Agent System*, *8*, 203–236. doi:10.1023/B:AGNT.0000018806.20944.ef

Breu, R., Burger, K., Hafner, M., Jürjens, J., Popp, G., Lotz, V., & Wimmel, G. (2003). Key Issues of a Formally Based Process Model for Security Engineering. *In:* International Conference on Software and Systems Engineering and their Applications, 2003.

Buecker, A., Ashley, P., Borrett, M., Lu, M., Muppidi, S., & Readshaw, N. (2007). *Understanding SOA Security Design and Implementation. IBM Redbooks*. IBM.

Cheng, B. H. C., Konrad, S., Campbell, L. A., & Wassermann, R. (2003). *In* (pp. 13–22). Monterey Bay, CA, USA: Using Security Patterns to Model and Analyze Security Requirements.

Clements, P., & Northrop, L. (2002). *Software Product Lines: Practices and Patterns*. Addison-Wesley.

CWM, O. M. G. (2003). Common Warehouse Metamodel (CWM).

Delessy, N. A., & Fernandez, E. B. (2008). A pattern-driven security process for SOA applications. *In:* SAC '08: Proceedings of the 2008 ACM symposium on Applied computing, 2008 Fortaleza, Ceara, Brazil. ACM, 2226-2227.

Devanbu, P., & Stubblebine, S. (2000). Software engineering for security: a roadmap in: A. Finkelstein. *The Future of Software Engineering, ACM Press*, 227-239.

Djebbi, O., Salinesi, C., & Fanmuy, G. (2007). Industry Survey of Product Lines Management Tools: Requirements, Qualities and Open Issues. *15th IEEE International Requirements Engineering Conference (RE'07)*, *15*, 301 - 306.

Endrei, M., Ang, J., Arsanjani, A., Chua, S., Comte, P., Krogdahl, P., et al. (2004). *Patterns: Service-Oriented Architecture and Web Services* [Online]. Available: http://www.redbooks.ibm.com/abstracts/sg246303.html [Accessed].

Faegri, T. E., & Hallsteinsen, S. (2006). A Software Product Line Reference Architecture for Security. In Käkölä, T., & Dueñas, J. C. (Eds.), *Software Product Lines: Research Issues in Engineering and Management*. Springer.

Fernandez, E. B., Cholmondeley, P., & Zimmermann, O. (2007). Extending a Secure System Development Methodology to SOA. *In:* DEXA '07: Proceedings of the 18th International Conference on Database and Expert, 2007 Regensburg, Germany. IEEE Computer Society, 749-754.

Fernández-Medina, E., Jurjens, J., Trujillo, J., & Jajodia, S. (2009). Model Driven Development for Secure Information Systems. *Information and Software Technology, 51,* 809–814. doi:10.1016/j.infsof.2008.05.010

Fernández-Medina, E., & Piattini, M. (2005). Designing Secure Databases. *Information and Software Technology, 47,* 463–477. doi:10.1016/j.infsof.2004.09.013

Fernández-Medina, E., Trujillo, J., & Piattini, M. (2007a). Model Driven Multidimensional Modeling of Secure Data Warehouses. *European Journal of Information Systems, 16,* 374–389. doi:10.1057/palgrave.ejis.3000687

Fernández-Medina, E., Trujillo, J., Villarroel, R., & Piattini, M. (2006). Access Control and Audit Model for the Multidimensional Modeling of Data Warehouses. *Decision Support Systems, 42,* 1270–1289. doi:10.1016/j.dss.2005.10.008

Fernández-Medina, E., Trujillo, J., Villarroel, R., & Piattini, M. (2007b). Developing secure data warehouses with a UML extension. *Information Systems, 32,* 826–856. doi:10.1016/j.is.2006.07.003

Ferrari, E., & Thuraisingham, B. (2000). Secure Database Systems. In Piattini, M., & Díaz, O. (Eds.), *Advanced Databases: Technology Design.* London: Artech House.

Firesmith, D. G. (2003). Engineering Security Requirements. *Journal of Object Technology, 2,* 53–68.

Firesmith, D. G. (2004a). Specifying Reusable Security Requirements. *Journal of Object Technology, 3*(1), 61–75. doi:10.5381/jot.2004.3.1.c6

Firesmith, D. G. (2004b). Specifying Reusable Security Requirements. *Journal of Object Technology,* 61-75.

Flechais, I., Mascolo, C., & Sasse, M. A. (2007). Integrating security and usability into the requirements and design process. *International Journal Electronic Security and Digital Forensics, 1,* 12–26. doi:10.1504/IJESDF.2007.013589

Gamma, E., Helm, R., Johnson, R., & Vlissides, J. (1994). *Design Patterns: Elements of Reusable Object-Oriented Software.* Addison-Wesley.

Garlan, J., & Anthony, R. (2002). *Large-Scale Software Architecture.* John Wiley & Sons.

Ghosh, A., Howell, C., & Whittaker, J. (2002). Building Software Securely from the Ground Up. *IEEE Software, 19,* 14–16. doi:10.1109/MS.2002.976936

Giorgini, P., Mouratidis, H., & Zannone, N. (2007). Modelling Security and Trust with Secure Tropos. In Mouratidis, H., & Giorgini, P. (Eds.), *Integrating Security and Software Engineering: Advances and Future Visions.* Idea Group Publishing.

Graham, D. (2006). *Introduction to the CLASP Process* [Online]. OWASP CLASP Project http://www.owasp.org/index.php/Category:OWASP_CLASP_Project. Available: https://buildsecurityin.us-cert.gov/daisy/bsi/articles/best-practices/requirements/548.html [Accessed].

Gutiérrez, C., Fernández-Medina, E., & Piattini, M. (2004). A Survey of Web Services Security. *In:* AL., L. E., ed. Workshop on Internet Communications Security 2004 (WICS 2004), in conjunction with the 2004 International Conference on Computational Science and Its Applications (ICCSA 2004), 2004 Assisi (PG), Italy. Springer-Verlag, 969-977.

Gutiérrez, C., Fernández-Medina, E., & Piattini, M. (2006). Towards a Process for Web Services Security. *Journal of Research and Practice in Information Technology*, 38, 57–67.

Gutiérrez, C., Fernández-Medina, E., & Piattini, M. (2007). Web Services-based Security Requirement Elicitation. *IEICE Transaction on Information and Systems. E (Norwalk, Conn.)*, 90-D, 1374–1387.

Gutiérrez, C., Rosado, D., & Fernández-Medina, E. (2009). The Practical Application of a Process for Eliciting and Designing Security in Web Service Systems. *Information and Software Technology*, 51, 1712–1738. doi:10.1016/j.infsof.2009.05.004

Hafner, M., & Breu, R. (2009). Security Engineering for Service-Oriented Architectures. *Springer*, 248.

Hafner, M., Breu, R., Agreiter, B., & Nowak, A. (2006). SECTET: An Extensible Framework for the realization of Secure inter-organizational Workflows. *Internet Research*, 16, 491–506. doi:10.1108/10662240610710978

Haley, C. B., Laney, R., Moffet, J. D., & Nuseibeh, B. (2008). Security Requirements Engineering: A Framework for Representation and Analysis. *IEEE Transactions on Software Engineering*, 34, 133–153. doi:10.1109/TSE.2007.70754

Haley, C. B., Laney, R. C., & Nuseibeh, B. (2004). Deriving security requirements from crosscutting threat descriptions. *In:* 3rd International Conference on Aspect-Oriented Software Development (AOSD), March 22-24, 2004 2004 Lancaster, UK. 112-121.

Haley, C. B., Moffet, J. D., Laney, R., & Nuseibeh, B. (2006). *A Framework for Security Requirements Engineering*. Software Engineering for Secure Systems Workshop, 2006 Shanghai. *China*, 35–42.

Harmon, P. (2004). *The OMG's Model Driven Architecture and BPM*. Newsletter of Business Process Trends.

IEEE. (1990). *IEEE Standard 610.12–1990 IEEE Standard Glossary of Software Engineering Terminology*. New York, NY, USA: Institute of Electrical and Electronics Engineers.

Inmon, H. (2002). *Building the Data Warehouse*. New York: John Wiley & Sons.

ISO/IEC. (2005a). *ISO/IEC 15408 (Common Criteria v3.0)*. Information Technology Security Techniques-Evaluation Criteria for IT Security.

ISO/IEC (2004). ISO/IEC 13335 Information technology - Security techniques - Management of information and communications technology security.

ISO/IEC (2005b). ISO/IEC 27001. Information technology - Security techniques - Information security management systems - Requirements.

Jürjens, J. (2002). UMLsec: Extending UML for secure systems development. In: JÉZÉQUEL, J., HUSSMANN, H. & COOK, S. (eds.) *UML 2002 - The Unified Modeling Language, Model engineering, concepts and tools*. Dresden, Germany: Springer. LNCS 2460.

Jürjens, J. (2005). *Secure Systems Development with UML*. New York: Springer.

Jürjens, J. (2008). A Domain-specific Language for Cryptographic Protocols based on Streams. *Journal of Logic and Algebraic Programming, Special issue on Streams and Algebra*.

Jürjens, J., & Houmb, S. H. (2004). Risk-Driven Development Of Security-Critical Systems Using UMLsec. In: Boston, S., ed. IFIP International Federation for Information Processing, 21-53.

Jürjens, J., Schreck, J., & Bartmann, P. (2008a) *Model-based Security Analysis for Mobile Communications*. In: International Conference on Software Engineering, 2008a Leipzig, Germany. IEEE Computer Society.

Jürjens, J. & Shabalin, P.(2007). Tools for Secure Systems Development with UML. *Invited submission to the FASE 2004/05 special issue of the International Journal on Software Tools for Technology Transfer,* 9, 527-544.

Jürjens, J., Schreck, J. & Yu, Y. (2008b). Automated Analysis of Permission-Based Security Using UMLsec. *Fundamental Approaches to Software Engineering (FASE 2008), held as part of the Joint European Conferences on Theory and Practice of Software (ETAPS 2008),* 292-295.

Kam, S. H. (2005). Integrating the Common Criteria Into the Software Engineering Lifecycle. *IDEAS,* 05, 267–273.

Kang, K., Cohen, S., Hess, J. A., Novak, W. E., & Peterson, S. A. (1990). *Feature-Oriented Domain Analysis (FODA) Feasibility Study.* Software Engineering Institute, Carnegie-Mellon University.

Kienzle, D. M. & Elder, M. C. (2005). *Final Technical Report: Security Patterns for web Application Development.*

Kim, J., Kim, M. & Park, S. (2005). Goal and scenario bases domain requirements analysis environment. *The Journal of Systems and Software.*

Kotonya, G., & Sommerville, I. (2000). *Requirements Engineering Process and Techniques.* John Willey & Sons.

Kruchten, P. (2000). *The Rational Unified Process: An Introduction.* Reading, MA: Addison-Wesley Pub Co.

Lampson, B. W. (2004). Computer Security in the Real World. *IEEE Computer,* 37(6), 37–46.

Lee, J., Lee, J., Lee, S., & Choi, B. (2003). A CC-based Security Engineering Process Evaluation Model. *27th Annual International Computer Software and Applications Conference (COMPSAC'03),* 130-.

Lodderstedt, T., Basin, D., & Doser, J. (2002). SecureUML: A UML-based modeling language for model-driven security. *In:* UML 2002. The Unified Modeling Language. Model Engineering, Languages Concepts, and Tools. 5th International Conference, 2002 Dresden, Germany. Springer, 426-441.

Lonjon, A. (2004). Business Process Modeling and Standardization. *BPTrends,* http://www.bp-trends.com/.

López, F., Amutio, M. A., Candau, J., & Mañas, J. A. (2005). *Methodology for Information Systems Risk Analysis and Management.* Ministry of Public Administration.

Luján-Mora, S., Trujillo, J., & Song, I.-Y. (2006). A UML profile for multidimensional modeling in data warehouses. *Data & Knowledge Engineering,* 59, 725–769. doi:10.1016/j.datak.2005.11.004

McDermott, J., & Fox, C. (1999) *Using Abuse Case Models for Security Requirements Analysis.* In: 15th Annual Computer Security Applications Conference, Phoenix, Arizona. IEEE Computer Society, 55-66.

MDA. (2003). *O. M. G.* Model Driven Architecture Guide.

Mead, N. R., & Hough, E. D. (2006). *Security Requirements Engineering for Software Systems: Case Studies in Support of Software Engineering Education.* CSEE&T.

Mead, N. R., & Stehney, T. (2005). *Security Quality Requirements Engineering (SQUARE) Methodology.* In: Software Engineering for Secure Systems (SESS05), ICSE 2005 International Workshop on Requirements for High Assurance Systems, May 15-16, 2005 2005 St. Louis.

Mellado, D., Fernández-Medina, E., & Piattini, M. (2006a). Applying a Security Requirements Engineering Process. *11th European Symposium on Research in Computer Security (ESORICS 2006)*, Springer LNCS 4189, 192-206.

Mellado, D., Fernández-Medina, E., & Piattini, M. (2006b). A Comparative Study of Proposals for Establishing Security Requirements for the Development of Secure Information Systems. *The 2006 International Conference on Computational Science and its Applications (ICCSA 2006)*, *Springer LNCS 3982*, 3, 1044-1053.

Mellado, D., Fernández-Medina, E., & Piattini, M. (2006c). A Comparison of the Common Criteria with Proposals of Information Systems Security Requirements. *"First International Conference on Availability, Reliability and Security" (ARES '06)*, 654-661.

Mellado, D., Fernández-Medina, E., & Piattini, M. (2007). A Common Criteria Based Security Requirements Engineering Process for the Development of Secure Information Systems. *Computer Standards & Interfaces*, 29, 244–253. doi:10.1016/j.csi.2006.04.002

Mellado, D., Fernández-Medina, E., & Piattini, M. (2008a). Security Requirements Engineering Process for Software Product Lines: A Case Study. *The Third International Conference on Software Engineering Advances" (ICSEA 2008)*, 1-6.

Mellado, D., Fernández-Medina, E., & Piattini, M. (2008b). *Towards security requirements management for software product lines: a security domain requirements engineering process*. Computer Standards & Interfaces.

Mellado, D., Rodríguez, J., Fernández-Medina, E., & Piattini, M. (2009). Automated Support for Security Requirements Engineering in Software Product Line Domain Engineering. *The Fourth International Conference on Availability, Reliability and Security (ARES 2009)*, accepted.

Mouratidis, H. (2004). A Security Oriented Approach in the Development of Multiagent Systems: Applied to the Management of the Health and Social Care Needs of Older People in England, *PhD Thesis*, University of Sheffield

Mouratidis, H., & Giorgini, P. (2006). *Integrating Security and Software Engineering: Advances and Future Vision*. Hershey, PA: Idea Group Publishing.

Mouratidis, H., & Giorgini, P. (2007). Secure Tropos: A Security-Oriented Extension of the Tropos methodology [IJSEKE]. *International Journal of Software Engineering and Knowledge Engineering*, *17*(2), 285–309. doi:10.1142/S0218194007003240

Mouratidis, H., & Giorgini, P. (2007b). *Security Attack Testing (SAT)-Testing the Security of Information Systems at Design Time. Information Systems 32(8)* (pp. 1166–1183). Elsevier.

OMG (Object Management Group). (2003). *Model Driven Architecture Guide Version 1.0.1* [Online]. Available: http://www.omg.org/mda/ [Accessed].

OMG (Object Management Group). (2005). MOF QVT final adopted specification.

OMG (Object Management Group). (2007). *Unified Modeling Language: Superstructure Version 2.1.1 (formal/2007-02-05)* [Online]. Available: http://www.omg.org/docs/formal/07-02-05.pdf [Accessed].

Opdahl, A. L., & Sindre, G. (2008). (in press). Experimental comparison of attack trees and misuse cases for security threat identification. [*Corrected Proof.*]. *Information and Software Technology*.

Pohl, K., Böckle, G., & Linden, F. V. D. (2005). *Software Product Line Engineering. Foundations, Principles and Techniques*. Berlin, Heidelberg: Springer.

Popp, G., Jürjens, J., Wimmel, G., & Breu, R. (2003). Security-Critical System Development with Extended Use Cases. 10th Asia-Pacific Software Engineering Conference.

Priebe, T., & Pernul, G. (2001) A Pragmatic Approach to Conceptual Modeling of OLAP Security. *In:* 20th International Conference on Conceptual Modeling (ER 2001), Yokohama, Japan. Springer-Verlag.

Ramachandran, J. (2002). *Designing Security Architecture Solutions*. John Wiley & Sons.

Rodriguez, A., Fernandez-Medina, E., & Piattini, M. (2007). An MDA Approach to Develop Secure Business Processes through a UML 2.0 Extension. *Computer Systems. Science and Engineering, 22*, 307–319.

Rodríguez, A., Fernández-Medina, E., & Piattini, M. (2007) *Towards CIM to PIM transformation: from Secure Business Processes defined by BPMN to Use Cases*. 5th International Conference on Business Process Management (BPM), 24-28 September 2007 2007d Brisbane, Australia. 408-415.

Rodríguez, A., Fernández-Medina, E., & Piattini, M. (2007a) Analysis-Level Classes from Secure Business Processes through Models Transformations. In: 4th International Conference on Trust, Privacy and Security in Digital Business (Trust-Bus), September 3 – 7 Regensburg, Germany. 104-114.

Rodríguez, A., Fernández-Medina, E., & Piattini, M. (2007b). A BPMN Extension for the Modeling of Security Requirements in Business Processes. *IEICE Transactions on Information and Systems. E (Norwalk, Conn.), 90-D*(4), 745–752.

Rodríguez, A., Fernández-Medina, E., & Piattini, M. (2007c). *M-BPSec: A Method for Security Requirement Elicitation from a UML 2.0 Business Process Specification*. 3rd International Workshop on Foundations and Practices of UML, 2007c Auckland, New Zealand. 106-115.

Rosado, G., Gutiérrez, C., Fernández-Medina, E., & Piattini, M. (2006). Security Patterns and Security Requirements for Web Services. *Internet Research*, 16.

Sachitano, A., & Chapman, R. O. & JR., J. A. H. (2004). Security in Software Architecture: A Case Study. *Workshop on Information Assurance*. United States Military Academy, West Point, NY: IEEE.

Schumacher, M., Fernandez, E. B., Hybertson, D., & Buschmann, F. (2005). *Security Patterns*. New York: John Wiley & Sons.

Schumacher, M., & Roedig, U. (2001) *Security Engineering with Patterns*. 8th Conference on Patterns Lnaguages of Programs, PLoP 2001, July 2001 Monticello, Illinois, USA.

Sindre, G., & Opdahl, A. L. (2005). Eliciting security requirements with misuse cases. *Requirements Engineering, 10*(1), 34–44. doi:10.1007/s00766-004-0194-4

Soler, E., Trujillo, J., Blanco, C., & Fernández-Medina, E. (2009). Designing Secure Data Warehouses by using MDA and QVT. *Journal of Universal Computer Science, 15*, 1607–1641.

Soler, E., Trujillo, J., Fernández-Medina, E., & Piattini, M. (2008). Building a secure star schema in data warehouses by an extension of the relational package from CWM. *Computer Standards & Interfaces, 30*, 341–350. doi:10.1016/j.csi.2008.03.002

Steel, C., Nagappan, R., & Lai, R. (2005a). *Core Security Patterns: Best Practices and Strategies for J2EE™, Web Services, and Identity Management*. Upper Saddle River, NJ: Prentice Hall PTR / Sun Microsystems.

Steel, C., Nagappan, R., & Lai, R. (2005b). *The Alchemy of Security DesignMethodology, Patterns, and Reality Checks. Core Security Patterns: Best Practices and Strategies for J2EE™, Web Services, and Identity Management*. Prentice Hall PTR / Sun Microsystems.

Thuraisingham, B., Kantarcioglu, M., & Iyer, S. (2007). Extended RBAC-based design and implementation for a secure data warehouse. [IJBIDM]. *International Journal of Business Intelligence and Data Mining, 2*, 367–382. doi:10.1504/IJBIDM.2007.016379

Trujillo, J., Soler, E., Fernández-Medina, E., & Piattini, M. (2009a). An Engineering Process for Developing Secure Data Warehouses. *Information and Software Technology, 51*, 1033–1051. doi:10.1016/j.infsof.2008.12.003

Trujillo, J., Soler, E., Fernández-Medina, E., & Piattini, M. (2009b). A UML 2.0 Profile to define Security Requirements for DataWarehouses. *Computer Standards & Interfaces, 31*, 969–983. doi:10.1016/j.csi.2008.09.040

Vela, B., Fernandez-Medina, E., Marcos, E., & Piattini, M. (2006). Model Driven Development of Secure XML Databases. *SIGMOD Record, 35*, 22–27. doi:10.1145/1168092.1168095

Villaroel, R., Fernández-Medina, E., Trujillo, J., & Piattini, M. (2006). UML 2.0/OCL Extension for Designing Secure Data Warehouses. *Journal of Research and Practice in Information Technology, 38*, 31–43.

Villarroel, R., Fernández-Medina, E., & Piattini, M. (2005). *Secure information systems development- a survey and comparison.* Computers & Security.

Vinoski, S. (2004). WS-NonexistentStandards. *IEEE Internet Computing, 8*, 94–96. doi:10.1109/MIC.2004.73

Weiss, M., & Mouratdis, H. (2008). *Selecting Security Patterns that Fulfill Security Requirements.* Proceedings of the 16th IEEE International Conference on Requirements Engineering (RE'08), IEEE Computer Society, pp. 169-172

Yoder, J., & Barcalow, J. Year. Architectural Patterns for Enabling Application Security. *In:* 4th Conference on Patterns Language of Programming (PLoP'97), 1997 Monticello, Illinois.

Yu, E. (1997)Towards modelling and reasoning support for early-phase requirements engineering. *In:* 3rd IEEE International Symposium on Requirements Engineering (RE'97), 1997 Washington, DC. 226-235.

Yu, E., Liu, L. & Mylopoulos (2007). A Social Ontology for Integrating Security and Software Engineering. *Integrating Security and Software Engineering: Advances and Future Visions.* Hershey, PA: Idea Group Publishing.

Chapter 6
Balancing Security and Performance Properties During System Architectural Design

Siv Hilde Houmb
Telenor GBDR Platform for Service Innovation Group, Norway

Geri Georg
Colorado State University, USA

Dorina C. Petriu
Carleton University, Canada

Behzad Bordbar
University of Birmingham, UK

Indrakshi Ray
Colorado State University, USA

Kyriakos Anastasakis
University of Birmingham, UK

Robert B. France
Colorado State University, USA

ABSTRACT

Developers of critical systems need to address several quality properties, such as security and performance, in the early stages of the development cycle to ensure that the system under construction meets its requirements. Sometimes quality properties conflict with each other and/or with the system's functionalities, so the developers need to make trade-off decisions. Unreasonable costs, added developer resources and tight project schedules may be other reasons for having to trade-off between alternative solutions. In the context of Model-Driven Development, the analysis of quality properties is done by

DOI: 10.4018/978-1-61520-837-1.ch006

transforming software design models into different analysis models based on various formalisms, which are then analyzed with existing tools. A major challenge is to integrate different models, transformations and tools into a consistent and coherent process. In this chapter the authors present a methodology called Aspect-Oriented Risk Driven Development (AORDD), which integrates the analysis of two quality properties, namely security and performance, into the development process of critical systems. Each quality property is analyzed separately, and then all results are input to a trade-off analysis that identifies conflicts between the properties. Trade-off analysis aims at supporting designers and developers in choosing the security and performance solutions that best fit their needs, without introducing unacceptable development delays or costs. The security analysis consists of identifying the assets (critical components, such as sensitive information) of an application and the attacks that can compromise these assets, and formally analyzing whether these attacks are actually possible using the tools UML2Alloy and Alloy Analyzer. If the system is vulnerable to the attack, some security solution, modeled as an aspect according to Aspect Oriented Modeling (AOM), is added to the system. The analysis must be repeated to ensure that the resulting system is secure. Performance analysis is accomplished using Layered Queuing Network (LQN) models. Annotated system models are transformed into LQN models and performance experiments are executed on them. If the performance results are unacceptable, the system design has to be changed and the analysis repeated. Finally, the results of the security and performance analysis are input to the system quality property trade-off analysis, which is implemented as a Bayesian Belief Network (BBN) topology, and which also takes as input external parameters, such as time to market and budget constraints. The results of the trade-off analysis help identify how well a particular design meets performance, security and other project goals, which, in turn, can guide the developer in making informed design decisions. The approach is illustrated using a transactional web e-commerce benchmark (TPC-W) originally developed by the Transaction Processing Performance Council.

INTRODUCTION

Developers of critical systems need to address several quality properties in the early stages of the development cycle, to ensure that the system under construction meets its requirements. Basing design decisions on quality analysis results early during system design can help avoid drastic and expensive changes in later development stages. In the context of Model-Driven Development, the analysis of quality properties is done by transforming software design models into different analysis models based on various formalisms, which are then analyzed with existing tools. The challenge consists in integrating different models, transformations and tools into a coherent development process.

Sometimes quality properties conflict with each other and/or with the system's functionalities, so the developers need to make trade-off decisions. For example, security and performance qualities were conflicting in the redesign of the Secure Sockets Layer (SSL) protocol proposed in Apostolopoulos et al. (1999). The proposed version achieved its goal of reducing SSL server performance cost, but violated the goal of providing a secure connection (see Jürjens (2005) for more details).

Performance and security goals are often at odds with each other. Customers want easy, secure access to systems, and a delay-free experience. However, this may not be feasible, and designers must make trade-off decisions that optimize parts of the system for one quality property over the other, or balance the quality properties. Financial considerations play a major role in these decisions since development resources and budget most often are limited. Software development approaches that support systematic trade-off analysis are most likely to produce flexible, robust architectural designs that meet both security and performance goals over the lifetime of the software.

In this chapter we present a methodology called Aspect-Oriented Risk Driven Development (AORDD), which integrates the analysis of two quality properties, security and performance, into the development process of critical systems. Each quality property is modeled and analyzed separately, and then all results are input to a system quality property trade-off analysis. The modeling language used is UML (OMG (2007) and OMG (2007-1)). Our approach uses Aspect-Oriented Modeling (AOM) techniques (see France et. al. (2004), Georg et. al. (2008)), to model security concerns separately as aspects, and to systematically experiment with alternative ways of addressing them. AOM techniques enable designers to quickly change the system design to incorporate additional or alternative security treatment designs prior to security analyses. Designers can therefore more easily search for a solution design that provides adequate protection (France et al. (2004-1), Straw et al. (2004), and Woodside et al. (2009)).

AORDD security analysis is carried out to determine how resilient a system design is to various attacks. The analysis involves transforming the UML models into Alloy (Bordbar and Anastasakis (2005) and Anastasakis et al. (2008)) and using the Alloy Analyzer (Alloy (2008)) to test security assertions. AORDD performance analysis of alternative designs is explored using the toolset developed by the Performance by Unified Model Analysis (PUMA) project, which takes as input UML models with performance annotations (Woodside et al. (2005) and Petriu and Woodside (2004)). Although the toolset can transform annotated UML models into different types of performance models, we use it to create Layered Queuing Network (LQN) models which allow us to analyze the system from a capacity viewpoint (e.g. mean response time for a given

workload), rather than a strict deadline viewpoint (which requires scheduling analysis).

The result of both security and performance analyses are used as input, together with financial, project, and development constraints, to a quality property trade-off analysis technique. Trade-off analysis in AORDD uses a Bayesian Belief Network (BBN) topology computation to derive fitness scores of alternative designs, and thus provides design decision support. Our previous work used this technique to compare how well alternative security mechanism designs meet security goals (as obtained from formal security analysis), and also other project goals such as time-to-market, budget, business goals, etc. In this chapter we add performance analysis data to trade-off analysis. This allows a designer to compare design alternatives from a performance point of view. A user of the trade-off analysis tool provides security, performance, and project goal information and also prioritizes the various goals. Since the analysis uses a flexible BBN topology, new goals can be added, and goal priorities can easily be changed.

The work described in this chapter is part of a larger research effort by the authors to integrate methodologies and tools that support the analysis and tradeoff of security, performance, and other quality property goals early in the software lifecycle. The AORDD methodology builds on our previous work in designing secure and dependable complex systems where there are competing project, financial, and quality goals. We have described the methodology in previous papers (see Houmb (2007) and Houmb et al. (2005) for details), and incorporated two types of formal security analysis into it (Georg et al. (2008) and Houmb et al. (2007)).

The chapter is structured as following. A description of our methodology is presented in the section *AORDD Methodology*. We demonstrate the various steps of the methodology in the sections *Demonstration of the AORDD Methodology, Security Analysis with Alloy Analyzer, Perfor-*

mance Analysis Using PUMA, and *Balancing Performance and Security*. We use a transactional web e-Commerce benchmark example in the demonstration. Specifically, *Demonstration of the AORDD Methodology* walks through initial steps of the methodology using the benchmark example. *Security Analysis with Alloy Analyzer* discusses the security analysis technique, and *Performance Analysis Using PUMA* discusses the performance analysis technique. *Balancing Performance and Security* presents the trade-off analysis portion of the methodology. A discussion of the AORDD methodology and its place in the context of concurrent system property analysis is presented in the section titled *Discussion*. The section titled *Related Work* looks into other related works and how the AORDD methodology compares to these, and *Conclusions* presents our closing remarks.

AORDD METHODOLOGY

This section gives an overview of the AORDD methodology, describes the iterative nature and the iteration mechanism of the underlying process, and provides a short introduction to the AORDD trade-off analysis, which is a combination of a system quality property conflict resolver and trade-off analysis. The AORDD methodology allows developers to treat security and performance issues in parallel, independent of formalisms and tools. The tools and techniques presented in this chapter are used to demonstrate the various steps of the methodology, but alternative analysis tools that produce output compatible with the inputs to trade-off analysis can also be used. The methodology itself can be looked upon as having multiple layers, where each layer works independently (e.g. security modeling and analysis versus performance modeling and analysis), but where the type and format of input and output moving across layers are compatible (e.g. from security or performance analysis to trade-off analysis).

Overview

Since cost is a restrictive development boundary, AORDD ensures that system quality properties are integrated at design, i.e., as early as possible. This promotes a consistent and coherent system design, and avoids expensive security or performance add-ons during later stages of development, or even after the system has been deployed. AORDD provides support with its step-by-step iterative process, which makes it possible for developers to deal with one challenge at a time. The methodology helps designers identify potential conflicts introduced by security or performance solutions. It provides data to aid the designer in selecting a solution that fits with the existing quality properties and requirements, and that is within the budget and development schedule boundaries.

The underlying process of AORDD is iterative and the iterations move the development and analysis forward using a set of *iteration* rules. There are two core iteration rules that guide the developer and designer through the quality property design, analysis and conflict resolution activities. The first rule is that no quality property conflicts should remain, so the process iterates until all conflicts are resolved. If conflicts cannot be completely resolved, the developer is asked to prioritize the requirements in order to solve the conflict. For example, the developer can choose to weaken the security requirements to ensure that performance issues are properly addressed. The second rule is that other project constraints, such as, budget and development schedule, should not be violated. These constraints are checked in the last part of the trade-off analysis.

Development with AORDD starts by examining the system core functional requirements and properties and using them to create an initial system functional design. Part of this design will also include some information relevant to security and performance, such as initial security requirements, risk acceptance criteria and performance demands. The design models are next analyzed

Figure 1. AORDD methodology including data (rectangles) and steps (ovals)

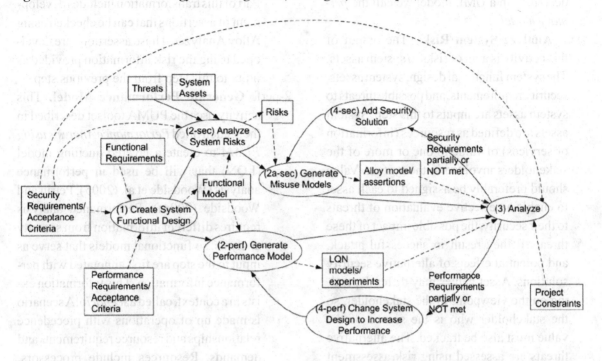

to identify the critical assets (parts or components of the system with value to one or more stake-holders) and potential threats to them. If there are no security demands, then the process can move directly to conflict and trade-off analysis. In case of security needs, modeling and analysis targeted towards fulfilling security requirements is performed. Security analysis may indicate that a security treatment is required. If so, the solution design is added to the system design and security analysis is repeated.

Similarly, modeling and analysis aimed at understanding the performance needs are also carried out. In cases where the performance needs are not met, changes must be introduced and the analysis executed again. In cases where performance needs are shown to be met, the process moves on to conflict and trade-off analysis. Performance and security modeling and analysis can be carried out simultaneously, and represent instances of iteration in AORDD. Once these iterations produce acceptable results for each system quality property,

conflict and trade-off analysis is performed. The results of trade-off analysis can cause additional security or performance iterations if the outcome is not acceptable.

The AORDD methodology is shown in Figure 1. Ovals represent activities or steps and rectangles represent data. Arrows represent data flow (dashed) and control flow (solid). Flow labels represent conditions under which the path is taken. The activities and their inputs and outputs are described below:

1. **Create System Functional Design.** This activity produces a functional design of the system. Its inputs are functional and quality requirements that are derived from their respective goals. The quality concerns currently supported in AORDD are security and performance. AORDD does not require the use of a particular method for this first activity, but it requires core functionality be

described in a UML model we call the *primary model*.

2-sec. **Analyze System Risks.** The output of this activity is a set of risks to system assets. The system functional design, system assets, security requirements, and possible threats to system assets are inputs to this step. System assets are defined as resources (information or services) of value to one or more of the stakeholders involved in the system. Value should preferably be assigned to each asset to enable an effective evaluation of threats to their security, the possible impact of these threats if they result in successful attack, and potential effects of alternative security solutions. Asset values may differ depending on the viewpoint of the stakeholder, so the stakeholder who is the source of the value must also be tracked. The alternative threats are assessed using risk assessment techniques, which may identify additional potential threats. Risk assessment involves human-intensive tasks; however, some techniques, such as CORAS (CORAS (2003), Houmb et al. (2008)), are computer-assisted.

2a-sec. **Generate Misuse Models.** The output of this activity is a *system misuse model*, ready for security analysis. Attacks associated with unacceptable risk are modeled as aspects in a set of *misuse models*. Misuse models specify the unwanted events or incidents that make up a security risk, the frequency of the events, and their impact on the system and its environment if they are successful. A misuse model is composed with the system model to create a *system misuse model*. A *system misuse model* represents the system under a specific attack, and illustrates the degree to which an asset can be compromised by the given attack. In our example we use the UML2Alloy tool described in the section titled *Security Analysis with Alloy Analyzer* to transform the system misuse model into an Alloy model suitable for security analysis.

Part of this transformation includes development of assertions that can be checked using Alloy Analyzer. These assertions are developed using the risk information provided as input to this step from the previous step.

2-perf. **Generate Performance Model.** This activity uses the PUMA toolset described in the section titled *Performance Analysis using PUMA* to create a layered queuing model (LQN) that will be used in performance analysis (Woodside et al. (2005), Petriu and Woodside (2004)). Performance analysis requires different information from security analysis, so functional models that serve as input to the step are first annotated with performance information. This information exists in a context, called a *scenario*. A scenario is made up of operations with precedence relationships and resource requirements and demands. Resources include processors, other devices, software components, processes and logical resources, while demands describe how many requests are made by an operation, or how much CPU processing is demanded. Each scenario has an associated workload that defines the arrivals of requests to execute the scenario. Annotated models are input to the PUMA tools to create the performance model. Another output of this step is a set of experimental questions that will be answered during performance analysis.

3. **Analyze.** Both security and performance analysis are part of this activity, as is trade-off analysis. Input to this step are system asset information, security and performance acceptance criteria (derived from their respective requirements), project constraints (e.g. time to market, budget, financial goals, etc.), the Alloy system misuse model and assertions, and the performance model. This step is shown in more detail in Figure 2. Output from the *Analyze* step can cause iteration to change/add security treatments

(step 4-sec) or to change the system design to increase performance (step 4-perf).

4-sec Add Security Solution. Potential security mechanism aspects are composed with the primary model to create a *security-treated* system model if a security analysis (performed in activity 3) provides unacceptable results. The security-treated model specifies the system in which a security mechanism has been incorporated, and which should now be resistant to the attack. The process moves back to step 2a-sec where the attack model is composed with this new system model and prepared for another security analysis (step 3). This iteration (steps 2, 3 and 4 and back to step 2 again) continues until successful results are achieved in step 3.

4-perf ChangeDesigntoIncreasePerformance. If a performance problem is discovered in the analysis in activity 3, changes must be made to the design to cope with this inefficiency.

This sometimes results in changes to the physical or logical architecture. Output of this step is a changed system design. This means that when leaving this step, the process iterates back to activity (2-perf) and then to activity (3) for further analysis. The resulting iteration steps are 2, 3, and 4, and back to step 2 until successful results are achieved.

AORDD Analysis

Figure 2 shows the flow of data between AORDD activities and the components of the *Analyze* activity (activity 3 in Figure 1). Here we only briefly describe the flow; details are provided in later sections. As in Figure 1, activities or steps are shown as ovals and data as rectangles. Dashed arrows indicate data flow while solid arrows show control flow. The major outputs of the Analyze activity are indicated by bold arrows.

Figure 2. Analyze step with major (dashed bold) and optional (solid bold) outputs

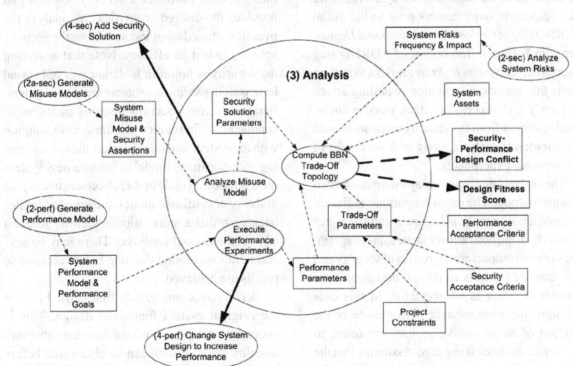

The AORDD *Analyze* step consists of three sub-steps. Performance and security analysis may be performed in parallel, but both must precede trade-off analysis as computed by the BBN topology. The numbered steps in Figure 2 (e.g. *2a-sec* and *2-perf*) correspond to AORDD activities shown in Figure 1.

Input to security analysis (*Analyze Misuse Model* in Figure 2) is an Alloy system misuse model that was created as part of step 2a-sec along with security assertions that can be tested by Alloy Analyzer.

Input to performance analysis (*Execute Performance Experiments* in Figure 2) is a performance model that was created as part of step 2-perf along with experimental questions to be answered regarding system performance.

Inputs to the trade-off analysis are obtained from many sources. Project constraints include goals such as time-to-market (TTM), budget, business goals, laws and regulations, and any other goals or constraints pertinent to the project. Security and performance acceptance criteria are assumed to be those that were derived from their respective requirements prior to the initial AORDD step of *Create System Functional Design,* step 1 in Figure 1. The output of AORDD step 2-sec, *Analyze System Risks,* is the risks to system assets that include information regarding attack frequency and successful attack consequences. Finally, output from the security analysis is used in the trade-off analysis, along with the results of performance experiments.

The analysis step has two major outputs and two optional outputs. The major outputs are indicated by dashed bold arrows in Figure 2, and the minor outputs by solid bold arrows in the same diagram. The optional outputs are the results of security and performance analysis causing a design-analyze iteration if either is unacceptable. In this case a design change to enhance performance or the addition of an alternative security treatment to counteract an attack is required. Assuming that the analyses produce acceptable results, the first major

output of the trade-off analysis can be computed. This is the Security-Performance Design Conflict score that reflects the extent to which the security and performance designs compromise each other's goals. The trade-off topology then computes an overall Design Fitness score that reflects the ability of the design to meet all the trade-off parameter goals, including both performance and security goals. This score may lead to additional iterations of the design-analyze cycle, which we discuss next.

The Iterative Design-Analyze Cycle

The first core iteration rule, that no quality property conflicts should remain in the system design, drives iteration design-analysis cycles for security, performance, and conflict analysis. We next discuss each of these three possible cycles.

Security analysis is performed on a system misuse model. Alloy Analyzer gives evidence as to whether the security assertions developed earlier are true for the system misuse model. If some desired security assertion does not hold, then we must introduce a security solution that provides the desired properties. We analyze the overall system design incorporating the security solution to test its efficacy. Note that analyzing the security solution in isolation will not reveal how well the solution protects the given system. Iterations through security analysis are therefore conducted by first composing the security solution with the system functional design, then recomposing with the attack model to create a new system misuse model. If undesirable effects are uncovered in the system misuse model, the process iterates back such that a more suitable security solution can be chosen and analyzed. There may be several iterations around the loop before acceptable results are achieved.

Performance analysis is first carried out on the original system functional design. This is necessary so that any bottlenecks in the core functionality of the system can be discovered before analyzing the impact of any security solutions that are added to the system. This helps avoid confusion regarding whether a security solution introduced a bottleneck or whether the bottleneck existed all along in the initial system design. Performance analysis begins by transforming the UML model into Core Scenario Model (CSM), which is then transformed into a Layered Queuing Network (LQN) model. The designer must also develop performance goals to be answered using experiments on the LQN model. If the results of these experiments are not acceptable, the system design is changed to improve performance to the point where the goals can be met. This can also be an iterative process, where different changes are made to finally produce a system design that meets performance goals.

Successful completion of both the performance and security iterative processes produce a base system model that performs as needed and a security-treated model that provides solutions to the identified security risk represented by the misuse model during security analysis. However, we do not yet know whether all the security and performance requirements can be met, since we have not integrated the security solutions with the performance-acceptable system design. AOM composition techniques are used to integrate the security aspect model into the performance-acceptable system design model and create what we call an *aggregated design* model. This model is a new security-treated system model. Performance analysis must be run on this model, and security analysis must be run on a new system misuse model created by composing the attack aspect model with the new security-treated system model. Results of these two analyses are input to conflict analysis, which computes the extent to which security and performance properties conflict.

A benefit of this step-wise process is that at any point in time it is possible to roll back to the last known good stage if the integrated security solutions degrade performance to an unacceptable level. The security analysis of the integrated system is used to ensure that no undesired ef-

fects have been introduced through performance enhancements, and performance analysis is used to uncover any bottlenecks that might have been introduced by security solutions. If the conflict analysis uncovers a problem, it can be resolved in several possible ways:

1. introduce an alternative security solution which aims to enhance performance,
2. keep the aggregated design as is, and change performance requirements so that the results of performance analysis are acceptable,
3. keep the security solution and change the design to meet performance requirements,
4. keep the aggregated design as is, and change the security requirements such that the results of security analysis are acceptable, or
5. remove both the security solution and any performance enhancing changes made and restart the process.

In practice, conflict resolution is influenced by considerations such as budget, time-to-market constraints, stakeholder goals, asset values, etc. For example, if a system asset is highly valued by a large set of influential stakeholders, security considerations may take precedence over performance goals, resulting in the relaxation of performance requirements (resolution type *b*)

We elaborate on performance, security, and conflict analysis iterations in the sections titled *Security Analysis with Alloy Analyzer, Performance Analysis Using PUMA*, and *Balancing Performance and Security.*

Trade-Off Analysis Using BBNs

The second core iteration rule, that project constraints should not be violated, drives iterations caused by trade-off analysis. The AORDD trade-off analysis is implemented as a BBN topology (Jensen, (1996/2001)), as shown in Figure 3. A BBN is a directed acyclic graph with an associated set of probability tables. The graph consists of

Figure 3. AORDD trade-off analysis top-level BBN topology

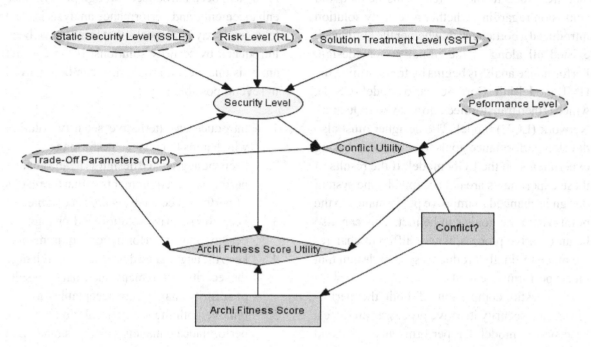

nodes representing variables, and arcs representing dependencies between these variables. Nodes are defined as stochastic or decision variables and multiple variables may be used to determine the state of a node. Each state of a node is expressed using probability density functions (pdf). These functions represent confidence in the various outcomes of the set of variables connected to a node. Node states depend conditionally on the status of the parent nodes of incoming edges. These directed arcs between nodes denote the causal relationship between their underlying variables.

There are three types of nodes in the graph: (i) target, (ii) observable (or leaf), and (iii) intermediate (between target and observable) nodes. Target nodes hold the assessment of the network and are the objectives of a computation. They can be either directly influenced by parents nodes, or be decision nodes. The state of a decision node is computed from an accompanying utility function. The utility function is a probability function used to calculate the expected usefulness of each possible decision the node represents. Target nodes

in the AORDD trade-off analysis topology are decision nodes.

Evidence or information is entered at the observable nodes and propagated through the network using the causal relationships and a propagation algorithm based on the underlying computational model of BBN (Pourret et al. (2008)). Furthermore, the status of the network is continually updated as information is entered, and propagated backward and forward along the edges. Evidence can be hard, meaning that we are certain that the state of a node is set into a particular value, as when, for example, a value is given to us. Hard evidence is also called instantiation and it blocks the node such that it does not receive any new evidence. In practice this means that the value can never be relaxed unless the original evidence is retracted. The alternative is soft evidence, which allows the probability values of node states to be updated. These values are updated based on values from incoming nodes and the current probability values, which are called prior probability values. Probability functions can determine the state of a target node if it is influenced directly by its parents, in which case the functions are called Node Probability Tables (NPT).

The AORDD BBN topology is implemented using the HUGIN™ (Hugin Version 6.8, (2007)) tool. All HUGIN BBN diagrams shown in this chapter display stochastic variables as ovals, decision variables as rectangles, and the associated utility functions supporting the decision variables are displayed as diamonds.

The AORDD topology shown in Figure 3 consists of several sub-networks, shown as ovals outlined with a dotted line. The target of the topology is computation of the fitness of a system design in terms of its ability to meet security, performance, and other trade-off parameters. As a result there are three components for dealing with security, performance and other trade-off parameters. The topology uses multiple sub-networks to compute a security level and one sub-network to compute the performance level of a system. A conflict decision node and associated utility function are used to determine how chosen security and performance solution designs conflict with each other and with the other trade-off parameters.

Initial population of the subnet variable probability density functions (either NPT or utility functions) can come from different sources (Houmb (2007)). For example, project stakeholders can be the source of initial system asset valuations or trade-off parameter pdfs, while organizational experience, security experts, national security postings, etc. can provide initial pdfs for security-related variables. Organizational experience or expert knowledge can also be used to provide initial pdfs for performance-related variables. Initial pdf sources and their affect on subnet calculations are discussed in detail in the sections titled *Demonstration of the AORDD Methodology, Security Analysis with Alloy Analyzer, Performance Analysis Using PUMA,* and *Balancing Performance and Security.*

DEMONSTRATION OF THE AORDD METHODOLOGY

The example we use in this chapter comes from a benchmark e-commerce system originally developed by the Transaction Processing Performance Council (TCP-W (2002)). This benchmark system describes a transactional retail system for books, including multiple on-line browsing sessions, shopping, purchasing, and shipping actions. The system includes database interactions and dynamic page generation. The system is divided into different kinds of workloads (shopping, browsing, and web-based ordering) whose ratio can be varied to simulate different environments for performance experimentation purposes. Each workload is subject to response time and resource constraints. The benchmark system includes a high-level design and user/system scenarios. These specifications were used to create UML class, deployment, and sequence diagrams for the scenarios. We use the scenario related to purchasing a book as our running example, since there are both security and performance requirements associated with it. We show the use of AORDD on this example. Steps in the methodology relating to Figure 1 are indicated in the section titles.

Create System Functional Design: AORDD Step 1

Figure 4 shows the main *GetBuyConfirmPage* sequence, and its referenced sequence called *Checkout.* The overall sequence is constrained by performance considerations, while only the interactions between *:EB* and *:WebServer* objects are constrained by security considerations. The assets associated with message between these objects, *PayInfo, ShippingInfo,* and *buyConfirmPage,* must be protected.

Figure 4. E-commerce example scenario

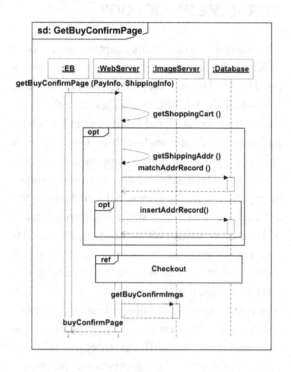

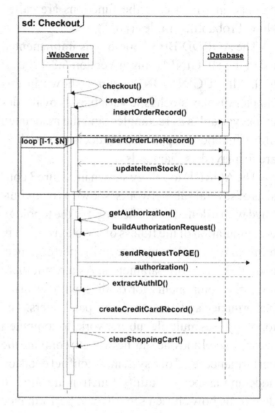

Analyze System Risks: AORDD Step 2-sec

The risk analysis portion of the AORDD methodology identifies system assets, values them according to system stakeholders, identifies risks to them and determines the consequences of successful attacks. This information is used to populate the first sub-network of the trade-off topology we will discuss, the Static Security Level (SSLE) subnet. The subnet topology is shown in Figure 5. For our example, we will assume that there are two stakeholders of interest, the company providing the e-commerce application, and a customer making a purchase. We will also assume that the customer has more influence on asset valuation than the company, since the customer can easily use a different company to make purchases, whereas

it may be difficult for the company to attract new customers. This influence is represented in the *Stakeholder Weight* variable of the subnet, which is used to prioritize between the identified assets, and can be tailored to each case.

In our example, we assume that both the company and customer highly value information about payment, such as credit card numbers (*PayInfo* in Figure 4). We further assume that the customer values information regarding shipping, such as land and email addresses more highly than the company (*ShippingInfo* in Figure 4), and that the company values information sent back to the user at the close of the transaction, such as order confirmations, more highly than the customer (*buyConfirmPage* in Figure 4). Each of these assets is associated with a variable in the SSLE subnetwork. Note that this subnet is therefore flexible

Figure 5. SSLE sub-network

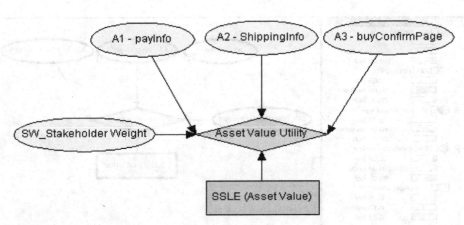

in that the number of asset variables depends on the particular system.

In the top-level trade-off topology (Figure 3) the SSLE subnet is associated with the static security level decision variable *SSLE* shown in Figure 5. This decision variable (shown as a rectangle) is used to feed information from the sub-network into the top-level network.

The *Asset Value Utility* node represents a utility function that is generated from a set of logic statements describing the relations between the variables in the subnet. We use a qualitative data scale (*low*, *medium*, and *high*) for all asset value variables. The utility function can be changed when needed, as for example, when a new stakeholder is added. We define the customer stakeholder weight as *high* and the e-commerce company stakeholder weight as *low*. This will ensure that the customer has precedence over the company when valuing assets. (A stakeholder weight of *medium* indicates that both stakeholders have equal influence in asset valuation.)

While we can specify asset value as soft evidence, i.e., a distribution over low, medium and high (e.g. (low=0.1, medium=0.5, high=0.4)), in this example, we use hard evidence. This allows us to present a simplified version of the asset value prioritizing logic. The logic used to create the utility function is as follows:

1. if the stakeholder weight is *low* then, when all three asset values are *low*, the resulting SSLE asset value is also *low* when two of the asset values are *high* and the third value is *low*, the resulting SSLE asset value is set to the median of the three ordinal values otherwise the resulting SSLE asset value takes the value of the '*buyConfirmPage*' value

2. if the stakeholder weight is *medium*, the resulting SSLE asset value is set to be a weighted distribution of the three asset values (for example, if two of the asset values are in the *high* state and one in the *low* state, the weighted distribution becomes *low=0.25*, *medium=0* and *high=0.75*)

3. if the stakeholder weight is *high*, then when the '*buyConfirmPage*' value is in the *high* state, the resulting SSLE asset value is set to be a weighted distribution of the three asset values otherwise the resulting SSLE asset value is set to that of the '*PayInfo*'

For example, if the stakeholder weight is *high*, this indicates that the information is provided by the customer stakeholder. The customer is more concerned about the '*PayInfo*' and '*ShippingInfo*' assets than the '*buyConfirmPage*' asset, which is more important to the company than the '*ShippingInfo*' asset. This does not mean that the result-

Figure 6. Updated results from the SSLE computation

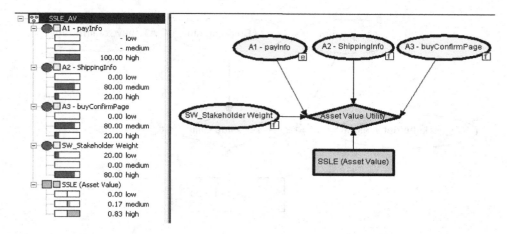

ing SSLE asset value is *high* in all cases where '*ShippingInfo*' is in the *high* state, but that the distribution is skewed towards *high*. Since this example has only three assets, the asset value average is derived as the median of the three values. This simplification is applicable since there are few asset variables and stakeholders.

The rules described above provide the prior probability distribution for all nodes in the SSLE network, that is, the probability distribution before any information from the stakeholders has been inserted and propagated (computed in the BBN). For our example, these prior probability distributions are first updated with information from the customer stakeholder and then with information from the company stakeholder. For both sets of information this is done in a two-step procedure: (i) first evidence or information is inserted into the relevant observable nodes in the network, and (ii) then this information is propagated along the edges of the network from the observable nodes via the directed arcs and to the target node using the propagation algorithm in the HUGIN tool. In our example, we use the propagation algorithm sum normal (Jensen (2001)), which allows us to say that the two sets of information are aggregated using the above-defined rules.

Figure 6 shows the HUGIN tool output after all the information has been inserted and propagated for the SSLE subnet. The prior probability distributions are initially uniformly distributed. This indicates that we have no prior belief on how the two stakeholders will value the assets. (Typically, the prior probability distributions are updated during the analysis process as more insight into both the stakeholder priorities and the possible misuses becomes available.) In our example, the first set of stakeholder values becomes the prior probability distribution of the second set and so forth when aggregating information using the sum normal algorithm.

The information given by the two stakeholders is shown on the left side of Figure 6, together with the stakeholder weights and the resulting asset value or SSLE value. There are two types of information that can be inserted into the network: (i) evidence and (ii) probability distribution. The probability and the type of evidence are noted on the associated node on the right side of the figure (i.e. the network side). An '*e*' next to a node denotes hard evidence, while an '*f*' denotes a probability distribution, or soft evidence.

Figure 7. Security analysis process

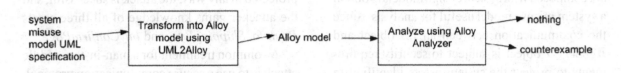

SECURITY ANALYSIS WITH ALLOY ANALYZER: AORDD STEP 3

AORDD uses the Alloy Analyzer tool to analyze security assertions of models written in UML and OCL, which are automatically transformed into the Alloy language. Alloy is a fully declarative first-order logic language that is designed to model complex systems. An Alloy model consists of a number of *signature* declarations that specify entities used to model the system, and *relation* declarations that specify dependencies between entities. The Alloy Analyzer is the associated constraint solver, which is fully automated. The solver translates the model and assertions about the model into a Boolean expression, and uses embedded SAT-solvers to analyze it. The domain of model elements is bounded by a user-supplied *scope*. This bound allows the tool to create finite formulas for evaluation by the SAT-solver. The result of using Alloy Analyzer can be a counterexample, which indicates that an instance of the model was produced that violates the assertions associated with that model. However, if no counterexample is produced, this does not mean that the model always adheres to its assertions. Rather, we can only assume that for the specified scope, all instances conform to the assertion. No counterexample therefore adds to the confidence in the correctness of the model. The larger a scope that is used, the more confidence is provided, but the analysis takes longer.

The "small scope hypothesis" defined by Jackson (Jackson (2006)) emphasizes that design flaws are often discovered using small scopes. Both the

system problem domain and the security property of interest must be used to determine the appropriate scope since there are no general-purpose scope guidelines that exist. However, if Alloy Analyzer does not produce a counterexample, and the situation calls for a high degree of confidence in the system design, other techniques such as model checking or theorem provers can be used to ensure the security properties of interest are present in the design. These techniques are more time-consuming and resource-intensive than Alloy Analyzer, so using the Alloy approach initially can save both time and resources to rapidly discover initial flaws.

Details of the tools used in security analysis, including their inputs and outputs, are shown in Figure 7.

We next demonstrate using Alloy in the context of the running example. First, a system misuse model must be created and security assertions developed. These are transformed into an Alloy model and assertions that can be analyzed with the Alloy Analyzer. Results are then used to populate variables that compute the Security Level (SL) subnet in Figure 3.

Creating System Misuse Models

We will discuss two system misuse models in this section, one created from the original system model, and one created from a security-treated version of the system model. Both were converted to Alloy and analyzed by Alloy Analyzer.

Recall from AORDD step 2a-sec (Figure 1), that misuses of the system are identified from risk analysis of system assets, and that misuse models are composed with system design models to obtain a system misuse model useful for analysis. Since the communication between an *EB* object and *WebServer* object is subject to security requirements to protect the system assets identified in the section titled *Demonstration of the AORDD Methodology*, this is the part of the system where misuses could occur. One such misuse is the well-known man-in-the-middle attack where the attacker eavesdrops on the communication, in an attempt to discover valuable information. This kind of attack can be modeled by inserting an *Attacker* object between the *EB* and *WebServer* objects, and forcing all messages between *EB* and *WebServer* to pass through *Attacker*. *Attacker* has the ability to delete, insert, or change messages prior to passing them onto the intended receiver.

We must first create an aspect model of the attack, and then use AOM techniques to compose it with the system design model. Aspects are defined independently of the application in which they may be used, as *generic* models. A generic aspect defines parameters (indicated with a '|' preceding the parameter name); one generic aspect may be integrated in a system design in multiple locations through multiple mappings of its parameters to specific model elements of the system design. Our techniques create *context-specific* aspects through instantiation of a generic aspect using bindings from system model elements to corresponding parameterized elements. Tools create default elements for parameters that are not specified as part of the instantiation bindings. Automated model composition makes it easy to incorporate different security mechanism designs into the system design.

A generic aspect attack model describing the man-in-the-middle attack can be instantiated into a context-specific aspect model and composed with the original primary model to create the system misuse model. This system misuse model is shown in Figure 8. Note that all communication between *:EB* and *:WebServer* pass through the added object

:Attacker. Thus, since the communications are not protected in any way, the attack is successful, and the attacker gains knowledge of all three assets *PayInfo*, *ShippingInfo*, and *buyConfirmPage*.

A common treatment for a man-in-the-middle attack is to use a secure communication protocol, and Secure Sockets Layer (SSL) is one such protocol (TLSWG (1996)). SSL is the most common authentication protocol used for web-based secure transactions (Menascé (2003)). It handles mutual or one-way authentication and preserves the integrity and confidentiality of data exchanged between clients and servers. SSL has two phases: a handshake phase and a data transfer phase. Each phase represents a different functionality that must be inserted in the primary model at the proper locations. The handshake must be composed once with the primary model prior to any communication between the client (*:EB*) and server (*:Web-Server*). The data transfer must be composed after successful completion of the handshake. The data transfer consists of a sender and receiver, so it must be composed once with the *:EB* element as the sender and the *:WebServer* element as the receiver for the first communication that needs to be protected (*getBuyConfirmPage* message in Figure 4), and once with the elements in the opposite roles for the second communication that needs to be protected (*buyConfirmPage* message in Figure 4). We next discuss the transfer portion of SSL and its composition with the primary model.

Figure 9 shows the SSL transfer sequence as a generic aspect with parameterized elements (names beginning with the "|" character). SSL transfers occur as follows. First, the sender SSL breaks the message into fragments, the number of which depends on the length of the message. A fragment is encrypted using a symmetric session key computed independently by the client and server using a shared secret, as part of the SSL handshake. The encrypted fragment is put into a record and sent to the receiver SSL, which decrypts it. The receiver SSL validates the frag-

Figure 8. Original system misuse model including man-in-the-middle attack

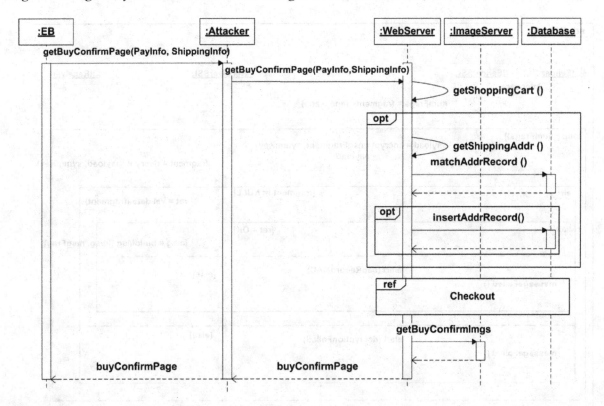

ment and adds it to the message that is being built. Once the entire message is complete, the receiver SSL forwards the message to the target receiver. If the decryption fails to recover a non-NULL fragment, or the validation fails, the receiver SSL sends an alert to the sender SSL indicating the failure type. Depending on how the application is implemented (which is independent of the SSL protocol), the sender may attempt to re-send the record or terminate.

The generic SSL aspect must be instantiated in the context of the e-commerce application and composed with the application primary model to create a security-treated system model. The composed model is presented in Figure 10, and it represents a security-treated system model. The SSL authorization handshake and transfer sequences are referenced in the composed model. A note accompanying the reference shows the bindings that were used to instantiate the refer-

enced sequence. For example, in the *SSLauthHS* sequence, the parameter:|*Client* is bound to *:EB*, and:|*Server* is bound to *:WebServer*. The parameter |*message* in the *SSLxfer* sequence is bound to *getBuyConfirmPage(PayInfo,ShippingInfo)*.

A new system misuse model is created by once again instantiating the generic man-in-the-middle attack model into a context-specific aspect model and composing it with the security-treated system model. The result is similar to the system misuse model shown in Figure 8, and is not included in this chapter: all communication between the *:EBSSL* and *:WebServerSSL* elements in the security-treated misuse model passes through an *Attacker* element.

Informally, in the case of the security-treated system, a successful attack can only occur if the attacker has the symmetric key used to encrypt the message. If the attacker has this key, then the

Figure 9. Portion of SSL transfer sequence generic aspect

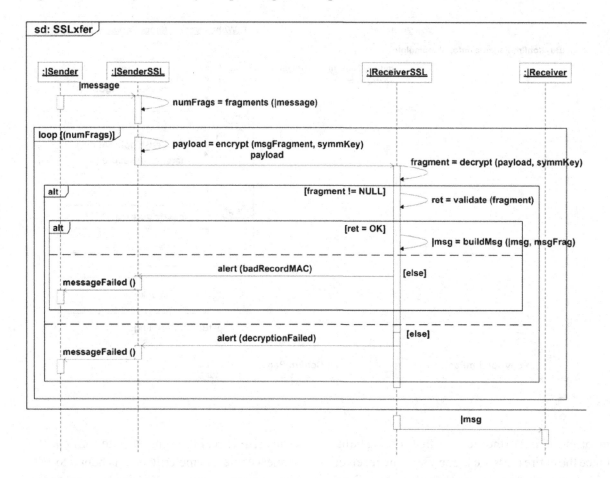

message can be decrypted to obtain the system assets *PayInfo*, *ShippingInfo* and *buyConfirmPage*.

Analyzing UML Models Using Alloy

Alloy Analyzer tests whether assertions can be derived from a system model. We must therefore develop assertions regarding system assets that need protection, in the context of the system misuse model that will be transformed to Alloy. In the case of the original system misuse model, an attacker should not know the *PayInfo* or *ShippingInfo* of the *EB* object and the attacker should not receive the *buyConfirmPage*. In the case of the security-treated misuse model, the attacker can only gain knowledge of these assets if it can

decrypt the messages that contain them, so the attacker should not gain access to the session symmetric key.

There are two steps involved in transforming a UML model into Alloy in order to analyze its security properties. In the first step the model is simplified to remove elements that are not essential to analyzing the security properties of interest. The second step is to translate this output to Alloy using the UML2Alloy tool (Anastasakis et al. (2008), Georg et al. (2008), and UML2Alloy (2005)).

There are also two steps involved in model analysis with Alloy Analyzer. The first step is to simulate the model to generate a random instance that conforms to the *whole* specification. This ensures that there are no conflicting statements in the

Figure 10. SSL security-treated system model

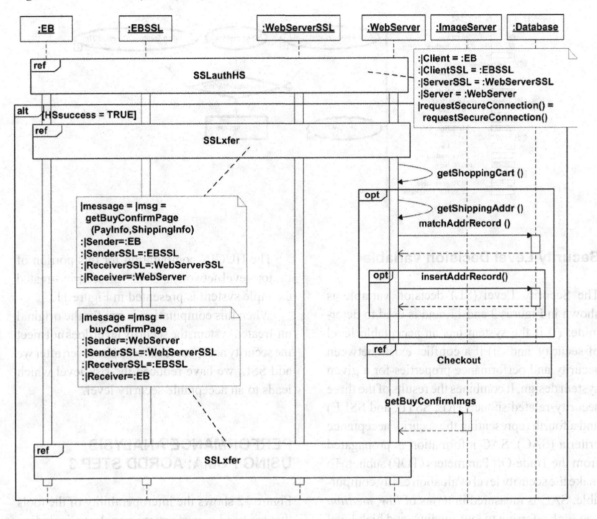

model. If an instance cannot be created, there are conflicting statements in the model and this must be corrected. The next step is to run the analyzer to automatically check the security property assertions. If any of these assertions fail, the analyzer produces a counterexample. The counterexample can be used to determine the source of the failure.

When Alloy Analyzer is run on the original system misuse model that does not have SSL protection, it produces a counterexample. The counterexample shows an instance of an attacker having access to the client payment information, the shipping information, and the confirmation

page. When the analyzer is run on the security-treated system misuse model, the analyzer does not produce any counterexamples to the assertion. This indicates that the attacker does not have access to the sensitive information.

The information obtained from the analysis, i.e. whether the assertions are false or not, is used to populate portions of the BBN trade-off analysis topology. In particular, this information flows into the RL and SSTL subnets (see Figure 3), which in turn influence the computed value of the Security Level (SL) decision variable. This variable is discussed in the next section.

Figure 11. HUGIN computation of security level for security-treated example system

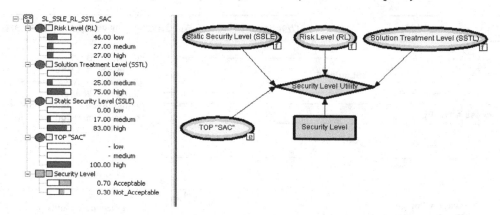

Security Level Decision Variable

The Security Level (SL) decision variable is shown in Figures 3 and 11, and is used to determine: (i) if the system has an acceptable level of security, and (ii) if a conflict exists between security and performance properties for a given system design. It combines the results of the three security-related subnets (RL, SSTL, and SSLE) and a fourth representing the security acceptance criteria (SAC). SAC information is propagated from the Trade-Off Parameters (TOP) subnet. To make the security level evaluation easily computable, SAC is measured in terms of *low*, *medium* and *high* referring to low, medium and high level of security, respectively.

Since the security level is modeled as a decision node/utility function pair, the "rules" defining an acceptable security level are part of the utility node. We use a simple schema to determine security level acceptance in our example. In general, the security level is acceptable if the qualitative average of SSLE and SSTL values is equal or higher than the required security level expressed in the SAC variable after taking the risk level (RL) into consideration. Specifically, either SSLE or SSTL must equal *TOP "SAC"* and the lowest value of SSLE and SSTL cannot be lower than that of RL.

The HUGIN computation for this portion of the top-level network and our SSL security-treated example system is presented in Figure 11.

When this computation is run for the original un-treated system, the security level does not meet the security acceptance criteria. However, after we add SSL, we have reduced the risk level which leads to an acceptable security level.

PERFORMANCE ANALYSIS USING PUMA: AORDD STEP 3

Figure 12 shows the interoperability of the tools that are used in performance analysis, including their inputs and outputs.

In a similar fashion to security analysis, system models must be transformed into performance models. The first step of this process is adding annotations that are specific to performance. The PUMA toolset extracts relevant information into a projection that can be transformed into different types of performance models. The target performance model (LQN) is created next and experiments are run. Analysis output drives design-analyze iteration cycles, and eventually provides data for the Performance Level (PL) subnet of Figure 3.

Figure 12. Tools used in performance analysis

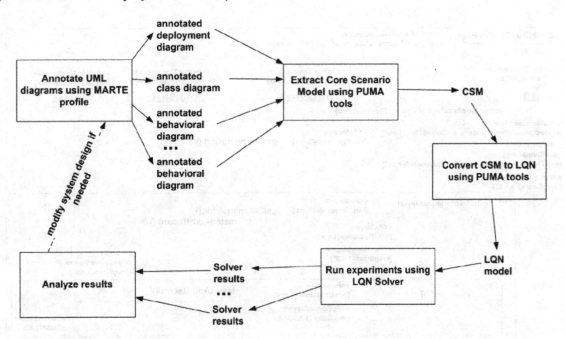

Annotating UML Models with Performance Information

We first add performance-related annotations to UML static and behavioral descriptions of the system model (class and deployment diagrams and either activity or sequence diagrams). The diagrams are annotated using the OMG Modeling and Analysis of Real-Time Embedded systems (MARTE) profile (OMG-MARTE (2008)). We illustrate these annotations using our example system.

The main abstraction used in performance analysis is a *scenario*. Scenarios define response paths through a system and may have attached performance requirements expressed in terms of response time or throughput. Usually, a set of key scenarios are of interest for performance analysis in the system, and these are specified using multiple behavioral diagrams. The MARTE performance sub-profile defines the stereotype *<<GaPerformanceContext>>* to allow a set of scenarios to be identified as belonging to the same

analysis context. This stereotype is used in Figure 13, and includes a tag indicating parameters that will be used across multiple scenarios, in this case *$Nusers, $ThinkTime, $Images,* and *$N.* Scenarios are executed according to a *workload*, which is either *open* (requests arrive in a pre-determined pattern) or *closed* (requests arrive based on a fixed number of active users or jobs). The stereotype *<<GaWorkloadEvent>>* is used to specify the workload for a scenario. For example, in Figure 13, the workload is closed, with a fixed number of users (*$Nusers*).

Scenarios consist of *steps*, (indicated by the stereotype *<<PaStep>>),* which have performance specifications, including quantitative resource demands. Most of the steps in Figure 13 have associated resource demands on a host computing device, as shown by the *hostDemand* tag. The first step also has requirements for response time. Each step corresponding to an *opt* combined fragment has a probability of execution. Communication steps (indicated by *<<PaCommStep>>)* correspond usually to messages that

Figure 13. Performance-annotated sequence diagram: GetBuyConfirmPage scenario

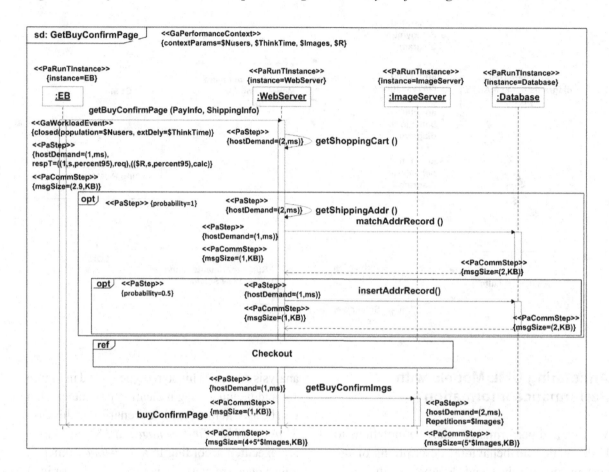

utilize communication resources and their specification includes the size of the message.

Resources are another basic abstraction for performance analysis, and can be active or passive, each with their own attributes including capacity, overheads, and maximum number of instances. For example, physical resources are represented by nodes in an annotated deployment diagram, such as Figure 14. Resources can be dedicated to communication, as specified by the <<*GQAM::gaCommHost*>> stereotype, or computation, as specified by the <<*GQAM::gaExecHost*>> stereotype. Some of the performance specifications of a communication host are shown in Figure 14, including blocking time and capacity. Execution hosts can

have communication overhead specified for transmission and receipt, and the maximum number of instances can also be specified. Loadable modules, or files, are included in the diagram, shown as elements that are *deployed* on the resources, and they in turn *manifest* software classes, or source code.

Choosing the values to be assigned to performance parameters is not a simple task; some difficulties are related to performance evaluation issues rather than to UML modeling. In general, it is difficult to estimate quantitative resource demands for each step in the design phase, when an implementation does not exist and measurements have not been performed. Several approaches are used by performance analysts to come up with reasonable estimates in early design

Figure 14. Performance-annotated example system deployment diagram

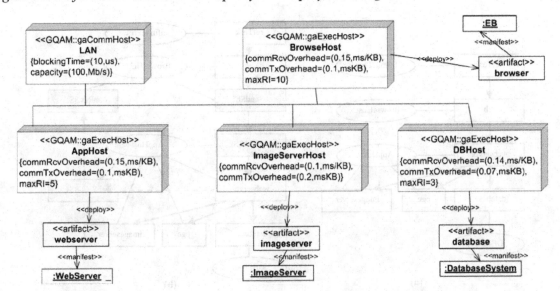

stages: expert experience with previous versions or with similar software, understanding of the algorithm complexity, measurements of reused software, measurements of existing libraries, or using time budgets. As the project advances, early estimates can be replaced with measured values for the most critical parts. However, this is not to say that performance analysis should be deferred until late in the lifecycle, when the system is implemented and can be measured, because then it may be too late to correct costly performance mistakes realized in the implementation.

Generating the Performance Model

In PUMA, different structural and behavioral UML views are transformed first into an intermediate model called Core Scenario Model (CSM), a kind of projection from the UML model into the performance domain, which captures the use of resources by the system behavior (Petriu and Woodside (2004)). CSM filters out design information irrelevant to performance analysis, and contains, by design, performance attributes obtained from MARTE annotations. A CSM may be derived from different kinds of UML diagrams and supports the

generation of different performance formalisms (such as queuing networks, Petri nets, stochastic process algebra, and simulation). In this research, we generate Layered Queuing Network (LQN) models from CSM.

A Queuing Network model represents physical resources as servers, where jobs are queuing for service; after a job is served, it moves to another server. A Layered Queuing Network (LQN) model allows for nested services, meaning that, while serving a job, a server may request nested services from other servers. Since the resources can be held in a nested fashion, this leads to layered queues. An LQN model consists of a set of servers, called tasks, which represent either software resources (drawn as rectangles) or hardware resources (as ovals). Each server has an associated queue. Software tasks may require nested services from other software or from hardware tasks. Tasks may offer different services, which are called entries. Interactions can be blocking, in that they may consist of requests and replies, or non-blocking. The LQN model for the example system is shown in Figure 15(a). Solid arrows indicate synchronous calls, dotted arrows asynchronous calls and lighter-weight lines without arrows between

Figure 15. LQN model for example system: (a) primary model; (b) composed model

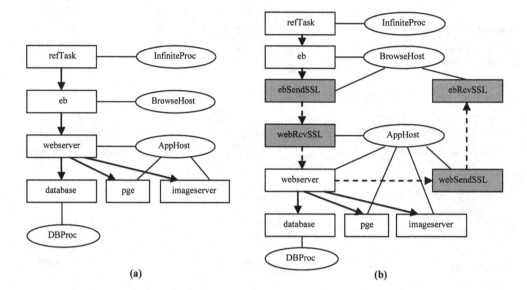

(a)　　　　　　　　　　　　　(b)

tasks and processors show deployment of tasks on particular processors.

In addition to creating the model, we must formulate performance requirements in a way that can be explored using LQN models. LQN experiments are able to explore capacity types of questions, not strict deadlines (schedulability analysis is needed for these), so we must create capacity-related performance requirements.

For our example, we consider two separate scenarios that require secure communication: *GetCustomerRegistrationPage* and *GetBuyConfirmPage*. We express the performance requirements in terms of mean response time for a given workload (expressed as the number of concurrent users executing the same scenario simultaneously). For the first scenario, we would like to insure that the mean response time is no more than 500ms for 600 concurrent users, while for the second no more than 1000 ms for 170 concurrent users. The LQN analytic algorithms used by the PUMA solver are based on Markov Chains and exponential distributions that are not bounded. The simulation solver uses soft deadline capabilities to determine what percentage of samples are below particular

values. The performance analysis results for this model are discussed along with those of improved variations, in the sub-section titled *Performance Analysis Results*.

Composing Security Aspects into a Primary Model

There are two ways of composing the security aspects with the primary model: at the UML level, as in (Petriu et. al. (2007)) or at the CSM level (Woodside et al. (2009)). Since we can compose aspects at the CSM level, aggregation actually takes place as part of the performance analysis process once all UML aspect models have been annotated using the MARTE profile.

The CSM meta-model consists of a smaller set of elements than the UML meta-model, so the resulting model is simpler. As a result, composition of CSMs is also simpler. For this reason we are able to transform both the primary and aspect models into CSMs and then compose them more easily than if the complete UML versions of the models were composed.

Figure 16. Performance results for the two scenarios

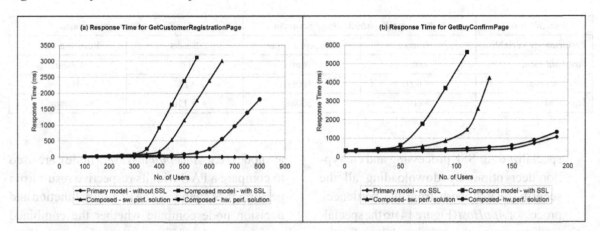

However, no matter whether the aspect composition takes place at the UML or CSM level, the resulting CSM that corresponds to the composed model can be converted into an LQN just like the primary model, by using the PUMA toolset. The resulting LQN that represents the security-treated *GetBuyConfirmPage* scenario is shown in Figure 16(b). The nodes of the LQN that correspond to SSL aspect elements are shaded in the figure.

Performance Analysis Results

The results of the LQN experiments for the two scenarios are shown in the graph of Figures 16 (a) and (b). The performance behavior of the two scenarios is similar, even if the numerical values are different. The four curves represent the response time versus the number of users for the following designs/configurations:

a. The lowest curve on each graph corresponds to the primary model for the respective scenario, without security enhancements. The first scenario is shorter, making fewer resource demands, which is reflected in the shorter response times. In both cases, the concurrency level of the software tasks have been chosen such that the system gives

the maximum performance for the given hardware configuration.

b. The highest curve corresponds to the composed model with the SSL aspects, for the configuration obtained immediately after the aspect composition, without any attempt to optimize for performance. The response time has a typical non-linear form with a knee around 300 users for the first scenario and 60 users for the second, after which it grows very fast due to the saturation of the system. The performance requirements are not satisfied by far.

c. The second highest curve corresponds to the composed system after performance analysis, with an improved software configuration. The problem before this improvement is that the software task charged with security functions, introduced by the aspect, becomes saturated even though the hardware resources are not used at maximum capacity. This is known as "software bottleneck". The solution is to introduce more threads for the bottleneck task, in order to use the available capacity of the hardware resources. The response time is improved, but the performance requirements are not met yet.

d. The last performance improvement is a hardware solution: introduce a processor

Table 1. Qualitative performance scale values

Scenario Name	*GetCustomerRegistrationPage* Scenario		*GetBuyConfirmPage* Scenario	
Performance variable	Nusers	Response Time	Nusers	Response Time
threshold value	600	500ms	170	1000ms
lower interval	< 600	< 500ms	<170	< 1000ms
higher interval	> 600	> 500ms	> 170	> 1000ms

specialized for SSL processing and encryption/decryption. By downloading all the security-related work from the bottleneck processor *AppHost* (Figure 14) to the specialized processor, the queuing delays for the tasks running on *AppHost* are considerably reduced and the response time meets the performance requirements.

The Performance Sub-Network

Figure 3, the top-level trade-off analysis BBN topology, contains a subnet dedicated to performance. The outcome of this subnet, Performance Level, is used to evaluate the performance level, to help identify performance and security conflicts, and in the overall trade-off analysis.

As for the other subnets, we use qualitative value scales for all nodes in the subnet. We define a qualitative scale *{lower, threshold, higher}* for performance, and assign meaning to each value as a quantitative interval. Interval values are based on the particular scenarios we have analyzed. For our example, two scenarios were evaluated (*GetCustomerRegistrationPage* and *GetBuyConfirmPage*), and their requirements stated in the section titled *Generating the Performance Model*. We use these requirements to set threshold values and to map intervals for *lower* and *higher*. The resulting intervals are shown in Table 1.

As in the case for security, we define performance acceptance criteria (PAC), based on the requirements developed for performance analysis. The PL subnet shown in Figure 17 contains two PAC variables: *PAC_U* for number of users and *PAC_RT* for response time. Associated intermediate nodes (e.g. *Acceptable Nusers* node), are used to compare a PAC with its respective result from performance analysis. The PL utility function and decision node compute whether the combined performance level for number of users and response time is acceptable or not.

Figure 17 and Figure 18 present the resulting BBN computations for the *GetBuyConfirmPage* scenario, showing the composed model with SSL in both cases. The computation in Figure 17 is for the original and software-improved systems, cases (b) and (c) in the sub-section titled *Performance Analysis Results*. The computation in Figure 18 is for the hardware-improved system, case (d) in the sub-section titled *Performance Analysis Results*.

BALANCING PERFORMANCE AND SECURITY: AORDD STEP 3

Balancing security and performance properties of a system begins by comparing how well a proposed system design meets both sets of acceptance criteria. The design must ultimately be compared against the other project criteria as well. We begin balancing with just the performance and security criteria, as reflected in the *Conflict* decision node and its associated *Conflict Utility* function shown in the top-level trade-off topology (Figure 3).

Identifying Performance and Security Conflicts

Identifying that performance and security properties are in conflict is non-trivial as there are no

Figure 17. Performance Level subnet computation for SSL-treated system with software improvements for GetBuyConfirmPage scenario

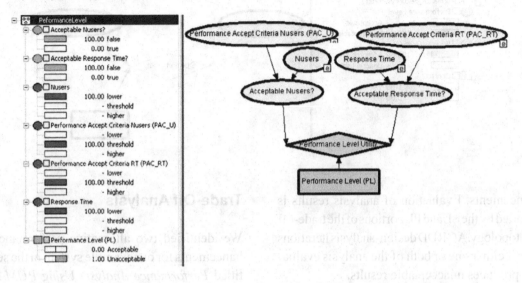

Figure 18. Performance Level subnet computation for SSL-treated system with hardware improvements for GetBuyConfirmPage scenario

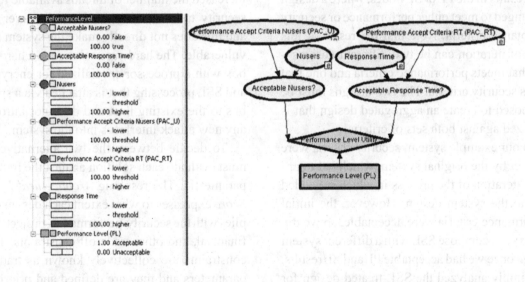

general rules that can be used to detect a performance violation caused by a security solution or vice versa. For this reason, whenever a system design is changed to better meet either security criteria or performance criteria, both analyses must be performed and produce acceptable results before moving on to overall trade-off analysis.

To carry out a successful conflict identification and analysis, it is important that security and performance analyses based on the original system model are available. This is to avoid confusion about whether a security or performance issue existed in the initial design, or whether it was introduced due to security or performance

Figure 19. Performance and security conflict detection

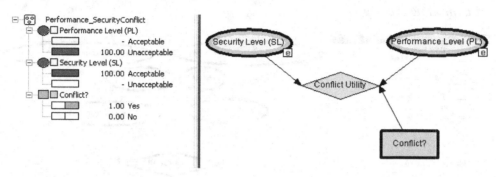

enhancements. Evaluation of analysis results is supported by the SL and PL portions of the trade-off BBN topology. AORDD design-analysis iterations occur if either one or both of the analysis evaluations produces unacceptable results.

Recall that design-analyze iterations can occur in two places in AORDD analysis. The first design-analyze iteration is triggered by unacceptable results in the PL or SL nodes, where a design is changed to meet either performance or security acceptance criteria. Note that the result of this level of iteration can be two different designs – one that meets performance criteria and one that meets security criteria. The two designs must be composed to create an aggregated design that is analyzed against both sets of criteria.

In our example system, security criteria were not met by the original system, which led to another iteration of the process in which we added SSL to the system design. However, the initial performance criteria were acceptable, so we did not have to compose SSL with a different system design once we had acceptable PL and SL results. We simply analyzed the SSL-treated design for performance properties, and obtained the results shown in Figure 16 (b), the connected rectangle line. When this data is given as input to the BBN topology, the PL node becomes unacceptable as shown in Figure 17, and a conflict is detected, as shown in Figure 19. Once a conflict is identified, trade-off analysis is used to provide a rationale for its resolution. Trade-off analysis in the context of our example system is discussed in the next section.

Trade-Off Analysis

We identified two alternative performance enhancements for our example system in the section titled *Performance Analysis Using PUMA*, one based on software changes and one based on hardware additions. There are no security implications of either solution. The software solution simply increased the number of threads available for the security tasks running on the web server side, and this does not directly make the system more vulnerable. The hardware solution is a hardware box with a processor specialized for encryption and SSL processing that is attached via a special bus to the existing host and does not introduce any new attack interfaces into the system.

To decide between the two alternatives we must evaluate each solution against the trade-off parameters. The resulting *Architectural Fitness Score* expresses to what extent each design complies with the security, performance, project, time, financial, and other trade-off constraints. These constraints are collectively known as trade-off parameters and they are defined and prioritized in the Trade-Off Parameter (TOP) subnet.

TOP Subnet

The trade-off parameters that we consider in this chapter are budget (BU), resources (RES), time-to-market (TTM), priorities (PRI), and TOP_Cost. BU, RES, and TTM each represent how much of the item is available to incorporate the performance and security solution into the system, rather than the amount of the item available over the entire project. BU represents the financial means available, RES the hours or effort that personnel have available, and TTM the time available to incorporate the solution(s) being evaluated. PRI is used to prioritize between these trade-off parameters. The TOP_Cost node has an associated subnet that is used to determine its state. It holds and propagates the result of the overall cost evaluation: a score for the return on investment of the performance and security solutions currently being evaluated.

The TOP_Cost subnet consists of six variables: misuse cost, SAC, security solution cost, security rank, PAC, performance cost, and performance rank. Misuse cost represents the indirect and direct cost that can be caused by the misuse initially used to create the system misuse models analyzed by Alloy Analyzer. Misuse cost can include financial aspects, damage to reputation, loss in normal production, etc. SAC are the same security acceptance criteria as those used in the SL computation. Security solution cost includes both direct and indirect costs of incorporating the security solution under consideration into the system. This cost is evaluated against the SAC to derive a security rank. This rank represents the return on security investment. For example, if the security rank is high, this means that there is a high potential that the security solution represents a good investment in terms of its cost and how well it ensures security.

In a similar fashion, PAC and performance cost are evaluated against each other to produce a performance rank that represents the return on performance investment. PAC in this subnet is an aggregation of the PAC_U and PAC_RT variables discussed in the section titled *Performance Analysis Using PUMA*. Performance cost denotes the direct and indirect costs of a performance solution, including procurements cost, cost of incorporating the solution, and cost related to maintaining it. The TOP_Cost subnet is then computed using security and performance ranks and the misuse cost.

The costs we associate with the two performance alternatives for the example system are as follows. We assume the software solution has *low* cost, while the hardware solution is evaluated as having a *medium* cost. The reason for this is that procurement and incorporation of the proposed software changes to the *ServerSSL* resource is relatively inexpensive since it simply consists of increasing the number of available threads. Furthermore, there is no additional maintenance of the Server SSL resource, so the maintenance cost is also *low*. We set the cost of the hardware performance solution to *medium*, since there is a procurement cost for the hardware itself, some cost associated with incorporating the solution into the system, and a slightly higher maintenance cost relative to the software solution. (Details on how to evaluate and aggregate these cost-related variables are in Houmb (2007)). Once TOP_Cost is computed, it can be prioritized against the other trade-off parameters to compute the TOP subnet.

Overall Trade-Off Analysis

The last part of the trade-off analysis is to propagate the TOP subnet computation results to the top-level BBN, along with all other subnets. The result of this computation is an architectural fitness score, or how well the combined performance and security enhancements to the system design fit all the project criteria represented by the trade-off parameters. The results of this computation may trigger another design-analyze iteration as described in the AORDD analysis discussion of the section titled *AORDD Methodology*.

In our example, we consider the software and hardware performance-enhancing alternatives to demonstrate how BBN trade-off analysis can be used to experiment with design alternatives. Figure 20 shows the results of the computation for the software performance solution when all emphasis is put on the trade-off parameter *TOP_Cost*, meaning that we care most about the return on investment of the performance and security so-

Figure 20. Architectural fitness of software solution regarding return on investment

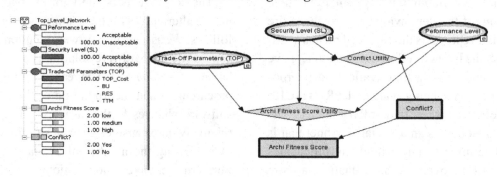

Figure 21. Architectural fitness of hardware solution regarding return on investment

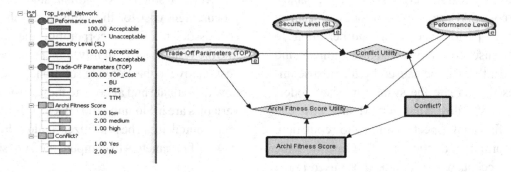

lutions. The results show that the chance of the architectural fitness score being *low* is two times more than it being *medium* or *high*.

If the hardware solution is analyzed with *TOP_Cost* as the highest priority, there is twice the chance that the fitness score is *medium* rather than *low* or *high*, as shown in Figure 21. The reason is that even though the hardware solution is more costly, the system performance is acceptable for this solution. However, the fitness score is not certain to be *high* since the cost of the hardware solution is *medium* and not *low*.

These examples show that by changing the priorities of the trade-off parameters, designers can see how decisions involving security and performance designs compare against each other. As the project progresses and these priorities change, their impact can also be determined.

The trade-off analysis presented in this section performs simultaneous evaluation of security and

performance solutions. However the *TOP_Cost* subnet only contains one set of variables associated with a performance design and one set associated with a security design. Thus, only one security/performance solution pair can be evaluated at the same time. We address this issue through multiple uses of AORDD design and analysis. A typical application is to gradually build up a system design that incorporates multiple security solutions, added to prevent their associated misuses, with each security addition being evaluated for performance effects and those effects addressed with performance enhancements to the design. Such an incremental approach to security is needed to ensure that a solution added to prevent one misuse does not break a solution previously added that prevents a different misuse. We apply this approach by composing the system design with all misuse models previously considered each time a new security solution is added to the system, and then performing a security analysis of the resulting system misuse model.

DISCUSSION

The AORDD approach combines a number of techniques to help designers balance non-functional properties, such as performance and security, in their designs. The focus is on the early phases of software development, since security and performance changes tend to be less costly and use fewer resources at stages where the system architecture is still flexible. Both analysis types start from the same UML models, but use completely different techniques and tools and produce different kinds of results. The process is not light-weight, and is intended to be used in situations where the effort involved is offset by the potential cost of making cross-cutting and potential architectural changes in later stages of design.

Using AOM

We use AOM techniques to compose different types of aspects into our system designs. Both primary and aspect models must be specified at the same level of abstraction in order to produce a meaningful composition. Since our tools and methods do not require any particular level of abstraction, designers are free to use different levels of abstraction depending on the final usage of the composed model. However, this generality also creates an additional expectation, in that the designer must supply models of the appropriate level of abstraction for use in the different steps of AORDD.

Integrating Disparate Information

The output of security, performance, and trade-off analyses are different; some are qualitative and some are quantitative. Furthermore, both syntactically and semantically the results are different and

cannot be directly compared. We use the BBN technology to compare these disparate types of information after essentially translating results so that they can be compared. This translation is performed by specifying the relationship among variables in the BBN topology via probability density functions and utility functions. Syntactic relationships are specified simply through the topology itself – the fact that certain stochastic, decision, and utility nodes are connected and the directions of those relationships. The semantic relationships reside in the probability functions. BBN allows us to easily specify these relationships and to change them. In addition, we can resolve the relationships through BBN computation using Bayes theorem. This is done automatically in the HUGIN tool, which also offers optimized algorithms for solving large-scale conditional probability expressions.

Variables in the topology are derived as quantitative values. These are then mapped to probability distributions over ordinal qualitative scales (e.g. *{low, medium, high}*) before being inserted in the network. The main disadvantage of such a translation is that the level of precision in the result is reduced, and the results are subject to interpretation. However, the translation to a qualitative scale makes it possible to develop a generic and reusable BBN topology, where the qualitative scale is assigned a specific meaning for each instance and computation of the network. Hence, the model does not change between cases, only the mapping between quantitative values and the associated qualitative scales.

Extensibility

The BBN topology has been developed in a layered fashion, with subnets handling different areas of interest (e.g. performance level, security level, trade-off parameters). It is therefore fairly easy to evolve different portions further, provided that the relations between the parts do not change. However, for cases where a change affects the utility node between the different parts of the network, a substantial change to the semantic specification of the relationships between the affected parts may be required. Trade-off analysis can in principle be extended to include additional non-functional properties. This will require a mapping between the results produced from the new non-functional property analysis and both security and performance analysis results. The challenge lies in comparing results, specifying the relationships between the non-functional properties, and specifying the process of identifying potential conflicts, as well as how to solve these. This may require a simple addition of a new non-functional part to the trade-off BBN topology, in addition to updating the comparison utility functions and the TOP subnet, but it might also require re-structuring several parts of the topology, depending on the type of results produced, the relationships involved and which trade-off parameters are relevant.

RELATED WORK

Security and Risk Management Standards

There are many standards and methodologies for identifying and assessing risks. Standards provide tools for evaluating the security controls of systems. One example is ISO 15408:2007 Common Criteria for Information Technology Security Evaluation (ISO 14508, 2007), which includes schemas for certification of IT Products, in addition to security best practices. Another example is the ISO/IEC 27000 series, which includes ISO/IEC 27002:2005 Information technology - Security techniques - Code of Practice for Information Security Management (ISO/IEC 27002, 2005) within the security domain, and IEC 61508:1998 Functional safety of electrical/electronic/programmable electronic safety-related systems (IEC 61508, 1998) within the safety domain. However, most standards-based evaluations consist of qualitative and subjective activities that can be biased by the evaluator even though they follow a standard. The AORDD methodology and trade-off analysis also uses qualitative data, but focuses on aggregating all possible estimation sources as it accepts and tackles both hard and soft evidence. The AORDD methodology is not an alternative to the above-mentioned standards, but rather a supportive tool. It follows the same way of thinking when evaluating security, but gives explicit and detailed recommendations on how to execute these activities from the developer and designer point of view. It also takes both security and performance properties into consideration and can help designers balance these concerns during system design.

Risk assessment was initially developed within the safety domain, but was later adapted to security critical systems in the form of security risk assessments. The two most relevant approaches are CCTA Risk Analysis and Management Methodology (CRAMM) (Barber and Davey, 1992) and the CORAS framework (Stølen et al., 2002, CORAS Project, 2003). CRAMM targets healthcare information systems and is asset-driven. The CORAS framework is inspired by CRAMM and has adapted the asset-driven strategy of CRAMM. The main deficiency of the current security risk assessment approaches is that the focus is not on calculated risks, meaning that there is no activity that determines what risks are acceptable, based on some cost-benefit strategy. Calculated risk assessment requires knowledge regarding potential attack paths, cost of attacks for the attacker and the system owner, the probability or frequency of attacks, and the potential impact attacks might have on the strategic level. The AORDD methodology supports calculated risk assessment with its tool-based security analysis. The methodology also provides data to help designers balance security with performance concerns, in the context of other project and system considerations.

Risk and Misuse Modeling and Analysis

In recent years several researchers have studied how to model misuses or attacks in the early phases of system development. One of the earliest attempts is a misuse case-driven approach that elicits security requirements (Sindre and Opdahl (2005)). Here, a visual link is established between use cases and misuse cases. This link is used to guide the analysis of functional requirements against security requirements and the threat environment. As it can be labor intensive to model and analyze misuse cases, Whittle et al. (Whittle et al. (2008)) have developed an executable misuse case modeling language which allows modelers to specify misuse case scenarios in a formal yet intuitive way, and to execute the misuse case model in tandem with a corresponding use case model. In this chapter we present tools that use the Alloy analyzer to perform security analysis, but AORDD does not preclude the use of other types of security analysis. We only require that security analyses produce output compatible with the trade-off analysis tool.

Performance Analysis

Software Performance Engineering (Smith and Williams (2002)) is a methodology that promotes the integration of performance analysis models into the software development process through predictive performance from the early stages and continuing throughout the whole software life cycle. A significant body of work has been done in the past twenty years to integrate performance analysis into the software development process by using different performance modeling formalisms: queuing networks, Petri nets, stochastic process algebras, and simulation (Balsamo et al. (2004)). In the past ten years, there have been efforts to define performance annotations for UML models, which led to the standardization of two UML profiles, OMG SPT (2005), and OMG MARTE (2008).

UML performance annotations have been used to generate many different kinds of performance models, but most of these transformations are specific to one kind of UML behavior diagram and one kind of performance model. PUMA (Woodside et al. (2005)) attempts to unify the use of arbitrary combinations of design diagrams and of performance models by using the CSM intermediate model. As in the case of security analysis, AORDD does not prohibit the use of alternative performance analysis methods. We only require that these methods produce results that can be mapped into the input required by our trade-off analysis.

Trade-off Analysis

There is little related work on security solution design trade-off analysis or system quality property trade-off analysis. Elahi and Yu (Elahi and Yu (2007)), examine how conceptual modeling can provide support for analyzing security trade-offs, using an extension to the i* framework (Yu (1997)). Furthermore, Flechais et al. (Flechais et al. (2007)), present an approach which integrates security and usability into the requirements and design process, based on a UML meta-model for defining and reasoning over the system's assets. Security trade-off analysis, as discussed by Houmb et al. (Houmb et al. (2005) and Houmb et al. (2007)), looks at security from a cost-benefit perspective with respect to financial and project factors, such as budget and time-to-market. However, the challenge still remains to measure risk level in an accurate manner and to balance security with other system quality properties as well as cost, schedule and resources. A BBN-based model for more accurately estimating risk is discussed by Houmb and Franquira (Houmb and Franquira (2009)). This model uses the Common Vulnerability Scoring System (CVSS) to assist in estimating risk event frequency and impact estimation, i.e. misuses or security threats (CVSS (2007)). The AORDD trade-off analysis has been extended to incorporate performance considerations. We have constructed the topology to be extensible, and have identified issues associated with further extending the technique to incorporate other system quality property concerns.

CONCLUSION

This chapter describes an approach to balancing security and performance goals in the early and critical phases of software development. Often, security and performance goals conflict with each other and sometimes it is not possible to satisfy both. Furthermore, such conflicts are often only discovered after the fact; that is, very late in development, when it is too costly and resource demanding to solve the problem, even if it is technically feasible. In addition, a performance problem may grow over time if not solved early, and a security challenge may get out of hand if not treated, so it is important to address and at least be aware of any potential or actual conflicts. Thus, the aim of this chapter is to show how to balance security and performance properties along with other project constraints in early development stages.

Our approach uses a system quality property (performance and security) trade-off analysis that is supported by Aspect-Oriented Modeling (AOM) techniques. We use AOM to specify security and performance concerns separately as UML aspect models, and to systematically experiment with alternative designs of a UML system model. Our analysis process is iterative in that security and performance issues are analyzed by security and performance analyses carried out on the system model, and issues are addressed independently before being combined and re-analyzed. The additional analysis is used to investigate whether changes introduce new security and performance problems and to identify and resolve any security and performance conflicts. Security analyses are supported by the Alloy Analyzer and performance analysis is supported by the toolset developed

by the Performance by Unified Model Analysis (PUMA) project. The quality property conflict and trade-off analysis is supported by a BBN trade-off topology that takes security requirements, performance requirements and project, development and financial constraints as input and produces a relative fitness score for a design alternative as output. This score can be compared across a set of design alternatives, providing evidence for design decisions. Our approach is demonstrated on an e-commerce shopping example.

Our approach uses different analysis tools (e.g. Alloy Analyzer and LQN solvers), and therefore different toolsets, to accomplish its aims. A current limitation of the approach is the limited integration of these tools. We use the UML2Alloy tool and PUMA toolset to alleviate integration issues, however, opportunities for integration improvement still exist. Similarly, integration of analysis results into the BBN topology currently consists of manually applying a set of translators (with rule sets). The first phase of active integration of analysis tools and the BBN topology is to automate the manual translator tasks and to build APIs to the BBN topology for automating the input of analysis results. Another critical facet of our future work involves refining and extending the relationship between security and performance properties in the trade-off topology, and extending how analysis deals with performance properties that are of interest in different types of systems, such as throughput in switching and routing systems.

ACKNOWLEDGMENT

This work was partially supported by AFOSR under Award No. FA9550-07-1-0042.

REFERENCES

Alloy (2008). Alloy. Retrieved from <http://alloy.mit.edu>.

Anastasakis, K., Bordbar, B., Georg, G., & Ray, I. (2008). *On Challenges of Model Transformation from UML to Alloy.* accepted for publication in Journal on Software and Systems Modeling (SOSYM) special issue of extended papers from the MODELS 2007 conference, *on-line first:* DOI 10.1007/s10270-008-0110-3.

Apostolopoulos, V., Peris, V., & Saha, D. D (1999). Transport layer security: How much does it really cost? *Conference on Computer Communications (IEEE Infocom),* New York, pp. 717-725.

Balsamo, S., DiMarco, S. A., Inverardi, P., & Simeoni, M. (2004). Model-based Performance Prediction in Software Development. *IEEE Transactions on Software Engineering, 30*(5), 295–310. doi:10.1109/TSE.2004.9

Barber, B., & Davey, J. (1992). *The Use of the CCTA Risk Analysis and Management Methodology CRAMM in Health Information Systems.* In K.C. Lun, P. Degoulet, T.E. Piemme, & O. Rienhoff (editors): Proceedings of MEDINFO'92, North Holland Publishing Co, Amsterdam, pp. 1589–1593.

Bordbar, B., & Anastasakis, K. (2005). *MDA and Analysis of Web Applications.* In Trends in Enterprise Application Architecture (TEAA) 2005, volume 3888 of Lecture notes in Computer Science, pages 44-55, Trondheim, Norway, 2005.3

CORAS. (2003). IST-2000-25031.Retrieved from http://sourceforge.net/projects/coras.

CVSS. (2007). *Common Vulnerability Scoring System (CVSS-SIG).*Retrieved from http://www.first.org/cvss/.

Elahi, G., & Yu, E. (2007). *A goal oriented approach for modeling and analyzing security trade-offs.* In ER 2007. In *Lecture Notes in Computer Science* (*Vol. 4801*, pp. 375–390). Springer-Verlag.

Flechais, I., Mascolo, C., & Sasse, M. A. (2007). Integrating security and usability into the requirements and design process. *International Journal of Electronic Security and Digital Forensics, 1*(1), 12–26. doi:10.1504/IJESDF.2007.013589

France, R. B., Kim, D.-K., Ghosh, S., & Song, E. (2004). A UML-Based Pattern Specification Technique. *IEEE Transactions on Software Engineering, 3*(30), 193–206. doi:10.1109/TSE.2004.1271174

France, R. B., Ray, I., Georg, G., & Ghosh, S. (2004). (2004-1). Aspect-Oriented Approach to Design Modeling. *IEE Proceedings. Software, 4*(151), 173–185. doi:10.1049/ip-sen:20040920

Georg, G., Ray, I., Anastasakis, K., Bordbar, B., Toahchoodee, M. & Houmb, S.H. (2008). An Aspect-Oriented Methodology for Designing Secure Applications, *Information and Software Technology,* Special Issue on Model Based Development for Secure Information Systems, doi:10.1016/j.infsof.2008.05.004.

Houmb, S. H. (2007). *Decision Support for Choice of Security Solution: The Aspect-Oriented Risk Driven Development (AORDD) Framework.* PhD thesis, Norwegian University of Science and Technology (NTNU), NTNU-Trykk, Trondheim, Norway, November 2007. ISBN 978-82-471-4588-3.

Houmb, S. H., Franqueira, V. N. L., & Engum, E. A. (2008). *Estimating Impact and Frequency of Risks to Safety and Mission Critical Systems Using CVSS.* In ISSRE 2008 Supplemental Proceedings: 1st Workshop on Dependable Software Engineering, 11 November 2008, Seattle, US. IEEE CS Conference Proceedings. IEEE Computer Society Press.

Houmb, S. H., & Franquira, V. N. L. (2009). *Estimating ToE Risk Level using CVSS. To be published in the Proceeding of the Forth International Conference on Availability, Reliability and Security (ARES 2009),* IEEE Computer Society, Fukuoka, Japan, March 16-19, 8 pages.

Houmb, S. H., Georg, G., Jürjens, J., & France, R. B. (2007). An Integrated Security Verification and Security Solution Trade-Off Analysis. In Mouratidis, H., & Giorgini, P. (Eds.), *Integrating Security and Software Engineering: Advances and Future Vision.* (pp. 190–219). Hershey, PA: Idea Group.

Houmb, S. H., Georg, G., France, R., Bieman, J. M. & Jürjens (2005). *Cost-Benefit Trade-Off Analysis Using BBN for Aspect-Oriented Risk-Driven Development.* Proceedings of the Tenth IEEE International Conference on Engineering of Complex Computer Systems (ICECCS 2005), pp. 195-204.

IEC 61508(1998) Functional safety of electrical/electronic/programmable electronic safety-related systems.

ISO 15408 (2007) *Common Criteria for Information Technology Security Evaluation*, Version 3.1, Revision 2, CCMB-2007-09-001, CCMB-2007-09-002 and CCMB-2007-09-003.

ISO/IEC 27002: (2005). Information technology - Security techniques - Code of Practice for Information Security Management.

Jackson, D. (2006). *Software Abstractions: Logic, Lanaguage, and Analysis.* London, England: MIT Press.

Jensen, F. (1996). *An introduction to Bayesian Network.* University College London: UCL Press.

Jensen, F. V. (2001). *Bayesian Networks and Decision Graphs.* New York: Springer-Verlag.

Jürjens, J. (2005). *Secure Systems Development with UML.* Berlin, Heidelberg, New York: Springer-Verlag.

Lite Version, H. U. G. I. N. 6.8 (2007). Hugin Expert A/S, Alborg, Denmark. http://www.hugin.com. Downloaded April 19 2007.

Menascé, D. (2003). Security Performance. *IEEE Internet Computing, 7*(3), 84–87. doi:10.1109/MIC.2003.1200305

OMG. (2007). *Unified Modeling Language: Superstructure Version 2.1.2 Formal/07/11/02.* http://www.omg.org/docs/formal/07-11-02.pdf.

OMG. (2007-1). *Unified Modeling Language: Infrastructure Specification V2.1.2.* http://www.omg.org/docs/formal/07-11-04.pdf.

OMG MARTE. (2008). UML Profile for Modeling and Analysis of Real-Time Embedded systems (MARTE). *BETA Bulletin of Experimental Treatments for AIDS, 2*, http://www.omg.org/docs/ptc/08-06-08.pdf.

OMG SPT (2005) *UML Profile for Schedulability, Performance, and Time*, Version 1.1, OMG document formal/05-01-02.

Petriu, D. B., & Woodside, C. M. (2004). *A Metamodel for Generating Performance Models from UML Designs.* in Proc UML 2004, LNCS 3273, pp. 41-53, Springer.

Petriu, D. C., Shen, H., & Sabetta, A. (2007). Performance Analysis of Aspect-Oriented UML Models. *Software and Systems Modeling, 6*(4), 453–471. doi:10.1007/s10270-007-0053-0

Pourret, O., Naïm, P., & Marcot, B. (2008). *Bayesian Networks: A Practical Guide to Applications (Statistics in Practice).* John Wiley & Sons Ltd.

Sindre, G., & Opdahl, A. L. (2005). Eliciting security requirements with misuse cases. *Requirements Engineering Journal, 10*(1), 34–44. doi:10.1007/s00766-004-0194-4

Smith, C. U., & Williams, L. G. (2002). *Performance Solutions.* Reading, MA: Addison-Wesley.

Stølen, K., den Braber, F., Dimitrakos, T., Fredriksen, R., Gran, B., & Houmb, S. H. (2002). *Model-based Risk Assessment in a Component-Based Software Engineering Process: The CORAS Approach to Identify Security Risks.* Chapter in: *Business Component-Based Software Engineering* (pp. 189–207). Kluwer.

Straw, G., Georg, G., Song, E., Ghosh, S., France, R. B., & Bieman, J. M. (2004). *Model Composition Directives. Ed. A. Moreira and S. Mellor.* Proceedings of the UML 2004. Springer, pp. 84-97.

TCP-W. (2002). *Transaction Processing Performance Council benchmark TPC-W=*.Retrieved from http://www.tpc.org/tpcw/

TLSWG. (1996). *SSL 3.0 Specification.* Retrieved from http://www.mozilla.org/projects/security/pki/nss/ssl/draft302.txt

UML2Alloy (2005). *UML2Alloy website*: http://www.cs.bham.ac.uk/~bxb/UML2Alloy.html

Whittle, J., Wijesekera, D., & Hartong, M. (2008). *Executable misuse cases for modeling security concerns.* In ICSE '08: Proceedings of the 30th international conference on Software engineering, pp. 121–130, ACM, New York, NY, USA, 2008.

Woodside, C. M., Petriu, D. C., Petriu, D. B., Shen, H., Israr, T., & Merseguer, J. (2005). *Performance by Unified Model Analysis (PUMA).* In Proc. 5th Int. Workshop on Software and Performance WOSP'2005, pp. 1-12, Palma, Spain, 2005.

Woodside, C. M., Petriu, D. C., Petriu, D. B., Xu, J., Israr, T., Georg, G., & France, R. B. (2009). a,Bieman, J. M., Houmb, S. H. & Jürjens, J. (2009). Performance Analysis of Security Aspects by Weaving Scenarios Extracted from UML Models. *Journal of Systems and Software, 82*, 56–74. doi:10.1016/j.jss.2008.03.067

Yu, E. (1997). *Towards Modelling and Reasoning Support for Early-Phase Requirements Engineering.* In Proc of the 3rd IEEE Int. Symposium. on Requirements Engineering (RE'97) Jan. 6-8, 1997, Washington D.C., USA. pp. 226-235.

Chapter 7
State Model Diagrams:
A Universal, Model Driven Method for Network System Configuration and Management

S. P. Maj
Edith Cowan University, Australia

ABSTRACT

The Internet is an integral part of business communications, however it was based on open standards without due regard to security issues consequently security threats are not only persistent but also increasing. The Computer Security Institute (CSI) 2007 reported a doubling of average annual loss by US companies. There are three primary network security threats: policy, technology, and configuration. This chapter is primarily concerned with the configuration and management of network devices. There are a number of different network management tools currently available, however typically it is problematic to concurrently display configuration data from devices and protocols whilst maintaining a navigational context. This chapter demonstrates how the State Model Diagram method is not only a universal model-driven network tool but also useful for the configuration and management of complex security protocols and devices.

NETWORK DEVICE CONFIGURATION AND MANAGEMENT

Configuring devices, even for routine end users applications such as Internet Explorer, may be problematic (Furnell, 2007) (Furnell, 2005). This problem is exacerbated for dedicated devices such as firewalls which are not only complex devices within themselves but also difficult to configure. Configuring a firewall is considered to be of paramount importance (Rubin, 1997). A firewall employs directional; rule based stateful packet analysis for inbound and outbound packets. According to Bartal,

This is a crucial task ... The bottom line, however, is that the security of the whole intranet depends upon the exact content of the rule-base, with no level of abstraction available. Since the syntax

DOI: 10.4018/978-1-61520-837-1.ch007

and semantics of the rules and their ordering depend upon the firewall product/vendor, this is akin to the dark ages of software, where programs were written in assembly language so that the programmer had to know all the idiosyncrasies of the target processor. (Bartal, Mayer, Nissim, & Wool, 2004)

Firewall configuration is via either a text based Command Line Interface (CLI) or a Graphical User Interface (GUI). The syntactic and semantic complexities of the Cisco PIX firewall CLI have, to some extent, been progressively addressed. Check Point can be configured using either the GUI or the INSPECT language. The INSPECT language is a powerful but complex low level-language. The Check Point GUI is designed to address the problems associated with configuring directional, rule-based filtering. However, according to Wool direction-based filtering remains problematic,

Most firewall vendors (exemplified by Cisco and Lucent) seem to be unaware of the usability issues related to direction-based filtering. These vendors simply expose the raw and confusing direction based filtering functionality to the firewall administrator. A notable exception is Check Point. In order to avoid the usability problem, Check Point chooses to keep its management interface simple, and hide the direction-based filtering functionality in such a way that most users are essentially unable to use it. (Wool, 2004)

In effect the human factor is a significant aspect of security. According to Shultz security is primarily a people issue and hence a usability problem, *'People, for example, are almost invariably involved in installing, configuring and maintaining technology, something that leaves ample opportunity for human error that can result in exposures that can allow those who are intent on evildoing to bypass or defeat this technology.'* (Shultz, 2005)

Based on a heuristic evaluation method Nielson developed criteria for a successful human interface (Nielsen & Molich, 1990), (Nielsen). These criteria may be used to evaluate security related interfaces (Furnell, 2007). To address issues specific to interfaces for security purposes Johnston proposed criteria for a security Human Computer Interface (HCI-S) (Johnston, Eloff, & Labuschagne, 2003). HCI-S criteria are defined as: convey features; visibility of system status; learnability; aesthetic and minimalist design; errors; satisfaction and trust. Despite advances in GUI development, administrators continue to use the CLI (Takayama, 2006).

The problems associated with security device management are further exacerbated by the need to configure, integrate and manage a wide range of heterogeneous technologies such as routers, and switches. Van den Akker (van den Akker, 2001) makes the point, *'Other security breaches caused by user error can be attributed to the complexity of modern systems. Users must be able to used and clearly understand the system in order to use it effectively.'* Wireless technologies may be especially problematic. According to Solms, *'Insecure wireless networks can cause very serious risks to companies, and before installing any such networks, all these risks must be identified, evaluated, and based on the results, the necessary counter measures must be installed to secure the network.'* (Solms & Marais, 2004).

Commercial Network Management Tools

There are a range of both simple and more advanced Windows and Linux based tools for manually testing network connectivity that include: ping, traceroute, whois, nslookup, dig, netsat and nbstat, all of which are typically based on the text-based Command Line Interface (CLI) with associated pull down menus. The syslog protocol allows network devices to automatically send unacknowledged notification messages to event message collectors called syslog servers. Windows and Linux based syslog servers typically provide a CLI with associated pull down menus. In addition, GUIs are available for displaying time dependent information such as Syslog statistics.

An operational network must be monitored to determine the availability of network resources, create trending reports and identify and correct issues in real time. There are a variety of Windows and Linux based network monitoring tools, typically based on the Internet Control Message Protocol (ICMP) Echo request-reply (i.e. PING), that include: Spong, Nagios/Netsaint, Open NMS and NIMIS. These tools typically provide a CLI with associated pull down menu and also web based GUI. A variety of SNMP based tools, both Windows and Linux based are available that include: Multi-Router Traffic Grapher (MRTG); Round Robin Database Tool (RRDTool), Cacti and Cricket. These tools typically provide a CLI with associated pull down menu and also web based GUI.

There are a number of different vendor based software tools designed for network configuration and management such as Ciscoworks, Cisco netManager, Security Device Manager, WhatsUp Gold, OpenNMS, IBM Tivoli and Novell Zenworks. Some of these products are designed to provide entire systems solutions and hence address the problems associated with the convergence of different technologies such as Voice, wireless, data, public, private etc and also the persistent problem of network security.

Each of the different vendor based network management tools has strengths, weaknesses and limitations (table 1) and no vendor can provide a complete solution (Paquet, 1997). It has been commented that Cisco Systems' success is based on marketing rather than technical excellence (Fabbi, 2005). Furthermore, according to Schluting,

Many large NM tools are complex and expensive packages even thought they have the basic features network engineers look for, but lack usability; for instant, HP OpenView and IBM's Tivoli are cost-prohibitive to most, and to others, simply too complex to use. (Schluting, 2005)

However, these tools are typically lacking in two important areas:

- It is difficult to concurrently display real-time data from multiple devices and protocols.
- The CLI is inherently sequential and requires multiple commands.

STATE MODEL DIAGRAMS

Complexity may be controlled by abstraction. Models based on abstraction control detail by means of hierarchical top-down decomposition – only details specific to a given context are presented to the user. According to Gilbert,

A model is a simplified representation of a system, which concentrates attention on specific aspects of the system. Moreover, models enable aspects of the system i.e. objects, events, or ideas which are either complex or on a different scale to that which is normally perceived, or abstract to be rendered with visible or more readily visible. (Gilbert, 1995)

The ACM/IEEE list abstraction as a fundamental concept in computer science (Tucker et al., 1991). State Model Diagrams (SMDs) were proposed as a model for configuring and managing network devices and associated protocols (S.P Maj & Kohli, 2004). According to Maj,

Using the models it is relatively easy to understand the purpose and structure of the devices. The models include implementation details, derived from the CLI commands, hence it is possible to verify and validate device operation. (S.P Maj, Kohli, & Murphy, 2004)

Table 1. Network management tools (Source. C. Nuangjamnong, 2009)

Ciscoworks		
Characteristics	**Advantages**	**Disadvantages**
• Simplifying the configuration, administration, monitoring, and troubleshooting of Cisco networks • Improving the accuracy and efficiency of the network operations staff • Increasing the overall availability of the network by simplifying configuration and quickly identifying and fixing network problem • Maximizing network security through integration with access control services and audit of network-level changes	• A centralised system for sharing device information across all network applications, improving manageability, and increasing system-wide awareness of network changes • Network discovery, topology views, end-station tracking • Real-time network fault analysis • Hardware and software inventory management, centralised configuration • Monitoring and tracking of network response time availability • Web-based interface for launching and navigating network functionality	• A Cisco-based computer network only can be used • Very expensive • Consumes a huge amount of computer resources. • Requires high performance networking equipment to run it because it has become such a large and complete management system • Not suitable to update network configuration when it is required immediately • As many network management protocols have been used, they create a lot of network traffic
WhatsUp Gold		
Characteristics	**Advantages**	**Disadvantages**
• Web-based interface • Full reporting features • Supports Both SNMP and WMI • Real-time monitoring all critical network devices and services	• Discovers and maps all network devices • Notifies when problems happen on the network • Gathers network information over time and generates reports • Real-time network monitoring	• Consumes a huge of computer resources. • Requires high performance networking equipment to run it because it has become such a large and complete management system • As many network management protocols have been used, they create a lot of network traffic • Not suitable to update network configuration when it is required immediately • Very expensive

The use of SMD modeling will be illustrated by firstly comparing the output of a simple network managed using the CLI and the same network managed using SMDs. Then progressively more complex networks will be modeled using SMDs.

The Command Line Interface

Networking devices are typically configured and managed using the CLI. For a two router network four different CLI commands are typically needed: show running-config, show arp, show interface fa0/1 and show interface fa0/0. As can be seen CLI output is text based and verbose.

```
Router1#show running-config
Building configuration...
!
interface FastEthernet0/1
 ip address 192.168.1.1 255.255.255.0
 duplex auto
 speed auto
!
interface Ethernet0/0
 ip address 192.168.10.1
255.255.255.0
 duplex auto
 speed auto
!
Router1#show arp
Protocol  Address          Age (min)
```

```
Hardware Addr   Type   Interface
Internet  192.168.1.1              -
000c.30e2.e501 ARPA    FastEthernet0/1
Internet  192.168.1.2           24
0001.6c81.644c ARPA    FastEthernet0/1
Internet 192.168.1.3          26
0001.6c81.678a ARPA FasteEthernet0/1
Router1#show int fa0/1
FastEthernet0/0 is up, line protocol
is up
   Hardware is AmdFE, address is
000c.30e2.e501 (bia 000c.30e2.e501)
IP address 192.168.1.1/24
MTU 1500 bytes, BW 100000 Kbit, DLY
100 usec,
      reliability 255/255, txload
1/255, rxload 1/255
   Encapsulation ARPA, loopback not
set
   Keepalive set (10 sec)
   Full-duplex, 100Mb/s, 100BaseTX/FX
   ARP type: ARPA, ARP Timeout
04:00:00
   Last input 00:01:02, output
00:00:25, output hang never
   Last clearing of "show interface"
counters never
   Input queue: 0/75/0/0 (size/max/
drops/flushes); Total output drops: 0
   Queueing strategy: fifo
   Output queue:0/40 (size/max)
   5 minute input rate 0 bits/sec, 0
packets/sec
   5 minute output rate 0 bits/sec, 0
packets/sec
      5301 packets input, 806014 bytes
      Received 5239 broadcasts, 0
runs, 0 giants, 0 throttles
      0 input errors, 0 CRC, 0 frame,
0 overrun, 0 ignored
      0 watchdog
      0 input packets with dribble
condition detected
      12722 packets output, 1150037
```

```
bytes, 0 underruns
      0 output errors, 0 collisions, 7
interface resets
      0 babbles, 0 late collision, 0
deferred
      10 lost carrier, 0 no carrier
      0 output buffer failures, 0 out-
put buffers swapped out
Router1#show int fa0/0
FastEthernet0/0 is up, line protocol
is up
   Hardware is AmdFE, address is
000c.30e2.e500 (bia 000c.30e2.e500)
IP address 192.168.10.1/24
   MTU 1500 bytes, BW 100000 Kbit, DLY
100 usec,
      reliability 255/255, txload
1/255, rxload 1/255
   Encapsulation ARPA, loopback not
set
   Keepalive set (10 sec)
   Full-duplex, 100Mb/s, 100BaseTX/FX
   ARP type: ARPA, ARP Timeout
04:00:00
   Last input 00:01:02, output
00:00:25, output hang never
   Last clearing of "show interface"
counters never
   Input queue: 0/75/0/0 (size/max/
drops/flushes); Total output drops: 0
   Queueing strategy: fifo
   Output queue:0/40 (size/max)
   5 minute input rate 0 bits/sec, 0
packets/sec
   5 minute output rate 0 bits/sec, 0
packets/sec
      5301 packets input, 806014 bytes
      Received 5239 broadcasts, 0
runs, 0 giants, 0 throttles
      0 input errors, 0 CRC, 0 frame,
0 overrun, 0 ignored
      0 watchdog
      0 input packets with dribble
condition detected
```

```
     12722 packets output, 1150037
bytes, 0 underruns
     0 output errors, 0 collisions, 7
interface resets
     0 babbles, 0 late collision, 0
deferred
     10 lost carrier, 0 no carrier
     0 output buffer failures, 0 out-
put buffers swapped out
```

In addition to this two PC configuration commands (ipconfig) are needed.

```
PC1
C:\>ipconfig /all
Windows IP Configuration
     Host Name. .. .. .. .. .. .:
Ethernet adapter Local Area Connec-
tion:
     Connection-specific DNS Suf-
fix  .:
     Description. .. .. .. .. .
.: Intel(R) PRO/100+ Server Adapter
(PILA8470B)
     Physical Address.. .. .. ..
.: 0001.6c81.644c
     Dhcp Enabled.. .. .. .. ...... .:
No
     IP Address.. .. .. .. .. .. .:
192.168.1.2
     Subnet Mask. .. .. .. .. . .:
255.255.255.0
     Default Gateway. .. .. .. .
.:192.168.1.1
PC2
C:\>ipconfig /all
Windows IP Configuration
     Host Name. .. .. .. .. .. .. .:
Ethernet adapter Local Area Connec-
tion:
     Connection-specific DNS Suf-
fix  .:
     Description. .. .. .. .. .. .
.: Intel(R) PRO/100+ Server Adapter
```

```
(PILA8470B)
     Physical Address.. .. .. ..
.: 0001.6c81.678a
     Dhcp Enabled.. .. .. .. .. .:
No
     IP Address.. .. .. .. .. .. .:
192.168.1.3
     Subnet Mask. .. .. .. .. .. .:
255.255.255.0
     Default Gateway. .. .. .. .
.:192.168.1.1
```

SMD: Secure OSI Layer 3 Devices

The above network can also be managed using the SMD model as follows. A level 0 SMD represents the topology of the network under consideration i.e. all the named network devices, interfaces, connections and IP addresses (Figure 1).

From the level 0 SMD it is possible to select a specific device, such as a Router 1, and obtain a level 1 SMD (Figure 2). The level 1 SMD of Router1 extracts data from the device and displays it in the context of the OSI model. OSI layer 1 is concerned with the interface line status (either up or down). The OSI layer 2 represents interface MAC address and line protocol (either up or down). The OSI layer 3 represents the interface IP addresses and layer 3 protocols such as Address Resolution Protocol (ARP), routing and security protocols.

The ARP protocol automatically maps physical (MAC) to logical (IP) addresses in order to encapsulate layer 3 packets into layer 2 frames. The ARP box may be expanded using a level 2 SMD (figure 3).

Significantly this single SMD (figure 3) represents the output of four router CLI commands (show running-config, show ARP, show interface fa0/1 and show interface fa0/0) and two PC text commands (ipconfig) - but does so concurrently. Concurrency provides the ability to directly observer protocol interactions. For example ARP

Figure 1. Level 0 SMD

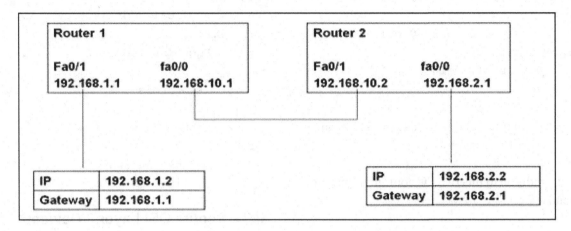

Figure 2. Level 1 SMD

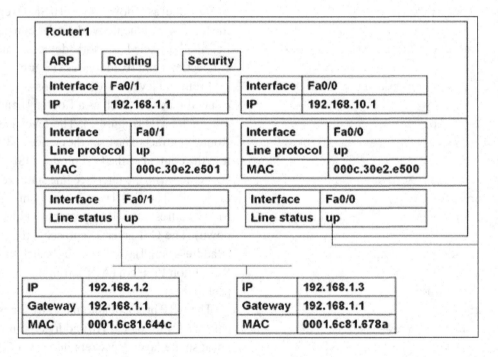

has mapped the PC IP address (192.168.1.2) to the associated MAC address (001.6c81.644c).

SMD table construction is configurable and may be defined by the user. Hence tables may be simplified or even expanded to include further details. For example the table for interface fa0/1 may be expanded to include details such as Full-duplex, 100Mb/s etc. Similarly it is possible to select and expand the 'Routing' box in order to

determine which routing protocol has been configured and the associated operational details.

An unprotected router is a relatively easy target for hackers by means of eavesdropping and spoofing. Authentication and update filtering can be applied to routing protocols, such as Enhanced Interior Gateway Routing Protocol (EIGRP), in order to protect routing table integrity by means of neighbor authentication using Message Digest

Figure 3. Level 2 SMD with ARP table expanded

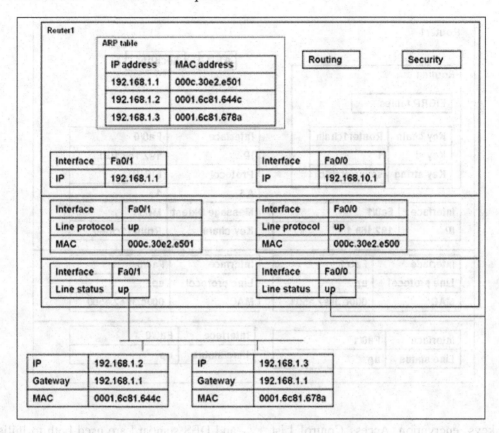

Algorithm 5 (MD5) which is easily displayed using an SMD model (Figure 4). Expanding the routing box displays that the routing protocol EIGRP has been configured – further expansion is possible to display the EIGRP neighbor, topology and routing tables. Key chain details (name, id and key-string) correspond to the authenticated interface fa0/0 (protocol, Autonomous System, message digest and key chain).

Significantly, research has demonstrated that SMDs may be used to manage a network,

SMDs also provide top down decomposition thereby enabling a large complex network to be partitioned into independent units of an amenable size. Using SMDs it is possible to examine the overview of an entire network and also obtain increasing levels of detail while still maintaining

links and interfaces between the different levels. (S. P. Maj & Tran, 2006)

Furthermore SMDs may be used to represent even complex protocols, or even multiple protocols, operating on a single device (S.P. Maj & Veal, 2007). In effect SMDs are universally applicable for all networking devices and protocols. They may be especially useful for the configuration of complex protocols security protocol suites (C. Nuangjamnong, Maj, S. P., Veal, D., 2007).

Cisco Encryption Technology

Complex security protocols and devices may also be modelled using SMD diagrams. Router 1 has been configured for the Cisco Encryption Technology (CET) protocol suite (Figure 5). The level 2 SMD represents CET as four functional

Figure 4. SMD level 3, EIGRP Routing method authentication

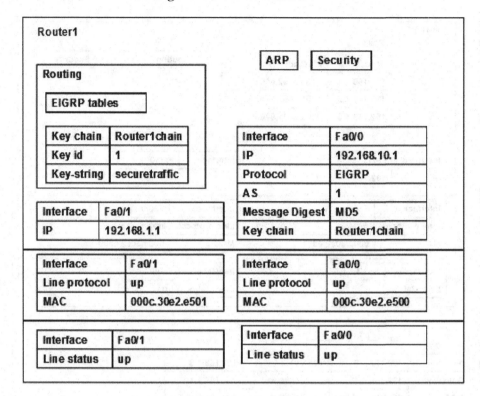

areas – keys, encryption, Access Control List (ACL) and mapping.

The four CET functional areas (keys, encryption, ACL and mapping) can each be expanded and represented as an SMD (Figure 6). However in order to ensure the correct screen 'foot print' it is necessary to minimize the 'foot print' of other protocols. It is now possible to concurrently observe the configuration details for CET not only within a specific device but also the peer device. For CET encryption to work properly it is necessary to coordinate the configuration of peer devices. During the setup of each encrypted session, peer devices attempt mutual authentication. If either authentication fails an encrypted session cannot be established and hence encrypted sensitive data cannot be sent.

CET implements the following standards: Digital Signature Standard (DSS), the Diffie-Hellman (DH) public key algorithm, and Data Encryption Standard (DES). The DH algorithm and DES standard are used both to initiate and conduct encryption. The DSS keys are unique for each router: a unique DSS public key, and a unique DSS private key (Router1 Private key). The DSS private key is stored in private non-volatile RAM (NVRAM) and is not distributed to other devices and normally cannot be viewed by the administrator. The DSS public key is distributed to the peer device (or devices) and must be verified. CET employs out-of-band voice authentication for key exchange. As illustrated in figure 6, the SMD displays identification for both the public key of Router1 (E416EDA2) and the peer device (A2114072). Without correct public key exchange encryption cannot occur. The public key is then used to authenticate the peer and also generate a temporary DES key called a session key which is used for encryption.

After peer authentication and session key generation data can be encrypted. However peer devices must employ the same encryption algo-

Figure 5. SMD of router with Cisco encryption technology

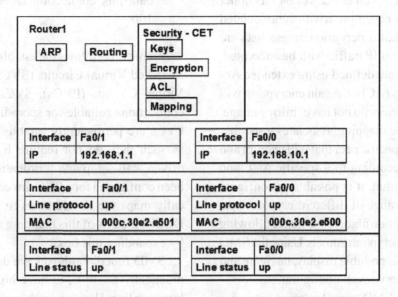

Figure 6. SMD router with Cisco encryption technology

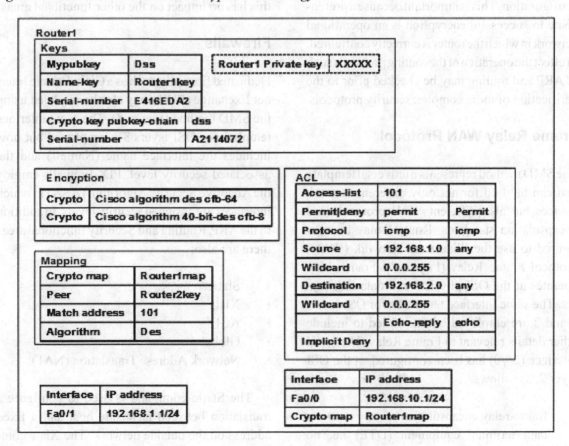

rithms such as DES with either 8 or 64 bit Cipher Feedback (CFB) or encryption with the associated decryption will fail. Encryption access lists are used to define what IP traffic with be encrypted. Such access lists are defined using extended Access Control Lists (ACLs). Again encryption will fail if the peer devices do not have 'mirror image' ACLs. Finally the mapping associates a specific interface with a specific peer that will encrypt and decrypt traffic according to a specific ACL and encryption algorithm. It is possible to configure a device with a range of different crypto maps, ACLs and encryption algorithms hence allowing multiple secure encryption tunnels. Using the SMD representation it is possible display, navigate and concurrently observe such configurations.

Significantly SMD representation allows a systematic approach to the verification of valid configuration. This is important because a prerequisite to successful encryption is an operational network in which the router is correctly configured. In effect the operation of the routing protocols such as ARP and routing may be checked prior to the verification of more complex security protocols.

Frame Relay WAN Protocol

The SMD method represents a universal template that can be used for not only different network devices but also different WAN protocols and encapsulation standards. Router1 may be configured to use the Wide Area Network (WAN) protocol Frame Relay (Figure 7). Frame relay operates at the OSI physical and data link layers. The same interface templates for OSI levels 1 and 2 are employed but expanded to include other details relevant to Frame Relay. The serial interface (S0/0) has been configured, at the OSI layer 2, as follows:

- frame-relay encapsulation
- data terminal equipment (DTE) i.e. no clocking

- data link connection identifier (DLCI) of 100

Frame relay allows the establishment of either Switched Virtual Circuits (SVCs) or Permanent Virtual Circuits (PVCs). SVCs are temporary connections suitable for sporadic data transfers. PVCs are permanently established connections as such they do not require frequent, demand driven, call setup and termination. Router1 has been configured for a PVC. Inverse ARP dynamically maps the IP addresses to the OSI layer 2 DLCIs. Details of this mapping may be obtained by expanding this box.

SMD functional boxes are designed, as far a practically possible, to have high cohesion and low coupling. Hence even though an interface has been configured with an entirely different protocol this has no impact on the other functional areas.

Firewalls

Dedicated firewalls, such as a Cisco Private Internet Exchange (PIX), may also be modeled using the SMD method (Figure 8). The same interface template for OSI layers 3 is employed but now includes the interface name (Nameif) and the associated security level. PIX firewalls employ the Adaptive Security Algorithm (ASA) in which interfaces are assigned security levels. In addition to the ARP, Routing and Security functional areas there are also:

- Static
- Xlate
- ACL
- Global
- Network Address Translation (NAT)

The Static command is used to configure a translation between an inside host and a fixed address on the outside network. The Xlate command displays the current and maximum number of translations through the PIX device. A trans-

Figure 7. SMD router with security and frame relay

Router1
ARP
Routing
Security
Frame relay
Inverse ARP
Interface
Fa0/1
IP
192.168.1.1
Interface
S0/0
IP
192.168.10.1
Frame relay
PVC
Interface
Fa0/1
Line protocol
up
MAC
000c.30e2.e501
Interface
S0/0
Encapsulation
Frame-relay
Intf type
DTE
DLCI
100
Line protocol
up
Interface
Fa0/1
Line status
up
Interface
S0/0
Line status
up

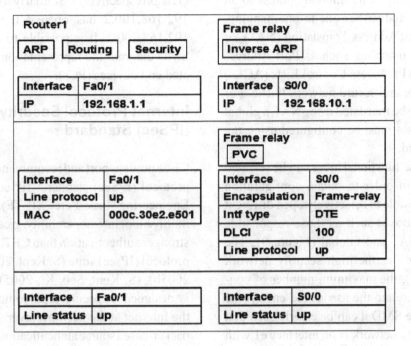

Figure 8. SMD of PIX firewall

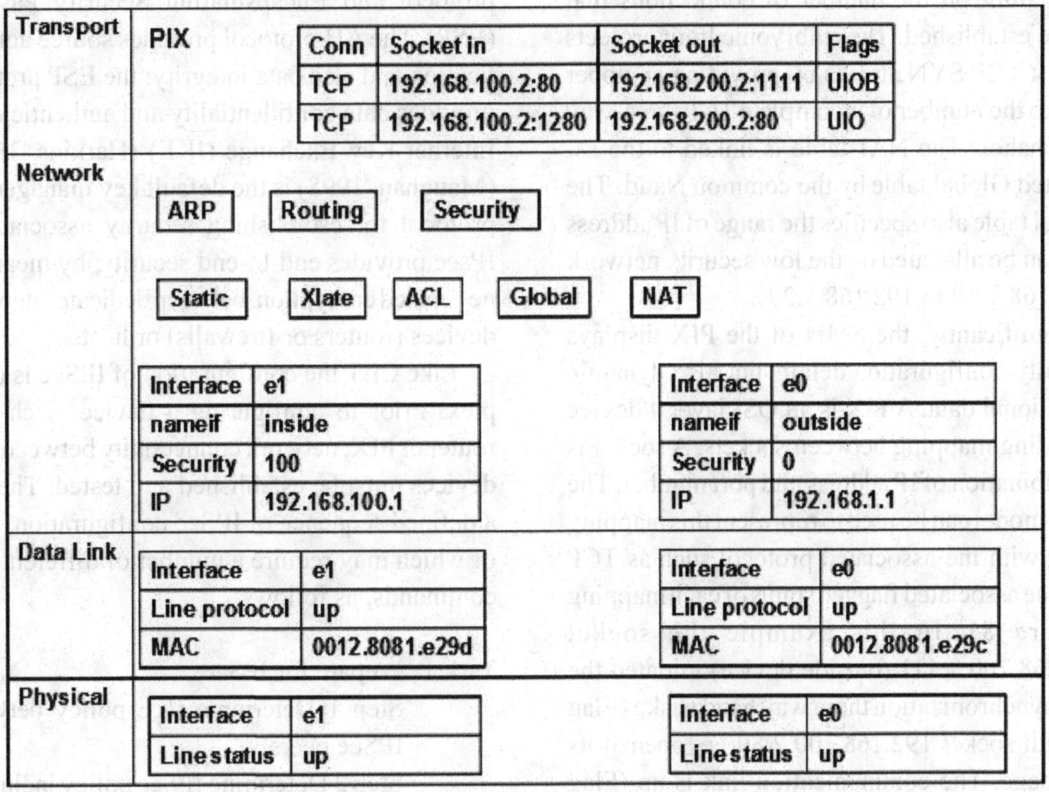

Transport
PIX
Conn
Socket in
Socket out
Flags
TCP
192.168.100.2:80
192.168.200.2:1111
UIOB
TCP
192.168.100.2:1280
192.168.200.2:80
UIO
Network
ARP
Routing
Security
Static
Xlate
ACL
Global
NAT
Interface
e1
nameif
inside
Security
100
IP
192.168.100.1
Interface
e0
nameif
outside
Security
0
IP
192.168.1.1
Data Link
Interface
e1
Line protocol
up
MAC
0012.8081.e29d
Interface
e0
Line protocol
up
MAC
0012.8081.e29c
Physical
Interface
e1
Line status
up
Interface
e0
Line status
up

lation is a mapping of an internal address to an external address and can be a one-to-one mapping, such as Network Address Translation (NAT), or a many-to-one mapping, such as Port Address Translation (PAT). Access Control Lists (ACLs) are used to filter and secure network traffic. For an inside host to be translated using NAT, a global pool of addresses must be configured using the global command.

Each of these functional areas can be selected and expanded in order to obtain configuration details. It is possible to selectively open different SMD security boxes such as those responsible for dynamic NAT and Global (Figure 9). The NAT table specifies the high security network (192.168.100.0), the maximum number of connections allowed and the associated embryonic limits. From the SMD it can be clearly seen that this high security network is on interface e1 with a nameif of "inside" and a security level of 100. The maximum number of connections places an upper limit on the number of connections that can be established. The embryonic limit protects against TCP SYN attacks by providing an upper limit to the number of incomplete TCP three-way handshakes. The NAT table is linked to the associated Global table by the common Natid. The Global table also specifies the range of IP address that can be allocated on the low security network (192.168.1.10 to 192.168.1.20).

Significantly, the SMD of the PIX displays not only configuration details but also dynamic operational data. A PIX is an OSI layer 4 device providing mapping between sockets. A socket is a combination of IP address and port number. The SMD model can be used to represent this mapping along with the associated protocol such as TCP with the associated flagged status of each mapping (Figure 8). In this example the socket 192.168.200.2:111 (outside device) initiated the TCP synchronization three way hand shake (Flag B) with socket 192.168.100.2:80 i.e. opened its web page. The communication link is up (Flag U) and there is inbound and outbound data (I and

O flags respectively). Similarly it can be seen that 192.168.100.2 has opened the web page of 192.168.200.2. It is possible to include on this SMD diagram the representations of the associated end devices (PCs).

Internet Protocol Security (IPSec) Standard

Cisco now support and recommend the IP security protocol (IPSec) standard. IPSec is an Internet Engineering Task Force (IETF) standard with multivendor interaoperability, greater security and stronger authentication than CET. The IP security protocol (IPsec) suite (S. Kent, 2005a), (S. Kent, 2005b), (S. Kent, Seo, K., 2005), (Piper, 1998) is designed to secure data communications on the Internet at the network layer. IPSec provides packet-based source authentication, data confidentiality and integrity. There are two main protocols in the IPSec suite – Authentication Header (AH) protocol and Encapsulating Security Payload (ESP). The AH protocol provides source authentication and also data integrity; the ESP protocol provides data confidentiality and authentication. Internet Key Exchange (IKE) (Harkins, 1998), (Maughan, 1998) is the default key management protocol for establishing security associations. IPsec provides end-to-end security, by means of negotiated encryption, between dedicated network devices (routers or firewalls) or hosts.

Like CET the configuration of IPSec is complex. Prior to configuring a device, such as a router or PIX, network connectivity between peer devices must be established and tested. There is a defined sequence of IPSec configuration, each of which may require a number of different CLI commands, as follows:

Task 1. Prepare for IPSec
      Step 1 Determine IKE policy between IPSec peers
      Step 2 Determine IPSec policy including IPSec peer details

Figure 9. SMD of PIX firewall with NAT and Global

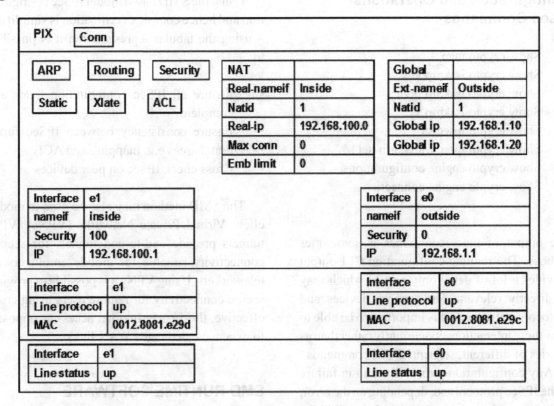

Step 3 Check current device configurations

Step 4 Ensure network connectivity

Task 2. Configure Internet Key Exchange (IKE) for pre-shared keys

Step 1 Enable IKE

Step 2 Create IKE policies

Step 3 Configure pre-shared keys

Step 4 Verify IKE configurations

Task 3. Configure IPSec

Step 1 Configure crypto access lists

Step 2 Configure transform set suites

Step 3 Configure global IPSec security association lifetimes (optional)

Step 4 Configure crypto maps

Step 5 Apply crypto maps to interface

Step 6 Verify IPSec

Task 4. Test and verify IPSec

In order to determine that a PIX device, configured with IPSec, has been configured correctly and is also operating correctly requires numerous different CLI commands that include:

Configuration CLI Commands

1. Show running-config
2. Show routing
3. Show static
4. Show global
5. Show nat

Dynamic Operational CLI Commands

1. Show arp
2. Show conn
3. Show xlate
4. Show interface inside
5. Show interface outside

Configuration and Operational IPsec Commands

1. Show crypto map
2. Show crypto isakmp key
3. Show crypto isakmp policy
4. Show crypto isakmp sa
5. Show crypto ipsec sa
6. Show crypto ipsec transform-set
7. Show crypto engine configurations
8. Show crypto engine connections

The output of these commands is sometimes verbose. The running-configuration CLI output provides a lot of detail only part of which may be directly relevant. Furthermore devices and protocols interact and it is important to be able to view these interactions concurrently rather than as a series of different, sequential CLI commands.

Any configuration error will result in failure of the IPSec protocol and, depending on the error, fault diagnosis may be complex. Like CET the IPSec fields on peer devices must correspond; peer devices must employ the same encryption algorithms such as ESP transform with DES 56 bit cipher (esp-des) and ESP transform using HMAC-MD5 authentication (esp-md5-hmac) or encryption with the associated decryption will fail; peer devices must have mirror image ACL's. Finally the mapping associates a specific interface with a specific peer that will encrypt and decrypt traffic according to a specific ACL and encryption algorithm.

The IPSec protocol can be modeled using the SMD method. Similar to the CET protocol suite, the PIX SMD level 2 represents IPSec as four functional areas – keys, encryption, Access Control List (ACL) and mapping. The four IPSec functional areas can each be expanded and represent an (Figure 10). However in order to ensure the correct screen foot print it is necessary to minimize other protocols.

Using the SMD based model IPSec configuration and hence complex verification is simplified – using the tabular representation it is possible to:

- Ensure all IPSec configuration fields are complete
- Ensure consistency between IPSec functional areas e.g. mapping and ACL
- Cross check IPSec on peer devices

The SMD method may also be used to model client Virtual Private Networks (VPNs). VPN tunnels provide end-to-end tunnels for secure connectivity suitable for mobile employers or teleworkers. Using VPNs it is possible to provide secure connectivity for remote users using cost-effective, third-party Internet access as opposed to expensive dedicated WAN links.

SMD RUNTIME SOFTWARE

The original SMD model was entirely paper based – data was collected from the devices by means of CLI commands and entered into tables by hand. This manual method was evaluated as a network management tool and was found to be as useful as the CLI for all aspects of network management, and significantly, more useful than the commercial product Ciscoworks used in these trials (S. P. Maj & Tran, 2006).

The SMD model has been converted to a run-time model, called Sopwith, which can be used to validate network behavior in real-time (S. P. Maj, Cooper, J. R., Carter, J., 2009). The program uses a combination of Simple Network Management Protocol (SNMP) and PING in order to populate the SMD tables. SNMP is a client-server application layer protocol with three main components: managed devices (a switch, router, firewall, PC or printer), software agents on the managed devices, and a network manager. The software agents on

Figure 10. Level 3 SMD of PIX firewall with IPSec

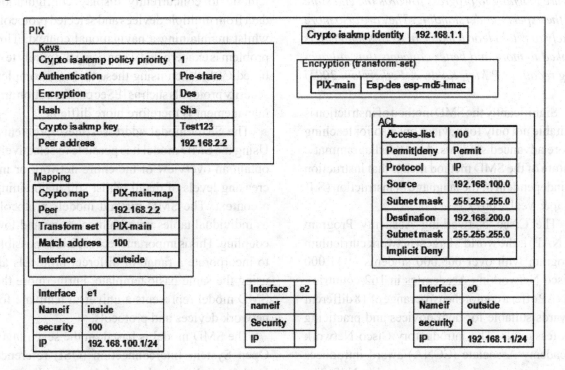

each device will gather specific information about the state of the device into data structures called Management Information Bases (MIBs), which the network manager can interrogate. Sopwith further assists in fault diagnosis by color changes. If a network interface develops a fault, it's on-screen representation changes from black to red. Unlike other network management tools Sopwith allows the user to add sub diagrams and tables to the SMD as it runs. An interface is provided to enable configuration of the tables. The user is able to define, and extend SMD tables as follows:

- Which table columns to display
- How to name the columns
- Conditions indicating that a row should not be shown
- Color scheme for error conditions

To date no evaluation of how resource intensive Sopwith is compared to other network management tools.

SMDs as a Pedagogical Tool

Paper-based SMDs have been extensively evaluated as the pedagogical foundation of network technology curriculum. SMD based curriculum it was found that,

Postgraduate students, whose learning was based upon the state models, demonstrated a comprehension of devices comparable to a qualified and experienced expert in this field. Furthermore these students performed significantly better that other students. (S.P Maj & Kohli, 2004)

A more extensive study concluded,

This indicates that both groups of students learnt the required material equally well. However from the diagrams of the state model students it can be inferred that they have richer conceptual understandings and these were aligned with those of an expert. Consequently they will be more able in

future learning to progress towards the end state of the expert's understanding. They are also more likely to retain learnt material as this material is linked to more and better concepts thus enhancing recall. (S.P Maj, Kohli, & Fetherston, 2005)

Significantly the SMD method of instruction is suitable not only for novices but also for teaching more advanced students. Also the diagrammatic nature of the SMD method means that instruction is independent of the language of instruction (S.P. Maj & Veal, 2007).

The Cisco Networking Academy Program (CNAP) is the world's largest network curriculum program with over 600,000 students in 11,000 Cisco Networking Academies in 162 countries. CNAP offer a comprehensive range of 18 different awards suitable for both novices and practicing professionals. The introductory Cisco Network Academy Associate (CCNA) award introduces students to networking concepts such as NAT. The more advanced Cisco Network Academy Professional (CCNP) course consists of four different units. The unit Implementing Secure Converged Wide Area Networks is primarily concerned with designing secure enterprise networks suitable for teleworkers based on the IPSec standard.

SMD modeling principles are in the process of being incorporated into the Cisco Network Academy Program (CNAP) network simulation and visualization tool, Packet Tracer. This work is in conjunction with the Networking Academy Learning Systems Development (NALSD) Group of Cisco Systems.

CONCLUSION AND FUTURE RESEARCH DIRECTIONS

The different network management tools currently available have relative strengths and weaknesses. It is hard to argue that one single product meets the requirements of all users in all circumstances. However typically, when using them, it is prob-

lematic to concurrently display configuration data from multiple devices and selected protocols whilst maintaining a navigational context. This problem is exacerbated when using the purely text based CLI. When using these tools for complex security protocols such as IPSec configuration and management is therefore more difficult.

The SMD model addresses these problems. Using the SMD model it is possible to selectively obtain an overview of the entire network or increasing levels of detail whilst still maintaining a context. The SMD method models protocols as individual tables with high cohesion and low coupling. This is important because it then possible to incorporate a range of different protocols all using the same basic template. Furthermore the SMD model represents a universal template for network devices and protocols.

The SMD model is based on the seven layer Open System Interconnection (OSI) reference model. High cohesion and low coupling are intrinsic in the OSI model – each of the seven layers is self-contained so that functions provided by protocols in each layer can be implemented independently. For example, for a router interface the 'Line Status' protocols is an OSI layer 1 function; the 'Line Protocol' and MAC address are OSI layer 2 functions whereas IP addressing, ARP, routing etc are all OSI layer 3 functions (figure 3). Because the OSI organizes network protocols into different layers solutions offered by one layer may be updated without affecting the other layers. For example a router's interface may be modified in the OSI layer to 3 include EIGRP encryption; however this has no effect on the other OSI layers (figure 4).

There are a number of advantages to the SMD method when compared to other network management tools that include:

- SMDs are universally applicable to all network devices and protocols
- A single SMD equivalent to output from numerous different CLI commands

- SMDs allow user to observe concurrent interactions
- SMDs simultaneously display both configuration and runtime data
- SMDs allow the user to navigate between different levels of details
- Possible to simultaneously display SMD representations of different devices
- Possible to simultaneously display SMD representations of peer devices
- Aids network device configuration and verification
- Aids fault diagnosis

There is considerable research evidence demonstrating that there are advantages to using even the paper-based SMD method not only for network configuration and management but also as the pedagogical foundation of network curriculum.

An evaluation of the network management tools CLI, Ciscoworks and SMD clearly indicated that: both the CLI and SMD to be useful; the SMD method was more useful than the CLI; Ciscoworks was of little value. (S. P. Maj & Tran, 2006). However further work is needed.

The recently developed SMD runtime model requires further development to incorporate a more extensive portfolio of different network devices and protocols. Furthermore the current version of software does not allow users to configure network devices and protocols. This software has yet to be fully tested, documented and evaluated. Trials will consist of using this software for configuration and management of a range of different networks of increasing complexity all restricted to an experimental context. It is then planned to conduct trails on operational networks.

When the SMD software is integrated with Packet Tracer the NALSD group will assist in establishing a network of academics and students for global trials in order to evaluate the pedagogical value of this runtime software.

REFERENCES

Bartal, Y., Mayer, A., Nissim, K., & Wool, A. (2004). Firmato: A Novel Firewall Management Toolkit. *ACM Transactions on Computer Systems*, *22*(4), 381–420. doi:10.1145/1035582.1035583

IP Encapsulating Security Payload (ESP), RFC 4303 C.F.R. (2005b).

Fabbi, M., Ahlawat, R., Allen, N., Blood, S., Dulaney, K., Goodness, E., et al. (2005). *Cisco Systems: A Detailed Review* (Publication. Retrieved January 2009, from Gartner. Furnell, S. (2005). Why users cannot use security. *Computers & Security, 24*, 274-279.

Furnell, S. (2007). Making security usable: Are things improving? *Computers & Security, 26*, 434–443. doi:10.1016/j.cose.2007.06.003

Gilbert, J. (1995). *The role of models and modelling in some narrative science learning.* Paper presented at the Annual meeting of the American Educational Research Association, San Francisco, CA.

Internet Security Association and Key Management Protocol (ISAKMP), ROC 2408 C.F.R. (1998).

IP authentication header, RFC 4302 C.F.R. (2005a).

Johnston, J., Eloff, J. H. P., & Labuschagne, L. (2003). Security and human computer interfaces. *Computers & Security, 22*(8), 675–684. doi:10.1016/S0167-4048(03)00006-3

Maj, S. P., Cooper, J. R., Carter, J. (2009). State Model Diagrams – A Universal Runtime Network Management Method. *Manuscript submitted for publication.*

Maj, S. P., & Kohli, G. (2004). A New State Models for Internetworks Technology. *Journal of Issues in Informing Science and Information Technology, 1*, 385–392.

Maj, S. P., Kohli, G., & Fetherston, T. (2005). *A Pedagogical Evaluation of New State Model Diagrams for Teaching Internetwork Technologies.* Paper presented at the 28th Australasian Computer Science Conference (ACSC2005), Newcastle, Australia.

Maj, S. P., Kohli, G., & Murphy, G. (2004). *State Models for Internetworking Technologies.* Paper presented at the IEEE, Frontiers in Education, 34th Annual Conference, Savannah, Georgia, USA.

Maj, S. P., & Tran, B. (2006, 2007). *State Model Diagrams - a Systems Tool for Teaching Network Technologies and Network Management.* Paper presented at the International Joint Conferences on Computer, Information and Systems Sciences, and Engineering, University of Bridgeport.

Maj, S. P., & Veal, D. (2007). State Model Diagrams as a Pedagogical Tool - An International Evaluation. *IEEE Transactions on Education, 50*(3), 204–207. doi:10.1109/TE.2007.900028

Nielsen, J. Ten Usability Heuritics. Retrieved December, 2008, from http://www.useit.com/papers/heuristic/heuristic_list.html

Nielsen, J., & Molich, R. (1990). *Heuristic evaluation of user interfaces.* Paper presented at the Human Factors in Computing Systems, Seattle, WA.

Nuangjamnong, C. (2009). *An Investigation into Network Management.* Perth: Edith Cowan University.

Nuangjamnong, C., Maj, S. P., & Veal, D. (2007). *Network Security Devices and Protocols Using State Model Diagrams.* Paper presented at the 5th Australian Information Security Management Edith Cowan University, Perth, Western Australia.

Paquet, R., Strovink, K. (1997). *The risks of network and systems management technology investments* Publication. Retrieved January, 2009.

Rubin, A. D., Geer, D., & Ranum, M. J. (1997). *Web Security Sourcebook.* John Wiley & Sons.

Schluting, C. (2005). Chose the Right Network Management Tool. Retrieved January 2009, from http://www.enterprisenetworkingplanet.com/netos/article.php/3465921

Security architecture for the Internet protocol, RFC 4301 C.F.R. (2005).

Shultz, E. (2005). The human factor in security. *Computers & Security, 24,* 425–426. doi:10.1016/j.cose.2005.07.002

Solms, B., & Marais, E. (2004). From secure wired networks to secure wireless networks - what are the extra risks? *Computers & Security, 23,* 633–637. doi:10.1016/j.cose.2004.09.005

Takayama, L., & Kandogan, E. (2006). *Trust as an Underlying Factor of System Adminstrator Interface Choice.* Paper presented at the CHI'06 Montreal, Quebec, Canada.

The Internet IP security domain of interpretation for ISAKMP, RFC 2407 C.F.R. (1998).

The Internet Key Exchange (IKE), RFC 2409 C.F.R. (1998).

Tucker, A. B., Barnes, B. H., Aiken, R. M., Barker, K., Bruce, K. B., & Cain, J. T. (1991). A Summary of the ACM/IEEE-CS Joint Curriculum Task Force Report, Computing Curricula 1991. *Communications of the ACM, 34*(6).

van den Akker, T., Snell, O. Q., & Clement, M. J. (2001). *The YGuard Access Control Model: Set-Based Access Control.* Paper presented at the Sixth ACM Symposium on Access Control Models and Technologies, Chantilly, VA.

Wool, A. (2004). The use and usability of direction-based filtering in firewalls. *Computers & Security, 23,* 459–468. doi:10.1016/j.cose.2004.02.003

Section 3
Privacy and Trust

Chapter 8
Designing Privacy Aware Information Systems

Christos Kalloniatis
University of the Aegean, Greece

Evangelia Kavakli
University of the Aegean, Greece

Stefanos Gritzalis
University of the Aegean, Greece

ABSTRACT

A major challenge in the field of software engineering is to make users trust the software that they use in their everyday activities for professional or recreational reasons. Trusting software depends on various elements, one of which is the protection of user privacy. Protecting privacy is about complying with user's desires when it comes to handling personal information. Users' privacy can also be defined as the right to determine when, how and to what extend information about them is communicated to others. Current research stresses the need for addressing privacy issues during the system design rather than during the system implementation phase. The aim of this chapter is to elevate the modern practices for ensuring privacy during the software systems' design phase. Through the presentation of the modern methods, the basic privacy requirements that should be considered during system analysis are introduced. Additionally, a number of well known methods that have been introduced in the research area of requirements engineering which aim on eliciting and analyzing privacy requirements during system design are introduced and analyzed. Finally, a comparative analysis between these methods is presented.

INTRODUCTION

In the online world every person has to hold a number of different data sets so as to be able to have access to various e-services and take part in specific economical and social transactions. Such

data sets require special consideration since they may convey personal data, sensitive personal data, employee data, credit card data etc. Recent surveys (Business, 1998; PricehouseCoopers, 2001) have shown that people feel that their privacy is at risk from identity theft and erosion of individual rights. Therefore, it is obvious that privacy violation is an issue of great importance

DOI: 10.4018/978-1-61520-837-1.ch008

these days especially for the active online users that daily accomplish transactions in the new digital world. Another issue of great importance is the degree of trust that online users have on the information systems they use.

One of the main criteria that formulate users' trust regarding the use of an information system is the way that that their privacy is protected. The aforementioned issues along with the issue of handling privacy as a design criterion during the design and not the implementation phase of an information system consist the basic concerns of recent researches (Anton, 1996; Kalloniatis et al., 2009; Mouratidis et al., 2003a).

Research efforts aiming to the protection of user privacy fall in two main categories: security-oriented requirement engineering methodologies and privacy enhancing technologies. The former focus on methods and techniques for considering security issues (including privacy) during the early stages of system development and the latter describe technological solutions for assuring user privacy during system implementation. The main limitation of security requirement engineering methodologies is that they do not link the identified requirements with implementation solutions. Understanding the relationship between user needs and the capabilities of the supporting software systems is of critical importance. Privacy enhancing technologies, on the other hand, focus on the software implementation alone, irrespective of the organizational context in which the system will be incorporated. This lack of knowledge makes it difficult to determine which software solution best fits the organizational needs.

The aim of this chapter is to elevate the modern practices for ensuring privacy during the software systems' design phase. Through the presentation of the modern methods, the basic privacy requirements that should be considered during system analysis are introduced. Additionally, a number of techniques are mentioned for incorporating these requirements on the processes of the developing systems.

Specifically, in section 2, the term privacy along with the basic privacy requirements as they are formed from recent research are defined. In section 3, a number of well-known methods and techniques, proposed in the fields of requirements engineering and security engineering, which support the elicitation and management of security and privacy requirements during the early stages of system development, are mentioned. In section 4, a comparative analysis between these methods is presented along with the analysis of the comparison results. Finally, in section 5, the chapter concludes by addressing issues regarding the incorporation of privacy during system development.

PRIVACY AND PRIVACY REQUIREMENTS

In this section the basic concepts of privacy are presented. Additionally, the need for protecting privacy during the system design phase is stressed out and the basic privacy requirements during the analysis and design of information systems are presented.

Privacy

When a user types a text using a typical text editor he/she usually does not think if someone is close enough to observe and see the text being written. When the same user surfs the Internet is like walking in the middle of a Rolling Stone's Concert while hundreds of people can see what he/she doing or listen what he/she says (Cannon, 2004).

Most people use the Internet for its services either for personal or for recreational reasons. Internet and email services are offered from the Internet Service Providers (ISPs). These providers use servers that keep logs of Internet traffic, typically for tuning, performance monitoring etc. Also personal data are stored for various reasons like faster access to sources already been visited, history track, personalized services etc. These logs are always available to server administrators for reading and processing purposes.

The use of World Wide Web and email services is two of the most commonly services used by the Internet users today. By using these services, users leave a lot of personally identifiable information without even knowing it thus, putting their privacy into danger. How well do Internet users know the risk their personal data are involved to regarding the possible exposure to unknown third parties?

Privacy as a social and legal issue, traditionally, has been the concern of social scientists, philosophers and lawyers. However, the extended use of various software applications in the context of basic e-services sets additional technology-related requirements for protecting the electronic privacy of individuals.

Most e-services are relying on stored data for identifying customers, their preferences and previous record of transactions. Combining such data constitutes in many cases, an invasion of privacy. Protecting privacy is especially important in e-applications, since the greater collection and storage of personal data, the lower the trust of users using the specific applications. Towards the development of a global information society and with the rapid development of new information infrastructures among various states, a number of threats are created regarding privacy protection of the users using these resources and systems.

Privacy as a fundamental human right recognised in the UN Declaration of Human Rights, the International Convenant on Civil and Political Rights and in many other international and regional treaties has to be protected in a democratic society (Privacy International, 1999).

In general, privacy protection can be undertaken by:

- privacy and data protection laws promoted by governments

- self-regulation for fair information practices by codes of conducts promoted by businesses
- privacy-enhancing technologies adopted by individuals
- privacy education of consumers and IT professionals

The first definition of privacy was given by Warren and Brandeis in their article "The Right to Privacy" (Warren & Brandeis, 1890). The two American lawyers defined privacy as *"the right to be left alone"*. More recently, Alen Westin defined privacy as *"The claim of individuals, groups and institutions to determine for themselves, when, how and to what extent information about them is communicated to others"* (Westin, 1967).

In general the concept of privacy incorporates three aspects (Holvast, 1993; Rosenberg, 1992):

- Territorial Privacy, by protecting the close physical area surrounding a person
- Privacy of the person, by protecting a person against undue interference
- Informational privacy, by controlling whether and how personal data can be gathered, stored, processed or selectively disseminated

Personal data means any information concerning the personal or material circumstances of an identified or identifiable person (the data subject). Data protection is the protection of personal data in order to guarantee privacy and is only a part of the concept of privacy. However, privacy is not an unlimited or absolute right, as it can be in conflict with other rights or legal values, or because individuals cannot participate fully in society without revealing personal data (Fischer-Hubner, 2001).

In a networked society as the one we live today privacy is endangered and cannot be protected solely by laws and regulations. Developers and information system specialists must consider privacy as a technical requirement in the system under construction and more specifically it has to be considered early from the design phase of the development cycle as a separate design criterion.

For accomplishing the aforementioned goal and transform privacy from a general concept to a technical requirement the following privacy requirements have been defined (Fischer-Hubner, 2001; Koorn et al., 2004; Pfitzmann & Hansen, 2007):

- Authentication
- Authorisation
- Identification
- Data Protection
- Anonymity
- Pseudonymity
- Unlinkability
- Unobservability

These requirements cover different aspects of privacy during the use of an information system. Depending on the way that a system needs to be protected, regarding privacy, one or more of the aforementioned requirements are implemented.

In the following sections an analytical description of these requirements is presented, providing a clear definition of each concept, showing how they contribute to the realization of user privacy as a wider design goal.

Authentication

Authentication is the process of determining whether someone or something is, in fact, who or what is declared to be. In private and public computer networks (including the Internet), authentication is commonly done through the use of logon passwords.

Authentication is basically a security requirement rather than a privacy one. However, it plays a great role in the realisation of privacy as well. Specifically, when an entity requires access to a specific service offered by an information system, depending on the service authentication may be

mandatory or not. By examining each service both the entity requesting access and the personal information that are stored in the information system are protected since only eligible users can access restricted services while for simple services users are not forced to supply personal information for gaining access.

Authorisation

Authorisation is the process of giving specific access rights to an entity for accessing a service or a set of services in an information system. In a system with many multiple users, the administrator is responsible for assigning to each user specific rights depending on their roles and obligations in the system.

Authorisation, like authentication, is basically a security requirement. However, authorisation plays a critical role in privacy protection since in a system only authorised users must be able to access other users' personal information. By protecting the way users access personal information part of their privacy is also protected.

Authorisation usually follows authentication since an entity must be positively authenticated into a system and then to be allocated with the proper rights based on its role in the system.

Identification

Identification can realise privacy in two different ways. From the external's entity point of view, the lack of identification can protect its privacy while accessing a specific service. On the contrary, identification can protect the personal information stored in the system by identifying the entities which try to gain access on them.

Specifically, for the external entity, identification assists privacy protection by checking whether or not the required service demands authentication and authorisation or not. In case that there is no need for identifying the entity, the request for accessing the service is satisfied while the external entity does not provide any personal information to the system.

On the other hand, the private information that are stored to the system are fully protected since none unauthorised entity can gain access to them. Thus identification protects the stored data as well and so the data subjects' privacy.

Data Protection

The aim of the data protection privacy requirement is the protection of personal data from being processed and handled in a way opposite to the one described in current regulation and in the 95/46/ Directive of the European Union regarding *the protection of individuals with regard to the processing of personal data and on the free movement of such data* (EU Directive, 1995).

The main objectives of the Directive is on one hand the protection of privacy as a fundamental right, which is increasingly endangered in the networked society and on the other hand the requirement of a uniform minimum standard of privacy protection for preventing restrictions on free flow of personal data between EU member states for reasons of privacy protection.

The basic privacy principles addressed by related laws and the aforementioned Directive which are required so as to be guaranteed that the proper privacy protection exists when personal data is collected or processed, are the following (Fischer-Hubner, 2001):

- *Principle of lawfulness and fairness* (personal data should be collected and processed in a fair and lawful way)
- *Principle of the purpose specification and purpose binding* (The purposes for which personal data is collected and processed should be specified and legitimate. The subsequent use of personal data is limited to those specified purposes, unless there is an informed consent by the data subject

- *Principle of necessity of data collection and processing* (The collection and processing of personal data should only be allowed, if it is necessary for the tasks falling within the responsibility of the data processing agency)
- *Information notification and access rights of the data subjects* (Data subjects have the right to information, to notification and the right to correction, erasure or blocking of incorrect or illegally stored data. These rights should not be excluded or restricted by a legal transaction)
- *Principle of security and accuracy* (Appropriate technical and organisational security mechanisms have to be taken to guarantee the confidentiality, integrity and availability of personal data. Personal data has to be kept accurate, relevant and up to date)
- *Supervision and sanctions* (An independent data protection authority has to be designed and should be responsible for supervising the observance of privacy provisions. In the event of violation of the provisions of privacy legislation, criminal or other penalties should be predicted)

For the proper understanding and realization of the aforementioned principles, a number of basic privacy concepts are also defined in the Directive 95/46/EC as follows (EU Directive, 1995):

- *Data Subject* (The natural person participating in a communication)
- *Personal data* (any information relating to an identified or identifiable natural person (' data subject')
- *Identifiable Person* (one who can be identified, directly or indirectly, in particular by reference to an identification number or to one or more factors specific to his physical, physiological, mental, economic, cultural or social identity)

- *Processing of personal data* (any operation or set of operations which is performed upon personal data, whether or not by automatic means)
- *Personal data filing system* (any structured set of personal data which are accessible according to specific criteria)
- *Controller* (the natural or legal person, public authority, agency or any other body which alone or jointly with others determines the purposes and means of the processing of personal data)
- *Processor* (a natural or legal person, public authority, agency or any other body which processes personal data on behalf of the controller)
- *Third party* (any natural or legal person, public authority, agency or any other body other than the data subject, the controller, the processor and the persons who, under the direct authority of the controller or the processor, are authorized to process the data)
- *Recipient* (a natural or legal person, public authority, agency or any other body to whom data are disclosed, whether a third party or not; however, authorities which may receive data in the framework of a particular inquiry shall not be regarded as recipients)
- *The data subject's consent* (any freely given specific and informed indication of his wishes by which the data subject signifies his agreement to personal data relating to him being processed)

Anonymity

One of the basic privacy requirements is anonymity. Anonymity ensures that a user may use a resource or service without disclosing the user's identity (Fischer-Hubner, 2001). In 1990 Pfitzmann (Pfitzmann, 1990) defined anonymity in a formal way. Specifically, let R_U denote the event that an entity U (e.g. a user) performs a role R (e.g. as a sender or receiver of a message) during an event E (e.g. business transaction). Let A denote an attacker, and let NC_A be the set of entities that are not cooperating with A.

According to Pfitzmann an entity U is called anonymous in role R for an event E against an attacker A, if for each observation B that A can make, the following relation holds:

$$\forall U' \in NC_A : 0 < P(R_{U'}|B) < 1$$

However, anonymity for an entity U in the role R can only be guaranteed if the value P(RU|B) is not too close to the values 1 and 0.

Depending on the role that a user is performing during an event, the following types of anonymous communication properties exist. Firstly, the *sender anonymity* is defined, which means that the user is anonymous in the role of the sender of a message, while the receiver may be not. Secondly, the *receiver anonymity* is defined, which means that the user is anonymous in the role of the receiver of the message.

An entity U, in a role R for an event E against an attacker A is defined as *perfectly anonymous* if for each observation B that A can make,

$$\forall U' \in NC_A : P(R_{U'}) = P(R_{U'}|B)$$

observations give an attacker no additional information.

For an entity that potentially sends/receives during a communication the role of *perfect sender/ perfect recipient* exists, which means that the attacker cannot distinguish the situations where the sender/receiver actually sends/receives during the communication and which he/she does not.

In 2007 Pfitzmann (Pfitzmann & Hansen, 2007) defined anonymity as "*Anonymity of a subject from an attacker's perspective means that the attacker cannot sufficiently identify the subject within a set of subjects, the anonymity set*". The set contains all entities that participate in the communication and can potentially be identified by the possible attackers.

Pseudonymity

Pseudonymity has characteristics similar to anonymity in that an entity is not identifiable to third parties. When pseudonymity is applied users use pseudonyms for protecting the reveal of their real identity. Pfitzmann defines pseudonym as an identifier of a subject other than one of the subject's real names (Pfitzmann & Hansen, 2007).

In (Fischer-Hubner, 2001) pseudonymity is defined as the requirement that ensures that a user acting under one or more pseudonyms may use a resource or service without disclosing his identity. However, under certain circumstances it is possible to translate the pseudonyms into the user identities. Pseudonymity should be enforced if anonymity cannot be guaranteed, for instance because the user has to be still accountable for his actions.

Pfitzmann, Waiden and Pfitzmann (Pfitzmann et. al, 1990) provide a classification of pseudonyms according to the degree of protection that they offer. The categories are: a) Personal pseudonyms and b) role-pseudonyms.

A pseudonym is called *personal pseudonym* if it is related to an individual and used by its holder for various business transactions over some time period. Thus, a personal pseudonym is an alias for a user's name.

A pseudonym is called *role pseudonym* when it is not related to an individual but to the role that the individual is currently performing. Role pseudonyms offer higher degree of protection than personal pseudonyms because there are valid only for a specific role on a specific communication.

Unlinkability

Unlinkability expresses the inability to link related information. In particular, unlinkability is successfully achieved when an attacker is unable to link specific information with the user that processes that information. Also unlinkability can be successfully achieved between a sender and a recipient. In that case unlinkability means that though the sender and recipient can both be identified as participating in some communication, they cannot be identified as communicating with each other (Cannon, 2004).

In 1990 Pfitzmann (Pfitzmann, 1990) defined unlinkability in a formal way. Let $X_{E,F}$ denote the event that events E and F have a corresponding characteristic X. Two events E and F are unlinkable in regard of a characteristic X for an attacker A, if for each observation B that A can make, the probability that E and F are corresponding in regard of X given B is greater than zero and less than one:

$$0 < P(X_{E,F}|B) < 1$$

A stricter requirement for unlinkability is:

$$0 \ll P(X_{E,F}|B) \ll 1$$

E and F are *perfectly unlinkable* if for every observation B of the attacker A:

$$P(X_{E,F}|B) = P(X_{E,F})$$

which means that the attacker does not receive any information from the observation of the transactions E and F.

In 2007 Pfitzmann (Pfitzmann & Hansen, 2007) defined unlinkability as "Unlinkability of two or more items of interest (IOIs, e.g., subjects, messages, actions,...) from an attacker's perspective means that within the system (comprising these and possibly other items), the attacker cannot sufficiently distinguish whether these items of interest are related or not".

The ability to link transactions could give a stalker an idea of your daily habits or an insurance company an idea of how much alcohol your family consumes over a month. Ensuring unlinkability is vital for protecting user's privacy.

Unobservability

Unobservability protects users from being observed or tracked while browsing the Internet or accessing a service. Unobservability is similar to unlinkability in the sense that the attacker aims to reveal users identifiable information by observing rather than linking the information he/she retrieves.

In 1990 Pfitzmann (Pfitzmann, 1990) defined unobservability in a formal way. An event E is unobservable for an attacker A if for each observation B that A can make, the probability of E given B is greater than zero and less than 1.

$$0 < P(E|B) < 1$$

A stricter requirement for unlinkability is:

$$0 << P(E|B) << 1$$

meaning that if for each possible observation B that A can make, the probability of an event E is equal to the probability of E given B, that is P(E)= P(E|B), then E is called *perfectly unobservable*.

In 2007 Pfitzmann (Pfitzmann & Hansen, 2007) defined unobservability as "Unobservability of an item of interest (IOI) means: i) undetectability of the IOI against all subjects uninvolved in it and b) anonymity of the subject(s) involved in the IOI even against the other subject(s) involved in that IOI".

SECURITY AND PRIVACY REQUIREMENTS ENGINEERING METHODS

In the following sections a number of well-known security and privacy requirements engineering methods are presented. These methods have been proposed from the research fields of requirements engineering and information systems security. Most of these methods can be considered as standard requirements engineering frameworks which

support not only the elicitation and management of functional requirements but also of non-functional requirements during the early stages of the system design process.

The reason that this section focuses on the specific methods is because they take into account relevant concepts for clearly representing security requirements (which also include privacy requirements) and they define the way that these requirements can be transformed in specific policies for the system under construction.

The methods examined in this section are the following:

- The *NFR* (Non-Functional Requirement Framework) method (Chung, 1993)
- The *i** method (Yu, 1993)
- The *Secure Tropos* method (Mouratidis et.al, 2003a) (Mouratidis & Giorgini 2007)
- The *KAOS* method (Letier & van Lamsweerde, 2002b)
- The *GBRAM* (Goal-Based Requirements Analysis Method) method (Anton & Earp, 2000)
- The *RBAC* (Role-Based Access Control) method (He & Anton, 2003)
- The *M-N* (Mofett-Nuseibeh Framework) method (Moffett & Nuseibeh, 2003)
- The *B-S* (Bellotti-Sellen Framework) method (Belloti & Sellen, 1993)
- The *STRAP* (STRuctured Analysis for Privacy) method (Jensen et al., 2005)
- The *PriS* (Privacy Safeguard) method (Kalloniatis et al, 2008)

The NFR Method

NFR provides a systematic way of representing and recording the system design process in terms of interdependent design decisions on how to best satisfy non-functional requirements such as security, accuracy, performance and cost (Chung, 1993; Chung et. al., 2000). Non-functional requirements are treated as *softgoals* to be achieved, i.e., they are special type of goals which need to be clarified, disambiguated, prioritized, elaborated upon, etc. Although the NFR method might be applied in all phases of system development it has mostly been used in the early stages of system requirements specification.

The NFR operation can be seen as the incremental and interactive construction, elaboration and revision of a softgoal interdependency graph (SIG). The graph records the developer's consideration of softgoals and shows the interdependencies among softgoals. Interdependencies show refinements of general softgoals downwards into more specific (operational) softgoals. They also show the contribution of softgoals upon meeting other softgoals which may be at the same or higher level. To determine whether softgoals are achieved an evaluation procedure which considers interdependencies as well as developer claims. Finally, operationalised softgoals are linked to the system functional requirements thus, showing how they constrain the system implementation.

An important aspect of the NFR method is that the construction of the softgoal graph can be guided by previous experience recorded in the form of softgoal type classification catalogues (guiding softgoal refinement), correlation catalogues (guiding the identification of negative/positive contributions among softgoals) and method catalogues (guiding the identification of appropriate operationalisations).

Specific NFR catalogues have been constructed for security requirements also considering privacy (as part of the confidentiality security requirement), which makes NFR a useful tool for defining privacy requirement and identifying possible design alternatives.

The functionality of the NFR method is based on a formal model. In addition, a case tool namely the NFR Assistant (extending the previous Organization Modeling Environment (OME)) has been developed, which offers a graphical interface for building NFR models and guides developers in each step of the NFR way-of-working.

The *i** Method

The *i** method focus on the early stages of system design and aims on mapping organization's logic and context (Chung et. al, 2000; Yu, 1993; Yu, 1997). It is agent-oriented in the sense that it focus on systems agents and their social interdependencies. *i** was initially designed as tool for modeling, analyzing and redesigning organization processes. Recently, it has been used for modeling security and privacy requirements, as well (Liu et.al, 2002; Liu et al., 2003; Yu & Cysneiros 2002; Yu & Cysneiros, 2003). Similarly to the NFR method, modeling security requirements in *i** is based in the notion of *softgoal*. However, *i** does not focus on overall system goals rather on individual goals of system actors (active entities of the system into consideration). In fact, system actors are interdependent since the accomplishment of their goals depends on tasks performed by other actors or on resources shared by other agents.

Following an initial construction of a domain model, in terms of the actors involved and their dependencies, security analysis takes place using a number of analysis techniques. In particular, attacker analysis helps identify potential system abusers and their malicious intents (threats). Dependency vulnerability analysis helps detect vulnerabilities in terms of organizational relationships among stakeholders. Countermeasure analysis supports the dynamic decision-making process of addressing vulnerabilities and threats. This results into further refinement of actor softgoals. When all actors are considered an evaluation procedure is applied in order to decide whether the impact of threats and vulnerabilities has been eliminated to an acceptable level. Finally, role-based access control analysis further details actor roles in terms of the tasks they perform and the resources they depend upon thus, getting closer to a system design.

The *i** method meta-model is formally defined and is supported by the OME tool indicated previously in NFR.

The Secure Tropos Method

Secure Tropos is based on Tropos, which is a method for describing organizational systems and their environment (Mouratidis et al., 2003a; Mouratidis et. al., 2003b; Perini et al., 2001). It is applied in all stages of system development, adopting a homogeneous analysis from requirements analysis, to system design and implementation. Tropos organizational model is based on *i** adopting its basic concepts such as actors, goals, tasks and social dependencies. Additionally, Secure Tropos defines the term *secure entity* to describe any goals and tasks related to the security of the system. A secure goal represents the strategic interests of an actor with respect to security. A secure task is defined as a task that represents a particular way for satisfying a secure goal. A secure dependency introduces security constraint(s) on the relations between actors.

The security process in Secure Tropos is one of analyzing the security needs of the stakeholders and the system in terms of security constraints imposed to the stakeholders (early requirements analysis) and the system (late requirements analysis), identifying secure entities that guarantee the satisfaction of the security constraints, and assigning capabilities to the system (architectural design) to help towards the satisfaction of the secure entities. These capabilities are subsequently specified in AUML notation -- a UML extension of actor modeling (detailed design).

The Secure Tropos method is supported by formal models. In addition, a software tool (namely secTro) has been developed for designing the method's models as well as for analyzing these models.

The KAOS Method

KAOS is a goal-oriented framework, which focuses on the elaboration and specification of the system requirements (Anton & Earp, 2000; Dardenne et al. 1993; Dardenne et al. 1996; Letier & van Lamsweerde, 2002a); van Lamsweerde et. al., 1995; van Lamsweerde et. al., 1998; van Lamsweerde et. al., 2000). To this end, it provides a specification language for defining system requirements, as well as an elaboration method for eliciting such requirements.

From a methodological perspective, KAOS uses a goal elaboration method for capturing security requirements from high-level organizational *security goals*. Firstly the goal AND/OR structure is developed by defining goals and their refinement links until assignable goals are reached. Subsequently, the objects involved in goal formulation are defined (object capture). In a similar manner, operation capture identifies the objects state transitions that are meaningful to the goals and operationalisation derives pre/post/trigger conditions on operations ensuring that all terminal goals are met. Finally, responsibility assignment identifies all alternative responsibilities for terminal goals, makes decisions among refinements and assigns operations to agents, guaranteeing the terminal goals selected.

During the elaboration process *obstacles* and *anti-goals* preventing security goals from being met are also taken into consideration and a refinement procedure is followed until these obstacles are overcome.

KAOS offers to system designers a formal representation language, requirements engineering strategies as well as support through a software tool which assists designers in defining requirements derived from more abstract-generic goals.

The GBRAM Method

GBRAM (Anton & Earp, 2000) is another goal-oriented method. It provides a methodical approach for identifying and refining the goals that software systems must achieve, managing trade-offs among the goals, and converting them into operational requirements.

GBRAM has also been used to analyze privacy policies of e-applications and to systematically extract the requirements and goals underlying organizations' privacy practices. This process, called 'goal-mining', makes use of a *privacy taxonomy* that classifies the extracted requirements as either *protection goals* or *vulnerabilities*. Protection goals express the effort declared by an organization to honor/respect its customers' privacy. Vulnerabilities reflect potential threats to customer privacy as derived from current organization practices such as information collection, storage and transfer. The privacy goals are subsequently operationalised into system requirements, using a number of techniques including scenario analysis, identification of goal obstacles and constraints and refinement strategies via heuristics, guidelines and recurring question types.

Finally, the degree of compliance between requirements and policy statements is assessed and possible conflicts and ambiguities are resolved, thus aligning privacy requirements to organizations' privacy policy statements.

GBRAM is not supported by formal models. A software tool called SMaRT (Scenario Management and Requirements Tool) has been developed in order to support the GBRAM goal analysis. The tool also incorporates the privacy taxonomy.

The RBAC Method

He and Antón present an agent oriented framework for modeling privacy requirements as the as the contexts and obligations of Role-Based Access Control (RBAC) entities and relationships, thus linking privacy requirements to organizational access control policies (He & Anton, 2003).

It includes a context-based data model for representing roles that have permissions to access data objects and *privacy elements* linked to these objects. Three privacy elements are recognised namely purpose for accessing a data object, conditions that must be satisfied before a data access request can be permitted, and obligations i.e., actions that must be carried out if a request to access data is granted.

In addition, it provides a goal-driven role engineering process for eliciting and modeling these privacy elements. This process consists of two phases: Role Permission Analysis (RPA) and Role Permission Refinement (RPR). RPA uses goal-oriented, scenario analysis to identify the tasks to be performed by each role and associated RBAC permissions. In particular, the events of each scenario are modeled as RBAC permissions and the actors of the events are modeled as RBAC roles. The set of roles and permissions candidates generated from is further refined during the RPR phase in order to identify associated privacy elements.

RBAC is not supported by formal models. A guiding framework has been defined for expressing the relations between the roles and their restrictions on organisation's assets. Finally, a software tool has been developed but it does not cover the whole method since it does not support role analysis.

The M-N Method

The objective of this method is to elicit and analyze security requirements during the early stages of system design. It provides a meta-model in the spirit of the KAOS conceptual model (Moffett & Nuseibeh, 2003) but suggests an alternative way-of-working for dealing with security requirements.

In addition it adopts the security engineering concept of *asset* (anything valuable for the organisation, e.g. the backup files, the main server, etc.), together with *threats* of harm to those assets. Security goals aim to protect assets from those threats and are operationalised into security requirements.

The M-N way of working includes two steps. In the first step security risk analysis and management techniques are applied in order to identify and evaluate the risks to a system and make the decisions for the appropriate security measures. This step identifies assets and their valuation against relevant threats for those assets. In the second step, high-level security goals are defined in the sense of "what we are aiming to achieve". The determination of each security goal comes from each threat defined in step 1. Refinement of these security goals into security constraints is accomplished using KAOS goal refinement method.

M-N method is not supported by formal models nor software tools.

The B-S Method

Belloti and Sellen (Belloti & Sellen, 1993) developed the method B-S, which main objective is the elicitation of privacy requirements during system design phase and specifically during requirements specification.

Privacy requirements in B-S are represented as *privacy criteria* which designers should follow in order to define organization's vulnerabilities so as to be able to suggest a number of possible solutions for overcoming the identified vulnerabilities.

B-S elicits privacy requirements in the following way. Firstly, the designers evaluate the organization based on a list of privacy criteria defined by the method. Designers can also ask a number of questions (also defined by the method) to organization's employees in order to acquire the relevant knowledge and understand the organization's status in a faster and more reliable way. When designers receive the answers from the above mentioned process, the vulnerabilities of the system are noted and the designers decide how they will represent those vulnerabilities.

The method proposed in Hong, Lederer and Landay (Hong et. al., 2004) extends B-S by increasing the number and the quality of questions being asked as well as the criteria list on which the proposed solutions are based.

The B-S method is not supported formally. Also it does not offer any software tool for assisting developers during late design phases.

The STRAP Method

The STRAP method (STRuctured Analysis of Privacy) (Jensen et al., 2005) was developed with the objective of eliciting and analyzing privacy requirements during system design phase. In STRAP privacy requirements are represented as *vulnerabilities*. STRAP builds a goal-model which represents all functional requirements and vulnerabilities have the form of obstacles between the goals and the subgoals in the goal-model.

The method's way of working comprises of the following steps: a) Analysis, b) Refinement, c) Evaluation and d) Iteration. During the analysis phase, firstly all the system goals are analyzed. The result of this phase is the identification of all goals, the active entities and the basic system components. Additionally, relevant information is gathered regarding the context of the developing system and the first set of privacy requirements are elicited and recorded. Like B-S method, STRAP uses a number of questions for every goal and subgoal identified by the previous step. The result of the questions leads to the identification of various system vulnerabilities regarding privacy protection. Vulnerabilities then are recorded in the goal-model as obstacles between the goals and the relevant subgoals. Moreover, the identified vulnerabilities are categorised based on the Fair Information Practices list (Welfare, 1973). Before the categorisation an analysis on the vulnerabilities set is conducted in order to eliminate similar ones thus narrowing the set and facilitating the solutions suggestion phase.

During the refinement phase, designers eliminate and narrow the set of vulnerabilities by deleting all those vulnerabilities for which a solution is easy to implement. Specifically, for the vulnerabilities belonging to this category, designers immediately suggest a specific solution and they delete them from the vulnerabilities set.

In the next phase, the evaluation, the suggested design scenarios for the developing system are evaluated. All these suggestions are evaluated based on a number of criteria. The first criterion evaluates the proposed suggestions by examining the way each suggestion overcomes the identified vulnerabilities. The best scenario is the one that eliminates the most vulnerabilities thus decreasing the risk and assuring the proper privacy protection. STRAP suggests a number of criteria that guide the evaluation phase.

Finally, in the iteration phase the aforementioned steps are repeated since the system needs to be redesigned for including all possible alterations conducted during the previous phases. Particularly, the goal structure is re-examined, the necessary alterations take place, the vulnerabilities are redefined, the new scenarios are evaluated etc. The iteration phase ends when no alterations take place in the previous three steps.

STRAP is not supported by formal models. Also, no software tool has been implemented for guiding the designers and for the graphical representation of the method's models.

The Pris Method

PriS (Kalloniatis et al., 2008) is a security requirements engineering method, which incorporates privacy requirements early in the system development process. PriS considers privacy requirements as organizational goals that need to be satisfied and adopts the use of privacy process patterns as a way to: (a) describe the effect of privacy requirements on business processes; and (b) facilitate the identification of the system architecture that best supports the privacy-related business processes.

Pris method models privacy requirements as a special type of goal, the *privacy goal*, which constraints the causal transformation of organizational goals into processes. In particular, eight types of privacy goals are recognised namely a) authentication, b) authorisation, c) identification, d) data protection, e) anonymity, f) pseudonymity, g) unlinkability and h) unobservability.

From a methodological perspective reasoning about privacy goals in PriS comprises of the following activities. The first step concerns the elicitation of the privacy goals that are relevant to the specific organization. This task usually involves a number of stakeholders and decision makers who aim to identify the basic privacy concerns and interpret the general privacy requirements with respect to the specific application context into consideration. In addition, existing privacy requirements already forming part of the organization's goals are identified. The second step consists of two stages. In the first stage the impact of privacy goals on the organizational goals is identified and analyzed. In the second stage, the impact of the privacy goals on the relevant processes that realize these goals is examined and the processes that realize the privacy-related goals are identified and characterized as privacy-related processes. Having identified the privacy-related processes the next step is to model them, based on the relevant *privacy process patterns*. Business process patterns are usually generalized process models, which include activities and flows connecting them, presenting how a business should be run in a specific domain (Kavakli et al., 2007). The last step is to define the system architecture that best supports the privacy-related process identified in the previous step. Once again, process pattern are used to identify the proper implementation technique(s) that best support/implement corresponding processes.

PriS assists in the application of privacy requirements in the organizational context as well as in providing a systematic way of locating a number of system architectures that can realize these requirements. PriS way of working assumes that privacy goals are generic-strategic organizational goals thus being mentioned high in the goal model hierarchy.

PriS metamodel has a formal definition and graphical representation. Also, a software tool has been developed for guiding designers as well as for automating its way of working (Kalloniatis et al., 2009).

Figure 1. Comparison framework

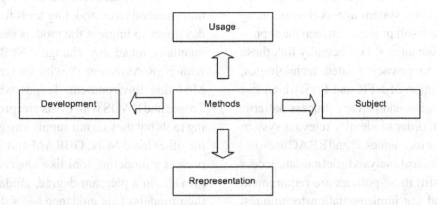

ANALYSING PRIVACY REQUIREMENT METHODS

The Analysis Framework

This section provides a critical analysis of the different strands of privacy-oriented RE research, based on a common framework for understanding privacy-oriented approaches.

This takes into account a number of different views, as they are expressed in the following questions: in which stage of the RE process are they applied *(usage)*; what type of privacy issues do they address *(subject)*; what mechanisms do they offer for expressing privacy issues *(representation)*; what kind of support do they provide to designers in applying proposed way-of-working *(development)*.

The analysis framework is presented in figure 1.

Analysis

Regarding the *usage perspective*, despite the fact that there is no common definition of the RE process, three general tasks to be performed have been identified: requirements elicitation, requirements specification and requirements validation. All methods provide suitable concepts for specifying privacy requirements (softgoals, security goals, etc) as well as a number of relationships among

them (AND/OR refinement, support / conflict relationship, obstacles) and other organizational concepts (actors, tasks, objects, processes). Specification of privacy goals is greatly affected by work in the area of goal modeling. This is natural since privacy requirements are non-functional (quality) requirements, and goals have long been used as a way to handle NFRs in Requirements Engineering. A great number also deals with the elicitation of privacy goals and their relationships, offering a number of techniques, including privacy taxonomies, security ontologies (which might be generic or linked to a specific domain), privacy requirement catalogues, risk analysis and scenario analysis. Few consider the requirements validation and mainly as qualitative goal-reasoning technique aiming to evaluate the degree to which privacy goals are satisfied (NFR, *i**, Tropos and KAOS). They are based on the identification of conflicts between privacy issues or obstacles that hinder their achievement. However, few actually offer techniques for eliminating / resolving such obstacles (e.g., scenario analysis used in STRAP). RBAC is the only method that validates privacy requirements against organizational privacy statements.

Regarding the *subject view*, most methodologies consider privacy requirements as overall system goals derived from business or organization goals, which constrain the system functional requirements. *i** and Tropos consider the privacy goals of individual system agents thus defining privacy as a trade-off process between the aspirations of different agents. Few actually link these requirements to privacy related technologies, with the exception of NFR and PriS which use method catalogues and privacy process patterns respectively in order to identify relevant system implementation techniques. *i** and RBAC use role-based access control analysis to define data access policies, but still these policies are requirement statements and not implementation techniques. GBRAM in addition, considers the relation between privacy requirement to business privacy policies, thus ensuring the compliance between system operation and business rules.

Regarding the *representation view*, most methods use a graphical notation of representing their models. NFR, *i**, Tropos, KAOS and PriS use decomposition techniques for representing the hierarchy among privacy goals and their subgoals. Beside the graphical notation these methods also use a formal language for formally representing their models. NFR and *i** use the Telos language. Tropos uses Formal Tropos specification language. Formal Tropos complements *i** by defining a textual notation for *i** models and allows the description of dynamic constraints among the different elements of the specification in a first order linear-time temporal logic. In KAOS security goals are formalized according to the pattern of behavior they require, using temporal logic. PriS way of working has also been expressed formally. M-N, B-S, STRAP and GBRAM do not use a formal language or a graphical notation for representing their models. M-N, B-S and STRAP use an informal textual approach for expressing its models. GBRAM defines tables where each goal is assigned with specific obstacles identified and scenarios for solving those obstacles. RBAC, does not use any graphical notation or formal language. Boolean expressions are used only for modeling the conditions specified in a privacy policy.

Finally, regarding the *development view*, most methods use modeling tools for helping the developer to impress the models generated or to manually make any changes. NFR framework with NFR Assistant, *i** with its Organizational Modeling Environment, Tropos with graphical Tropos and KAOS with Observier provide modeling tools but they do not supply any guidance. On the other hand M-N, GBRAM and RBAC don't present a modeling tool like Observier but they provide, in a pleasant degree, guidance through their models. This guidance helps the developer to resolve any possible conflicts between security goals or other security issues or even change the way the model is manipulating security requirements so far. NFR, *i**, Tropos and KAOS are very restricted since the developer can only achieve a good representation of the model without getting any suggestions on how to resolve impending problems. PriS uses a software tool for assisting its designers on creating its models. Models are represented in tree view but users cannot change this view to a more graphic one. Additionally, PriS guides its users throughout the whole usage of the specific tool starting from the elicitation of privacy requirements and continuing until the suggestion of the relevant implementation techniques.

The comparison results are shown in table 1.

DISCUSSION

Privacy is recognized internationally as a human right which has to be protected in the societies in which people participate and interact. Daily, more and more people use Internet since the services it offers improve their way and quality of living. This rapid development of Internet users led the service providers to increase the number of products and services they offer in order to improve the quality of services for the users and also to manage to remain in the market aiming for better profits.

Table 1. Comparison results

		NFR	i*	Secure Tropos	KAOS	GBRAM	RBAC	M-N	B-S	STRAP	PriS
Usage	Requirements Elicitation	✓	✓		✓	✓	✓	✓	✓	✓	✓
	Requirements Specification	✓	✓	✓	✓	✓	✓	✓		✓	✓
	Requirements Validation	✓	✓	✓	✓	✓				✓	
Subject	Overall Business Privacy Goals	✓			✓	✓	✓	✓	✓	✓	✓
	Privacy Goals of collaborating actors		✓	✓							
	Privacy enabling technologies	✓									✓
	Privacy Policies		✓				✓		✓		
Representation	Graphical notation	✓	✓	✓	✓						✓
	Formal language	✓	✓	✓	✓						✓
Development	Guidance Processes						✓	✓	✓	✓	✓
	Modeling Tools	✓	✓	✓	✓	✓					✓

This chapter defines the basic privacy requirements and presents a number of methods in the field of requirements engineering that incorporate concepts for clearly representing security & privacy requirements during system design and also study ways for transforming these requirements into specific system policies. The common theme in all these approaches is the realization that security and privacy requirements must be analyzed early during the system design phase and not later in the implementation phase since the time and cost needed for resolving any vulnerabilities in the later phase is much greater than in the design phase. The aim of the analysis presented in this chapter is to provide an overall picture of privacy-related RE research, enabling researchers to position current research efforts identify possible extensions.

Indeed, as can be seen in Table 1, security and privacy issues are not considered with equal significance during the various phases of system design. Many methods stop the analysis before reaching the implementation phase thus failing to successfully guide the designer throughout the whole phases of system development. The tendency for a holistic confrontation of security and privacy requirements from the early stages of system design through its implementation phase is expressed in the latest research methods (e.g. PriS).

To this end, requirement engineering methods could benefit from parallel research in the software engineering field and particularly in the area of privacy process patterns as a way to deal with specific privacy requirements during system development. For example, Romanosky et al. (2006) introduce privacy patterns interactions, distinguishing between patterns for system architecture issues and patterns for end-user support. Every pattern is described in terms of five fields namely a) context, b) problem, c) solution, d) Known Uses and e) Consequences. The patterns introduced are i) Informed consent for Web-Based transactions, ii) masked online traffic and iii) Minimal Information Asymmetry. The goal of these patterns is to describe how users can protect their privacy by both revealing less about themselves, and acquiring more information from the party with whom they are communicating. Sharing the same logic, a number of privacy patterns have been presented like Schumacher (Schumacher, 2002; Schumacher et al., 2006) and Schummer (2004).

Furthermore, the analysis framework presented in this chapter can assist requirements engineers in understanding and accordingly selecting the best fit for usage method, determined by the functionality needed (e.g., elicitation of privacy requirements, aligning privacy requirements to organizational policies, selecting appropriate privacy technologies, etc).

The applicability of a particular method is also determined by other nonfunctional or *situational factors*, relevant to the particular project. For example, even if elicitation of privacy requirements is needed in two projects, depending on the synthesis and culture of the design team, a more explorative approach based on the examination of alternative scenarios could be more appropriate in one case, whilst an approach based on interviews and consultations of business experts might better fit the other.

Other situational factors that affect the applicability of a method may include the use of appropriate tools that facilitate method execution and the familiarity of requirement engineers with the applied method.

To be able to compare the effectiveness of different methods a framework should take into consideration all these aspects, and this is the subject matter of our future efforts.

REFERENCES

Antón, A. & Earp, J. (2000). *Strategies for developing policies and requirements for secure electronic commerce systems*. 1st Workshop on security and privacy in e-commerce. ACM.

Antón, A. (1996). *Goal-based requirements analysis. ICRE'96*. Colorado Springs, Colorado, USA, IEEE 136-144.

Bellotti, V., & Sellen, A. (1993). *Design for privacy in ubiquitous computing environments*. Proceedings of the third european conference on computer supported cooperative work (ECSCW 93). G. In Michelis, Simone, C., Schmidt, K. 93-108.

Business, W. (1998). A Little Net Privacy, Please. Available at: www.businessweek.com last accessed: 17/12/2007.

Cannon, J. C. (2004). *Privacy, What developers and IT professionals should know*. Reading, MA: Addison-Wesley.

Chung, L. (1993). *Dealing with security requirements during the development of information systems*. The 5th international conference of advanced information systems engineering, CAiSE'93, Paris, France. *Springer Verlag LNCS*, *685*, 234–251.

Chung, L., & Nixon, B. Yu. E., & Mylopoulos, J., (2000). *Non-Functional requirements in software engineerin.*, Kluwer Academic Publishers.

Dardenne, A., & van Lamsweerde, A. (1996). *Formal refinement patterns for goal-driven requierements elaboration*. 4th ACM SIGSOFT International Symposium on the Foundations of Software Engineering pp: 179-190.

Dardenne, A., van Lamsweerde, A., & Fickas, S. (1993). Goal-directed requirements acquisition. *Science of Computer Programming*, *20*, 3–50. doi:10.1016/0167-6423(93)90021-G

EU, Directive (1995). *Directive 95/46/EC on the protection of individuals with regard to the processing of personal data and the free movement of such data*.

Fischer-Hubner, S. (2001). *IT-security and privacy-Design and use of privacy enhancing security mechanisms*. 5th International Conference on Applications of Natural Language to Information Systems, Versailles, France, Lecture Notes in Computer Science 1958, pp: 35-106 June 2000.

He, Q. & Antón, A., (2003). *A framework for modeling privacy requirements in role engineering.* International workshop on requirements engineering for software quality (REFSQ). Klagenfurt/Verden, Austria.

Holvast, J. (1993). *Vulnerability and Privacy: Are We on the Way to a Risk-Free Society?* Elsevier Science Publishers B.V. (North-Holland) IFIP-WG9.2 340 References Conference.

Hong, J., Ng, J., Lederer, S., & Landey, J. (2004). *Privacy risk models for designing privacy-sensitive ubiquitous computing systems. Symposium on Designing Interactive Systems archive.* Proceedings of the 2004 conference on Designing interactive systems: processes, practices, methods, and techniques. Acm-Press. Cambridge, MA, USA 91-100.

Jensen, C., Tullio, J., Potts, C., & Mynatt, E., (2005). *STRAP: A Structured Analysis Framework for Privacy.* GVU Technical Report, Georgia Institute of Technology, GIT-GVU-05-02.

Kalloniatis, C., Kavakli, E., & Gritzalis, S. (2008). Addressing privacy requirements in system design: The PriS method. [New York: Springer.]. *Requirements Engineering, 13*(3), 241–255. doi:10.1007/s00766-008-0067-3

Kalloniatis, C., Kavakli, E., & Kontellis, E. (2009) *PriS Tool: A Case Tool for Privacy-Oriented RE.* Proceedings of the MCIS 2009 4th Mediterranean Conference on Information Systems (MCIS 2009)", 27 September 2009, Athens, Greece

Kavakli, E., Gritzalis, S., & Kalloniatis, C. (2007). Protecting Privacy in System Design: The Electronic Voting Case. *Transforming Government: People. Process and Policy, 1*(4), 307–332.

Koorn, R., van Gils, H., Hart, J., Overbeek, P., & Tellegen, R. (2004). *Privacy Enhancing Technologies-White paper for decision makers.* the Netherlands: Ministry of the Interior and Kingdom Relations.

Letier, E., & van Lamsweerde, A. (2002a). Agent-based tactics for goal-oriented requirements elaboration. *24th International Conference on Software Engineering (ICSE '02)* pp: 83-93.

Letier, E., & van Lamsweerde, A. (2002b). *Deriving operational software specifications from system goals.* 10th ACM SIGSOFT International Symposium on the Foundations of Software Engineering pp: 119-128.

Liu, L., Yu, E., & Mylopoulos, J. (2002). *Analyzing security requirements as relationships among strategic actors.* SREIS'02. Raleigh, North Carolina.

Liu, L., Yu, E., & Mylopoulos, J. (2003). *Security and privacy requirements analysis within a social setting. IEEE, 11th international requirements engineering conference (RE '03).* California, USA: Monterey Bay.

Moffett, D. & Nuseibeh, B., (2003). *A framework for security requirements engineering. Department of computer science,* University of York, YCS 368.

Mouratidis, H., & Giorgini, P. (2007). Secure Tropos: A Security-Oriented Extension of the Tropos methodology. [IJSEKE]. *International Journal of Software Engineering and Knowledge Engineering, 17*(2), 285–309. doi:10.1142/S0218194007003240

Mouratidis, H., Giorgini, P., & Manson, G. (2003a). *Integrating security and systems engineering: Towards the modelling of secure information systems. LNCS 2681* (pp. 63–78). Berlin, Heidelberg: Springer-Verlag.

Mouratidis, H., Giorgini, P., & Manson, G. (2003b). *An ontology for modelling security: The tropos project. Proceedings of the KES 2003 invited session ontology and multi-agent systems design (OMASD '03)*-Lecture Notes in Artificial Intelligence 2773. V. Palade, R. Howlett and L Jain. United Kingdom, University of Oxford, Springer-Verlag 1387-1394.

Perini, P., Bresciani, P., Giorgini, P., Giunchiglia, F., & Mylopoulos, J. (2001). *Towards an agent-oriented approach to software engineering,* Modena-Italy.

Pfitzmann, A. (1990). *Diensteintegrierende, Kommunikationsmnetze mit teilnehmeruberprufbaren Datenschutz. Informatik-Fachberichte 234.* Berlin, Heidelberg, New York: Springer-Verlag.

Pfitzmann, A., & Hansen, M. (2007). *Anonymity, Unlinkability, Undetectability, Unobservability, Pseudonumity and Identity Management-A Consolidated Proposal for Terminology v.029.* TU Dresden ULD Kiel, 31 July 2007, Dresden.

Pfitzmann, B., Waidner, M., & Pfitzmann, A. (1990). *Rechsicherheit trotz Anonymitat in offenen digitalen Systemen. Datenschutz und Datensicherheit (DuD), No 6 (Part 1)* pp. 243-253, No 7 (Part 2) pp. 305-315.

PricewaterhouseCoopers. (2001). *Privacy: a weak link in the cyber-chain.* New York: E-Business Leadres Series, PricewaterhouseCoopers.

Privacy International, Electronic Privacy Information Center (1999). *Privacy and Human Rights - An International Survey of Privacy Laws and Developments.*

Romanosky, S., Acquisti, A., Hong, J., Cranor, L., & Friedman, B. (2006). *Privacy Patterns for Online Interactions.* Int. Conf. on Pattern Languages of Programs Conference (PLOP). New York, NY, USA.

Rosenberg, R. (1992). *The Social Impact of Computers.* New York: Academic Press.

Schumacher, M. (2002). *Security Patterns AND Security Standards.* European Conf. on Pattern Languages of Programs (EuroPLoP), Kloster Irsee, Germany

Schumacher, M., Fernandez-Buglioni, E., Hybertson, D., Buschmann, F., & Sommerlad, P. (2006). *Security Patterns: Integrating Security and Systems Engineering.* John Wiley & Sons.

Schummer, T. (2004). *The Public Privacy–Patterns for Filtering Personal Information in Collaborative Systems, (Tech. Rep).* Hagen, Germany: FernUnivesität in Hagen.

van Lamsweerde, A., Darimont, R., & Letier, E. (1998). Managing conflicts in Goal-driven requirements engineering. *IEEE Transactions on Software Engineering, 24*(11), 908–925. doi:10.1109/32.730542

van Lamsweerde, A., Darimont, R., & Massonet, P. (1995). Goal-directed elaboration of requirements for a meeting scheduler: Problems and lessons learnt. *2nd IEEE International Symposium on Requirements Engineering* pp: 194-203.

van Lamsweerde, A., & Letier, E. (2000). Handling obstacles in goal-oriented requirements engineering. *IEEE Transactions on Software Engineering, 26,* 978–1005. doi:10.1109/32.879820

Warren, S., & Brandeis, L. (1890). The Right to Privacy. *Harvard Law Review, 5,* 193–220. doi:10.2307/1321160

Welfare, US Department of Health Education and Code of Fair Information practises (The).

Westin, A. (1967). *Privacy and Freedom.* The Bodley Head Ltd.

Yu, E. (1993). *Modeling organisations for information systems requirements engineering.* 1st IEEE International Symposium on Requirements Engineering pp: 34-41.

Yu, E. (1997). Towards Modelling and reasoning support for early phase requirements engineering. *3rd IEEE International Symposium on Requirements Engineering* pp: 226-235.

Yu, E., & Cysneiros, L. (2002). Designing for privacy and other competing requirements. *2nd Symposium on Requirements Engineering for Information Security (SREIS'02)*

Yu, E., & Cysneiros, L. (2003). Designing for Privacy in a Multi-Agent World. Trust, Reputation and Security:Theories and Pactice. *Springer Verlag LNCS, 2631*, 209–223.

Chapter 9
Privacy Aware Systems:
From Models to Patterns

Alberto Coen-Porisini
Università degli studi dell'Insubria, Italy

Pietro Colombo
Università degli studi dell'Insubria, Italy

Sabrina Sicari
Università degli studi dell'Insubria, Italy

ABSTRACT

Enterprises have adopted various strategies to protect customers' privacy and to make public their policies. This chapter presents a conceptual model for supporting the definition of privacy policies. The model, described by means of UML, introduces a set of concepts concerning privacy and defines the existent relationships among those concepts along with the interfaces for the definition of privacy related mechanisms. The chapter also illustrates how the conceptual model can be used to build design solutions for three recurrent requirements for privacy aware systems concerning the definition of anonymity, the acquisition of the informed consent, and privacy policies enforcement. The proposed problems are separately illustrated and a solution based on the conceptual model is described for each of them. Finally, in order to assess the model and the design solutions, this chapter presents an example concerning the health domain.

INTRODUCTION

Nowadays privacy is a key issue and has received increasing attention from consumers, companies, researchers and legislators. Legislative acts, such as the European Union Directive[1] for personal data, the Health Insurance Portability and Accountability Act[2] for healthcare and the Gramm Leach Bliley Act[3] for financial institutions, require

governments and enterprises to protect the privacy of their citizens and customers, respectively. Although enterprises have adopted various strategies to protect customers privacy and to make public their privacy policies (e.g., publishing a privacy policy on web-sites possibly based on P3P[4]), none of these approaches include systematic mechanisms to describe how personal data are actually handled after they are collected.

This chapter proposes a conceptual model that provides a sound foundation for the definition of

DOI: 10.4018/978-1-61520-837-1.ch009

privacy policies. The model, which extends the work proposed by Coen-Porisini & al. (2007), is defined using UML[5] and represents a general schema that can be easily adopted in different contexts.

A privacy policy defines the way in which data referring to individuals can be collected, processed and diffused according to the rights that individuals are entitled to. Thus, the model introduces the concepts, such as users, data, actions, that are needed in order to define a privacy policy along with the existing relationships among them.

Although the model introduces all the elements that are required for the definition of privacy aware systems, it operates at a conceptual level with a very high level of abstraction. The main benefit of this approach is represented by the fact that the model is domain independent and it can be used in different contexts. In this way analysts and designers can describe privacy related features/requirements and then they can integrate them at design time in new or existing systems exploiting the visibility and usability of UML.

In addition to presenting the above mentioned model, this chapter introduces a design solution to some privacy related requirements that are common to most privacy aware systems. The way in which such design solutions are provided is by means of design patterns (Gamma et al. 1994), which constitute a set of design guidelines and schemes that can drive the designer towards the specification of a privacy aware system.

In this chapter, for space reasons, we focus on the following three requirements: anonymity, informed consent acquisition and privacy policy enforcement. Notice that other privacy related requirements such as pseudonymity, unobservability and so on can be addressed in the same way by developing appropriate design patterns.

Anonymity is an important requirement for a privacy aware system that aims at protecting the identity of the individuals whose data are handled by the system. In general, data can be categorized into different classes. Among them, one class includes data, referred to as *sensitive data*, concerning the private life, political or religious creed and so on, while another class contains data that describes the identity of individuals (e.g., first name, family name, etc.). A privacy aware system must assure that only authorized users can view the existing relationship between sensitive data and the identity of the individuals.

Informed consent is another important requirement for privacy aware systems that aims at assuring individuals that the system will use their data according to their will. For instance many legislations require that individuals must be informed of both the reasons for which the system will handle their data and the way in which data processing is performed. In such cases every individual has to provide an explicit consent before any data processing can occur.

Privacy policies enforcement requires that the activities performed within a system are checked against the privacy policy in order to avoid any privacy violation.

Finally, in order to test the effectiveness of the conceptual model and of the proposed design solutions, we discuss their application by means of an example concerning the healthcare domain.

In the last few years, hospitals, clinics, surgeries, and diagnostic centers have increasingly adopted Information Technology-supported healthcare solutions in order to manage health-related information and to provide a (semi)automated administration of clinical functions. As a consequence, due to its critical nature, the healthcare domain represents an ideal field for experimenting the definition of privacy mechanisms.

The rest of the chapter is organized in the following way: Section 2 provides an overview of the main related works concerning privacy; Section 3 introduces the privacy model and discusses its main features; Section 4 illustrates how the proposed model can be used for defining design solutions that achieve specific requirements such as the anonymity, the informed consent and the enforcement of privacy policies; Section 5 presents an application scenario in the healthcare domain; finally, Section 6 draws some conclusions.

BACKGROUND

While research on security is a well-established field, the issues that arise when dealing with privacy have been under thorough investigation only in the recent years. The research efforts aiming at the protection of individuals privacy can be partitioned in two main categories: Security-oriented Requirement Engineering (SRE) methodologies and Privacy Enhancing Technologies (PETs).

The former focuses on methods for taking into account security and privacy issues during the early stages of systems development, while the latter describes techniques to ensure privacy.

Several existing requirement engineering methodologies, such as Kaos (Lamsweerde & al. 2000), Tropos (Liu & al., 2002), Secure Tropos (Mouratidis & al., 2003a; Mouratidis & al., 2003b; Mouratidis & Giorgini, 2007), NFR (Chung, 1993; Mylopolulos & al., 1992) and GBRAM (Anton, 1996), can be used to take into account security issues at design level.

All the above methodologies address the problem of how to state as clearly as possible the requirements that an information system must satisfy in order to be considered secure (with respect to a set of given security policies). This is different from our goal, which is to define a conceptual model for representing privacy policies.

Kalloniatis & al. (2008) present a methodology, called PRIS, to incorporate privacy requirements into the system design process. PRIS is a requirement engineering methodology focused on privacy issues rather than on security requirements although it can be applied to the latter as well. It is based on the Enterprise Knowledge Development (EKD) framework, which is a systematic approach for developing and documenting organisational knowledge.

PRIS considers privacy requirements as organisational goals that need to be satisfied and adopts the use of privacy-process patterns as a way to: (1) analyse the impact of privacy requirement(s) on organisational goals, sub-goals and processes; and (2) facilitate the identification of the best system architecture supporting privacy-related business processes.

Thus, PRIS provides a complete view of the system including both the enterprise and privacy goals and refines the latter to identify a set of privacy requirements.

Instead, our approach introduces a set of concepts concerning privacy such as users, data, actions, and it defines the existent relationships among them, providing in this way a high level conceptual model, described in UML, that can be used to model privacy policies, which can be used to satisfy specific privacy requirements. In fact, in our approach, privacy requirements are addressed by introducing design patterns derived from the conceptual model. More specifically, our design patterns represent a set of design guidelines and schemes that can drive the designer towards the specification of a privacy aware system. In this way analysts and designers can describe privacy related features/requirements and then they can integrate them at design time in new or existing systems exploiting the visibility and usability of UML.

Agrawal & al. (2005) provide extensions to a RBDMS in order to express P3P privacy policies, at schema definition level. Furthermore, the authors define mechanisms for translating P3P privacy policies into a properly extended SQL-like data definition language. This is different from our approach, since what we propose is a conceptual model for the definition of privacy policies (not necessarily expressed in P3P) and for the specification of the needed functional modules of an application in order to enforce such policies.

Finally, in the field of SRE methodologies, several techniques have been proposed in order to protect private data from unauthorized accesses. Typical examples are anonymizing techniques based on data suppression or randomization (Mielikinen, 2004; Narayanan & Shmatikov, 2005). However, these techniques do not require the definition of any privacy policies; rather they can be used as building blocks for realizing them.

The literature also reports many works that propose patterns and design guidelines for addressing the requirements imposed by specific security and privacy problems.

Many security patterns were defined to address enterprise, architectural and user-level security (Yoder & al. 1997; Blakley & al. 2004; Chung & al., 2004; Steel & al., 2005; Schumacher & al., 2006), while, presently, only few contributions concerning privacy have been defined. Chung & al. (2004) define privacy patterns for ubiquitous computing domain.

Schummer (2004) describes the privacy masquerade pattern, i.e., a pattern that specifies how it is possible to prevent personal information from being improperly transmitted.

Schumacher (2002) describes two privacy patterns, named Pseudonymous Email and Protection against Cookies, respectively. The former specifies mechanisms for hiding the sender of an email message; while the latter describes how to control the cookies in a web browser. Romanosky & al. (2006) introduce privacy patterns for online interactions, distinguishing between patterns for system architecture issues and patterns for end-user support. Hafiz (2006) defines anonymity design patterns for various types of online communication systems, online data sharing, location monitoring, voting and electronic cash management.

All the just mentioned patterns, however, address specific application domain issues, while the solution that we propose in the following sections is more general and can be applied to different contexts.

MODELLING PRIVACY

In order to model privacy policies it is necessary to introduce concepts such as users, data, actions and so on. The rest of the chapter adopts the terminology introduced by the EU directive, which is summarized in what follows:

- *personal data* means any information relating to an identified or identifiable natural person (referred to as data subject or subject).
- *processing of personal data (processing)* means any operation or set of operations which is performed upon personal data, whether or not by automatic means, such as collection, recording, organization, storage, adaptation or alteration, retrieval, consultation, use, disclosure by transmission, dissemination or otherwise making available, alignment or combination, blocking, erasure or destruction;
- *controller* means the natural or legal person, public authority, agency or any other body which alone or jointly with others determines the purposes and means of the processing of personal data;
- *processor* means a natural or legal person, public authority, agency or any other body which processes personal data on behalf of the controller;
- *the data subject's consent (consent)* means any freely given specific and informed indication of his/her wishes by which the data subject signifies his/her agreement to personal data relating to him/her being processed.

Moreover, as a distinctive feature of a privacy policy, the processor is allowed to execute given processing actions only under explicit *purposes* and *obligations*. A purpose describes for what aims data are processed, and it can be defined either as a high-level activity (e.g., "marketing", "customer satisfaction") or as a set of actions (e.g., "compute the average price", "evaluate the customer needs"). An obligation is a set of actions that the processor guarantees to perform, after the data have been processed, that is after the execution of processing actions. Controllers define processing actions, as well as purposes and obligations and are required to verify that the former are executed according to the latter.

Subjects, whenever their data are collected, must grant their consent before any processing can be done and must be informed of the purposes and of the obligations related to any processing. Notice that, the consent can be given selectively that is, a subject can grant the consent for one purpose, while denying it for another one.

Starting from the previously presented terms we introduce several concepts and refinement. More specifically, data handled by a system are categorized into different classes. Among them, one class includes *sensitive data*, that is data concerning the private life, political or religious creed, health conditions and so on. Another class contains *identifiable data*, that is, data describing the identity of individuals (e.g., first name, family name, address, telephone, etc.).

Finally, we define the concepts of *role* and *function*. The role (Ni & al., 2007) specifies whether an individual is a subject, a controller or a processor, while the function represents the task performed by an individual within an organization. Thus, role is a cross cutting concept that is domain independent, while function strictly depends on the application domain. For example, in the context of a hospital information system we may have different functions, such as doctor, nurse, head-nurse, employee, and so on. Notice that, a function implicitly defines the set of actions that can be executed by an individual. For instance, a doctor is allowed to prescribe therapies and access patients' case histories, while an employee is allowed to make an appointment for a medical examination.

Figure 1. The privacy policy class diagram

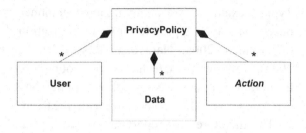

Therefore, given an application scenario, each individual is characterized by a pair function-role, which specifies his/her behavioral profile with respect to a privacy policy.

THE UML MODEL

In the following we introduce a UML model that specifies the concepts occurring in a privacy policy along with their relationships. First of all we describe the static aspects of the model, by introducing all the structural elements involved by means of Class diagrams. Then, we describe by means of several Sequence diagrams the behavioral aspects of the model by specifying the basic interactions occurring among the previously introduced structural elements.

Figure 1 depicts a class diagram that provides a high level view of the basic structural elements of the model.

A privacy policy is represented by means of class *PrivacyPolicy*, which is composed of three different classes named *User*, *Data* and *Action*, respectively. Thus, an instance of *PrivacyPolicy* is characterized by specific instances of *User*, *Data* and *Action*.

Let us focus on the classes introduced by the diagram:

- *User* represents an actor either interested in processing data or involved by such a processing. Users are characterized by functions and roles. More specifically *Function* represents the employment of a user in an application domain, while *Role* characterizes users with respect to privacy. As a consequence, *Role* is extended by three distinct classes to represent the different roles: *Subject*, which is anyone whose data are referred to, *Processor*, which is anyone who asks for processing data by performing some kind of action on them and *Controller*, which defines the allowed actions that can be performed by processors.

- *Data* represents the information referring to subjects that can be handled by processors. *Data* is extended by means of *Identifiable* data and *Sensitive* data. The former represents the information that can be used to uniquely identify subjects, while the latter represents information that deserves particular care and that should not be freely accessible. Moreover, *Data* is a complex structure composed of basic information units named *Field*. Class *Field* contains the attributes *name* and *content*. The former represents an identifier used to identify the information contained in the field, while the latter describes the information itself.

- *Action* represents any operation performed by *User* (usually *Processor*). Since in a privacy aware scenario a processing is executed under a purpose and an obligation, *Action* is defined as an abstract class that is extended by classes *Obligation*, *Processing* and *Purpose*. Moreover, *Processing* specifies an aggregation relationship with *Purpose* and *Obligation* so that each action can be recursively composed of other actions allowing the definition of complex actions in term of simpler ones. Finally, instances of *Action* are created by instances of *Controller* by means of the services provided by class *FactoryAction*.

Figure 2 provides a complete view of the aforementioned classes along with their relationships. For instance, the dependency relationship between *Action* and *Data* states that data are processed by actions, while the association between *Subject* and *Data* represents data ownership.

Notice that this model can be extended in order to support the definition of policies related to different application domains. For example, to specify privacy policies compliant with the Italian privacy legislation[6], it is necessary to extend the model introducing the concept of "judicial data". Such an extension can be easily obtained by introducing a class *Judicial* that extends class *Data*.

Furthermore, several interfaces have been introduced to model the flow of information among the instances of the different classes. In fact, an interface defines the services that a class can either implement or use (invoke).

The interface *ActionBehavior*, provided by class *Action*, is introduced in order to model action execution. *ActionBehavior* can be used by classes *Processor* and *Controller* that can invoke the method *run()* to represent the execution of an action. Notice that, each class extending *Action* inherits interface *ActionBehavior* and therefore may provide a specific implementation of method *run()*.

The interface *ConsentRequest*, provided by class *Subject*, is used to notify subjects of both the purposes and the obligations of any processing of their data. Thus, an instance of class *Controller*, taken its *id* and an instance of *Processing*, invokes the method *notify()* of interface *ConsentRequest* to notify a given instance of *Subject* that a processing on his/her data may occur. Interface *ConsentAcquisition*, provided by class *Controller*, is used by class *Subject* to allow its instances to grant or deny the consent to data processing. More specifically, the interface provides the method *setAgreement()*, that taken an instance of *Processing*, the *id* of *Subject* and a boolean value, notifies the controller whether the subject has granted or denied the consent to data processing.

Figure 2. The class diagram that describes the conceptual model

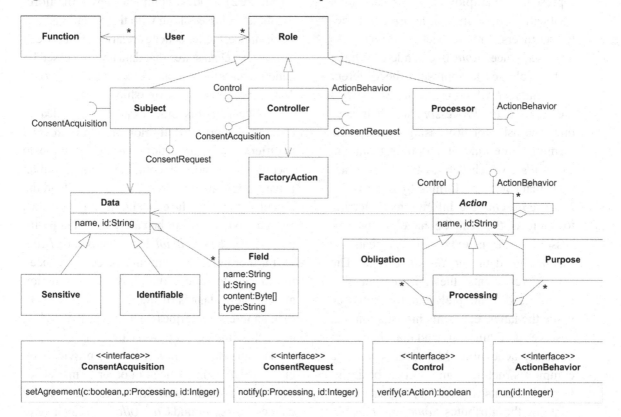

Finally, interface *Control*, defined by class *Controller*, is used by class *Action* to verify whether a given action can be executed, that is whether the subjects involved have granted the consent. Thus, interface *Control* provides the method *verify()* that, taken an instance of *Action*, returns whether the latter is authorized that is, the consent has been granted.

Notice that this model is meant to describe all the activities related to privacy even though some of them may occur outside the system. For example let us suppose that a new customer wants to open a checking account in a traditional bank. In this case he/she may interact with a bank employee who will provide the customer with all the information concerning the privacy policy. Before actually registering the new customer in the system, the employee asks him/her to sign a statement in which the customer grants the consent

Figure 3. The general scenario

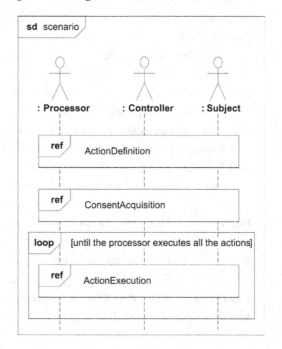

to data processing. Such an interaction is not supported by the system since it takes place by oral explanations and documents reading. However, from our point of view this corresponds to having the employee invoking the method *notify()* of *ConsentRequest* and then the customer invoking the method *setAgreement()*.

On the contrary, if we consider a new customer of an on-line bank the system will support all the interactions needed to get the informed consent. In both cases the way in which the interaction is modeled does not change, the difference being to which extent the activities are directly supported by the system rather than being specified by human executed procedures.

Although the class diagram of Figure 2 faithfully represents the components of privacy policies, it does not express any dynamic aspect. This can be done by means of UML Sequence diagrams and therefore in what follows we present some Sequence diagrams modeling general interaction schemes that are common to any privacy aware system. Notice that such diagrams can be specialized and extended for specific needs.

The sequence diagram of Figure 3 reports a general scenario that introduces the main actors along with the basic activities that can occur in a privacy aware system. The scenario refers to three different tasks, named *ActionDefinition*, *ConsentAcquisition* and *ActionExecution*, each of which is represented by means of a Sequence diagram. According to the semantics of UML Sequence diagram, such internal scenarios are sequentially executed.

The first task, named *ActionDefinition*, describes how it is possible to define new actions. Notice that actions can be exclusively defined by users characterized by the role of *Controller*, using the services provided by class *FactoryAction*.

Class *FactoryAction* provides several methods to allow controllers to create new actions. In particular the class allows the definition of the following basic actions:

- Data creation. The method *defData(Data obj, String fieldName, String fieldType, String fieldId)* returns a new basic action whose execution creates an instance of class *Field* associated with *obj*. For instance *defData(d1, "family name", "String", "001")*, inserts a new data field named "family name" of type String into d1 (an instance of class *Data*).

- Data writing. The method *defWrite(Field f, Byte[] content)* returns an action whose execution updates the content of field *f*. For instance, the method *defWrite()* allows one to initialize the content of the previously created field, representing the family name, to the value "Smith".

- Data reading. The method *defRead(Field f)* returns an action whose execution reads the content of the field *f*.

The definition of basic actions is described in the Sequence diagram, named *BasicActionDefinition*, shown in Figure 4.

Such basic actions represent the behavioral unit for the definition of *Processing*, *Obligation* and *Purpose*. Once all the required basic actions are defined, the controller defines a new complex action by invoking the method *defAction(...)*, provided by *FactoryAction (seeFigure 5)*. The method *defAction(...)* takes as input the list of actions composing the new action along with its type (i.e., *Purpose*, *Obligation* or *Processing*). Notice that a *Processing* action is defined by composing instances of *Purpose* and *Obligation*, hence the purpose and the obligation associated with any instance of *Processing* can be easily retrieved.

Actions definition can be carried out by means of two different scenarios. The first one, shown in Figure 6, represents the most common scenario in which, all the needed actions are predefined by a controller.

In fact, for each application domain it is possible to identify a set of actions that almost every

Figure 4. The basic actions definition scenario

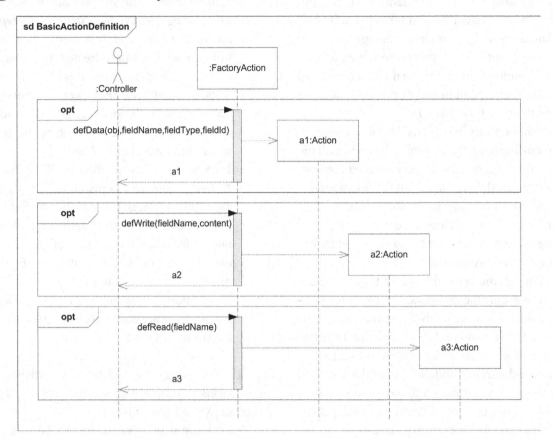

processor will try to execute in order to carry out his/her duty. Such actions represent the services that the company provides to its customers (subjects). In this case the subject consent is acquired *a priori*. As an example, let us consider the case of a potential bank customer that wants to open a checking account. The customer is informed that if he/she will request to make a domestic bank transfer, his/her data will be processed for the purpose of complying with his/her request under the obligation of notifying national authorities whenever the transferred amount exceeds a given threshold. Notice that in this scenario the customer is informed and required to grant consent even if he/she will never request any bank transfer to be made.

In the second scenario, shown in Figure 7, the action definition is triggered by a processor that

needs to execute a not yet defined action. Therefore, this scenario describes a situation in which specific actions are built in order to fulfill a specific request coming from a processor; in this case the subject is required to grant consent for any action for which the consent was not granted *a priori*. In this case, the processor interacts with the controller in order to define the purpose, the obligation and the needed processing. In particular, the processor sends his/her *Id* to the controller, which, in turn, instantiates three actions (a purpose, an obligation and a processing) requested for processing the data. Notice that *Processing* represents the intention to perform a specific data processing, which can be carried out only after the involved subject has granted the consent.

As an example, let us consider the case of an actual bank customer requesting to make an in-

Figure 5. The action definition scenario

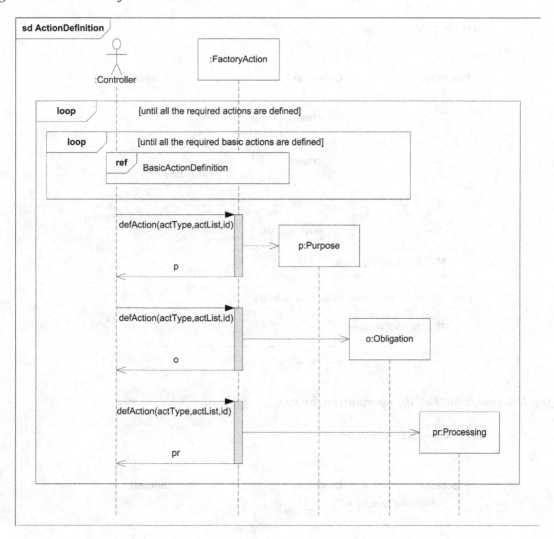

ternational bank transfer. Since international bank transfers are less common than domestic ones, the customer was not informed nor he/she granted the consent when he/she opened the checking account. Therefore, when the customer requests the international bank transfer, he/she is informed that his/her data will be processed for the purpose of complying with his/her request under the obligation of notifying the National Security Agency. Notice that in this scenario the customer is informed and required to grant consent only when he/she requests for the first time to make an international bank transfer.

In both scenarios before action execution the *Subject* has been notified of the processing and, as described in Figure 8, he/she can grant or deny the consent.

Finally, the scenarios terminate with the execution of the authorized actions (if any). As specified by the loop construct, depending on the processor needs, actions once authorized, can be executed multiple times.

Figure 6. Action definition, the most typical scenario

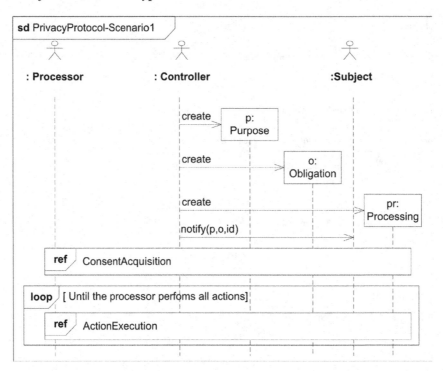

Figure 7. Action definition, the alternative scenario

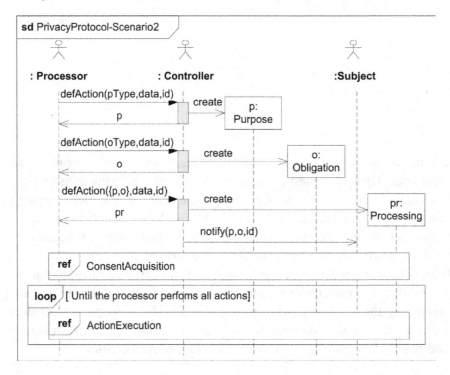

Figure 8. The consent acquisition scenario

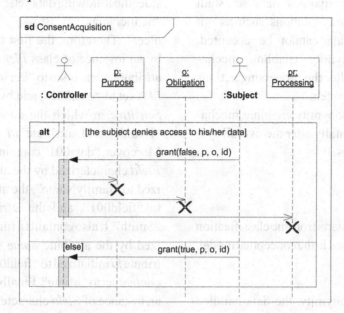

TOWARDS DESIGN SOLUTIONS

Anonymity, informed consent acquisition and enforcement of privacy policies are fundamental requirements for privacy aware systems that can be used both to test the effectiveness of the model and to introduce design solutions based on extensions/refinements of the model itself. In what follows we present three different design patterns providing a design solution for each of the above mentioned requirements. The same approach is used to provide solutions to other privacy requirements such as pseudonymity, unobservability and so on. Therefore, privacy requirements can be satisfied by providing appropriate design patterns providing the needed extensions to the conceptual model. Notice that such extensions should be viewed as being part of a development process in which one starts from a high level description and moves towards the solution by adding details concerning the different aspects of a privacy aware system.

Anonymity

Anonymity states that sensitive data managed by a system, cannot be used to retrieve the identity

of the data owner, that is the subject to whom data refer, without an explicit authorization. For example, let us consider a hospital information system that stores both health related data (sensitive data) and personal data of hospital patients. Hospital doctors may be allowed to access both kinds of data when they have to make a diagnosis, while if the hospital staff is conducting some statistics, the may be allowed to access only sensitive data without being able to retrieve the identity of patients.

The aim of this pattern is to introduce a domain independent solution schema that drives the construction of anonymity assurance mechanisms, which prevent the identification of individuals starting from their data.

Requirements

Several requirements must be taken into account when defining anonymity assurance mechanisms (Hafiz, 2006):

- Identity masking. Anonymity enabling mechanisms shall mask the identity of subjects.

- Usability. An anonymous data set shall be usable. Extreme solutions such as not releasing any data cannot be accepted. Moreover, anonymity enabling mechanisms shall not alter the processing actions performed by a system.

- Performance. Anonymity enabling mechanisms shall minimally alter the overall system performances.

Solution

The proposed solution starts from the classification of data and users proposed in the conceptual model.

Data Structure

In order to define anonymity, the data handled by a system need to be suitably structured. Data are composed of fields that, depending on their characteristics, are grouped into sensitive and identifiable subsets. Moreover, a data type may be characterized by a hierarchical structure composed of other data types possibly classified as sensitive or identifiable.

In order to keep the link between identifiable and sensitive data, we introduce a reference field to the data structure used for identifiable data. This is done by means class *RefField*, which extends class *Field* of the conceptual model, as shown in Figure 9. The (inherited) attributes of Class *RefField* are used in the following way: the attribute *name* is set to the name of the data to which it refers, while the attribute *content* is set to the value of the attribute *id* of the instance of *Data* to which it refers.

For example, let us consider the definition of a data structure composed of the fields "familyName", "city" and "disease". Fields "familyName" and "city" identify the data owner, while "disease" represents a sensitive information. As a consequence two different data types are defined. The former, named "Person", is composed of the identifiable fields, while the latter, named "Health", contains the sensitive one. Let us con-

sider the following data sets: 1) "Smith", "Milan", "hemicranias"; 2) "Brown", "New York", "gastric ulcer". Therefore, the first triplet is represented by an instance of class *Identifiable* in which the attribute *name* is set to "Person", and the attribute *id* is set to "data001", and by an instance of class *Sensitive* in which the attribute *name* is set to "Health" and attribute *id* is set to "data003". Moreover, "data001" contains an instance of class *Field* characterized by the attribute *name* initialized to "familyName", the attribute *id* initialized to "field001", and the attribute *content* set to "Smith". It also contains a further *Field* characterized by the attribute *name* set to "city", the attribute *id* initialized to "field002", and the attribute *content* set to "Milan". Finally, "data003" contains an instance of *Field* characterized by the attribute *name* initialized to "Disease", the attribute *id* initialized to "field005", and the attribute *content* set to "hemicranias". In order to represent the link between the identifiable data represented by "data001" and the sensitive data represented by "data003", "data001" contains an instance of *RefField* in which the attribute *name* is set to "Health", the attribute *id* is set to "ref001" and the attribute *content* is set to "data003". Figure 10 reports the structure of such data sets by means of a Composite Structure Diagram.

In order to prevent the identification of data owners starting from their sensitive data, instances of *Identifiable* may own references to instances of *Identifiable* or *Sensitive*, while instances of *Sensitive* can own only references to instances of *Sensitive*. In other words, instances of *Sensitive* cannot own any reference to instances of *Identifiable*.

A second issue that must be taken into account concerns the possibility that starting from identifiable data one can access the associated sensitive data, by following the reference fields. However, the system should prevent non authorized users of the system to follow such references, that is there may be some users that can access identifiable data without being authorized to access sensitive data.

Figure 9. Extensions of the conceptual model to support anonymity

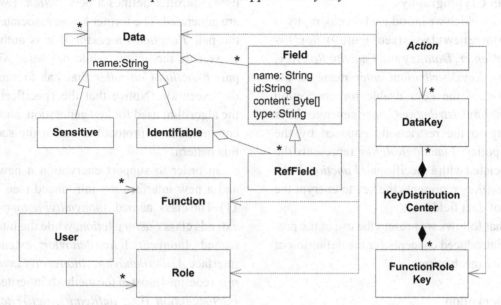

Figure 10. The composite structure diagram that describes the example

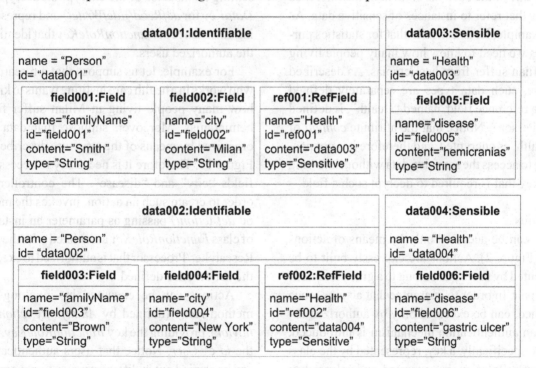

The way in which we prevent non authorized accesses to sensitive data is based on cryptography. Notice that at this level we do not need to choose any particular encryption technique (e.g., public key, symmetric key, etc.), since the needed extensions of the conceptual model are independent from encryption techniques.

Handling Cryptography

The way in which we introduced cryptography is based on three new classes (see Figure 9): *KeyDistributionCenter*, *DataKey* and *FunctionRoleKey*. The class *KeyDistributionCenter* manages the generation of the keys usable for encryption purposes. *KeyDistributionCenter* generates keys according to the restrictions imposed by the privacy policy. *FunctionRoleKey* represents the key associated with a specific pair *Function-Role*, while *DataKey* represents the key to encrypt the content of data fields.

In what follows we present the use of the previously introduced concepts for the definition of anonymity mechanisms.

Data Encryption

A key, named *DataKey*, is generated to encrypt the value of the attribute *content* of the reference fields that refer to instances of sensitive data. As an example, let us consider that for statistics purposes we need to know how many people living in Milan suffer from hemicranias. As described above, such data types are separately defined and a reference field, named "Health", is defined on "Person". Notice that the attribute *content* of "Health" is encrypted, and therefore it is not possible to access the sensitive data without knowing the key that is required to decrypt such a field.

Actions

Data can be accessed only by means of actions (see Figure 2). Actions are expressly built to be executed by users that belong to a given function-role pair. In order to guarantee that actions, once defined, can be executed only by authorized users, an authentication mechanism is introduced. More specifically, a key, represented by the class *FunctionRoleKey*, is generated and released to the authorized users.

FunctionRoleKey instances are handled by *KeyDistributionCenter*, which provides generation and secure communication mechanisms like the ones proposed by Kerberos[7]. Whenever a user-controller defines a new *Action*, two keys are generated. The former key is associated with the pair *Function-Processor* that is authorized to execute the action, while the latter with the pair *Function-Controller* that has to supervise the execution. Notice that the specification of the algorithm used for key generation, and of the communication protocol is out of the scope of this pattern.

In order to support encryption a new class and a new interface are introduced (see Figure 11). The class, named *AnonymityFactoryAction*, extends class *FactoryAction*, while the interface, named *AnonymityActionBehavior*, extends the interface *ActionBehavior*. *AnonymityFactoryAction* redefines most of the methods inherited from *FactoryAction* (i.e., *defRead()*, *defWrite()* and *defAction()*) by adding a new parameter representing an instance of the encryption/decryption *DataKey* for *defRead()/defWrite()* and representing an instance of *FunctionRoleKey* that identifies the authorized users.

For example, let us suppose that a researcher who works in a health care institute wants to know how many people living in Milan suffer from hemicranias. Moreover, suppose that data are organized by means of the structure described in Figure 10. Therefore it is necessary to access the fields "city" and "disease". The controller, in order to create such an action, invokes the method *defAction()* passing as parameter an instance of class *FunctionRoleKey* associated with the pair Researcher/Processor that is authorized to execute the action once defined.

Actions can be executed by invoking the method *run()* (defined by *AnonymityActionBehavior*), providing the key *FunctionRoleKey*, and the *id* of *User*. Notice that users authentication can be carried out in different ways. For example, the first task of method *run()* may check whether the function-role key provided by the user is the same key that was set at action definition time.

Figure 11. Extensions of the conceptual model to support anonymity

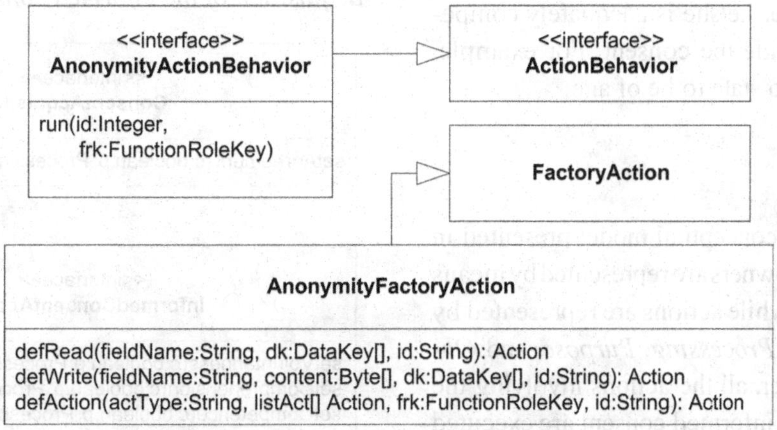

Consequences

The pattern has the following benefits.

- Privacy. The separation of sensitive data from identifiable data, and the adoption of encryption techniques makes it more difficult to associate sensitive data with the identity of data owners.
- Minimal user involvement. The users are not required to modify their normal activities.

A not properly defined implementation of this pattern may suffer from the following weaknesses.

- Usability. A too high granularity level of encryption mechanisms can undermine the usefulness of data. As an example, in the case of database applications, if all the data entries are encrypted, the resultant dataset may be hardly used even by authorized users.
- Overhead and delay. The application of encryption mechanisms requires adequate computational resources. Hence, the overall system performances may worsen, and delays and/or overheads can be generated. In order to guarantee an adequate level of

usability and privacy, it is necessary to balance the usage of encryption techniques.

Informed Consent

Informed consent states that individuals (i.e., data owners) must be informed on the purposes of any processing involving their data. Therefore, the goal of this pattern is to provide a basic schema to deal with the acquisition of the informed consent.

Requirements

Several requirements need to be taken into account in order to define informed consent acquisition mechanisms:

- Disclosure. The data owner has to be informed of the processing purposes, before processing can take place.
- Agreement. The data owner has to reply to the requests to access his/her data by specifying whether he/she agrees upon.
- Comprehension. The data owner has to state whether he/she understood how the requested information will be used.
- Voluntariness. The data owner has to ensure whether his/her consent is given without any coercion or external influence.

- Competence. The data owner has to declare whether he/she is adequately competent to provide the consent. For example, he/she has to state to be of age.

Solution

According to the conceptual model presented in this chapter, data owners are represented by means of class *Subject*, while actions are represented by means of classes *Processing*, *Purpose*, and *Obligation*. Moreover, all the actions involving the acquisition of the informed consent are executed by an instance of class *Controller*. Therefore, the acquisition of the informed consent requires user-subjects and user-controllers to communicate among them using the method of the interface *ConsentAcquisition* provided by class *Controller*. However, in order to deal with the requirements of competence, voluntariness and comprehension it is necessary to extend the interface *ConsentAcquisition* introducing a new interface, named *InformedConsentAcquisition* (see Figure 12).

Such an extension satisfies all the previously introduced requirements, as discussed in what follows:

- Disclosure. In order to inform *User-Subject* of the processing purpose, *User-Controller* invokes the method *notify()* of the interface *ConsentRequest* by specifying the purpose of the processing and under which obligation the action will be executed.
- Agreement. In order to reply to the request of *User-Controller*, *User-Subject* invokes the method *setAgreement()* by specifying whether he/she granted the consent for processing his/her data.
- Comprehension. The *User-Subject*, in order to confirm whether he/she understood how the requested information will be used, invokes the method *setComprehension()*.
- Voluntariness. The *User-Subject*, in order to ensure whether his/her consent is given

Figure 12. The extensions required to support the acquisition of the informed consent

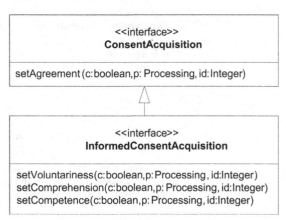

without any coercion or external influence, invokes the method *setVoluntariness()*.
- Competence. The *User-Subject*, in order to declare whether he/she is adequately competent to provide the consent, invokes the method *setCompetence()*.

The UML Sequence diagram of Figure 13 describes a consent acquisition scenario. Notice that the sequence of actions proposed is only one of the many scenarios that can be defined. In other words, *Subject* has to invoke all the methods of the interface *InformedConsentAcquisition*. In case *Subject* does not grant his/her consent, all the actions that were defined for accessing his/her data are destroyed.

Consequences

This pattern offers the following benefits:

- Trust: the exchange of clear and complete information increases the individuals confidence in the system.
- Protocol: the proposed pattern, besides defining the fundamental interactions among the actors involved in a consent acquisition scenario, supports the definition of different interaction protocols.

Figure 13. The consent acquisition scenario

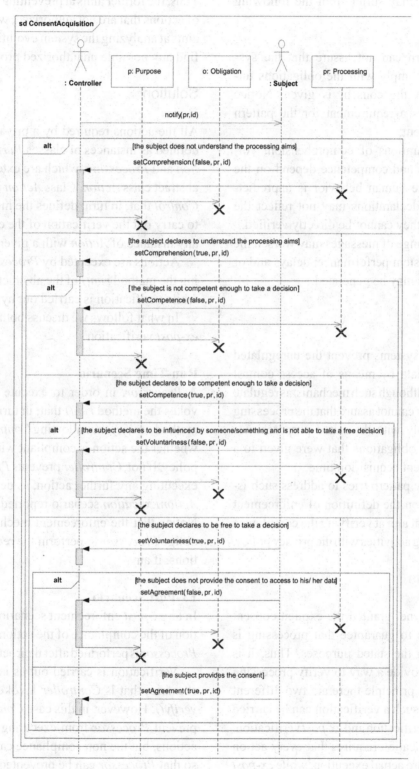

This pattern may suffer from the following weaknesses:

- The pattern can not assure that the system will comply with the obligations under which the consent is given. Notice that this is a requirement for the pattern Enforcement.
- The declarations of comprehension, voluntariness and competence depend on the user. Since human behavior is unpredictable, the declarations may not reflect the truth and they cannot be directly verified.
- The exchange of messages may worsen the overall system performance: delays and/or overheads may be generated.

Enforcement

Privacy aware systems prevent the unregulated disclosure of data by means of access control mechanisms. Although such mechanisms regulate data access they cannot assure that the processing activities comply with the stated purposes, nor with the stated obligations that were given to a *Subject* at consent acquisition time.

This privacy pattern tries to address such issues, focusing on the definition of enforcement mechanisms that aim at verifying the compliance of the processing activities with the privacy policy.

Requirements

Once a data owner granted the explicit consent the system has to guarantee that processing is compliant with the stated purposes. Thus, it is necessary to provide a way to verify processing compliance. In principle there are two different ways in which such a verification can be carried out: run-time verification and *ex-post* verification. Run-time verification requires that every action is checked before actual execution, while *ex-post* verification requires that actions are verified once they are executed (e.g., audit-based mechanisms).

Thus, the former aims at preventing the execution of actions that are not authorized, while the latter aims at analyzing the system evolution in order to find any possible unauthorized processing.

Solution

All the actions required by a privacy policy are defined as instances of classes *Purpose*, *Obligation* and *Processing*, which are extensions of the abstract class *Action*. Class *Action* uses interface *Control* that, in turn, defines the method *verify()* to carry out the verification of the compliance of any instance of *Action* with a given policy.

Actions are executed by *Processor* by invoking the method *run()* of the abstract class *Action*, while verification is carried out by *Controller*.

In what follows we discuss both run-time and *ex-post* verification.

Run-Time Scenario

A *Processor*, in order to execute an action invokes the method *run()* that, in turn, invokes the method *verify()* thus allowing *Controller* to check whether the action is compliant with the privacy policy. If not, *Controller* prevents *Processor* from executing any further action, as described in the *ActionExecution* scenario reported in Figure 14. Notice that the enforcement mechanism cannot oblige *Processor* to perform the required obligations, if any.

Ex-Post Scenario

In an *ex-post* enforcement scenario, the verification of the compliance of the actions executed by *Processor* is performed after their actual execution.

Verification is carried out as in the run-time scenario, that is *Controller* invokes the method *verify()*. However, in this case *Controller* cannot prevent *Processor* from executing unauthorized actions, but the non compliance can be recorded so that *Processor* can be prevented from executing other actions.

Figure 14. Enabling run-time enforcement

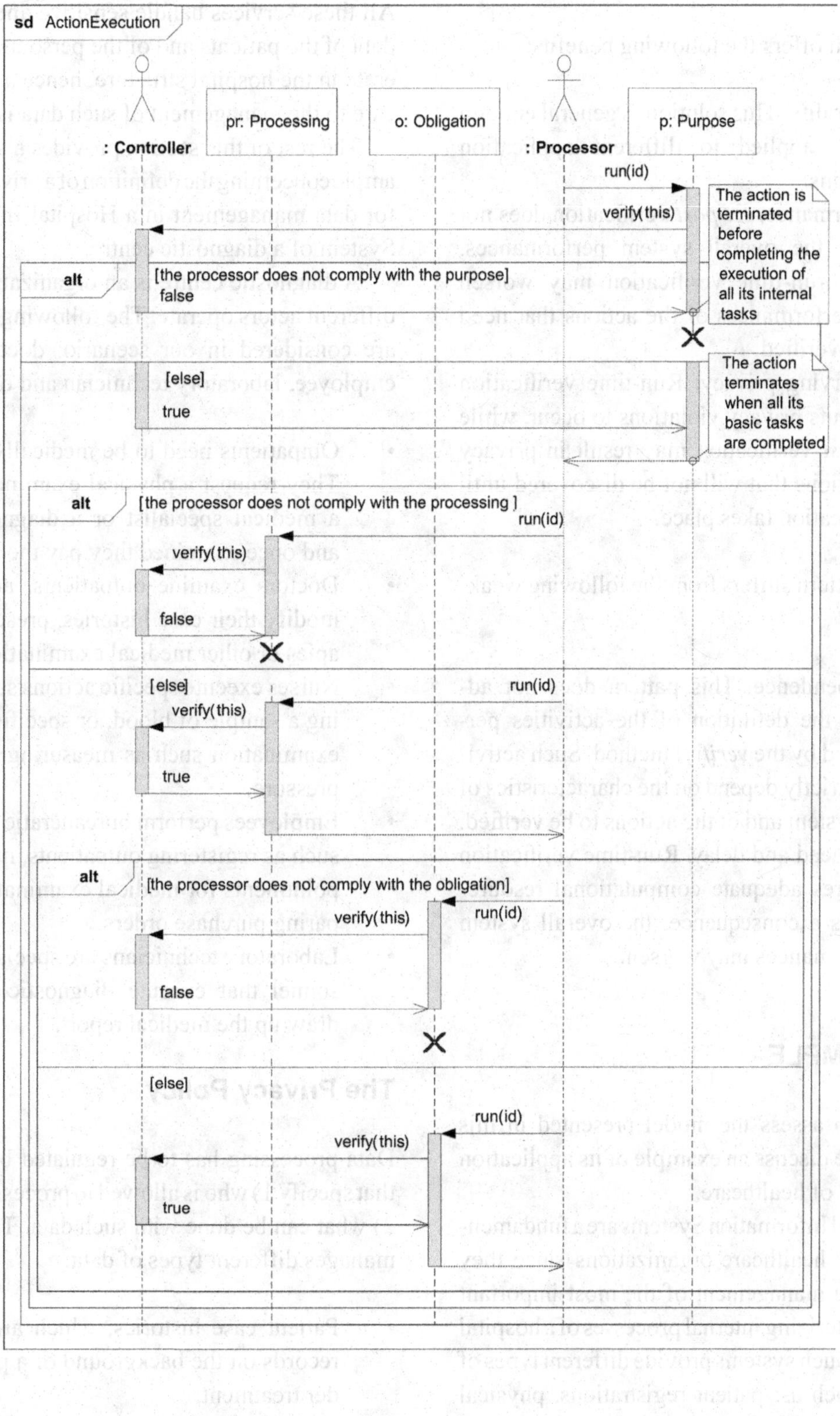

Consequences

This pattern offers the following benefits:

- Generality. This solution is general enough to be applied to different application domains.
- Performance. *Ex-post* verification does not affect the overall system performances, while run-time verification may worsen the performances of the actions that need to be verified.
- Preserving privacy: Run-time verification prevents privacy violations to occur, while *ex-post* verification may result in privacy violations that will not be discovered until verification takes place.

This pattern suffers from the following weaknesses:

- Independence. This pattern does not address the definition of the activities performed by the *verify()* method. Such activities strictly depend on the characteristics of the system and of the actions to be verified.
- Overhead and delay. Run-time verification requires adequate computational resources. As a consequence, the overall system performances may worsen.

AN EXAMPLE

In order to assess the model presented in this chapter, we discuss an example of its application in the field of healthcare.

Hospital Information Systems are a fundamental tool for healthcare organizations since they support the management of the most important and characterizing internal processes of a hospital structure. Such systems provide different types of services such as: patient registrations, physical examination reservations, patients' admission, etc. All these services handle sensitive and personal data of the patients and of the personnel that operate in the hospital structure, hence a particular care to the management of such data is required.

The rest of this section provides a simple example concerning the definition of a privacy policy for data management in a Hospital Information System of a diagnostic centre.

A diagnostic centre is an organization where different actors operate. The following functions are considered in our scenario: doctor, nurse, employee, laboratory technician and outpatient.

- Outpatients need to be medically assisted. They request a physical examination with a medical specialist or a diagnostic test, and once examined they pay the fee
- Doctors examine outpatients, access and modify their case histories, prescribe therapies or other medical examinations.
- Nurses execute specific actions such as taking a sample of blood, or specific physical examination such as measuring the blood pressure.
- Employees perform bureaucratic activities: such as registering outpatients, making appointments for medical examinations, preparing purchase orders.
- Laboratory technicians are specialized personnel that execute diagnostic tests and draw up the medical report.

The Privacy Policy

Data processing has to be regulated by policies that specify 1) who is allowed to process data, and 2) what can be done with such data. The system manages different types of data:

- Patient case histories, which are detailed records on the background of a person under treatment.

- Medical examination prescriptions: the requests of thorough diagnostic tests.
- Medical examination results: the results of the diagnostic tests.
- Identifiable data: identifiable data associated with patients
- Administrative data: the payment state for medical examinations and treatments.

In what follows we consider one of the activities that are usually supported by a HIS, namely blood tests management.

Let us consider that an outpatient needs to contact the diagnostic center to request an appointment for a blood test.

The following scenario sketches the involved actors and actions:

- An employee makes the appointment for the medical examination;
- The outpatient goes to the appointment, and a nurse takes a sample of his/her blood;
- The outpatient pays the fee at the payment office;
- A laboratory technician executes the blood test and stores the results of the patient in the system;
- The patient picks up the results.

The privacy policy that we wants to model must satisfy the following requirements:

- Outpatients must be informed of the processing purposes of the diagnostic centre.
- The processing of the data of the outpatients is exclusively allowed under their explicit consent.
- The system has to prevent the identification of outpatients starting from their health related data.
- The processing actions can be exclusively executed by authorized users

Modeling the Example

The actors involved in the proposed scenario are represented by means of instances of the classes *User*, *Function* and *Role*. Notice that in a real scenario users may be characterized by multiple function-role associations, but in this example we do not consider this situation for the sake of simplicity.

Employees are instances of *User* characterized by a *Function* that specify the task of "Employee" and by the role *Processor*, since employees process the data of the patients. Similarly, doctors are characterized by the *Function* "Doctor" and the role of *Processor*, while technicians are characterized by the *Function* "Laboratory Technician" and the role of *Processor*. Finally, outpatients are the data owners whose data will be processed by doctors, laboratory technicians and employees. Therefore, outpatients are characterized by the role of *Subject* and no *Function* is associated with them.

Data

The data managed by the system concern outpatients, appointments, costs, payments and the results of diagnostic tests. Moreover, the system should keep track of which laboratory technician executes a diagnostic test for a given outpatient.

First of all it is necessary to model the data structure and to classify the different *Data* instances as sensitive or identifiable. In particular the following data types (i.e. instances of class *Data*) are introduced:

- "Person": composed of fields such as "first name", "family name", "birth date", "address", "telephone number", "social security number", which identify an outpatient.
- "Physical examination", "Diagnostic test": composed of fields such as: "date", "time", "place", "examination type", "examination description", which provide information on the examination/test.

- "Price list": composed of fields such as "examination type" and "price", which describe the price associated with each examination.
- "Result": composed of fields that describe the results of the examination / test.
- "Processor trace": composed of fields that keep track of the users that performed the examination / test.
- "Payment information": composed of fields that keep track of the payment of the examinations/tests.

"Person" is an identifiable data type that stores references to instances of sensitive data such as "Diagnostic test" / "Physical examination". Moreover, "Physical examination"/ "Diagnostic test" stores a reference to further sensitive data named "Result", "Processor trace" and "Payment information". "Price list" is neither sensitive not identifiable data type.

Actions

In what follows we introduce the actions needed to model blood tests management.

- "Registration": registers a new outpatient into the information system of the diagnostic centre
- "Physical examination reservation" / "Diagnostic test reservation": makes a reservation for an examination / diagnostic test
- "Log Processor": keeps track of the processor that executes specific actions
- "Record Result": stores the tests result of the outpatient
- "Pay the bill": stores the payment of the fee associated with a test or with an examination
- "Check payment": verifies that a fee was paid

- "Print result": prints out the results of an examination

In order to assure anonymity we assume that actions are executed only by authorized users. Moreover, we assume that a key distribution centre and a key management service exist so that encryption keys can be created and distributed to each pair function-role that operates the system. In particular, the keys are used to encrypt/decrypt the reference fields needed to access sensitive data. The choice of a specific encryption/decryption algorithm is not discussed being out of the scope of this chapter.

For each action it is necessary to specify: 1) the data types and the fields that need to be accessed; 2) the keys that are needed to access reference fields; and 3) which pair *Function-Role* can execute the action along with the needed keys.

Scenarios

In the following we introduce several scenarios, each of which describes the way in which the interactions between the different actors and the system occur. In particular, the scenarios taken into account concern:

- The acquisition of the informed consent from the outpatient.
- The registration of the outpatient.
- The way in which appointment for blood tests are made.
- The way in which the blood sample is taken from the outpatient.
- How the outpatient pays the fee.
- The activities related to the blood test examination.

Acquiring the Consent

Before any processing concerning the outpatient data can take place, he/she has to grant the informed consent. Therefore an explanation of the processing purposes must be provided to outpatients. Notice that this scenario follows the Informed Consent Pattern.

Whenever a new outpatient enters the diagnostic centre, an employee at the registration desk asks the patient to provide the consent to process his/her data. Thus the employee acts as *Processor*, while the outpatient acts as *Subject*.

The employee informs the patient by means of the method *notify()* provided by interface *ConsentRequest*. Once done, the outpatient is informed of the actions (processing, purpose and obligations) that the system of the diagnostic center may execute on his/her data.

Then, the outpatient interacts with the information system by specifying his/her comprehension, competence, voluntariness and agreement by means of the methods *setComprehension()*, *setCompetence()*, *setVoluntariness()* and *setAgreement()* provided by interface *InformedConsentAcquisition*. Since no action can be executed on the data of an outpatient if he/she does not grant the consent, the following scenarios can take place only if the consent was granted.

Registering the Outpatient

The employee records the data of the outpatient by means of the method *run()* of the action "Registration". In order to execute the method *run()* the employee has to specify his/her *id* and his/her *FunctionRoleKey*. In order to verify that the employee is authorized to execute the action, the method *run()* checks whether the provided *FunctionRoleKey* equals the one introduced at action definition time. If the key is the same the action is executed and the data of the outpatient are stored in the system, that is a new instance of "Person" is created, its attribute *id* is initialized and the value is communicated to the outpatient. Otherwise the execution is aborted since the employee is not authorized to execute the action.

Notice that this check can be considered as a run-time enforcement in which the role of the controller is played by the system rather than by a physical person.

Making the Appointment

Once the outpatient is registered, the employee can make an appointment for the blood test by executing the action "Diagnostic test reservation". This action is composed of multiple basic actions (data writing/data reading) involving some of the fields of "Person", "Price list" and "Diagnostic test". More specifically, the action requires to access the fields "first name", "family name", "birth date" and "social security number" of "Person" and the fields "examination type" and "price" of "Price list".

The action defines a new instance of "Diagnostic test" and initializes the fields "date", "time", "place", "examination type" and "examination description". The action requires the employee to provide his/her function-role-key, so that the keys required to access the reference fields of the involved data sets ("Diagnostic test" of "Person", and "Payment information", "Result" and "Processor trace" of "Diagnostic test") can be automatically retrieved from the key distribution centre. Therefore the action is executed by means of the method *run()* by specifying the identifier of the employee, his/her *FunctionRoleKey*, the identifier of the outpatient, the type and a description of the diagnostic test, the date, the time and the place of the examination. As in the previous scenario, the system checks whether the employee is allowed to execute the action. The action creates a new instance of "Diagnostic test", whose *id*, once encrypted using the key associated with the sensitive data "Diagnostic test", is stored in the homonymous reference of the instance of "Person" representing the outpatient. The action also creates an instance of "Payment information", "Result", and "Processor trace". "Payment information" specifies the total amount due for the examination, while "Result" will be used by the laboratory technician to store the results of the examination. Finally, "Processor trace" is used to keep track of the examination executors. Notice that this action initializes only the field *id* of "Result" and "Processor trace", and the fields *id* and *total* of "Payment information" while all the other fields will be set during the execution of other actions.

The values of *id* are encrypted with the keys associated with sensitive data "Payment information", "Result" and "Processor trace", respectively, and the resulting values are stored in the homonymous reference fields of "Diagnostic test".

When the execution completes, the diagnostic test is booked.

Taking a Sample of Blood

The outpatient gives the *id* of the reservation to the nurse in charge of taking the blood sample. Once the blood sample is taken the nurse labels the test tube with the *id* of the test (i.e., the value of the attribute *id* of "Diagnostic test"). Then he/she registers the test by invoking the action "Log Processor", which creates an instance of "Processor trace" and initializes the value of the field "executor" with the *id* of the nurse.

Notice that also in this scenario the system checks whether the action is executed by an authorized member of the staff (i.e., the nurse). As usual this is done by means of the key associated with the pair *Nurse-Processor* that has to be provided when executing the action.

Paying the Fee

The outpatient has to pay the fee for the execution of diagnostic test. Hence, he/she provides the *id* of the reservation to the payment office employee that, in turn, registers the payment by invoking

the action "Pay the bill". This action accesses the field "examination type" of "Diagnostic test" and the fields "examination type" and "price" of "Price list". The value of the field "examination type" of "Diagnostic test" is used to calculate the price associated with the examination. The resulting value is used to update the field "paid" of "Payment information".

Examining the Sample

The laboratory technician executes the diagnostic test on the sample of blood. Once done, he/she executes the action "Log Processor" to keep trace of the technician who did the test. The action uses the *id* written on the label of the test tube and the *id* of the technician. Finally, the technician stores the results of the test by executing the action "Record test results", which sets the values of all the fields of the data type "Result".

At this point the outpatient may get the results by providing the *id* of the "Diagnostic test" to the employee. The employee checks whether the outpatient paid the fee by means of the action "Check payment". During action execution the key to decrypt the field "Payment information" of "Diagnostic test" is retrieved. Once decrypted, the value is used to verify whether the outpatient has paid the amount due. If this is the case, the employee invokes the action "Print Results", otherwise he/she notifies the outpatient that he/she still owes some money to the diagnostic centre.

Action "Print Results" decrypts the reference field "Result" of "Diagnostic test" to access the instance of "Result" so that the complete report can be printed and handed to the outpatient.

CONCLUSION

Privacy is becoming more and more important in many aspects of every day life, and therefore it is becoming a fundamental requirement in the development of systems that handle individuals data.

In this chapter we presented an UML-based conceptual model for the definition of general privacy policies, allowing one to define the concepts needed to deal with privacy-related information. The choice of using UML is motivated by the fact that it is well known by a wide range of analysts, modelers and programmers and therefore the model can be easily understood. Moreover, UML supports a model centric development process and thus the different diagrams introduced in this chapter provide different views showing the main aspects of the whole model. Finally, UML can be used for representing concepts at different levels of abstraction. Even though the presented model has a high level of abstraction, it can be easily extended and adapted for specific application domains;

This chapter also describes some design solutions for specific privacy related recurrent problems. More specifically, the chapter presents a general solution to implement anonymity, to support the informed consent and to define enforcement mechanisms.

The model provides the conceptual foundations that are required by such problems, such as the separation of sensitive from identifiable data, and the classification of roles and actions. The proposed solutions, represented by means of design patterns, consist in concepts and guidelines that drive the modeler towards the definition of privacy aware systems. The solutions extend the conceptual model by adding the elements, such as data encryption, needed to support the above mentioned requirements.

An example concerning the healthcare domain presents the application of the patterns. The example drives the reader through the classification of users and actions, and shows how it is possible to integrate the encryption mechanisms in order to define anonymity and how it is possible to support the informed consent and the enforcement.

REFERENCES

Agrawal, R., Bird, P., Grandison, T., Kiernan, J., Logan, S., & Rjaibi, W. (2005). Extending Relational Database Systems to Automatically Enforce Privacy Policies. *Int. Conf. on Data Engineering (ICDE 2005)*, (pp. 1013-1022). IEEE Computer Society.

Anton, A. (1996). Goal-Based Requirements Analysis. *IEEE Int. Conf. on Requirements Engineering (ICRE 96)*, (pp. 136-144). Colorado Springs CO.

Blakley, B., & Heath, C. (2004). *Security Design Patterns*. Technical Guide, The Open Group.

Chung, E. S., Hong, J. I., Lin, J., Prabaker, M. K., Landay, J. A., & Liu, A. L. (2004). Development and evaluation of emerging design patterns for ubiquitous computing. *Int. Conf. on Designing Interactive Systems*, New York: ACM Press.

Chung, L. (1993). Dealing with Security Requirements during the Development of Information System. *Int. Conference on Advanced Information System Engineering (CAiSE '93)*, Paris (France).

Coen-Porisini, A., Colombo, P., Sicari, S., & Trombetta, A. (2007). A Conceptual Model for Privacy Policies. In Proc. of *Software Engineering Application (SEA '07)*. Cambridge, MS.

Gamma, E., Helm, R., Johnson, R., & Vlissides, J. M. (1994). *Design Patterns: Elements of Reusable Object Oriented Software*. Reading, MA: Addison-Wesley.

Hafiz, M. (2006). A collection of privacy design patterns. *Int. Conf. on Pattern Languages of Programs Conference (PLOP)*. New York, NY, USA.

Kavakli, E., Kalloniatis, C., Loucopoulos, P., & Gritzalis, S. (2008). Addressing Privacy Requirements in System Design: the PriS Method. [New York: Springer]. *Journal Requirements Engineering, 13*(3), 241–255. doi:10.1007/s00766-008-0067-3

Lamsweerde, A. V., & Letier, Handling, E. (2000). Obstacles in Goal-Oriented Requirement Engineering. *IEEE Transactions on Software Engineering, 26,* 978–1005. doi:10.1109/32.879820

Liu, L., Yu, E., & Mylopoulos, J. (2002) Analyzing Security Requirements as Relationships among Strategic Actors. *Symposium on Requirements Engineering for Information Security (SREIS '02).* Raleigh, North Carolina, USA.

Mielikinen, T. (2004). Privacy Problems with Anonymized Transaction Databases. *Int. Conf. on Discovery Science (DS 2004),* Vol 3245 of Lecture Notes in Computer Science 3245, Springer.

Mouratidis, H., & Giorgini, P. (2007). Secure Tropos: A Security-Oriented Extension of the Tropos methodology. [IJSEKE]. *International Journal of Software Engineering and Knowledge Engineering, 17*(2), 285–309. doi:10.1142/S0218194007003240

Mouratidis, H., Giorgini, P., & Manson, G. A. (2003b). An Ontology for Modelling Security: The Tropos Approach. *Int Conf. on Knowledge-Based Intelligent Information & Engineering Systems (KES 2003),* Vol. 2773 of Lecture Notes in Computer Science, (pp. 1387-1394). Springer.

Mouratidis, H., Giorgini, P., & Mason, G. A. (2003a). Integrating Security and Systems Engineering towards the Modelling of Secure Information System. *Int. Conf. on Advanced Information System Engineering (CAiSE '03),* Vol. 2681 of Lecture Notes in Computer Science, (pp. 63-78). Springer.

Mylopolulos, J., Chung, L., & Nixon, B. (1992). Representing and Using non Functional Requirements: a Process Oriented Approach. *IEEE Transactions on Software Engineering, 18,* 483–497. doi:10.1109/32.142871

Narayanan, A., & Shmatikov, V. (2005). Obfuscated Databases and Group Privacy. *ACM Int. Conference on Computer and Communications Security (CCS '05),* (pp. 102-111). New York, NY, USA. ACM Press.

Ni, Q., Trombetta, A., Bertino, E., & Lobo, J. (2007). Privacy-aware Role-Based Access Control. *ACM Symp. on Access Control Methods And Technologies (SACMAT '07).* Sophia Antipolis, France.

Romanosky, S., Acquisti, A., Hong, J., Cranor, L., & Friedman, B. (2006). Privacy Patterns for Online Interactions. *Int. Conf. on Pattern Languages of Programs Conference (PLOP).* New York, NY, USA.

Schumacher, M. (2002) Security Patterns AND Security Standards. *European Conf. on Pattern Languages of Programs (EuroPLoP),* Kloster Irsee, Germany

Schumacher, M., Fernandez-Buglioni, E., Hybertson, D., Buschmann, F., & Sommerlad, P. (2006). *Security Patterns: Integrating Security and Systems Engineering.* John Wiley & Sons.

Schummer, T. (2004). *The Public Privacy–Patterns for Filtering Personal Information in Collaborative Systems, (Tech. Rep).* Hagen, Germany: FernUnivesität in Hagen.

Steel, C., Nagappan, R., & Lai, R. (2005). *Core Security Patterns: Best Practices and Strategies for J2EE, Web Services, and Identity Management.* Prentice Hall.

Yoder, J., & Barcalow, J. (1997). Architectural Patterns for Enabling Application Security. *Int. Conf. on Pattern Languages of Programs Conference (PLOP).* Monticello, Illinois, USA.

ENDNOTES

[1] Directive 95/46/EC of the European Parliament and of the Council of 24 October 1995 on the protection of individuals with regard to the processing of personal data and on the free movement of such data. Official Journal of the European Communities of 23 November 1995 No L. 281 p. 31

[2] http://www.hipaa.org

[3] http://www.glba.org

[4] The Platform for Privacy Preferences 1.1 (P3P1.1) Specification. W3C Working Group Note, 2006 - http://www.w3.org/TR/P3P11/

[5] OMG. Unified Modeling Language: Infrastructure, 2007. Ver. 2.1.1, formal/2007-11-04 and OMG. Unified Modeling Language: Superstructure, 2007. Ver. 2.1.1, formal/2007-11-02 - http://www.omg.org/spec/UML/2.1.2/

[6] Decreto Legislativo n. 196, 30 Giugno 2003, Codice in materia di protezione dei dati personali, Gazzetta Ufficiale n.174 del 29-7-2003 - Suppl. Ord. n. 123.

[7] http://web.mit.edu/kerberos

Chapter 10
Incorporating Social Trust into Design Practices for Secure Systems

Piotr Cofta
BT (British Telecom), UK

Hazel Lacohée
BT (British Telecom), UK

Paul Hodgson
BT (British Telecom), UK

ABSTRACT

Companies are increasingly dependent on modern information and communication technology (ICT), yet the successful adoption of ICT systems stubbornly hovers at only around 50%, adding disappointment to business losses. Trust (both inter-personal and technology-related) has significant explanatory power when it comes to technology adoption, but only as part of a systematic methodology. Therefore, understanding more fully the interaction between human process and technology by adding the richness of socio-technical considerations to the design process of ICT systems should significantly improve adoption rates. At the same time, trust-based design has to demonstrate the (often neglected) business value of trust. 'Designing for trust', discussed in this chapter, is a design framework that consolidates trust governance and security management. Trust governance is a complete proposition that makes trust relevant to business practices, including the design and deployment of ICT systems. Trust governance incorporates the business justification of trust with an analytical framework, and a set of relevant tools and methods, as well as a maturity model. This chapter discusses how 'designing for trust' leverages trust governance into the design practices of ICT systems by complementing security-based methodologies, demonstrating the value of this approach.

DOI: 10.4018/978-1-61520-837-1.ch010

1. INTRODUCTION

Throughout their industrial experience, the authors have seen several examples of systems where security suffered due to a lack of proper consideration for the complexity of an inter-play between technical systems and their social environment. Further, the authors can see that even within the confines of a large technical system, its security depends not only on purely technical measures or mastery of technical designs, but also on the ability and willingness of design and support personnel to engage at a deeper level. The authors' current work concentrates on improving industrial practices, using elements of a proposition presented here.

In the continuous fight to improve on offerings and decrease costs, companies are increasingly dependent on complex information and communication technology (ICT) systems. While the design and deployment of such systems represents a challenge in itself, the fact is that up to 50% of those systems do not live up to their original expectations (Lippert & Davis, 2006) adding frustration and damaged reputation to lost investment and missed revenues.

While analysing the reasons for such a lack of success, it is apparent that failures can often be attributed to the lack of social adoption of such new systems. This lack of adoption often originates in inappropriately designed and applied security measures (Cranor and Garfinkel, 2005), that are either too lax (so that they expose vulnerabilities) or too stringent (so that they inspire creative rejection), or finally, they may be appropriate in strength but entirely ignore established practices. Note that quite often such security measures are designed in full accordance with requirements or specifications, yet they miss the importance of the social context of practical application (Lippert & Davis, 2006).

A system that fails to achieve adoption represents a business loss, but a system that is not fully or willingly adopted represents a significant security vulnerability, specifically if users of such a system are set to circumvent security controls by means of creative social practices. For example, even the most sophisticated access control does not provide security if users choose to use their access cards according to their perception of social relationships (and value systems) rather than according to security policies (Collins, 2007), or if a PIN code for a credit card is shared (Lacohée, Cofta, Phippen, and Furnell, 2008).

This phenomenon of 'unintended consequences' can be best described in terms of affordance, coined by Gibson (1986) and popularised in the field of HCI and design by Norman (1988) who applied the concept to everyday artefacts. Norman defined affordance as "the perceived and actual properties of the thing, primarily those fundamental properties that determine just how the thing could possibly be used." Affordance, therefore, determines what an ICT system can be used for, following the intentions of its users, while specification and design concentrates on how the system is intended to be used by its original designers. The disparity between both intentions creates tension that eventually undermines system adoption.

While the 'answer' to such 'user challenges' of 'unintended consequences' may lie partly in better education, improved usability or more stringent supervision, the underlying truth is that the deployment of an ICT system is a cause and enabler of a planned change (Lippert & Davis, 2006) that should be designed with its immediate social environment in mind. Successful technologies owe a large part of their success to the fact that they fulfil or enhance an existing human need, or fit well into an already well established social context. In common with other types of change, any unsubstantiated demand that requires a radical change of social practices will be met with rejection and creative re-use or even abuse. Therefore, a successful socio-technical approach to design should take into account social relationships and practices that surround a given system, leading to improvements in acceptance rates.

Considering established software development practices, best design practice (Anderson, 2001) stresses that features such as security should be designed into the system as early as possible. This is corroborated by general observations that changes in the design stage can be made easier, faster and cheaper than changes undertaken later in the system's lifetime (Boehm, 1981). Such approaches are well accepted and there are existing tools and methodologies to support them (e.g. Mouratidis & Giorgini, 2007). However, addressing security alone does not allow for the proper modelling of relationships between social agents and relationships between such agents and technology, where assurance can be resolved by means other than control.

Adding the richness of social considerations (specifically the notion of affordance) to the design process of ICT systems should therefore significantly improve design considerations, thus decreasing potential security vulnerabilities as well as improving system adoption. It has been identified that trust (both inter-personal and technology-related) has significant explanatory power when it comes to technology adoption (Lippert & Davis, 2006). Therefore, of several social constructs that may have an impact in this context, trust seems to be best positioned to complement control-based considerations in designing secure ICT systems. This is further reinforced by the characteristics of trust that are complementary to security and that allow for modelling unsystematic risk. Furthermore, security reflects well desired functionality (thus constraining social behaviour) while trust reflects social behaviour that relates to affordance.

Analysis of trust should not be undertaken in isolation, it should be integrated together with security. Owing to the complementary (but very different) properties of both components, such an integration requires a complete fields of study to be created (Mouratidis & Cofta, 2010), based

upon a coherent methodology (Hodgson & Cofta, 2009), (Cofta & Lacohée, 2010) to convert what might be described as 'warm yet fuzzy' trust into design practices that are comparable with security. Such a field of study goes beyond designing or modelling tools, to understanding what trust is and how trust satisfies business objectives - again in a manner that is similar to security.

This chapter presents an approach that allows trust to be incorporated into design practices in a close relationship with security. The framework of 'designing for trust' unifies established principles of security management with a novel approach of trust governance. Trust governance is a complete proposition (even though it is still a work in progress) that incorporates business justifications of trust with an appropriate methodology, a set of tools and a maturity process in order to make trust relevant to business objectives.

This chapter starts with a discussion of a key difference in ICT design driven by technology requirements and design driven by the understanding of social reactions to ICT systems. Next, the way trust and such a socio-technical interaction is reflected in secure design is briefly discussed. The chapter then provides an overview of trust in the context of business to identify the types of trust that should be incorporated into design. From there, trust is explained in terms of its business relevance. The discussion then leads to a unifying paradigm and an assessment of methodology. This is followed by observations on methods to improve trust and achieve greater maturity, with concluding comments closing the chapter.

2. AFFORDANCE

It has already been noted that one of the key reasons for the failure of ICT systems is the fact that users tend to creatively ignore, bend or circumvent best-wished policies and countermeasures set by developers. If users always behaved exactly as desired (i.e. followed policies, entered correct data, used tools only for intended designed purposes etc.), or could be constrained to behave in such a manner (e.g. as security measures often demand) the development of technology (including ICT systems) would be much easier.

But of course, users of technology do not behave as we might like in an ideal security-driven ICT mediated environment, as they have a habit of adapting technology to suit their own needs and requirements. In short, they utilise what technological developments afford, creatively using the properties of a given technological artefact to achieve novel and unintended solutions to achieve goals as they perceive them in a given context.

For example, the use of Chip and PIN cards affords similar properties and similar infringements of intended security measures as those described in the access control example above. Lacohée, Cofta, Phippen and Furnell (2008) found that since Chip and PIN cards no longer require a signature, card holders exploit the (unintended) convenience of the system by telling trusted friends and family their PIN number, thus enabling them to make purchases on their behalf, even though this practice is an infringement of the terms and conditions laid down by the card issuer.

Affordance can be described as the properties of the environment that are compatible with and relevant to people's interactions, how we perceive something influences the way in which we respond to it and how we behave. The view of the system from the user's perspective of affordances may thus radically differ from the perspective of a system designer or application developer. In Norman's terms, if our goal is to pass through a door that has a handle, our perception and experience of the affordance of such an artefact (a door handle) leads us to expect that it will open if we push down on the handle and we trust that our action will be successful in achieving our goal. If we are confronted with a door with a flat hand plate but no handle we trust and expect that it will open if we push against the plate. It is the qualities of the artefact that determine and influence our interpretation,

expectation and action. To borrow from the often quoted Mark Twain in this context, "To a man with hammer, everything looks like a nail," and conversely we might say, "To a man with a nail, everything looks like a hammer."

Technology of course offers many unexpected affordances. Innovative, unanticipated, unpredicted and creative use of technology is commonplace and reflects human behaviour at its most fundamental level. Historically we have seen many examples of affordance; women appropriated the telephone, originally envisaged by its designers as a business tool, as a device for maintaining social relationships (Martin 1991), and video, also designed as a business tool, was quickly adopted by busy mothers as a childminding device.

SMS or text messaging offers an interesting and 'accidental' example of success born of affordance that took nearly everyone in the mobile industry by surprise; there was very little promotion or mention of SMS by network operators until after it had taken off. Designers envisaged SMS as a voice mail alerting service but the affordance it offers - that of low cost communication (and the fact that communication is fundamental to human relationships and a powerful means of social grooming), represents a user triumph, one that the industry has been able to effectively and successfully exploit. Such affordances illustrate the importance of the interaction between the intended use of technology and what it might afford in a particular social or cultural environment and the ways in which this might impact on successful adoption and uptake.

In its broadest terms affordance is the relationship between an object in the world and the intentions, perceptions and capabilities a person has towards that object. Therefore affordance-related analysis complements design specifications in the sense that it discusses what is technically possible and socially desirable rather that what is technically desirable and socially possible. Furthermore, in the context of this chapter the concept of affordance is best thought of not as a one-to-one relationship between a user and a technological artefact, but as a broader concept that encompasses an interaction between the cultural and social aspects of the environment in which technology is used and the users of that technology.

3. SECURE SYSTEMS

A secure system is usually understood as a system that demonstrates sufficient resilience under adverse conditions (e.g. attacks). Such a system may include its software component (secure software), but it has to be stressed that the security of the software alone does not translate directly into the security of the system. Therefore, what we are concerned with here is the design of socio-technical systems that stress the inter-dependence of the technical and non-technical components of such systems. Consequently, approaches to software engineering are presented here from this socio-technical standpoint

When it comes to designing and developing software for secure systems, four different approaches can be taken, resulting in preferences for different methodologies and different tools. Those approaches are briefly discussed below, to indicate the position of the one we describe in this paper. The approaches described here are non-exclusive and may co-exist throughout the design and development of the software. For each approach, we will illustrate how trust-related considerations can be (or already are) incorporated in a way that clearly demonstrates benefits to the security of the system.

3.1. Early Capture

This approach stresses the importance of early capture of security-related considerations. It focuses on capturing security requirements, with the intention of bringing them into the development process. Methods such as misuse cases or

attack trees (Mauw and Oostdijk, 2005) allow for identifying the most important cases while a more complete methodology, e.g. Threat Modelling (Microsoft, 2009) brings security specific requirements into the design practice.

It is an existing practice to capture trust relationships during the requirement analysis, either explicitly (e.g. in a form of trust models) or indirectly, e.g. by excluding certain areas from consideration. Neither method satisfies the complexity of real situations. Trust models correctly identify that trust precedes security, but then fail to expose the dynamic relationship between both, as well as failing to address the richness and the variety of trust-based relationships. Excluding certain areas form consideration introduces unnecessary vulnerabilities into the design as such salient assumptions may fail, and -without being properly documented - their failure may pass unnoticed.

Trust governance addresses these shortcomings by allowing us to record the co-existence of trust and security within a single conceptual framework, throughout the lifetime of the system. Trust governance is particularly useful at capturing requirements and at the design stage, for both new systems and modifications to existing socio-technical systems.

3.2. Quality of Expression

Even the best capture is insufficient if security needs cannot be expressed in a manner that allows for the richness of expression, precision and automation, so that they can be validated and taken into the development process, to be eventually used to generate acceptance criteria. This is particularly true for large systems where security considerations may include tens of policies applied to hundreds of co-operating systems and sub-systems.

Security modelling plays an important role here, as it substitutes imprecise and ambiguous natural language description with formal methods. There are a variety of methodological frameworks and tools (see e.g. Kearney, 2009 for an overview). They either leverage existing modelling frameworks by introducing elements of security (e.g. UML), or introduce frameworks that focus on security-related requirements.

Trust governance addresses the quality of expression by extending Secure Tropos (Mouratidis and Giorgini, 2007) framework to address trust-based relationships within a unifying paradigm. This allows for security and trust to be exposed, described and processed in a consistent way throughout the whole system development process.

3.3. Deficiency of Practice

It is widely recognised that security can be compromised by the deficiency of appropriate practices, whether these are operational or design based. There are several methods to improve design practices of the software, ranging from appropriate certification to design practices to formal verification. However, those methods introduce vulnerabilities that must be (yet are usually not) captured into the system design.

The complete socio-technical system is as much about technology as about social practices. Methodologies that improve on technical design often rely on salient social assumptions. For example, designer certification relies on an appropriate certification process, peer review relies on group dynamics etc. Trusted computing (Pearson, S. et al, 2002) relies on technology and processes that are 'somewhere else', even if they directly impact on the security of the particular system. If not taken into account, those dependencies only shift vulnerabilities, rather than contributing to desired improvements in security.

Trust governance takes on the socio-technical stance from the very beginning, thus allowing us to expose such dependencies, and include them into the system design. It has already been noted that the lack of a socio-technical approach to security leads to significant deficiencies; hence trust governance fills an important gap. Further, as several improvements to security practice rely on trust (as opposed to control), trust governance allows us to capture, express and reason about these elements so that they do not disappear out of sight.

3.4. Acceptance of Fallibility

The final approach to secure systems is to accept their inherent fallibility and to offer solutions that allow for certain minimum resilience. Technical measures (such as redundancy) and non-technical measures (such as disaster recovery procedures) are equally applicable here. Software components are thus allowed to fail, provided that failure of individual components does not overly endanger the security of the system as a whole. Similarly, people are allowed to fail (make improper decisions) because the software supports them in a rapid recovery rather than strong prevention.

Such an approach clearly demonstrates alternative approaches that are based on control or trust, both applicable, and both have their relative merits. Should a system fail, a trusted person can stand in. Should a person fail, a trusted system can identify the problem and support the correction.

Trust governance however, allows for a more complete view of the system, thus showing different methods to achieve desired levels of resilience. Further, it allows us to integrate 'alternative' methods that are increasingly gaining popularity while not being, as yet, fully incorporated into the body of security design practices. Methods such as trust-based access control (Dimmock et al., 2005), reputation-based schemes (Chang, Dillion and Hussain, 2006) and similar are better expressed as jointly analysing trust and control, rather than focussing on control alone.

4. THREE DISCUSSIONS ON TRUST

There is wide agreement that trust is important to all aspects of our lives. As human beings we have a natural propensity to trust and we extend this to a lesser or greater degree towards our dealings with technology. However, our trust is not always well-placed of course but neither is trust necessarily blind, it requires transparency, accountability and credible ways of signalling its justification along with certain 'scaffolding' for the mechanisms of trust to function effectively.

In the wider context, trust is essential both to an effective civil society and to economic prosperity but in today's climate public trust in business, financial and political arenas has never been lower. We urgently need to turn this around if we are to regain the ground we have lost because modern society cannot function unless people can have faith in the corporate world and in societal institutions

Discussions about trust are significantly impaired by the fact that trust encompasses up to 17 meanings (McKnight & Chervany, 1996), thus being particularly hard to reason, agree upon or even detect. At the same time, trust is pervasive (Luhmann, 1979) and intuitively obvious (Petland & Heibeck, 2008). For a more detailed analysis of different meanings and aspects of trust, please refer to (Cofta, 2007) or (Abdul-Rahman, 2005).

Trust is not simply a 'like to have' virtue perceived of as 'good thing', it can become a tangible artefact that can be incorporated into design to achieve unparalleled levels of measurable trustworthiness. In order to incorporate trust into design practices, one should be able to express trust in terms that are understood by the design community so that trust-related design decisions can be enabled. Security, for example, is understood and measured in terms of the risk of potential losses to business that can be contained by deploying instruments of security. By quantifying risk and cost, businesses can calculate potential cost savings arising from security measures and can justify investment.

In the case of trust, the current state of discussion is much more fragmented and can be structured into three main streams, each one highlighting significantly different aspects of trust, and each differently relating to practices. These aspects are briefly discussed below, in an intentionally contrasting manner. The everyday practice of trust usually combines certain elements of all three, so that the authors believe that only by properly incorporating all three aspects of trust into a business context can trust be properly evaluated so that it becomes at least as relevant to business as security.

4.1. Trust as *Fides*

The Latin word *fides* can be translated as 'trust', but it implies a notion of trust that is similar to our modern understanding of fiduciary obligations, i.e. the relationship (not necessarily symmetric, but co-dependent) between a trustee and a beneficiary. Relationships between friends, between parents and children, an investor and his bank, an employee and a company etc. can be best described in terms of fides.

Fides does not imply that both parties have to depend on each other to the same extent, or that they have to trust each other in the same way. While both parties share a common purpose, their roles are usually different. Also, the type of trust is usually different for example, a parent's trust in a child differs from a child's trust in a parent.

Trust as fides focuses on the development of trust within the relationship, including recovery from breaches of trust and from distrust. Such a development requires the cooperation of both parties, despite occasional glitches, including actions such as regret, forgiveness or restitution (Marsh & Briggs, 2008).

The concept of trust as fides is discussed widely within philosophical discourse (e.g. as a moral virtue in Potter, 2002), as well as in politics (e.g. as a civic duty in Hardin, 2002), law (e.g. fiduciary obligation in Birks, 1997), social science (e.g. as a social capital - Fukuyama, 1996), and organisational science (e.g. as change enabler in Saunders and Thornhill, 2003) etc.

4.2. Trust as Credere

In contrast, trust as *credere* (closely related to the modern word 'credit') concentrates on the unilateral assessment of trustworthiness. Such an assessment can be conducted e.g. by a bank in order to determine the creditworthiness of a loan applicant; by an employer while performing a background check of a new employee, or by a merchant who is checking the reputation of a new supplier.

The concept of *credere* is unilateral and relates to the current situation of a trustee, i.e. the assessment is about 'here' and 'now', with certain disregard to the development potential of a relationship. The assessor assumes that if an assessment results in an unsatisfactory outcome he can choose another trustee (e.g. move to another supplier) without any negative consequences.

Credere is a key concept that is relevant to the modern economy and finance industry (in the form of creditworthiness), but it is also closely related to the concept of brand (as encapsulated in trustworthiness in Lassar, Mittal, and Sharma 1995), reputation (e.g. in reputation-based systems in Chang, Dillion, and Hussain, 2006), and social networks (e.g. web of trust, in Golbeck, 2008) etc.

4.3. Trust as Externality

Trust is considered as an *externality* if it is an essential enabler of a system, but not a part of it. Such an approach is particularly evident within the modern approach to security (including information security). From a security perspective, trust is a component that is essential in every security assurance, yet it is external to security design or implementation.

In fact, the very definition of a trusted component (e.g. Anderson, 2001) of a security system implies that breaking such a component may invalidate security policies - but very little is said of how to create and maintain such trust. Trust in certain components of the system (technology, individuals, companies) is desired, assumed and implied, but once such a need for trust is established, the upkeep of that trust is delegated to best practices, encapsulated in the process of assurance (e.g. Flowerday and von Solms, 2006)

While trust is external to control-driven security, trust governance can learn from the transition that information security undertook during the last couple of decades: from an arcane domain associated with military operations to acceptance as an essential part of business strategy; from knowledge known to a few to a popular conversation subject; from a closed community to a profession.

Furthermore, from a business perspective trust and control are not in conflict. While trust advocates can opt for an all-trusting future, business leaders know that both trust and control have their place in organisations and products, and that they complement each other. Therefore trust governance brings trust into the business domain in strict conjunction with security.

5. TRUST GOVERNANCE IN 'DESIGNING FOR TRUST'

This chapter is concerned with a discussion about the methodology of 'designing for trust' that unifies an approach inspired by security management with one driven by trust governance to introduce trust into design practices. As security management and its implications on design are widely known (Anderson, 2001), this chapter intentionally concentrates on trust governance and its implications for the design of ICT systems.

However, the purpose and applicability of both trust governance and 'designing for trust' differ. Designing for trust addresses the design phase of socio-technical systems (with special focus on ICT systems) and offers a systematic approach that should result in the incorporation of trust and security into the design process. Trust governance is a component framework that brings trust much closer to business practices and that can be used (partly or in its entirety) by 'designing for trust'

The foundations of trust governance are informed by the three streams of discussion about trust described here that relate differently to business practices (such as the development of ICT systems) and provide different justifications for investing in trust - including the incorporation of trust in design practices. Relational trust as *fides* is desired for long-term relationships, but *credere* is more appropriate for new or transitional contacts. Finally, *externality* of trust combines it with another business instrument - control.

Those three approaches are not in conflict but they do demonstrate the different roles that trust can to have within the system. While trust as *fides* is fundamental to the long-term success of the system, it is its proper assessment (as *credere*) that warrants reciprocity and it is its usage as *externality* that facilitates short-term relationships.

From the design perspective, trust as *externality* is usually addressed by security considerations that require trust to be present and assume its existence (but do not guarantee it). Trust as *credere* can be incorporated by methods adopted from 'computing with trust' (Golbeck, 2008) such as reputation-based systems, webs of trust etc., but trust as *credere* is directed mostly towards the dynamic properties of a system, i.e. towards its operation, not its design. This leaves trust as *fides* as the area that is under-represented but potentially most relevant to the design phase because it links the structure of the system with the structure of the social environment where the system is going to be deployed.

Against this background, this chapter advocates an approach that focuses on trust as *fides*, but that integrates it closely with business needs, security considerations and design practices. Such

an approach will be referred to here as '**trust governance**' and the remaining part of this chapter discusses the various components that comprise this approach.

Trust governance can be defined as (Definition 1.)

Definition 1. Trust governance is a comprehensive framework of tools, methods and processes that act as a guide towards an increased maturity of trust assurance regarding the location, extent and type of trust.

Trust governance is a pragmatic approach to designing and operating systems in such a way that the appropriate level and type of trust is assured (i.e. justified trust), according to long term business needs. While trust governance concentrates on trust as fides, one can also see the value of the operational role of credere or the complementing role of trust as externality. In the latter case, trust is seen as an essential complement to control-based practices, not as a solution that is superior to them.

Trust governance complements security management by bringing trust into consideration within a unifying framework. In a natural way, it extends, enhances and complements various aspects of security management that are relevant to design. The following discussion about trust governance is structured into five areas that reflect its five main components, as presented in Figure 1.

The relationship between trust governance and security management differs, depending on the area, as illustrated in Figure 1. In some areas (e.g. business proposition), trust governance strongly complements security management, which is illustrated by the jagged line between them. The paradigm, in turn, unifies both, while the assessment framework starts from a unifying approach but then separates trust and security into complementary streams. Such a portfolio of trust-related methods complements security to eventually develop into a separate proposition, so that the trust-related maturity model has no common points

Figure 1. Trust governance vs. security management

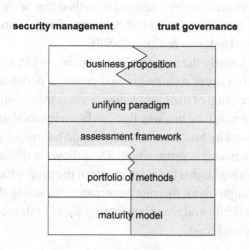

with one that is security-based. We now move to a discussion of the areas that are greyed in Fig 1 as they relate to trust.

Note that while this discussion is naturally concentrated on trust, it uses a methodology and vocabulary that is familiar to security practitioners and in many cases clearly demonstrates the link between security and trust. However, depending on the area, the relationship between trust governance and security management is slightly different.

In regard to business propositions, trust governance strongly complements security because it addresses those needs that are natural weaknesses of security, while at the same time building on security wherever appropriate. This unifying framework naturally consolidates trust governance with security management, and this consolidation is also visible throughout the assessment framework. However, within this framework, at certain points, trust governance concentrates solely on trust-related issues. The growing separation is increasingly visible when it comes to the portfolio of methods and the maturity model.

Trust governance is a relatively new concept, and the integration of trust governance and security management is not complete, so that much of the

work presented here is still in progress. Hence it is advisable to gain updates on progress before embarking on any particular activity related to trust governance at this stage of development.

Reverting back to the discussion of 'designing for trust' methodology and trust governance framework, it is now possible to demonstrate how 'designing for trust' can use different components of trust governance to support the design process. 'Designing for trust' suggests the following approach for the analysis of new systems. Alternative approaches can be developed for an analysis of existing systems (specifically in the case of their failure), analysis of potential updates, decommissioning etc.

1. Capture system requirements using the unifying paradigm, in the form of goals, as described by system designers (and would-be system operators), but expressed from the position of users of the future system.

2. Follow the unifying paradigm to determine dependencies by speculating on affordance, to anticipate a variety of potential scenarios of users satisfying goals in several different ways. This step effectively simulates the behaviour of future users and must go beyond that which is expected or desired, but should not cover openly malicious or fraudulent use.

3. Continue with the paradigm by defining each dependency in terms of confidence, structuring it into trust and control, to establish a graph of trust and control relationships of a satisfying granularity.

4. Apply the assessment framework to such a graph to anticipate problems related to the way future users may satisfy their dependencies. Use different assessment methods depending on the purpose of analysis.

5. From the portfolio of methods, select and design appropriate technical and social means to remove, constrain or minimise identified problems. Apply security-related controls

or methods offered by trust governance, depending on needs, constraints and desired effect.

6.   Use business propositions from trust governance to perform a business analysis and argue for the trust-related portion of the proposed solution; use security-related business propositions to argue for security-related solutions.

7.   Iterate through the process to achieve higher maturity in understanding the value and limitations of trust, as suggested by the maturity model.

6. TRUST AND BUSINESS

Trust governance brings trust closer to business practices, thus allowing for an analysis of the business value of trust as well as the benefit of using trust-based design. The business proposition for trust, as discussed here, can be used by 'designing for trust' to analyse and argue the business case for trust-related components of the system.

In becoming more worthy of trust, businesses can potentially create more effective collective and co-ordinated action and can lower transaction costs. The commercial value of trust is increasingly appreciated, evidence shows an approximate 8% increase in profit margin (Resnick, 2006) and/ or 40% cost savings on outsource management (Willcocks & Cullen, 2006). At the same time, trust is often considered too 'fuzzy' or 'soft' to be regularly incorporated into business practices, and too often it is relegated or restricted to intangibilities such as culture or individual development. In contrast, ICT security has found a way to demonstrate its commercial value to business in a consistent form. But trust is not the 'soft' and 'fuzzy' concept that belongs only to the domain of the social sciences, showing why trust evolved and the purpose it serves in human organisations;

it is fast becoming part of 'hard' science' as positivist and soft systems (interpretivist) methods are combined to give a scientific method that bridges the human and technical domains of understanding. (Hodgson & Cofta, 2009)

Clearly the corporate world needs to catch up and in order to increase and enable a better appreciation of trust in business settings trust should be positioned in a way that can be understood and valued by business, i.e. trust should be structured as a business proposition. The following discussion highlights the main points of the proposition brought about by trust governance, stressing the similarity and complementary role of both security *and* trust.

6.1. Trust is a Business Tool

Trust is not a remedy for all ills within business; rather it is one of several tools in a business toolbox that support particular business objectives. Furthermore, trust is not 'good' by its own virtue, but rather it is good if it is aligned with such objectives. Conversely, distrust is not automatically 'bad', as it may actually benefit the company (e.g. Seppanen and Blomqvist 2006).

What companies usually need is an appropriate type and extent of trust, aligned with objectives. For example, too little trust means that opportunities can be missed, but too much trust can make a company unnecessarily vulnerable. Similarly, over-investment in trust may damage cash flow, while under-investment may negatively affect long-term survival.

From the 'designing for trust' perspective, it has to be understood that an ICT system is not developed to satisfy a need for trust, but that trust embedded in such a system has to satisfy business objectives. Therefore, a trust-based approach should be considered only if there is a business case for it, in a manner similar to an economic analysis of security.

Table 1. Complements of trust and control

Characteristic	Trust	Control
activity	passive	active
volatility	volatile	predictable
internality	internal	external
contextuality	holistic	contextual
temporality	gradual	instant
measurability	qualitative	quantitative

6.2. Trust Complements Control

Trust complements control and security so that several problems can be resolved either through control or through trust, or (most likely) through a combination of both. The diametrically different characteristics of trust, as compared with control, (Cofta, 2007), make trust particularly interesting as a complement that can be utilised in places where control cannot bring the expected results, due e.g. to its cost, inflexibility, timescales, or uncertainty etc.

From the perspective of system design ('designing for trust') the complementary nature of trust and control call for a non-partisan approach where the relative benefits and shortcomings of both should be compared, discussed and decided.

6.3. Trust is an Asset

Trust bears several characteristics of a capital asset because, similar to land, buildings or machinery, it requires investment and maintenance, it delivers value only in a longer timeframe, and it cannot be rapidly disposed of without accepting a significant loss in value etc. Several researchers recognise these characteristics of trust and qualify it as a social capital (Fukuyama, 1996) that can be gradually earned and then used when circumstances change. This approach is visible e.g. in organisational science where trust can be earned during normal operation, and used at the time of change, uncertainty or failing quality.

This approach to trust allows for the inclusion of trust-related investment into the balance sheet (together with some other intangible assets such as innovation portfolio, brand value etc. such that, one may eventually venture to estimate trust equity within the company, i.e. the total value of trust assets held throughout the company. It has already been noted that for some companies the 'brand value' (that represents the value of trust as credere) may exceed their book value (that represents mostly tangible assets). Furthermore, the value of trust in the company itself cannot be under-estimated, as it warrants its long-term existence (Nooteboom, 2002).

While the notion of trust does not conform to the narrowly understood economic thinking of rational, utility-driven behaviour, it is actually a pre-requisite for the existence of the market itself (Ashraf, Camerer, and Loewenstein, 2005). Therefore, trust may not populate next quarter balance sheets, but it should concern those responsible for strategic growth. Fostering trust and collaboration (rather than selfish greed) may not bring immediate benefits, but should be a part of any long-term modelling.

Trust governance is less concerned with the absolute growth of such trust equity, and more concerned with an appropriate allocation of warranted (justified) trust (and distrust, if necessary) throughout the organisation. Similar to capital investment, excessive investment in trust generates expenditures while contributing little if any) to the bottom line in any obvious or measurable manner.

'Designing for trust' should therefore use justified trust as *fides* for long-term cases where its benefits outweigh initial costs, using trust as an *externality* to satisfy other dependencies. However, this does not imply that trust has to be minimised and contained (as suggested by security management), if there is a business case for a large deployment of trust.

6.4. Trust and ROI

Trust governance acknowledges the qualitative and subjective nature of trust, and relies for its quantitative assessment of trust not on the strength of one's belief, but on the strength of trust, in terms of its resistance to a potentially unfavourable course of events.

From a capital investment perspective, different classes of trust entail different risks, require different levels of investment and generate different returns. For example, shallow trust can be established at a relatively low cost, but then its value is quite limited because it will diminish at the first signs of trouble. In contrast, deep trust may require years to develop but it can withstand a wide range of difficulties.

The pragmatics of trust governance suggest that the strength of trust that should be present at a given place and time should match expected returns, i.e. strong trust should be reserved for those cases that may deserve it over the course of time, while weak trust can be more appropriate for casual, short-term relationships.

'Designing for trust' suggests that organisations should not overspend on trust if there is no expectation that such trust will eventually be useful in the future - i.e. the possibility that the return on investment could actually be negative. For example, they should not invest in developing deep trust with casual customers, but rather reserve such efforts for those of longstanding loyalty.

6.5. Maturity of Trust

Trust is quite often relegated from a business perspective as being soft and thus inappropriate, indicating the low level of maturity in most companies' approach to trust. It is desirable that companies develop a more mature approach to trust, where initial disorganised approaches will become more structured and subject to systematic, optimising processes.

It is not expected that all companies will achieve such high degrees of maturity in their approaches to trust, or that every company will apply the same level of maturity throughout its organisation (even though such an outcome is highly desirable). However, an increased growth in the maturity of trust is the most desirable outcome for all companies who wish to avail themselves of the full benefits of adopting trust into their business practices.

'Designing for trust' uses the maturity model from trust governance to indicate the stage of the discussion about trust. While indicative, this model allows companies to achieve a certain understanding of their position and the potential benefits of a better understanding of trust.

7. UNIFYING PARADIGM

Paradigms provide a unifying 'view of the world' that structures and informs the overall framework. In the case of trust governance, the paradigm aims to incorporate not only trust, but also security (control), in ways that complement each other. Furthermore, it is a socio-technical paradigm because it incorporates both the ICT system and the social agents that are an integral part of the system.

The paradigm employed by both trust governance and by 'designing for trust' is inspired by TROPOS (Giunchiglia, Mylopoulos and Perini 2001) and Secure Tropos (Mouratidis and Giorgini, 2007), as well as the discussion of the duality of trust and control (Mollering, 2005), in its more pragmatic approach (Cofta, 2007), and it directly relates to the complementary role of trust and security. The paradigm consists of the following elements, as illustrated in Figure 2.

The unifying paradigm attempts to model the conflicting requirements of designers of an ICT system and the users of such a system, described from the perspective of a user (whether actual user or a would-be user of a future system).

Figure 2. Unifying paradigm

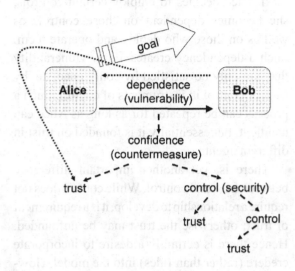

Therefore, it models what 'is' rather than what 'should be'. In this sense, the paradigm addresses both affordance and functionality, i.e. the way the system is used and the way the system is intended to be used.

The context in which the paradigm should be considered is as follows. The user has been given (or will be given) an ICT system that has certain technical functionalities that are likely to be a reflection of the intentions of its designers and developers. For example, the system may allow a user to enter data into a healthcare database. However, the goal of users of such a system is only partly related to such functionality (e.g. their goal is to provide quality healthcare). They depend on the system to satisfy some parts of such goals, but they are able to bypass, circumvent or ignore some functionalities through social practices (within the affordance of the system), if they do not support their goals. In this process, they depend on each other, as well as on the system.

7.1. Agents

For the purpose of our unifying paradigm the ICT system and its social environment are modelled in terms of intentional, goal-seeking agents. An agent is an abstraction used to model anything that makes decisions such as a human being, a company or a software entity. For example, a person, company role (such as IT support), an element of an ICT system (such as an application or a server) can all be considered to be an agent. The number and type of agents depends on the purpose of the analysis. Different agents may have different understanding of the number, structure and roles of other agents.

Humans are natural candidates for such intentional, goal-seeking agents, however, organisations or inanimate objects can be also treated as intentional agents (Dennett, 1989), especially when the details of their internal operations are not immediately or obviously available to another agent. In fact, the perception of intentionality of such agents serves as a mental stance that is grounded in the rationality of human beings who developed, deployed or operate a particular technology.

The abstraction level of agents depends on the purpose of the analysis and on the perception of the world, as viewed by particular users. Some agents may represent more abstract concepts, for as long as they are attributed with intentionality, e.g. 'the world', or 'the Internet'. Such coarse-grained agents can reveal their inner structure through a deeper analysis, but such an analysis may not be always necessary. For example, a customer may view the call centre as a single agent, but the manager of such a call centre can see its internal complexity.

It is a requirement that agents should seek goals otherwise they are not dependent on others in any meaningful way. Human agents are natural goal-seekers and their goals can be captured either through formal analysis (e.g. from codified business objectives) or through informal means (e.g. through interviews). In the case of inanimate agents such as computers or systems, the goals of such agents are determined by the goals of their creators and operators, as perceived by users.

7.2. Dependency and Confidence

Agents are dependent on other agents in achieving their goals, and this dependence represents a vulnerability because it exposes an agent (e.g. Alice) to the behaviour of others (e.g. Bob), where Bob's behaviour is not always predictable. This dependence makes Alice concerned about achieving her desired outcome (her goals) because her goals are contingent upon Bob's (uncertain) actions). Furthermore, if Alice wants to consider all possible outcomes she is bound by the cognitive complexity of this process (Hodgson & Cofta 2008).

The vulnerability of dependency can be countermeasured by the confidence that Alice has in the future actions of Bob. This confidence allows Alice to contain the complexity of possible outcomes by mentally concentrating only on those where Bob acts in a manner that is beneficial, predictable and trustworthy!

7.3. Duality of Trust and Control

Alice can reason (e.g. by self-reflection on her own situation) that Bob's future actions depend on two factors: his intentions and his constraints, i.e. that he may have the intention and willingness to act in a way that is beneficial to Alice, or he may be forced by certain constraints to act against his intentions. The first way to satisfy Alice's confidence is related to trust, the alternative is to control.

Therefore Alice can be confident about Bob's actions because she trusts him (and hopefully her trust is justified) or she can be confident because she has control over his actions. One can expect that in the majority of cases Alice would apply a mix of trust and control to achieve her confidence. Such a combination is usually driven by prudence (e.g. Alice lets Bob keep her account books but also employs an auditor) or by controls that constrain Alice's decisions (e.g. Alice lets Bob drive her car but she has to take out an insurance policy).

If Alice decides to employ certain controls, she becomes dependent on those controls as well as on those who deploy and operate them. Such a dependency creates a new vulnerability that can only be satisfied by confidence, i.e. by trust or control in instruments of control. Such a process can be repeated for as long as Alice can handle it, but essentially it is founded on trust in different agents.

There is, yet another important difference between trust and control. While control does not require a relationship to develop, it is a requirement of trust; otherwise the trust may be unfounded. Hence there is certainly a desire to incorporate credere (rather than fides) into the model. However, several forms of trust as credere should be understood here in terms of control rather than trust. Specifically, reputation can be seen as an instrument of social control that holds Bob hostage to his reputation, but that requires Alice to trust sources that report such a reputation (Cofta, 2007). The only form of credere that definitely is not related to control is Alice's own assessment of Bob's trustworthiness - but then its is quite likely that Alice is already in a relationship with Bob - even though the relationship is a shallow one.

8. ASSESSMENT FRAMEWORK

Reasoning about trust and control is quite simple and intuitive for small systems but the growth in size and complexity of ICT systems makes it necessary to utilise tools and methods that facilitate the reasoning process i.e. the assessment framework. The problem that analysis faces is the combination of the sheer amount of data that must be taken into account with semantic variations of the sources of such information. They can solicit certain local and expert knowledge about dependencies but the amount of data, combined with its semantic incompatibility make reasoning almost impossible.

Following the paradigm, the framework jointly analyses trust and control, and it is not intended to analyse trust in isolation (even though it is of course possible). The assessment framework can be used in many different ways throughout the life of an ICT system. While this chapter concentrates on incorporating trust into the design phase, it is important to remember that the phenomenon of trust is pervasive and should be addressed throughout all the phases, as listed below:

1. During the requirements phase it supports the capture of declarative statements regarding trust and control that express preferences and affordances of different actors, beyond what is directly related to the actual operating system. In a manner similar to the one above, such statements will be captured in a way that is potentially intra-subjective and quantitative.

2. During the specification phase, it facilitates global reasoning about trust and control across potentially incompatible domains of understanding. This is specifically important for large systems where the co-dependence of several actors from incomparable backgrounds is essential for the successful operation of the system.

3. During design, it allows for the detection of risk factors such as anomalies and deficiencies of relationships of trust and control, e.g. circular reference, single point of failure, excessive responsibility etc. Such anomalies and deficiencies can be attributed to significant risk factors and their elimination or reduction should greatly decrease the risk.

4. During the maintenance phase the framework facilitates the capture of local knowledge regarding trust and control within the system that is actually in operation and its immediate environment, as perceived by different actors related to the system ('I can be dependent on X because...').

5. During all phases, it allows for speculative 'what-if' scenarios to be tested before the deployment of particular updates, extensions or new products, greatly decreasing risk associated with the continuity and growth of the system.

There are several ways in which the resulting dependency graph can be analysed, and the exact method depends on the desired outcome. Therefore, subsequent sections should be read as illustrative examples, not as prescriptive methods. While they attempt to consolidate best theoretical and practical aspects of trust-related analysis, the complete analytical framework is still under development. However, for several practical cases a simple (even overly simplistic) approach is often sufficient to identify significant deficiencies, and methods presented below have been used to study such cases.

8.1. Structural Analysis

The core component of the framework is a dependency graph that allows for the capture and representation of existing dependencies and perceived ways of dealing with them. Figure 3 presents a simplified version of a graph that has been used to analyse the social adoption of a particular identity management system (Cofta, 2009). For simplicity, this example only analyses trust relationships (thus ignoring control) and uses a simple bi-nominal scale of trust: either an agent is trusted or distrusted. Despite this apparent over-simplification, the analysis conducted with the help of this graph has been extremely useful in determining potential deficiencies.

In general, agents, both technical and social, are represented as nodes and the dependencies between them are represented as directed thick solid lines. The declared confidence between them (unilateral trust, mutual trust, distrust) is represented as a light (solid or dashed) directed line. For example, A is dependent on X with regard to

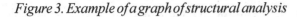

Figure 3. Example of a graph of structural analysis

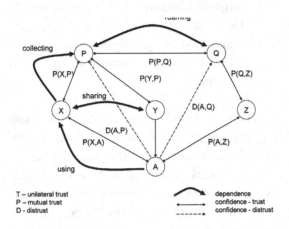

usage (thick solid line) and there is a mutual trust between A and X (light solid line).

The graph is a result of individual agents expressing their understanding of dependencies and confidence in the surrounding world. While constructing a graph, it is necessary to determine at least the following for each agent:

1. Agent's view on dependencies within the system, not only his own but also other agents, specifically technical agents.
2. Agent's understanding of context and temporal characteristics of a particular dependency (what it is about and how it may change over time).
3. Agent's reasoning about confidence regarding a given dependency and the composition of trust and control that delivers such confidence.
4. Agent's perception of the strength of trust and control that contribute to the degree of confidence.
5. If an analysis uncovers new dependencies (e.g. because an agent is dependent on an instrument of control), the above should be repeated recursively.

The finished graph is a compromise between the subjectivity of an individual's perception of the world and the objectivity that is necessary for analysis. There are several methods that facilitate the creation of a graph that strikes a reasonable balance between subjectivity and objectivity. For example, while it is desirable to engage with a large group of social agents (to achieve a complete view of the problem), it is necessary to use moderators that are responsible for the gradual convergence of subjective perspectives.

8.2. Strength of Trust

Measuring trust is a key challenge, yet without measuring little can be done in terms of reasoning. Existing approaches (see e.g. Cofta, 2007 for a review) range from formal scales of trust (e.g. Marsh, 1994), feedback-based reputation (Golbeck, 2008), to measuring trust through its outcome (Keser, 2003) to the acknowledgement of the complex, qualitative, subjective and generally non-measurable nature of trust (Castelfranchi and Falcone 2000).

Trust governance takes a pragmatic approach, trying to quantify what may be essentially subjective and qualitative for the purpose of assessing its contribution to confidence. The proposal acknowledges the variety of natures and sources of trust (Lewicki & Bunker, 1996) and rather than seeking exactness it looks for differentiation that is sufficient for design purposes and can inform the choice of an appropriate set of tools.

The starting point for this discussion is the difference between the roles of trust and control (security) when it comes to satisfying confidence. While the assessment of control relates to the ability to enforce a specific behaviour through external pressure (or the threat of it), trust attempts to assess intentions that are fully exhibited only if there is no external pressure. Trust, therefore, is an assessment of trustworthiness, where such trustworthiness is related to intentions rather than behaviour - thus being impossible to observe directly, and accessible only through the interpretation of an assessor.

The assessment of trustworthiness is therefore inherently subjective, where the mental attitude of an assessor is a part of the assessment - they collectively form the frame of mind (Nooteboom, 2005) that redefines the interpretation of any evidence available to an assessor. The same evidence can therefore be interpreted differently (even drastically differently) depending on the frame of mind, leading to diametrically different outcomes of assessment. In contrast, security-related assessment of behaviour can be undertaken from the position of an external observer, informed by policies, in an almost objective manner, leaving little to subjective interpretations and eventually providing better foundations for introducing numerical values into an assessment.

However, the relationship of trust goes through a series of distinctive frames of mind that are universally shared and can be reliably recognised (McAllister, Lewicki, & Chaturvedi, 2006). Each frame determines why one trusts (and why one is considered trustworthy) and what kind of evidence can support such an assessment. Such a sequence of frames of mind can be used to determine the relative strength of trust within such a relationship, as they are correlated with the resistance of trust to errors, lapses and misinterpretations, i.e. to the strength of trust.

Within each frame, it is possible to apply an appropriate methodology to determine (and possibly quantify as a numerical value) the relative strength of trust, but such quantification is valid only within such a frame. Quantified values are incomparable between frames, as they relate to different states of mind and are likely to be determined by different methodologies. Later, when it comes to working with trust, different frames call for different instruments to improve or contain trust.

For practical analysis it may often be more important to determine the exact frame of mind rather than the exact value within such a frame,

Figure 4. The strength of trust

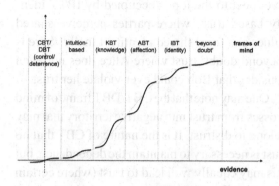

and for every analysis the determination of an actual frame of mind should be made before attempting to assess the value. Similarly, for practical reasons, it may be more important to make a coarse assessment of trust versus distrust than to achieve an exact measurement.

Figure 4 illustrates the assumed relationship between available evidence of trustworthiness and the perceived strength of trust. It is necessary to stress that this is a proposition and the shape of the S-curve composed of disjointed S-curves may not exactly reflect the relationship, only showing its general nature. Every disjointed element of a main S-curve represents a distinctively different frame of mind, ordered according to their relative strength. Within each frame, the curve repeats itself, reflecting the (generally quantitative) growth of a relationship between qualitative discontinuations.

The lowest level of trust belongs to the frame identified as CBT/DBT (control-based trust or deterrence-based trust). It is the position where trust does not exist but has been compensated for by control and deterrence. Moving towards a stronger degree of trust, there is an instinctive trust that one can assess subconsciously, through the neuropsychological mechanism (Petland & Heibeck, 2008), followed by KBT - knowledge-based trust that is built rationally out of knowledge and reputation. Further up in the hierarchy is ABT

- affection-based trust that acts on emotions. The level next to the top is occupied by IBT - identity based trust, where parties perceive shared values and form shared identity. Finally, there is 'beyond doubt' trust where Alice does not even consider that Bob could ever violate her trust.

One may note that the CBT/DBT frame of mind crosses from trust into negative territory that may belong to distrust. It is the nature of CBT that no trust is necessary to maintain the dependence, but this may equally well lead to trust (where certain controls allow for safe experimentation to meet demands). Alternatively it may lead to distrust (where excessive control is considered to be a sign of a lack of trust that should be reciprocated).

It may be possible to construct a symmetric structure of frames of mind that lead to distrust, starting from a certain intuition and ending at distrust beyond repair. The construct of distrust (Cofta, 2006; Hardin, 2004), is unfortunately even more complex than the construct of trust, so that this chapter will not discuss the strength of distrust further, saying only that the strength of distrust can be understood symmetrically to the strength of trust - as an effort that is needed to overcome such a distrust.

8.3. Reasoning

One can quickly determine from Figure 3 that the dependency graph is not complete as not all confidence levels are reported. For example, there is no explicit information about confidence between X and Y, even though there is a mutual dependency related to information sharing.

Reasoning rules enable the assessment of confidence on the basis of existing observations if a direct report about such confidence is not available. While there can be several different reasoning schema (Alcalde & Mauw 2009), the one below has been found useful as an example, discussed here. It is worth noting that for different application areas, different schema may be more

suitable, and that the one below should be treated only as an illustration of a concept.

The schema lists six simple rules that allow reasoning about missing confidence or to determine anomalies. The schema should be interpreted as follows. In order to determine the confidence that is not present in the graph, reasoning rules can be applied to existing information until such a confidence can be determined. Note that such reasoning may not yield any result (if there is not enough information) or it may yield conflicting results (if two different sequences of rules bring different outcomes).

1. $T(x, y), T(y, z) \rightarrow T(x, z)$ (transitivity)
2. $T(x, a), T(x, b) \rightarrow P(a, b)$ (delegation)
3. $T(x, y), T(y, x) \rightarrow P(x, y)$ (consolidation)
4. $T(x, y), D(y, z) \rightarrow D(x, z)$ (pruning)
5. $T(x, a), D(x, b) \rightarrow D(a, b)$ (conflict)
6. $T(x, y), D(x, y) \rightarrow D(x, y)$ (distrust)

For example, while assessing confidence between X and Y, it is possible to reason that because there is $P(X, P)$ and $P(Y, P)$ then (rule 2) there should be $P(X, Y)$. Note that reasoning may lead to several different assessments of the same relationship or may lead to an assessment that conflicts with a direct observation. Either is an anomaly that should be somehow addressed.

8.4. Anomaly Detection

As an evocative example, let's consider a simple information system that is being used by only three people: Alice, Bob and Carol. While all of them depend on the system to carry out their duties, none of them has a global understanding of relationships of trust that are relevant to the system. Several important defects can exist unnoticed, for example:

1. Structural defects. If Alice trusts (i.e. relies on) Bob to take care of the system, Bob trusts Carol and Carol trusts Alice, all of

them seem to be reassured that the system is taken care of, yet no-one is actually doing it.

2. Quantitative defects. If Alice trusts Carol a lot while Bob trusts her only a little (in the same context), then either their judgement is impaired or Carol is actually not trustworthy.

3. Contextual deficiencies. If Carol relies on Alice (e.g. to manage a database) and Alice trusts Bob (to manage backups), then Carol may be misled in relying on Bob to manage the database on the basis of Alice's trust, that is in fact placed in a different context.

4. Objectivity deficiencies. Alice may believe that she has to trust Carol to have the system working properly while Bob believes that he can trust Carol for the same purpose. While both use the term 'trust', their reasoning may not be compatible.

All the examples above relate to trust only and serve to illustrate the novel components of the framework. The assessment framework allows for the detection of at least some anomalies with regard to trust alone, and an even larger number of such anomalies when trust and control are analysed together. Such a joint analysis is important, as dependencies are usually satisfied by the combination of trust and control, and only a joint analysis can uncover deficiencies and anomalies.

Referring back to Figure 3, it is possible to note that while A mutually trusts X and X mutually trusts P, there is a distrust between A and P - the potential quantitative defect. For as long as there is no direct dependency between A and P, such a situation is manageable because X can take the responsibility for maintaining both trust relationships. However, if P desires to substitute X in the relationship (e.g. by becoming a preferred point of contact or by operating the system), the dependency will not be compensated for.

8.5. Portfolio of Methods

It is of little value to detect anomalies if it is not possible to act on them. Certainly, a designer can redesign the system so that certain anomalies or defects are removed. Furthermore, a designer can capitalise on identified relationships of trust to improve on the overall design, introducing trusted intermediaries, trusted third parties, and deregulation of tasks etc. It is possible to develop a catalogue of transitions to the original graph of structural analysis that introduces improvements to the distribution and usage of trust, thus removing some of the defects.

However, it is also quite likely that a defect cannot be removed yet the need for trust has to be satisfied, for example, when a particular group of people has to work together or a particular person has to be trustworthy. Such dependencies call for an alternative approach that can be used in situations where the actual strength of trust does not satisfy needs. In the case of security, controls (such as firewalls, policies, access control etc.) can be designed and deployed to deliver the desired effects. Trust, however, cannot be guaranteed or enforced, but it can be enabled or enhanced.

Enablers capitalise on the natural human propensity to trust (i.e. the trait of choosing trust over distrust), by improving communication between people. There is an expectation that such improved communication will eventually expose the real intentions of both parties, and will enable trust, but it may also enable distrust if parties find themselves in disagreement.

Technical support for enablers are in the form of improved communication means, ranging from telephone to e-mail, shared web spaces, messaging, virtual worlds, shared game spaces etc. It is specifically important for enablers to clearly communicate evidence of trust (or distrust) to the other party without unnecessary processing but in a form that is most easily understood. Certain forms of reputation ratings (e.g. eBay's PowerSeller, see Cofta, 2007) provide a good example of enablers.

Enhancers aim to develop trust where it is desired, by demonstrating to both parties the possibility, potential for, and benefits of trust, in the expectation that this will eventually positively affect intentions. Enhancers can be used to both improve trust and to recover loss of trust, and potentially even recover from the position of distrust. While enhancers capitalise on the natural human propensity to trust, they also provide technical support for the two main techniques that are useful in trust development of the 'soft' game of trust (Ullmann-Margalit, 2003) and rituals of regret and forgiveness (Marsh and Briggs, 2008).

Technology can support trust enhancers by providing non-threatening collaborative spaces where trust can be gradually built (e.g. Dwyer, 2009) or by introducing those two techniques to existing interaction systems.

9. MATURITY MODEL

Business approaches to trust need to evolve from the inability to deal with trust (that we commonly observe today, Lewicki & Bunker, 1996) to a conscious, controlled investment in trust equity throughout a company, including the development of appropriate systems. Following the widely used CMM model (e.g. Persse, 2001), one can identify five stages of the maturity model.

1. Initial (chaotic). Trust is treated as a 'soft' and 'fuzzy' entity and decisions related to trust are individual and subjective. There may be some local standards or initiatives to deal with trust, but trust is not a part of the corporate agenda. While designing or procuring ICT systems, trust is not a part of the requirements.
2. Repeatable (disciplined). The company understands that there is value in trust (even though it may have problems in quantifying it) and establishes certain processes related to trust. For example, a trustworthy provider

may be preferred to one that is cheaper etc. Trust appears as a non-functional requirement, but is not quantified.
3. Defined (standard). There are established (yet possibly not complete) standards of trust and trustworthiness throughout the company, such as expected quality of service (QoS), team development process etc. For ICT systems, the company can express its needs, usually in the form of testable quality of service requirements that span functional and non-functional requirements.
4. Managed (quantified). The value of trust is understood by the business and the company actively manages its expectations regarding different aspects of trust. There is a process to assess and improve trust (if necessary) and the value of long-term investment in trust is recognised. ICT systems are designed with social trust in mind, possibly using the methodology presented here.
5. Optimizing (improvement). The company can reflect on its approach to trust and can improve upon it addressing the deficiencies of its own actions. There is an investment in implementing and improving trust governance for the benefit of the company. ICT systems are part of an overall approach to trust.

10. CONCLUSION

This chapter discusses some aspects of 'designing for trust', a design methodology that incorporates trust into the design practice. This methodology is heavily based on trust governance, a complete proposition that makes trust relevant to business practices, including the design and deployment of ICT systems, in close relationship with well recognised security practices. Trust governance is a five-part proposition that incorporates the business justification of trust with an analytical framework, and a set of relevant tools and methods, as well as a maturity model, to make trust relevant to business objectives.

We have discussed how 'designing for trust' allows trust to be incorporated into the design practices of ICT systems by incorporating trust governance and by complementing security-based methodologies. However, the value of 'designing for trust' and trust governance exceeds the scope of ICT system design. The methodology incorporated into trust governance can be used in several contexts, where trust and security-based control both shape reliance and cope with dependencies. For example, organisational science will find it beneficial to use trust governance to study relationships of trust within organisations, in relation to group building, knowledge sharing etc. Similarly, Web Science can benefit from this approach while analysing webs of trust or trust-related behaviours while customer-facing organisations may use it to analyse customer behaviour and improve upon existing practices.

The current research effort concentrates on two directions. First, a set of tools that supports the methodology is being developed, together with the associated logic for reasoning and anomaly detection. Second, a series of small exercises are being undertaken to verify the practical usefulness and practicality of the proposition. In the future, large scale projects will be undertaken.

REFERENCES

Abdul-Rahman, A. (2005) *A Framework for Decentralised trust Reasoning*. PhD Thesis. Available at: http://www.cs.ucl.ac.uk/ staff/ F.AbdulRahman/ docs/ thesis-final.pdf.

Alcalde, B., & Mauw, S. (2009) *An algebra for trust dilution and trust fusion*. Accepted for the 2009 World Congress on Privacy, Security, Trust and the Management of e-Business.

Anderson, R. (2001). *Security Engineering: A Guide to Building Dependable Distributed Systems*. New York: John Wiley & Sons Inc.

Ashraf, N., Camerer, C. F., & Loewenstein, G. (2005). Adam Smith, Behavioral Economist. *The Journal of Economic Perspectives, 19*(3). doi:10.1257/089533005774357897

Birks, P. (1997). *The Classification of Obligations*. Clarendon Press.

Boehm, B. (1981). *Software Engineering Economics*. Upper Saddle River, NJ: Prentice-Hall.

Castelfranchi, C., & Falcone, R. (2000) Trust is much more than subjective probability: Mental components and sources of trust. Proc. *of the 33rd Hawaii Int. Conf. on System Sciences (HICSS2000). Vol. 6*, 2000.

Chang, E., Dillion, T., & Hussain, F. K. (2006). *Trust and Reputation for Service-Oriented Environments: Technologies for Building Business Intelligence and Consumer Confidence*. New York: John Wiley & Sons, Ltd. doi:10.1002/9780470028261

Cofta, P. (2006) *Distrust. In: Proc. of Eight Int. Conf. on Electronic Commerce ICEC'06*, Fredericton, Canada. pp. 250-258.

Cofta, P. (2007). *Trust, Complexity and Control: Confidence in a Convergent World*. New York: John Wiley and Sons.

Cofta, P. (2009). Towards a better citizen identification system. *Identity in the Information Society, 1*(1), 39–53. doi:10.1007/s12394-009-0006-6

Cofta, P. (2009). Designing for Trust. In Whitworth, B., & de Moor, A. (Eds.), *Handbook of Research on Socio-Technical Design and Social Networking Systems. Information Science Reference*. IGI Global.

Cofta, P., & Lacohée, H. (2010). Trust in identification systems: from empirical observations to design guidelines. In Yan, Z. (Ed.), *Trust Modelling and management in Digital Environments: From Social Concepts to System Development.* New York: Information Science Reference. doi:10.4018/978-1-61520-682-7.ch019

Collins, T. (2007) NHS security dilemma as smartcards shared. *Computer Weekly,* January 30, 2007.

Cranor, L., & Garfinkel, S. (2005) *Security and Usability: Designing Secure Systems that People Can Use.* O'Reilly Media, Inc.

Dennett, D. C. (1989). *The Intentional Stance.* New York: Bradford Books.

Dimmock, N., Bacon, J., Ingram, D., & Moody, K. (2005). Risk Models for Trust-Based Access Control (TBAC). In Herrmann, P. (Ed.), *iTrust2005, LNCS 3477* (pp. 364–371).

Dwyer, N. (2009) *Enabling Trust in Virtual Teams.* BT STRF Research Report.

Flowerday, S., & von Solms, R. (2006). Trust: An Element of Information Security. In Fischer-Hubner, S., Rannenberg, K., Yngstrom, L., & Lindskog, S. (Eds.), *IFIP Int. Federation for Information Processing, Security and Privacy in Dynamic Environments.* Boston: Springer.

Fukuyama, F. (1996). *Trust: The Social Virtues and the Creation of Prosperity.* Touchstone Books.

Gibson, J. J. (1986). *The Ecological Approach to Visual Perception.* Houghton Mifflin Company USA.

Giunchiglia, F., Mylopoulos, J., & Perini, A. (2001) *The Tropos Software Development Methodology: Processes, Models and Diagrams.* Technical Report DIT-02-008, Informatica e Telecomunicazioni, University of Trento

Golbeck, J. (2008). *Computing with Social Trust.* New York: Springer.

Hansen, M. T. (2009). When Internal Collaboration is Bad for Your Company. *Harvard Business Review,* (April): 83–88.

Hardin, R. (Ed.). (2002). *Trust and trustworthiness.* Russel Sage Foundation.

Hardin, R. (Ed.). (2004). *Distrust.* Russell Sage Foundation.

Hodgson, P., & Cofta, P. (2008) Society as an information network. *International journal of technology, knowledge and society,* Boston.

Hodgson, P., & Cofta, P. (2009) *Towards a methodology for research on trust.* In: Proceedings of the WebSci'09: Society On-Line, 18-20 March 2009, Athens, Greece. (In Press)

Isham, J. (2000). *The Effect of Social Capital on Technology Adoption: Evidence from Rural Tanzania.* Opportunities in Africa: Micro-evidence on Firms and Households. Retrieved 18 October, 2007, from http://www.csae.ox.ac.uk/conferences/2000-OiA/pdfpapers/isham.PDF

Kearney, P. (2009) *Preliminary specification and design of graphical workbench.* Deliverable M3.2.1 EU MASTER project.

Keser, C. (2003). Experimental games for the design of reputation management systems. *IBM Systems Journal, 42*(3). doi:10.1147/sj.423.0498

Lacohée, H., Cofta, P., Phippen, A., & Furnell, S. (2008). *Understanding Public Perceptions: Trust and Engagement in ICT Mediated Services.* International Engineering Consortium.

Lassar, W., Mittal, B., & Sharma, A. (1995). Measuring customer-based brand equity. *Journal of Consumer Marketing, 12*(4), 11–19. doi:10.1108/07363769510095270

Lewicki, R. J., Bunker, B, B. (1996) Developing and maintaining trust in work relationships. In Trust in Organisations: Frontiers of theory and Research

Lippert, S, K., Davis, M. (2006). A conceptual model integrating trust into planned change activities to enhance technology adoption. *Journal of Information Science*, 32.

Luhmann, N. (1979). *Trust and Power*. New York: John Wiley & Sons.

Marsh, S., & Briggs, P. (2008). Examining Trust, Forgiveness and Regret as Computational Concepts. In Golbeck, J. (Ed.), *Computing with Social Trust*. New York: Springer.

Marsh, S. P. (1994) *Formalising Trust as a Computational Concept*. University of Stirling PhD thesis.

Martin, M. (1991). *"Hello, Central?" Gender, technology and Culture in the Formation of Telephone Systems*. Montreal: McGill-Queen's University Press.

Mauw, S., & Oostdijk, M. (2005). Foundations of Attack Trees. Information Security and Cryptology - ICISC 2005. *Springer Lecture Notes in Computer Science*, 3935, 186–198. doi:10.1007/11734727_17

McAllister, D. J., Lewicki, R. J., & Chaturvedi, S. (2006). Trust in developing relationships: From theory to measurement. In Weaver, K. M. (Ed.), *Academy of Management Best Papers Proceedings*.

McKnight, D. H., & Chervany, N. L. (1996) *The Meanings of Trust*. In University of Minnesota, http://www.misrc.umn.edu/ wpaper/ wp96-04. htm.

Microsoft. (2009) *The Microsoft SDL Threat Modelling Tool*. Available: http://msdn.microsoft. com/en-us/security/dd206731.aspx

Mollering, G. (2005) The Trust/Control Duality: An Integrative Perspective on Positive Expectations of Others. In: *Int. Sociology, September 2005, Vol. 20*(3): 283–305. 2005.

Mouratidis, H., & Cofta, P. (2010). *Practitioner's challenges in designing trust into online systems*. Manuscript.

Mouratidis, H., Giorgini, P. (2007) Secure Tropos: A Security-Oriented Extension of the Tropos methodology, *International Journal of Software Engineering and Knowledge Engineering (IJSEKE) 17(*2) pp. 285-309, World Scientific, 2007.

Nooteboom, B. (2002). *Trust: Forms, Foundations, Functions, Failures and Figures*. Edward Elgar.

Nooteboom, B. (2005) *Framing, attribution and scripts in the development of trust. In. Proc. of symposium on 'Risk, trust and civility'*, Victoria College, University of Toronto, 6-8 May 2005.

Norman, D. A. (1988). *The Psychology of Everyday Things*. New York: Basic Books.

Pearson, S. (2002). Trusted Computing Platforms: TCPA Technology. In *Context*. Upper Saddle River, NJ: Prentice-Hall.

Persse, J. R. (2001). *Implementing the Capability Maturity Model*. New York: Wiley.

Petland, S., & Heibeck, T. (2008, Fall). Understanding 'Honest Signals' in Business. *MIT Sloan Management Review., 50*(1), 70–75.

Potter, N. N. (2002). *How Can I Be Trusted?: A Virtue Theory Of Trustworthiness*. Rowman & Littlefield Publishers.

Resnick, P. (2006, Jun). The value of reputation on eBay: a controlled experiment. *Experimental Economics, 9*(Issue 2), 79–101. Available at http:// www.si.umich.edu/ ~presnick/ papers/ postcards/ PostcardsFinalPrePub.pdf. doi:10.1007/s10683-006-4309-2

Saunders, M. N. K., & Thornhill, A. (2003). Organisational justice, trust and the management of change: An exploration. *Personnel Review, 32*(3), 360–375. doi:10.1108/00483480310467660

Seppanen, R., & Blomqvist, K. (2006) It is not all About Trust-The Role of Distrust in Inter-Organizational Relationships. In: *Network-Centric Collaboration and Supporting Frameworks, proc. of IFIP TC5 WG 5.5 Seventh IFlP Working Conference on Virtual Enterprises, 25'27 September 2006*, Helsinki, Finland. Springer Boston.

Ullmann-Margalit, E. (2003) *Trust out of distrust*. Available at: www.law.nyu.edu/ clppt/program2001/ readings/ ullman_margalit/ Trust%20 out%20of%20Distrust.pdf

Venkatesh, V., Morris, M. G., Davis, G. B., & Davis, F. D. (2003). User acceptance of information technology: Toward a unified view. *Management Information Systems Quarterly, 27*(3), 425–478.

Willcocks, L. P., & Cullen, S. (2006) *The Outsourcing Enterprise: The Power of Relationships*. Available: http://www.logicacmg.com/ pSecured/ admin/ countries/ assets/ serve_asset. asp?id=3252.

Section 4
Secure Code Analysis

Chapter 11
Static Program Analysis of Multi–Applet Java Card Applications

Alexandros Loizidis
Aristotle University of Thessaloniki, Greece

Vasilios Almaliotis
Aristotle University of Thessaloniki, Greece

Panagiotis Katsaros
Aristotle University of Thessaloniki, Greece

ABSTRACT

Java Card provides a framework of classes and interfaces that hide the details of the underlying smart card interface and make it possible to load and run on the same card several applets, from different application providers with complex trust relationships. This fact paves the way for new business applications, but the card issuer has to secure absence of malicious or faulty card applets. He has to be able to check that (i) applets do not cause illicit method invocations that violate temporal restrictions of inter-applet communication, (ii) applets protect themselves from unwanted information flow to third parties and (iii) it is not possible for an unhandled Java Card API exception to leave an applet in an unpredictable state that is potentially dangerous for the application's security. The authors explore recent advances in theory and tool support of static program analysis and they present an approach for automatic verification of smart card applications that by definition are security critical.

INTRODUCTION

In this work, we propose program analysis techniques implemented in the FindBugs open source framework (Hovemeyer & Pugh, 2004; The Find-Bugs project site, 2009), for statically verifying

important security properties of interacting Java Card applets.

Static program analysis has the potential to become a credible technique for automatic verification of smart card applications that by definition are security critical. There is a large collection of well established analysis techniques and recent research developments, as well as versatile analy-

DOI: 10.4018/978-1-61520-837-1.ch011

sis frameworks like FindBugs that open excellent prospects to exploit the provided support and the already implemented error detectors. Current article introduces error detectors adapted to the security requirements of the Java Card multi-applet environment, in order to highlight the perspectives and the limitations of the discussed alternative.

The most significant virtue is the use of a single verification technique, in place of existing verification approaches that require highly specialized formal analysis skills, for the different Java Card security verification tasks. In our case, analysis assumes only basic Java programming skills, but the analysis precision is restricted by the current limitations of the analysis support provided by FindBugs. We highlight these limitations and we discuss recent research work that aims at improved analysis precision, based on requirements that may be fulfilled in future versions of FindBugs.

Our analysis addresses the security concerns caused by the fact that Java Card allows several applets to load and run on the same card, from different application providers with complex trust relationships and partnerships. The Java Card platform controls cooperation of interacting applets through a firewall mechanism that enforces applet isolation and allows communication only through explicitly declared shareable interfaces including the explicitly permitted method invocations. This sort of checks is static in nature, i.e. one method call is either allowed in all cases or it is never allowed. Thus, the built-in Java Card protection cannot impose temporal restrictions on inter-applet communications.

In a scenario, where several independent application providers have applets on a single card, the aforementioned weakness generates a serious security risk for illicit method invocations between the interacting applets. Let us consider the typical case of a multi-applet smart card with one purse applet and two loyalty applets that are notified when card transactions occur, in order to award bonus points. Loyalty applets are communicated to by calls to methods declared in shareable in-

terfaces. Temporal restrictions for secure applet interaction include the requirement of recursion freeness for the methods of the shareable interfaces and the absence of transitive communications that span the contexts of the two loyalty applets. In the more complex case, where a loyalty applet shares bonus points through some agreed loyalty applet to loyalty applet communication, secure interaction requires additional temporal restrictions besides those mentioned.

Apart from temporal safety, it is also important to assure that the allowed communication between the three applets does not imply unwanted information flow from one loyalty applet to the other. This is the only way to guarantee that secret and potentially commercial data produced in one applet cannot be leaked to another applet, while at the same time applets of one application cannot be crashed by other applet's corrupt data.

Other sources of security risk are the misused Java Card API calls in combination with the multiple-entry-point program structure. Since applets run forever and their execution is suspended when the card is removed from the reader, a potentially unhandled exception that reaches the invoked entry point may leave an applet in an unpredictable state that can be dangerous for the application's security.

Next section presents the current state of the art in security verification of Java Card multi-applet applications. We highlight the problems faced and we examine the available alternatives for static program analysis techniques that focus on the described Java Card security problems. In the subsequent section, we introduce basic concepts of static program analysis with the Find-Bugs framework. The provided analysis support is exploited in the developed FindBugs security bug detectors that are presented in the following section. Our bug detectors belong to a category of static program analysis techniques, which are commonly referred to as typestate tracking. These techniques are appropriate for the first and the third mentioned security problems. In separate sections, we discuss state of the art program analysis techniques that improve analysis precision, as well as techniques for the second mentioned security problem. Finally, we conclude with a critical view of the shown security verification approach and we discuss its anticipated impact.

BACKGROUND

Static Analysis

Static analysis can be effective in verifying the behavior of a program against a partial specification that represents the absence of a security error. By the term static analysis we refer to any approach for assessing code without executing it. This broad definition includes fully-automated model checking techniques, semi-automated formal analyses that involve logical inference and program analyses that are based on abstract interpretation or alternatively on dataflow facts over the control-flow graph of the source program.

In the Java Card multi-applet environment, security errors may be attributed to illegal applet interactions that are not caught by the Java Card firewall or to misused and therefore dangerous calls of Java Card API methods. The static analyses found in the related bibliography are based on established formal techniques that aim in precise program verification (Burdy et. al., 2003; Beckert & Mostowski, 2003; Marché et. al., 2004; Meyer & Poetzsch-Heffter, 2000; Jacobs et. al., 2004; Van den Berg & Jacobs, 2001; Breunesse et. al., 2005), but they are not fully automated. It is important to note that there is no single technique that can cope with all kinds of security errors in Java Card applications.

For detecting unwanted information flows to third parties we refer to the following alternatives:

- The type inference approach proposed in (Akdemir, 1998), which essentially intro-

duces changes in the original type inference algorithm of the Java Card platform.

- The assume-guarantee model checking approach of (Bieber et. al., 2002), which is based on abstracting the byte codes of the methods of a Java Card application to interconnected SMV modules.

Overall, complete static verification may have to be based on a combination of techniques that will cover all sources of security violations in the Java Card multi-applet environment. Efficient use of these techniques requires highly specialized formal analysis skills that cannot be found in most software engineers.

The aforementioned limitations illustrate the need for an easier way to apply fully automated static analysis techniques, perhaps at the cost of affordable lower precision in the provided verification results. Static program analyses are neither sound nor complete verification approaches meaning that in the general case there is no guarantee that they will detect all security violations, if any (yielding false negatives). Moreover, there is no guarantee for the absence of false positives. In most cases, we can usually afford a relatively small number of false positives, but we require the analysis to exclude all possibilities of false negatives.

Program Analysis

Abstract interpretation is one of the proposed static program analyses for Java Card applets (The Java Verifier project, 2009). It lies on a semantics-based description of all possible executions by the use of abstract values in place of the actual computed values. Unfortunately, there are no published works with qualitative results on abstract interpretation of Java Card applets and there is no evidence that this technique is appropriate for analyzing security guarantees in multi-applet applications.

A well known static program analysis for Java Card applications (Catano & Huisman, 2002), introduces the use of ESC/Java (2), a static analysis tool for proving specifications, without requiring the analyst to interact with the back-end theorem prover (called Simplify). The provided analysis is neither sound nor complete, but has been found effective in proving absence of runtime exceptions and in verifying relatively simple correctness properties.

In (Almaliotis et. al., 2008) we introduced a static program analysis for temporal safety of Java Card API calls, which is based on computing dataflow facts over the control-flow graph of a Java Card applet. Our approach is implemented in the form of bug detector plugins for the FindBugs tool (Hovemeyer & Pugh, 2004; The FindBugs project site, 2009) and in contrast to (Catano & Huisman, 2002) it does not require annotations in the applet source code. This reduces the verification cost to the applet developers, since they do not have to make explicit all implicit assumptions needed for correctness (e.g. the non-nullness of buf in many Java Card API calls). FindBugs bug detector plugins may be distributed together with the Java Card Development kit or by an independent third party. Applet developers use the bug detectors as they are, but they can also extend their open source code in order to develop bug detectors for custom properties. In ESC/Java (2), user-specified properties assume familiarization, (i) with the Java Modeling Language (JML), (ii) with the specificities of the "design by contract" specification technique and (iii) with the corresponding JML based Java Card API specification (Meijer & Poll, 2001). On the other hand, development of new FindBugs bug detectors assumes only Java programming skills that most software engineers already have.

We aim at a holistic fully-automatic verification approach with the only requirement of basic Java programming skills, perhaps at the cost of a few false positives in the provided results. The most important consequence is the use of a single verification technique for the three types of security errors that we mentioned.

Recent developments in the theory of static program analysis create promising prospects towards minimizing the number of false positives in the obtained results. However, as we will see in the following sections the current version of FindBugs does not offer the necessary support for implementing the most advanced analyses published in the related work.

Static Program Analysis Basics

Static program analyses, in general, explore the different execution paths that can take place, when the program is executed. In fact, they are based on a control flow graph (CFG) representation of the analyzed program, where the nodes of the graph are basic blocks, i.e. sequences of instructions that will always be executed without the possibility that any instruction(s) will be skipped. Edges in the control flow graph are directed and represent potential control flow paths between basic blocks. Back edges in a control flow graph represent potential loops.

A call graph represents potential control flow between methods. Nodes in the graph represent methods and directed edges represent the potential for one method to invoke another.

Dataflow analyses examine the way data move through a program by traversing a method's control flow graph, in order to estimate conservative approximations about facts that are true at each node of the graph. Facts are mutable, but they have to form a lattice.

An advanced static program analysis consists of at least two major parts: an intraprocedural analysis component for analyzing an individual method and an interprocedural analysis component that operates across an entire program, flowing information from the caller to its callees and vice versa. FindBugs does not offer direct support for interprocedural analyses, which is a basic requirement for analyzing multi-applet applications. However, as we will see it was eventually possible to overcome this problem.

Interprocedural analysis in the FindBugs framework is still a challenging problem, if we want to reduce the number of false positives we currently get. The reason is that the behavior of each method is dependent upon the context in which it is called and the current version of Find-Bugs does not provide support for determining the circumstances and conditions under which a method runs. Another aspect related to context sensitivity is the fact that the number of paths through the code grows exponentially with the number of conditionals and for this reason when explicitly gathering facts along each path this may result in an unacceptably slow analysis. Advanced static program analyses try to alleviate this problem by allowing paths to share information about common subpaths, as well as by techniques that allow for implicit enumeration of paths.

Typestate Tracking & Tainted Object Propagation

The analysis techniques presented here focus on the use of FindBugs for the three types of security errors that need to be checked in a Java Card multi-applet application. Also, we discuss recent developments towards advanced context-sensitive analyses with high precision, which can be potentially implemented in future versions of FindBugs that will provide appropriate support. Static program analyses for security errors with a particular interest for the Java Card environment lie into two broad categories, namely:

- typestate tracking (Strom & Yemini, 1986), for illicit method invocations spanning the contexts of different applets, as well as for violations of temporal safety in Java Card API calls and

- taint propagation (Livshits & Lam, 2005; Sabelfeld & Myers, 2003; Haldar et. al. 2005) for unwanted information flows to third parties.

Temporal safety of API calls, as well as applet interactions must conform to specific rules about their ordering that are possibly associated with constraints on the data values visible at the boundary of the interacting parties. Temporal safety violations are typically detected by typestate tracking. The typestate is a refinement of the concept of type: whereas the type of a data object determines the set of operations ever permitted on the object, typestate determines the subset of these operations, which are performed in a particular context. Typestate tracking aims to statically detect syntactically legal, but semantically undefined execution sequences.

On the other hand, a tainted object propagation problem consists of a set of source descriptors and sink descriptors. To represent the fact that data can be trusted for some purposes but not for others, different varieties of tainted data can be modeled as carriers of different taint flags. Source descriptors define program locations, where tainted data enter the applet and the different source descriptors introduce data with different taint flags. Sink descriptors define program locations that should not receive tainted data or data carrying a certain type of taint. Taint propagation analyses aim at detecting information flows, such as the variation of "confidential" or "high" input to some applet that is caused by the variation of "public" or "low" output. This occurs when the flow of taint terminates in a sink point, as a consequence of not having stopped the propagation between objects by some sanitization method. Typically, sanitization may be performed by creating a new fresh sanitized object.

STATIC ANALYSIS WITH THE FINDBUGS FRAMEWORK

FindBugs is a tool and framework that applies static analysis techniques on the Java (Java Card) bytecode in order to detect bug patterns, i.e. to detect "places where code does not follow correct practice in the use of a language feature or library API" (Hovemeyer & Pugh, 2004). In general, FindBugs bug detectors behave according to the Visitor design pattern: each detector visits each class and each method in the application under analysis. The framework comes with many analyses built-in and classes and interfaces that can be extended to build new analyses. In our work, we exploit the already provided intra-procedural control flow analysis that transforms the analyzed bytecode into control flow graphs (CFGs), in order to support the property analyses that we present in next sections.

The bug pattern detectors are implemented using the Byte Code Engineering Library - BCEL (Dahm, 2001), which provides the appropriate infrastructure for analyzing and manipulating Java class files. In essence, BCEL offers data types for inspection of binary Java (Java Card) classes. One can obtain methods, fields, etc. from the main data types, JavaClass and Method. The project source directories are used only for mapping the reported warnings back to the Java source code.

Bug pattern detectors are packaged into FindBugs plugins that can use any of the built-in FindBugs analyses and in effect extend the provided FindBugs functionality without any changes to its code. A plugin is a jar file that contains detector classes, analysis classes and the following meta-information: (i) the plugin descriptor (findbugs. xml) that declares the bug patterns, the detector classes, the detector ordering constraints and the analysis engine registrar, (ii) the human-readable messages (in messages.xml), which are the localized messages generated by the detector. Plugins are easily activated in the analyst's FindBugs installation by copying the jar file into the proper location of the user's file system.

FindBugs applies the loaded detectors in a series of AnalysisPasses. Each pass executes a set of detectors selected according to declared detector ordering constraints. In this way, Find-Bugs distributes the detectors into AnalysisPasses and forms a complete ExecutionPlan, i.e., a list of AnalysisPasses specifying how to apply the loaded detectors to the analyzed application classes. When a project is analyzed, FindBugs follows the following steps:

1. Reads the project
2. Finds all application classes in the project
3. Loads the available plugins with the detectors
4. Creates an execution plan
5. Runs the FindBugs algorithm to apply detectors to all application classes

The basic FindBugs algorithm in pseudo-code is:

```
for each analysis pass in the execu-
tion plan do
  for each application class do
    for each detector in the anal-
    ysis pass do
      apply the detector to the
      class
    end for
  end for
end for
```

All detectors use a global cache of analysis objects and databases. An analysis object (accessed by using a ClassDescriptor or a MethodDescriptor) stores facts about a class or method, for example the results of a null-pointer dataflow analysis on a method. On the other hand, a database stores facts about the entire program, e.g. which methods unconditionally dereference parameters. All detectors implement the Detector interface, which includes the visitClassContext() method that is

Figure 1. A purse applet and two loyalty applets that award bonus points

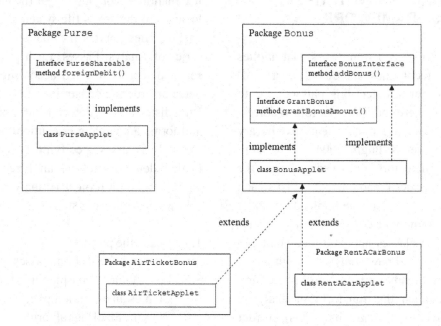

invoked on each application class. Detector classes (i) request one or more analysis objects from the global cache for the analyzed class and its methods, (ii) inspect the gathered analysis objects and (iii) report warnings for suspicious situations in code. When a Detector is instantiated its constructor gets a reference to a BugReporter. The Detector object uses the associated BugReporter, in order to emit warnings for the potential bugs and to save the detected bug instances in BugCollection objects for further processing.

STATIC VERIFICATION OF JAVA CARD APPLICATIONS BY TYPESTATE TRACKING

Static verification of interacting applets is illustrated with an example application that includes a purse applet and two loyalty applets that award bonus points. The purse applet keeps a balance that is updated upon requests from the environment that allow the card owner to purchase goods.

The interface method foreignDebit() is invoked by the loyalty applets that reside in separate packages, in order to transfer according to some fixed rate, part of the bonus points back to the purse. We consider two loyalty applets, namely the AirTicketBonus and the RentACarBonus that basically implement the same interfaces. The interface method addBonus() is invoked by the purse applet, whenever there is a need to notify a loyalty applet for an occurred balance update. Finally, we consider the possibility for a loyalty applet to have an agreement with other loyalty applets, in order to share bonus points. This is achieved by a direct loyalty applet to loyalty applet communication using the interface method grantBonusAmount(). Figure 2 introduces the class diagram for the discussed application.

Typestate Tracking for Verifying Temporal Restrictions of Inter-Applet Communication

Temporal restrictions of inter-applet communication concern rules about the ordering of method

Figure 2. Class diagram for the application of the purse with the two loyalty applets

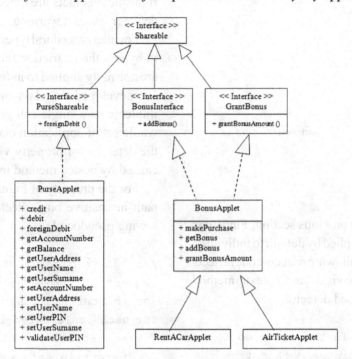

invocations, which span the contexts of different applets. Typestate tracking makes it possible to detect such illicit method calls that – as we already noted - cannot be caught by the Java Card firewall.

Bug detectors for verifying inter-applet communication track the state of the property of interest and at the same time track what we call execution state, i.e. the values of all program variables. In the considered application, example properties are the following:

- Methods declared in shareable interfaces are neither transitive nor recursive. Thus, the method addBonus() is not allowed to cause a direct or indirect call to addBonus() for the same or for a different loyalty applet.
- Method foreignDebit() is called at most once within a transaction.
- The method grantBonusAmount() is invoked only through a call to addBonus() for some loyalty applet and it is never called directly from the purse applet.

Correctness properties of inter-applet communication are captured in appropriate state machines that recognize finite execution traces with improper use of the methods declared in shareable interfaces. Figure 3 introduces the state machine for the first mentioned property. Accurate tracking of the execution state can be very expensive, because this implies tracking every branch in the control-flow, in which the values of the examined variables differ along the branch paths. The resulted search space may grow exponentially or even become infinite.

Bug detectors have to take into account two distinct cases of property violations:

1. Intraprocedural property violations can be detected by simple bytecode scanning or CFG-based analyses that basically follow the states of the property state machine.

2. Interprocedural property violations can be detected by extending the CFG-based and call graph analysis functions provided in FindBugs.

Figure 3. Transitive or recursive invocation of a loyalty applet method

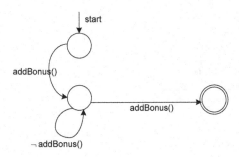

As we saw in the previous section, FindBugs static analyses are applied by default to individual class contexts. The following pseudo-code reflects the functionality of the visitClassContext() method of a typical CFG-based detector.

```
for each method in the class do
request a CFG for the method from the
ClassContext
request one or more analysis objects
on the method from the ClassContext
    for each location in the method
    do
        get the dataflow facts at the
        location
        inspect the dataflow facts
        if a dataflow fact indicates
        an error then
            report a warning
        end if
    end for
end for
```

The basic idea is to visit each method of the analyzed class in turn, requesting some number of analysis objects. After getting the required analyses, the detector iterates through each location in the CFG. A location is the point in execution just before a particular instruction is executed (or after the instruction, for backwards analyses). At each location, the detector checks the dataflow facts to see if anything suspicious is going on.

If suspicious facts are detected at a location the detector issues a warning.

For interprocedural typestate tracking, we have to bypass the restriction that FindBugs analyses are normally applied to individual class contexts. We developed the class InterCallGraph, which implements a single call graph structure for the whole set of application classes and thus allows the detection of property violations that may be caused by nested method invocations.

For the property of Figure 3 we introduce the path-insensitive bug detector shown in the following pseudocode.

```
//populate black list
request all implemented interfaces
for the current class
for each implemented interface do
    request all extended interfaces
    (parent interfaces)
    for each parent interface do
        if parent interface is "Share-
        able" then
            add all methods of imple-
            mented interface in the
            blacklist
        end if
    end for
end for

//construction of the call graph
request all methods of all classes
create nodes for these methods
for each class in the program do
    for each method in class do
        scan for calls and make a link
        for each call between methods-
        nodes
    end for
end for
for each method in the blacklist do
for each method in the class do
    start a Depth First Search from
    the corresponding graph node:
```

```
if method of the node is the cur-
rent blacklist method then
    if the same method is visited
    again then
        report the detected bug
    end if
end if
end for
end for
```

The bug detector first creates a black list, which is used to record all methods declared in implemented interfaces that inherit from "ShareableInterface". This allows to statically verifying the property of Figure 3, for all methods declared in shareable interfaces. The bug detector discovers both intraprocedural and interprocedural property violations. Repeated calls of methods that bypass the application firewall may also occur as a method invocation enclosed in a basic block of for/while or a do... while loop. Method CFGs are inspected for this particular CFG pattern and when detected, this causes a transition to the final state of the property violation automaton. For an occurred state transition from the initial state, the bug detector starts a depth first search from the current node of the instantiated InterCallGraph, in order to detect potential recursive or transitive calls to the black listed method. Figure 4 shows the FindBugs response for a transitive call to the method addBonus().

Typestate Tracking for Verifying Temporal Safety of Java Card API Calls

Contrary to ordinary Java programs that have a single main() entry point, Java Card applets have several entry points, which are called when the card receives various application (APDU) commands. These entry points roughly match the different phases that an applet can be in: (i) loading, (ii) installation, (iii) personalization, (iv) selectable, (v) blocked and (vi) dead.

In a Java Card, any exception can reach the top level, i.e. the applet entry point invoked by the Java Card Runtime Environment (JCRE). In this case, the currently executed command is aborted and the command, which in general is not completed yet, is terminated by an appropriate status word: if the exception is an ISOException, the status word is assigned the value of the reason code for the raised exception, whereas in all other cases the reason code is 0x6f00 corresponding to "no precise diagnosis".

An exception in an applet's entry point can reveal information about the behavior of the application and in principle it should be forbidden. In practice, whereas an ISOException is usually explicitly thrown by the applet code using throw, a potentially unhandled exception is implicitly raised when executing an API method call that causes an unexpected error. This may result in leaving the applet in an unpredicted and ill state that can possibly violate the application's security properties.

Unhandled exceptions are detected by looking for an exception thrower block preceding the instruction by which typestate tracking reaches the final state (Figure 5). Access to an exception handler block (if any) is possible through a handled exception edge. In FindBugs, method isExceptionThrower() detects an exception thrower block and method isExceptionEdge() determines whether a CFG edge is a handled exception edge.

Potentially unhandled exceptions are usually caused by violations of temporal restrictions in the use of Java Card API calls. Temporal safety violations are captured by typestate tracking based on an appropriate state machine, which recognizes finite execution traces with improper calls. In (Almaliotis et. al., 2008) we introduced a FindBugs bug detector that detects unhandled instances of APDUException, for improper use of the setOutgoing() API call.

Figure 4. A method declared in a shareable interface triggers an indirect call to itself

```
232    public void addBonus(short amount){
233        byte[] PURSE_AID = {
234            (byte) 0xA0, (byte) 0x00, (byte) 0x00, (byte) 0x00,
235            (byte) 0x62, (byte) 0x03, (byte) 0x01, (byte) 0x0C,
236            (byte) 0x08, (byte) 0x01
237        };
238        if (amount <= 0) ISOException.throwIt(SW_BAD_ARGUMENT);
239
240        if(amount>MAX_TRANSACTION) ISOException.throwIt(SW_TRANSACTION_OVERFLOW);
241
242        if ((short) (bonus - amount) < 0) ISOException.throwIt(SW_UNDERFLOW);
243
244        AID PurseAID = new AID(PURSE_AID,(short)0, (byte)0x0A);
245        PurseShareable sio = (PurseShareable) JCSystem.getAppletShareableInterfaceObj
246
247        JCSystem.beginTransaction();
248        bonus += amount;
249        sio.foreignDebit((short) 2);
250        JCSystem.commitTransaction();
251
252
253    }
```

Found in Purse.PurseApplet.foreignDebit(short)
At PurseApplet.java:[line 353]
In method Purse.PurseApplet.foreignDebit(short) [Lines 337 - 354]

```
336    public void foreignDebit(short amount){
337        byte[] BONUS_AID = {
338            (byte) 0xA0, (byte) 0x00, (byte) 0x00, (byte) 0x00,
339            (byte) 0x62, (byte) 0x03, (byte) 0x01, (byte) 0x0C,
340            (byte) 0x05, (byte) 0x01
341        };
342        if (amount <= 0) ISOException.throwIt(SW_BAD_ARGUMENT);
343
344        if(amount>MAX_TRANSACTION) ISOException.throwIt(SW_TRANSACTION_OVERFLOW);
345
346        if ((short) (balance - amount) < 0) ISOException.throwIt(SW_UNDERFLOW);
347
348        JCSystem.beginTransaction();
349        balance -= amount;
350        JCSystem.commitTransaction();
351        AID bonusAID = new AID(BONUS_AID,(short)0, (byte)0x0A);
352        BonusInterface bon = (BonusInterface) JCSystem.getAppletShareableInterfaceOb
353        bon.addBonus ((short) 2);
354    }
```

Illegal call
A method in shareable interface implements transitive call

Constraints on Data Values Visible at the Boundary of the Interacting Parties

Dataflow analysis is the basic means to statically verify the correctness of the called methods' arguments and it is necessary, when temporal safety involves constraints on the data values accessed at the boundary of the interacting parties (communicating applets or an applet interacting with the Java Card API). In this case, the described static program analyses are combined with dataflow analyses like the one shown here.

A dataflow analysis estimates conservative approximations about facts that are true in each location of a CFG. Facts are mutable, but they have to form a lattice. In FindBugs, the DataflowA-

Figure 5. CFG pattern to find unhandled exception edges

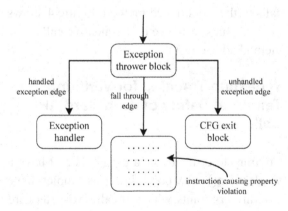

nalysis interface, which is shown in Figure 6 is the super-type of all concrete dataflow analysis

Figure 6. FindBugs base classes for dataflow analyses

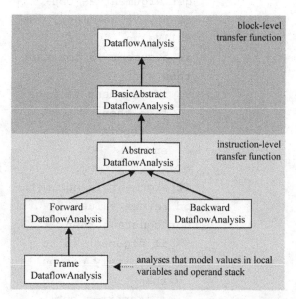

classes. It defines methods for creating, copying, merging and transferring dataflow facts. Transfer functions take dataflow facts and model the effects of either a basic block or a single instruction depending on the implemented dataflow analysis. Merge functions combine dataflow facts when control paths merge. The Dataflow class and its subclasses implement: (i) a dataflow analysis algorithm based on a CFG and an instance of DataflowAnalysis, (ii) methods providing access to the analysis results.

We are particularly interested in the Frame-DataflowAnalysis class that forms the base for analyses which model values in local variables and the operand stack. Dataflow facts for derived analyses are subclasses of the class Frame, whose instances represent the Java stack frame at a single CFG location. In a Java stack frame, both stack operands and local variables are considered to be "slots" that contain a single symbolic value.

The built-in frame dataflow analyses used in static verification of the called methods arguments are:

- The TypeAnalysis that performs type inference for all local variables and stack operands.
- The ConstantAnalysis that computes constant values in CFG locations.
- The IsNullValueAnalysis that determines which frame slots contain definitely-null values, definitely non-null values and various kinds of conditionally-null or uncertain values.
- The ValueNumberAnalysis that tracks the production and flow of values in the Java stack frame.

The class hierarchy of Figure 6 and the aforementioned built-in dataflow analyses form a generic dataflow analysis framework, since it is possible to create new kinds of dataflow analyses that will use as dataflow facts objects of user-defined classes.

A bug detector exploits the results of a particular dataflow analysis on a method by getting a reference to the Dataflow object that was used to execute the analysis. There is no direct support for interprocedural dataflow analysis, but there are ways to overcome this restriction. More precisely, analysis may be performed in multiple passes. A first pass detector will compute method summaries (e.g. method parameters that are unconditionally dereferenced, return values that are always non-null and so on), without reporting any warnings and a second pass detector will use the computed method summaries as needed. However, this approach is not convenient for implementing context-sensitive interprocedural dataflow analyses.

In the following paragraphs, we present a bug detector for unhandled API exceptions regarding the correctness of arguments in method calls. Consider the following Java Card method:

```
short arrayCopy (byte[] src, short
srcOff, byte[] dest, short destOff,
short length)
```

A NullPointerException is raised when either src or dest is null. Also, when the copy operation accesses data outside the array bounds the ArrayIndexOutOfBoundsException is raised. This happens either when one of the parameters srcOff, destOff and length has a negative value or when srcOff+length is greater than src.length or when destOff+ length is greater than dest.length. We provide the pseudo-code of the visitClassContext() method for the detector of unhandled exceptions raised by invalid arrayCopy arguments:

```
for each method in the class do
    request a CFG for the method
    get the method's ConstantDataflow
    from ClassContext
    get the method's ValueNumberData-
    flow from ClassContext
    get the method's IsNullValueData-
    flow from ClassContext
    for each location in the method
    do
        get instruction handle from
        location
        get instruction from instruc-
        tion handle
        if instruction is not instance
        of invoke static then
            continue
        end if
        get the invoked method's name
        from instruction
        get the invoked method's sig-
        nature from instruction
        if invoked method is arrayCopy
        then
            get ConstantFrame (fact) at
            current location
            get ValueNumberFrame (fact) at
            current location
            get IsNullValueFrame (fact) at
            current location
            get the method's number of
            arguments
```

```
            for each argument do
                get argument as Con-
                stant, ValueNumber, Is-
                NullValue
                if argument is constant
                then
                    if argument is nega-
                    tive then
                        report a bug
                    end if
                else
                if argument is not meth-
                od return value
                nor constant then
                    if argument is not
                    definitely not null
                    then
                        report a bug
                    end if
                end if
            end for
        end if
    end for
end for
```

Figure 7 demonstrates how the detector responds in two different property violation cases. In the first case, PurseApplet calls arrayCopy with the parameter accountNumber as null. It is important to note that it is not possible to determine by static analysis the correctness of the method call for all of the mentioned criteria, because buffer gets its value at run time by the Java Card Runtime Environment (JCRE). However, a complete FindBugs bug detector could generate a warning for the absence of an appropriate exception handler. In the second test case, parameter offset is assigned an unacceptable value.

TAINTED OBJECT PROPAGATION

In multi-applet Java Card applications, the leakage of sensitive data to third parties is an information

Figure 7. Illegal use of arrayCopy detected with (a) null value parameter and (b) unacceptable constant value parameter

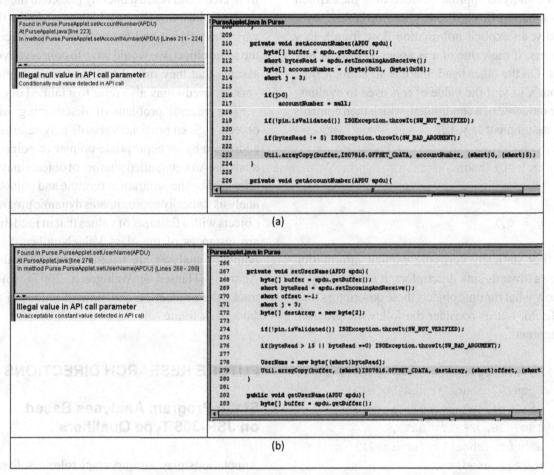

flow analysis problem. The basic idea behind using tainted object propagation for detecting information flow is to statically check that flow of information between variables is consistent with the trust relationships of the application providers. Although the accurate detection of information flow is undecidable, static analysis can over-approximate information flows, in order to ensure absence of sensitive data leakage.

Tainted object propagation can be formulated as a dataflow analysis problem and can be solved efficiently using an iterative algorithm. We consider only two possible lattice values, namely TAINTED and NOT TAINTED. On the lattice, the greatest lower bound of the two elements is

defined such as anything that meets a tainted value becomes tainted. An appropriate static analysis will include the following steps:

1. Consider all variables as NOT TAINTED.
2. Annotate the sensitive applet source points as TAINTED.
3. Propagate the tainted values through the applet code. If a tainted value is used in an expression, mark the result of the expression as TAINTED.
4. Repeat step 3 until a fixed point is reached.
5. Find all TAINTED sink descriptors and report them.

It is important to note that the aforementioned static analysis approach detects only the explicit information flows. For any two variables, say x and y, an explicit information flow from x to y occurs, if the value of x is assigned to y, as in y = x. On the other hand, there is an implicit flow from x to y, if the value of x is used to evaluate the outcome of a conditional, which then controls an assignment to y, i.e.

```
if (x > 0) then
    y = 1
else
    y = 0;
```

For statically verifying explicit information flows towards sink descriptors, it is necessary to know what runtime objects these descriptors may refer to. Let us consider the following program fragment:

```
1  byte[] buffer = apdu.getBuffer();
2  byte[] amount = new byte[2];
3  Util.arrayCopy(buffer,(short)
   ISO7816.OFFSET_CDATA,
   amount,(short)0,(short)2);
4  byte[] credit;
   .......
5  short creditS = (short)(credit[1]
   & 0x0F);
6  creditS += (short)(credit[1] &
   0xF0);
7  creditS += (short)(credit[0]<<8);
8  BonusInterface sio= (BonusIn-
   terface)JCSystem.getAppletShar
   eableInterfaceObject(bonusAID,
   (byte)0x00);
9  sio.addBonus((short)creditS);
```

In the shown example, apdu.getBuffer() returns the reference buffer to some tainted data, i.e. the data contained in the binary array buffer with the APDU command. Also, amount becomes tainted, because it is derived from buffer by a call

to arrayCopy (line 3). Finally, creditS is derived from credit and is subsequently passed to the sink method addBonus (line 9). Unless we know that variables amount and credit may never refer to the same object, we would have to conservatively assume that they may. Since amount is tainted, variable credit may also refer to a tainted object.

The general problem of determining what objects a given program variable may refer to is addressed by an appropriate pointer or points-to analysis. An unbounded number of objects may be allocated by the program at runtime and points-to analysis statically approximates dynamic program objects with a finite set of values that in FindBugs are instances of the class ValueNumber. Thus, points-to analyses are based on ValueNumber-Analysis (Hansen & Wahlgreen, 2007), which tracks the production and flow of values in the Java stack frame.

FUTURE RESEARCH DIRECTIONS

Static Program Analyses Based on JSR-305 Type Qualifiers

Annotations play an important role in software defect detection especially in problems, where there is a need to specify requirements about what the code is supposed to do. Java Specification Request 305 (Hovemeyer & Pugh, 2007) defines standard annotations that allow designers/ developers to describe design intents in a way that will make them amenable to program analysis by FindBugs and other tools. JSR-305 annotations are being proposed for inclusion as standard in Java 7 (Harold, 2008).

Such a design intent, which can be specified by an annotation language like JSR-305 is the requirement for a non-null parameter in all calls of some specific method. For this purpose, FindBugs provides the annotation type @NonNull that may be applied into some field, method, parameter or local variable.

Regarding JSR-305, one of the most interesting aspects is that it provides meta-annotations, which allow developers to define type qualifiers (Foster et. al., 1999). Type qualifiers extend the language type rules, in order to model the flow of qualifiers through the program, where each qualifier or set of qualifiers comes with additional type constraints that capture its semantics.

The latest version of FindBugs includes support for type qualifier dataflow analyses in the form of an abstract class. The functionality of abstract class TypeQualifierDataflowAnalysis is based on points-to information provided by a ValueNumberAnalysis, as well as on an appropriate structure that stores facts for source-to-sink mappings. There is also a CFG-based bug detector that exploits the provided support for checking user-defined type qualifiers.

For security properties that are formulated as information flow problems, JSR-305 introduces the following annotations:

- @Tainted
- @Untainted
- @Detainted

In a Java Card multi-applet application, data from outside of an applet will be marked as @ Tainted, as opposed to data from inside the applet that will be marked @Untainted. Tainted data that has been sanitized e.g. by passing it to some sort of escaping function can be annotated as @ Detainted. These annotations are necessary for a tainted object propagation analysis, in order to follow the path of data through the applet towards ensuring that tainted data never reaches a method invoked into another applet through a shareable interface:

```
private void function(@Tainted APDU
apdu){
.......
BonusInterface sio= (BonusInterface)
JCSystem.getAppletShareableInterfaceO
```

```
bject(bonusAID, (byte)0x00); sio.ad-
dBonus(@Untainted (short)creditS);}
```

Limitations of FindBugs

In FindBugs interprocedural dataflow analyses may be implemented by multiple-pass bug detectors, where the first pass computes method summaries.

The precision of an interprocedural analysis depends on whether it is path-sensitive and context-sensitive. A path-sensitive analysis ignores the invalid program paths and generates a reduced number of false positives. In commercial static analysis tools this feature is usually provided by less efficient bug detectors that implement decision procedures for whether a path is feasible or not.

A context-sensitive analysis processes the program's methods by taking into account all global variables as well as the passed parameter values for each method call instance. This feature further eliminates the generated false positives.

When using FindBugs, the real challenge towards effective use of the discussed program analysis techniques is to exploit the benefits and the extensibility prospects of the FindBugs open source support and at the same time to look for new ways to implement sophisticated and precise analyses that reduce false positives and at the same time scale to real Java Card programs. The most prominent limitation of the currently available FindBugs support is the implemented method call and return structure, which can be exploited in multiple-pass bug detectors. This structure does not provide obvious possibilities for implementing truly path-sensitive and context-sensitive program analysis techniques.

FindBugs was initially developed as a framework where developers could build highly efficient and usable bug detectors, whereas analysis precision was a second priority concern. With the improved support for interprocedural analysis in the latest versions of FindBugs we realize that analysis precision becomes an equally important concern. In the near future, we believe that mature static analysis techniques will allow a tradeoff between analysis precision and efficiency and we expect FindBugs to improve the current support towards this perspective.

Precise and Scalable Static Program Analysis Techniques

Static program analysis can provide automated verification solutions for the whole range of security properties that arise in Java Card multi-applet applications.

For typestate tracking, an interesting source of inspiration is the SAFE project (The SAFE project, 2009) at the IBM Research Labs. The heuristics applied in SAFE are reported in (Fink et. al., 2006). In that work the authors propose a composite verifier built out of several composable verifiers of increasing precision and cost. In this setting, the composite verifier stages analyses, in order to improve efficiency without compromising precision. The early stages use the faster verifiers to reduce the workload for later, more precise, stages. Prior to any path-sensitive analysis, the first stage prunes the verification scope using an extremely efficient path-insensitive error path feasibility check.

CONCLUSION

We explored static program analyses with Find-Bugs, which can provide an automatic verification approach for the security concerns raised in Java Card multi-applet applications. When compared with existing security verification alternatives, our approach does not require specialized formal analysis skills to the application developer, but basic Java programming skills that most software engineers already have. Moreover, it provides a single fully-automatic verification prospect for all the three types of security problems discussed, in place of diverse costly approaches, for the different verification tasks.

FindBugs provides an open source analysis support that may be exploited in the development of new pluggable bug detectors, which can be easily installed in the static analysis tool suite. The presented bug detectors are available online in (The S-OMA SMART CARDS Project, 2009). Bug detector plugins may be distributed together with the Java Card Development kit or by an independent third party. Applet developers are still able to extend the bug detectors open source code, in order to develop bug detectors for custom properties.

All these attractive features open a new perspective for verifying Java Card multi-applet applications that by definition are security critical. We highlighted current restrictions in the proposed verification approach, but we believe that due to the prospects for extending the current open source support these restrictions will be eliminated in the foreseeable future.

REFERENCES

Akdemir, I. O. (1998). *An implementation of secure flow type inference for a subset of Java.* Unpublished Master thesis, Naval Postgraduate School, Monterey, California.

Almaliotis, V., Loizidis, A., Katsaros, P., Louridas, P., & Spinellis, D. (2008). Static program analysis for Java Card applets. In G. Grimaud & F.-X. Standaert (Ed.), *Proc. of the 8th IFIP Smart Card Research and Advanced Application Conference (CARDIS)* (pp. 17-31), Springer LNCS 5189.

Beckert, B., & Mostowski, W. (2003). A program logic for handling Java Card's transaction mechanism. *Proc. of 6th Int. Conference on Fundamental Approaches to Software Engineering (FASE'03)* (pp. 246-260), Springer LNCS 2621.

Bieber, P., Cazin, J., Girard, P., Lanet, J.-L., Wiels, V., & Zanon, G. (2002). Checking secure interactions of smart card applets: extended version. *Journal of Computer Security, 10*, 369–398.

Breunesse, C. B., Catano, N., Huisman, M., & Jacobs, B. (2005). Formal methods for smart cards: an experience report. *Science of Computer Programming, 55*, 53–80. doi:10.1016/j.scico.2004.05.011

Burdy, L., Requet, A. & Lanet, J. L. (2003). Java applet correctness: a developer-oriented approach. *Proc. of Formal Methods Europe (FME)*, Springer LNCS 2805.

Catano, N., & Huisman, M. (2002). Formal specification and static checking of Gemplus's electronic purse using ESC/Java. In G. Goos, J. Hartmanis & J. van Leeuwen (Ed.), *Proc. of Formal Methods Europe (FME '02)* (pp. 272-289), Springer LNCS 2391.

Dahm, M. (2001). *Byte code engineering with the BCEL API* (Tech. Rep. B-17-98). Freie University of Berlin, Institute of Informatics, Germany.

Fink, S., Yahav, E., Dor, N., Ramalingam, G., & Geay, E. (2006). Effective typestate verification in the presence of aliasing. *Proc. of the Int. Symp. on Software Testing and Analysis (ISSTA)* (pp. 133-144), New York: ACM Press.

Foster, J. S., Fähndrich, M., & Aiken, A. (1999). A theory of type qualifiers, *Proc. of the ACM SIGPLAN Conference on Programming language design and implementation (PLDI)* (pp. 192-203), New York: ACM Press.

Haldar, V., Chandra, D., & Franz, M. (2005). Dynamic taint propagation for Java. In D. Thomsen (Ed.), *Proc. of the 21st Annual Computer Security Applications Conference (ACSAC)* (pp. 303-311), Washington, DC: IEEE Computer Society.

Hansen, T. J., & Wahlgreen, B. (2007). *Static analysis of concurrent Java programs* (Tech. Rep. IMM-B.Sc-2007-11). Technical University of Denmark, Denmark.

Harold, E. R. (2008, September). *The Open Road: javax.annotation.* java.net: The Source for Java Technology Collaboration, online: http://today.java.net/ pub/a/today/2008/09/11/jsr-305-annotations.html

Hovemeyer, D., & Pugh, W. (2004). Finding bugs is easy. *SIGPLAN Notices, 39*(12), 92–106. doi:10.1145/1052883.1052895

Hovemeyer, D., & Pugh, W. (2007). *Status report on JSR-305: Annotations for software defect detection. Proc. of Object Oriented Programming Systems Languages and Applications (OOPSLA)* (pp. 799–800). ACM Press.

Jacobs, B., Marche, C., & Rauch, N. (2004). Formal verification of a commercial smart card applet with multiple tools. *Proc. 10th Int. Conference on Algebraic Methodology and Software Technology (AMAST 2004)* (pp. 241-257), Springer LNCS 3116.

Livshits, V. B., & Lam, M. S. (2005). Finding security vulnerabilities in Java applications with static analysis. *Proc. of the 14th Conference on USENIX Security Symposium* (pp. 271-286).

Marché, C., Paulin-Mohring, C., & Urbain, X. (2004). The KRAKATOA tool for certification of JAVA/JAVACARD programs annotated in JML. *Journal of Logic and Algebraic Programming, 58*(1-2), 89–106. doi:10.1016/j.jlap.2003.07.006

Meijer, H., & Poll, E. (2001). Towards a full formal specification of the JavaCard API. In G. Goos, J. Hartmanis & J. van Leeuwen (Ed.), *Proc. of the Int. Conf. on Research in Smart Cards: Smart Card Programming and Security (E-smart)* (pp. 165-178), Springer LNCS 2140.

Meyer, J., & Poetzsch-Heffter, A. (2000). An architecture for interactive program provers. *Proc. of Tools and Algorithms for the Construction and Analysis of Systems (TACAS)* (pp. 63-77), Springer LNCS 1785.

Sabelfeld, A., & Myers, A. C. (2003). Language-based information-flow security. *IEEE Journal on Selected Areas in Communications*, *21*(1), 5–19. doi:10.1109/JSAC.2002.806121

Strom, R. E., & Yemini, S. (1986). Typestate: A programming language concept for enhancing software reliability. *IEEE Transactions on Software Engineering*, *12*(1), 157–171.

The, S. A. F. E. (Scalable And Flexible Error detection) project. (n.d.). Accessed February 28, 2009, http://www.research.ibm.com/safe/

The FindBugs project site,(n.d.). Accessed February 18, 2009, in http://findbugs. sourceforge.net

The Java Verifier project. (n.d.). Accessed February 28, 2009. in http://www.inria.fr /actualites/ inedit/inedit36_partb.en.html

The Security in Open Multi-Application Smart Cards (S-OMA SMART CARDS) Project. Accessed February 28, 2009, http://mathind.csd. auth.gr/ smart/

Van den Berg, J., & Jacobs, B. (2001). The LOOP compiler for Java and JML. *Proc. of Tools and Algorithms for the Construction and Analysis of Systems (TACAS)* (pp. 299-312), Springer LNCS 2031.

Chapter 12
Automatic Timed Automata Extraction from Ladder Programs for Model-Based Analysis of Control Systems

Kézia de Vasconcelos Oliveira
Federal University of Campina Grande, Brazil

Kyller Gorgônio
Federal University of Campina Grande, Brazil

Angelo Perkusich
Federal University of Campina Grande, Brazil

Antônio Marcus Nogueira Lima
Federal University of Campina Grande, Brazil

Leandro Dias da Silva
Federal University of Alagoas, Brazil

ABSTRACT

Control Systems are used to produce a certain result with little or no human supervision. The principal aim of such systems is to ensure that resources are used efficiently and that the desired product quality is achieved. Moreover for critical systems such as oil and gas plants, it is important to guarantee the safety and dependability of the operation. Therefore, it is necessary to verify whether what is running in the device is in accordance with what was defined in the specification documents. The goal of this chapter is to present a method that automatically generates the timed automata models from the specification ISA 5.2 Binary Logic Diagrams, and the implementation Ladder programs, for model-based analysis, in order to increase the confidence in the behavior of critical Control Systems. This approach is based on the use of the Uppaal tool and the Uppaal-TRON testing tool.

DOI: 10.4018/978-1-61520-837-1.ch012

INTRODUCTION

The development of new technologies raised the complexity level of modern industrial control and automation systems. In order to overcome the challenge of guarantee the dependability of the process and the safety of equipments, installation and employees, new methods, techniques and tools have to be adopted (Neves, Duarte, Viana, & Lucena, 2007). Dependability means the probability that a device will function properly for a defined period of time under the influence of specific environmental and operational conditions (ISO, 1997).

In order to overcome the challenges mentioned above, verification techniques have been increasingly used in Control Systems. Control Systems (Wescott, 2006) are widely used in industries and have the following objectives: to reduce production costs; to increase the quality level of products; to minimize the material and energy losses; and, furthermore, should ensure that the program executes as expected or designed.

The usual development scenario is as follow. First, the interested company generates a set of requirements that constitute the specification. Once the specification is completed, the software company develop the software using some of the IEC 61131-3 language (PLCopen, 2004; John & Tiegelkamp, 2001). Finally, the program is compiled to run in a given Programmable Logic Controller (PLC) (Parr, 2003). It is important to note that the company does not have a formal guarantee that the final implementation corresponds to its original specification. Even considering the fact that there is an important phase of acceptance tests, it is impossible to guarantee the conformance because the number of inputs, events, timing, and their combinations.

In this context, it is essential to analyze if the system is correct. It is necessary to check whether what is executing in the device is in accordance with what is defined in the specification documents. One possibility to achieve this is executing conformance testing to validate the implementation against its specification.

The objective in this chapter is to introduce a method to increase the dependability and safety in the operation of Control Systems. The proposed method consists in the translation of ISA 5.2 Binary Logic Diagrams (ISA, 1992), for the specification, and Ladder programs, for the implementation, in eXtensible Markup Language (XML) files. These files represent the timed automata model automata (Alur & Dill, 1994; Bengtsson & Yi, 2003) in the Uppaal tool (Behrmann, David & Larsen, 2004) internal representation. After the generation of timed automata models for the specification and implementation, the conformance test is performed. These test consists of generation and execution of test cases to validate the correctness of the system. This is done using the Uppaal-TRON tool (Larsen, Mikucionis, Nielsen, & Skou, 2005).

BACKGROUND

In this section the theoretical basis necessary for the understanding of this chapter is presented. The main concepts related to ISA 5.2 Binary Logic Diagrams (ISA, 1992), Programmable Logic Controllers (PLC), Ladder and timed automata are introduced.

ISA 5.2 Binary Logic Diagrams

The ISA 5.2 standard is used to describe the specification binary systems, and aims to improve communication between parties involved in the development systems through the use of symbols that represent operations processes (ISA, 1992). This standard facilitates the understanding of the functioning of modeled system. Some of the symbols used by this standard are illustrated in Table 1.

Table 1. ISA 5.2 Symbols

Symbol	Description
inputName HS	Represents an input to ISA 5.2 Diagram.
outputName AC	Represents an output to ISA 5.2 Diagram.
AND	Represents a Boolean AND operation on an ISA 5.2 Diagram.
OR	Represents a Boolean OR operation on an ISA 5.2 Diagram.
Di pt	Delay Initiation of output: Represents a timer element. It energizes the output after a set period of time (time = pt) when there exists logic 1 in input.
Dt pt	Delay Termination of output): Represents a timer element. It energizes the output when there is logic 1 at the input. When the logic in the input pass to 0 the output is energized after a period of time (time = pt).
Po pt	Pulse Output: Represents a timer element. Energizes the output during a period of time (time = pt) when exist logic 1 at the input. Even if there is logic 0 on input, the output remains activated during the default time (time = pt).

PLC and IEC 61131-3

Programmable Logic Controllers (PLCs) are computers widely used in industries such as manufacturing, oil and gas, chemical, energy and nuclear plants for process control and automation.

Programs for PLCs can be written in one of the languages from the IEC 61131-3 standard and are executed in cycles with three main steps. First, the inputs of the system are read and their values stored in memory. After that, the program is executed using the stored input values, and all computed values of outputs are also stored. In the last step, all outputs are activated based on their values stored in memory.

The five programming languages defined by standard IEC 61131-3 are the following:

- Instruction List (IL) is a textual language, it resembles assembly;
- Ladder Diagram (Ladder) is based on the graphical representation of Relay Ladder Logic;
- Function Block Diagram (FBD) expresses the behavior of a controller as a set of interconnected graphic blocks;
- Structured Text (ST) is a very powerful high-level language that is close to Pascal;
- Sequential Function Chart (SFC) is a graphical programming language. The elements are defined for structuring the internal organization of programmable controllers programs and function blocks.

In this chapter the focus is on the Ladder language. It is called Ladder because its representation resembles a ladder. This language is composed by two rails, left and right, representing respectively the hot rail and neutral (grounded) rail. These rails are connected by the control logic that is the rungs. The rung is compound by a set of elements (contacts, coils, timers, functions, function blocks, procedures and others) that form the control logic. Elements are either connected in series, parallel, or some combination to obtain the desired control logic. The control logic should be programmed so that the instructions are energized for the power flow between the two rails, from left to right and from top to bottom.

In Table 2, some of the main elements of the Ladder language are shown.

In Figure 1(a), a Ladder program is illustrated. The reading of a Ladder program is from left to right and from top to bottom. The variables input1, input2 and input3 are called contacts and output

Table 2. Elements of Ladder Language

Symbol	Description
inputName ─┤ ├─	Normally Open Contact: Represents an input to the control logic. A PLC examines the specified bit corresponding to this symbol and it returns logic 0 if that bit is 0 or logic 1 if that bit is 1.
inputName ─┤/├─	Normally Closed Contact: Represents an input to the control logic. A PLC examines the specified bit corresponding to this symbol and it returns logic 1 if that bit is 0 or logic 0 if that bit is 1.
outputName ( )	Output Coil: Represents an output. It is the actuator element, which is turned on or turned off by the logic control block.
TON IN Q PT	On-Delay Timer (TON/TMR): Represents a timer element. It energizes the output (Q = 1) after a set period of time (time = PT) when there exists logic 1 in IN (IN = 1).
TOF IN Q PT	Off-Delay Timer (TOF): Represents a timer element. It Energizes the output (Q = 1) when there exists logic 1 in IN (IN = 1). When output is logic 1 (Q = 1) and the input changes to 0 (IN = 0) it delays turning off the output by PT time.
TP IN Q PT	Pulse Output: Represents a timer element. Energizes the output during a period of time (time = PT) when exit logic 1 at the input. Even if there is logic 0 on input, the output remains activated during the default time (time = PT)

is called coil; input1 and input2 are connected in parallel (Boolean OR operation) and in series with input3 (Boolean AND operation): output = (input1 OR input2) AND input3. In the Figure 1(b) is illustrated the truth table of this Ladder program.

In Figure 2(a), another example of a Ladder program is illustrated. The variables input1 and input2 are connected in parallel (Boolean OR operation). The variable TEMPO01 represents a TMR with base time equal to 1 second. The value of output depends on timer TMR. If the logic operation input1 OR input2 = 1, then TEMPO01 will start timing; when this time arrives in 20s (time base x const) output is ON (logic value 1). In the Figure 2(b) is illustrated the truth table of this Ladder program.

Timed Automata and Tools

Timed automata are state machines with time constraints associated with its edges and states, and are designed to model the behavior of real-time systems (Alur, 1999; Alur & Dill, 1994; Bengtsson & Yi, 2004). The constraints are built from the timed variables, called clocks. These clocks progress synchronous and are declared as real values, because time is considered continuous.

In Figure 3, an example of timed automata network modeled, simulated and verified with the Uppaal tool is presented. In Figure 3(a) a timed automata modeling a faucet is shown. This faucet posses the automatic triggering of the flow of water when the hands press it. The automata has two locations: off and on. The expressions of color green represented guards, and the expressions purple represented assigns. If the user presses a faucet (hands == 1), then the clock, represented by c, is initialized (c = 0) and faucet is turned on. At this location two situations can occur: the user continues pressing the faucet (hands == 1), so that it remains turned on; or the user stop pressing the faucet and two seconds have passed (hands == 0 && c >= 2), then the faucet is turned off. The user model is shown in Figure 3(b).

The following formal definition will facilitate the comprehension of the syntax and semantics of timed automata.

Timed automata is a tuple (L, l_0, C, A, E, I), where:

- L is a set of locations;
- l_0 is the initial location;
- C is a set of clocks;
- A is set of actions;
- E is a set of edges between locations with an action, a guard and a set of clocks to be reset, where $E \subseteq L \times A \times B(C) \times 2^c \times L$. B(C) is the set of conjunctions over simple conditions of the form $x \vartriangleleft\vartriangleright c$ or $x - y \vartriangleleft\vartriangleright c$, where x, y $\in$ C, c $\in$ N e $\vartriangleleft\vartriangleright \in \{<, >, <=, >=, =\}$;

Figure 1. Example of the rung of Ladder program

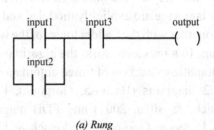

(a) Rung

input1	input2	input3	output
0	0	0	0
0	0	1	0
0	1	0	0
0	1	1	1
1	0	0	0
1	0	1	1
1	1	0	0
1	1	1	1

(b)Truth table

Figure 2. Example of a Ladder rung with timer

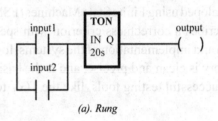

(a). Rung

input1	input2	output
0	0	0
0	1	0 – antes 20 s 1 – depois 20 s
1	0	0 – antes 20 s 1 – depois 20 s
1	1	0 – antes 20 s 1 – depois 20 s

(b).Truth table

Figure 3. The Faucet modeling with timed automata

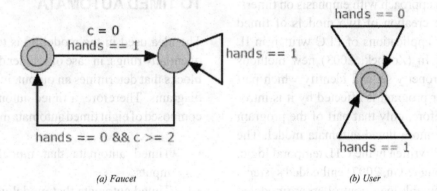

(a) Faucet

(b) User

- I is the assignment of an invariant to each location (define a time interval for which the system can remain in a state), where I → B(C).

Besides Uppaal, the Uppaal-TRON is also used in this work. Uppaal-TRON is an online testing tool, based on the Uppaal engine, for black-box conformance testing of real-time embedded systems. Test cases are generated, executed and checked event by event. This tool generates a set

of traces from the timed automata that represent an environment and uses those traces to test the implementation.

RELATED WORK

This section outlines the relevant work done in the field of control program analysis and verification. In (Heiner & Menzel, 1998), an approach to translate Instruction List (IL) programs into

Petri nets is presented. Temporal logic formulae are used to prove functional and safety requirements. In (Bender, Combemale, Crégut, Farines, Berthomieu & Vernadat, 2008), a model driven approach is shown. In this approach, Ladder Diagram programs are models that must conform to the LD metamodel. This metamodel is translated to Timed Petri Nets that input format of the Tina tool, where this input is simulated and verified using properties represented in LTL formulae.

In (Rossi & Schnoebelen, 2000), a method to transform Ladder programs into a system transition for the verification in the Symbolic Model Verifier (SMV) tool is shown. In (Canet, Couffin, Lesage, Petit, & Schnoebelen, 2000), IL programs are translated to a transition system as input to the SMV tool. In (Moon, 1994), safety and operability of PLCs are verified. The method consists of a system model, assertions, and a model checker that verifies if the system model satisfies the assertions.

Regarding timed automata, in (Mader & Wupper, 1999) an approach with emphasis on timers, based on the creation of two models of timed automata for applications of PLC written in IL is presented. In (Zoubek, 2003) new methods to verify a property set and identify which part of the Ladder program is affected by it is introduced. Therefore, only that part of the program is translated into a timed automata model. The properties are written in the CTL temporal logic. In (Wang, Song & Gu, 2007) embedded systems with programmable logic controllers are modeled by timed automata. These models are synchronized by passing signals through channels. The safety and time constraint requirements are validated by Uppaal tool with the use of CTL temporal logic.

The main difference of the method proposed in this work is the use of conformance testing instead of model checking or theorem proof and automatic model extraction. This is because a usual system has more than a thousand variables. Therefore, the use of model checking is impractical because of the state space explosion problem. Moreover,

it is necessary to deal with time in a quantitative way. In this chapter, the time elements from the Ladder language are explicitly modeled and analyzed together with the Ladder logic for the whole program. In a previous work, the algorithms for the automatic extraction of timed automata from ISA 5.2 diagrams (Barbosa, Gorgônio, Lima, Perkusich, & Silva, 2007) and FDB diagrams (Silva, Barbosa, Gorgônio, Perkusich & Lima, 2008) were defined.

In (Bijl, 2004), the formal testing based on the ioco-test theory is presented. This theory is developed using Finite State Machines (FSM) and describes a correctness criterion with specification and implementation of the systems. Ioco-test theory is clean and precise, and is the basis used in successful testing tools, like the TGV tool.

FROM LADDER PROGRAM AND ISA 5.2 DIAGRAMS TO TIMED AUTOMATA

The idea used in the modeling is to execute sequentially rungs, in case of Ladder diagrams, and blocks that determines an output, in case ISA 5.2 diagrams. Therefore, a timed automata network composed of eight timed automata models is built:

- Timed automata that modeling boolean inputs;
- Timed automata that modeling the process of reading input values;
- Timed automata that modeling the processing of input signals;
- Timed automata that modeling the behavior of timed elements;
- Timed automata that modeling the execution of logic program;
- Timed automata that modeling the process of evaluation of output states;
- Timed automata that modeling the processing of output signals;

Figure 4. Timed Automata than represent inputs

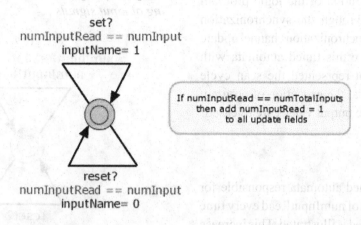

Figure 5. Timed Automata than represent reading input values

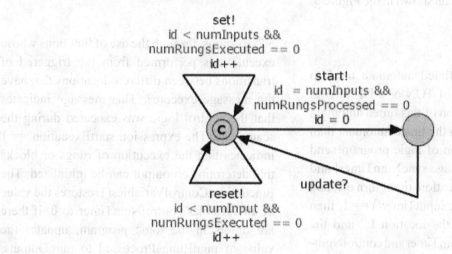

- Timed automata that modeling the scan cycle of PLC.

In the following subsections the details of these models of timed automata are presented.

Inputs

In the Figure 4 the modeling of inputs as single state automata is illustrated. The boolean variable numInputRead used as guard, is used to determine what input is to be updated. When the last input is updated the value of numInputRead is initial-

ized to 1. In this way, in the next scan cycle the input values can be sequentially updated again. One important fact to be mentioned is that the feedback variables and variables than are of input and output at the same time, are not modeled as timed automata, because they are used to store values resulting of a control logic of a program.

Reading Inputs

In the Figure 5 a timed automata what reading, in sequence, the values of inputs is shown. After all are updated, in other words, id ==

numInputs, the execution of the logic program can be initialized through the synchronization channel start. The synchronization channel update is used to sincronize this timed automata with timed automata that reprsented the scan cycle of PLC, indicates that the execution of program is completed and the output values are released.

Input Signals

In Figure 6, the timed automata responsible for increasing the value of numInputRead every time that input was updated is illustrated. This increase is accomplished through receiving of messages set! or reset! of timed automata shown in the Figure 5.

Timers

In the Figure 7, the timed automata used to represent the behavior of TON or a DI timer is illustrated. The execution of this timed automata occur as follows. When the timed automata than represents the execution of logic program send a synchronization message syncNumTimer! and the timer is in the L1 location, timer turn off, and your input is energized, inputTimer() == 1, then the model changes to the location L2 and the variables numCyclesNumTimer and controlNum-Timer are initialized. If equality inputTimer()== 0 is established, then the timer is turned off. Case equality numCyclesNumTimer == 0 is obtained and a timer remains energized (inputTimer() == 1) then the transition of the location L2 to location L3 is triggered and the output timer to logical value 1 is released. If the timer is turned on and an input timer is not energized the transition of the location L3 to location L1 is triggered and the timer is restarted.

Execution of Logic Program

The idea used in the modeling is to executed sequentially rungs, in case of Ladder diagrams, and blocks that determines an output, in case ISA

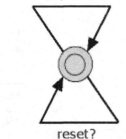

5.2 diagrams, through the use of functions whose execution is performed from the triggered of transitions between different locations that have the message execute?. This message indicates that the control logic was executed during the scan cycle. The expression startExecution == 1 indicates that the execution of rungs or blocks that determine an output can be initialized. The function setControlVariables() restores the value of all variables controlNumTimer to 0, if there are timers in the logic program, updates the value of numRungsProcessed to numOutputs, informant that all rungs or blocks that determine an output were processed and updates the value of startExecution to 0, stating that the program has been finalized. When all the rungs or blocks that determine an output were executed the message end! is sent to the timers of the program, if any, stating that their executions could no longer be held in this scan cycle. For the method, two types of rungs or blocks that determine an output are considered:

- Rungs or blocks that determine an output which control logic does not contain tim-ers: they are modeled by a transition be-

Figure 7. Timed Automata than represent TON or DI timers

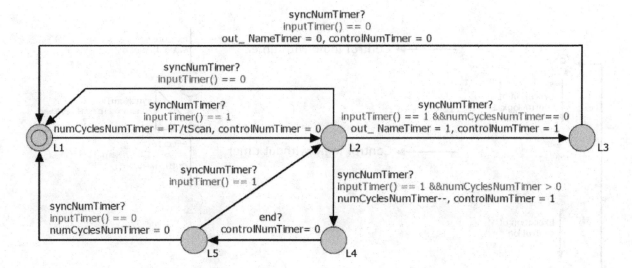

tween two consecutive locations with labels execute? and value_NameCoil().

- Rungs or blocks that determine an output which control logic contain timers: they are modeled by two transitions and two locations. The first transition occurs between the same location and has labels syncNumtimer! and checkExecutionNameTimer(). The second transition occurs between two consecutive locations with labels follow execute?, evaluateOuputNameTimer() and outNameTimer().

The function checkExecutionNameTimer() identifies whether a timer or is not able to executed. It is specific to each type of timer. For a timer type TON or DI it behaves as follows:

```
bool checkExecutionNameTimer(){
return (IN == 1 &&  control-
Numtimer == 0 && out_NameTimer
== 0) || (IN == 0 && controlNumtimer
== 0 && out_NameTimer == 1) ||(IN ==
0 && controlNumtimer == 0 && numCy-
clesNumTimer > 0)
}
```

Where, the first logical expression indicates that a timer is activated and it runs. The second logical expression indicates that the timer is executed and its input has to be false, then it must be reset. The third indicates that the timer is still to run more cycles before its exit was released, but its input has been disabled and it will have to be reset.

The function evaluateOuputNameTimer() has the goal of de- synchronize the model that represents a timer of the model that represents the execution of logic program. It is specific to each type of timer. For a timer type TON or DI it behaves as follows:

```
bool evaluateOuputNameTimer(){
return (IN == 1&& controlNumTimer ==
1) || (IN == 1 && out_NameTimer ==
1) || (IN == 0 && controlNumTimer ==
0 && out_NameTimer == 0 && numCycle-
sNumTimer == 0);
}
```

Where the first and second logical expression indicating that the timer can no longer perform even its input will be energized, as it has done its execution during the pre-set time (Present Time).

Figure 8. Timed Automata than represent the execution of logic program

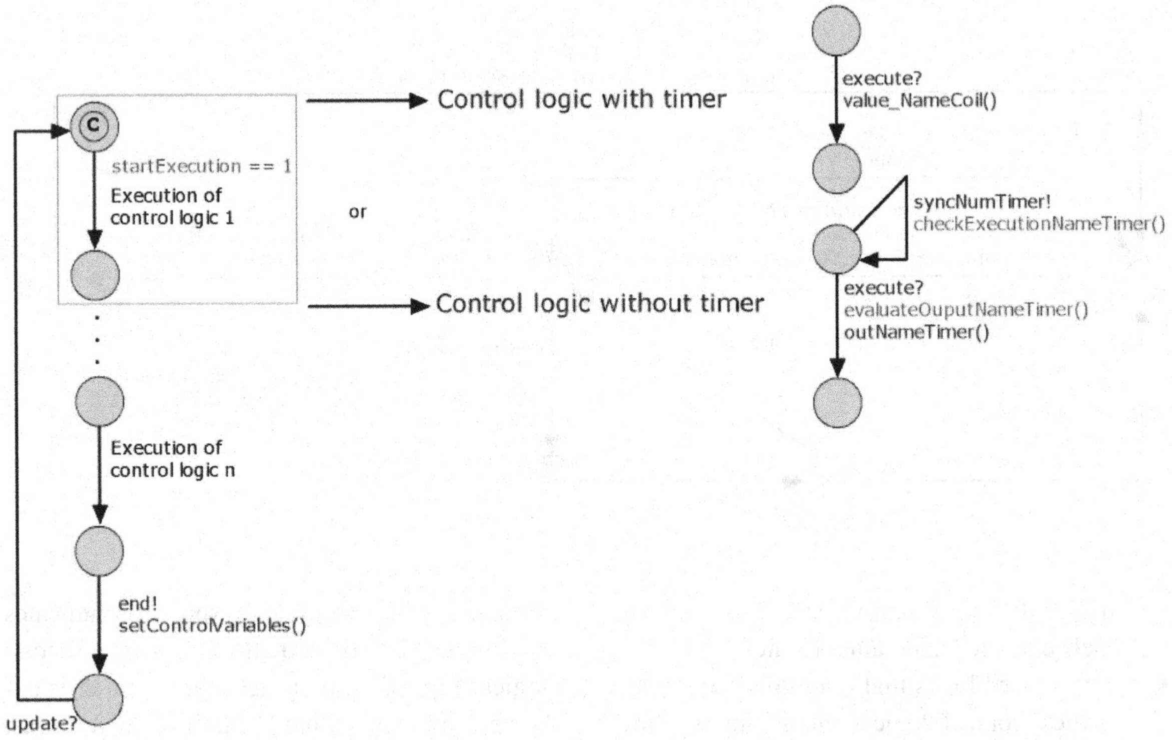

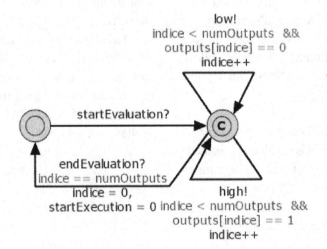

Figure 9. Timed Automata than represent the evaluation of outputs states

Figure 10. Timed Automata than represent processing of output signals

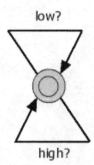

low?

high?

The third logical expression indicates that a timer is turned off, then it is not execute.

Evaluation of Output States

Output Signals

In the Figure 10 the timed automata that processes the outputs states is shown. This processing is performed by receiving messages high! or low! for timed automata shown in the Figure 9.

Scan Cycle

In the Figure 11 is illustrated the scan cycle of PLC. The execution of this timed automata occur as follows. After the updates of the input are made, the timed automata that represents the process of reading input values sends a message start! To the scan cycle timed automata stating that the execution program can be initialized. Then, the transition of the L1 location to L2 location is triggered and the variable startExecution is initialized to logical value 1. This variable is intended to inform that the execution program can be started. The second step of the scan cycle is performed through the sends a message execute! by this timed automata to timed automata that represents the execution of logic program. While each step is executed the value of the variable numRungsExecuted is incremented. This processing step should not exceed the scan time (time <= tScan). When all rungs are completed and the scan time for reaching then the outputs values are released and the timer value is restored. After this step, the evaluation of the outputs states is performed by sending the message startEvaluation! for the timed automata

Figure 11. Timed Automata than represent the scan cycle

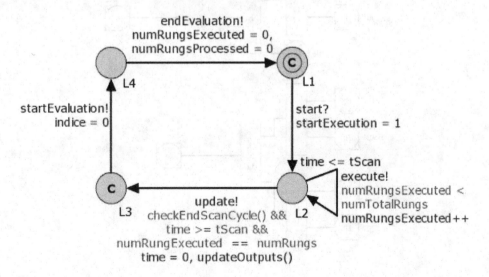

Figure 12.ISA 5.2 Diagram for bottles filler system

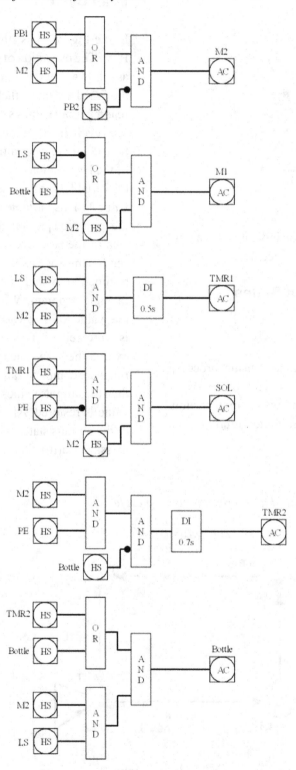

that represents the evaluation of outputs states. When all the states of the outputs are evaluated a message endEvaluation! is sent to the timed automata before, stating that the evaluation of outputs states must be terminated. The function updateOutputs() is released the outputs of the system that have not yet been released during the execution of program. The function check-EndScanCycle() evaluates whether all timers are no longer running ($\forall$ controlNumTimer $\in$ logic programa $\rightarrow$ controlNumTimer == 0) and if the execution of program has been completed (startExecution == 0).

CASE STUDY

In Figures 12 and 13 the modeling of the bottles filler system as ISA 5.2 Diagrams and Ladder Diagrams are illustrated, respectively. The operation of this system is as follows. Since the start button (PB1) is pressed, the auto motor feedback (M2) is connected. This engine will remain on until the stop button (PB2) is triggered. The motor M1 is activated once the system is started (on M2), and will stop when the sensor (LS) detect a bottle in position. When bottle is in position and 0.5 seconds is elapsed, the solenoid (SOL) will open the valve to release the coolant and filling take place until the photo eye (PE) detect an appropriate level of refrigerant in the cylinder. After being filled, the bottle will remain in this position for 0.7 seconds. Then, the motor M1 is started. This will remain on until the sensor detects another bottle.

Modeling of Bottles Filler System with Timed Automata Network

In the Figures 14 to 22 the modeling the behavior of bottles filler system as a timed automata network is illustrated.

In the Figures 14(a), 14(b), 14(c) and 14(d) the modeling of inputs, PB1, PB2, LS and PE as timed automata is shown. The variables M2,

TMR1, TMR2 and Bottle are not modeled as timed automata, because they are used to store values resulting of a control logic of a program.

In the Figure 15 a timed automata what reading, in sequence, the values of inputs is shown. The variable numInputs should be initialized with value 4, for four input variables were modeled as timed automata. In the Figure 16 the timed automata responsible for increasing the value of numInputRead every time that input was updated is illustrated.

In the figure 17 the timed automata used to represent the behavior of the TON timer called Timer1 is illustrated. This timer is a first timer found in the execution program, then the suffix NumTimer for this timer will have value 1. Therefore, variables such as controlNumTimer will be transformed into control1. The value of PT (Present Time) corresponds to 500 microseconds thus the expression numCyclesNumTimer = PT / tScan be transformed into numCycles1 = 500/tScan. The function inputTimer() is declared as follows:

```
bool inputTimer() {
return (LS and M2);
}
```

In the figure 18 the timed automata used to represent the behavior of the TON timer called Timer2 is illustrated. This timer is a second timer found in the execution program, then the suffix NumTimer for this timer will have value 2. Therefore, variables such as controlNumTimer will be transformed into control2. The value of PT (Present Time) corresponds to 700 microseconds thus the expression numCyclesNumTimer = PT / tScan be transformed into numCycles2 = 700/tScan. The function inputTimer() is declared as follows:

```
bool inputTimer() {
return ((PE and M2) and (!Bottle));
}
```

In the Figure 19 is shows the modeling of the execution of logic program as a timed automata. The implementation of the rungs or blocks that

Figure 13. Ladder Program for bottles filler system

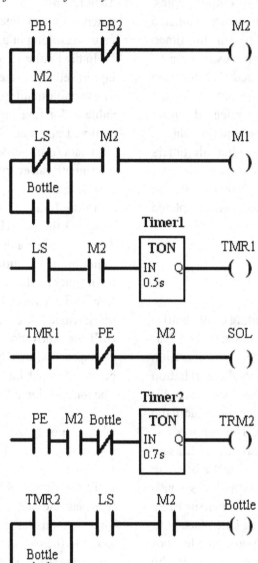

determine an output occur sequentially through the firing of transitions between different locations that have the message execute?. The functions used to model such a timed automata are:

As the rungs or blocks that determine an output containing the coils M2, M1, SOL and Bottle not have timed elements, then the value of each control logic that composed such rungs or blocks that determine an output is determined by the performance of functions labeled by value_Na-

meCoil(), where the suffix represents the Name-Coil behalf of the coil contained in the rungs or blocks that determine an output that is being processed. These functions are illustrated below:

```
void value_M2(){
M2 = ((PB1 or M2) and !PB2);
outputs[0] = M2;
}
void value_M1(){
```

Figure 14. Timed automata that representing the modeling of inputs to the bottles filler system

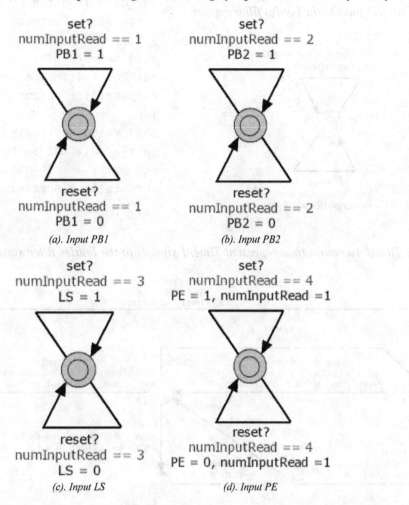

set?
numInputRead == 1
PB1 = 1

reset?
numInputRead == 1
PB1 = 0

(a). Input PB1

set?
numInputRead == 2
PB2 = 1

reset?
numInputRead == 2
PB2 = 0

(b). Input PB2

set?
numInputRead == 3
LS = 1

reset?
numInputRead == 3
LS = 0

(c). Input LS

set?
numInputRead == 4
PE = 1, numInputRead =1

reset?
numInputRead == 4
PE = 0, numInputRead =1

(d). Input PE

Figure 15. Timed Automata than represent reading input values to the bottles filler system

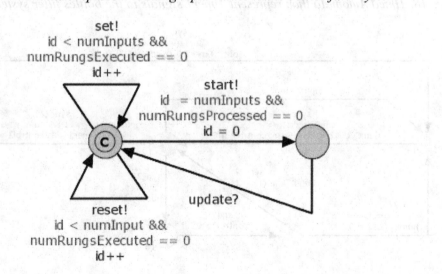

set!
id < numInputs &&
numRungsExecuted == 0
id++

start!
id = numInputs &&
numRungsProcessed == 0
id = 0

update?

reset!
id < numInput &&
numRungsExecuted == 0
id++

Figure 16. Timed Automata than represent processing of input signals to the bottles filler system

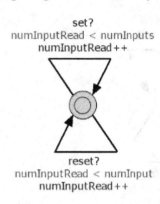

```
out_M1 = ((Bottle or !LS) and M2);
outputs[1] = output_M1;
}
void value_SOL(){
out_SOL = ((TMR1 and !PE) and M2);
outputs[3] = output_SOL;
}
void value_Bottle(){
Bottle = ((TMR2 or Bottle) and (LS
and M2));
outputs[5] = Bottle;
}
```

Figure 17. Timed Automata than represent Timer1 signals to the bottles filler system

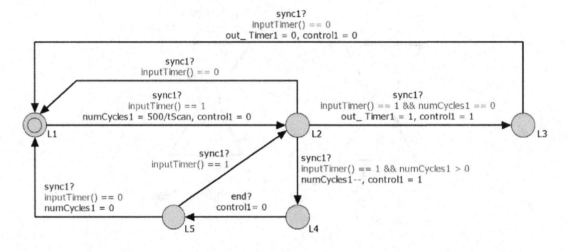

Figure 18. Timed Automata than represent Timer1 signals to the bottles filler system

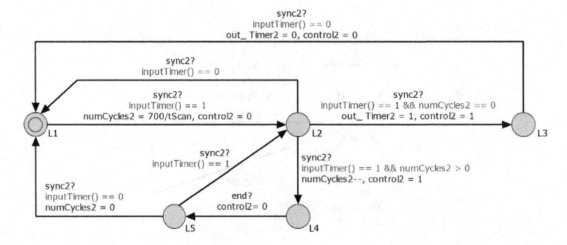

Figure 19. Timed Automata than represent the execution of logic program to the bottles filler system

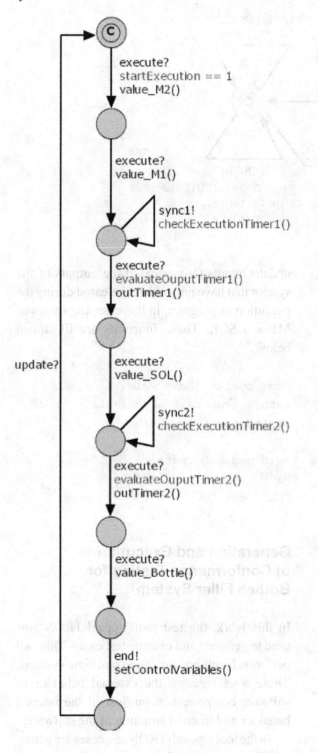

As the rungs or blocks that determine an output that contains the colis TMR1 and TMR2 have TON timer, then the performance of functions labeled by checkExecutionNameTimer(), evaluateOuput-NameTimer() and outNameTimer() determine the value of the control logic of the rungs or blocks that determine an output represented by such coils. These functions are illustrated below:

```
void outTimer1(){
TMR1 = (out_Timer1);
outputs[2] = TMR1;
}
bool checkExecutionTimer1(){
return((LS and M2) == 1 && control1
== 0 && out_Timer1 == 0) || ((LS and
M2) == 0 && control1 == 0 && out_Tim-
er1 == 1) || ((LS and M2) == 0 &&
control1 == 0 && numCycles1 > 0);
}
bool evaluateOuputTimer1(){
return  (out_Timer1 == 1 && (LS and
M2) == 1) ||
((LS and M2) == 0 && control1 == 0 &&
out_Timer1 == 0 && numCycles1 == 0)
|| (control1 == 1 && (LS and M2) ==
1);
}
void outTimer2(){
TMR2 = (out_Timer2);
outputs[4] = TMR2;
}
bool checkExecutionTimer2(){
return ((((PE and M2) and !Bottle) ==
1 && control2 == 0 && out_Timer2 ==
0) || (((PE and M2) and !Bottle) == 0
&& control2 == 0 && out_Timer2 == 1)
|| (((PE and M2) and !Bottle) == 0 &&
control2 == 0 && numCycles2 > 0);
}
bool evaluateOuputTimer2(){
return (out_Timer2 == 1 && ((PE  and
M2) and !Bottle) == 1) || (control2
== 1 && ((PE and M2) and !Bottle) ==
```

Figure 20. Timed Automata than represent the evaluation of outputs states to the bottles filler system

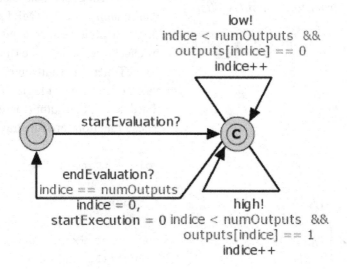

Figure 21. Timed Automata than represent processing of output signals to the bottles filler system

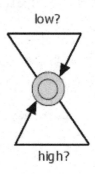

```
1) || (out_Timer2 == 0 && ((PE  and
M2) and !Bottle) == 0 &&  numCycles2
== 0);
}
```

In the Figure 20 is presented the timed automata that evaluate the outputs states (output energized or de-energized). In the Figure 21 the timed automata that processes the outputs states is shown.

In the Figure 22 is illustrated the scan cycle. The function checkEndScanCycle() used in the modeling of such automata, evaluates whether all timers are no longer running, control1 == control2 == 0, and if the execution of program has been completed, startExecution == 0. The function

updateOutputs () is released the outputs of the system that have not yet been released during the execution of program, in this case, the values of M1 and SOL. These functions are illustrated below:

```
bool checkEndScanCycle(){
return (control1 = control2 = 0) &&
startExecution == 0;
}
void updateOutputs(){
M1 = out_M1;
SOL = out_SOL;
}
```

Generation and Execution of Conformance Testing for Bottles Filler System

In this work, the test tool Uppaal-TRON was used to generate and execute test cases. This tool performs black-box testing in real-time systems. These tests measure the external behavior of software component, regardless of the internal behavior and internal structure of the software.

In the tool Uppaal-TRON test cases are generated from the model that represents the specifica-

Figure 22. Timed Automata than represent the scan cycle to the bottles filler system

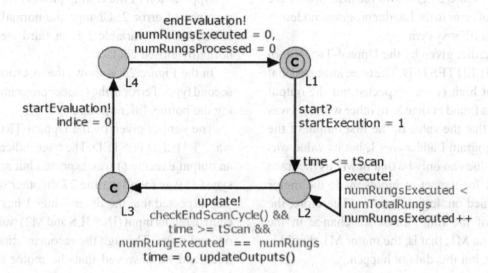

tion (environmental model) and the execution of these test cases are made by the model that represents the implementation (IUT - Implementation Under Test). After the execution of test cases a verdict is given.

For the testing process is performed three files are necessary, the model represents the specification, the model represents the implementation and a configuration file that contains the following information: events that are characterized as input events that are categorized as output, time precision necessary for implementation of each event and total units of time for implementation of events.

For this case study, the configuration and partitioning model were made as follows:

- Inputs: set(), reset(), start(), end(), sync1(), sync2(), low(), high();
- Outputs: execute(), update(), evaluation(), out_evaluation();
- Precision: 1;
- Timeout: 300;

The first implementation model to be tested was a model whose representation is faithful to the specification, i.e. the timed automata network

representing the Ladder program illustrated in the Figure 12. The verdict given by the tool Uppaal-TRON was: "TESTED PASSED: time out for testing". Thus, during the time scheduled for the tests, 300 units of time, no abnormality related to behavior of the model of implementation was detected. Therefore, implementation is faithful to the specification.

To illustrate the validity of the method, by detecting errors in the implementation, the following errors were entered into the Ladder program that represents the bottles filler system:

- Error 1: Change the order of execution of rungs, i.e., the second rung is executed and then the first rung is executed;
- Error 2: Change a normally open contact of a normally closed contact, in the case, for the third rung, the variable LS will be represented by a normally closed contact;
- Error 3: Change the value of PT of Timer1 to 0.3 second.

Application of the testing process for the occurrence of error 1: The second rung is executed and then the first rung is executed.

In the Figure 23 is shows the insertion of the first type of error in the Ladder program modeling the bottles filler system.

The verdict given by the Uppaal-TRON tool was: "FAILED TESTED. The trace indicated that the output high () was expected but the output low () was found at time 8. In other words, it was expected that the value of the first output of the Ladder program Ladder was 1, but its value was 0. This value can only be that of M1 as the trace generated for the set of inputs made the motor M2 is turned on, logical value 1. Therefore, the reversal of the rungs caused a change in the value of the M1, that is, the motor M1 should is turned on, but this did not happen.

Application of the testing process for the occurrence of error 2: Change the normally open contact of the variable LS, in third step, by a normally closed contact.

In the Figure 24 is shows the insertion of the second type of error in the Ladder program modeling the bottles filler system.

The verdict given by the Uppaal-TRON tool was: "FAILED TESTED. The trace indicated that an output execute () was expected but an output sync1 () was found at time 27. In other words, it was expected that the timer Timer 1 has not executed, but its input (IN = !LS and M2) was turned on, and it ran. Through the reconstruction of the trace can be observed that the motor M2 was

Figure 23. Insertion of error 1 in the Ladder program to the bottles filler system

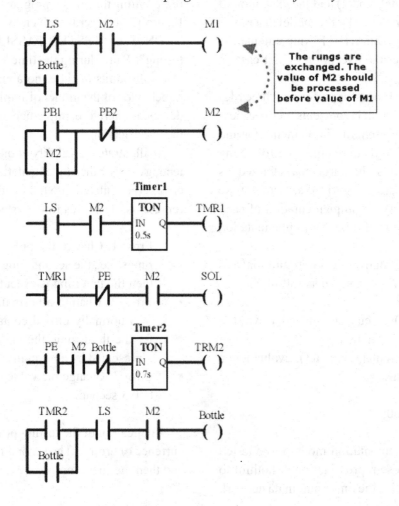

turned on and LS sensor was not enabled, then a possible explanation for the occurrence of this fact is to change the normally open contact to the normally closed contact represented by the input LS.

Application of the testing process for the occurrence of error 3: Change the value of PT of Timer1 to 0.3 second.

In the Figure 25 is shows the insertion of the third type of error in the Ladder program modeling the bottles filler system.

The verdict given by the tool Uppaal-TRON was: "FAILED TESTED. The trace indicated that

an output sync1 () was expected, but an output execute () was found at time 53. In other words, it was expected that the timer Timer1 continue to run, because running two cycles were still needed for their output on was released, but the output activated timer Timer1 has already been released.

FUTURE RESEARCH DIRECTIONS

As a future work more Ladder elements have to be considered. Also, function block extensions such as *add* and *move* can be considered. As a

Figure 24. Insertion of error 2 in the Ladder program to the bottles filler system

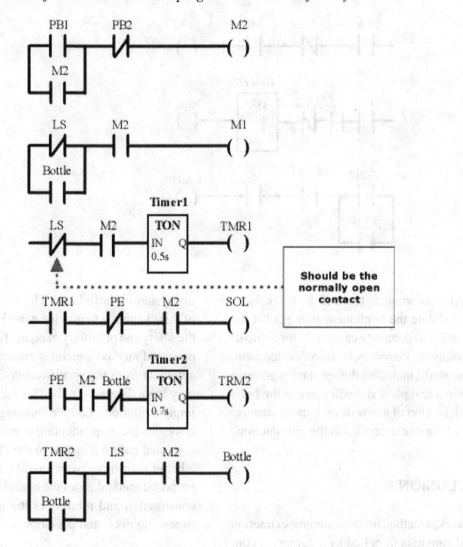

Figure 25. Insertion of error 3 in the Ladder program to the bottles filler system

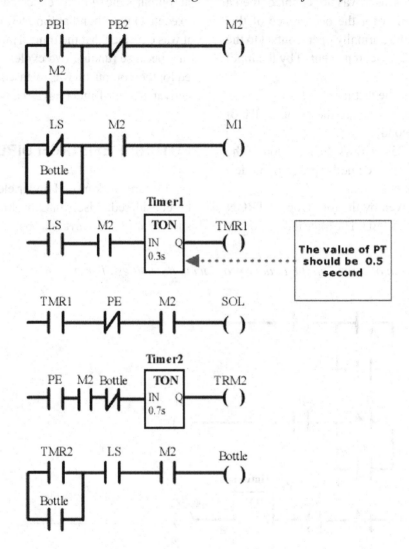

next step, conformance test will be extensively used to validate the implementation against the specification. A complete case study for a brazilian oil company, Petrobras, is under development. This case study, including the test stage is going to be used in a real plant and will serve as the basis for the definition of a new development scenario instead of the one described in the introduction.

CONCLUSION

In this work, a method for the automatic extraction of timed automata from Ladder programs of con-

trol systems is introduced. The main contribution of this chapter is to provide a method to increase the safety and reliability of control programs. The proposed method generates automatically timed automata from the specification documents, binary logic diagrams in the ISA 5.2 standard, and implementation, Ladder language. Therefore, errors in the implementation are detected and corrected before it is sent to the PLC, achieving a better control software quality. Moreover, the proposed method hides the complexity of model construction and minimizes the interaction between engineers and developers.

REFERENCES

Alur, R. (1999). Timed automata. Lectures Notes in Computer Science. *In 11th International Conference on Computer-Aided Verification*. 1633 (pp. 8–22). Spinger Verlag.

Alur, R., & Dill, D. (1994). A theory of timed automata. *Theoretical Computer Science, 126*(2), 183–235. doi:10.1016/0304-3975(94)90010-8

Barbosa, L. P. A., Gorgônio, K., Lima, A. M. N., Perkusich, A., & Silva, L. D. (2007). *On the automatic generation of timed automata models from isa 5.2 diagrams*. IEEE Conference on Emerging Technologies and Factory Automation ETFA. IEEE Conference (pp. 406–412). Patras, Greece.

Behrmann, G., David, A., & Larsen, K. G. (2004). A tutorial on uppaal. Bernardo and F. Corradini, editors. *Formal Methods for the Design of Real-Time System: 3185. In LCNS* (pp. 200–237). Springer Verlag.

Bender, D. F., Combemale, B., Crégut, X., Farines, J.-M., Berthomieu, B., & Vernadat, F. (2008). Ladder Metamodeling and PLC Program Validation through Time Petri Nets. *ECMDA-FA '08: Proceedings of the 4th European conference on Model Driven Architecture*, (pp. 121-136). Berlin, Germany.

Bengtsson, J., & Yi, W. (2003). *Timed automata: Semantics, algorithms and tools* (pp. 87–124). Lectures on Concurrency and Petri Nets.

Bijl, M. V. D., Rensink, A., & Tretmans, J. (2004). *Compositional Testing with IOCO. Formal Approaches to Software Testing* (pp. 86–100). Berlim, Germany: FATES. doi:10.1007/978-3-540-24617-6_7

Canet, G., Couffin, S., Lesage, J.-J., Petit, A., & Schnoebelen, Ph. (2000). Towards the automatic verification of PLC programs written in Instruction List. *IEEE International Conference on Systems, Man and Cybernetics (SMC 2000)* (pp. 2449–2454) Nashville, Tennessee: Argos Press.

Heiner, M., & Menzel, T. (1998). A petri net semantics for the PLC language instruction list. *IEEE Workshop on Discrete Event Systems* (pp. 161–165). Cagliari, Italy.

ISA. (1992). *Binary Logic Diagrams for Process Operations. ISA 5.2-1976 (R1992)*. ISA - The Instrumentation, Systems, and Automation Society.

ISO/IEC. (1997). Information technology – Vocabulary – Part 14: Reliability, maintainability and availability. *ISO Standards*. Retrieved January 30, 2009, from: http://www.iso.org/

John, K.-H., & Tiegelkamp, M. (2001). *IEC 61131-3: Programming Industrial Automation Systems*. Berlin, Germany: Springer.

Larsen, K. G., Mikucionis, M., Nielsen, B., & Skou, A. (2005). Testing real-time embedded software using uppaal-tron: an industrial case study. *In EMSOFT '05: Proceedings of the 5th ACM international conference on Embedded software*, (pp. 299–306), New York: ACM Press.

Mader, A., & Wupper, H. (1999). Timed automata models for simple programmable logic controllers. *Euromicro Conference on Real-Time Systems*, York, UK.

Moon, I. (1994). Modeling programmable logic controllers for logic verification. *IEEE Control Systems Magazine, 14*(2), 53–59. doi:10.1109/37.272781

Neves, C., Duarte, L., Viana, N., & Lucena, V. (2007, Novembro*). The ten biggest challenges of industrial automation: the perspectives for the future. (Os dez maiores desafios da automação industrial: as perspectivas para o futuro)*. Paper presented at the II Congress of Research and Innovation of Network North Northeast of Technological Education, João Pessoa, Paraíba, Brazil.

Parr, E. A. (2003). *Programmable Controllers: An engineer's guide* (3rd ed.). London, England: Newnes.

PLCopen for efficiency in automation (2004). IEC 61131-3: a standard programming resource. *Technical Committee 1 Standards*. Retrieved November 10, 2008, from: http://www.plcopen. org/pages/tc1_standards/downloads/

Rossi, O., & Schnoebelen, Ph. (2000). Formal modeling of timed function blocks for the automatic verification of Ladder Diagram programs. Engell, S., Kowalewski, S., & Zaytoon, J., editors, *Proceedings of the 4th International Conference on Automation of Mixed Processes: Hybrid Dynamic Systems (ADPM 2000)* (pp. 177–182). Dortmund, Germany: Shaker Verlag.

Silva, L. D., Barbosa, L. P. A., Gorgônio, K., Perkusich, A., & Lima, A. M. N. (2008). On the automatic generation of timed automata models from function block diagrams for safety instrumented systems. *IEEE International Conference on Industrial Electronics*, Orlando, Florida, USA.

Wang, R., Song, X., & Gu, M. (2007). Modelling and verification of program logic controllers using timed automata. *Software, IET, 1*(4), 127–131. doi:10.1049/iet-sen:20070009

Wescott, T. (2006). *Applied Control Theory for Embedded Systems (Embedded Technology)*. Newnes.

Zoubek, B. (2002). *Automatic verification of programs for control systems.*

Zoubek, B. (2003). *Towards automatic verification of ladder logic. IMACS Multiconference on Computational Engineering in Systems Applications* (pp. 9–12). CESA.

Compilation of References

Abdul-Rahman, A. (2005) *A Framework for Decentralised trust Reasoning*. PhD Thesis. Available at: http://www. cs.ucl.ac.uk/ staff/ F.AbdulRahman/ docs/ thesis-final. pdf.

Agrawal, R., Bird, P., Grandison, T., Kiernan, J., Logan, S., & Rjaibi, W. (2005). Extending Relational Database Systems to Automatically Enforce Privacy Policies. *Int. Conf. on Data Engineering (ICDE 2005)*, (pp. 1013-1022). IEEE Computer Society.

Aiello, M., & Giorgini, P. (2004). Applying the Tropos Methodology for Analysing Web Services Requirements and Reasoning about Qualities of Services. *UPGRADE*, *5*, 20–26.

Akdemir, I. O. (1998). *An implementation of secure flow type inference for a subset of Java*. Unpublished Master thesis, Naval Postgraduate School, Monterey, California.

Alcalde, B., & Mauw, S. (2009) *An algebra for trust dilution and trust fusion*. Accepted for the 2009 World Congress on Privacy, Security, Trust and the Management of e-Business.

Alexander, I. (2003). Misuse cases: use cases with hostile intent. *IEEE Software*, *20*(1), 58–66. doi:10.1109/MS.2003.1159030

Alexander, C., Ishikawa, S., & Silverstein, M. (1977). *A pattern language: towns, builings, construction*. New York: Oxford University Press.

Alexander, I. (2002). Initial industrial experience of misuse cases in trade-off analysis. *Proceedings of IEEE Joint International Conference on Requirements Engineering*.

Allen, J. H., Barnum, S., Ellison, R. J., Mcgraw, G., & Mead, N. R. (2008). *Software Security Engineering: A Guide for Project Managers*. Addison Wesley Professional.

Almaliotis, V., Loizidis, A., Katsaros, P., Louridas, P., & Spinellis, D. (2008). Static program analysis for Java Card applets. In G. Grimaud & F.-X. Standaert (Ed.), *Proc. of the 8th IFIP Smart Card Research and Advanced Application Conference (CARDIS)* (pp. 17-31), Springer LNCS 5189.

Alur, R., & Dill, D. (1994). A theory of timed automata. *Theoretical Computer Science*, *126*(2), 183–235. doi:10.1016/0304-3975(94)90010-8

Alur, R. (1999). Timed automata. Lectures Notes in Computer Science. *In 11th International Conference on Computer-Aided Verification*. 1633 (pp. 8–22). Spinger Verlag.

Anastasakis, K., Bordbar, B., Georg, G., & Ray, I. (2008). *On Challenges of Model Transformation from UML to Alloy*. accepted for publication in Journal on Software and Systems Modeling (SOSYM) special issue of extended papers from the MODELS 2007 conference, *on-line first*: DOI 10.1007/s10270-008-0110-3.

Anderson, R. (2001). *Security Engineering: A Guide to Building Dependable Distributed Systems*. New York: John Wiley & Sons Inc.

Anton, A. (1996). Goal-Based Requirements Analysis. *IEEE Int. Conf. on Requirements Engineering (ICRE 96)*, (pp. 136-144). Colorado Springs CO.

Antón, A. & Earp, J. (2000). *Strategies for developing policies and requirements for secure electronic commerce systems.* 1st Workshop on security and privacy in e-commerce. ACM.

Apostolopoulos, V., Peris, V., & Saha, D. D (1999). Transport layer security: How much does it really cost? *Conference on Computer Communications (IEEE Infocom),* New York, pp. 717-725.

Arciniegas, J. L., Dueñas, J. C., Ruiz, J. L., Cerón, R., Bermejo, J., & Oltra, M.A. (2006). Architecture Reasoning for Supporting Product Line Evolution: An Example on Security. In Käkölä, T., & Dueñas, J. C. (Eds.), *Software Product Lines: Research Issues in Engineering and Management.* Springer.

Arlow, J. (1998). Use cases, UML visual modelling and the trivialisation of business requirements. *Requirements Engineering, 3*(2), 150–152. doi:10.1007/BF02919976

Artelsmair, C., & Wagner, R. (2003).Towards a Security Engineering Process. *In:* Nagib Callaos, W. L., Belkis Sánchez, Elizabeth Hansen (eds.), The 7th World Multiconference on Systemics, Cybernetics and Informatics, July 27-30,2003 2003 Orlando, Florida, USA. 22-27.

Ashraf, N., Camerer, C. F., & Loewenstein, G. (2005). Adam Smith, Behavioral Economist. *The Journal of Economic Perspectives, 19*(3). doi:10.1257/089533005774357897

Association of Computing Machinery. (2001) *Computer Science Body of Knowledge.* Retrieved January 2009 from Online at http://www.sigcse.org/cc2001/cs-csbok.html

Atluri, V. (2001). Security for Workflow Systems. *Information Security Technical Report, 6*(2), 59–68. doi:10.1016/S1363-4127(01)00207-2

Bachmann, F., Bass, L., Carriere, J., Clements, P., Garlan, D., Ivers, J., Little, R. & Nord, R. (2000). Software Architecture Documentation in Practice: Documenting Architectural Layers CMU/SEI-2000-SR-004.

Balsamo, S., DiMarco, S. A., Inverardi, P., & Simeoni, M. (2004). Model-based Performance Prediction in Software Development. *IEEE Transactions on Software Engineering, 30*(5), 295–310. doi:10.1109/TSE.2004.9

Barber, B., & Davey, J. (1992). *The Use of the CCTA Risk Analysis and Management Methodology CRAMM in Health Information Systems.* In K.C. Lun, P. Degoulet, T.E. Piemme, & O. Rienhoff (editors): Proceedings of MEDINFO'92, North Holland Publishing Co, Amsterdam, pp. 1589–1593.

Barbosa, L. P. A., Gorgônio, K., Lima, A. M. N., Perkusich, A., & Silva, L. D. (2007). *On the automatic generation of timed automata models from isa 5.2 diagrams.* IEEE Conference on Emerging Technologies and Factory Automation ETFA. IEEE Conference (pp. 406–412). Patras, Greece.

Bartal, Y., Mayer, A., Nissim, K., & Wool, A. (2004). Firmato: A Novel Firewall Management Toolkit. *ACM Transactions on Computer Systems, 22*(4), 381–420. doi:10.1145/1035582.1035583

Basin, D., Doser, J., & Lodderstedt, T. (2006). Model Driven Security: from UML Models to Access Control Infrastructures. *ACM Transactions on Software Engineering and Methodology, 15,* 39–91. doi:10.1145/1125808.1125810

Basin, D., Doser, J., & Lodderstedt, T. (2003) Model Driven Security for Process-oriented Systems. *In:* ACM Symposium on Access Control Models and Technologies, 2003 Como, Italy. ACM Press, 100-109.

Bass, L., Clements, P., & Kazman, R. (1998). *Software Architecture in Practice* (1st ed.). Reading, MA: Addison-Wesley.

Bass, L., Bachmann, F., Ellison, R. J., Moore, A. P., & Klein, M. (2004). *Security and Survivability Reasoning Frameworks and Architectural Design Tactics.* SEI.

Bass, L., Clements, P., & Kazman, R. (2003). *Software Architecture in Practice.* Addison-Wesley.

Beckert, B., & Mostowski, W. (2003). A program logic for handling Java Card's transaction mechanism. *Proc. of 6th Int. Conference on Fundamental Approaches to Software Engineering (FASE'03)* (pp. 246-260), Springer LNCS 2621.

Behrmann, G., David, A., & Larsen, K. G. (2004). A tutorial on uppaal. Bernardo and F. Corradini, editors. *Formal Methods for the Design of Real-Time System: 3185. In LCNS* (pp. 200–237). Springer Verlag.

Bellotti, V., & Sellen, A. (1993). *Design for privacy in ubiquitous computing environments*. Proceedings of the third european conference on computer supported cooperative work (ECSCW 93). G. In Michelis, Simone, C., Schmidt, K. 93-108.

Bender, D. F., Combemale, B., Crégut, X., Farines, J.-M., Berthomieu, B., & Vernadat, F. (2008). Ladder Metamodeling and PLC Program Validation through Time Petri Nets. *ECMDA-FA '08: Proceedings of the 4th European conference on Model Driven Architecture*, (pp. 121-136). Berlin, Germany.

Bengtsson, J., & Yi, W. (2003). *Timed automata: Semantics, algorithms and tools* (pp. 87–124). Lectures on Concurrency and Petri Nets.

Best, B., Jürjens, J., & Nuseibeh, B. (2007). Model-Based Security Engineering of Distributed Information Systems Using UMLsec. In *Proceedings of the 29th International Conference on Software Engineering* (pp. 581-590). New York: ACM.

Bieber, P., Cazin, J., Girard, P., Lanet, J.-L., Wiels, V., & Zanon, G. (2002). Checking secure interactions of smart card applets: extended version. *Journal of Computer Security, 10,* 369–398.

Bijl, M. V. D., Rensink, A., & Tretmans, J. (2004). *Compositional Testing with IOCO. Formal Approaches to Software Testing* (pp. 86–100). Berlim, Germany: FATES. doi:10.1007/978-3-540-24617-6_7

Birks, P. (1997). *The Classification of Obligations*. Clarendon Press.

Blakley, B., & Heath, C. The Open Group. (2004). *Technical Guide*. Security Design Patterns.

Blakley, B., & Heath, C. (2004). *Security Design Patterns*. Technical Guide, The Open Group.

Blanco, C., García-Rodríguez de Guzmán, I., Rosado, D., Fernández-Medina, E., & Trujillo, J. (2009). Applying QVT in order to implement Secure Data Warehouses in SQL Server Analysis Services. *Journal of Research and Practice in Information Technology, 41,* 135–154.

Boehm, B. (1981). *Software Engineering Economics*. Upper Saddle River, NJ: Prentice-Hall.

Bordbar, B., & Anastasakis, K. (2005). *MDA and Analysis of Web Applications*. In Trends in Enterprise Application Architecture (TEAA) 2005, volume 3888 of Lecture notes in Computer Science, pages 44-55, Trondheim, Norway, 2005.3

BPMN. (2006). *Business Process Modeling Notation Specification* [Online]. OMG Final Adopted Specification, dtc/06-02-01. Available: http://www.bpmn.org/Documents/OMG%20Final%20Adopted%20BPMN%201-0%20Spec%2006-02-01.pdf [Accessed].

Braber, I. F., Hogganvik, M. S. L., Stølen, K., & Vraalsen, F. (2007). Model-based security analysis in seven steps - a guided tour to the CORAS method, (pp. 101-117). *BT Technology Journal, 25*(1). doi:10.1007/s10550-007-0013-9

Braz, F., Fernandez, E. B., & VanHilst, M. (2008). Eliciting security requirements through misuse activities. In *Proceedings of the 19th International Workshop on Database and Expert Systems Applications* (pp. 328-333). Los Alamitos, CA: IEEE Computer Society.

Bresciani, P., Perini, A., Giorgini, P., Giunchiglia, F., & Mylopoulos, J. (2004). Tropos: An Agent-Oriented Software Development Methodology. *Autonomous Agents and Multi-Agent Systems, 8*(3), 203–236. doi:10.1023/B:AGNT.0000018806.20944.ef

Breu, R., Burger, K., Hafner, M., Jürjens, J., Popp, G., Lotz, V., & Wimmel, G. (2003). Key Issues of a Formally Based Process Model for Security Engineering. *In:* International Conference on Software and Systems Engineering and their Applications, 2003.

Breunesse, C. B., Catano, N., Huisman, M., & Jacobs, B. (2005). Formal methods for smart cards: an experience report. *Science of Computer Programming, 55,* 53–80. doi:10.1016/j.scico.2004.05.011

Buecker, A., Ashley, P., Borrett, M., Lu, M., Muppidi, S., & Readshaw, N. (2007). *Understanding SOA Security Design and Implementation. IBM Redbooks*. IBM.

Burdy, L., Requet, A. & Lanet, J. L. (2003). Java applet correctness: a developer-oriented approach. *Proc. of Formal Methods Europe (FME)*, Springer LNCS 2805.

Buschmann, F., Meunier, R., Rohnert, H., Sommerlad, P., & Stal, M. (1996). Pattern-Oriented Software Architecture: *Vol. 1. A System of Patterns*. West Sussex, England: John Wiley & Sons.

Business, W. (1998). A Little Net Privacy, Please. Available at: www.businessweek.com last accessed: 17/12/2007.

Cabot, J., & Zannone, N. (2008). *Towards an Integrated Framework for Model-driven Security Engineering*. Proceedings of the Workshop on Modeling Security (MODSEC08), Toalose, France.

Canet, G., Couffin, S., Lesage, J.-J., Petit, A., & Schnoe-belen, Ph. (2000). Towards the automatic verification of PLC programs written in Instruction List. *IEEE International Conference on Systems, Man and Cybernetics (SMC 2000)* (pp. 2449–2454) Nashville, Tennessee: Argos Press.

Cannon, J. C. (2004). *Privacy, What developers and IT professionals should know*. Reading, MA: Addison-Wesley.

Castelfranchi, C., & Falcone, R. (2000) Trust is much more than subjective probability: Mental components and sources of trust. Proc. *of the 33rd Hawaii Int. Conf. on System Sciences (HICSS2000). Vol. 6*, 2000.

Castroa, J., Kolp, M., & Mylopoulos, J. (2002). Towards requirements-driven information systems engineering: the Tropos project. *Information Systems, 27*(6), 365–389. doi:10.1016/S0306-4379(02)00012-1

Catano, N., & Huisman, M. (2002). Formal specification and static checking of Gemplus's electronic purse using ESC/Java. In G. Goos, J. Hartmanis & J. van Leeuwen (Ed.), *Proc. of Formal Methods Europe (FME'02)* (pp. 272-289), Springer LNCS 2391.

Chandramouli, R., & Blackburn, M. (2004). *Automated Testing of Security Functions using a combined Model & Interface driven Approach*. Proceedings of the 37th Hawaii International Conference on System Sciences.

Chang, E., Dillion, T., & Hussain, F. K. (2006). *Trust and Reputation for Service-Oriented Environments: Technologies for Building Business Intelligence and Consumer Confidence*. New York: John Wiley & Sons, Ltd.doi:10.1002/9780470028261

Cheng, B. H. C., Konrad, S., Campbell, L. A., & Wassermann, R. (2003). *In* (pp. 13–22). Monterey Bay, CA, USA: Using Security Patterns to Model and Analyze Security Requirements.

Choppy, C., Hatebur, D., & Heisel, M. (2005). *Architectural patterns for problem frames. IEEE Proceedings - Software, Special Issue on Relating Software Requirements and Architecture* (pp. 198–208). Washington, DC: IEEE Computer Society.

Choppy, C., Hatebur, D., & Heisel, M. (2006). Component composition through architectural patterns for problem frames. *In Proceedings of the Asia Pacific Software Engineering Conference (APSEC)* (pp. 27-34). Washington, DC: IEEE Computer Society.

Chung, L. (1993). *Dealing with security requirements during the development of information systems*. The 5th international conference of advanced information systems engineering, CAiSE'93, Paris, France. *Springer Verlag LNCS, 685*, 234–251.

Chung, E. S., Hong, J. I., Lin, J., Prabaker, M. K., Landay, J. A., & Liu, A. L. (2004). Development and evaluation of emerging design patterns for ubiquitous computing. *Int. Conf. on Designing Interactive Systems*, New York: ACM Press.

Chung, L., & Nixon, B. Yu. E., & Mylopoulos, J., (2000). *Non-Functional requirements in software engineerin.*, Kluwer Academic Publishers.

Clements, P., & Northrop, L. (2002). *Software Product Lines: Practices and Patterns*. Addison-Wesley.

Coen-Porisini, A., Colombo, P., Sicari, S., & Trombetta, A. (2007). A Conceptual Model for Privacy Policies. In Proc. of *Software Engineering Application (SEA '07)*. Cambridge, MS.

Cofta, P. (2007). *Trust, Complexity and Control: Confidence in a Convergent World*. New York: John Wiley and Sons.

Cofta, P. (2009). Towards a better citizen identification system. *Identity in the Information Society*, *1*(1), 39–53. doi:10.1007/s12394-009-0006-6

Cofta, P. (2009). Designing for Trust. In Whitworth, B., & de Moor, A. (Eds.), *Handbook of Research on Socio-Technical Design and Social Networking Systems. Information Science Reference*. IGI Global.

Cofta, P., & Lacohée, H. (2010). Trust in identification systems: from empirical observations to design guidelines. In Yan, Z. (Ed.), *Trust Modelling and management in Digital Environments: From Social Concepts to System Development*. New York: Information Science Reference. doi:10.4018/978-1-61520-682-7.ch019

Cofta, P. (2006) *Distrust. In: Proc. of Eight Int. Conf. on Electronic Commerce ICEC'06*, Fredericton, Canada. pp. 250-258.

Collins, T. (2007) NHS security dilemma as smartcards shared. *ComputerWeekly*, January 30, 2007.

Coplien, J. O. (1992). *Advanced C++ programming styles and idioms*. Reading, MA: Addison-Wesley.

CORAS. (2003). IST-2000-25031.Retrieved from http://sourceforge.net/projects/coras.

Côté, I., Hatebur, D., Heisel, M., Schmidt, H., & Wentzlaff, I. (2008). A systematic account of problem frames. *In Proceedings of the European Conference on Pattern Languages of Programs (EuroPLoP)* (pp. 749-767). Universitätsverlag Konstanz.

Cranor, L., & Garfinkel, S. (2005) *Security and Usability: Designing Secure Systems that People Can Use*. O'Reilly Media, Inc.

CVSS. (2007). *Common Vulnerability Scoring System (CVSS-SIG)*.Retrieved from http://www.first.org/cvss/.

Dahm, M. (2001). *Byte code engineering with the BCEL API* (Tech. Rep. B-17-98). Freie University of Berlin, Institute of Informatics, Germany.

Dardenne, A., van Lamsweerde, A., & Fickas, S. (1993). Goal-directed requirements acquisition. *Science of Computer Programming*, *20*, 3–50. doi:10.1016/0167-6423(93)90021-G

Dardenne, A., & van Lamsweerde, A. (1996). *Formal refinement patterns for goal-driven requierements elaboration*. 4th ACM SIGSOFT International Symposium on the Foundations of Software Engineering pp: 179-190.

Davidson, M. A. (2006). *The case for information assurance*. Edinburgh: Keynote Address.

Delessy, N., & Fernandez, E. B. (2008). A pattern-driven security process for SOA applications. In *Proceedings of the 3rd International Conference on Availability, Reliability, and Security* (pp. 416-421). Washington DC: IEEE Computer Society.

Deng, Y. & Wang, J. & Tsai, J. J. P. & Beznosov, K. (2003). An approach for modeling and analysis of security system architectures, (pp. 1099 - 1119). *IEEE Transactions on Knowledge and Data Engineering*, *15*(5). Washington, DC: IEEE Computer Society.

Dennett, D. C. (1989). *The Intentional Stance*. New York: Bradford Books.

Devanbu, P., & Stubblebine, S. (2000). Software engineering for security: a roadmap in: A. Finkelstein. *The Future of Software Engineering, ACM Press*, 227-239.

Dimmock, N., Bacon, J., Ingram, D., & Moody, K. (2005). Risk Models for Trust-Based Access Control (TBAC). In Herrmann, P. (Ed.), *iTrust2005, LNCS 3477* (pp. 364–371).

Djebbi, O., Salinesi, C., & Fanmuy, G. (2007). Industry Survey of Product Lines Management Tools: Requirements, Qualities and Open Issues. *15th IEEE International Requirements Engineering Conference (RE'07)*, *15*, 301 - 306.

Dwyer, N. (2009) *Enabling Trust in Virtual Teams*. BT STRF Research Report.

Elahi, G., & Yu, E. (2007). *A goal oriented approach for modeling and analyzing security trade-offs*. In ER 2007. In *Lecture Notes in Computer Science* (*Vol. 4801*, pp. 375–390). Springer-Verlag.

Endrei, M., Ang, J., Arsanjani, A., Chua, S., Comte, P., Krogdahl, P., et al. (2004). *Patterns: Service-Oriented Architecture and Web Services* [Online]. Available: http://www.redbooks.ibm.com/abstracts/sg246303.html [Accessed].

ENISA (European Network and Information Security Agency). (2009). Retrieved January 2009 from http://www.enisa.europa.eu/

EU, Directive (1995). *Directive 95/46/EC on the protection of individuals with regard to the processing of personal data and the free movement of such data.*

European Future Internet Portal. (2009). Retrieved January 2009 from http://www.future-internet.eu//-projects.html

European Future Internet Portal. (2010). Retrieved January 2009 from http://www.future-internet.eu//-projects.html

Fabbi, M., Ahlawat, R., Allen, N., Blood, S., Dulaney, K., Goodness, E., et al. (2005). *Cisco Systems: A Detailed Review* (Publication. Retrieved January 2009, from Gartner. Furnell, S. (2005). Why users cannot use security. *Computers & Security, 24,* 274-279.

Faegri, T. E., & Hallsteinsen, S. (2006). A Software Product Line Reference Architecture for Security. In Käkölä, T., & Dueñas, J. C. (Eds.), *Software Product Lines: Research Issues in Engineering and Management*. Springer.

Failure-Divergence Refinement (FDR) 2 by Formal Systems (Europe) Limited.(n.d.). Retrieved June 24, 2009, from http://www.fsel.com/index.html.

Fernandez, E., Ballesteros, J., Desouza-Doucet, A., & Larrondo-Petrie, M. (2007). Security Patterns for Physical Access Control Systems. *Data and Applications Security, XXI,* 259–274. doi:10.1007/978-3-540-73538-0_19

Fernandez, E. B., Larrondo-Petrie, M. M., Sorgente, T., & VanHilst, M. (2006). A Methodology to Develop Secure Systems Using Patterns. In Mouratidis, H., & Giorgini, P. (Eds.), *Integrating Security and Software Engineering: Advances and Future Vision* (pp. 107–126). Hershey, PA: IDEA Group.

Fernandez, E. B., Larrondo-Petrie, M. M., Sorgente, T., & Vanhilst, M. (2007). In Mouratidis, H., & Giorgini, P. (Eds.), *Integrating security and software engineering: Advances and future visions* (pp. 107–126).

Fernandez, E. B., & la Red, M. D. L. & Forneron, J. & Uribe, V. E. & Rodriguez G., G. (2007). A secure analysis pattern for handling legal cases. *In Latin America Conference on Pattern Languages of Programming (SugarLoafPLoP)* (2007). Retrieved June 24, 2009, from http://sugarloafplop.dsc.upe.br/wwD.zip.

Fernandez, E. B., & Pernul, G. (2006). Patterns for session-based access control. In *Proceedings of the Conference on Pattern Languages of Programs*. Hillside Group. Retrieved November 25, 2009, from http://hillside.net/plop/2006/.

Fernandez, E. B., & Pan, R. (2001). *A pattern language for security models*. Proceedings of 8th Conference on Pattern Languages of Programs (PLoP), Monticello, Illinois, USA.

Fernandez, E. B., & Yuan, X. Y. (2007). Securing analysis patterns. In D. John and S.N. Kerr (Eds.) *Proceedings of the 45th ACM Southeast Conference* (pp. 288-293), New York: ACM.

Fernandez, E. B., Cholmondeley, P., & Zimmermann, O. (2007). Extending a Secure System Development Methodology to SOA. *In:* DEXA '07: Proceedings of the 18th International Conference on Database and Expert, 2007 Regensburg, Germany. IEEE Computer Society, 749-754.

Fernandez, E. B., Jürjens, J., Yoshioka, N., & Washizaki, H. (2008). Incorporating database systems into a secure software development methodology. In *Proceedings of the 2008 19th International Conference on Database and Expert Systems Application* (pp. 310-314). Washington DC: IEEE Computer Society.

Fernandez, E. B., Pelaez, J. C., & Larrondo-Petrie, M. M. (2007). Attack patterns: A new forensic and design tool. In P. Craiger & S. Shenoi (Eds.) *Advances in Digital Forensics III: Proceedings of the Third Annual IFIP WG 11.9 International Conference on Digital Forensics* (pp. 345-357). Berlin, Germany: Springer.

Fernandez, E. B., Pernul, G., & Larrondo-Petrie, M. M. (2008). Patterns and pattern diagrams for access control. In S. Furnell; S.K. Katsikas, & A. Lioy (Eds.) *LNCS 5185: Trust, Privacy and Security in Digital Business: 5th International Conference on Trust and Privacy in Digital Business* (pp. 38-47). Heidelberg, Germany: Springer.

Fernandez, E. B., Washizaki, H., Yoshioka, N., Kubo, A., & Fukazawa, Y. (2008). Classifying security patterns., In Y. Zhang, G. Yu, & E. Bertino (Eds.) *LNCS 4976 Progress in WWW Research and Development: Proceedings of the 10th Asia-Pacific Web Conference* (pp. 342-347). Heidelberg, Germany: Springer.

Fernandez, E. B., Yoshioka, N., Washizaki, H., & Jürjens, J. (2007). Using security patterns to build secure systems. *Proceedings of the 1st International Workshop on Software Patterns and Quality*, Retrieved November 25, 2009, from http://apsec2007.fuka.info.waseda.ac.jp/parts/W3SPAQu.pdf.

Fernandez, E., G. Pernul & M. Larrondo-Petrie (2008). Patterns and Pattern Diagrams for Access Control. *Trust, Privacy and Security in Digital Business*, 38-47.

Fernández-Medina, E., Jurjens, J., Trujillo, J., & Jajodia, S. (2009). Model-Driven Development for secure information systems. *Information and Software Technology*, *51*(5), 809–814. doi:10.1016/j.infsof.2008.05.010

Fernández-Medina, E., & Piattini, M. (2005). Designing Secure Databases. *Information and Software Technology*, *47*, 463–477. doi:10.1016/j.infsof.2004.09.013

Fernández-Medina, E., Trujillo, J., Villarroel, R., & Piattini, M. (2006). Access Control and Audit Model for the Multidimensional Modeling of Data Warehouses. *Decision Support Systems*, *42*, 1270–1289. doi:10.1016/j.dss.2005.10.008

Ferraiolo, D. F., Sandhu, R., Gavrila, S., Kuhn, D. R., & Chandramouli, R. (2001). Proposed NIST standard for role-based access control. *ACM Transactions on Information and System Security*, *4*(3), 224–274. doi:10.1145/501978.501980

Ferrari, E., & Thuraisingham, B. (2000). Secure Database Systems. In Piattini, M., & Díaz, O. (Eds.), *Advanced Databases: Technology Design*. London: Artech House.

Fink, S., Yahav, E., Dor, N., Ramalingam, G., & Geay, E. (2006). Effective typestate verification in the presence of aliasing. *Proc. of the Int. Symp. on Software Testing and Analysis (ISSTA)* (pp. 133-144), New York: ACM Press.

Firesmith, D. G. (2003). Engineering Security Requirements. *Journal of Object Technology*, *2*, 53–68.

Fischer-Hubner, S. (2001). *IT-security and privacy-Design and use of privacy enhancing security mechanisms*. 5th International Conference on Applications of Natural Language to Information Systems, Versailles, France, Lecture Notes in Computer Science 1958, pp: 35-106 June 2000.

Flechais, I., Mascolo, C., & Sasse, M. A. (2007). Integrating security and usability into the requirements and design process. *International Journal of Electronic Security and Digital Forensics*, *1*(1), 12–26. doi:10.1504/IJESDF.2007.013589

Flowerday, S., & von Solms, R. (2006). Trust: An Element of Information Security. In Fischer-Hubner, S., Rannenberg, K., Yngstrom, L., & Lindskog, S. (Eds.), *IFIP Int. Federation for Information Processing, Security and Privacy in Dynamic Environments*. Boston: Springer.

Foster, J. S., Fähndrich, M., & Aiken, A. (1999). A theory of type qualifiers, *Proc. of the ACM SIGPLAN Conference on Programming language design and implementation (PLDI)* (pp. 192-203), New York: ACM Press.

France, R. B., Kim, D.-K., Ghosh, S., & Song, E. (2004). A UML-Based Pattern Specification Technique. *IEEE Transactions on Software Engineering*, *3*(30), 193–206. doi:10.1109/TSE.2004.1271174

France, R. B., Ray, I., Georg, G., & Ghosh, S. (2004). (2004-1). Aspect-Oriented Approach to Design Modeling. *IEE Proceedings. Software, 4*(151), 173–185. doi:10.1049/ip-sen:20040920

Fukuyama, F. (1996). *Trust: The Social Virtues and the Creation of Prosperity*. Touchstone Books.

Furnell, S. (2007). Making security usable: Are things improving? *Computers & Security, 26*, 434–443. doi:10.1016/j.cose.2007.06.003

Gamma, E., Helm, R., Jonson, R., & Vlissides, J. (1996). *Design Patterns: Elements of Reusable Object Oriented Software*. Buam, Holland: Addison Wesley.

Garlan, J., & Anthony, R. (2002). *Large-Scale Software Architecture*. John Wiley & Sons.

Georg, G., Ray, I., Anastasakis, K., Bordbar, B., Toahchoodee, M. & Houmb, S.H. (2008). An Aspect-Oriented Methodology for Designing Secure Applications, *Information and Software Technology*, Special Issue on Model Based Development for Secure Information Systems, doi:10.1016/j.infsof.2008.05.004.

Ghosh, A., Howell, C., & Whittaker, J. (2002). Building Software Securely from the Ground Up. *IEEE Software, 19*, 14–16. doi:10.1109/MS.2002.976936

Gibson, J. J. (1986). *The Ecological Approach to Visual Perception*. Houghton Mifflin Company USA.

Gilbert, J. (1995). *The role of models and modelling in some narrative science learning.* Paper presented at the Annual meeting of the American Educational Research Association, San Francisco, CA.

Giorgini, P., Mouratidis, H., & Zannone, N. (2007). Modelling Security and Trust with Secure Tropos. In Mouratidis, H., & Giorgini, P. (Eds.), *Integrating Security and Software Engineering: Advances and Future Visions*. Idea Group Publishing.

Giorgini, P., Mylopoulos, J., Nicchiarelli, E., & Sebastiani, R. (2002). Reasoning with Goal Models. *Proceedings of the 21st International Conference on Conceptual Modeling*, Springer-Verlag: 167-181.

Giunchiglia, F., Mylopoulos, J., & Perini, A. (2001) *The Tropos Software Development Methodology: Processes, Models and Diagrams*. Technical Report DIT-02-008, Informatica e Telecomunicazioni, University of Trento

Global Watch Mission Report, D. T. I. (2006). *Changing nature of information security: A UK perspective on US experiences*. Anon.

Golbeck, J. (2008). *Computing with Social Trust*. New York: Springer.

Graham, D. (2006). *Introduction to the CLASP Process* [Online]. OWASP CLASP Project http://www.owasp.org/index.php/Category:OWASP_CLASP_Project. Available: https://buildsecurityin.us-cert.gov/daisy/bsi/articles/best-practices/requirements/548.html [Accessed].

Gürses, S., Jahnke, J. H., Obry, C., Onabajo, A., Santen, T., & Price, M. (2005). Eliciting confidentiality requirements in practice. *In Proceedings of the Conference of the Centre for Advanced Studies on Collaborative Research (CASCON)*, (pp. 101-116). New York: IBM Press.

Gutiérrez, C., Fernández-Medina, E., & Piattini, M. (2006). Towards a Process for Web Services Security. *Journal of Research and Practice in Information Technology, 38*, 57–67.

Gutiérrez, C., Fernández-Medina, E., & Piattini, M. (2007). Web Services-based Security Requirement Elicitation. *IEICE Transaction on Information and Systems. E (Norwalk, Conn.), 90-D*, 1374–1387.

Gutiérrez, C., Rosado, D., & Fernández-Medina, E. (2009). The Practical Application of a Process for Eliciting and Designing Security in Web Service Systems. *Information and Software Technology, 51*, 1712–1738. doi:10.1016/j.infsof.2009.05.004

Gutiérrez, C., Fernández-Medina, E., & Piattini, M. (2004). A Survey of Web Services Security. *In:* AL., L. E., ed. Workshop on Internet Communications Security 2004 (WICS 2004), in conjunction with the 2004 International Conference on Computational Science and Its Applications (ICCSA 2004), 2004 Assisi (PG), Italy. Springer-Verlag, 969-977.

Hafiz, M., Adamczyk, P., & Johnson, R. E. (2007). Organizing security patterns. *IEEE Software*, *24*(4), 52–60. doi:10.1109/MS.2007.114

Hafiz, M. (2006). A collection of privacy design patterns. *Int. Conf. on Pattern Languages of Programs Conference (PLOP)*. New York, NY, USA.

Hafner, M., Breu, R., Agreiter, B., & Nowak, A. (2006). SECTET: An Extensible Framework for the realization of Secure inter-organizational Workflows. *Internet Research*, *16*, 491–506. doi:10.1108/10662240610710978

Hafner, M., & Breu, R. (2009). Security Engineering for Service-Oriented Architectures. *Springer*, 248.

Haldar, V., Chandra, D., & Franz, M. (2005). Dynamic taint propagation for Java. In D. Thomsen (Ed.), *Proc. of the 21ˢᵗ Annual Computer Security Applications Conference (ACSAC)* (pp. 303-311), Washington, DC: IEEE Computer Society.

Haley, C. B., Moffet, J. D., Laney, R., & Nuseibeh, B. (2006). *A Framework for Security Requirements Engineering*. Software Engineering for Secure Systems Workshop, 2006 Shanghai. *China*, 35–42.

Haley, C. B. & Laney, R. & Moffett, J. & Nuseibeh, B. (2008). Security requirements engineering: A framework for representation and analysis, (pp. 133-153). *IEEE Transactions on Software Engineering, 34*(1). Washington, DC: IEEE Computer Society.

Haley, C. B., Laney, R., Moffett, J., & Nuseibeh, B. (2004). Picking battles: The impact of trust assumptions on the elaboration of security requirements. In C. D. Jensen & S. Poslad & T. Dimitrakos (Ed.), Proceedings of the International Conference on Trust Management (iTrust), (pp. 347-354). LNCS 2995. Springer Berlin / Heidelberg / New York.

Haley, C. B., Laney, R., Moffett, J., & Nuseibeh, B. (2005). Arguing security: Validating security requirements using structured argumentation. *In Proceedings of the Symposium on Requirements Engineering for Information Security (SREIS)*.

Haley, C. B., Laney, R. C., & Nuseibeh, B. (2004). Deriving security requirements from crosscutting threat descriptions. *In:* 3rd International Conference on Aspect-Oriented Software Development (AOSD), March 22-24, 2004 2004 Lancaster, UK. 112-121.

Halkidis, S. T. & Tsantalis, N. & Chatzigeorgiou, A. & Stephanides, G. (2008). Architectural risk analysis of software systems based on security patterns, (pp. 129 - 142). IEEE Transactions on Dependable and Secure Computing, 5(3). IEEE Computer Society.

Hall, J. G., Rapanotti, L., & Jackson, M. A. (2008). Problem Oriented Software Engineering: Solving the Package Router Control Problem. *IEEE Transactions on Software Engineering, 34*(2), 226–241. doi:10.1109/TSE.2007.70769

Hall, J. G., Jackson, M., Laney, R. C., Nuseibeh, B., & Rapanotti, L. (2002). Relating Software Requirements and Architectures using Problem Frames. *In Proceedings of IEEE International Requirements Engineering Conference (RE),* (pp. 137-144). IEEE Computer Society.

Hall, J. G., Rapanotti, L., & Jackson, M. (2007). *Problem Oriented Software Engineering: A design-theoretic framework for software engineering*. 5th IEEE International Conference on Software Engineering and Formal Methods.

Hansen, M. T. (2009). When Internal Collaboration is Bad for Your Company. *Harvard Business Review*, (April): 83–88.

Hansen, T. J., & Wahlgreen, B. (2007). *Static analysis of concurrent Java programs* (Tech. Rep. IMM-B.Sc-2007-11). Technical University of Denmark, Denmark.

Hardin, R. (Ed.). (2002). *Trust and trustworthiness*. Russel Sage Foundation.

Hardin, R. (Ed.). (2004). *Distrust*. Russell Sage Foundation.

Harmon, P. (2004). *The OMG's Model Driven Architecture and BPM*. Newsletter of Business Process Trends.

Harold, E. R. (2008, September). *The Open Road: javax. annotation.* java.net: The Source for Java Technology Collaboration, online: http://today.java.net/ pub/a/today/2008/09/11/jsr-305-annotations.html

Hatebur, D., & Heisel, M. (2005). Problem frames and architectures for security problems. In B. A. Gran & R. Winter & G. Dahll (Ed.), *Proceedings of the International Conference on Computer Safety, Reliability and Security (SAFECOMP)* (pp. 390-404). LNCS 3688. Springer Berlin / Heidelberg / New York.

Hatebur, D., Heisel, M., & Schmidt, H. (2006). Security engineering using problem frames. In G. Müller (Ed.), *Proceedings of the International Conference on Emerging Trends in Information and Communication Security (ETRICS)* (pp. 238-253). LNCS 3995. Springer Berlin / Heidelberg / New York.

Hatebur, D., Heisel, M., & Schmidt, H. (2007). A pattern system for security requirements engineering. *In Proceedings of the International Conference on Availability, Reliability and Security (AReS)* (pp. 356-365). IEEE Computer Society.

Hatebur, D., Heisel, M., & Schmidt, H. (2008). A formal metamodel for problem frames. *In Proceedings of the International Conference on Model Driven Engineering Languages and Systems (MODELS)* (pp. 68–82). LNCS 5301. Springer Berlin / Heidelberg / New York.

Hatebur, D., Heisel, M., & Schmidt, H. (2007). *A Security Engineering Process based on Patterns.* 18th International Conference on Database and Expert Systems Applications (DEXA), Regensburg, Germany.

He, Q. & Antón, A., (2003). *A framework for modeling privacy requirements in role engineering.* International workshop on requirements engineering for software quality (REFSQ). Klagenfurt/Verden, Austria.

Heiner, M., & Menzel, T. (1998). A petri net semantics for the PLC language instruction list. *IEEE Workshop on Discrete Event Systems* (pp. 161–165). Cagliari, Italy.

Heisel, M. (1998). Agendas - a concept to guide software development activities. In Proceedings of the IFIP TC2 WG2.4 working Conference on Systems Implementation: Languages, Methods and Tools (pp. 19-32). Chapman & Hall London.

Hoare, C. A. R. (1983). Communicating sequential processes. *Communications of the ACM, 26*(1), 100–106. doi:10.1145/357980.358021

Hoare, C. A. R. (1986). Communicating Sequential Processes. Prentice Hall. Retrieved June 24, 2009, from http://www.usingcsp.com.

Hodgson, P., & Cofta, P. (2008) Society as an information network. *International journal of technology, knowledge and society,* Boston.

Hodgson, P., & Cofta, P. (2009) *Towards a methodology for research on trust.* In: Proceedings of the WebSci'09: Society On-Line, 18-20 March 2009, Athens, Greece. (In Press)

Holvast, J. (1993). *Vulnerability and Privacy: Are We on the Way to a Risk-Free Society?* Elsevier Science Publishers B.V. (North-Holland) IFIP-WG9.2 340 References Conference.

Hong, J., Ng, J., Lederer, S., & Landey, J. (2004). *Privacy risk models for designing privacy-sensitive ubiquitous computing systems. Symposium on Designing Interactive Systems archive.* Proceedings of the 2004 conference on Designing interactive systems: processes, practices, methods, and techniques. Acm-Press. Cambridge, MA, USA 91-100.

Houmb, S. H., Georg, G., Jürjens, J., & France, R. B. (2007). An Integrated Security Verification and Security Solution Trade-Off Analysis. In Mouratidis, H., & Giorgini, P. (Eds.), *Integrating Security and Software Engineering: Advances and Future Vision.* (pp. 190–219). Hershey, PA: Idea Group.

Houmb, S. H. (2007). *Decision Support for Choice of Security Solution: The Aspect-Oriented Risk Driven Development (AORDD) Framework*. PhD thesis, Norwegian University of Science and Technology (NTNU), NTNU-Trykk, Trondheim, Norway, November 2007. ISBN 978-82-471-4588-3.

Houmb, S. H., & Franquira, V. N. L. (2009). *Estimating ToE Risk Level using CVSS. To be published in the Proceeding of the Forth International Conference on Availability, Reliability and Security (ARES 2009)*, IEEE Computer Society, Fukuoka, Japan, March 16-19, 8 pages.

Houmb, S. H., Franqueira, V. N. L., & Engum, E. A. (2008). *Estimating Impact and Frequency of Risks to Safety and Mission Critical Systems Using CVSS*. In ISSRE 2008 Supplemental Proceedings: 1st Workshop on Dependable Software Engineering, 11 November 2008, Seattle, US. IEEE CS Conference Proceedings. IEEE Computer Society Press.

Houmb, S. H., Georg, G., France, R., Bieman, J. M. & Jürjens (2005). *Cost-Benefit Trade-Off Analysis Using BBN for Aspect-Oriented Risk-Driven Development*. Proceedings of the Tenth IEEE International Conference on Engineering of Complex Computer Systems (ICECCS 2005), pp. 195-204.

Hovemeyer, D., & Pugh, W. (2004). Finding bugs is easy. *SIGPLAN Notices, 39*(12), 92–106. doi:10.1145/1052883.1052895

Hovemeyer, D., & Pugh, W. (2007). *Status report on JSR-305: Annotations for software defect detection. Proc. of Object Oriented Programming Systems Languages and Applications (OOPSLA)* (pp. 799–800). ACM Press.

Howard M. & Lipner S.(2006). *The Security Development Lifecycle*. Microsoft Publications Jun 28, 2006

Hu, J. H. Dirk C., Christoph M.(2004). A Virtual Laboratory for IT Security Education. In *Proceedings of the Conference on Information Systems in E-Business and EGovernment* (EMISA), Luxembourg, pp. 60-71

IEEE. (1990). *IEEE Standard 610.12–1990 IEEE Standard Glossary of Software Engineering Terminology*. New York, NY, USA: Institute of Electrical and Electronics Engineers.

Inmon, H. (2002). *Building the Data Warehouse*. New York: John Wiley & Sons.

International Organization for Standardization (ISO) and International Electrotechnical Commission. *(IEC)* (2006). Common evaluation methodology 3.1, ISO/IEC 18405. Retrieved June 24, 2009, from http://www.commoncriteriaportal.org.

Internet Security Association and Key Management Protocol (ISAKMP), ROC 2408 C.F.R. (1998).

Irvine, C. E. (1999) Amplifying Security Education in the Laboratory. In *Proceedings of the 1st World Conference on Information Security Education* (IFIP TCII WC 11.8), pp. 139-146.

ISA. (1992). *Binary Logic Diagrams for Process Operations. ISA 5.2-1976 (R1992)*. ISA - The Instrumentation, Systems, and Automation Society.

Isham, J. (2000). *The Effect of Social Capital on Technology Adoption: Evidence from Rural Tanzania*. Opportunities in Africa: Micro-evidence on Firms and Households. Retrieved 18 October, 2007, from http://www.csae.ox.ac.uk/conferences/2000-OiA/pdfpapers/isham.PDF

ISO 15408 (2007) *Common Criteria for Information Technology Security Evaluation*, Version 3.1, Revision 2, CCMB-2007-09-001, CCMB-2007-09-002 and CCMB-2007-09-003.

ISO/IEC (2004). ISO/IEC 13335 Information technology - Security techniques - Management of information and communications technology security.

ISO/IEC 27002: (2005). Information technology - Security techniques - Code of Practice for Information Security Management.

ISO/IEC. (1997). Information technology – Vocabulary – Part 14: Reliability, maintainability and availability. *ISO Standards*. Retrieved January 30, 2009, from: http://www.iso.org/

Jackson, M. (2001). *Problem Frames. Analyzing and structuring software development problems.* Reading, MA: Addison-Wesley.

Jackson, M. (1995). *Software Requirements and Specifications: A Lexicon of Practice, Principles and Prejudices.* London, United Kingdom: Addison-Wesley.

Jackson, D. (2006). *Software Abstractions: Logic, Lanaguage, and Analysis.* London, England: MIT Press.

Jackson, M., & Zave, P. (1995). Deriving Specifications from Requirements: an Example. In Proceedings of the Internation Conference on Software Engineering (SE) (pp. 15-24). New York: ACM Press.

Jacobs, B., Marche, C., & Rauch, N. (2004). Formal verification of a commercial smart card applet with multiple tools. *Proc. 10th Int. Conference on Algebraic Methodology and Software Technology (AMAST 2004)* (pp. 241-257), Springer LNCS 3116.

Jacobson, I. (1992). *Object-Oriented Software Engineering: A Use Case Driven Approach.* London, England: Addison-Wesley Professional.

Java Standard Edition, S. U. N. *6 API.*(n.d.). Retrieved June 24, 2009, from http://java.sun.com/javase/6/docs/api/overview-summary.html.

Jensen, F. V. (2001). *Bayesian Networks and Decision Graphs.* New York: Springer-Verlag.

Jensen, C., Tullio, J., Potts, C., & Mynatt, E., (2005). *STRAP: A Structured Analysis Framework for Privacy.* GVU Technical Report, Georgia Institute of Technology, GIT-GVU-05-02.

Jensen, F. (1996). *An introduction to Bayesian Network.* University College London: UCL Press.

John, K.-H., & Tiegelkamp, M. (2001). *IEC 61131-3: Programming Industrial Automation Systems.* Berlin, Germany: Springer.

Johnston, J., Eloff, J. H. P., & Labuschagne, L. (2003). Security and human computer interfaces. *Computers & Security*, 22(8), 675–684. doi:10.1016/S0167-4048(03)00006-3

Jurjens, J. (2004). *Secure Systems Development with UML.* Heidelberg: German, Springer-Verlag.

Jürjens, J. & Shabalin, P.(2007). Tools for Secure Systems Development with UML. *Invited submission to the FASE 2004/05 special issue of the International Journal on Software Tools for Technology Transfer,* 9, 527-544.

Jürjens, J. (2002). UMLsec: Extending UML for secure systems development. In: JÉZÉQUEL, J., HUSSMANN, H. & COOK, S. (eds.) *UML 2002 - The Unified Modeling Language, Model engineering, concepts and tools.* Dresden, Germany: Springer. LNCS 2460.

Jürjens, J. (2008). A Domain-specific Language for Cryptographic Protocols based on Streams. *Journal of Logic and Algebraic Programming, Special issue on Streams and Algebra.*

Jürjens, J., & Houmb, S. H. (2004). Risk-Driven Development Of Security-Critical Systems Using UMLsec. In: Boston, S., ed. IFIP International Federation for Information Processing, 21-53.

Kalloniatis, C., Kavakli, E., & Gritzalis, S. (2008). Addressing privacy requirements in system design: The PriS method. [New York: Springer.]. *Requirements Engineering*, 13(3), 241–255. doi:10.1007/s00766-008-0067-3

Kalloniatis, C., Kavakli, E., & Kontellis, E. (2009) *PriS Tool: A Case Tool for Privacy-Oriented RE.* Proceedings of the MCIS 2009 4th Mediterranean Conference on Information Systems (MCIS 2009)", 27 September 2009, Athens, Greece

Kam, S. H. (2005). Integrating the Common Criteria Into the Software Engineering Lifecycle. *IDEAS, 05*, 267–273.

Kang, K., Cohen, S., Hess, J. A., Novak, W. E., & Peterson, S. A. (1990). *Feature-Oriented Domain Analysis (FODA) Feasibility Study.* Software Engineering Institute, Carnegie-Mellon University.

Kavakli, E., Gritzalis, S., & Kalloniatis, C. (2007). Protecting Privacy in System Design: The Electronic Voting Case. *Transforming Government: People. Process and Policy*, 1(4), 307–332.

Kavakli, E., Kalloniatis, C., Loucopoulos, P., & Gritzalis, S. (2008). Addressing Privacy Requirements in System Design: the PriS Method. [New York: Springer]. *Journal Requirements Engineering, 13*(3), 241–255. doi:10.1007/s00766-008-0067-3

Kearney, P. (2009) *Preliminary specification and design of graphical workbench*. Deliverable M3.2.1 EU MASTER project.

Keser, C. (2003). Experimental games for the design of reputation management systems. *IBM Systems Journal, 42*(3). doi:10.1147/sj.423.0498

Kienzle, D. M. & Elder, M. C. (2005). *Final Technical Report: Security Patterns for web Application Development.*

Kim, J., Kim, M. & Park, S. (2005). Goal and scenario bases domain requirements analysis environment. *The Journal of Systems and Software.*

Kocher, P., & Joshua Ja, E. Benjamin Jun. (1999). *Differential Power Analysis*. Retrieved January 2009 from http://www.cryptography.com//./dpa/.pdf

Koorn, R., van Gils, H., Hart, J., Overbeek, P., & Tellegen, R. (2004). *Privacy Enhancing Technologies-White paper for decision makers*. the Netherlands: Ministry of the Interior and Kingdom Relations.

Kotonya, G., & Sommerville, I. (2000). *Requirements Engineering Process and Techniques*. John Willey & Sons.

Kruchten, P. (2000). *The Rational Unified Process: An Introduction*. Reading, MA: Addison-Wesley Pub Co.

Laboratories, R. S. A. (1999). *Password-Based Cryptography Standard PKCS #5 v2.0*. Retrieved June 24, 2009, from ftp://ftp.rsasecurity.com/pub/pkcs/pkcs-5v2/pkcs5v2-0.pdf

Lacohée, H., Cofta, P., Phippen, A., & Furnell, S. (2008). *Understanding Public Perceptions: Trust and Engagement in ICT Mediated Services*. International Engineering Consortium.

Lai, L., Lai, L., & Sanders, J. W. (1997). A refinement calculus for communicating processes with state. *In Proceedings of the Irish Workshop on Formal Methods: Electronic Workshops in Computing*. Berlin / Heidelberg / New York:Springer

Lampson, B. W. (2004). Computer Security in the Real World. *IEEE Computer, 37*(6), 37–46.

Lamsweerde, A. V., & Letier, Handling, E. (2000). Obstacles in Goal-Oriented Requirement Engineering. *IEEE Transactions on Software Engineering, 26*, 978–1005. doi:10.1109/32.879820

Larsen, K. G., Mikucionis, M., Nielsen, B., & Skou, A. (2005). Testing real-time embedded software using uppaal-tron: an industrial case study. *In EMSOFT '05: Proceedings of the 5th ACM international conference on Embedded software*, (pp. 299–306), New York: ACM Press.

Lassar, W., Mittal, B., & Sharma, A. (1995). Measuring customer-based brand equity. *Journal of Consumer Marketing, 12*(4), 11–19. doi:10.1108/07363769510095270

Lee, J., Lee, J., Lee, S., & Choi, B. (2003). A CC-based Security Engineering Process Evaluation Model. *27th Annual International Computer Software and Applications Conference (COMPSAC '03)*, 130-.

Letier, E., & van Lamsweerde, A. (2002a). Agent-based tactics for goal-oriented requirements elaboration. *24th International Conference on Software Engineering (ICSE '02)* pp: 83-93.

Letier, E., & van Lamsweerde, A. (2002b). *Deriving operational software specifications from system goals*. 10th ACM SIGSOFT International Symposium on the Foundations of Software Engineering pp: 119-128.

Lewicki, R. J., Bunker, B, B. (1996) Developing and maintaining trust in work relationships. In Trust in Organisations: Frontiers of theory and Research

Li, Z., Hall, J. G., & Rapanotti, L. (2008). From requirements to specifications: a formal approach. *In Proceedings of the International Workshop on Advances and Applications of Problem Frames (IWAAPF)* (pp. 65-70). New York: ACM Press.

Lin, L., Nuseibeh, B., Ince, D., & Jackson, M. (2004). Using abuse frames to bound the scope of security problems. *In Proceedings of IEEE International Requirements Engineering Conference (RE)* (pp. 354-355). Washington, DC: IEEE Computer Society.

Lin, L., Nuseibeh, B., Ince, D., Jackson, M., & Moffett, J. (2003). *Introducing abuse frames for analysing security requirements*. Proceedings of 11th IEEE International Requirements Engineering Conference.

Lippert, S, K., Davis, M. (2006). A conceptual model integrating trust into planned change activities to enhance technology adoption. *Journal of Information Science*, 32.

Lite Version, H. U. G. I. N. 6.8 (2007). Hugin Expert A/S, Alborg, Denmark. http://www.hugin.com. Downloaded April 19 2007.

Liu, L., Yu, E., & Mylopoulos, J. (2003). *Security and privacy requirements analysis within a social setting. IEEE, 11th international requirements engineering conference (RE'03)*. California, USA: Monterey Bay.

Liu, L., Yu, E., & Mylopoulos, J. (2003). *Security and privacy requirements analysis within a social setting*. 11th IEEE International Requirements Engineering Conference.

Liu, L., Yu, E., & Mylopoulos, J. (2002) Analyzing Security Requirements as Relationships among Strategic Actors. *Symposium on Requirements Engineering for Information Security (SREIS '02)*. Raleigh, North Carolina, USA.

Livshits, V. B., & Lam, M. S. (2005). Finding security vulnerabilities in Java applications with static analysis. *Proc. of the 14th Conference on USENIX Security Symposium* (pp. 271-286).

Lodderstedt, T., Basin, D., & Doser, J. (2002). SecureUML: A UML-based modeling language for model-driven security. *In:* UML 2002. The Unified Modeling Language. Model Engineering, Languages Concepts, and Tools. 5th International Conference, 2002 Dresden, Germany. Springer, 426-441.

Logan, P. Y. (1997). Crafting an Undergraduate Information Security Emphasis Within Information Technology. *Journal of Information Systems Education, 13*(3).

Lonjon, A. (2004). Business Process Modeling and Standardization. *BP Trends,* http://www.bptrends.com/.

López, F., Amutio, M. A., Candau, J., & Mañas, J. A. (2005). *Methodology for Information Systems Risk Analysis and Management*. Ministry of Public Administration.

Luhmann, N. (1979). *Trust and Power*. New York: John Wiley & Sons.

Luján-Mora, S., Trujillo, J., & Song, I.-Y. (2006). A UML profile for multidimensional modeling in data warehouses. *Data & Knowledge Engineering, 59*, 725–769. doi:10.1016/j.datak.2005.11.004

Mader, A., & Wupper, H. (1999). Timed automata models for simple programmable logic controllers. *Euromicro Conference on Real-Time Syste*ms, York, UK.

Maj, S. P., & Kohli, G. (2004). A New State Models for Internetworks Technology. *Journal of Issues in Informing Science and Information Technology, 1*, 385–392.

Maj, S. P., & Veal, D. (2007). State Model Diagrams as a Pedagogical Tool - An International Evaluation. *IEEE Transactions on Education, 50*(3), 204–207. doi:10.1109/TE.2007.900028

Maj, S. P., & Tran, B. (2006, 2007). *State Model Diagrams - a Systems Tool for Teaching Network Technologies and Network Management*. Paper presented at the International Joint Conferences on Computer, Information and Systems Sciences, and Engineering, University of Bridgeport.

Maj, S. P., Cooper, J. R., Carter, J. (2009). State Model Diagrams – A Universal Runtime Network Management Method. *Manuscript submitted for publication*.

Maj, S. P., Kohli, G., & Fetherston, T. (2005). *A Pedagogical Evaluation of New State Model Diagrams for Teaching Internetwork Technologies*. Paper presented at the 28th Australasian Computer Science Conference (ACSC2005), Newcastle, Australia.

Maj, S. P., Kohli, G., & Murphy, G. (2004). *State Models for Internetworking Technologies.* Paper presented at the IEEE, Frontiers in Education, 34th Annual Conference, Savannah, Georgia, USA.

Manna, Z., & Pnueli, A. (1992). *The Temporal Logic of Reactive and Concurrent Systems.* Springer Verlag.

Mantel, H. (2003). *A Uniform Framework for the Formal Specification and Verification of Information Flow Security.* Unpublished doctoral dissertation, Universität des Saarlandes, Saarbrücken, Germany.

Marché, C., Paulin-Mohring, C., & Urbain, X. (2004). The KRAKATOA tool for certification of JAVA/JAVA-CARD programs annotated in JML. *Journal of Logic and Algebraic Programming, 58*(1-2), 89–106. doi:10.1016/j.jlap.2003.07.006

Marsh, S., & Briggs, P. (2008). Examining Trust, Forgiveness and Regret as Computational Concepts. In Golbeck, J. (Ed.), *Computing with Social Trust.* New York: Springer.

Marsh, S. P. (1994) *Formalising Trust as a Computational Concept.* University of Stirling PhD thesis.

Martin, M. (1991). *"Hello, Central?" Gender, technology and Culture in the Formation of Telephone Systems.* Montreal: McGill-Queen's University Press.

Matulevicius, R., Mayer, N., Mouratidis, H., Dubois, E., Heymans, P., & Genon, N. (2008). Adapting Secure Tropos for Security Risk Management in the Early Phases of Information Systems Development. *Proceedings of the 20th international conference on Advanced Information Systems Engineering.* Montpellier, France, Springer-Verlag: 541-555.

Mauw, S., & Oostdijk, M. (2005). Foundations of Attack Trees. Information Security and Cryptology - ICISC 2005. *Springer Lecture Notes in Computer Science, 3935,* 186–198. doi:10.1007/11734727_17

Mayer, N., Heymans, P., & Matulevicius, R. (2007). *Design of a Modelling Language for Information System Security Risk Management.* 1st International Conference on Research Challenges in Information Science (RCIS), Ouarzazate, Morocco.

McAllister, D. J., Lewicki, R. J., & Chaturvedi, S. (2006). Trust in developing relationships: From theory to measurement. In Weaver, K. M. (Ed.), *Academy of Management Best Papers Proceedings.*

McDermott, J., & Fox, C. (1999) *Using Abuse Case Models for Security Requirements Analysis.* In: 15th Annual Computer Security Applications Conference, Phoenix, Arizona. IEEE Computer Society, 55-66.

McKnight, D. H., & Chervany, N. L. (1996) *The Meanings of Trust.* In University of Minnesota, http://www.misrc.umn.edu/ wpaper/ wp96-04.htm.

MDA. (2003). *O. M. G.* Model Driven Architecture Guide.

Mead, N. R., & Hough, E. D. (2006). *Security Requirements Engineering for Software Systems: Case Studies in Support of Software Engineering Education.* CSEE&T.

Mead, N. R., & Stehney, T. (2005). *Security Quality Requirements Engineering (SQUARE) Methodology.* In: Software Engineering for Secure Systems (SESS05), ICSE 2005 International Workshop on Requirements for High Assurance Systems, May 15-16, 2005 2005 St. Louis.

Meijer, H., & Poll, E. (2001). Towards a full formal specification of the JavaCard API. In G. Goos, J. Hartmanis & J. van Leeuwen (Ed.), *Proc. of the Int. Conf. on Research in Smart Cards: Smart Card Programming and Security (E-smart)* (pp. 165-178), Springer LNCS 2140.

Mellado, D., Fernández-Medina, E., & Piattini, M. (2007). A Common Criteria Based Security Requirements Engineering Process for the Development of Secure Information Systems. *Computer Standards & Interfaces, 29,* 244–253. doi:10.1016/j.csi.2006.04.002

Mellado, D., Rodríguez, J., Fernández-Medina, E., & Piattini, M. (2009). Automated Support for Security Requirements Engineering in Software Product Line Domain Engineering. *The Fourth International Conference on Availability, Reliability and Security (ARES 2009),* accepted.

Menascé, D. (2003). Security Performance. *IEEE Internet Computing, 7*(3), 84–87. doi:10.1109/MIC.2003.1200305

Meyer, J., & Poetzsch-Heffter, A. (2000). An architecture for interactive program provers. *Proc. of Tools and Algorithms for the Construction and Analysis of Systems (TACAS)* (pp. 63-77), Springer LNCS 1785.

Microsoft. (2009) *The Microsoft SDL Threat Modelling Tool.* Available: http://msdn.microsoft.com/en-us/security/dd206731.aspx

Mielikinen, T. (2004). Privacy Problems with Anonymized Transaction Databases. *Int. Conf. on Discovery Science (DS 2004)*, Vol 3245 of Lecture Notes in Computer Science 3245, Springer.

Moffett, D. & Nuseibeh, B., (2003). *A framework for security requirements engineering. Department of computer science,* University of York, YCS 368.

Mollering, G. (2005) The Trust/Control Duality: An Integrative Perspective on Positive Expectations of Others. In: *Int. Sociology, September 2005, Vol. 20*(3): 283–305. 2005.

Moon, I. (1994). Modeling programmable logic controllers for logic verification. *IEEE Control Systems Magazine, 14*(2), 53–59. doi:10.1109/37.272781

Moriconi, M., Qian, X., Riemenschneider, R. A., & Gong, L. (1997). Secure software architectures. *In Proceedings of the IEEE Symposium on Security and Privacy* (pp. 84 – 93). IEEE Computer Society.

Morriset, G. (2003). *Tutorial on language-based security,* given at the 2003 ACM PLDI San Diego. Retreived January 2009 from http://www.cs.cornell.edu/////pldi03.ppt#256,1,Tutorial on Language-Based Security

Morrison, P., & Fernandez, E. B. (2006). The credential pattern. In *Proceedings of the Conference on Pattern Languages of Programs.* Hillside Group. Retrieved November 25, 2009, from http://hillside.net/plop/2006/.

Mouratidis, H., & Giorgini, P. (2006). *Integrating Security and Software Engineering: Advances and Future Vision.* Hershey, PA: IGI Global.

Mouratidis, H., & Giorgini, P. (2007). Secure Tropos: A security-oriented extension of the Tropos methodology, (285-309). *International Journal of Software Engineering and Knowledge Engineering, 17*(2). doi:10.1142/S0218194007003240

Mouratidis, H., Weiss, M., & Giorgini, P. (2006). Modelling secure systems using an agent oriented approach and security patterns. [IJSEKE]. *International Journal of Software Engineering and Knowledge Engineering, 16*(3), 471–498. doi:10.1142/S0218194006002823

Mouratidis, H., Giorgini, P., & Manson, G. (2005). When security meets software engineering: a case of modelling secure information systems. *Information Systems, 30*(8), 609–629. doi:10.1016/j.is.2004.06.002

Mouratidis, H., & Giorgini, P. (2006). *Integrating Security and Software Engineering: Advances and Future Vision.* Hershey, PA: Idea Group Publishing.

Mouratidis, H. (2004). A Security Oriented Approach in the Development of Multiagent Systems: Applied to the Management of the Health and Social Care Needs of Older People In England (PhD Thesis), Department of Computer Science, University of Sheffield, Sheffield, UK.

Mouratidis, H., & Giorgini, P. (2004). Analysing security in information systems. Presented at the *Second International Workshop on Security in Information Systems*, Porto Portugal. Retrieved November 25, 2009, from http://www.dit.unitn.it/~pgiorgio/papers/ICEISWorkshop04.pdf

Mouratidis, H., Jürjens, J., & Fox, J. (2006). Towards a Comprehensive Framework for Secure Systems Development. In *LNCS 4001: Proceedings of the 18th Conference on Advanced Information Systems,* (pp. 48-62). Heidelberg, Germany: Springer.

Mylopolulos, J., Chung, L., & Nixon, B. (1992). Representing and Using non Functional Requirements: a Process Oriented Approach. *IEEE Transactions on Software Engineering, 18*, 483–497. doi:10.1109/32.142871

Nagaratnam, N., Nadalin, A., Hondo, M., McIntosh, M., & Austel, P. (2005). Business-driven application security: From modeling to managing secure applications. *IBM Systems Journal, 44*(4), 847–867. doi:10.1147/sj.444.0847

Narayanan, A., & Shmatikov, V. (2005). Obfuscated Databases and Group Privacy. *ACM Int. Conference on Computer and Communications Security (CCS '05)*, (pp. 102-111). New York, NY, USA. ACM Press.

Neves, C., Duarte, L., Viana, N., & Lucena, V. (2007, Novembro). *The ten biggest challenges of industrial automation: the perspectives for the future. (Os dez maiores desafios da automação industrial: as perspectivas para o futuro).* Paper presented at the II Congress of Research and Innovation of Network North Northeast of Technological Education, João Pessoa, Paraíba, Brazil.

Ni, Q., Trombetta, A., Bertino, E., & Lobo, J. (2007). Privacy-aware Role-Based Access Control. *ACM Symp. on Access Control Methods And Technologies (SACMAT '07).* Sophia Antipolis, France.

Nielsen, J. Ten Usability Heuritics. Retrieved December, 2008, from http://www.useit.com/papers/heuristic/heuristic_list.html

Nielsen, J., & Molich, R. (1990). *Heuristic evaluation of user interfaces.* Paper presented at the Human Factors in Computing Systems, Seattle, WA.

Nooteboom, B. (2002). *Trust: Forms, Foundations, Functions, Failures and Figures.* Edward Elgar.

Nooteboom, B. (2005) *Framing, attribution and scripts in the development of trust. In. Proc. of symposium on 'Risk, trust and civility',* Victoria College, University of Toronto, 6-8 May 2005.

Norman, D. A. (1988). *The Psychology of Everyday Things.* New York: Basic Books.

Nuangjamnong, C. (2009). *An Investigation into Network Management.* Perth: Edith Cowan University.

Nuangjamnong, C., Maj, S. P., & Veal, D. (2007). *Network Security Devices and Protocols Using State Model Diagrams.* Paper presented at the 5th Australian Information Security Management Edith Cowan University, Perth, Western Australia.

O'Hear, A. (1991). *An Introduction to the Philosophy of Science.* New York: Oxford University Press.

OASIS. (2009). Retrieved January 2009 from http://www.oasis-open.org//_home.php?wg_abbrev=emergency

OMG (Object Management Group). (2003). *Model Driven Architecture Guide Version 1.0.1* [Online]. Available: http://www.omg.org/mda/ [Accessed].

OMG (Object Management Group). (2005). MOF QVT final adopted specification.

OMG (Object Management Group). (2007). *Unified Modeling Language: Superstructure Version 2.1.1 (formal/2007-02-05)* [Online]. Available: http://www.omg.org/docs/formal/07-02-05.pdf [Accessed].

OMG MARTE. (2008). UML Profile for Modeling and Analysis of Real-Time Embedded systems (MARTE). *BETA Bulletin of Experimental Treatments for AIDS, 2,* http://www.omg.org/docs/ptc/08-06-08.pdf.

OMG SPT (2005) *UML Profile for Schedulability, Performance, and Time,* Version 1.1, OMG document formal/05-01-02.

Opdahl, A. L., & Sindre, G. (2008). (in press). Experimental comparison of attack trees and misuse cases for security threat identification. *[Corrected Proof.]. Information and Software Technology.*

OWASP. (n.d.). Retrieved January 2009 from http://www.owasp.org and threat modeling can be found at http://www.owasp.org/.php/Threat_Risk_Modeling#Alternative_Threat_Modeling_Systems

Paquet, R., Strovink, K. (1997). *The risks of network and systems management technology investments* Publication. Retrieved January, 2009.

Parr, E. A. (2003). *Programmable Controllers: An engineer's guide* (3rd ed.). London, England: Newnes.

Pearson, S. (2002). Trusted Computing Platforms: TCPA Technology. In *Context.* Upper Saddle River, NJ: Prentice-Hall.

Pelaez, J., Fernandez, E. B., & Larrondo-Petrie, M. M. (2009). Misuse patterns in VoIP. *Security and Communication Networks.* Wiley InterScience. Retrieved November 25, 2009 from http://www3.interscience.wiley.com/journal/122324463/abstract.

Peralta, K. P., & Alex, M. Orozco, Avelino F. Zorzo, Flavio M. Oliveira.(2008) Specifying Security Aspects in UML Models. In *Proceedings of the 2008 International Conference on Model Driven Engineering Languages and Systems.* Toulouse, France, September 28, 2008

Perini, P., Bresciani, P., Giorgini, P., Giunchiglia, F., & Mylopoulos, J. (2001). *Towards an agent-oriented approach to software engineering,* Modena-Italy.

Persse, J. R. (2001). *Implementing the Capability Maturity Model.* New York: Wiley.

Petland, S., & Heibeck, T. (2008, Fall). Understanding 'Honest Signals' in Business. *MIT Sloan Management Review.,* 50(1), 70–75.

Petriu, D. C., Shen, H., & Sabetta, A. (2007). Performance Analysis of Aspect-Oriented UML Models. *Software and Systems Modeling,* 6(4), 453–471. doi:10.1007/s10270-007-0053-0

Petriu, D. B., & Woodside, C. M. (2004). *A Metamodel for Generating Performance Models from UML Designs.* in Proc UML 2004, LNCS 3273, pp. 41-53, Springer.

Pfitzmann, A. (1990). *Diensteintegrierende, Kommunikationsmnetze mit teilnehmeruberprufbaren Datenschutz. Informatik-Fachberichte 234.* Berlin, Heidelberg, New York: Springer-Verlag.

Pfitzmann, A., & Hansen, M. (2007). *Anonymity, Unlinkability, Undetectability, Unobservability, Pseudonumity and Identity Management-A Consolidated Proposal for Terminology v. 029.* TU Dresden ULD Kiel, 31 July 2007, Dresden.

Pfitzmann, B., Waidner, M., & Pfitzmann, A. (1990). *Rechsicherheit trotz Anonymitat in offenen digitalen Systemen. Datenschutz und Datensicherheit (DuD), No 6 (Part 1)* pp. 243-253, No 7 (Part 2) pp. 305-315.

PLCopen for efficiency in automation (2004). IEC 61131-3: a standard programming resource. *Technical Committee 1 Standards.* Retrieved November 10, 2008, from: http://www.plcopen.org/pages/tc1_standards/downloads/

Pohl, K., Böckle, G., & Linden, F. V. D. (2005). *Software Product Line Engineering. Foundations, Principles and Techniques.* Berlin, Heidelberg: Springer.

Popp, G., Jürjens, J., Wimmel, G., & Breu, R. (2003). Security-Critical System Development with Extended Use Cases. 10th Asia-Pacific Software Engineering Conference.

Potter, N. N. (2002). *How Can I Be Trusted?: A Virtue Theory Of Trustworthiness.* Rowman & Littlefield Publishers.

Pourret, O., Naïm, P., & Marcot, B. (2008). *Bayesian Networks: A Practical Guide to Applications (Statistics in Practice).* John Wiley & Sons Ltd.

President's Information Technology Advisory Committee. (2007) *Cyber Security: A Crisis of Prioritization.*

PricewaterhouseCoopers. (2001). *Privacy: a weak link in the cyber-chain.* New York: E-Business Leadres Series, PricewaterhouseCoopers.

Priebe, T., & Pernul, G. (2001) A Pragmatic Approach to Conceptual Modeling of OLAP Security. *In:* 20th International Conference on Conceptual Modeling (ER 2001), Yokohama, Japan. Springer-Verlag.

Priebe, T., Fernandez, E. B., Mehlau, J. I., & Pernul, G. (2004). A pattern system for access control. In C. Farkas and P. Samarati (Eds.) *Research Directions in Data and Applications Security XVIII: Proceedings of the 18th. Annual IFIP WG 11.3 Working Conference on Data and Applications Security* (pp. 25-28). Amsterdam, Netherlands: Kluwer Academic Publishers.

Privacy International, Electronic Privacy Information Center (1999). *Privacy and Human Rights - An International Survey of Privacy Laws and Developments.*

Proceedings of. *14th International Symposium on Formal Methods. Hamilton, Canada,* (2006, August) LNCS. New York: Springer Berlin/Heidelberg

Proceedings of. *3rd ACM Workshop on Formal Methods in Security Engineering: From Specifications to Code.* (2005, November). Alexandria, VA, USA. Retrieved January 2009 from http://www.ti.informatik.uni-kiel.de/~kuesters//.html

Proceedings of. *6rd ACM Workshop on Formal Methods in Security Engineering.* (2008, October). Alexandria, VA, U.S.A. Retrieved January 2009 from http://www.cs.utexas.edu/~shmat//

Quality Assurance Agency. (n.d.). *Subject benchmark statements: Computing.* (undated) Retrieved January 2009 from http://www.qaa.ac.uk////.asp

Rajendra, G., & Madhura, H. *(n.d.). A New Approach to Application Security Testing Tool Design* Retrieved January 2009 from http://www.aztecsoft.com//_Whitepaper_Approach_to_Application_Security_Testing_Tool_Design.pdf

Ramachandran, J. (2002). *Designing Security Architecture Solutions.* John Wiley & Sons.

Rapanotti, L., Hall, J. G., Jackson, M., & Nuseibeh, B. (2004). Architecture Driven Problem Decomposition. *In Proceedings of IEEE International Requirements Engineering Conference (RE),* (73-82). Washington, DC: IEEE Computer Society.

Resnick, P. (2006, Jun). The value of reputation on eBay: a controlled experiment. *Experimental Economics, 9*(Issue 2), 79–101. Available at http://www.si.umich.edu/~presnick/papers/postcards/PostcardsFinalPrePub.pdf. doi:10.1007/s10683-006-4309-2

Rodriguez, A., Fernandez-Medina, E., & Piattini, M. (2007). An MDA Approach to Develop Secure Business Processes through a UML 2.0 Extension. *Computer Systems. Science and Engineering, 22,* 307–319.

Rodríguez, A., Fernández-Medina, E., & Piattini, M. (2007b). A BPMN Extension for the Modeling of Security Requirements in Business Processes. *IEICE Transactions on Information and Systems. E (Norwalk, Conn.), 90-D*(4), 745–752.

Rodríguez, A., Fernández-Medina, E., & Piattini, M. (2007) *Towards CIM to PIM transformation: from Secure Business Processes defined by BPMN to Use Cases.* 5th International Conference on Business Process Management (BPM), 24-28 September 2007 2007d Brisbane, Australia. 408-415.

Rodríguez, A., Fernández-Medina, E., & Piattini, M. (2007a) Analysis-Level Classes from Secure Business Processes through Models Transformations. In: 4th International Conference on Trust, Privacy and Security in Digital Business (TrustBus), September 3–7 Regensburg, Germany. 104-114.

Rodríguez, A., Fernández-Medina, E., & Piattini, M. (2007c). *M-BPSec: A Method for Security Requirement Elicitation from a UML 2.0 Business Process Specification.* 3rd International Workshop on Foundations and Practices of UML, 2007c Auckland, New Zealand. 106-115.

Romanosky, S., Acquisti, A., Hong, J., Cranor, L., & Friedman, B. (2006). *Privacy Patterns for Online Interactions.* Int. Conf. on Pattern Languages of Programs Conference (PLOP). New York, NY, USA.

Rosado, D. G., Gutierrez, C., Fernandez-Medina, E., & Piattini, M. (2006). Security patterns related to security requirements. In E. Fernandez-Medina and M. Inmaculada (Eds.) *Security in Informaiton Systems: Proceedings of the 4th International Workshop on Security in Information Systems.* Setúbal, Portugal: INSTICC Press.

Rosenberg, R. (1992). *The Social Impact of Computers.* New York: Academic Press.

Rossi, O., & Schnoebelen, Ph. (2000). Formal modeling of timed function blocks for the automatic verification of Ladder Diagram programs. Engell, S., Kowalewski, S., & Zaytoon, J., editors, *Proceedings of the 4th International Conference on Automation of Mixed Processes: Hybrid Dynamic Systems (ADPM 2000)* (pp. 177–182). Dortmund, Germany: Shaker Verlag.

Rubin, A. D., Geer, D., & Ranum, M. J. (1997). *Web Security Sourcebook.* John Wiley & Sons.

Sabelfeld, A., & Myers, A. C. (2003). Language-based information-flow security. *IEEE Journal on Selected Areas in Communications, 21*(1), 5–19. doi:10.1109/JSAC.2002.806121

Sachitano, A., & Chapman, R. O. & JR., J. A. H. (2004). Security in Software Architecture: A Case Study. *Workshop on Information Assurance.* United States Military Academy, West Point, NY: IEEE.

Salifu, M., Yu, Y., & Nuseibeh, B. (2007). *Specifying Monitoring and Switching Problems in Context.* Proceedings of the 15th IEEE International Conference in Requirements Engineering (RE '07), New Delhi, India.

Saltzer, J. H., & Schroeder, M. D. (1975). The protection of information in computer systems. *Proceedings of the IEEE, 63*(9), 1278-1308. Retrieved November 25, 2009 from http://web.mit.edu/Saltzer/www/publications/protection/index.html

Sandhu, R. S., Coyne, E. J., Feinstein, H. L., & Youman, C. E. (1996). Role-based access control models. *Computer, 29*(2), 38–47. doi:10.1109/2.485845

Santen, T. (2008). Preservation of probabilistic information flow under refinement, (pp. 213-249). *Information and Computation, 206*(2-4). doi:10.1016/j.ic.2007.07.008

Santen, T., Heisel, M., & Pfitzmann, A. (2002). Confidentiality-preserving refinement is compositional - sometimes. *In Proceedings of the European Symposium on Research in Computer Security (ESORICS),* (pp. 194-211). LNCS 2502. Springer Berlin / Heidelberg / New York.

Saunders, M. N. K., & Thornhill, A. (2003). Organisational justice, trust and the management of change: An exploration. *Personnel Review, 32*(3), 360–375. doi:10.1108/00483480310467660

Scandariato, R., Yskout, K., Heyman, T., & Joosen, W. (2008). *Architecting software with security patterns (Report No. CW515).* Katholieke Universiteit Leuven - Department of Computer Science.

Schluting, C. (2005). Chose the Right Network Management Tool. Retrieved January 2009, from http://www.enterprisenetworkingplanet.com/netos/article.php/3465921

Schmidt, H. (2009). Pattern-based confidentiality-preserving refinement. *In Engineering Secure Software and Systems - First International Symposium (ESSoS),* (pp. 43-59). LNCS 5429. Springer Berlin / Heidelberg / New York.

Schmidt, H., & Wentzlaff, I. (2006). Preserving software quality characteristics from requirements analysis to architectural design. *In Proceedings of the European Workshop on Software Architectures (EWSA),* (pp. 189-203). LNCS 4344/2006. Springer Berlin / Heidelberg / New York.

Schneier, B. (1999). *Attack trees.* Dr. Dobb's Journal. Retrieved June 24, 2009, from http://www.schneier.com/paper-attacktrees-ddj-ft.html.

Schumacher, M., Fernandez, E. B., Hybertson, D., Buschmann, F., & Sommerlad, P. (2006). *Security patterns: Integrating security and systems engineering.* Hoboken, NJ: John Wiley & Sons.

Schumacher, M. (2002). *Security Patterns AND Security Standards.* European Conf. on Pattern Languages of Programs (EuroPLoP), Kloster Irsee, Germany

Schummer, T. (2004). *The Public Privacy–Patterns for Filtering Personal Information in Collaborative Systems, (Tech. Rep).* Hagen, Germany: FernUnivesität in Hagen.

Sebastiani, R., P. Giorgini & J. Mylopoulos (2004). Simple and Minimum-Cost Satisfiability for Goal Models. *Advanced Information Systems Engineering*: 20-35.

Secure Systems Research Group. (2009). Florida Atlantic University. Retrieved November 25, 2009 from http://security.ceecs.fau.edu/

Seppanen, R., & Blomqvist, K. (2006) It is not all About Trust-The Role of Distrust in Inter-Organizational Relationships. In: *Network-Centric Collaboration and Supporting Frameworks, proc. of IFIP TC5 WG 5.5 Seventh IFIP Working Conference on Virtual Enterprises, 25'27 September 2006,* Helsinki, Finland. Springer Boston.

Shanahan, M. (1999). *The Event Calculus Explained. Artificial Intelligence Today: Recent Trends and Developments* (pp. 409–430). Berlin, Heidelberg: Springer.

Shaw, M., & Garlan, D. (1996). *Software Architecture - Perspectives on an Emerging Discipline*. Upper Saddle River, NJ: Prentice-Hall.

Shultz, E. (2005). The human factor in security. *Computers & Security*, *24*, 425–426. doi:10.1016/j.cose.2005.07.002

Silva, L. D., Barbosa, L. P. A., Gorgônio, K., Perkusich, A., & Lima, A. M. N. (2008). On the automatic generation of timed automata models from function block diagrams for safety instrumented systems. *IEEE International Conference on Industrial Electronics*, Orlando, Florida, USA.

Sindre, G., & Opdahl, A. L. (2005). Eliciting security requirements with misuse cases. *Requirements Engineering*, *10*(1), 34–44. doi:10.1007/s00766-004-0194-4

Smith, C. U., & Williams, L. G. (2002). *Performance Solutions*. Reading, MA: Addison-Wesley.

Sobel, A E Kelly & Clarkson, M R.(2002), Formal Methods Application: An Empirical Tale of Software Development. *IEEE Trans on Software Development, 28*(3).

Soler, E., Trujillo, J., Blanco, C., & Fernández-Medina, E. (2009). Designing Secure Data Warehouses by using MDA and QVT. *Journal of Universal Computer Science*, *15*, 1607–1641.

Soler, E., Trujillo, J., Fernández-Medina, E., & Piattini, M. (2008). Building a secure star schema in data warehouses by an extension of the relational package from CWM. *Computer Standards & Interfaces*, *30*, 341–350. doi:10.1016/j.csi.2008.03.002

Solms, B., & Marais, E. (2004). From secure wired networks to secure wireless networks - what are the extra risks? *Computers & Security*, *23*, 633–637. doi:10.1016/j.cose.2004.09.005

Spivey, M. (1992). *The Z Notation - A Reference Manual*. Upper Saddle River, NJ: Prentice Hall. Retrieved June 24, 2009, from http://spivey.oriel.ox.ac.uk/mike/zrm.

Steel, C., Nagappan, R., & Lai, R. (2005). *Core Security Patterns: Best Practices and Strategies for J2EE, Web Services, and Identity Management*. Prentice Hall.

Stølen, K., den Braber, F., Dimitrakos, T., Fredriksen, R., Gran, B., & Houmb, S. H. (2002). *Model-based Risk Assessment in a Component-Based Software Engineering Process: The CORAS Approach to Identify Security Risks*. Chapter in: *Business Component-Based Software Engineering* (pp. 189–207). Kluwer.

Straw, G., Georg, G., Song, E., Ghosh, S., France, R. B., & Bieman, J. M. (2004). *Model Composition Directives. Ed. A. Moreira and S. Mellor*. Proceedings of the UML 2004. Springer, pp. 84-97.

Strom, R. E., & Yemini, S. (1986). Typestate: A programming language concept for enhancing software reliability. *IEEE Transactions on Software Engineering*, *12*(1), 157–171.

Takayama, L., & Kandogan, E. (2006). *Trust as an Underlying Factor of System Adminstrator Interface Choice*. Paper presented at the CHI'06 Montreal, Quebec, Canada.

TCP-W. (2002). *Transaction Processing Performance Council benchmark TPC-W=*.Retrieved from http://www.tpc.org/tpcw/

The Security in Open Multi-Application Smart Cards (S-OMA SMART CARDS) Project. Accessed February 28, 2009, http://mathind.csd.auth.gr/ smart/

Thuraisingham, B., Kantarcioglu, M., & Iyer, S. (2007). Extended RBAC-based design and implementation for a secure data warehouse. [IJBIDM]. *International Journal of Business Intelligence and Data Mining*, *2*, 367–382. doi:10.1504/IJBIDM.2007.016379

TLSWG. (1996). *SSL 3.0 Specification*. Retrieved from http://www.mozilla.org/projects/security/pki/nss/ssl/draft302.txt

Tucker, A. B., Barnes, B. H., Aiken, R. M., Barker, K., Bruce, K. B., & Cain, J. T. (1991). A Summary of the ACM/IEEE-CS Joint Curriculum Task Force Report, Computing Curricula 1991. *Communications of the ACM, 34*(6).

Ullmann-Margalit, E. (2003) *Trust out of distrust*. Available at: www.law.nyu.edu/ clppt/program2001/ readings/ullman_margalit/ Trust%20out%20of%20Distrust.pdf

UML Revision Task Force, Object Management Group (OMG). (2007). OMG Unified Modeling Language: Superstructure. (n.d.). Retrieved June 24, 2009, from http://www.omg.org/spec/UML/2.1.2/.

UML Revision Task Force, Object Management Group (OMG) (2006). Object Constraint Language Specification. Retrieved June 24, 2009, from http://www.omg.org/docs/formal/06-05-01.pdf.

UML2Alloy (2005). *UML2Alloy website*: http://www.cs.bham.ac.uk/~bxb/UML2Alloy.html

van den Akker, T., Snell, O. Q., & Clement, M. J. (2001). *The YGuard Access Control Model: Set-Based Access Control.* Paper presented at the Sixth ACM Symposium on Access Control Models and Technologies, Chantilly, VA.

Van den Berg, J., & Jacobs, B. (2001). The LOOP compiler for Java and JML. *Proc. of Tools and Algorithms for the Construction and Analysis of Systems (TACAS)* (pp. 299-312), Springer LNCS 2031.

van Lamsweerde, A., Darimont, R., & Letier, E. (1998). Managing conflicts in Goal-driven requirements engineering. *IEEE Transactions on Software Engineering, 24*(11), 908–925. doi:10.1109/32.730542

van Lamsweerde, A., & Letier, E. (2000). Handling obstacles in goal-oriented requirements engineering. *IEEE Transactions on Software Engineering, 26*, 978–1005. doi:10.1109/32.879820

van Lamsweerde, A. (2004). Elaborating security requirements by construction of intentional anti-models. *In Proceedings of the International Conference on Software Engineering (ICSE)*, (pp. 148-157). Washington, DC: IEEE Computer Society.

van Lamsweerde, A., Darimont, R., & Massonet, P. (1995). Goal-directed elaboration of requirements for a meeting scheduler: Problems and lessons learnt. *2nd IEEE International Symposium on Requirements Engineering* pp: 194-203.

Vela, B., Fernandez-Medina, E., Marcos, E., & Piattini, M. (2006). Model Driven Development of Secure XML Databases. *SIGMOD Record, 35*, 22–27. doi:10.1145/1168092.1168095

Venkatesh, V., Morris, M. G., Davis, G. B., & Davis, F. D. (2003). User acceptance of information technology: Toward a unified view. *Management Information Systems Quarterly, 27*(3), 425–478.

Viega, J., & McGraw, G. (2001). *Building secure software: How to avoid security problems the right way.* Boston: Addison-Wesley.

Villaroel, R., Fernández-Medina, E., Trujillo, J., & Piattini, M. (2006). UML 2.0/OCL Extension for Designing Secure Data Warehouses. *Journal of Research and Practice in Information Technology, 38*, 31–43.

Villarroel, R., Fernández-Medina, E., & Piattini, M. (2005). *Secure information systems development- a survey and comparison.* Computers & Security.

Vinoski, S. (2004). WS-NonexistentStandards. *IEEE Internet Computing, 8*, 94–96. doi:10.1109/MIC.2004.73

Wang, R., Song, X., & Gu, M. (2007). Modelling and verification of program logic controllers using timed automata. *Software, IET, 1*(4), 127–131. doi:10.1049/iet-sen:20070009

Wang, Y., McIlraith, S. A., Yu, Y., & Mylopoulos, J. (2007). An automated approach to monitoring and diagnosing requirements. *Proceedings of the 22nd IEEE/ACM international conference on Automated software engineering.* Atlanta, Georgia, USA, ACM: 293-302.

Warmer, J., & Kleppe, A. (2003). *The object constraint language* (2nd ed.). Boston: Addison-Wesley.

Warren, S., & Brandeis, L. (1890). The Right to Privacy. *Harvard Law Review, 5*, 193–220. doi:10.2307/1321160

Washizaki, H., Fernandez, E. B., Maruyama, K., Kubo, A., & Yoshioka, N. (2009). Improving the classification of security patterns. In *Proceedings of the International Workshop on Database and Expert Systems Applications* (pp. 165-170). Los Alamitos, CA: IEEE Computer Society.

Weidenhaupt, K., Pohl, K., Jarke, M., & Haumer, P. (1998). *Scenario usage in system development: a report on current practice.* Proceedings of the 3rd International Conference on Requirements Engineering.

Weiss, M., & Mouratdis, H. (2008). *Selecting Security Patterns that Fulfill Security Requirements.* Proceedings of the 16th IEEE International Conference on Requirements Engineering (RE'08), IEEE Computer Society, pp. 169-172

Westin, A. (1967). *Privacy and Freedom.* The Bodley Head Ltd.

Whittle, J., Wijesekera, D., & Hartong, M. (2008). *Executable misuse cases for modeling security concerns.* In ICSE '08: Proceedings of the 30th international conference on Software engineering, pp. 121–130, ACM, New York, NY, USA, 2008.

Whyte, B. (2008). *The teaching of security issues to computing undergraduates in England: a cause for concern?* Retrieved January 2009 from http://www.ktn.qinetiq-

Whyte, B., & Harrison, J. (2008). *Secure Software Development: a White Paper (Software Security Failures: who should correct them and how).* Cyber Security Knowledge Transfer Network. Retrieved January 2009 from www. ktn.qinetiq-tim.net/content/files/groups/securesoft/SSD-SIG_softwareSecurityFailures.pdf

Willcocks, L. P., & Cullen, S. (2006) *The Outsourcing Enterprise: The Power of Relationships.* Available: http://www.logicacmg.com/ pSecured/ admin/ countries/ assets/ serve_asset.asp?id=3252.

Wing, J. M. (1998). *A Symbolic Relationship Between Formal Methods And Security.* Carnegie Mellon University report CMU-CS-98-118.

Woodside, C. M., Petriu, D. C., Petriu, D. B., Xu, J., Israr, T., Georg, G., & France, R. B. (2009). a,Bieman, J. M., Houmb, S. H. & Jürjens, J. (2009). Performance Analysis of Security Aspects by Weaving Scenarios Extracted from UML Models. *Journal of Systems and Software, 82,* 56–74. doi:10.1016/j.jss.2008.03.067

Woodside, C. M., Petriu, D. C., Petriu, D. B., Shen, H., Israr, T., & Merseguer, J. (2005). *Performance by Unified Model Analysis (PUMA).* In Proc. 5th Int. Workshop on Software and Performance WOSP'2005, pp. 1-12, Palma, Spain, 2005.

Wool, A. (2004). The use and usability of direction-based filtering in firewalls. *Computers & Security, 23,* 459–468. doi:10.1016/j.cose.2004.02.003

Yoder, J., & Barcalow, J. (1997). Architectural Patterns for Enabling Application Security. *Int. Conf. on Pattern Languages of Programs Conference (PLOP).* Monticello, Illinois, USA.

Yoshioka, N. (2006, March 29). A development method based on security patterns. Presented at National Institute of Informatics. Tokyo, Japan.

Yoshioka, N., H. Washizaki & K. Maruyama (2008). A survey on security patterns. *Progress in Informatics*(5): 35-47.

Yoshioka, N., Honiden, S., & Finkelstein, A. (2004) Security patterns: A method for constructing secure and efficient inter-company coordination systems. In *Proceedings of the Eighth IEEE International Enterprise Distributed Object Computing Conference* (pp. 84-97). Los Alamitos, CA: IEEE Computer Society.

Yu, E., & Cysneiros, L. (2003). Designing for Privacy in a Multi-Agent World. Trust, Reputation and Security:Theories and Pactice. *Springer Verlag LNCS, 2631,* 209–223.

Yu, E. (1993). *Modeling organisations for information systems requirements engineering.* 1st IEEE International Symposium on Requirements Engineering pp: 34-41.

Yu, E. (1997). *Towards Modelling and Reasoning Support for Early-Phase Requirements Engineering.* In Proc of the 3rd IEEE Int. Symposium. on Requirements Engineering (RE'97) Jan. 6-8, 1997, Washington D.C., USA. pp. 226-235.

Yu, E., & Cysneiros, L. (2002). Designing for privacy and other competing requirements. *2nd Symposium on Requirements Engineering for Information Security (SREIS'02)*

Yu, E., Liu, L. & Mylopoulos (2007). A Social Ontology for Integrating Security and Software Engineering. *Integrating Security and Software Engineering: Advances and Future Visions.* Hershey, PA: Idea Group Publishing.

Yu, Y., Kaiya, H., Washizaki, H., Xiong, Y., Hu, Z., & Yoshioka, N. (2008). Enforcing a security pattern in stakeholder goal models. *Proceedings of the 4th ACM Workshop on Quality of Protection.* Alexandria, VA: ACM, 9-14.

Zoubek, B. (2003). *Towards automatic verification of ladder logic. IMACS Multiconference on Computational Engineering in Systems Applications* (pp. 9–12). CESA.

Zoubek, B. (2002). *Automatic verification of programs for control systems.*

About the Contributors

Haralambos Mouratidis holds a B.Eng (Univ. of Wales, Swansea – UK); an MSc and a PhD (Univ. of Sheffield –UK). He is currently Principal Lecturer at the University of East London where he is leading the Secure Systems and Software Development Field at the School of Computing, IT and Engineering. Dr. Mouratidis has hold visiting researcher/academic positions with the University College London in the UK (20006/2007) and the National Institute of Informatics in Japan (2008) and a Research Fellowship with the British Telecom (2008/2009). His research interests are in secure software systems engineering, security requirements engineering and agent oriented software engineering. He has attracted funding as Principal Investigator from EPSRC, RAoE, British Telecom, ELC and the London Development Agency for research projects and from various national bodies and industrial partners for knowledge transfer projects. He is the co-editor of the *"Integrating Security and Software Engineering: Advances and Future Vision"* and he has more than 90 publications in refereed journals and conferences. He is the Editor in Chief of the International Journal of Computer Science and Security and the Programme Committee Chair of CAiSE 2011.

* * *

Vasilios Almaliotis is a postgraduate student in the Master of Science program of the Department of Informatics, Aristotle University of Thessaloniki (A.U.Th.), Greece. He holds a Diploma in Informatics from the same department. He has published a research article in conference proceedings, in the area of static program analysis for software security. For his master thesis, he researches the benefits of model checking in the software development cycle and more specifically in the automated generation of test cases based on the software requirements. He is also interested in the areas of open source software, software engineering and embedded systems.

Kyriakos Anastasakis received his PhD in Computer Science from the University of Birmingham, UK (2009). His doctoral thesis is entitled "A Model Driven Approach for the Automated Analysis of UML Class Diagrams". He also holds an MSc in Advanced Computer Science from the University of Birmingham (2004). His research is focused on software engineering, model based approaches for systems development and formal methods. Dr. Anastasakis has worked as an independent software consultant in Birmingham and as a software developer for Ulysses Systems prior to his postgraduate studies. He is a member of the ACM and the IEEE.

Arosha K. Bandara was appointed Lecturer in Computing at The Open University in October 2006. Previously he was a postdoctoral researcher at Imperial College London, where he was awarded a First Class MEng (Hons) in Information Systems Engineering (1998) and a PhD (2005). His research combines rigorous formal techniques with concrete implementations and applications of those techniques to practical problems. Dr. Bandara has served on the program committees of prestigious international conferences in network and systems management including POLICY 2004-09, NOMS 2006-10 and IM 2007-09. Additionally he co-chaired the programme committee for POLICY 2009. Dr. Bandara is a visiting researcher in the Department of Computing at Imperial College London. See http://mcs.open.ac.uk/akb235 for further details and selected publications.

Carlos Blanco has an MSc in Computer Science from the University of Castilla-La Mancha. He is currently a PhD student and a member of the Alarcos Research Group at the School of Computer Science at the University of Castilla-La Mancha (Spain), and his research activity is in the field of Security in Data Warehouses, MDA, Information Systems and Ontologies.

Behzad Bordbar is currently a lecturer at the School of Computer Science, University of Birmingham, UK, where he teaches courses in Software Engineering and Distributed Systems. Dr. Bordbar received a PhD in Pure Mathematics (1996) from the University of Sheffield, UK. He was a research fellow in Discrete Event Systems (1996–1997), at University of Ghent Belgium, Massively Distributed Manufacturing systems (1997–1998), Aston University, Birmingham and Distributed Multimedia Systems (1998–2000), University of Kent, UK., where he joined as a lecturer in 2000. He has close collaborative research with various academic and industrial organizations, among them Ghent University, Belgium; Osaka University, Japan; IT University of Copenhagen, Denmark; Colorado State University, US; BT Research Laboratory, IBM and Danske Bank. Bordbar was an IBM visiting research Scientist in Zurich Research Laboratory in 2007 and a BT research fellow in 2008. His research interests are in software tools and techniques for design, analysis and implementation of large distributed systems. In particular, he is currently interested in Model Driven Architecture, Domain Specific Languages, performance modeling and fault tolerance in Service Oriented Architectures.

Alberto Coen-Porisini received his Laurea degree in Electrical Engineering and his Ph.D in Computer Science from Politecnico di Milano in 1987 and 1992, respectively. He is Professor of Computer Science at Università degli Studi dell'Insubria since 2001. From 2006 he is Dean of the School of Science. Prior to that he was Visiting Scholar at University of California Santa Barbara, Assistant Professor at Politecnico di Milano and Associated Professor at Università degli Studi di Lecce. His research interests are in the field of software engineering and more specifically in specification of real time systems, middleware and privacy .

Piotr Cofta is with British Telecom (UK) as a Chief Transformational Security. He is responsible for strategic security improvements for one of BT mission-critical systems, being previously responsible in BT for strategic research in trust and security. Previously he has been working for many years for Nokia and more recently for Media Lab Europe, concentrating on the relationship between technology and society. Dr Cofta's is an author of his book "Trust, Complexity and Control: Confidence in a Convergent World" and has co-authored other books on trust and technology. He is an author of several patents and publications, from areas such as trust management, digital rights management and electronic commerce. Dr Cofta is a contributor to several international standards; he publishes and speaks frequently. Piotr Cofta received his PhD in computer science from the University of Gdansk, Poland. He is a CISSP and CEng and a member of BCS and IEEE. You can contact him at piotr.cofta@bt.com or at http://piotr.cofta.eu

Pietro Colombo is a post doctoral fellow in software engineering at the Department of Electrical and Computer Engineering of Concordia University, in Montreal, Canada. His main research interests concern methodologies to the modelling of software systems characterized by non functional properties like temporal properties and privacy. Dr.Colombo received his PhD degree in Computer Science from Università degli Studi dell'Insubria in Varese, Italy, with a thesis on an approach to requirements analysis and specification of real-time systems. He also got the Laurea degree (BS equivalent) in Computer Science and the Laurea Magistrale degree (MS equivalent) in Computer Science from Università degli Studi dell'Insubria, and a post graduate 2nd level master degree in Information Technologies from CEFRIEL- Politecnico di Milano.

Kyller Costa Gorgônio has graduation at computing science from Federal University of Paraiba (UFPB), in 1999 and master's at computing science by Federal University of Paraíba in 2001. Currently is of Federal university of Campina Grande, business associate of Paraiba Graphics Ltda., business associate of Nyx Tecnologia da Informação Ltda. and investor of Signove Tecnologia S/A. Has experience in the area of Computer Science, with emphasis on Methodology and Techniques of Computer. Focused, mainly, in the subjects: Petri nets, formal Methods, Automatic Verification of models, Software Engineering, Supervisory Control Theory and Discrete Event Systems.

Leandro Dias da Silva has a B.Sc. in Computer Science from Universidade Federal de Alagoas (1999), M.Sc. in Electrical Engineering from Universidade Federal da Paraíba (2002), Ph.D. in Electrical Engineering from Universidade Federal de Campina Grande (2006). Currently he is a Professor in the Universidade Federal de Alagoas. His research interests are Petri nets, model checking, software engineering, pervasive computing and embedded systems.

Eduardo B. Fernandez (Eduardo Fernandez-Buglioni) is a professor in the Department of Computer Science and Engineering at Florida Atlantic University in Boca Raton, Florida. He has published numerous papers on authorization models, object-oriented analysis and design, and security patterns. He has written four books on these subjects, the most recent being a book on security patterns. He has lectured all over the world at both academic and industrial meetings. He has created and taught several graduate and undergraduate courses and industrial tutorials. His current interests include security patterns and web services security and fault tolerance. He holds a MS degree in Electrical Engineering from Purdue University and a Ph.D. in Computer Science from UCLA. He is a Senior Member of the IEEE, and a Member of ACM. He is an active consultant for industry, including assignments with IBM, Allied Signal, Motorola, Lucent, and others. More details can be found at http://www.cse.fau.edu/~ed

Eduardo Fernández-Medina holds a PhD in Computer Science from the University of Castilla-La Mancha. His research activity is in the field of security in databases, data warehouses, web services and information systems, and also in security metrics. Fernández-Medina is co-editor of several books and book chapters on these subjects and has presented several dozens of papers at national and international conferences (DEXA, CAISE, UML, ER, etc.). He is the author of several manuscripts in national and international journals (DSS, ACM Sigmod Record, IS, IST, C&S, ISS, etc.) and belongs to various professional and research associations (AEC, ISO, IFIP WG11.3, etc.).

Robert France is a full professor in the Department of Computer Science at Colorado State University. His research interests include model-driven development (software modeling techniques, design patterns, and domain-specific modeling languages), aspect-oriented development, and formal methods. He received a PhD in computer science from Massey University, New Zealand. He is co-editor-in-chief of the Springer journal on Software and System Modeling (SoSyM), and is a past Steering Committee Chair of the MODELS conference series.

David García Rosado holds a PhD. in Computer Science from University of Castilla-La Mancha and has an MSc in Computer Science from the University of Málaga (Spain). His research activities are focused on security architectures for Information Systems and Mobile Grid Computing. He has published several papers in national and international conferences on these subjects. He is a member of the ALARCOS research group of the Information Systems and Technologies Department at the University of Castilla-La Mancha, in Ciudad Real, Spain.

Geri Georg is a research associate in Computer Science at Colorado State University. Her research interests include modeling and analysis of cross-cutting system properties in complex distributed systems. She is also interested in aspect-oriented modeling and model visualization of these properties. Dr. Georg received her MS and PhD degrees in Computer Science from Colorado State University, Fort Collins, Colorado. Prior to joining Colorado State University, she worked at the corporate research laboratories of Hewlett Packard Company and Agilent Technologies. She is an assistant editor of the Springer journal on Software and System Modeling (SoSyM), and is a member of the Steering Committee of the MODELS conference series.

Stefanos Gritzalis holds a BSc in Physics, an MSc in Electronic Automation, and a PhD in Information and Communications Security from the Dept. of Informatics and Telecommunications, University of Athens, Greece. Prof. Gritzalis is the Deputy Head of the Department of Information and Communication Systems Engineering, University of the Aegean, Greece and the Director of the Laboratory of Information and Communication Systems Security (Info-Sec-Lab). He has been involved in several national and EU funded R&D projects. His published scientific work includes 30 books or book chapters and more than 190 journal and international refereed conference and workshop papers. The focus of these publications is on Information and Communications Security and Privacy. He has acted as Guest Editor in 16 journal special issues, and has leaded more than 25 international conferences and workshops as General Chair or Program Commitee Chair. He has served on more than 170 Program Committees of international conferences and workshops. He is an Editor-in-Chief or Editor or Editorial Board member for 12 journals and a Reviewer for more than 35 journals. He was an elected Member of the Board (Secretary General, Treasurer) of the Greek Computer Society. He is a Member of the ACM, the IEEE, and the IEEE Communications Society "Communications and Information Security Technical Committee".

Carlos A. Guitiérrez has more than 10 years of professional experience, currently being in the position of IT & e-Business project manager at Correos Telecom (Madrid, Spain). He's been assistant professor of Software Engineering at the University of Castilla - La Mancha (Ciudad Real, Spain) within the period 2005-2009. Gutiérrez obtained his doctoral degree in computer sciences at the University of Castilla – La Mancha and his MSc in Computer Sciences at the Autonomous University of Madrid. He is postgraduate Expert in e-Business from the Technical University of Madrid, holds a postgraduate in Business Administration from the Madrid Chamber of Commerce and is certified in PMP by the PMI and in ITIL Foundations by Exin. Gutiérrez participates at the ALARCOS Research Group of the Department of Computer Science at the University of Castilla – La Mancha. His main research interests are security engineering, software security architectures and security in distributed systems.

Charles B. Haley is a Lecturer at The Open University, UK. His research interests include security requirements and their validation through formal and informal argumentation. His work has been published in prestigious venues such as IEEE Transactions on Software Engineering and IEEE Computer, and he has been invited to present lectures about his work to conferences in several countries. Before reentering the academic community in 1999, Dr. Haley worked for 25 years in the software industry at companies including Bell Laboratories, Rational Software, Bell Northern Research, and Sun Microsystems, holding positions ranging from Software Engineer to Director of Development. He obtained a PhD from the Open University, and MS and BA degrees from The University of California at Berkeley. See http://charles.the-haleys.org/ for more information.

John Harrison Director of LanditD, a UK company formed in 2003 providing consultancy to the UK government on Information Security and Telecommunications Resilience of the national infrastructure. Trusted information sharing projects for public private partnerships such as the UK www.warp.gov.uk model and a number of EC funded projects such as www.ms3i.eu are examples of his current work interests. John also chaired the Special Interest Group on Secure Software Development within the Cyber Security KTN for 2 years. This led to a Whitepaper published in 2008 and the creation of the UK Secure Software Development Panel (SSDP) to take the whitepaper recommendations forward. Before creating LanditD, John worked in the telecommunications industry for over 35 years, mainly in an R&D environment at BT Labs, Martlesham before leaving in 2000 to work in the SME sector for 2 years. John has an honours degree (1971) in Electrical and Electronic Engineering from the University of Wales

Denis Hatebur (denis.hatebur@uni-due.de) is a PhD student at University Duisburg-Essen in Germany and he is the CEO of ITESYS Institut f. technische Systeme GmbH in Dortmund/Germany since 2004. He worked in different industrial engineering projects as a consultant. In these safety and security projects he was responsible for specification and testing parts. His research interest is the field of dependability engineering considering requirements engineering, architectural design, and testing. In this area, he has authored numerous reviewed conference and workshop papers. He holds a Diploma degree in information technology from University of Applied Science in Dortmund/Germany and a Master degree in computer engineering from University Duisburg-Essen.

Shinpei Hayashi received a B.Eng. degree in information engineering from Hokkaido University in 2004. He also received M.Eng. and Dr.Eng. degrees in computer science from Tokyo Institute of Technology in 2006 and 2008, respectively. He is currently an assistant professor of computer science at Tokyo Institute of Technology. His research interests include software evolution and refactoring, software patterns, software development environment, and mining software repositories.

Maritta Heisel (maritta.heisel@uni-due.de) is a full professor for software engineering at University of Duisburg-Essen, Germany. Her research interests include the development of dependable software, pattern- and component-based software development, software architecture, and software evolution. She is particularly interested in incorporating security considerations into software development processes and in integrating the development of safe and secure software. She co-authored more than 70 refereed publications, including monographs, book chapters, journals and conference papers. She is member of various program committees and served as reviewer for a number of journals and conferences. Morevover, she is a member of the European Workshop on Industrial Computer Systems Reliability, Safety and Security (EWICS).

Paul Hodgson works for British Telecom (UK) as a Security Consultant on the Domain Management Platform. He is responsible for security management on 21C platforms. He joined BT in 1997 and previously worked in the Security Research Centre on defensive technologies and the Future Technologies group on applying nature inspired approaches to network security. His research interests include the technical and social aspects of creativity, trust and security with special reference to opportunities in convergent environments. Dr Hodgson is author of several publications and patents, from areas such as computational creativity, email anti-virus protection, mobile services encryption and trust management. Dr Hodgson is a contributor to several international journals and he publishes and speaks frequently. Paul Hodgson received his DPhil in cognitive science from the University of Sussex, UK. He is a CISSP, an ISO 27001 Lead Auditor, a fellow of the RSA and a visiting Research Fellow at the University of Sussex. You can contact him at paul.w.hodgson@bt.com

Siv Hilde Houmb is a researcher and security expert at Telenor R&I and a Telenor delegate in three standardization technical committees: ETSI TC TISPAN, ETSI TC IST and ETSI TC M2M. She also works as a Special Task Force security expert at the Telecommunication standardization organization ETSI (for Telenor) on security topics such as risk assessment, Common Criteria, data retention, and security requirements elicitation and tracing to design. Her research interests include decision support methodologies and techniques that allow architects to choose among sets of security solutions in security critical information systems taking all of security, development, project, and financial constraints into consideration. Dr. Houmb held a post-doctoral position in the department of Information Systems at the University of Twente, The Netherlands. She was a PhD Fellow and received her Ph.D. in Computer Science (security) from the Norwegian University of Science and Technology, Trondheim, Norway.

Jan Jürjens is a Professor at the Chair for Software Engineering (LS 14), Department for Computer Science, Technical University Dortmund (Germany), the Scientific Coordinator "Enterprise Engineering" and Attract research group leader at the Fraunhofer Institute for Software and Systems Engineering ISST (Dortmund), and a Senior Member of Robinson College (Univ. Cambridge, UK). He is currently supervising a research group consisting of 1 Postdoc and 8 PhD students. He is PI of several projects financed by Microsoft Research (Cambridge), British Telecom, and EPSRC, and Research Director of an Integrated Project financed by the EU within FP7, Future and Emerging Technologies Programme. Previously, he was a Senior Lecturer at The Open University (the British distance university), as well as Royal Society Industrial Fellow at Microsoft Research Cambridge and non-stipendiary Research Fellow at Robinson College (Univ. Cambridge). Before that, he organized the Competence Center for IT-Security at the chair for Software & Systems Engineering, TU Munich (Germany). Doctor of Philosophy in Computing from the University of Oxford and author of "Secure Systems Development with UML" (Springer, 2005; Chinese translation: Tsinghua University Press, Beijing, 2009) and various publications mostly on computer security and software engineering, totalling over 1500 citations (Google Scholar, Jan. 2009). Founding chair of the working group on "Formal Methods and Software Engineering for Safety and Security (FoMSESS)" within the German Society for Informatics (GI) and member of the executive board of the Division of Safety and Security within the GI, the executive board of the committee on Modeling of the GI, the advisory board of the Bavarian Competence Center for Safety and Security, the working group on e-Security of the Bavarian regional government, and the IFIP Working Group 1.7 "Theoretical Foundations of Security Analysis and Design". Much of his work is done in cooperation with industrial partners including Microsoft Research (Cambridge), O2 (Germany), BMW, HypoVereinsbank, Infineon, Deutsche Telekom, Munich Re, IBM-Rational, Deutsche Bank, Allianz. More information can be found at http://jurjens.de/jan.

Haruhiko Kaiya is an associate professor of Software Engineering in Shinshu University, Japan. He is also a visiting associate professor in National Institute of Informatics (NII), Japan.

Christos Kalloniatis holds a bachelor degree from the Department of Informatics of the Technological Institute of Athens (2000). In 2001 he took his master degree on Computer Science from the University of Essex, UK. In 2008 he finished his PhD at the Department of Cultural Technology and Communication of the University of the Aegean. The objective of his PhD was the protection of privacy during the design of Information Systems. From 2003 he teaches as an adjunct lecturer at the Department of Cultural Technology and Communication. His public scientific work includes almost 20 papers in journals and international refereed conferences. He is a member of Greek Computer Society, IEEE and ACM.

Panagiotis Katsaros is a Lecturer in the Department of Informatics, Aristotle University of Thessaloniki (A.U.Th.), Greece. He holds a Diploma in Mathematics, a Master of Science in Software Engineering from University of Aston in Birmingham, UK and a PhD in Computer Science from A.U.Th. He has published research articles in international journals and conference proceedings in the areas of software security, software dependability, fault tolerance and recovery, software verification by model checking and static program analysis, software architecture for quality design and simulation output analysis. He has coordinated national and international research projects in the aforementioned areas that were funded on a competitive basis. He is a member of the Program Committee of annual international conferences focused on the broader area of software engineering and he serves as referee for international journal publications.

Evangelia Kavakli is an assistant professor at the Department of Cultural Technology and Communication of the University of the Aegean. She has a BSc in Computer Science from the Computer Science Department of the University of Crete, an MSc by research and PhD in Computation from the Computation Department of the University of Manchester Institute of Science and Technology (UMIST). Her research interests lie in the area of goal-driven requirements engineering. Her research work has been financially supported by the UK Engineering and Physical Sciences and Research Council, the

Hellenic Secretariat of Research and Technology and the European Commission. Dr. Kavakli has played an active role in several Greek and European research projects. She has published over 40 papers in International Conferences and Journals.

Atsuto Kubo, born in 1981, received B.E. (2004), M.E. (2006) and PhD (2009) degrees in computer science from the Waseda University. He has worked as a research associate in Waseda University (2007-2009), and joined the National Institute of Informatics in Japan. He is a member of Information Processing Society of Japan and he is committing as a member of the SIGSE (Special Interests Group of Software Engineering) steering committee. He is interested in software engineering and knowledge engineering, especially software patterns. He introduced information retrieval technique to utilize software patterns.

Hazel Lacohée is a Principal Researcher at British Telecom (UK) undertaking qualitative social research for BT Innovate. She is responsible for investigation of the commercial, socio-economic and customer impact of ICT applications and systems and providing thought leadership on social and market implications. She is currently focused on issues concerning privacy, security and trust, and is lead author of the Trustguide report. Prior to joining BT in 1998 Dr. Lacohée spent two years with Hewlett Packard Laboratories undertaking user needs research in the UK, USA and Denmark followed by appointment as Senior Research Fellow at the University of the West of England for a BT funded project concerning the social aspects of software systems. Hazel Lacohée obtained an ESRC funded PhD in Psychology from the University of Bristol in 1996. She is author of a diverse range of publications and has contributed to a number of patents at BT.

Robin Laney is a Senior Lecturer at the OU, where he leads a research programme on software composition. Dr. Laney has contributed to research in this area from the perspective of feature and problem composition, software evolution, and support for music composition. His work has focused on bridging the gap between theoretical advances and the experience and problems of working software practitioners, investigating domains such as music, security, and, more broadly, applied computing. He has industrial experience as a software engineer working on programming language technology and graphics. He holds a First Class Honours BSc in Microcomputers and Applications from Westfield College, University of London, and a PhD in Computing from King's College, London.

Alexandros Loizidis is a postgraduate student in the Master of Science program of the Department of Informatics, Aristotle University of Thessaloniki (A.U.Th.), Greece. He holds a Diploma in Informatics from the Aristotle University of Thessaloniki. He has published one research article on static program analysis for Java Card applications, as a result of the collaborative work done for his graduation thesis. For the Master thesis, he has focused on the development of conformance testing theories and tools towards integration testing for software components. Other research interests include black-box testing and model checking.

Paul Maj is an Associate Professor in the School of Computer and Security Science at Edith Cowan University (ECU) in Perth, Western Australia. He has been highly successful in linking applied research with curriculum development to establish well-resourced environments and innovative approaches that significantly improve learning experiences and outcomes for students. Dr Maj was awarded an ECU Vice-Chancellor's Excellence in Teaching Award in 2002, and again in 2009. He also received a Carrick

Citation in 2006 for "the development of world class curriculum and the design and implementation of associated world-class network teaching laboratories". Dr Maj's ongoing work has been published in a range of prestigious journals and has attracted the attention of teachers, researchers and the professional IT community. His work on network curriculum has been recognized by the world's leading organization in this field, the Cisco Network Academy, and is being used to define international best practices.

Daniel Mellado holds a PhD in Software Engineering from the Castilla- La Mancha University (Spain) and a MSc in Computer Science from the Autonomous University of Madrid (Spain). He is part-time Assistant Professor of the Department of Information Technologies and Systems at the Universidad de Castilla- La Mancha at Toledo (Spain). He is civil servant at the Spanish Tax Agency (in Madrid, Spain), where he works as IT Auditor. His research activities are security requirements engineering, security in information systems, secure software process improvement, auditory, quality and product lines. He has several dozens of papers in national and international conferences and magazines on these subjects and co-author of several chapter books. He belongs to various professional and research associations (ISACA, ASTIC, etc.).

Armstrong Nhlabatsi worked as a post-doctoral researcher at the Open University between April and July 2009. He was awarded an MSc in Software Engineering (2005) from the University of the West of England, Bristol and a PhD (2009) from The Open University, Milton Keynes. His research interests include feature composition, feature interaction, inconsistency management, security requirements engineering, and software evolution.

Antonio Marcus Nogueira Lima (SM'94) was born in Recife, Brazil, in 1958. He received the B.S. and M.S. degrees in electrical engineering from the Federal University of Paraíba, Campina Grande, Brazil, in 1982 and 1985, respectively, and the Ph.D. degree from the Institut National Polytechnique de Toulouse, Toulouse, France, in 1989. From 1977 to 1982, he was with the Escola Técnica Redentorista, Campina Grande. From 1982 to 1983, he was a Project Engineer with Sul-Amárica Philips, Recife. From 1983 to 2002, he was with the Department of Electrical Engineering, Federal University of Paraíba. Since April 2002, he has been with the Department of Electrical Engineering, Federal University of Campina Grande, where he is currently a Professor of electrical engineering. His research interests are in the fields of electrical machines and drives, power electronics, electronic instrumentation, control systems, and system identification.

Bashar Nuseibeh is Chief Scientist at Lero – The Irish Software Engineering Research Centre, Professor of Software Engineering at the University of Limerick (Ireland), and Professor of Computing at The Open University (UK). He is also a Visiting Professor at Imperial College London (UK) and The National Institute of Informatics (Japan). His research interests are in requirements engineering & design, security & privacy, process modelling & technology, and technology transfer. He is Editor-in-Chief of IEEE Transactions on Software Engineering, Editor Emeritus of the Automated Software Engineering Journal, and Chair of IFIP Working Group 2.9 (Requirements Engineering). Previously, he was Chair of the Steering Committee of the International Conference on Software Engineering (ICSE), having served as programme chair for ICSE'05, RE'01, and ASE'98. He is an Automated Software Engineering Fellow, and a Fellow of the British Computer Society (FBCS) and the Institution of Engineering & Technology (FIET).

Mario Piattini has an MSc and a PhD in Computer Science from the Polytechnic University of Madrid. He is a Certified Information System Auditor from the ISACA (Information System Audit and Control Association). The author of several books and papers on databases, software engineering and information systems, Piattini leads the ALARCOS research group of the Department of Computer Science at the University of Castilla-La Mancha. His research interests include advanced database design, database quality, software metrics, object-oriented metrics and software maintenance.

Angelo Perkusich has a degree in Electrical Engineer from the Education Foundation of Barretos in 1982, Master's in Electrical Engineer from the Federal University of Paraíba in 1987 and Ph.D in Electrical Engineer from the Federal University of Paraíba in 1994. Currently is an adjunct professor at that Department of Electrical Engineering at the Federal University of Campina Grande. He has experience in computer science, with emphasis on Software Engineering and Pervasive Computing, acting on the following topics: Petri nets, software engineering, colored Petri nets, formal methods and object orientation.

Dorina C. Petriu is a full professor in the Department of Systems and Computer Engineering at Carleton University, Ottawa, Canada. She received a Dipl. Eng. degree in computer engineering from the Polytechnic University of Timisoara, Romania, and a Ph.D. degree in electrical engineering from Carleton University, Ottawa, Canada. Her main research interests are in the field of model-driven engineering, with emphasis on integrating performance analysis into the software development process. She was a contributor to two OMG standards for performance annotations, the "UML Profile for Schedulability, Performance and Time" (SPT) and the "UML Profile for Modeling and Analysis of Real-Time and Embedded Systems" (MARTE). Dr. Petriu is a Fellow of the Engineering Institute of Canada, a Senior Member of I.E.E.E. and a member of A.C.M.

Günther Pernul is full professor and head of the Department of Information Systems at the University of Regensburg, Germany. He got his academic education at the University of Vienna, Austria (with a PhD in 1989), and held PostDoc positions at University of Florida, Gainsville and Georgia Institute of Technology, Atlanta. Earlier positions include a professorship at University of Essen, Germany and a senior researcher position at University of Vienna, Austria. His research interests are web-based information systems, information systems security, and security of data centric applications. Günther Pernul is co-author of a text book, has edited or co-edited more than 15 books, published more than 100 papers in scientific journals and conference proceedings on various information systems topics and has participated as partner or coordinator in more than 10 European funded research projects under ESPRIT, ACTS and IST frameworks. He is a member of several professional associations, such as ACM, IEEE, the German Gesellschaft für Informatik (GI), and the Austrian OCG, member of the IFIP WG 11.3 and observer of the IFIP WG 11.8. He serves on the steering board of the Communications and Multimedia Security conference series and is founding editor of the conference series Electronic Commerce and Web Technologies (EC-Web, since 2000) and Trust and Privacy in Digital Business (Trustbus, since 2004).

Indrakshi Ray is an associate professor in the Computer Science Department at Colorado State University. Prior to joining Colorado State, she was a faculty at the University of Michigan-Dearborn. She obtained her PhD from George Mason University. Her research interests include security and privacy, database systems, e-commerce and formal methods in software engineering. She has published several refereed journal and conference papers in these areas. She served as the General Chair for SACMAT 2008, Program Chair for SACMAT 2006, and Program Co-Chair for IEEE/IFIP TSP 2008 and IFIP WG 11.3 DBSEC 2003. She has also been a member of several program committees such as EDBT, SACMAT, ACM CCS and EC-Web. She is a member of the ACM and the IEEE.

Alfonso Rodríguez is Associate Professor in the Computer Science and Information Technology Department of the University of Bio-Bio, Chillán, Chile. He received his PhD Degree in Computer Science from the University of Castilla-La Mancha, Spain and a Master's Degree in Business Administration from the University of Bio-Bio, Chile. His research interests are software engineering and information systems and his research activities are centered on security in business process and legacy information systems. He is author of papers in national and international conferences on these subjects.

Holger Schmidt (holger.schmidt@uni-due.de) is a PhD student at University Duisburg-Essen, Germany. He has authored papers and presented at numerous international conferences on the topics of requirements engineering, secure software engineering, and security requirements engineering. He holds a Diploma degree in mathematics from University Müunster, Germany. Moreover, he works for about two years as a freelancer in the area of security consultancy for software development and evaluation projects.

Sabrina Sicari received her master degree in Electronical Engineering, 110/110 cum laude, from the Università di Catania (Italy) in 2002. In March 2006 she got her Ph.d in Computer and Telecommunications Engineering at the same university. From September 2004 to March 2006 she was a research scholar at Politecnico di Milano under the guidance of Prof. Carlo Ghezzi. Since May 2006 she works at Università dell' Insubria in software engineering group. Her research interests are on wireless sensor network, risk assessment methodology and privacy policy models. She is a member of the Editorial Board of Computer Networks. She is the general co-chair of S-Cube'09, a steering committee member of S-Cube'10, guest editor of the ACM Monet Special Issue, "Sensor, system and Software", TPC member of Q2S Winet'09, of IEEE Globecom'10, of SESENA'10 and reviewer for many journals and conference such as Computer Network, Pervasive and Mobile Computing, IJCAT, ICC'09, ICC'10, WiOpt'09.

Thein Than Thun is a researcher in Requirements Engineering. He has held research and teaching positions at universities in Belgium and UK. His research interests include feature modelling, feature interaction, requirements inconsistency, requirements evolution, and failures of dependable systems.

Juan Trujillo is an Associate Professor at the Department of Software and Computing Systems in the University of Alicante (Spain), and he is the leader of the LUCENTIA Research Group at the same Department. His main research topics include bussiness intelligence applications, data warehouses development, data base conceptual modeling, multidimensional data bases, OLAP and data mining applications, object oriented analysis and design by using UML, MDA, data warehouses security and quality, etc. He has published more than a hundred research works in different national and international high impact conferences and journals, such as the ER, UML, ADBIS, CaiSE or WAIM, DKE, CS&I, DSS, ISOFT, IS, or JDBM. He has also participated as a PC member in different workshops, conferences, and JCR journals such us ER, DOLAP, DSS, y SCI, JDM, KAIS, ISOFT, JOD or DKE. Moreover, he has been Program Chair and Co-Chair in DOLAP'05, DAWAK'05-06 and FP-UML'05-'07 and BP-UML'08-'09.

Hironori Washizaki is an associate professor at Waseda University, and a visiting associate professor at National Institute of Informatics, Tokyo, Japan. He obtained his Doctor's degree in Information and Computer Science from Waseda University in 2003. His research interests include software architecture, reuse, quality assurance and patterns. He has published more than 35 research papers in refereed international journals and conferences. He received several awards including Yamashita Research Award 2008 and FIT2009 Best Paper Award from IPSJ. He has served as program co-chairs of SPAQu'07-09 and AsianPLoP 2010, workshop co-chair of ASE'06, publicity chair of APSEC'07, and Asian liaison of SEKE 2010. He has served as members of program committee for many international conferences including REP'04, ASE'06, Profes'04-10, APSEC'07-09, SNPD'08, SPattern'08-10, JCKBSE'06-10, PLoP'08-09, ICSOFT'09, and SEKE2010. He served as members of editorial board for several journals including Journal of Information Processing (JIP). He is a member of IEEE, ACM, IEICE, IEEJ, JSSST and IPSJ.

William ('Bill') Whyte has over 40 years experience in ICT research and product development, half of which has been devoted to hardware, software and business aspects of security, including 5 years as head of British Telecom's largest R&D security division, and 12 years university teaching in e-business and security. Was UK Department of Industry academic representative on 2006 USA mission to study the position of secure software development, and consultant to the subsequent secure software group of the UK Cyber-Security Knowledge Transfer Network. Independent consultancy to organizations including, BT, VDI-VDE, Mitre Corp, UK Centre for Protection of the Critical Infrastructure (CPNI), and the European Commission's European Network and Information Security Agency (ENISA). Published books: Multimedia telecommunications ed B Whyte. Springer-Verlag. Networked Futures W Whyte. Wiley Enabling eBusiness, W Whyte. Wiley. Plus various papers and consultancy reports.

Nobukazu Yoshioka is a researcher at the National Institute of Informatics, Japan. Dr. Nobukazu Yoshioka received his B.E degree in Electronic and Information Engineering from Toyama University in 1993. He received his M.E. and Ph.D. degrees in School of Information Science from Japan Advanced Institute of Science and Technology in 1995 and 1998, respectively. From 1998 to 2002, he was with Toshiba Corporation, Japan. From 2002 to 2004 he was a researcher, and since August 2004, he has been an associate professor, in National Institute of Informatics, Japan. His research interests include agent technology, object-oriented methodology, software engineering, and software evolution. He is a member of the Information Processing Society of Japan (IPSJ), the Institute of Electronics, information and Communication Engineers (IEICE) and Japan Society for Software Science and Technology.

Yijun Yu is a Senior Lecturer in Computing at the OU since 2006, also a Visiting Professor at the University of Trento, Italy (2008). Previously he was a postdoctoral researcher at the Department of Computer Science, University of Toronto, Canada (2003-2006) and Department of Electrical Engineering, Ghent University, Belgium (1999-2002). He graduated from the Department of Computer Science at Fudan University, China, with a BSc in 1992, an MSc in 1995, and a PhD in 1998. He is interested in investigating and developing automated techniques and tools to better support human activities in software development: from analysis and design, to implementation, testing, and maintenance. He received an ACM/SIGSOFT Distinguished Paper Award in 2007, and Best Paper awards at the International Workshop on the Design and Evolution of Autonomic Application Software at ICSE-2005, the International Conference on Parallel and Distributed Computing and Systems in 2002, and the International

Workshop of Visual Methods for Parallel and Distributed Programming in 2001. He is a Member of IEEE Computer Society (2003-2009) and Membership Secretary of Requirements Engineering Specialist Group at British Computer Society (2007-2009). He has served on programme committees including the International Conferences on Requirements Engineering (RE'10) and Software Maintenance (ICSM'09), and chaired the 1st International Workshop on Reverse Engineering to Requirements at the Working Conference on Reverse Engineering (WCRE'05).

Kézia de Vasconcelos Oliveira was born at Campina Grande, Brazil, 1983. She received his B.Sc. and M.Sc. in computing science from Federal University of Campina Grande (UFCG), in 2007 and 2009, respectively. She is currently a Ph.D. student at Federal University of Campina Grande. Her research interests are software engineering, formal methods and automatic verification of models.

Index